AF894328

ASCENT®

CENTER FOR TECHNICAL KNOWLEDGE

Creo Simulate 11.0
Structural and Thermal Analysis

Learning Guide

Edition 1.0

ASCENT - Center for Technical Knowledge®
Creo Simulate 11.0
Structural and Thermal Analysis
Edition 1.0

Prepared and produced by:

ASCENT Center for Technical Knowledge
630 Peter Jefferson Parkway, Suite 175
Charlottesville, VA 22911

866-527-2368
www.ASCENTed.com

Lead Contributor: Iouri Apanovitch

ASCENT - Center for Technical Knowledge (a division of Rand Worldwide Inc.) is a leading developer of professional learning materials and knowledge products for engineering software applications. ASCENT specializes in designing targeted content that facilitates application-based learning with hands-on software experience. For over 25 years, ASCENT has helped users become more productive through tailored custom learning solutions.

We welcome any comments you may have regarding this guide, or any of our products. To contact us please email: feedback@ASCENTed.com.

AS-CRS11-STA1-SG // RS-CRS11-STA1-SG

Contents

Preface

The *Creo Simulate 11.0: Structural and Thermal Analysis* guide covers the fundamentals of structural and thermal analysis in Creo Simulate. It provides you with the knowledge to effectively use Creo Simulate for finite element analysis, thereby reducing design time. Many concepts apply to both structural and thermal analysis; a portion of this guide is specifically dedicated to thermal analysis. This is an extensive hands-on guide, in which you have the opportunity to apply your knowledge through real-world scenarios and examples.

Topics Covered

- FEA fundamentals: P-elements and analysis convergence methods
- Basic modeling and analysis
- Types of loads and constraints
- Idealizations: shells and beams
- Sensitivity and optimization studies
- Assembly interfaces and contact analysis
- Thermal analysis
- Modal analysis
- Welds, springs, and masses
- Fasteners and rigid links
- Buckling analysis

Prerequisites

- Access to the Creo Simulate 11.0 software. The practices and files included with this guide might not be compatible with prior versions. Practice files included with this guide are compatible with the commercial version of the software, but not the student edition.
- Completion of the *Creo Parametric: Introduction to Solid Modeling* guide plus a minimum of 80 hours of Creo Parametric experience is recommended.

Note on Software Setup

This guide assumes a standard installation of the software using the default preferences during installation. Lectures and practices use the standard software templates and default options for the Content Libraries.

Note on Learning Guide Content

ASCENT's learning guides are intended to teach the technical aspects of using the software and do not focus on professional design principles and standards. The practices aim to demonstrate the capabilities and flexibility of the software rather than following specific design codes or standards.

Lead Contributor: Iouri Apanovitch

Iouri has been specializing in finite element analysis and simulation for over 30 years, with experience on multiple CAD and FEA systems, including Creo, CATIA, and Abaqus. Iouri uses his extensive knowledge and skills to develop instructor-led and web-based training products.

Iouri holds a Ph.D. degree in mechanical engineering from the National Academy of Sciences, Minsk, Belarus, as well as a Professional Engineer certification in Ontario, Canada.

Iouri Apanovitch has been the lead contributor for *Creo Simulate: Structural and Thermal Analysis* since 2013.

In This Guide

The following highlights the key features of this guide.

Feature	Description
Practice Files	The Practice Files page includes a link to the practice files and instructions on how to download and install them. The practice files are required to complete the practices in this guide.
Chapters	A chapter consists of the following: Learning Objectives, Instructional Content, and Practices. • **Learning Objectives** define the skills you can acquire by learning the content provided in the chapter. • **Instructional Content**, which begins right after Learning Objectives, refers to the descriptive and procedural information related to various topics. Each main topic introduces a product feature, discusses various aspects of that feature, and provides step-by-step procedures on how to use that feature. Where relevant, examples, figures, helpful hints, and notes are provided. • **Practice** for a topic follows the instructional content. Practices enable you to use the software to perform a hands-on review of a topic. It is required that you download the practice files (using the link found on the Practice Files page) prior to starting the first practice.

Practice Files

To download the practice files for this guide, use the following steps:

1. Type the URL *exactly as shown below* into the address bar of your Internet browser to access the Course File Download page.

   Note: If you are using the ebook, you do not have to type the URL. Instead, you can access the page by clicking the URL below.

   https://www.ascented.com/getfile/id/zewaldiaePF

2. On the Course File Download page, click the **DOWNLOAD NOW** button, as shown below, to download the .ZIP file that contains the practice files.

3. Once the download is complete, unzip the file and extract its contents.

   The recommended practice files folder location is:
   C:\Creo Simulate 11.0 Structural and Thermal Analysis Practice Files

   Note: It is recommended that you do not change the location of the practice files folder. Doing so may cause errors when completing the practices.

Stay Informed!
To receive information about upcoming events, promotional offers, and complimentary webcasts, visit:
www.ASCENTed.com/updates

Chapter

1

Introduction to Creo Simulate

Creo Simulate is a powerful software tool that enables you to simulate structural and thermal behavior of your design to understand and improve the design's performance.

Learning Objectives

- Understand the concept of FEA.
- Understand the concepts of H-refinement and P-refinement.
- Understand the advantages of P-elements.
- Understand solution convergence methods in Creo Simulate.
- Understand the analysis abilities of Creo Simulate.
- Understand the steps involved in a Creo Simulate analysis.
- Understand the recommendations for CAD model preparation.
- Understand the Creo Simulate modes of operation.

1.1 Finite Element Analysis (FEA)

Finite Element Analysis is a numerical mathematical method based on the following process:

- Discretize (i.e., divide) the model into smaller and more simplified volumes (tetrahedra, bricks, wedges, etc.) called *finite elements*. The collection of finite elements approximates the shape of the model, and is called *finite element mesh*, or just *mesh*. An example of a meshed model is shown in Figure 1–1.

*Note: Creo Simulate contains the **AutoGEM** tool, which automatically meshes a model.*

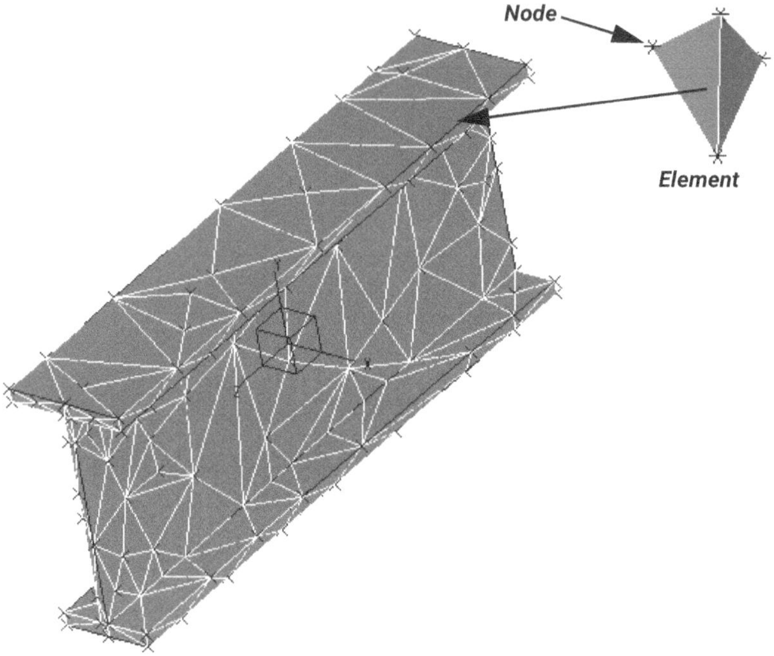

Figure 1–1

Note: In 2D models, finite elements are triangles or quadrilaterals. In 3D models, finite elements are 4-node tetra, 6 node wedge or 8-node bricks.

- Approximate the variation of the principal quantity of interest (such as displacement, stress, etc.), within each finite element with polynomials. These polynomials are typically called *local approximation functions* or *shape functions*.
- Connect the finite elements across the inter-element boundaries, thus effectively *sewing* elemental polynomials together. The *sewn* local polynomials now approximate a variation of the quantity of interest over the entire model, and therefore comprise the global approximation function in the form of a piece-wise polynomial.

- Solve the governing equations and boundary conditions for the global approximation function, and find the best fitting solution. In structural mechanics, the principle of minimum total potential energy is typically used to find the best fitting solution, which results in solving a large number (sometimes hundreds of thousands) of simultaneous linear equations.
- Present the results for this approximate solution.

Therefore, the key FEA concept is the use of piece-wise polynomials to approximate the sought field quantity in the model, which effectively replaces a continuum problem with an infinite number of degrees of freedom (DOF) by a discrete problem with a finite number of DOF (i.e., *finite elements* and *discretization*).

For example, consider how the FEA method works when applied to calculate deflections in a simple beam as shown in Figure 1–2. The beam is clamped at the left end, has a couple of supports in the middle, and is loaded by a couple of transversal forces and a moment. The bottom graph shown in Figure 1–2 represents the unknown true deflection of the beam, which you are trying to determine using the FEA method.

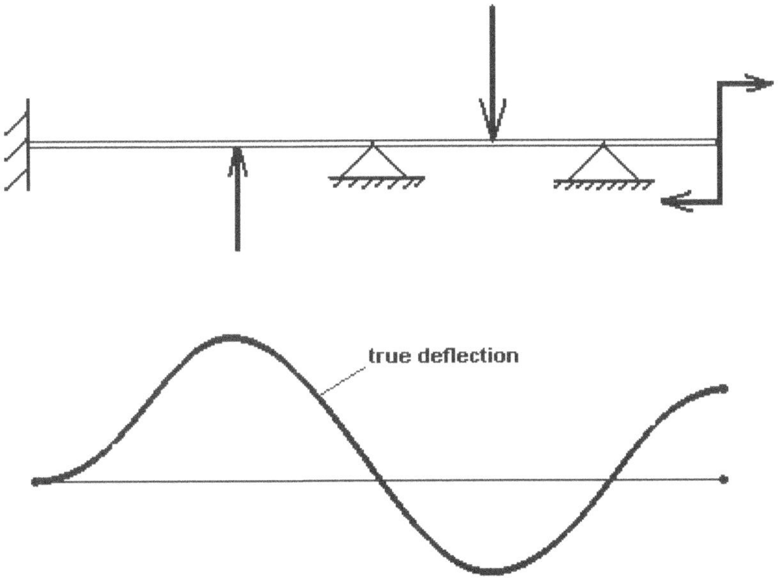

Figure 1–2

The first step in the process (shown in the example in Figure 1–3) is to mesh the beam by breaking it into a collection of shorter pieces (i.e., finite elements) connected at their ends (i.e., the nodes).

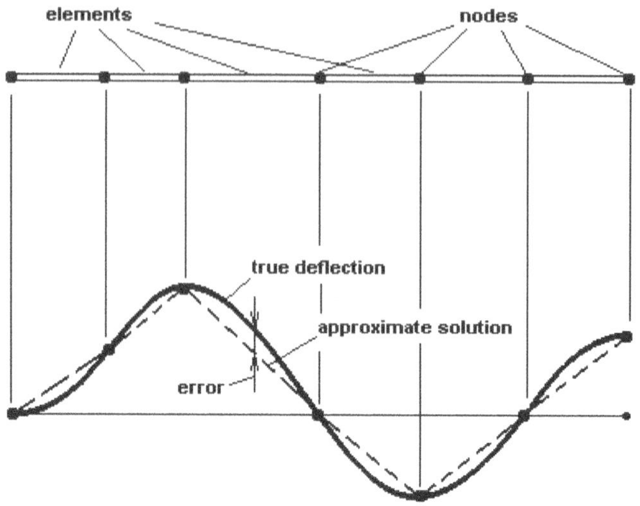

Figure 1–3

Next, the deflection **Y** within each finite element is approximated by a polynomial. In this example, you use linear polynomial **Y = a0 + a1X**, which means that deflection within each element is approximated by essentially a straight line.

Next, the local linear polynomials are sewn together at the nodes, creating a global approximation function in the form of a piece-wise linear polynomial, which is a polyline.

> ***Note:*** *Note that sewing local polynomials at the nodes ensures continuity of the global approximation function, and therefore of the FEA solution for the deflection over the entire beam.*

Finally, the global approximation function is best-fit to satisfy both the bending differential equations and beam boundary conditions (loads and constraints). The resulting function (the dashed line shown in Figure 1–3) now represents the FEA solution for the true deflection (the solid line shown in Figure 1–3) in the beam.

It is important to note that your FEA result contains a certain amount of error, which is the deviation between the true deflection (the solid line shown in Figure 1–3) and the FEA solution (the dashed line shown in Figure 1–3), and which is called a *discretization error*.

Any FEA solution is just an approximation, which means it always contains a discretization error. Therefore, in the FEA process, it is critical to know how to estimate, how to control, and how to reduce this unavoidable approximation error to acceptable levels.

1.2 FEA Solution Refinement

The process of bringing the FEA approximation error to acceptable levels is typically called *solution refinement*. There are two alternative ways in which an FEA solution can be refined.

The first option involves making the finite elements in the mesh progressively smaller while maintaining the order of polynomials within each element.

For example, consider the beam shown in Figure 1–3. If you make the finite elements smaller without changing anything else, the approximation error becomes smaller as well, as shown in Figure 1–4.

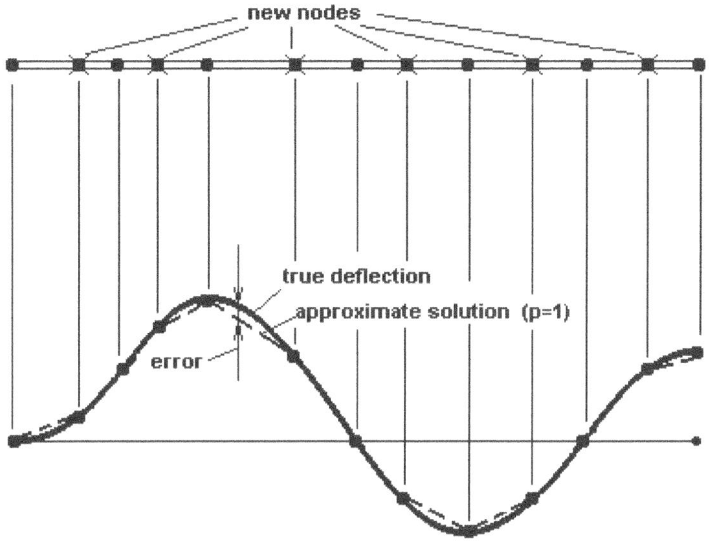

Figure 1–4

This approach is called *h-refinement* because the letter *h* in FEA literature typically refers to the size of the finite elements in the mesh. It is also worth noting that h-refinement requires re-meshing the model every time you need a more accurate solution.

The h-refinement approach is used by most FEA software systems that are commercially available today. However, this is not the only available option.

An alternative strategy involves increasing the order of polynomials within the finite elements, without changing the elements' sizes.

Again, consider the example of the beam shown in Figure 1–3. If you use second-degree polynomials $\mathbf{Y = a_0 + a_1X + a_2X2}$ to approximate the deflection within each element, this results in a more accurate solution, without needing to make the finite elements smaller, as shown in Figure 1–5.

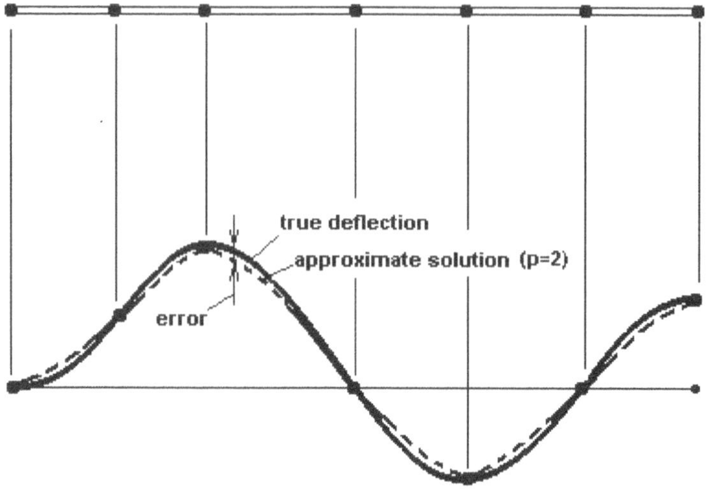

Figure 1–5

This approach is called *p-refinement*, because the letter *p* in FEA literature typically refers to the order of polynomials, and the process of progressively increasing the polynomial order is called *polynomial escalation*.

The p-refinement mathematical apparatus has been historically developed much later than the h-refinement. Today, the p-refinement approach is only used by a few commercial FEA software systems, one of which is Creo Simulate.

1.3 P-Elements

Creo Simulate exclusively uses p-elements and p-refinement technology to ensure the accuracy of the solution. The maximum polynomial order in Creo Simulate can be as high as 9. (The maximum polynomial order in the h-version of FEA is typically 2.)

The advantages of p-technology over h-technology are as follows:

- Solution accuracy can be improved without having to re-mesh the model.
- P-elements use hierarchical polynomials, which permits the use of different polynomial orders in different areas of the model for better efficiency.

  Note: *The rate of convergence refers to how quickly the refinement process converges to the true solution.*

- The rate of convergence to the true solution is greater than that of the h-technology.
- High stress gradients, such as in stress concentrators, are simulated extremely well.
- The restrictions on the shape of elements (aspect ratio, skewness, etc.) are less stringent. Therefore a p-mesh always contains fewer elements that an h-mesh.
- P-elements have curvilinear boundaries and tend to approximate CAD geometry very well.

1.4 Convergence Methods

Convergence in FEA (also called *adaptivity*) is a process of automatic solution refinement to achieve the required accuracy. In other words, the FEA software automatically *adapts* the solution parameters to better fit the true solution.

One of the key advantages of p-refinement over h-refinement is that p-elements permit an adaptive solution improvement without re-meshing the model. Instead, the maximum orders of polynomials used to approximate the solution are increased as required. The solution process can then be repeated on the same mesh, with the new increased polynomial orders. Such an adaptive step (called *pass* in Creo Simulate) can be repeated until the required accuracy is achieved.

In p-elements, the polynomial orders (called *P-levels* in Creo Simulate) can be assigned independently to each edge, face, or solid in the mesh. Using the convergence algorithm, Creo Simulate can pick P-levels independently for each mesh edge in the model, the goal being to select just the correct P-levels to achieve the required solution accuracy at minimum computational expense.

Multi-Pass Adaptivity (MPA) is the most commonly used convergence method in Creo Simulate. To identify the edges that warrant a P-level increase, the MPA algorithm compares displacements and element strain energies on the current solution pass with the corresponding values on the previous pass. Where the difference is larger than the user-specified percentage (i.e., convergence percentage), the P-level is increased and otherwise left unchanged. This process is repeated until the user-specified convergence percentage for the solution is met. The convergence criteria might include percentages on the default local and global quantities, such as displacement, strain energy, and RMS stress, but could also involve user-defined solution parameters.

The MPA convergence graphs can be visualized once the analysis has finished, as shown in Figure 1–6.

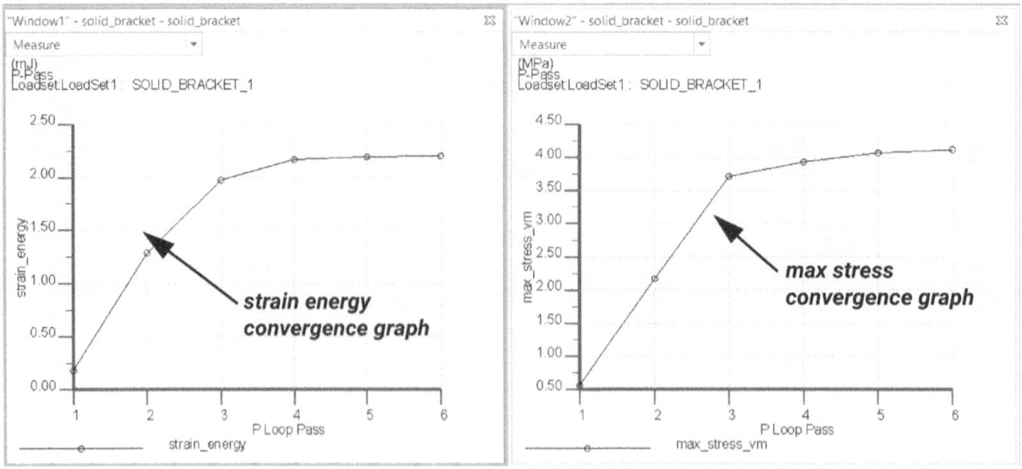

Figure 1–6

Since convergence percentage(s) are selected by the user, the MPA algorithm provides the user with maximum control, and is best used if the accuracy of the solution is critical.

The second convergence algorithm in Creo Simulate, called *Single-Pass Adaptivity* (SPA), uses a different theoretical foundation to reach an accurate solution.

The SPA algorithm is based on the fact that, although displacements in an FEA solution are continuous between elements, stresses are not, and the magnitude of stress jump at the discontinuity is a good indicator of the solution accuracy (i.e., the greater the stress jump, the less accurate the solution).

In the SPA algorithm, Creo Simulate first calculates the solution for P-level 3, assigned uniformly to all edges, and average stress discontinuities around each element (i.e. element error indicators) are computed. The P-levels of edges belonging to elements with large stress jumps are increased. Edges of elements with larger errors receive a higher P-level increase than edges of elements with lower errors. The solution is then repeated, and the result obtained at this point is taken as the final answer. The element error indicators are recomputed to indicate the overall stress accuracy.

Since only two convergence passes are performed in SPA, the computation time is typically much shorter than in MPA.

No convergence graphs are available in the SPA algorithm. Instead, the RMS stress error estimate is printed out to the Creo Simulate report file, as shown in Figure 1–7.

```
RMS Stress Error Estimates:

Load Set          Stress Error  % of Max Prin Str
----------------  ------------  -----------------
LoadSet1           1.26e+01       10.3% of   1.22e+02
```

Figure 1–7

The SPA algorithm has been optimized by PTC with the goal of obtaining as good or better result as using the MPA convergence with the default (10%) convergence percentage.

The SPA convergence method provides limited control over the accuracy of the solution. Therefore, it should be reserved for quick design-analysis iterations when solution accuracy is not critical.

The third convergence method in Creo Simulate is called *Quick Check*, and does not perform a convergence process. The model is only run once, with all of the P-levels fixed at 3. The results of a Quick Check should not be trusted. The intention of a Quick Check analysis is to quickly run the model through the solver to detect any potential modeling errors (such as in constraints), before committing to a more lengthy analysis run (such as when using MPA).

1.5 Types of Analysis in Creo Simulate

Creo Simulate analysis capabilities straddle two physics domains:

- **Structural:** Determines deformations, stresses, and strains in solid bodies caused by external forces, moments, and other types of loading.
- **Thermal:** Determines temperatures and heat fluxes in solid bodies due to heat sources and/or sinks.

The Structural part of Creo Simulate can perform the following types of analysis:

- Static (including nonlinear material models, large displacements, and contact)
- Pre-stress Static
- Buckling
- Fatigue
- Modal (Natural Vibrations)
- Pre-stress Modal
- Dynamic Time Response
- Dynamic Frequency Response
- Dynamic Random Response
- Dynamic Shock Response

The two options for the Thermal analysis are as follows:

- Steady State Thermal analysis
- Transient Thermal analysis

The models in Creo Simulate can be analyzed in 3D formulations (purely solids, or combinations of solids, shells, and beams) or 2D formulations (plane stress, plane strain, or axisymmetric).

1.6 FEA Process

A typical FEA analysis process in Creo Simulate consists of three principle steps, as shown in Figure 1–8:

- **Pre-processing:** All input data for the analysis is prepared, such as material properties, loads, and constraints.
- **Solution:** The convergence type and criteria are specified and the analysis computation is performed.
- **Post-processing:** The analysis results are reviewed and verified. A report is prepared.

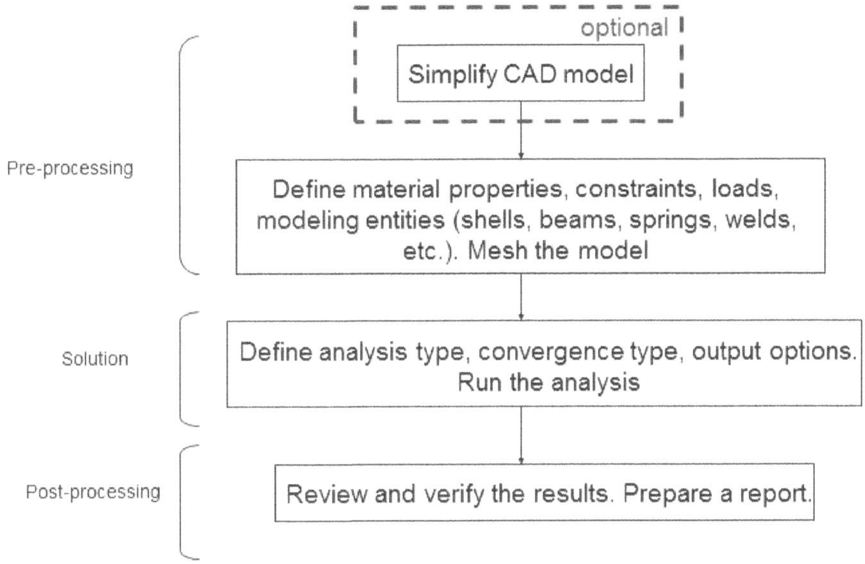

Figure 1–8

The CAD model simplification step is optional. It might not be required, depending on the complexity of the model.

1.7 CAD Model Preparation

A CAD model is developed to provide detailed information for manufacturing. All of the required information related to fillets, rounds, holes, and threads must be included. Processing steps and surface finishes are indicated and dimensions are fully specified.

An FEA model is developed to determine model behavior under a specific set of loading and boundary conditions. To analyze a model effectively, an FEA model is often different from a model developed for manufacturing. The symmetry of a model can often be used. Minor features, such as rounds, fillets, chamfers, and holes, can often be ignored unless they have a large effect on the result. Therefore, the general recommendation is to use the simplest model possible that is going to yield reliable results at the lowest computational time and cost.

In the example shown in Figure 1–9, the area of interest is the stress in the weld between two pipes due to high pressure. The FEA model within the component is shown on the right. In this case, the symmetry of the component (1/2 of the component) is used for the FEA model. The minor rounds, fillets, chamfers, and holes are ignored. The CAD model prepared for FEA would be different if the area of interest was the stress at the intersection of lips and pipes.

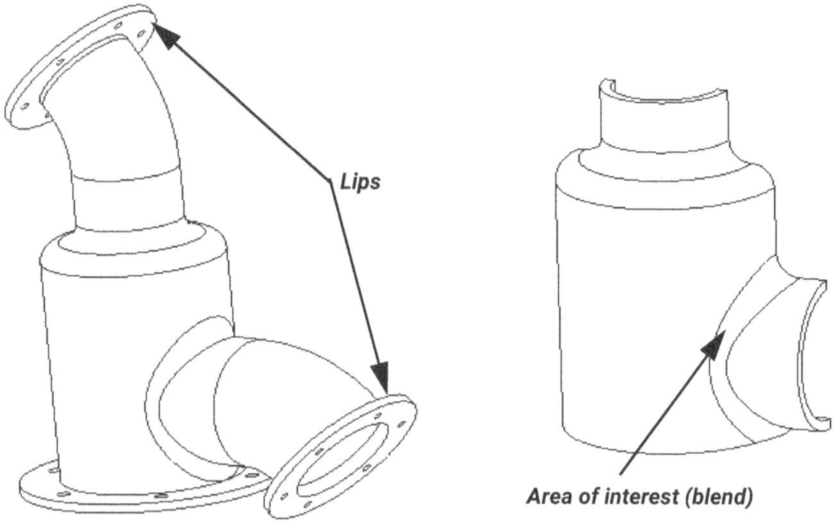

Figure 1–9

1.8 Creo Simulate Modes of Operation

Creo Simulate can operate in the following modes:

- **Integrated:** The simulation is fully integrated within the Creo Parametric design process (i.e., the models can be analyzed without ever leaving the Creo Parametric user interface). This is the most common way to use Creo Simulate.
- **Standalone:** Enables the loading of CAD models directly into Creo Simulate, without first loading Creo Parametric. This is useful if models originating from different software than Creo Parametric need to be analyzed.
- **FEM:** Provides pre- and post-processing capabilities only. The model has to be exported to a neutral file format and then solved by a third party FEA solver (ANSYS, NASTRAN, etc.). H-elements meshing is used.
- **Simulate Lite:** Limited model size of up to 200 surfaces and also has a limited user interface. Does not require a Simulate license.

This learning guide focuses on the Integrated mode, which provides the most streamlined approach to part or assembly simulation and optimization within the Creo environment.

Chapter 2

Basic Creo Simulate Modeling

You will learn about the tools and process required to set up your model for analysis. You will also learn how to set up and run an analysis and then view the results.

Learning Objectives

- Understand the Creo Simulate analysis steps and options.
- Launch Creo Simulate from Creo Parametric.
- Use the Creo Simulate user interface.
- Define the model type.
- Create idealizations.
- Apply material, constraints, and loads.
- Mesh the model.
- Create a design study and a structural analysis.
- Select a convergence method.
- Understand the files and directories created by Creo Simulate.
- Understand the concepts of result verification.
- Visualize analysis results.

2.1 Launching Creo Simulate

The Finite element analysis process contains three different components: pre-processing, analysis, and post-processing. Each component contains a number of steps, as shown in Figure 2–1.

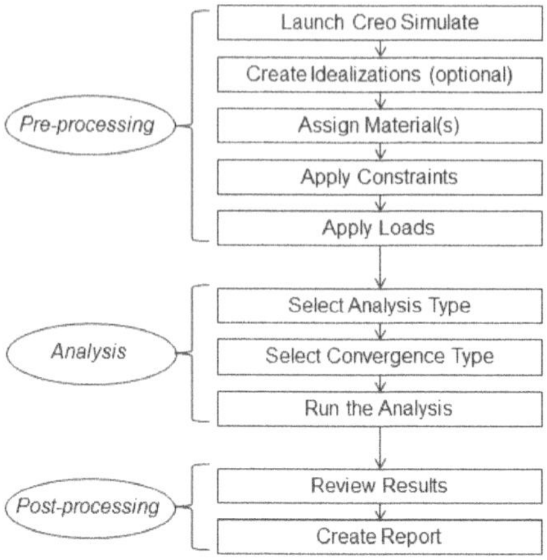

Figure 2–1

Each step in the structural analysis process requires a selection of the following options.

Model Analysis Steps	**Creo Simulate Structure Options**	
Model Type	3D Plane Stress Axisymmetric	Plane Strain 2D
Element Type	Shell Beams Solid	Springs Mass
Analysis Methods	Static Modal Buckling Prestress modal Prestress static	Dynamic Time Dynamic Frequency Dynamic Random Dynamic Shock Fatigue
Convergence Methods	Multi-Pass Adaptive Single-Pass Adaptive	Quick Check
Design Studies	Standard Optimization	Sensitivity

To launch Creo Simulate in Integrated mode, open the model in Creo Parametric, select the *Applications* tab, and click (Simulate). The Creo Simulate environment opens, the ribbon appearance changes as shown in Figure 2–2, and a coordinate system labeled **WCS** is automatically added to the model.

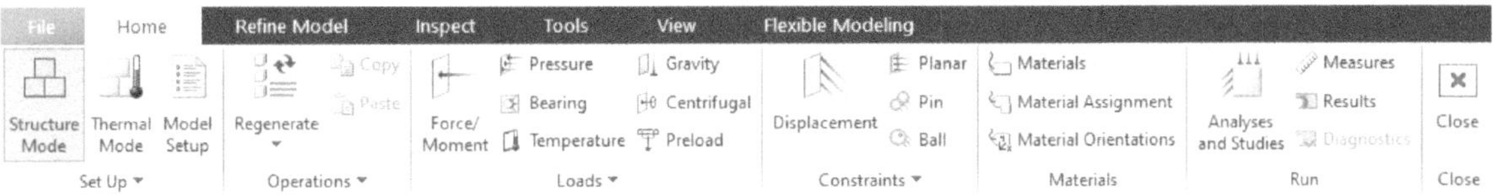

Figure 2–2

By default, Creo Simulate opens in Structure mode. To switch to Thermal mode if required, click (Thermal Mode).

Note that several options available in the ribbon are also available in the mini-toolbar, which displays after selecting entities on the model, as shown in Figure 2–3.

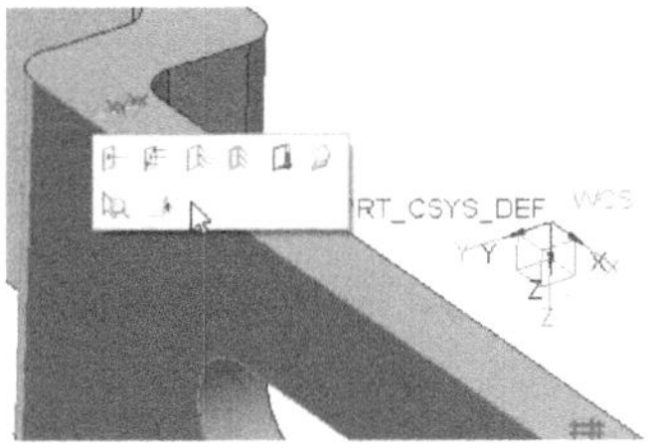

Figure 2–3

Structure Ribbon

The Structure mode ribbon contains several tabs, including *Home*, *Refine Model*, *Inspect*, *Tools*, *View*, and *Flexible Modeling*.

The *Home* tab (shown in Figure 2–2) contains all of the most frequently used analysis tools, such as model setup, loads, constraints, analysis setup, and access to the analysis results.

The *Refine Model* tab contains tools, such as idealizations, connections, regions, and meshing as shown in Figure 2–4.

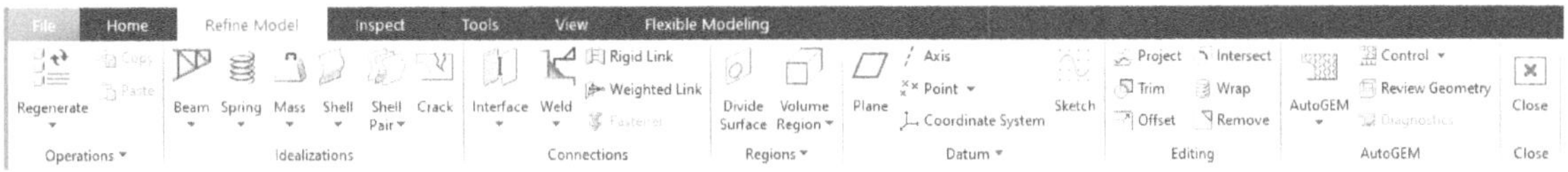

Figure 2–4

The *Inspect*, *Tools*, and *View* tabs contain common Creo tools, such as measurements, layers, views, appearances, etc.

2.2 Modeling Steps

Defining Model Type

By default, Creo Simulate assumes that the model you want to analyze is 3D. To change the analysis model type to 2D, click (Model Setup) and click **Advanced** to open the *Model Setup* dialog box, as shown in Figure 2–5.

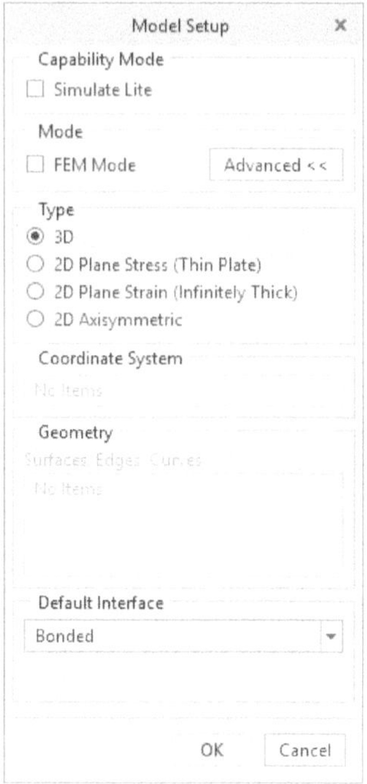

Figure 2–5

Creating Idealizations

Idealizations are tools that simplify your FEA model, resulting in a faster analysis. Idealizations are optional. If your model is not overly complex and solves in a reasonable time, Idealizations might not be required.

The following types of Idealizations are available in Creo Simulate, as shown in Figure 2–6:

- Beams
- Springs
- Masses
- Shells
- Cracks

Figure 2–6

Applying Material

In Creo Simulate, applying a material to your analysis model must be done in two steps:

- Import material definition into the model.
- Assign the imported material to your part.

If a material has already been applied to your part in Creo Parametric, it is automatically imported into the Creo Simulate model as well, but not assigned.

To assign the imported material, click (Material Assignment) to open the *Material Assignment* dialog box, as shown in Figure 2–7. Select **References**, select a material, and click **OK** to close the dialog box.

Figure 2–7

> ***Note:*** *The* ***Material Orientation*** *option only applies to non-isotropic materials, such as laminates, etc.*

If a material has not been applied in the Creo Parametric environment, you must import a material definition into your model from within the Creo Simulate environment.

To import a material definition, click (Materials) to open the *Materials* dialog box, as shown in Figure 2–8.

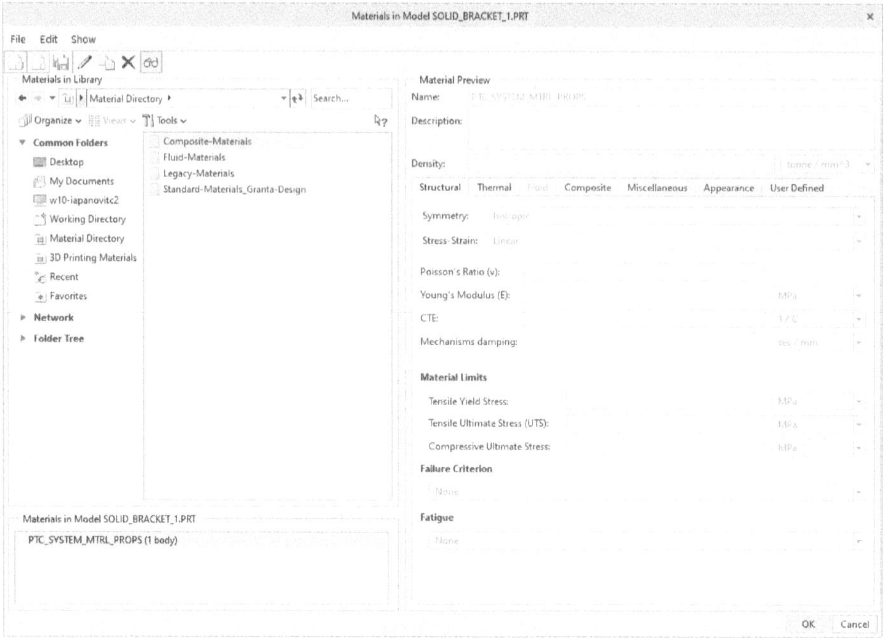

Figure 2–8

> ***Note:*** *The* ***PTC_SYSTEM_MTRL_PROPS*** *is the material applied in the Creo Parametric environment. If no material has been applied in Creo Parametric, the* ***PTC_SYSTEM_MTRL_PROPS*** *has no valid mechanical properties.*

Expand the **Legacy-Materials** or **Standard-Materials_ Granta-Design** folder and double-click on any available material. The material will be added to the *Materials in Model* field, as shown in Figure 2–9.

Figure 2–9

The material properties display in the *Material Preview* area of the *Materials* dialog box, as shown in Figure 2–10.

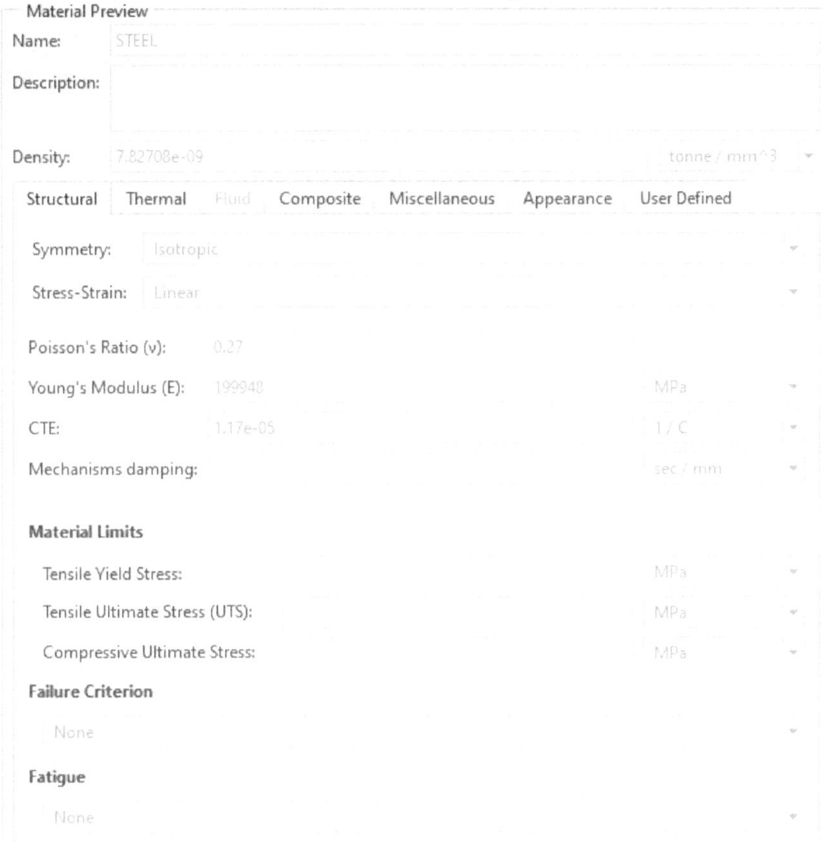

Figure 2–10

To edit the material properties, click (Edit).

Applying Constraints

Constraints simulate supports and other boundary conditions in your model. Constraints can be applied to the part's surfaces, edges/curves, or points.

The following types of constraints are available in Creo Simulate, as shown in Figure 2–11:

- Displacements
- Planar
- Pin
- Ball
- Symmetry

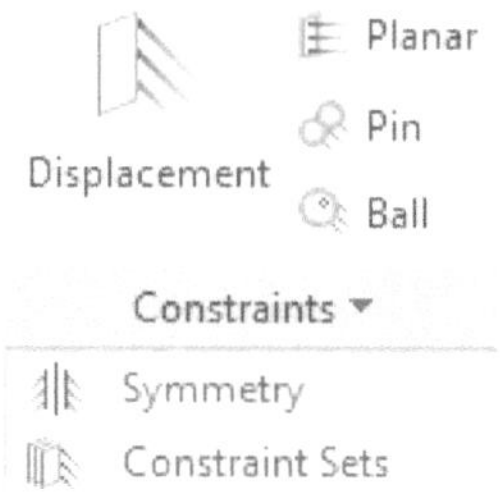

Figure 2–11

Applying Loads

Loads in your analysis are intended to simulate the actual loading conditions in your model.

The following types of loads are available in Creo Simulate, as shown in Figure 2–12:

- Force/Moment
- Pressure
- Bearing
- Temperature
- Gravity
- Centrifugal
- Preload

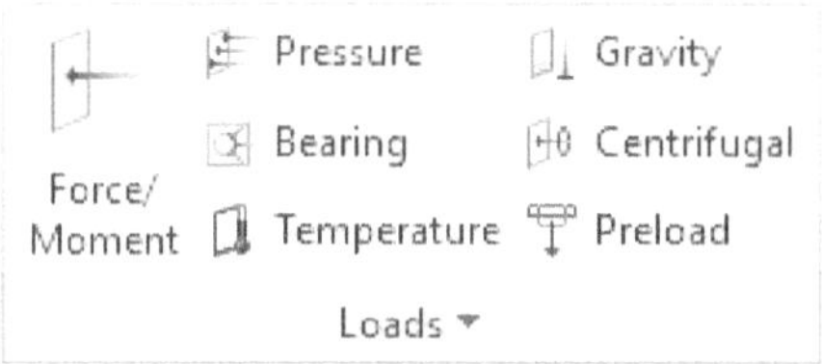

Figure 2–12

The type of geometry you can apply a load to depends on the type of load selected. For example, **Force/Moment** loads can be applied to surfaces, edges/curves, or points, while **Pressure** or **Bearing** loads can only be applied to surfaces.

Meshing the Model

Meshing the model before running the analysis is optional in Creo Simulate. If not pre-meshed, the model is automatically meshed during the analysis computation.

However, pre-meshing the model helps to indicate whether Creo Simulate can mesh your model successfully, and to roughly estimate the analysis runtime based on the number of elements in the mesh.

To mesh the model before the analysis, click (AutoGEM) in the *Refine Model* tab to open the *AutoGEM* dialog box, as shown in Figure 2–13.

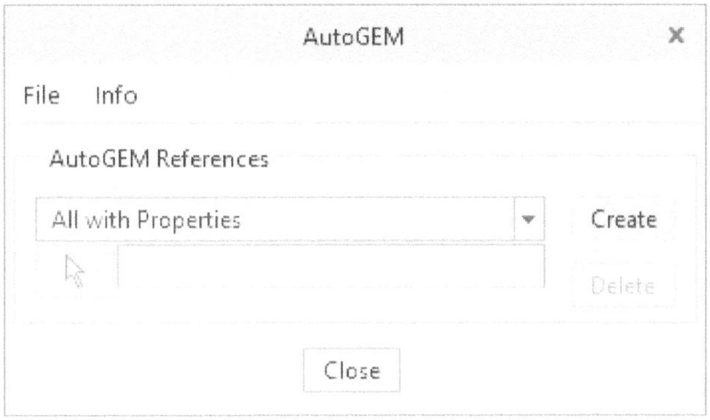

Figure 2–13

The options in the *References* drop-down list are as follows:

- **Volume:** Creates solid mesh for selected volumes.
- **Surface:** Creates shell mesh for selected surfaces.
- **Curves:** Creates beam mesh for selected curves.
- **All with Properties:** An all-in-one option, which automatically meshes all volumes with materials assigned, all surfaces with shell properties assigned, and all curves with beam properties assigned. This option is used if mesh is created during the analysis run.

In the *AutoGEM* dialog box, you can review, save, and highlight areas in which the mesh fails.

2.3 Analysis

Analysis Types

Creo Simulate can perform several types of structural analysis on a model. You select an analysis type based on the type of simulation that you want to perform. Click (Analyses and Studies) and select the appropriate option in the **File** menu, as shown in Figure 2–14.

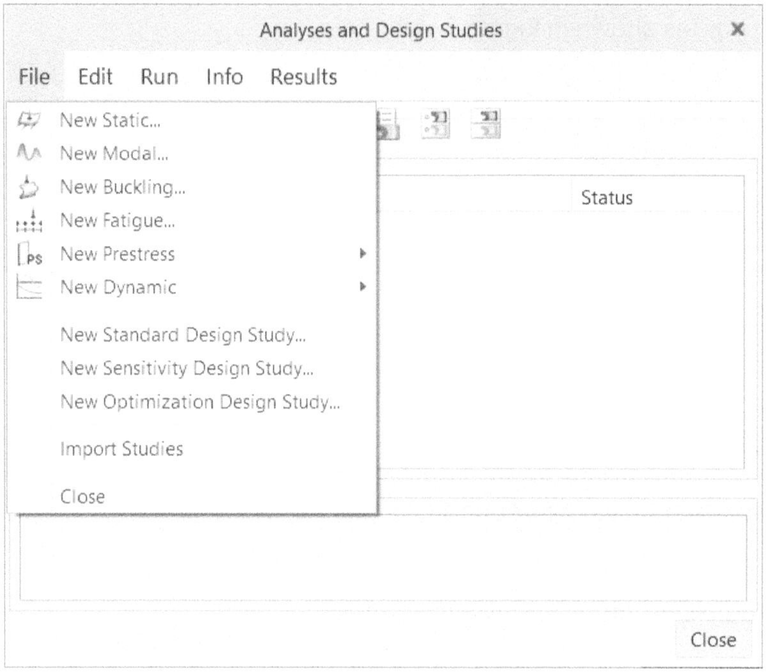

Figure 2–14

The types of structural analysis available in the *Analyses and Design Studies* dialog box are as follows:

Analysis Type	Description
New Static	Static analyses calculate the stresses and deformations in the model, that are caused by static loads.
New Modal	Modal analyses calculate the mode shapes (i.e., characteristic deformed shapes of natural frequencies) and natural frequencies of a model.
New Buckling	Buckling analyses calculate the Buckling Load Factor (BLF), a magnification factor of the applied load that causes buckling to occur. When applying a load of 1 unit to the model, the BLF equals the critical buckling load.

Analysis Type	Description
New Fatigue	Fatigue analyses calculate the effect of repeating or varying loads on a model.
New Prestress	• **Static:** Prestress Static analyses calculate the effect of a prestressed structure on a model's stresses, strains, and deformations. • **Modal:** Prestress Modal analyses calculate the effect of static loads on natural frequencies and modes.
New Dynamic	• **Time:** Dynamic Time analyses calculate displacements, velocities, accelerations, and stresses in response to a load that varies with time. • **Frequency:** Dynamic Frequency analyses determine the response of a system that is subjected to cyclical excitation (a frequency-dependent input). • **Random:** Dynamic Random analyses calculate the power spectral density (PSD) and the root mean square (RMS) values of displacements, velocities, accelerations, and stresses in a model subjected to a random loading. • **Shock:** Dynamic Shock analyses calculate the peak values of displacement and stresses in a model in response to a base excitation defined by a response spectrum curve. This type of analysis subjects a model to an earthquake-like motion.

Convergence Methods

The three analysis convergence options in Creo Simulate are as follows:

Option	Description	Uses
Quick Check	Runs a model through the solver to detect errors (e.g., in the constraints). The model is only run once for a single fixed low polynomial order. If an error occurs, Creo Simulate displays an error message prompting you with: *Run completed with a fatal error.*	• Use to determine whether an analysis has been set up correctly. • Use to generate proper elements. • Use to check problem areas in the model.
Single Pass Adaptive	Runs a model through the solver at a low polynomial order (default 3), evaluates the accuracy of the solution, and modifies the p-element values accordingly. The model is run through the solver a second time with the new p-element values. This provides reasonable results in a short computation time.	• Use for preliminary calculations. • Use when system resources are low.

Option	Description	Uses
Multi-Pass Adaptive	Runs a model through the solver in iterations (or *passes*), with the polynomial order of unconverged elements being increased with each pass. The passes continue until either the solution converges or the maximum order is reached (default 6 and maximum 9). Base your final decisions on the results obtained using this method.	• Use for accurate analysis. • Use when you have enough time and system resources.

Design Studies

Design studies enable you to find better design alternatives using simulation and analysis tools. Creo Simulate can run the following three types of design studies.

Study	Description
Standard	This study calculates the results for a standard analysis (e.g., Static analysis) for an alternative set of dimensions. Analogous to running a single *what if* scenario.
Sensitivity	This study calculates the results for several alternative sets of dimensions within a user-specified range. Analogous to running multiple *what if* scenarios.
Optimization	This study adjusts a model's parameters to meet a specified goal or to test the feasibility of a design. For this study, you assign a goal (e.g., minimum mass of the model) and one or more Creo Parametric dimensions (design variables), which can vary over assigned ranges.

2.4 Results

Files and Directories

Creo Simulate generates many output files that are written to an automatically created directory. The name of the result directory is the same as that of the analysis study. By default, the result directory is placed in the Creo working directory, which can be changed when you set up an analysis.

Create Simulate solver also creates many temporary files, which are only required when the solver is running, and which are automatically deleted on completion of the analysis run. The default location for the temporary files is in the Creo working directory, which can also be changed when you set up an analysis.

The typical files created by Creo Simulate in the result directory are as follows. The names *model*, *study*, and *filename* represent your specified names.

File Format	File/Directory Name	Description
Model Files	*model.mdb*	The .MDB file contains the last-saved model database.
Solver File	*/study/study.mdb*	The engine file contains the entire model database from the time a design study is started.
Solver Output Files	*/study/study.cnv* */study/study.hst* */study/study.res* */study/study.rpt* */study/study.ro1*	The .CNV file contains convergence information. The .HST file is a backup file that updates the model during optimization. The .RES file is a measure at each pass. The .RPT file is an output report that contains information about a run including measure values and warning messages. The .R01 file contains information about the resultant reaction of loads applied to the model.
Exchange Files	*filename.dxf* *filename.igs*	The exchange files are in formats that are used for the import or export of geometry information.
Temporary Files	*/study.tmp/*.tmp* */study.tmp/*.bas*	Temporary files contain the data that is required to solve analyses. They are deleted automatically on completion of the design.
Results Files	*filename.rwd*	The .RWD files store your Result Window plot window for later use.
AutoGEM Files	*model.agm*	The .AGM files store information about the most recent AutoGEM operation.
AutoMesh Files	*modelname.mmp* *modelname.mma*	This file stores a mesh database. The system allocates an .MMP extension to a part model mesh file and an .MMA extension to an assembly model.

Result Verification

Creo Simulate can produce several types of results to help determine the validity and soundness of your model. Take the following considerations into account when interpreting your results.

Result	Description
Reaction Verification	The resultant reaction of loads applied to the model is automatically generated in the .RO1 file. To satisfy the equilibrium criteria, the resultant reaction must equal the resultant loads applied to the model.
Model Integrity	Model integrity determines the integrity of your model by checking the model entities (i.e., material properties, constraints, loads, and unit systems), geometry, and part accuracy before starting the run. You can also use the **Check Model** option to check for errors in the model. If the model fails the check, the model entities were probably incorrectly defined.
Displacement Animation	Displacement animation verifies whether your model is deflecting correctly and that your constraints are correct. The animation simulates the effect of real-world conditions on the model and enables you to compare them to the applied boundary conditions.
Shape Animation	Shape animation (performed after a sensitivity or optimization study) takes the geometry through the entire range of relevant parameters. This ensures that no unexpected regeneration failures occur and that the design intent is sound.
Computational Solution Quality	Computational solution quality is the percentage of error that the system calculates on the maximum principle stress. A low percentage indicates that the model is sound. This error estimate can be found in the .RPT file in the analysis directory.
Convergence Criteria	Provides an idea of the accuracy of your results. Convergence results with specific limits set by the user can be found in the .RPT file. You can create graphs based on predefined measures for strain energy and displacement.

Result Visualization

Creo Simulate enables you to visualize many different types of results:

- Displacements
- Stresses
- Strains
- Reactions
- Strain Energy
- P-Levels

The results can be displayed as a fringe plot or as a graph along an edge or curve. Fringe plots can be animated for better understanding of the model deformation.

The results are visualized and manipulated in the Creo Simulate Results environment. An overview of the icons and options available in this environment is shown in Figure 2–15.

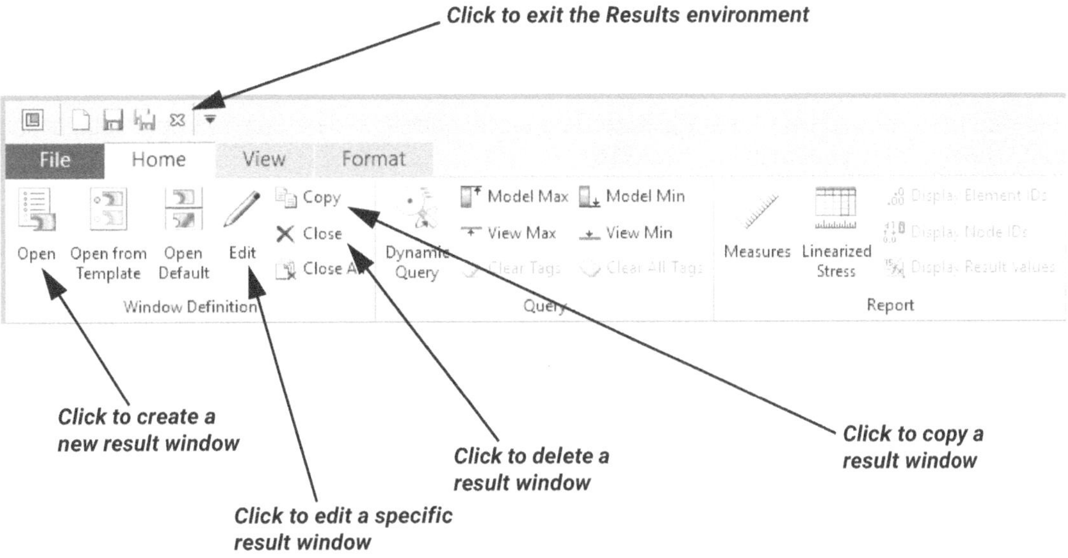

Figure 2–15

You can enter the Creo Simulate Results environment using one of the following options:

- Click (Review Results) in the *Analyses and Design Studies* dialog box.
- Click (Results) in the Creo Simulate interface, in the *Home* tab.
- Click (Simulate Results) in the Creo Parametric interface, in the *Applications* tab. This options enables you to open the Creo Simulate results without having to open a corresponding Creo Simulate model first.

Practice 2a
Static Stress Analysis of a Bracket

Practice Objectives

- Specify a 3D model type.
- Mesh the model.
- Set the loads, constraints, and material properties.
- Check the validity of the model.
- Set up and run a Quick Check analysis.
- Set up and run a Multi-Pass Adaptive analysis.
- Display the results.
- Animate and create sections through the part.

In this practice, you will mesh, set up, and run a static stress analysis on a simple solid bracket model. The model is shown in Figure 2–16.

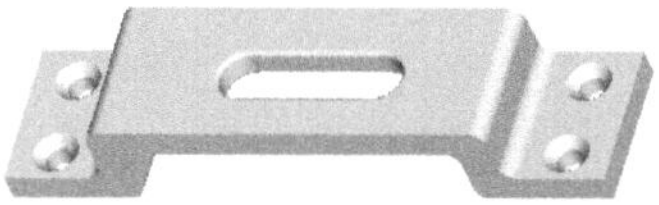

Figure 2–16

Modeling Tasks

In the following tasks, you will create the simulation entities required to analyze your model.

Task 1: Open the solid_bracket_1 part in Creo Parametric.

1. Set the working directory to **Chapter02**.
2. Open **solid_bracket_1.prt**.
3. Set the model display as follows:
   - *(Datum Display Filters)*: (Csys Display) Only
   - *(Spin Center)*: Off
   - *(Display Style)*: (Shading With Edges)

The part displays as shown in Figure 2–17.

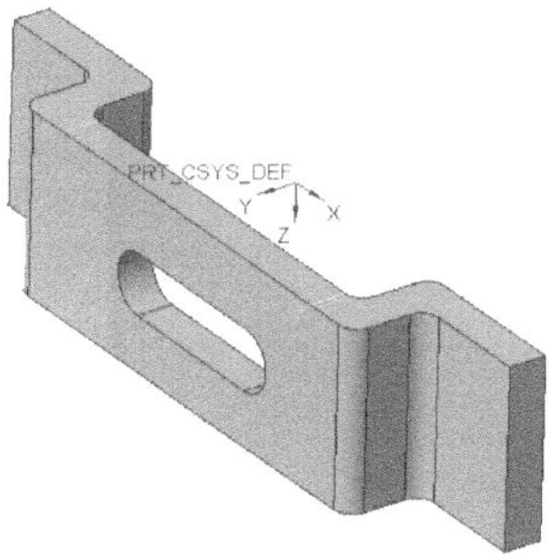

Figure 2–17

Note: The model has been defeatured. The rounds on the middle hole and bolt holes have been removed.

4. Select **File>Prepare>Model Properties** to check your unit system. The unit system for this practice is **mmNs**. Close the *Model Properties* dialog box.

Task 2: Launch Creo Simulate.

1. Select **Applications>Simulate** to launch the Creo Simulate environment.
2. Verify that (Structure Mode) is active. The model displays as shown in Figure 2–18. Verify that the datum coordinate system visibility is toggled on. Note that the WCS coordinate system displays in the model window.

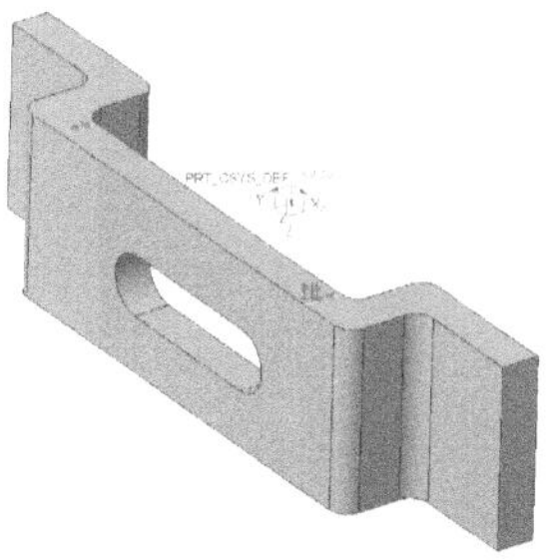

Figure 2–18

Note: WCS represents the World Cartesian System (the origin is at 0,0,0).

Task 3: Define the model type.

1. In the *Home* tab, click (Model Setup) and click **Advanced** to expand the *Model Setup* dialog box.
2. In the *Model Setup* dialog box, verify that the **3D** option is selected and click **OK**.

Task 4: Mesh the bracket part.

In this task, you will mesh the bracket, which enables you to check whether Creo Simulate can mesh your model before analysis. Using this option before applying simulation entities (e.g., loads or constraints) highlights the areas (geometry) where the mesh has failed in your model. This option speeds up the analysis run time.

1. Select the *Refine Model* tab, then expand the (AutoGEM) flyout and select **Settings**, as shown in Figure 2–19.

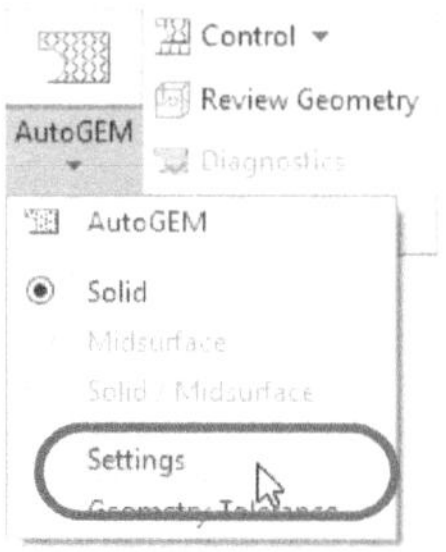

Figure 2–19

2. The *AutoGEM Settings* dialog box opens, as shown in Figure 2–20.

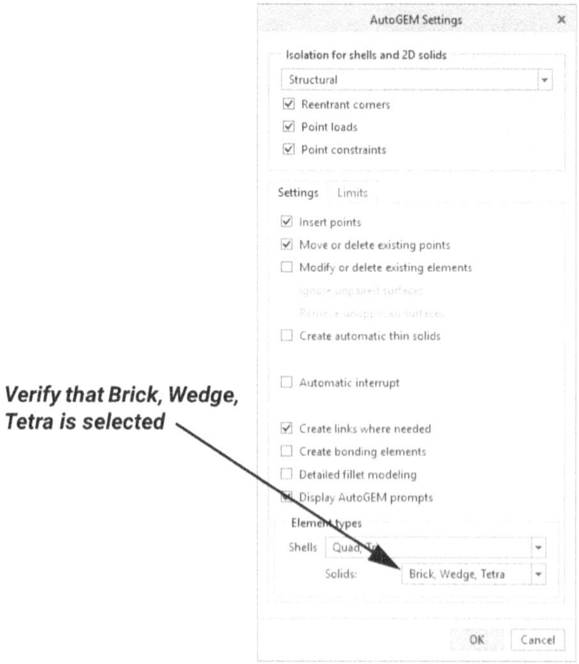

Figure 2–20

3. Select the *Limits* tab, as shown in Figure 2–21.

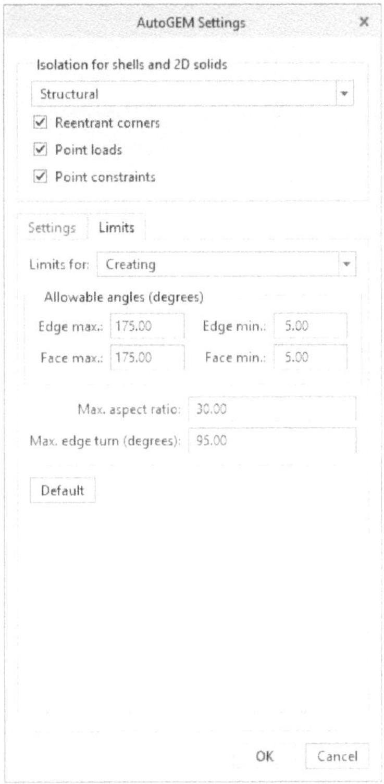

Figure 2–21

4. In the *AutoGEM Settings* dialog box, four types of settings display in *Limits* tab: **Edge Angles**, **Face Angles**, **Edge Turn**, and **Aspect Ratio**.
   - The allowable edge angles (**Edge Max** and **Edge Min**) between the edges of an element are shown in Figure 2–22.

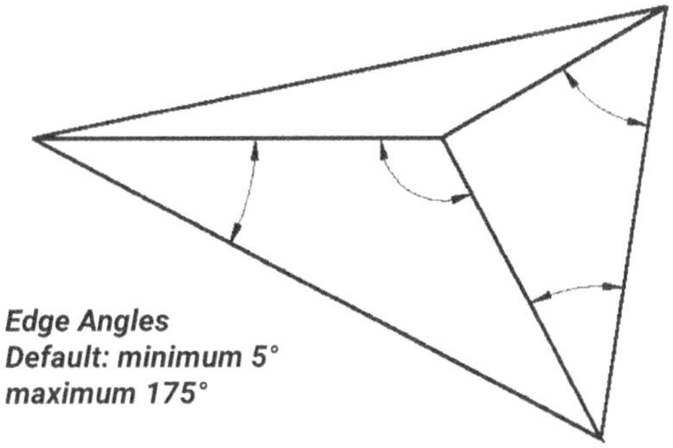

Figure 2–22

- The allowable face angles (**Face Max** and **Face Min**) between the faces of an element are shown in Figure 2–23.

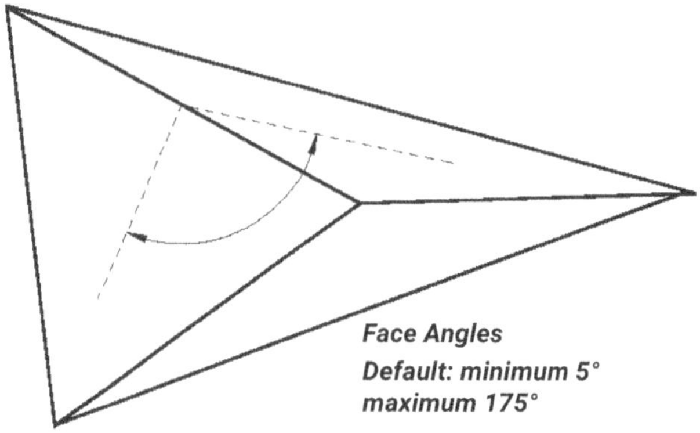

Figure 2–23

- The maximum allowable edge turns (**Max Edge Turn**) between 45° and 95° are shown in Figure 2–24. This limit has a valid range from 1° to 100°.

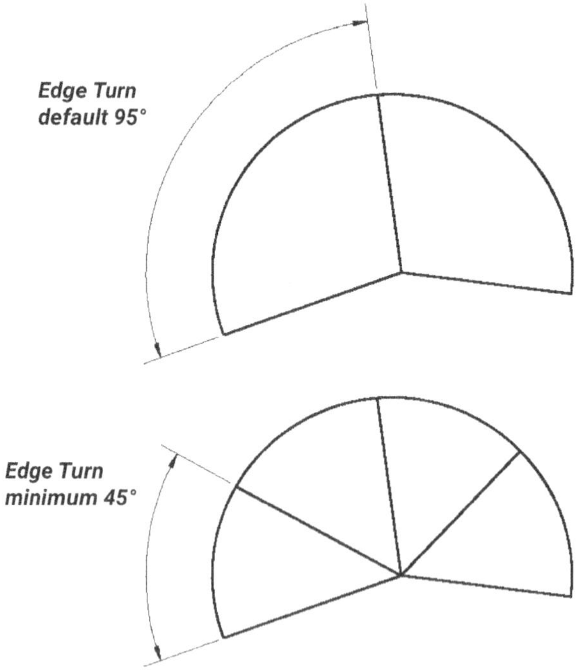

Figure 2–24

Note: *The maximum allowable Edge Turn enables you to create elements that better conform to the shape of the geometry on circles and cylinders.*

- The maximum allowable aspect ratio (**Max Aspect Ratio**), which is the ratio of length to width of an element, is shown in Figure 2–25.

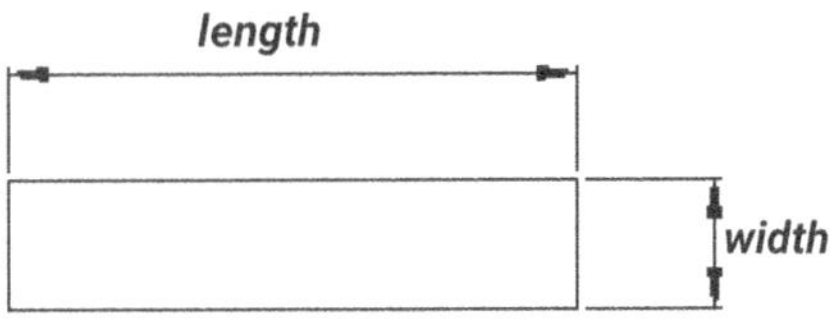

Figure 2–25

5. Click **OK** to close the *AutoGEM Settings* dialog box.

6. Click (AutoGEM). The *AutoGEM* dialog box opens, as shown in Figure 2–26.

Figure 2–26

7. Expand the *AutoGEM References* drop-down list and select **Volume**.

8. Click (Select Geometry) and select any surface on the model.
9. In the *Surface Selection* dialog box, click **OK** or click the middle mouse button.
10. Click **Create**.

    AutoGEM starts to pre-process the model and display these functions in the Creo message window. When initial processing is finished, AutoGEM creates and optimizes elements. The AutoGEM optimization process reduces the number of elements by 50% on average. If any of these functions (e.g., pre-processing or creating elements) takes more than 30 seconds, the system displays a message indicating their progress.

The message window for **solid_bracket_1** is shown in Figure 2–27.

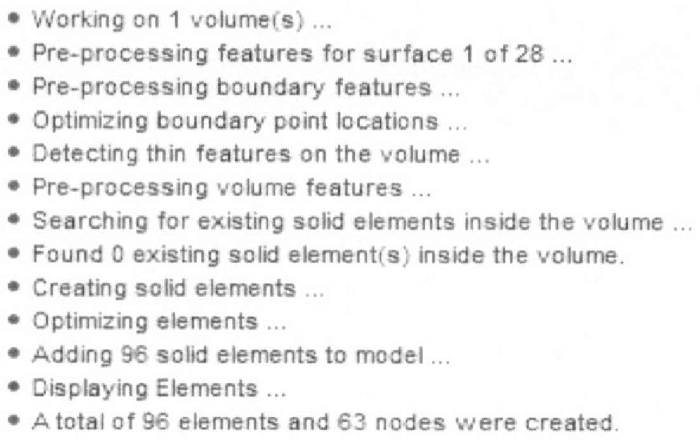

Figure 2–27

After a short time, the *AutoGEM Summary* and the *Diagnostics* dialog boxes open, as shown in Figure 2–28.

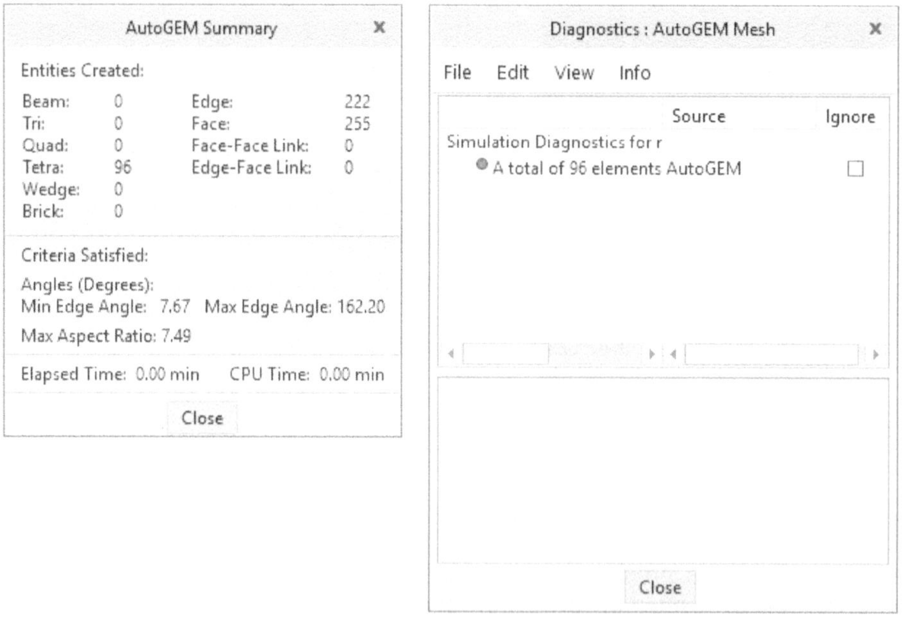

Figure 2–28

Examine the information in the boxes. For example, note that the system has discretized the volume into approximately 96 tetrahedron solid elements.

11. Close both the *AutoGEM Summary* and *Diagnostics* boxes, but do not close the *AutoGEM* dialog box yet. The model displays as shown in Figure 2–29.

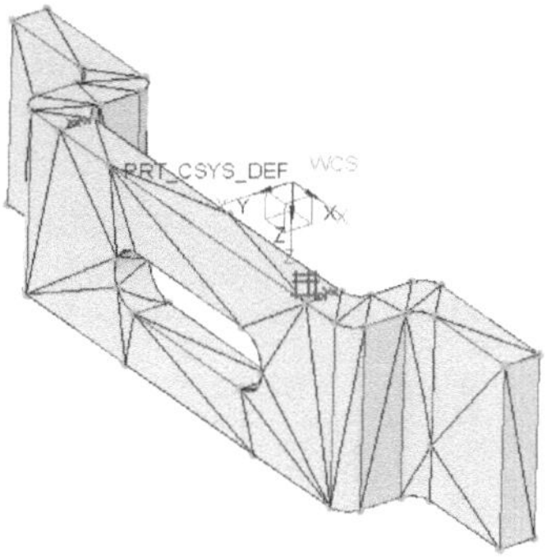

Figure 2–29

12. In the In-graphics toolbar, click (Simulation Display). The *Simulation Display* dialog box opens.
13. Select the *Mesh* tab. In the *Mesh Display* area, select the **Shrink Elements** option and increase the shrinkage value to 20%, as shown in Figure 2–30.

Figure 2–30

Note: *The* ***Shrink Elements*** *option does not affect the analysis. It is a visualization tool that helps you display the mesh clearly.*

14. Click **OK** to close the *Simulation Display* dialog box. The model displays as shown in Figure 2–31. Spin the model and review the elements in various areas of the model.

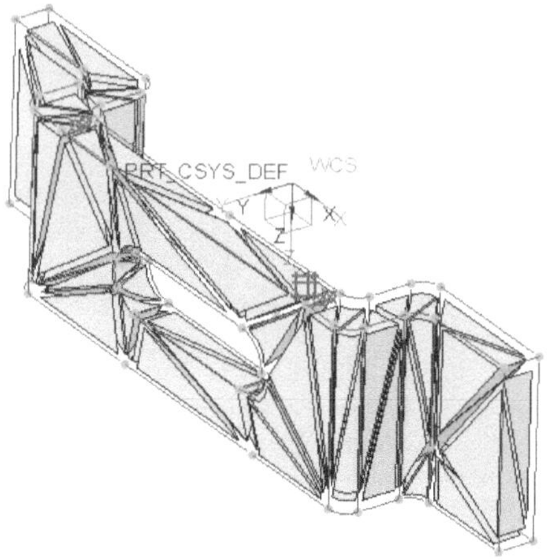

Figure 2–31

15. Click **Close** to close the *AutoGEM* dialog box, and the warning shown in Figure 2–32 will display.

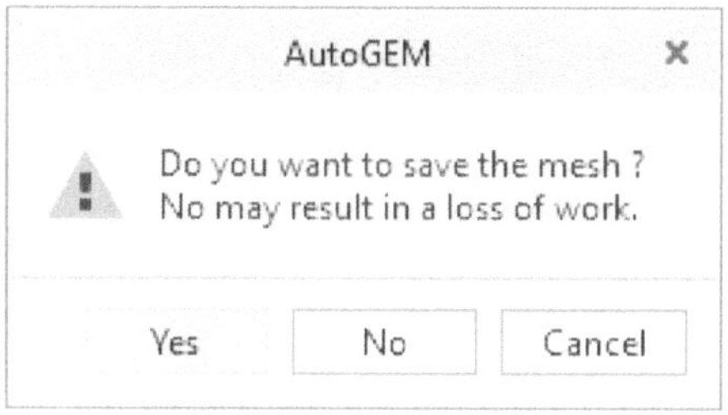

Figure 2–32

16. Click **Yes** to save the mesh.

The following three types of solid elements are commonly used:

Element	Description	Example
Hexahedron (brick)	Brick has 12 edges, 8 nodes, and 6 quad faces.	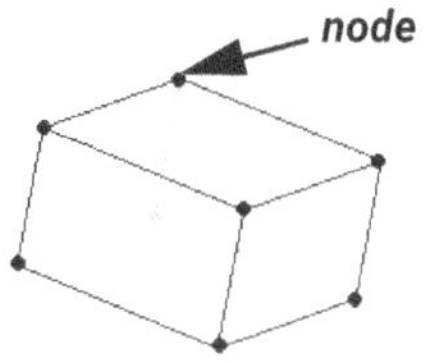
Pentahedron (wedge)	Wedge has 9 edges, 6 nodes, 2 triangular faces, and 3 quad faces.	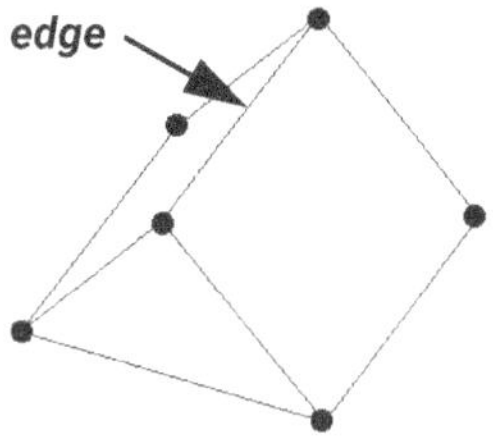
Tetrahedron (tetra)	Tetra has 6 edges, 4 nodes, and 4 triangular faces.	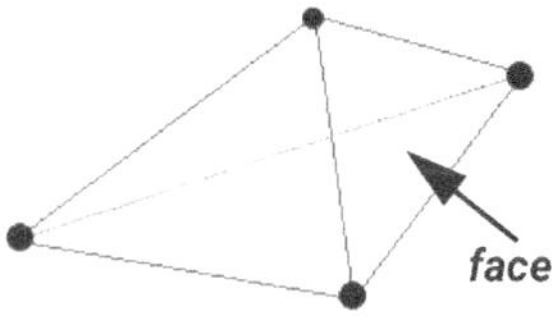

Task 5: Apply loads to the surface of the model.

In this task, you will apply loads to the surface of the model shown in Figure 2–33 to simulate the bracket loading. This task assumes that the bracket carries a load of 140kg (approx.) at 45° to vertical.

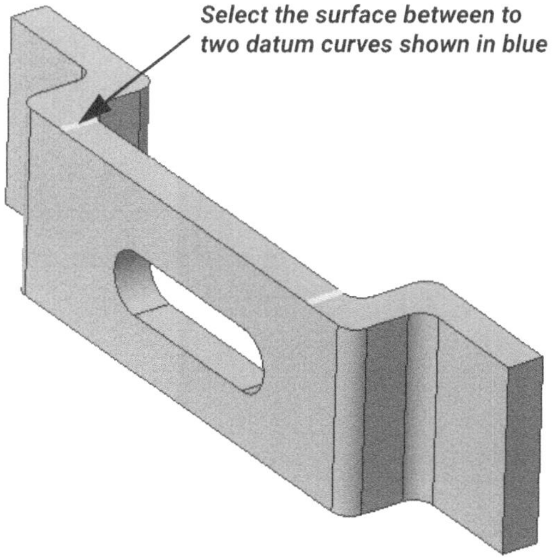

Figure 2–33

1. Select the *Home* tab and click (Force/Moment). The *Force/Moment Load* dialog box opens, as shown in Figure 2–34.

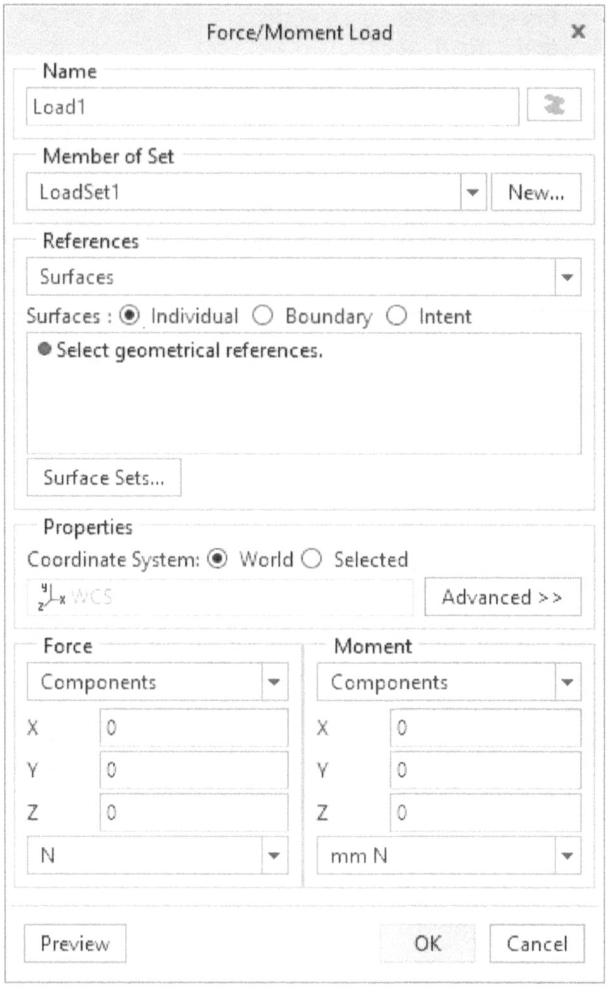

Figure 2–34

2. In the *Name* field, enter **surf_load**. For *Member of Set*, accept the default **LoadSet1** option.

3. Select the region of the surface between the two lines, as shown in Figure 2–35.

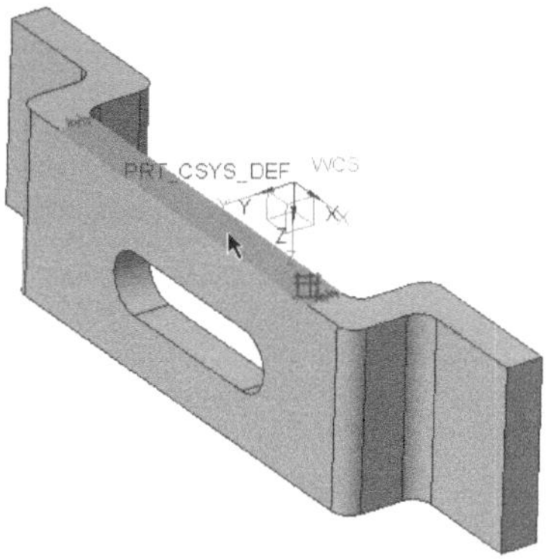

Figure 2–35

> ***Note:*** *You can also select the surface first and select (Force/Moment) from the mini-toolbar.*

4. In the *Force/Moment Load* dialog box, note that the loads are defined relative to the WCS coordinate system, as indicated in the *Properties* area.
5. Click **Advanced** to display the distribution and spatial variation options. Expand and examine the drop-down lists and accept the default options.
6. Ensure that the *Force* drop-down list displays the **Components** option.
7. In the *Force* area, in the *Y* field, enter **1000**.
8. In the *Force* area, in the *Z* field, enter **1000**.
9. Click **Preview** to display the applied load in the model.
10. Click **OK** to finish applying the load to the solid model. The load displays as shown in Figure 2–36.

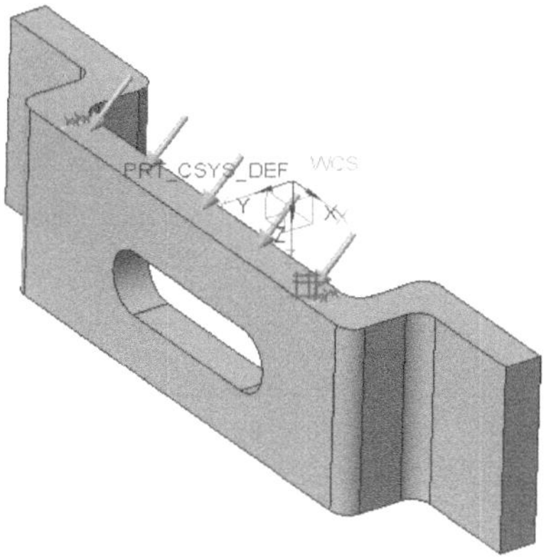

Figure 2–36

11. In the In-graphics toolbar, click (Simulation Display) to open the *Simulation Display* dialog box.

    Note: *Explore the different options in the Simulation Display dialog box.*

12. In the *Settings* tab, in the *Load and Constraint Display* area, enable the **Values** option.
13. Click **OK** to close the *Simulation Display* dialog box. The model displays as shown in Figure 2–37.

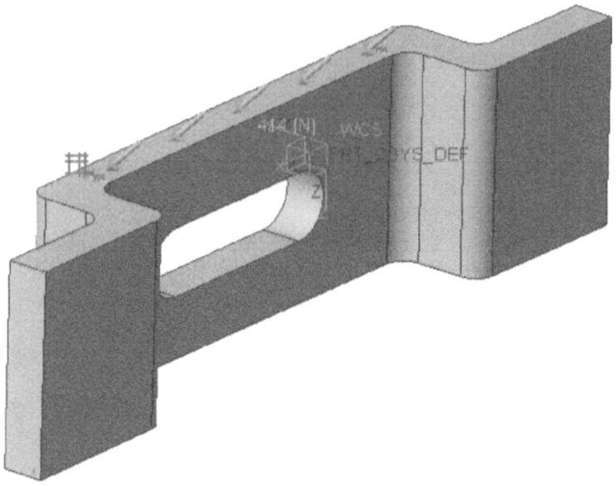

Figure 2–37

Task 6: Apply constraints to the surfaces of the model.

In this task, you will apply constraints to the entire end surfaces of the solid model, assuming that the load on the bracket is supported at the bracket flanges.

1. Select the surfaces shown in Figure 2–38 (hold <Ctrl> to select both surfaces).

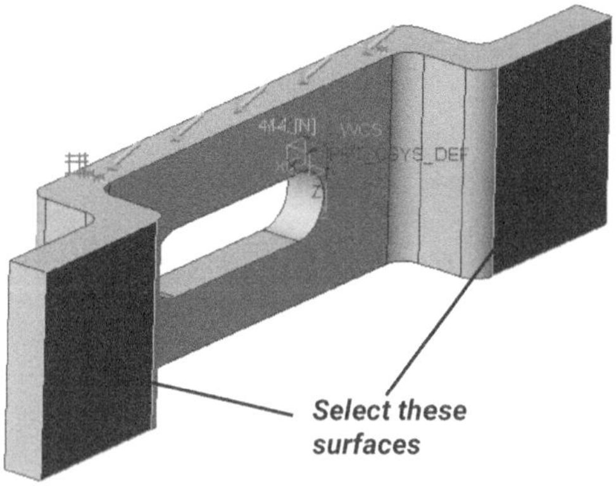

Figure 2–38

2. In the mini-toolbar, select (Displacement), as shown in Figure 2–39.

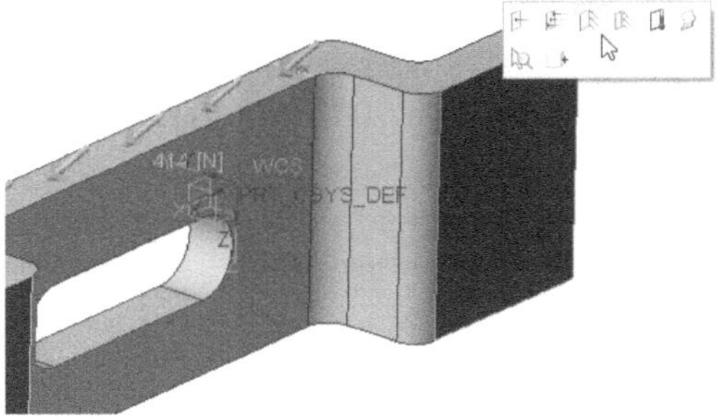

Figure 2–39

Note: You can also select (Displacement) *in the Home tab of the ribbon.*

3. The *Constraint* dialog box opens, as shown in Figure 2–40.

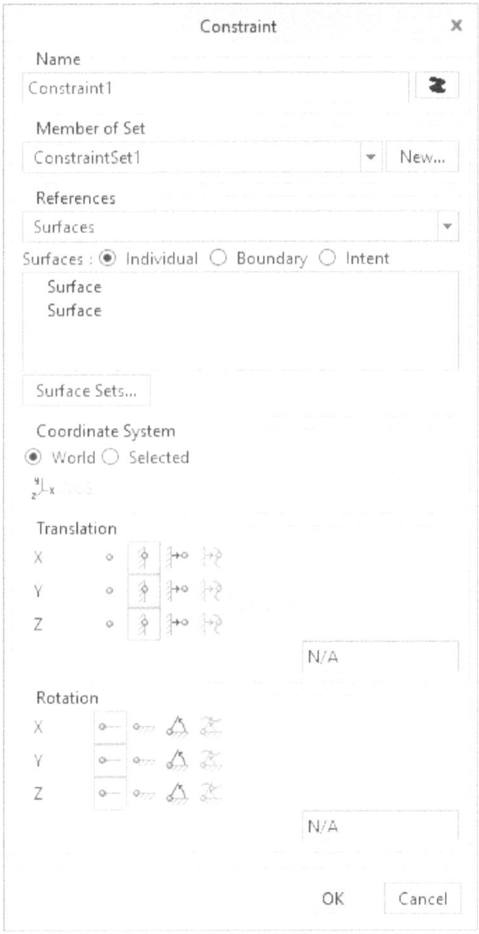

Figure 2–40

4. In the *Name* field, enter **fixed_faces**. For *Member of Set*, select **ConstraintSet1**.
5. The default coordinate system is WCS, as indicated in the *Coordinate System* area in the *Constraint* dialog box. Keep WCS as the coordinate system to be used.
6. Six possible constraints are available at the bottom of the *Constraint* dialog box: three translations and three rotations. The icons for these constraints are described below. Accept the default options for all of the translation and rotation directions.

Translation Icons	Rotation Icons	Description
		Enables the constrained feature to move or rotate freely in the related direction.
		Fixes the constrained feature so that it cannot move or rotate in the related direction.
		Forces the constrained feature to move or rotate in the related direction by a specified amount.

Note: Solid element nodes only have three translational degrees of freedom. The rotation of a node cannot be specified or calculated.

7. Click **OK** to finish applying the constraints. The model displays as shown in Figure 2–41.

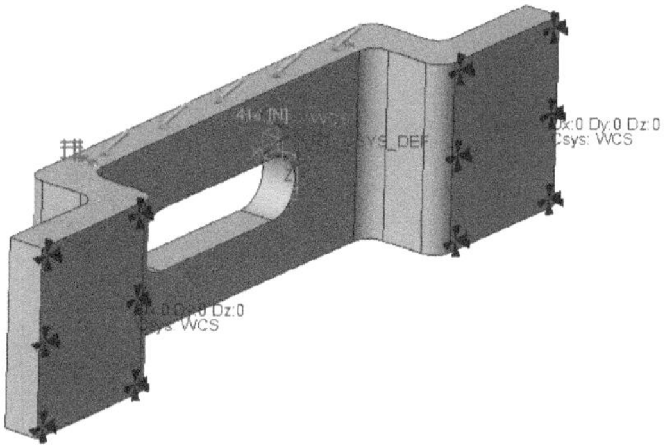

Figure 2–41

Note: *Depending on the orientation of your model, the load vectors might vary.*

Task 7: Apply the material.

In this task, you will select the material for the solid bracket.

1. In the *Home* tab, click (Materials). The *Materials* dialog box opens, as shown in Figure 2–42.

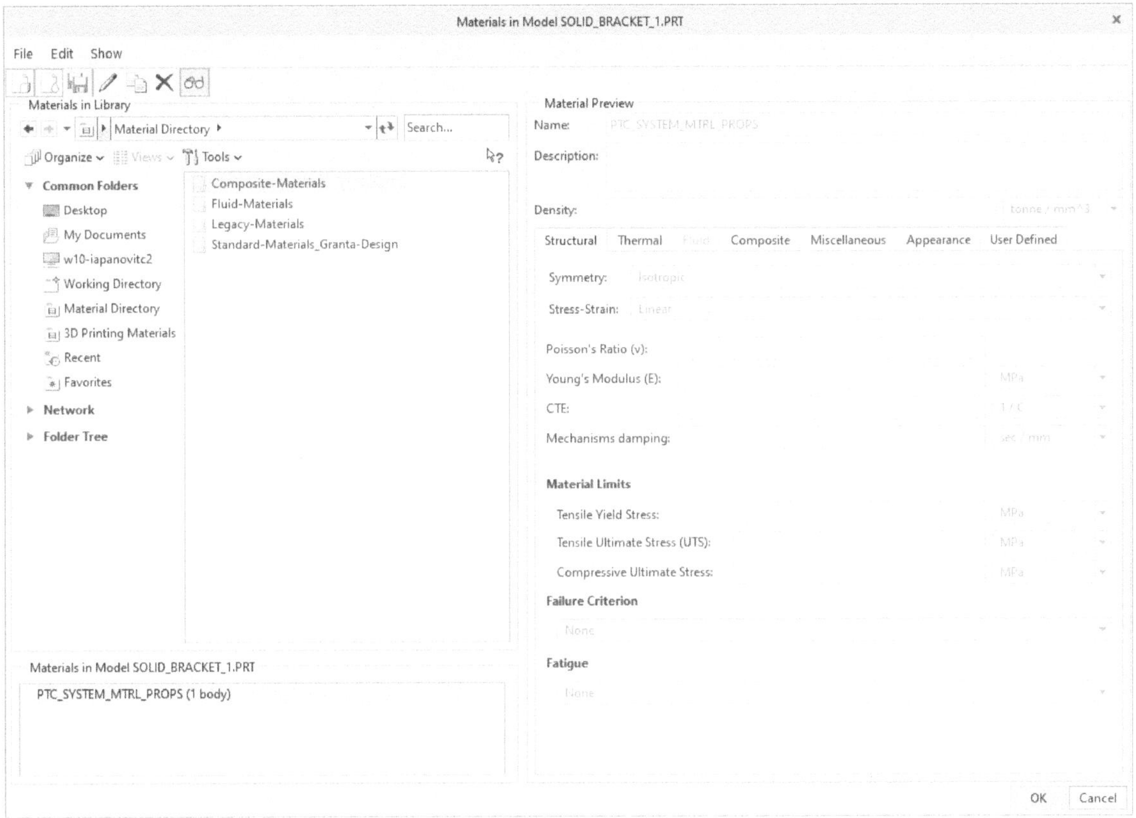

Figure 2–42

Note: *The* ***PTC_SYSTEM_MTRL_PROPS*** *is the material applied in the Creo Parametric environment. If no material has been applied in Creo Parametric, the* ***PTC_SYSTEM_MTRL_PROPS*** *has no valid mechanical properties.*

2. Double-click on the **Legacy-Materials** folder.
3. In the list of materials, double-click on **steel.mtl**.

4. The material is added to the *Materials in Model* area, as shown in Figure 2–43.

Figure 2–43

5. Note that **STEEL** has the following default material properties, as shown in Figure 2–44:
   - *Poisson's ratio:* **0.27**
   - *Young's modulus:* **199948 MPa**
   - *Coefficient of thermal expansion:* **1.17e-5 /C**
   - *Density:* **7.82708e-9 tonne/mm^3**

Figure 2–44

Note: *The model's material should be as stated.*

6. Click **OK** to close the *Materials* dialog box.

7. In the *Home* tab, click (Material Assignment). The *Material Assignment* dialog box opens, as shown in Figure 2–45.

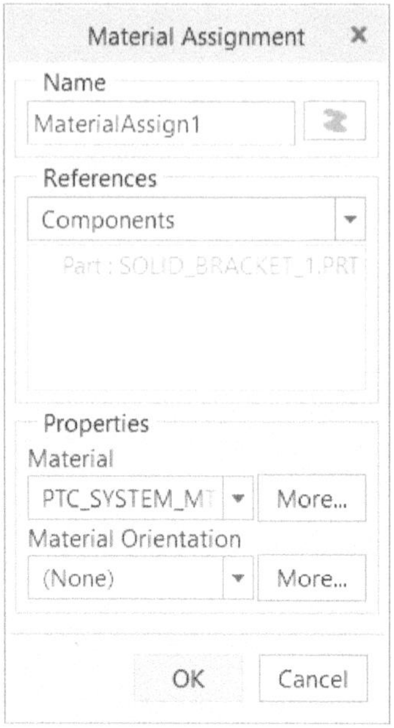

Figure 2–45

8. In the *Material* drop-down list, select **STEEL**.
9. Click **OK** to confirm the material assignment and to close the *Material Assignment* dialog box.

Analysis Tasks

In the following tasks, you will set the analysis type and convergence method, and then run the analysis.

Task 8: Set up and run the analysis.

In this task, you will specify the analysis type. First, the solid bracket is analyzed using the **Quick Check** convergence option to check for errors. The option gives you a general feel for the results and it indicates whether the model will behave as intended with the applied boundary conditions. The importance of this option increases with the size of your model.

1. In the *Home* tab, click (Analyses and Studies). The *Analyses and Design Studies* dialog box opens, as shown in Figure 2–46.

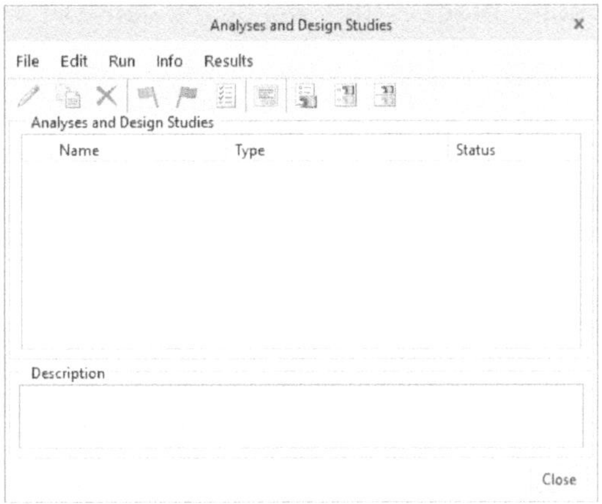

Figure 2–46

2. Select **File>New Static**. The *Static Analysis Definition* dialog box opens, as shown in Figure 2–47.

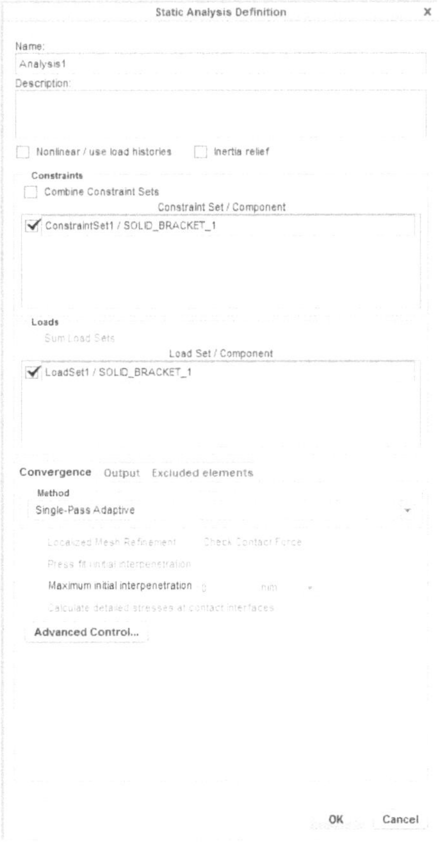

Figure 2–47

3. In the *Name* field, enter **solid_bracket** (this will be the name of a subdirectory containing all of your results files).
4. In the *Description* field, enter **Static analysis of a solid bracket**. This step is optional, but is helpful for identifying your analysis later.
5. For a static stress analysis, you need to specify or select the constraint and load sets. These are the ones you created in the previous steps. In this case, they are **ConstraintSet1** and **LoadSet1**. Ensure that they are highlighted.
6. For the type of convergence, expand the *Method* drop-down list and select **Quick Check**. This option enables you to determine whether the analysis has been set up correctly in your first run.
7. Click **OK** in the *Static Analysis Definition* dialog box.
8. Click (Settings) in the *Analyses and Design Studies* dialog box to set the locations for the temporary and output files, output files format, and RAM allocation. The *Run Settings* dialog box opens, as shown in Figure 2–48.

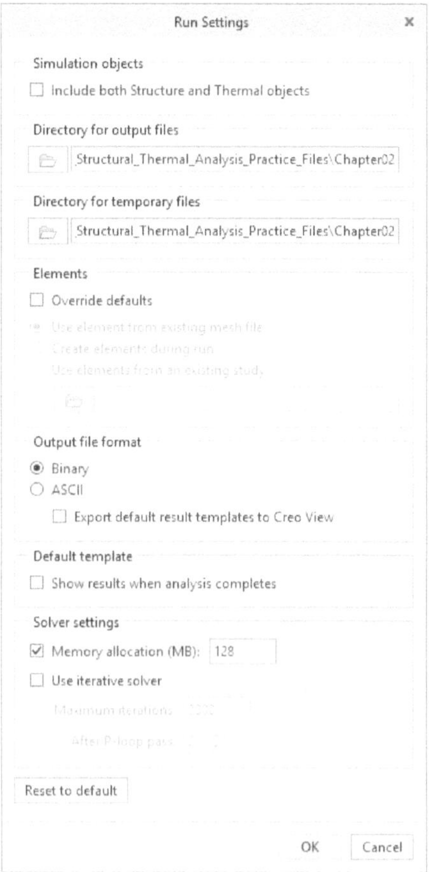

Figure 2–48

Note: By default, Creo Simulate files and directories are created in the Creo working directory. The recommended setting for the memory allocation is half the RAM in your computer.

Note the format for the output files in the *Output File Format* area. The **ASCII** option needs a much larger disk space. The advantage of ASCII output files is that they are portable between Unix and Windows operating systems.

9. Accept the remaining default values, including the **Use Element from Existing Mesh File** option.
10. Click **OK** to close the *Run Settings* dialog box.
11. Click **Info** and select **Check Model**. This command checks the validity of the simulation model. The *Information* dialog box opens (as shown in Figure 2–49), indicating that there are no errors.

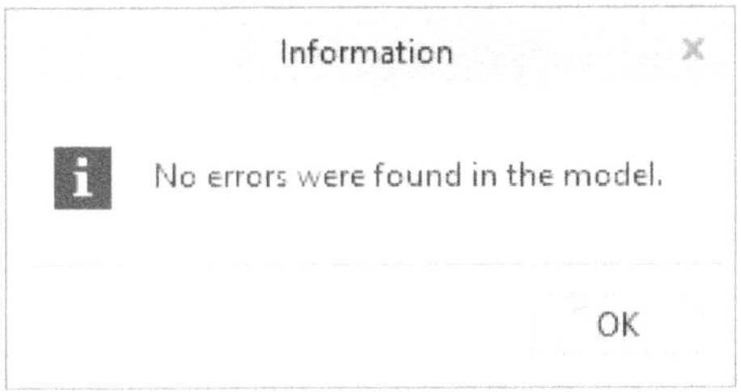

Figure 2–49

*Note: The **Check Model** option highlights any modeling errors (e.g., load-constraint conflicts or unassigned material properties) and errors from modeling edits.*

12. Click **OK** to confirm.
13. Click (Start) in the *Analyses and Design Studies* dialog box to start your analysis. The *Question* dialog box opens, as shown in Figure 2–50.

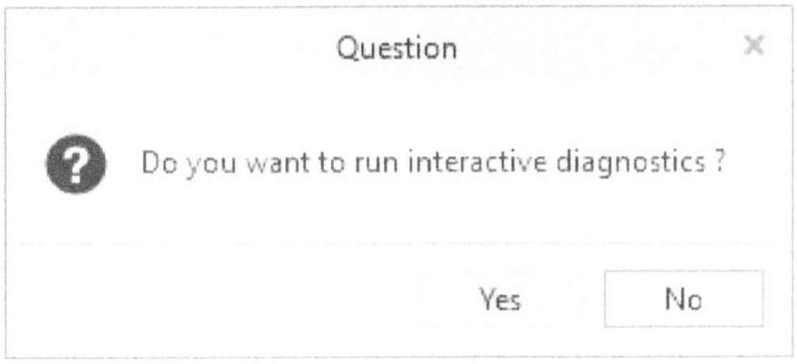

Figure 2–50

14. Click **Yes** in the *Question* dialog box. Creo Simulate solves the analysis. The *Run Status* dialog box opens, as shown in Figure 2–51, stating that the analysis run has been completed.

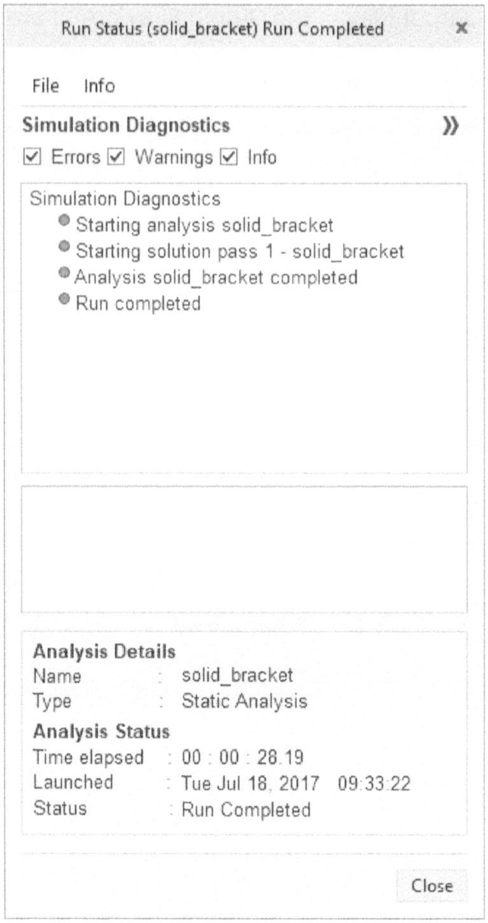

Figure 2–51

15. In the *Run Status* dialog box, click » (Show Summary Information) to expand it, displaying information regarding the analysis, such as the error estimates, mass moments of inertia, resultant loads, and so on, as shown in Figure 2–52.

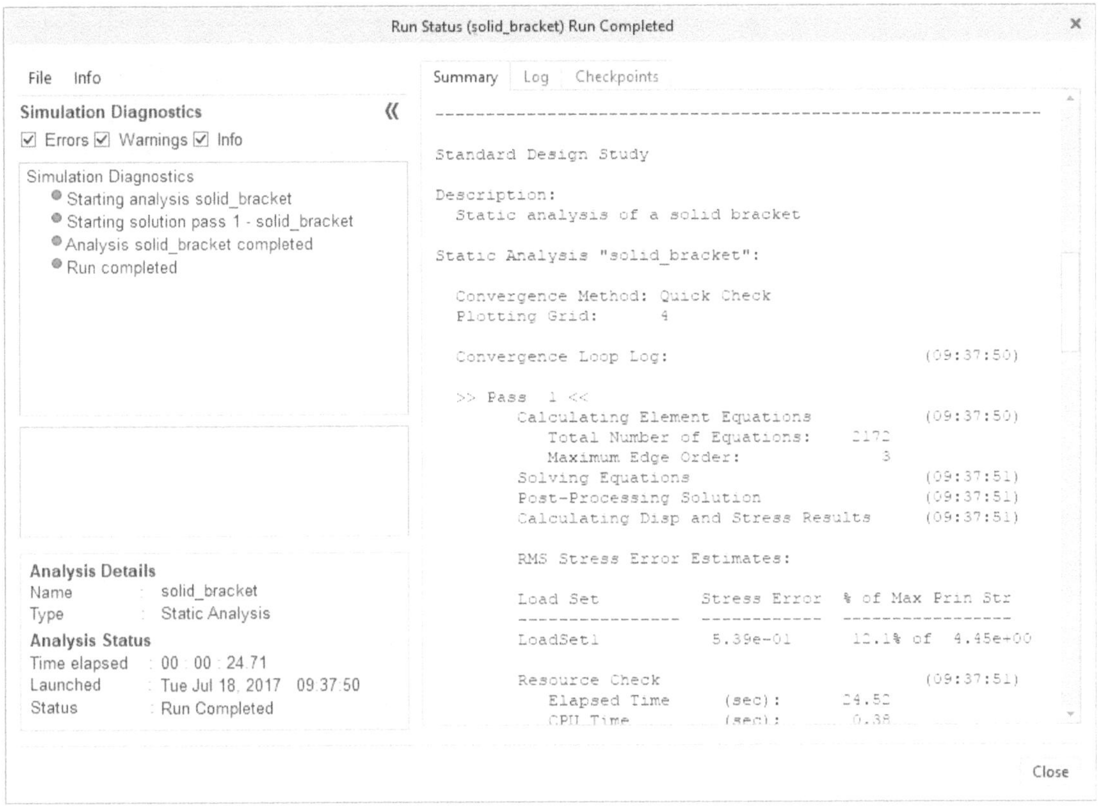

Figure 2–52

Note: *Note that if you close the Run Status dialog box, you can click (Status) in the Analysis and Design Study dialog box to display the status again.*

16. Click **Close** to close the *Run Status* dialog box.

17. Click **Close** in the *Analyses and Design Studies* dialog box. The **Quick Check** analysis is complete.

Task 9: Solve the solid bracket using the Multi-Pass Adaptive convergence option.

In this task, the model is run through the solver in multiple passes, with the element P-levels being increased with each pass. The passes continue until either the solution converges or the maximum polynomial order (default 6, maximum 9) is reached.

1. In the *Home* tab, click (Analyses and Studies). The *Analyses and Design Studies* dialog box opens, as shown in Figure 2–53.

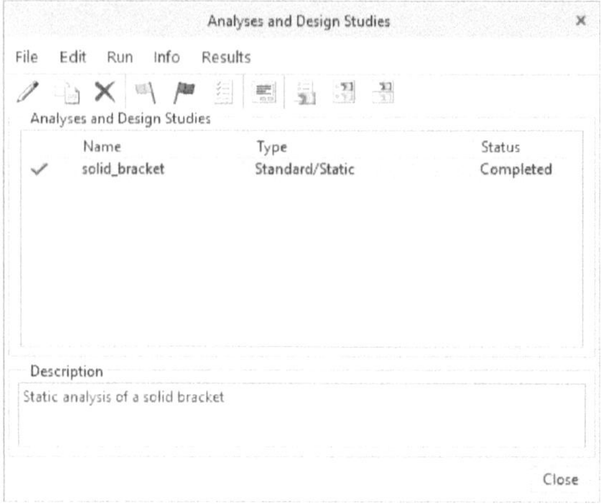

Figure 2–53

2. Highlight the **solid_bracket** analysis and click (Edit). The *Static Analysis Definition* dialog box opens, as shown in Figure 2–54.

Figure 2–54

3. Expand the *Method* drop-down list and select **Multi-Pass Adaptive**.
4. In the *Polynomial Order* area, for the *Maximum value*, select **9**.
5. In the *Limits* area, in the *Percent Convergence* field, enter **5**. The *Static Analysis Definition* dialog box displays as shown in Figure 2–55.

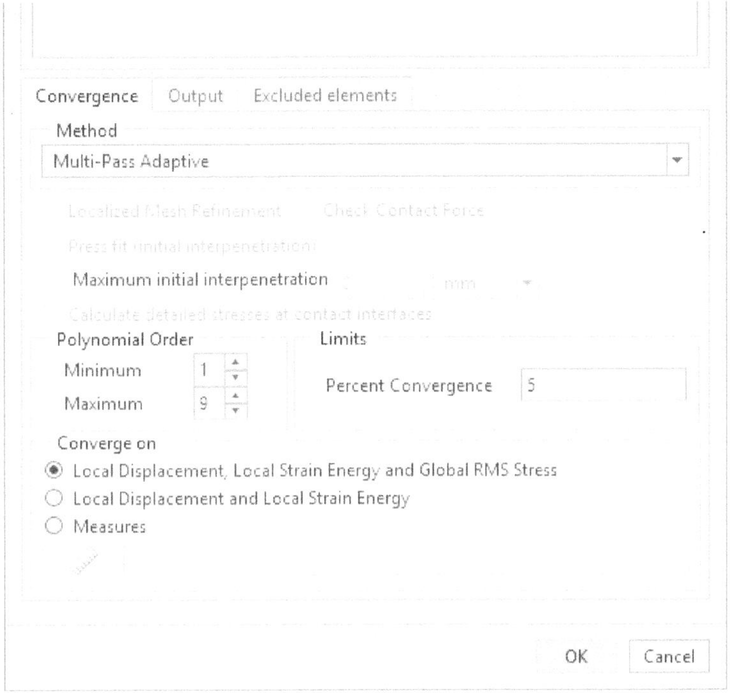

Figure 2–55

6. Click **OK** in the *Static Analysis Definition* dialog box.
7. Click (Start) in the *Analyses and Design Studies* dialog box to start the analysis. The *Question* dialog box opens, as shown in Figure 2–56.

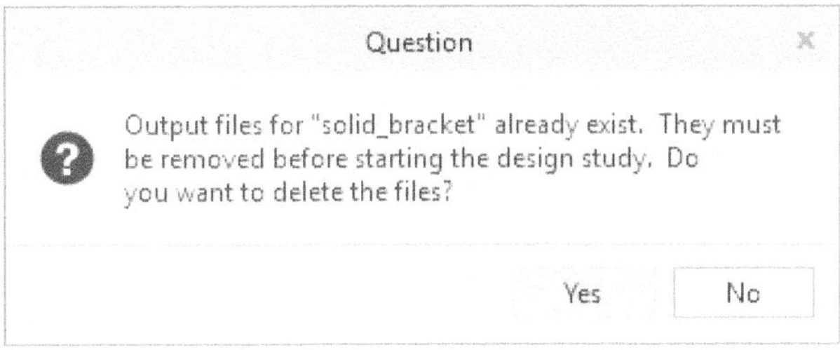

Figure 2–56

8. Click **Yes** in the *Question* dialog box.

9. Another *Question* dialog box opens, as shown in Figure 2–57.

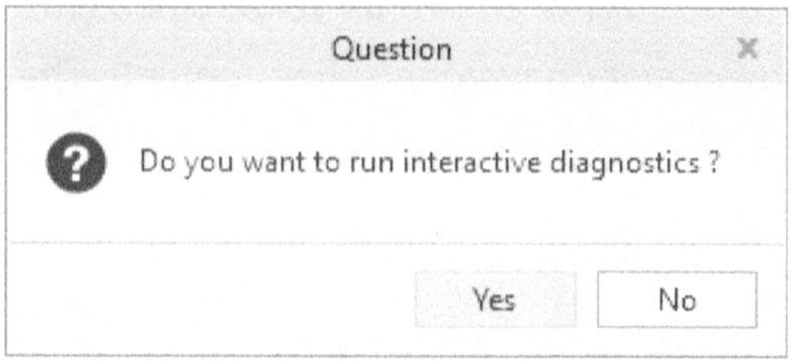

Figure 2–57

10. Click **Yes** in the *Question* dialog box. The message *The design study has started* displays in the Creo message window. Creo Simulate solves the problem. The *Diagnostics* dialog box opens, as shown in Figure 2–58, stating that the analysis run has been completed.

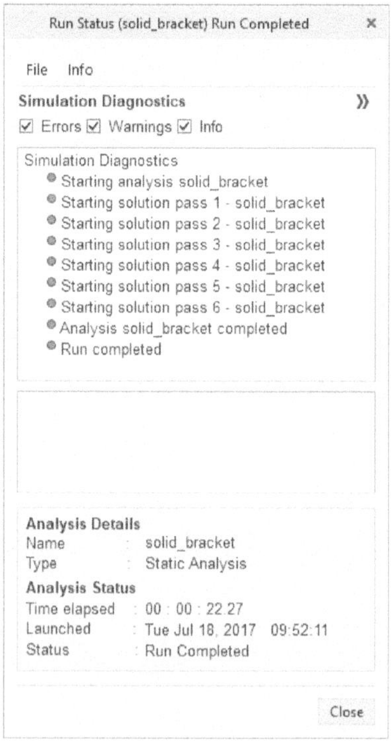

Figure 2–58

11. Click » (Show Summary Information) to expand the dialog box. Examine the information in the window. Note that the analysis took six solution passes, up to the maximum edge order 6, to converge within the requested 5%.
12. Click **Close** in the *Run Status* dialog box.
13. Do not close the *Analyses and Design Studies* dialog box.

Results Tasks

In the following tasks, you will display and interpret the results of this analysis.

Task 10: Display the results.

In this task, you will create and show a Von Mises stress plot.

1. Click (Review Results) in the *Analyses and Design Studies* dialog box. The *Result Window Definition* dialog box opens, as shown in Figure 2–59.

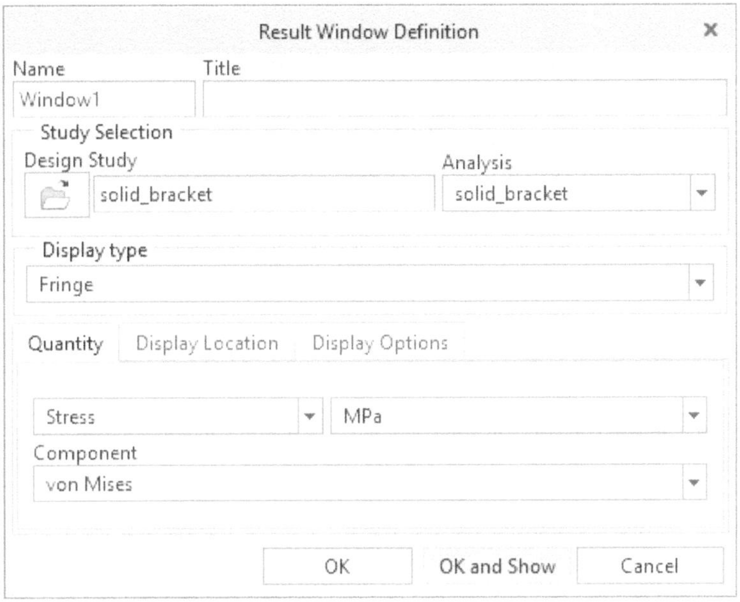

Figure 2–59

Note: *If Von Mises stress exceeds the yield strength, the material in that area is predicted to yield.*

2. In the *Name* field, accept the default **Window1** option.
3. In the *Title* field, enter **VM_Plot**.
4. Select the *Display Options* tab and select **Show Element Edges**.
5. Click **OK and Show**. The Creo Simulate Results environment opens, with the Von Mises Stress fringe plot displayed.

6. In the *View* tab, expand the *Appearance* drop-down list and select **Visibilities**. The *Visibilities* window displays, as shown in Figure 2–60.

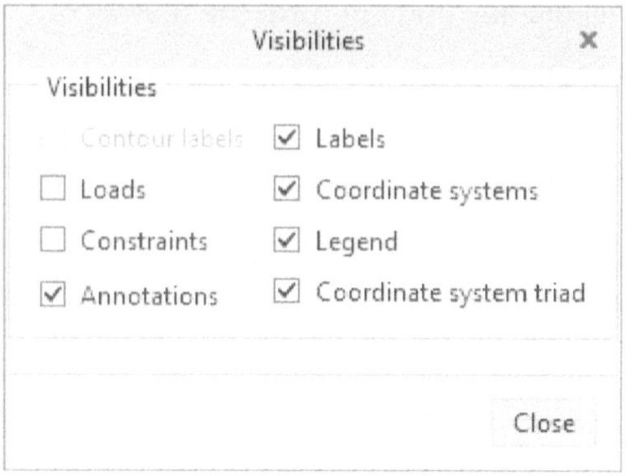

Figure 2–60

7. Enable the **Loads** and **Constraints** options and click **Close**.
8. Reorient the model until the results window displays as shown in Figure 2–61.

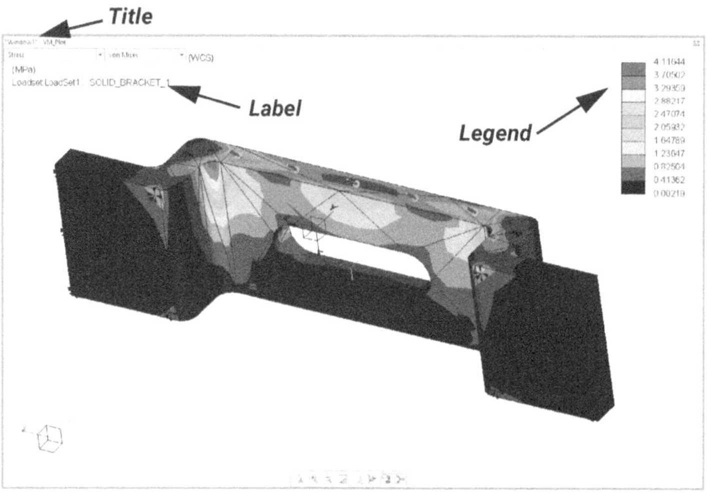

Figure 2–61

The stress values that you obtain when you run the analysis might be slightly different than those shown in Figure 2–61. This is because each new build of Creo Simulate produces slight variations in the creation of the mesh.

9. In the *Home* tab, click (Edit). The *Result Window Definition* dialog box opens. The *Display Options* tab is active, as shown in Figure 2–62.

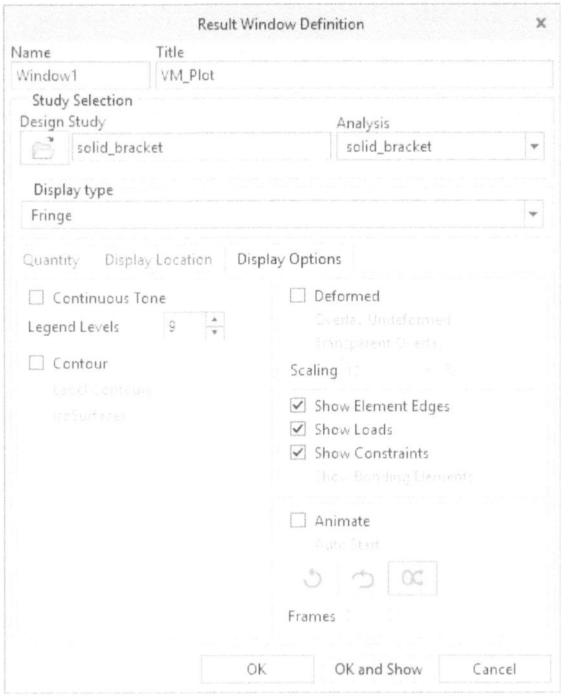

Figure 2–62

10. Select the **Continuous Tone** option and click **OK and Show**. **Window1** displays as shown in Figure 2–63.

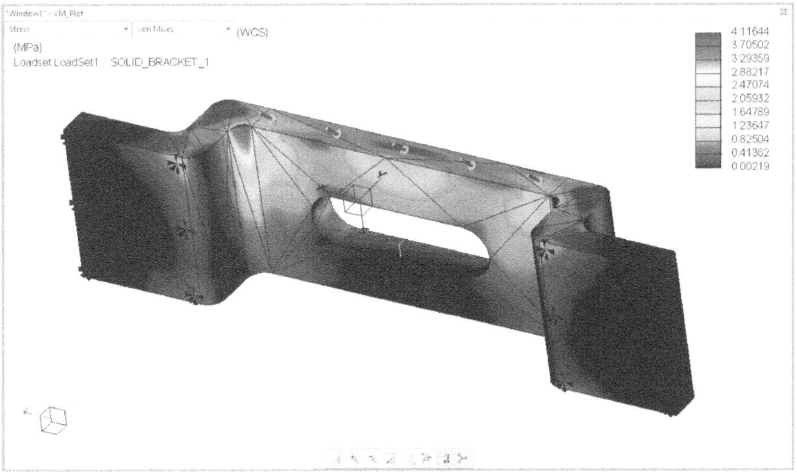

Figure 2–63

Task 11: Use predefined measures to study the convergence.

1. Click (Open) in the *Home* tab to create a new results window. The *Open Result Windows Definition* dialog box opens.
2. Select the **solid_bracket** study and click **Open**. The *Result Windows Definition* dialog box opens.
3. In the *Name* field, enter **Convm**, and in the *Title* field, enter **Convm**.
4. Expand the *Display Type* drop-down list and select **Graph**.
5. Expand the *Graph Ordinate (Vertical) Axis* drop-down list and select **Measure**.
6. Click (Measure). The *Measures* dialog box opens, as shown in Figure 2–64.

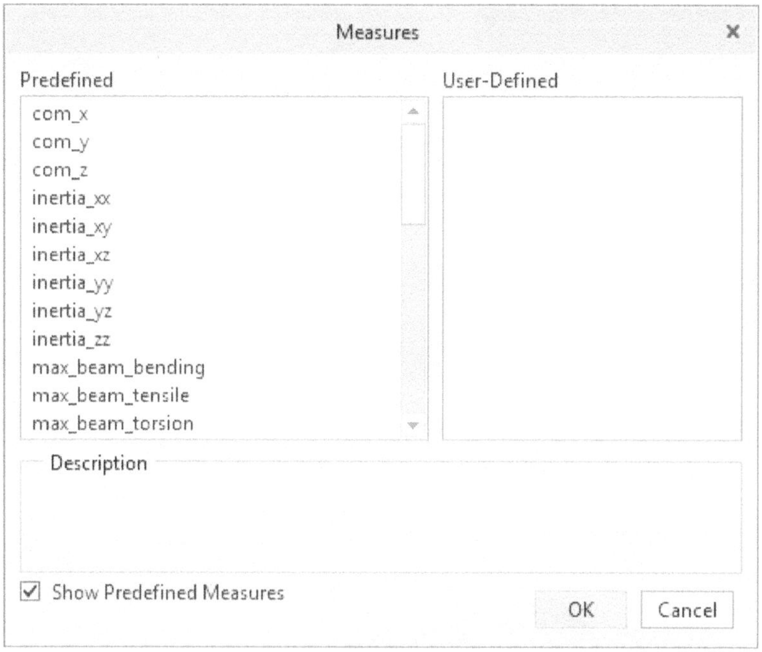

Figure 2–64

Note: *A measure is a "virtual gauge" attached to your model. For example, you can set a measure to obtain the stress at a specific point on a model.*

7. In the list of predefined measures, highlight **max_stress_vm** and click **OK**.
8. Click **OK** in the *Result Window Definition* dialog box to confirm the creation of the graph without actually displaying it.
9. Repeat the previous eight steps to create graph measures for **max_disp_mag** and **strain_energy**. Enter **max_disp_mag** and **strain_energy**, respectively, for the names of the result window definitions.

10. In the *View* tab, click (Show).The *Display Result Window* dialog box opens, as shown in Figure 2–65.

Figure 2–65

11. In the *Display Result Window* dialog box, highlight **Convm** only (disable any highlighting on others if required) and click **OK** to display **max_stress_vm**. The convergence plot displays as shown in Figure 2–66.

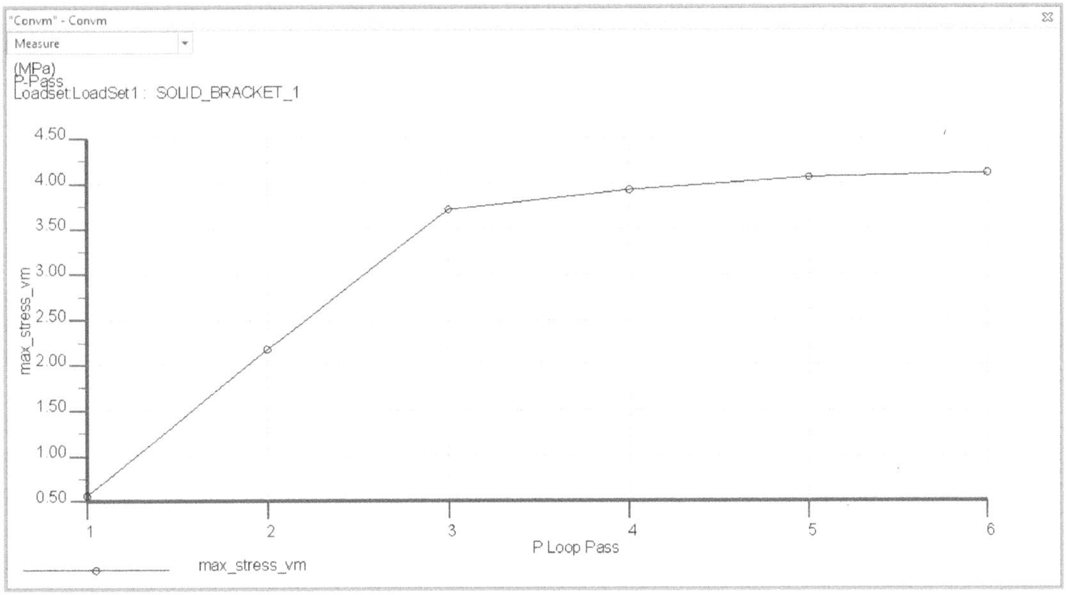

Figure 2–66

12. In the *Format* tab, select (Edit). The *Options* dialog box opens, as shown in Figure 2–67.

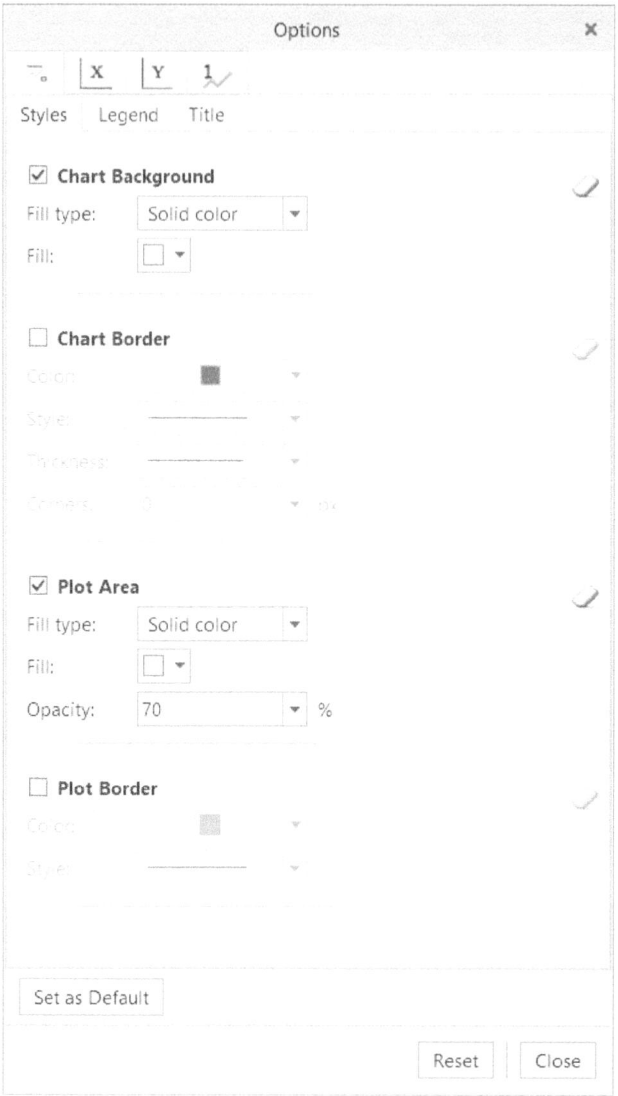

Figure 2–67

13. Explore the options in the *Options* dialog box by making changes to the graph shown in Figure 2–66. Click **Close** when finished.

14. In the *View* tab, click (Show). The *Display Result Window* dialog box opens.

15. Highlight only **max_disp_mag** in the dialog box and click **OK** to display the next graph. The convergence plot displays as shown in Figure 2–68.

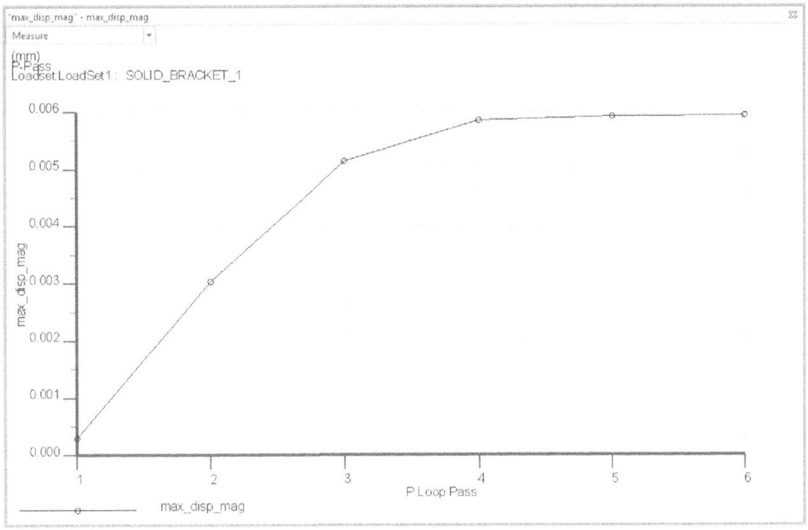

Figure 2–68

16. Repeat the previous two steps to display the **strain_energy** convergence plot, as shown in Figure 2–69.

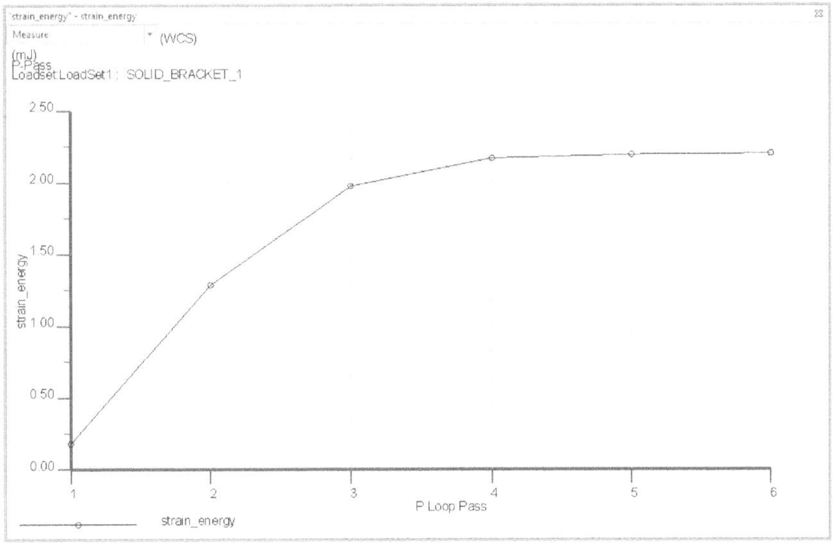

Figure 2–69

These plots indicate that the solution converges after six passes. The solution is practically unchanged after four passes.

Task 12: Study the P-Level plot.

1. In the *Home* tab, click (Open) to create a new results window. The *Open Result Windows* dialog box opens.
2. Select the **solid_bracket** study and click **Open**. The *Result Window Definition* dialog box opens.
3. In the *Name* field, type **PLevel**.
4. Expand the *Quantity* drop-down list and select **P-Level**.
5. Click **OK and Show**. Both strain energy convergence and P-Level plots display as shown in Figure 2–70.

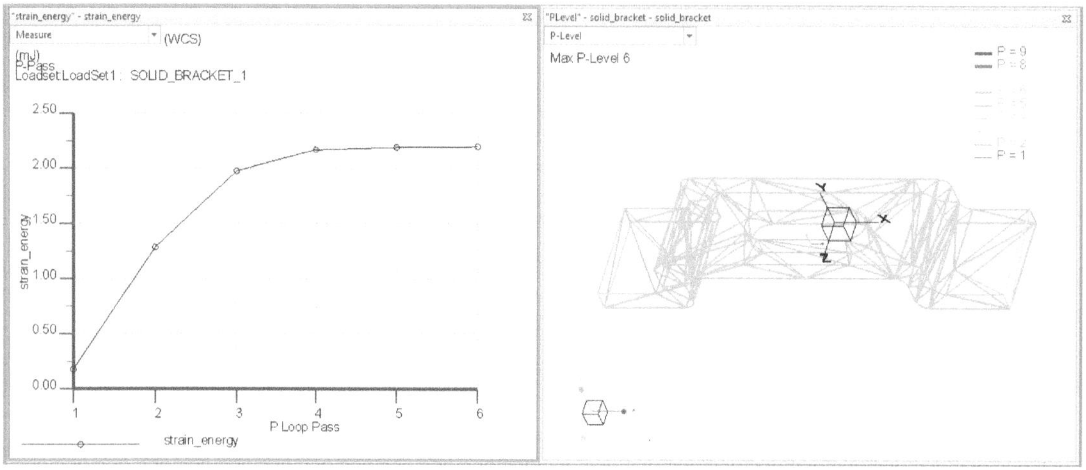

Figure 2–70

6. Examine the P-Level plot. Note that the maximum P-Level required to achieve convergence is **6**.

Task 13: Animate the Von Mises stress plot.

1. In the *View* tab, click (Show), highlight only **Window1** in the *Display Result Window* dialog box, and click **OK**. The Von Mises Stress fringe plot displays.

   Note: *Ensure that only* ***Window1*** *is selected in the Display Result Window dialog box.*

2. Right-click and select **Edit**. The *Result Window Definition* dialog box opens.
3. Select the *Display Options* tab and clear the **Continuous Tone** option. Select the **Deformed** option and accept the default Scaling value (10%).
4. Select the **Animate** option. Clear the **Auto Start** option and accept the default Frames value (8).

5. Click **OK and Show**.

6. In the *View* tab, click ▶ (Start) to start the animation. Click ■ (Stop) to stop the animation. Click ▶| (Step Forward) or |◀ (Step Back) to step through the animation frames.

Task 14: Determine the location of maximum stress.

In this task, you will locate the location and value of the maximum stress.

1. Right-click and select **Edit**. The *Result Window Definition* dialog box opens. Clear the **Deformed** and **Animate** options. Click **OK and Show**. The Von Mises stress plot displays.
2. Right-click and select **Model Max**. The location and value of maximum Von Mises stress displays, as shown in Figure 2–71. You can spin the model to display the location of the maximum Von Mises stress.

Location of maximum stress

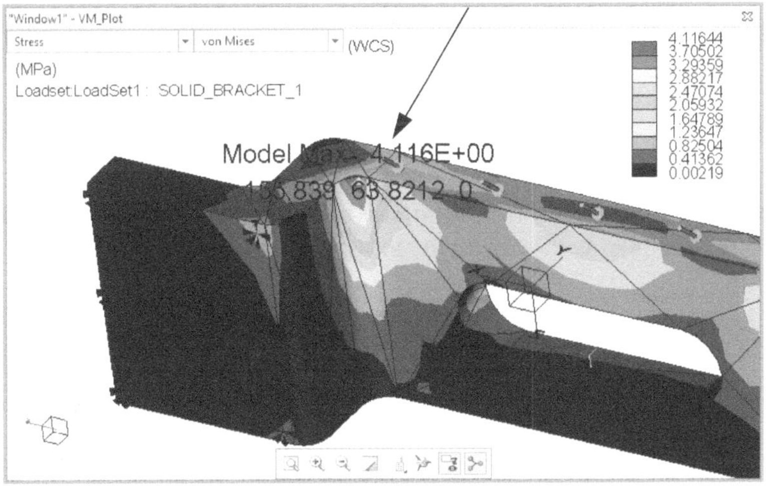

Figure 2–71

3. Investigate the other options in the *Query* group of the *Home* tab. For example, the **Dynamic Query** option displays the stress values at the cursor location. Mark a specific location with its stress level by selecting the location while the Dynamic Query is running. Select **Clear All Tags** when you are finished.

Task 15: Create sections through the solid bracket.

1. Select the *View* tab.

2. In the *Orientation* section, expand (Saved Orientations) and select **FRONT**.

   Note: *Select* ***View>Shaded*** *to remove any shading on the model.*

3. Select (Shaded) to remove the shade. The model displays as shown in Figure 2–72.

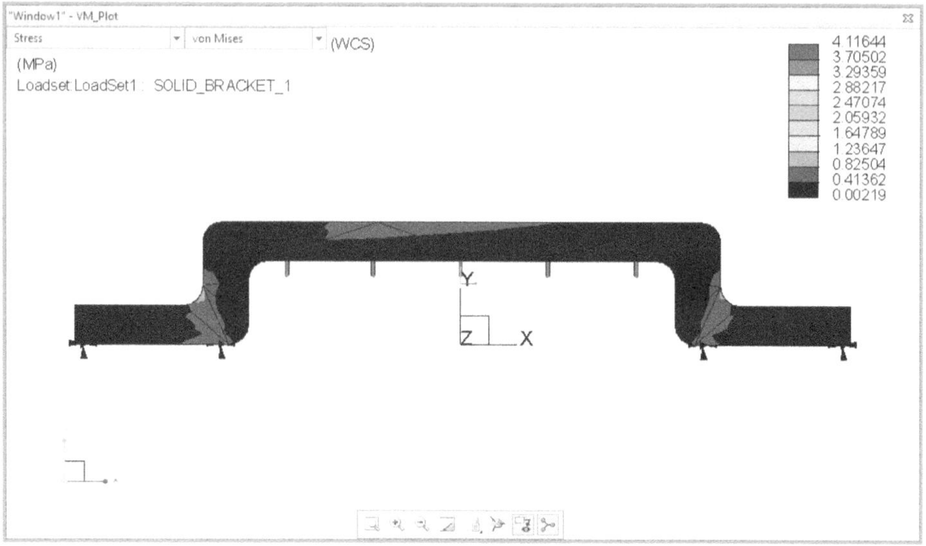

Figure 2–72

4. Select (New) in the **Capping & Cutting Surfs** section of the *View* tab.The *Results Surface Definition* dialog box opens, as shown in Figure 2–73.

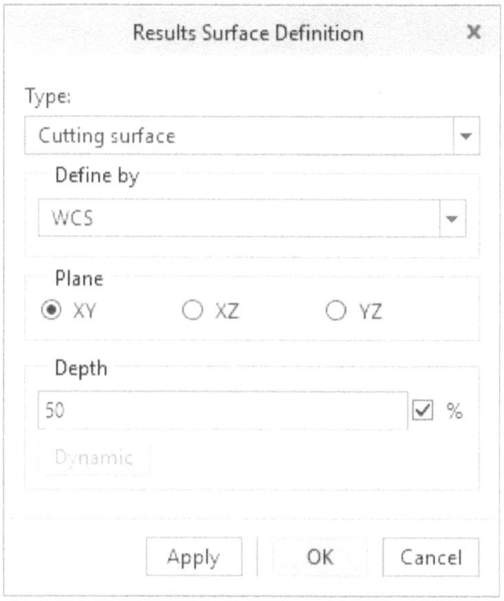

Figure 2–73

5. Select **YZ** in the *Plane* section of the *Results Surface Definition* dialog box.

6. Click **Apply** and reorient the model to display the section shown in Figure 2–74.

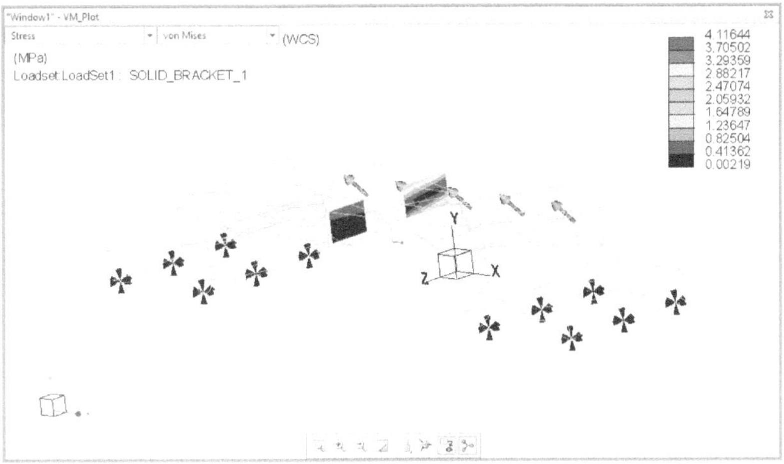

Figure 2–74

7. In the *Depth* field, enter **60** and click **Apply**. Note that the section moves along the part.
8. Click **Dynamic**. By holding the left mouse button and dragging the mouse up and down, you can move the section up and down in the model.
9. Click the middle mouse button to cancel the dynamic query.
10. Expand the *Type* drop-down list and select the **Capping Surface**.
11. Select **Below**.
12. In the *Depth* field, enter **50** and click **Apply**. The capped section displays as shown in Figure 2–75.

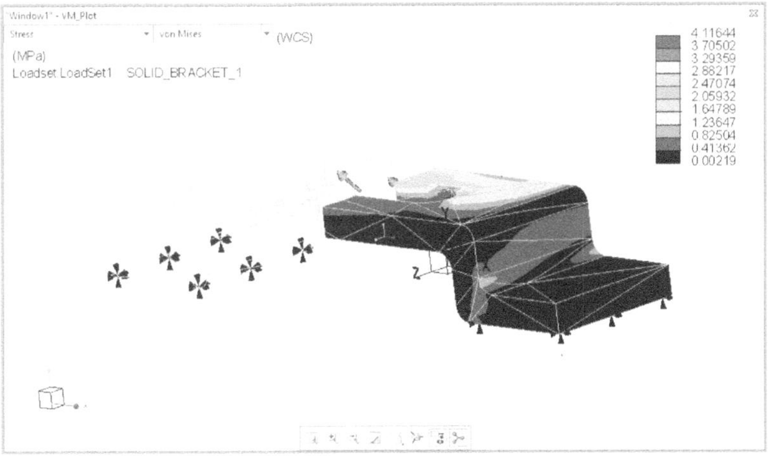

Figure 2–75

13. Click **OK** to close the *Results Surface Definition* dialog box.

14. In the *View* tab, click ✕ (Delete) to delete the capping surface.
15. Select **File>Close** or click (Close) to exit the Creo Simulate Results environment. Click **Don't Save** in the *Confirm Exit* window.
16. Close the *Analyses and Design Studies* dialog box.
17. Save the model and close the window.

End of practice

Practice 2b
Static Stress Analysis of a Bike Crank

Practice Objectives

- Apply loads, constraints, and material properties.
- Mesh the model.
- Check the validity of the model.
- Set up and run a Single-Pass Adaptive analysis.
- Display the results.
- Prepare the report.

In this practice, you will set up and run a static stress analysis on a bicycle crank assembly. The model is shown in Figure 2–76.

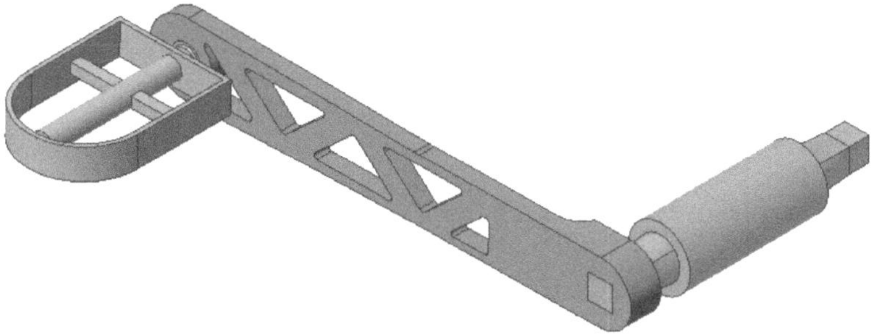

Figure 2–76

Modeling Tasks

In the following tasks, you will create the simulation entities required to analyze your model.

Task 1: Open the bike_crank assembly in Creo Parametric.

1. Set the working directory to **Chapter02**, if required.
2. Open **bike_crank.asm**.
3. Set the model display as follows:
   - *(Datum Display Filters)*: All Off
   - *(Spin Center)*: Off
   - *(Display Style)*: (Shading With Edges)

The model displays as shown in Figure 2–77.

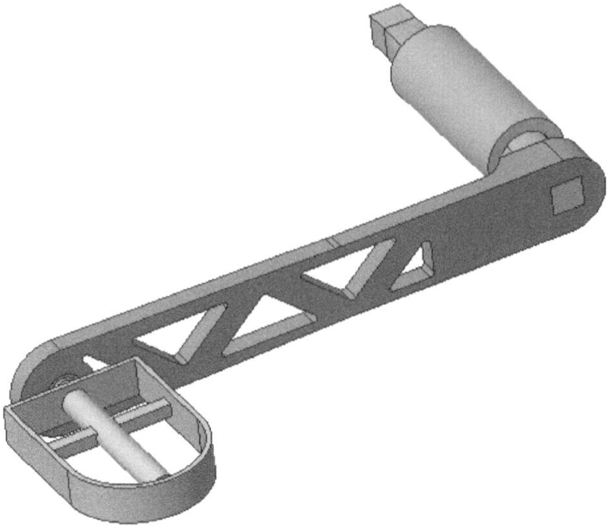

Figure 2–77

Task 2: Launch Creo Simulate.

1. Select **Applications>Simulate** to launch the Creo Simulate environment. Ensure that  (Structure Mode) is active.

Task 3: Apply materials.

In this task, you will select materials for the parts in the assembly.

1. In the *Home* tab, click (Materials). The *Materials* dialog box opens, as shown in Figure 2–78.

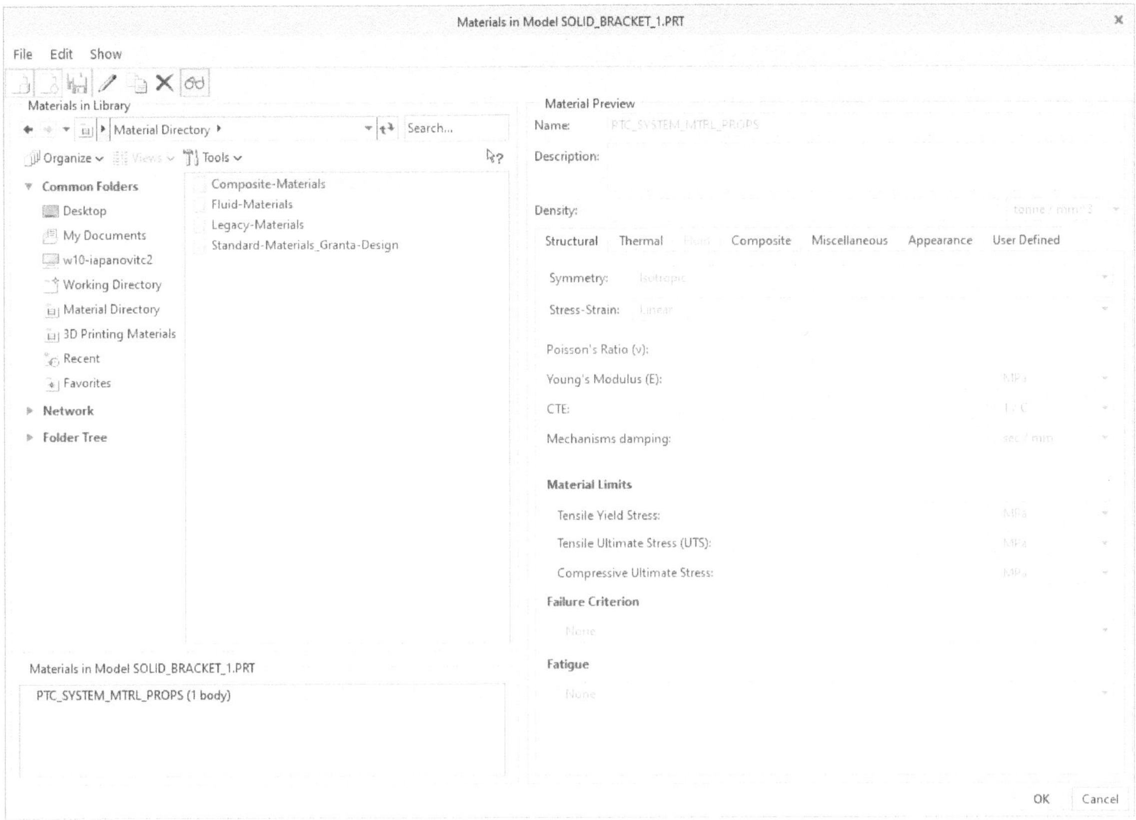

Figure 2–78

2. Double-click on **Legacy Materials** to view its contents, then double-click on **steel.mtl** to transfer **STEEL** to the *Materials in Model* area.

3. In the *Materials in Model* area, highlight **STEEL** and click (Edit) to edit the material.

4. In the *Material Definition* dialog box, make the following changes, as shown in Figure 2–79:
   - *Name:* **STEEL AISI 304**
   - *Tensile Yield Stress:* **215 MPa**
   - *Failure Criterion:* **Distortion Energy (von Mises)**

Figure 2–79

5. Click **OK** to close the *Material Definition* dialog box.
6. In the *Materials in Library* area, double-click on **AL6061** to transfer **AL6061** to the *Materials in Model* area.
7. In the *Materials in Model* area, highlight **AL6061** and click (Edit) to edit the material.

8. In the *Material Definition* dialog box, make the following changes, as shown in Figure 2–80:
    - *Name:* **AL6061 T4**
    - *Tensile Yield Stress:* **145 MPa**
    - *Failure Criterion:* **Distortion Energy (von Mises)**

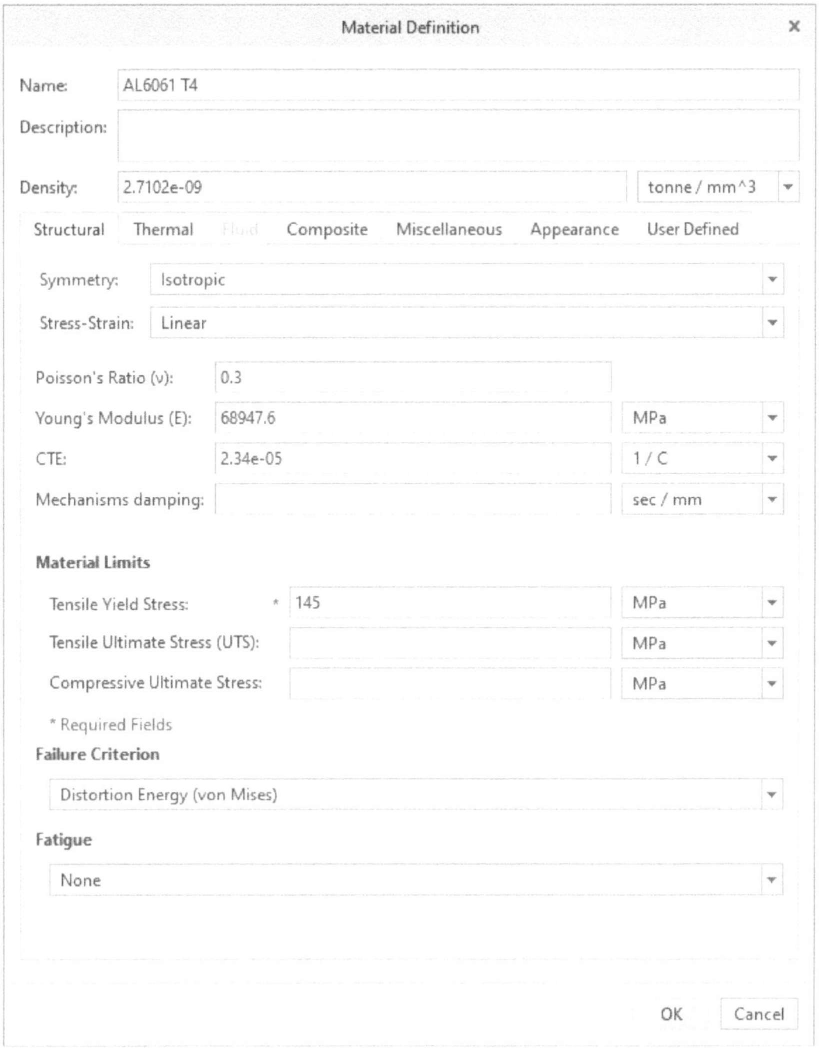

Figure 2–80

9. Click **OK** to close the *Material Definition* box.
10. Click **OK** to close the *Materials* dialog box.

11. In the *Home* tab, click (Material Assignment). The *Material Assignment* dialog box opens, as shown in Figure 2–81.

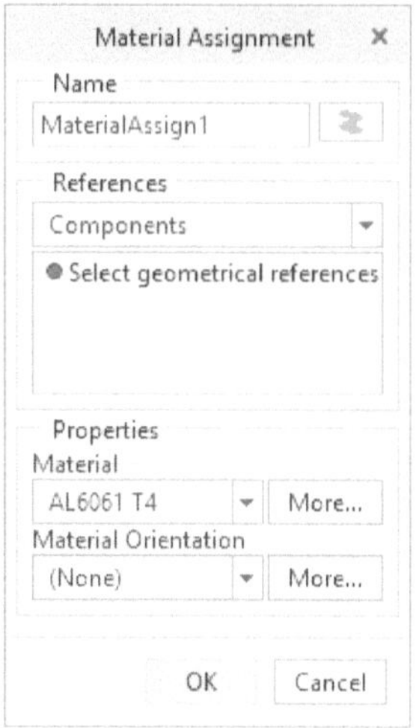

Figure 2–81

12. Select both **PEDAL** and **LHS CRANK** parts in the model (hold <Ctrl> for multiple selection) and click **OK** to assign **AL6061 T4** to both parts and close the *Material Assignment* dialog box.

13. In the *Home* tab, click (Material Assignment) again. In the model, select the **BOTTOM_BRACKET** part and in the *Properties* area, select **STEEL AISI 304**, as shown in Figure 2–82.

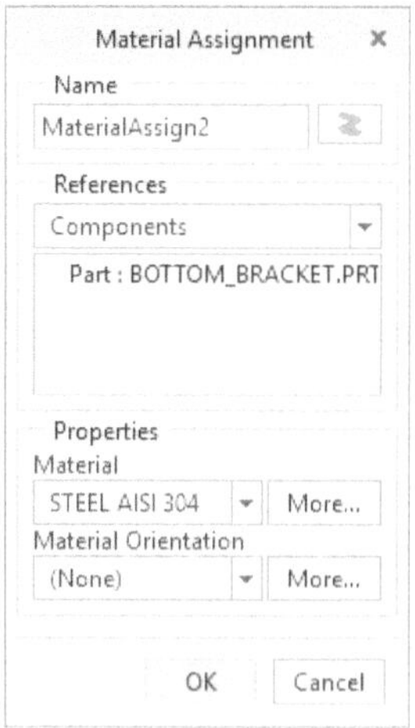

Figure 2–82

14. Click **OK** to close the *Material Assignment* dialog box.

Task 4: Apply constraints.

In this task, you will constrain the entire cylindrical surface of the **BOTTOM_BRACKET** part shown in Figure 2–83.

1. Press and hold <Ctrl> and select both surfaces of the cylinder shown in Figure 2–83 and select (Displacement) from the mini-toolbar.

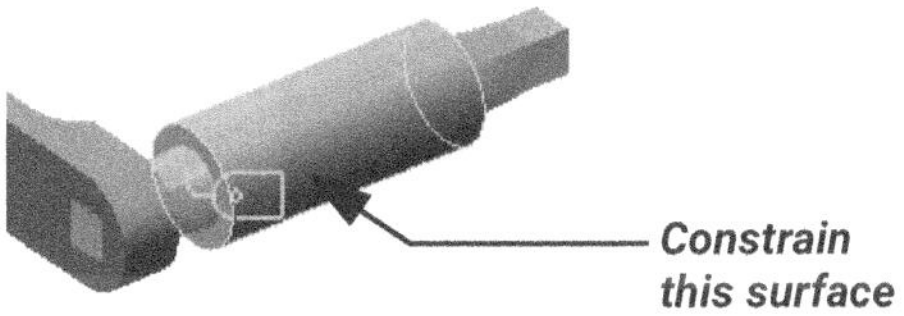

Figure 2–83

2. In the *Constraint* dialog box, rename the constraint as **fixed**, and accept the defaults for all of the other values. The dialog box should display as shown in Figure 2–84.

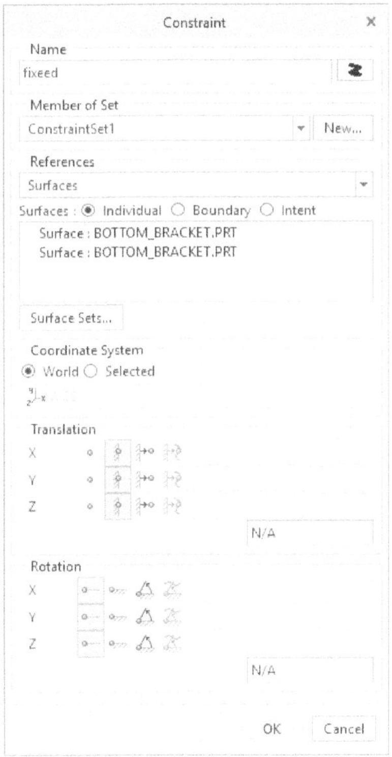

Figure 2–84

3. Click **OK** to close the *Constraint* dialog box. The model displays as shown in Figure 2–85.

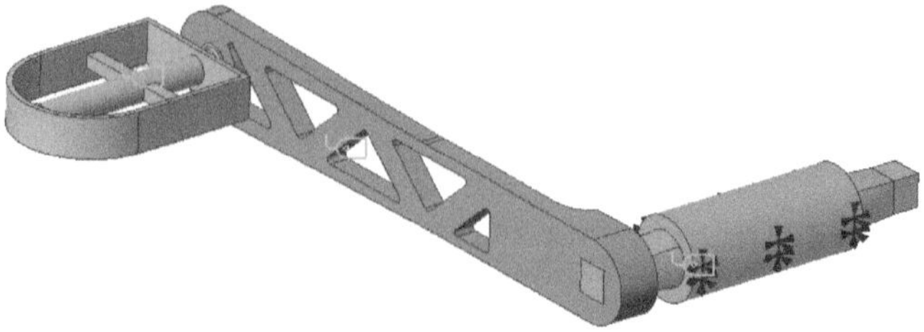

Figure 2–85

Task 5: Apply loads.

In this task, you will apply a 200N downward force to the top surface of the **PEDAL** part. The force simulates the average force a recreational bike rider applies to one pedal.

1. Select the surface shown in Figure 2–86 and select (Force/Moment) from the mini-toolbar.

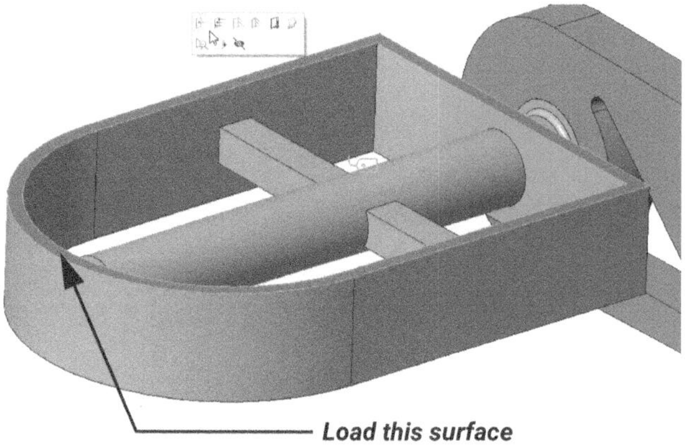

Figure 2–86

2. In the *Force/Moment* dialog box, enter the following values (as shown in Figure 2–87):
   - *Name:* **downward_force**
   - *Force Y:* **-200 N**

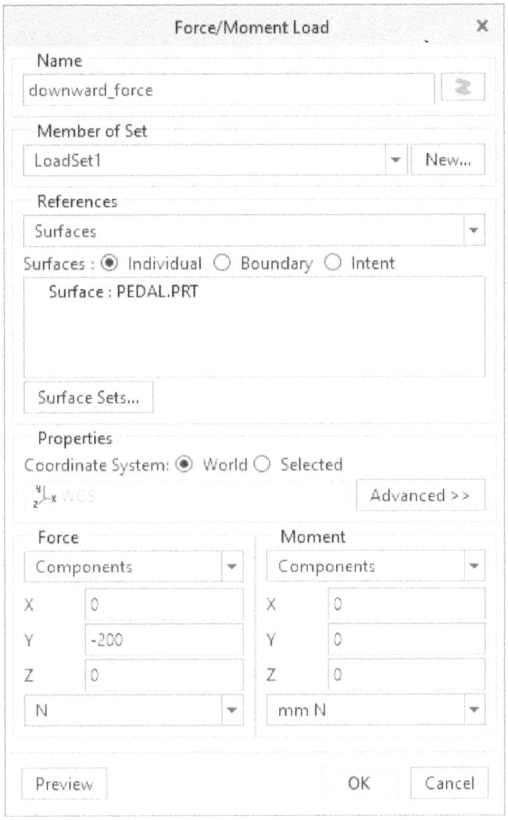

Figure 2–87

3. Click **OK** to close the *Force/Moment* dialog box. The model displays as shown in Figure 2–88.

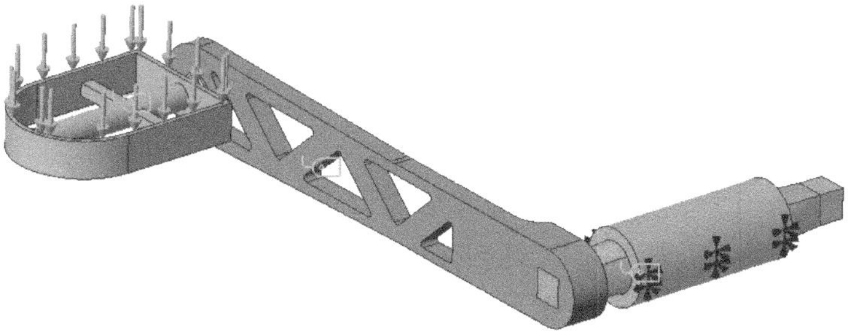

Figure 2–88

Task 6: Customize the simulation display.

1. In the In-graphics toolbar, click (Simulation Display). The *Simulation Display* dialog box opens.
2. In the *Settings* tab, in the *Load/Constraint Display* area, select **Values**. Set the *Distribution Density* to **3**, as shown in Figure 2–89.

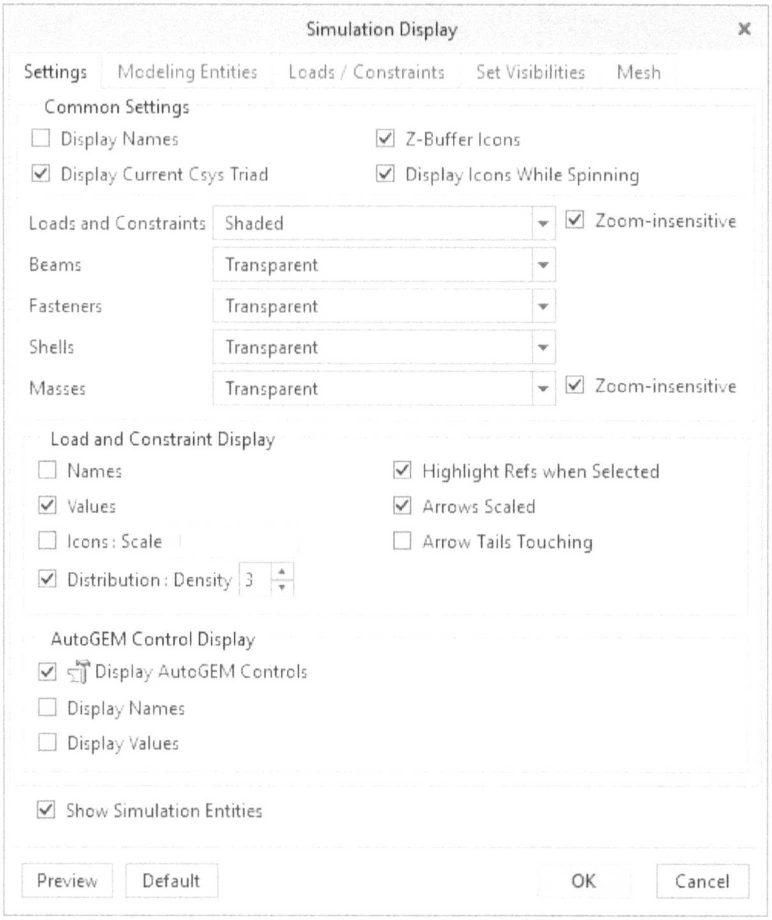

Figure 2–89

Note: *The* ***Distribution Density*** *option adjusts the number of force arrows displayed on the loaded surface. It does not affect the analysis results.*

3. In the *Modeling Entities* tab, clear the **Material Assignments** option, as shown in Figure 2–90.

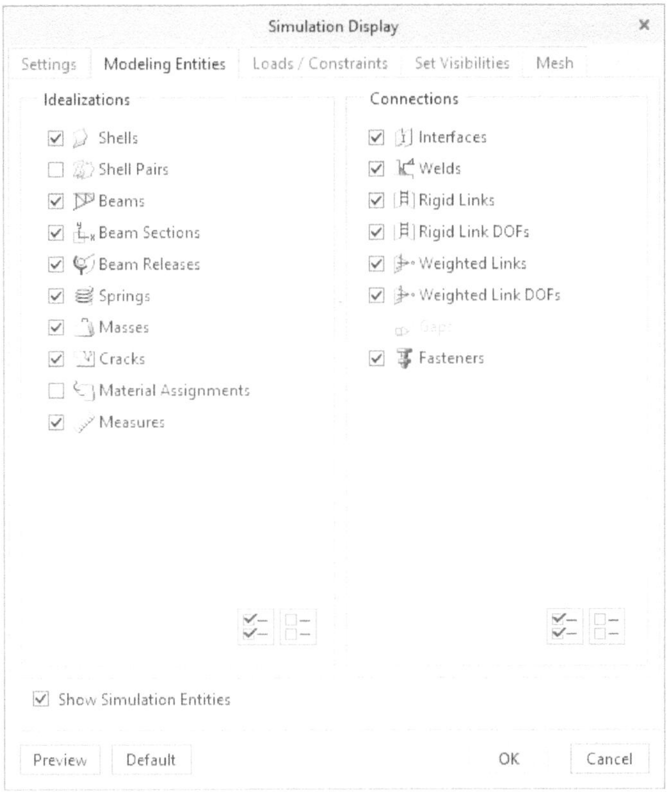

Figure 2–90

4. Click **OK** to close the *Simulation Display* dialog box. The model displays as shown in Figure 2–91. Note that the load magnitude (200N) is now shown and **Material Assignments** icons are now hidden.

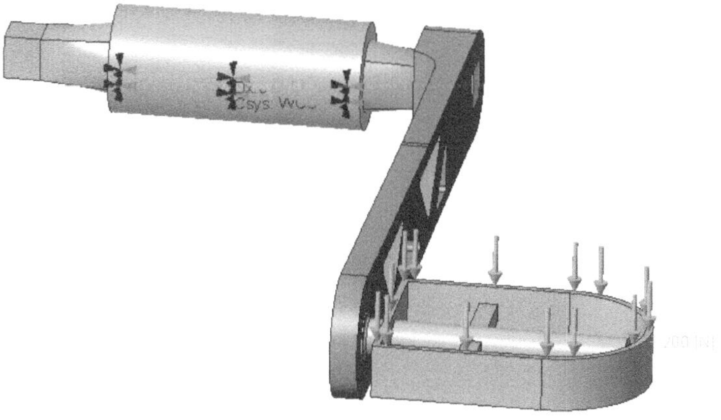

Figure 2–91

Task 7: Mesh the model.

1. In the *Refine Model* tab, click (AutoGEM). The *AutoGEM* dialog box opens, as shown in Figure 2–92.

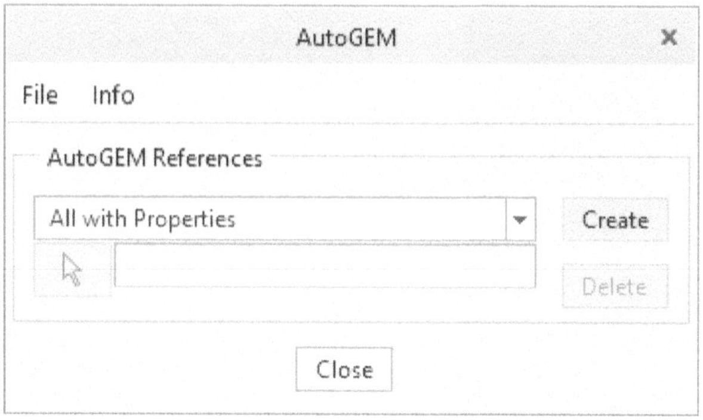

Figure 2–92

2. Ensure that the **All with Properties** option is active and click **Create**.

   Note: *The **All with Properties** option only meshes parts to which materials have already been assigned.*

3. The *AutoGEM Summary* and *Diagnostics* dialog boxes open, as shown in Figure 2–93. For this model, AutoGEM creates 1001 tetrahedral elements.

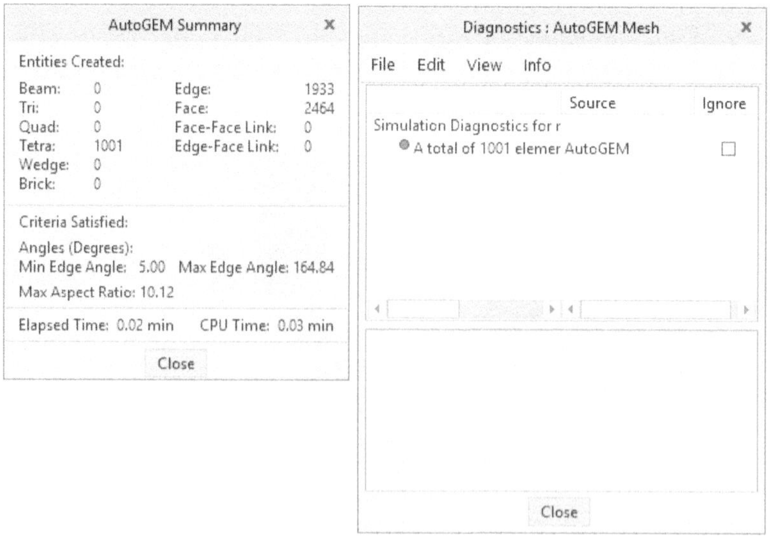

Figure 2–93

Note: *The number of elements might vary slightly, depending on the specific Creo build.*

4. Close the *AutoGEM Summary* and *Diagnostics* boxes, but do not close the *AutoGEM* dialog box. The model displays as shown in Figure 2–94.

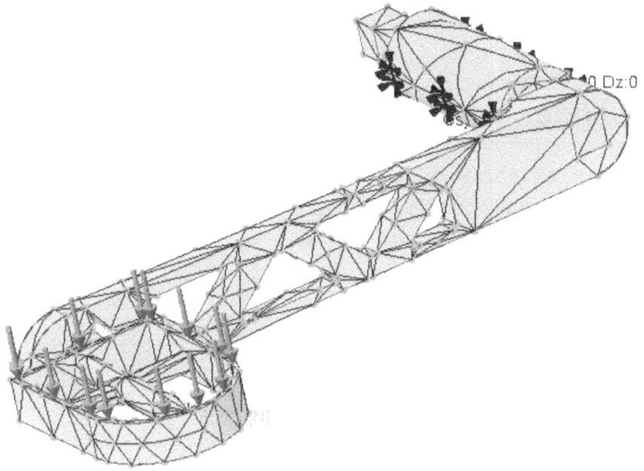

Figure 2–94

5. Click **Close** in the *AutoGEM* dialog box. The warning shown in Figure 2–95 displays.

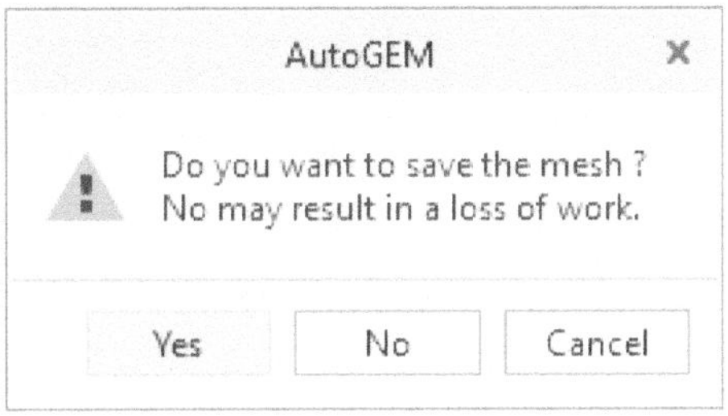

Figure 2–95

6. Click **No** to exit without saving the mesh.

The model will be meshed during the analysis run. Since meshing this model is fast, this will not impede the analysis runtime.

Analysis Tasks

In the following tasks, you will set the analysis type and convergence method, and then run the analysis.

Task 8: Set up the analysis.

1. In the *Home* tab, click (Analyses and Studies). The *Analyses and Design Studies* dialog box opens, as shown in Figure 2–96.

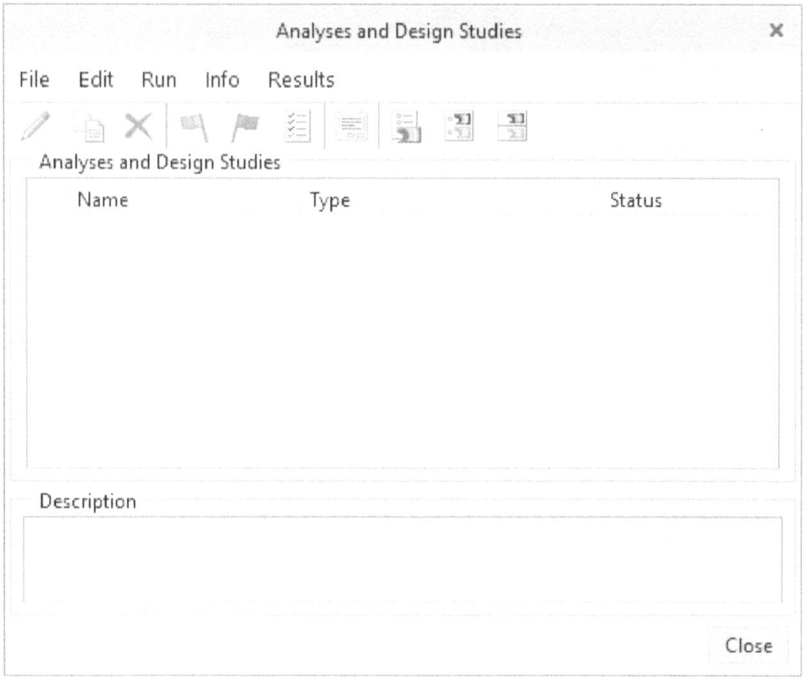

Figure 2–96

2. Select **File>New Static**. The *Static Analysis Definition* dialog box opens, as shown in Figure 2–97.

Figure 2–97

3. In the *Name* field, enter **bike_crank** (this will be the name of a subdirectory containing all of your results files).

4. For this analysis, you will use the **Single-Pass Adaptive** convergence method. Ensure that it is selected.

5. Click **OK** to close the *Static Analysis Definition* dialog box.

6. Click (Settings) in the *Analyses and Design Studies* dialog box. The *Run Settings* dialog box opens, as shown in Figure 2–98.

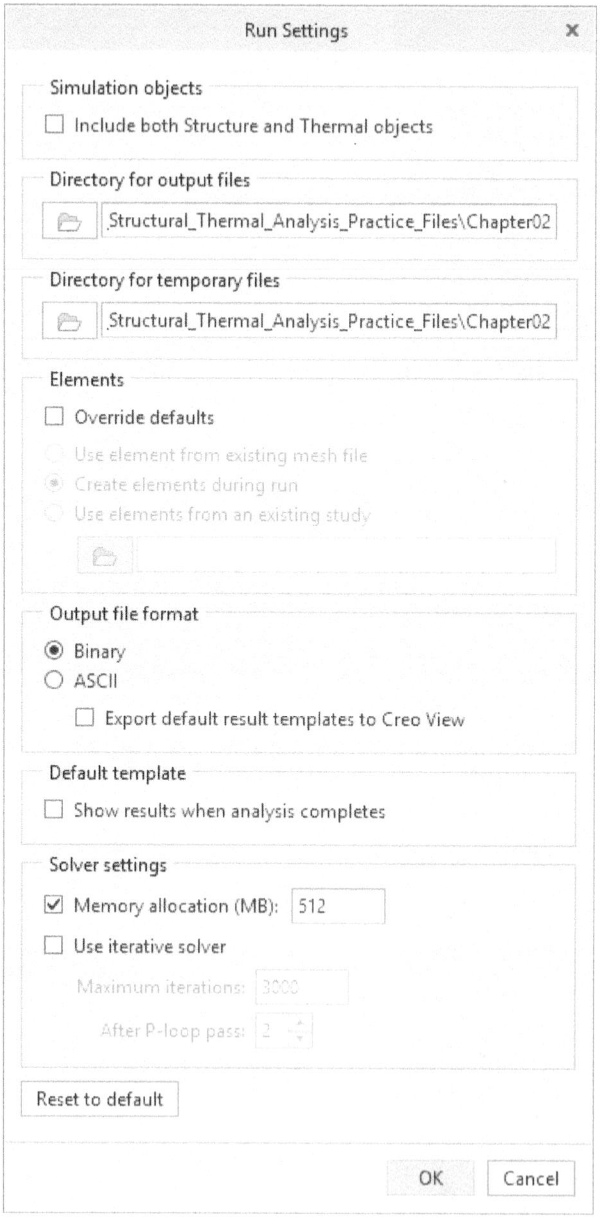

Figure 2–98

7. Note that, since you did not save the mesh file, the **Create Elements during Run** option is automatically selected in the *Elements* area.
8. Set *Memory Allocation* to **512Mb**.

   Note: *The recommended setting for the memory allocation is half the RAM in your computer.*

9. Click **OK** to close the *Run Settings* dialog box.
10. Expand the **Info** menu and select **Check Model**. This command checks the validity of the simulation model. The *Information* dialog box opens, as shown in Figure 2–99, stating that there are no errors.

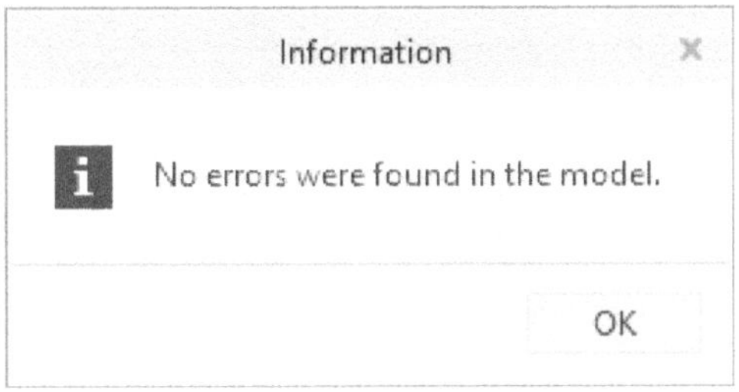

Figure 2–99

11. Click **OK** to confirm.

Task 9: Run the analysis.

1. Click (Start) in the *Analyses and Design Studies* dialog box to start your analysis. The *Question* dialog box opens, as shown in Figure 2–100.

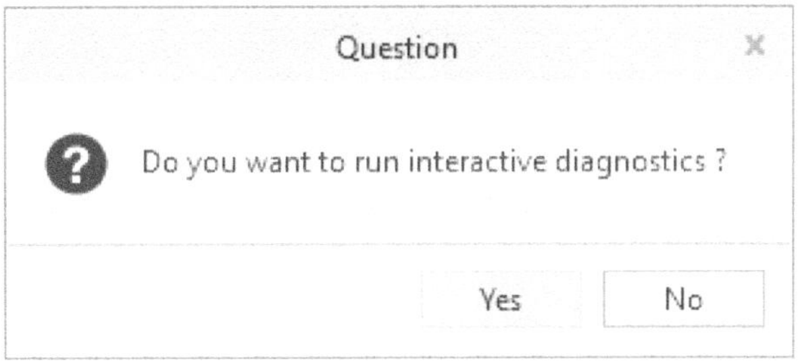

Figure 2–100

2. Click **Yes** in the *Question* dialog box. Creo Simulate solves the analysis. The *Diagnostics* dialog box opens, as shown in Figure 2–101, stating that the analysis run has been completed.

   Note that a warning message was issued during the analysis run, related to the yield condition being exceeded in AL6061 T4 material.

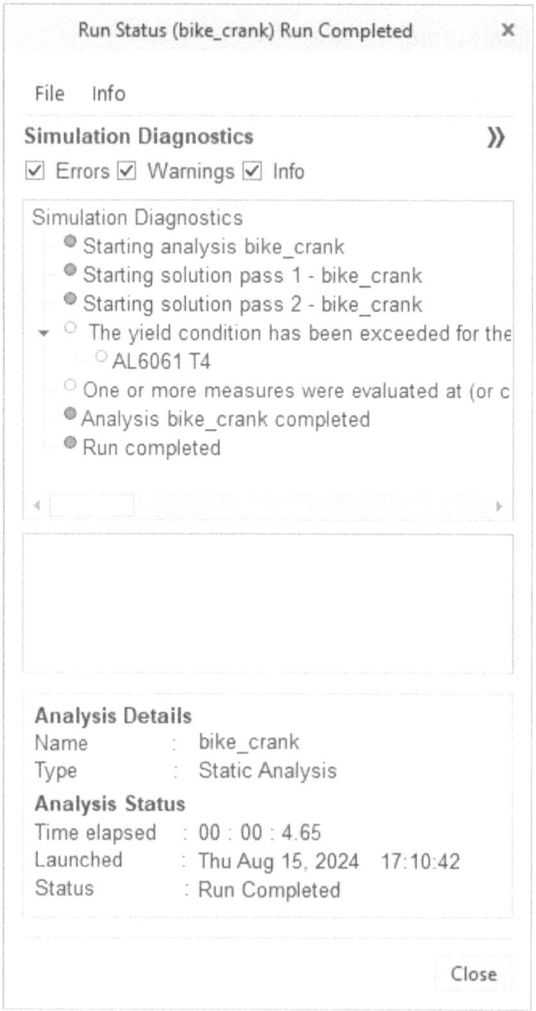

Figure 2–101

3. Click » (Show Summary Information) to expand the dialog box and display various information regarding the analysis as shown in Figure 2–102. Scroll up or down to the area that shows the RMS Stress Error Estimates and note that the estimated RMS stress error in this analysis is approximately 15.5 MPa, which is 8.3% of the maximum principal stress in the model.

   Since this is a preliminary analysis, which is only intended to check for gross design errors, you will accept this amount of analysis error. For a design validation analysis run, a more accurate **Multi-Pass Adaptive** convergence method would be recommended, with a target RMS stress error under 5%.

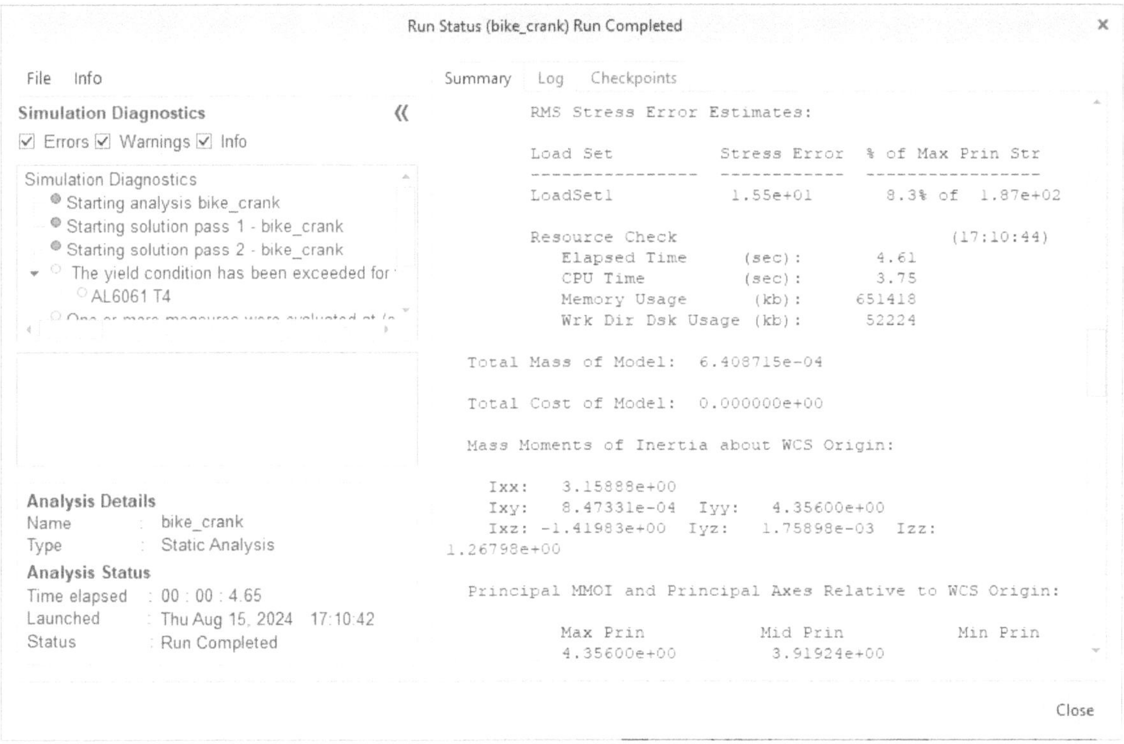

Figure 2–102

4. Click **Close** to close the *Run Status* dialog box, but do not close the *Analyses and Design Studies* dialog box yet.

Results Tasks

In the following tasks, you will display and interpret the results of this analysis.

Task 10: Display the results using the default template.

In this task, you will display the analysis results using the default template.

1. Click (Review Results from Default Template) in the *Analyses and Design Studies* dialog box (the tooltip on the icon should say *Review results of a design study from default template*). Creo Simulate takes a minute to prepare the visualization and then displays three result windows at once, as shown in Figure 2–103.

   The displayed result windows are as follows:

   - von Mises Stress Animation
   - Displacement Magnitude Fringe
   - Principal Stress Vectors

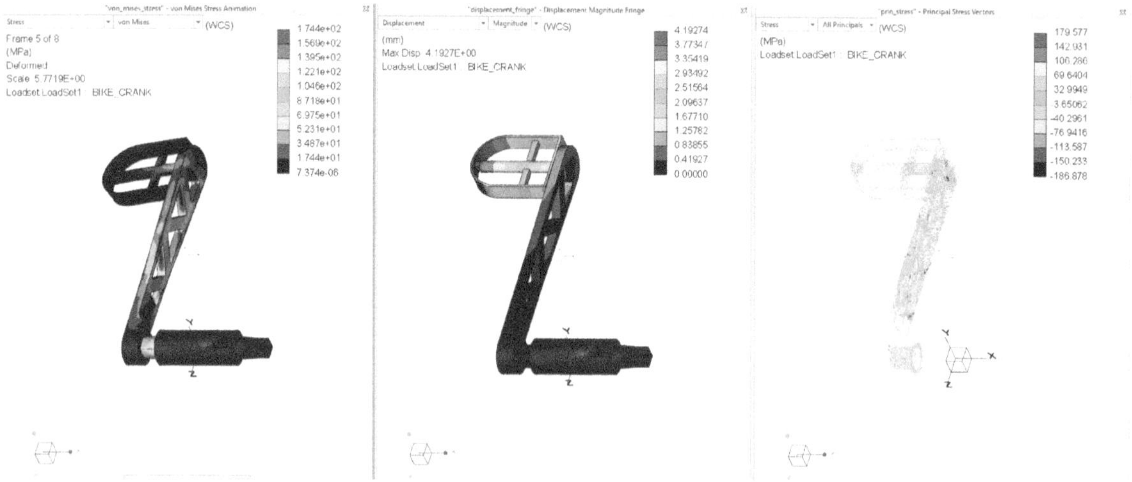

Figure 2–103

Task 11: Examine the Principal Stress results.

1. In the *View* tab, click (Show). The *Display Result Window* dialog box opens, as shown in Figure 2–104.

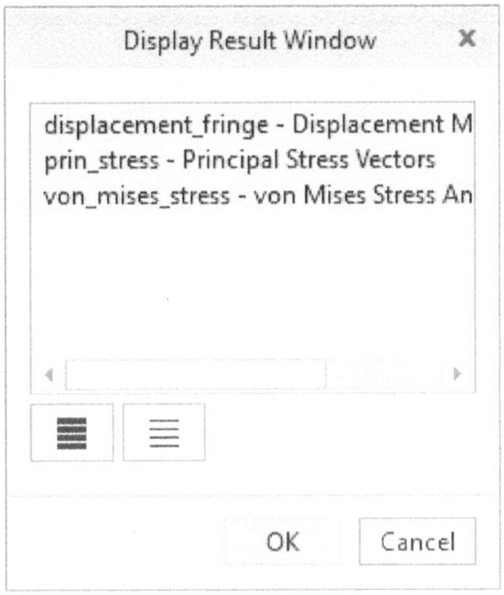

Figure 2–104

2. Clear the **displacement_fringe** and **von_mises_stress** options and click **OK**. Only the principal stress vector plot displays as shown in Figure 2–105.

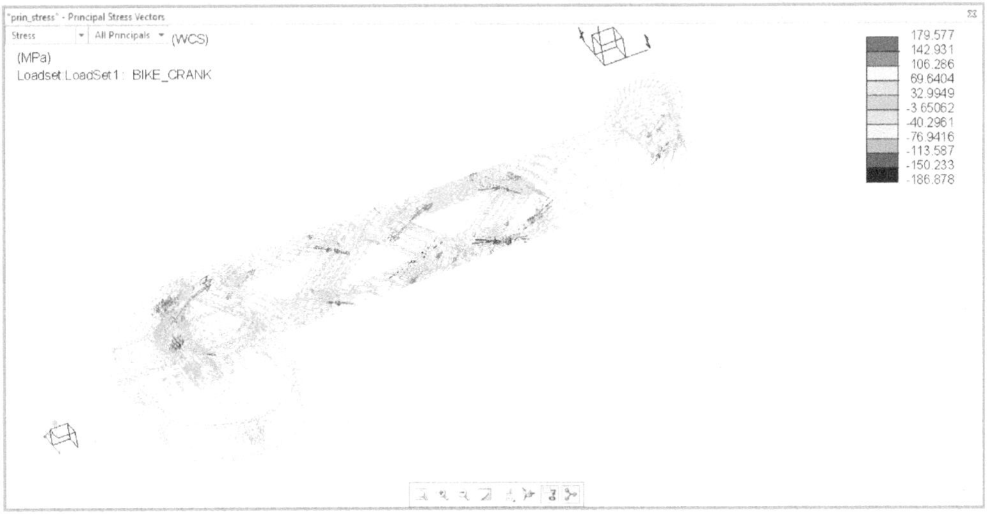

Figure 2–105

3. In the second drop-down list at the top-left corner of the window, select **Max Principal**, as shown in Figure 2–106.

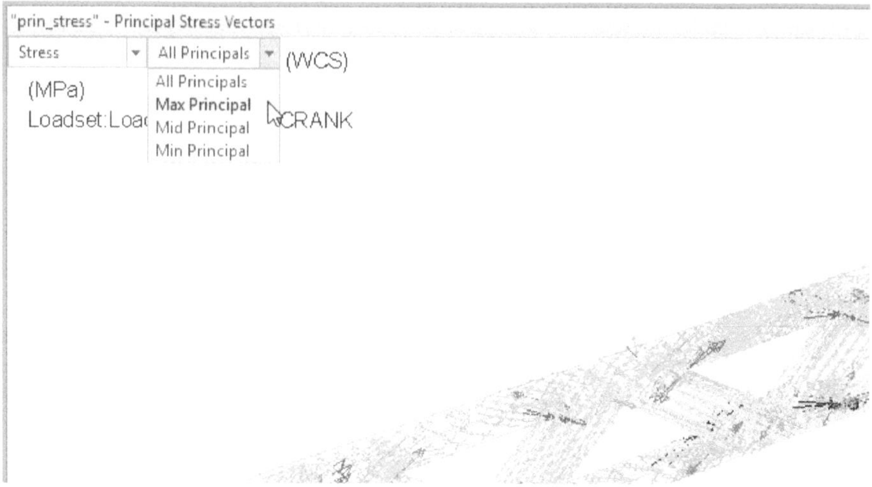

Figure 2–106

4. The result window now displays as shown in Figure 2–107.

   The maximum principal stress component is typically the tensile stress in the model, and is critical for predicting fatigue and brittle failures of the material. Use the **Rotate** and **Zoom** tools to examine the tensile stresses in the model.

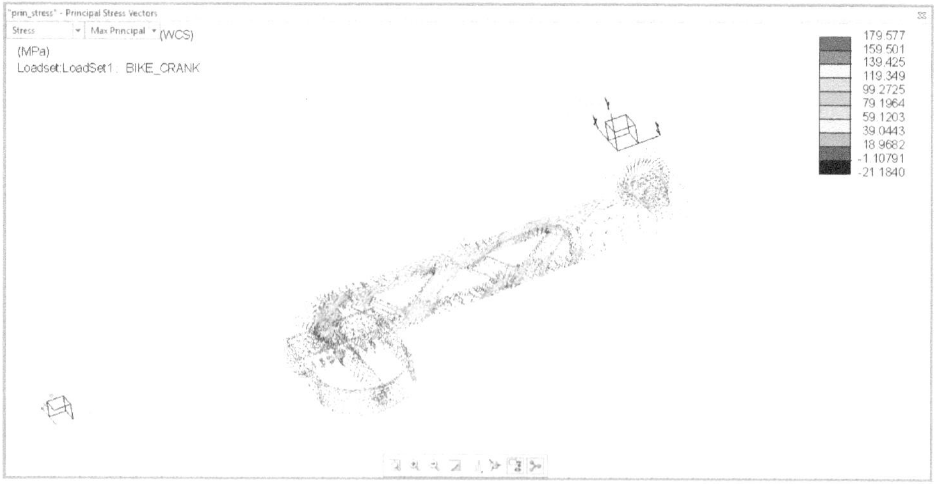

Figure 2–107

5. In the *View* tab, click (Show) to open the *Display Result Window* dialog box again. Clear the **prin_stress** option and click **OK** to hide all of the result windows for now.

Task 12: Display the Failure Index results.

In this task, you will display and examine the *Failure Index* result plot. The *Failure Index* is used to determine whether or not the material is predicted to fail under the given loading conditions:

- If the *Failure Index* is less than **1**, the material is not predicted to fail.
- If the *Failure Index* is equal to or greater than **1**, the material is predicted to fail.

> ***Note:*** *The Failure Index requires you to define a failure criterion. In Task 3, you defined* ***von Mises*** *as the failure criterion, which means the material is predicted to fail in the areas in which the* ***von Mises*** *stress exceeds the material's* ***Yield Stress****.*

1. In the *Home* tab, click (Open) to create a new results window. The *Open Result Windows* dialog box opens.
2. Select the **bike_crank** study and click **Open**. The *Result Window Definition* dialog box opens.
3. In the *Name* field, enter **fail_index_pedal**.
4. Expand the *Quantity* drop-down list and select **Failure Index**. The *Result Window Definition* dialog box should display as shown in Figure 2–108.

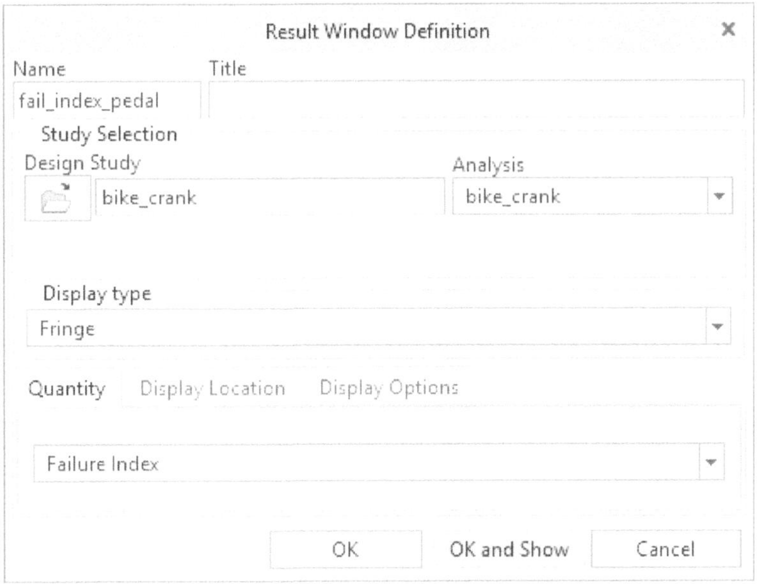

Figure 2–108

5. Click **OK and Show**. The result displays as shown in Figure 2–109.

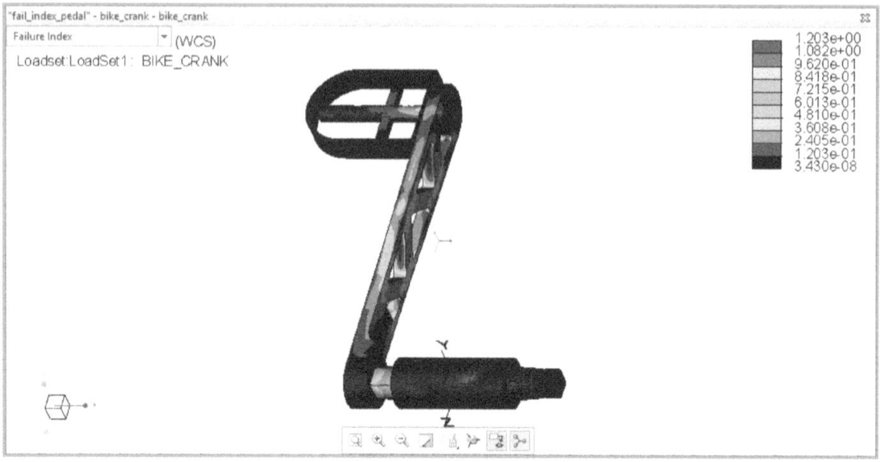

Figure 2–109

Note that the maximum failure index in the model is about 1.2, which is greater than 1, and means that in some areas in the model the material will fail under the given loading.

In the following steps, you will examine which areas in the model are predicted to fail.

6. In the *Home* tab, click (Edit). The *Result Window Definition* dialog box opens. Select the *Display Location* tab, as shown in Figure 2–110.

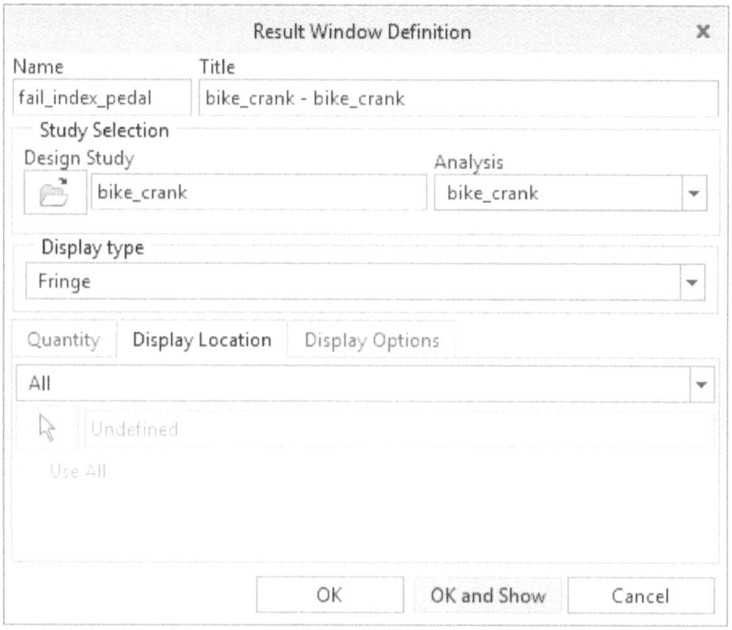

Figure 2–110

7. Expand the *Display Location* drop-down list and select **Components/Layers**. The *Component and Layer Visibility* dialog box opens, as shown in Figure 2–111.

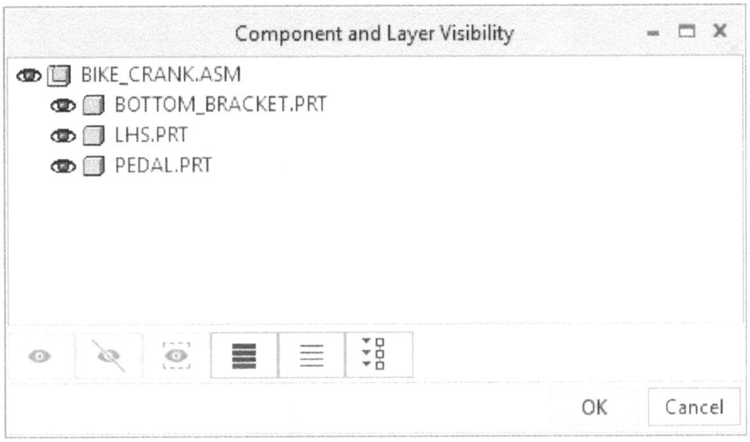

Figure 2–111

8. Set the visibility of **BOTTOM_BRACKET** and **LHS** to **Blanked**, as shown in Figure 2–112.

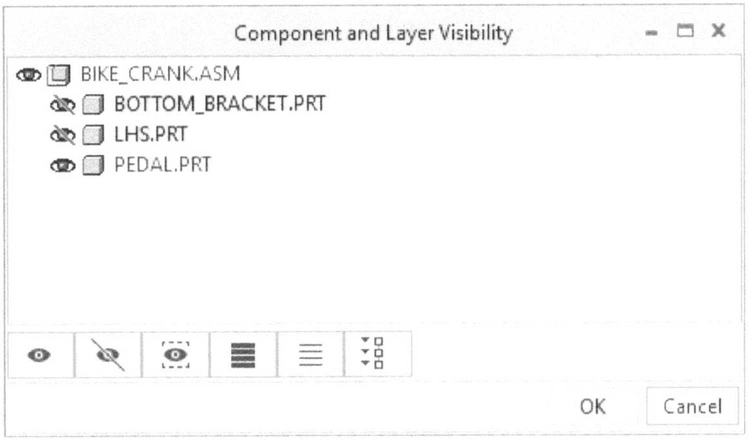

Figure 2–112

9. Click **OK** to close the *Component and Layer Visibility* dialog box and then click **OK and Show** to close the *Result Window Definition* dialog box. The result window displays as shown in Figure 2–113.

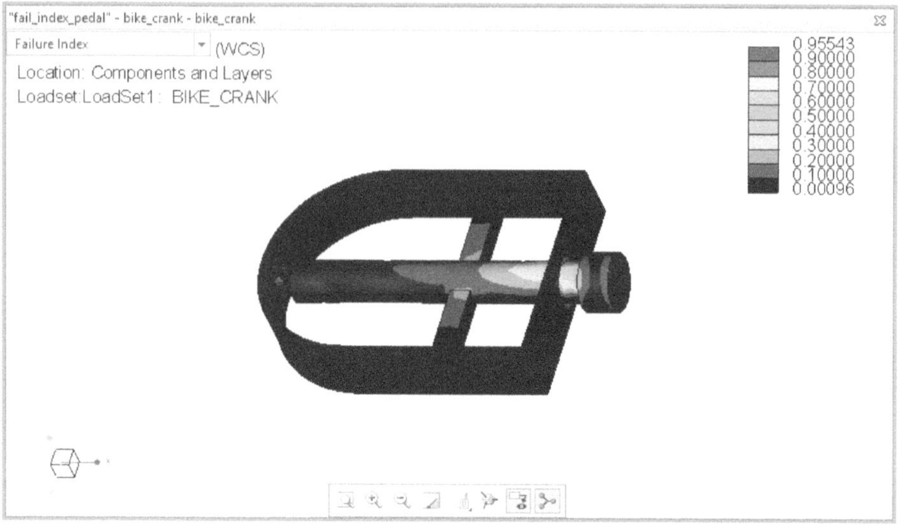

Figure 2–113

10. Right-click and select **Model Max** to locate the maximum failure index in the pedal, as shown in Figure 2–114.

The failure index in the fillet near the pedal's main thread is approximately 0.955. Therefore, the material in the pedal is not predicted to yield.

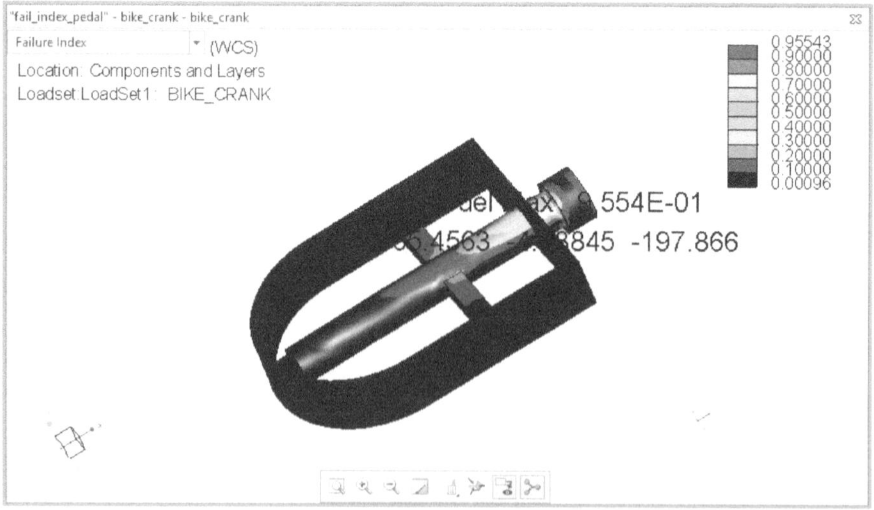

Figure 2–114

11. In the *Home* tab, click (Copy) to create a copy of the current result window. The *Result Window Definition* dialog box opens, as shown in Figure 2–115.

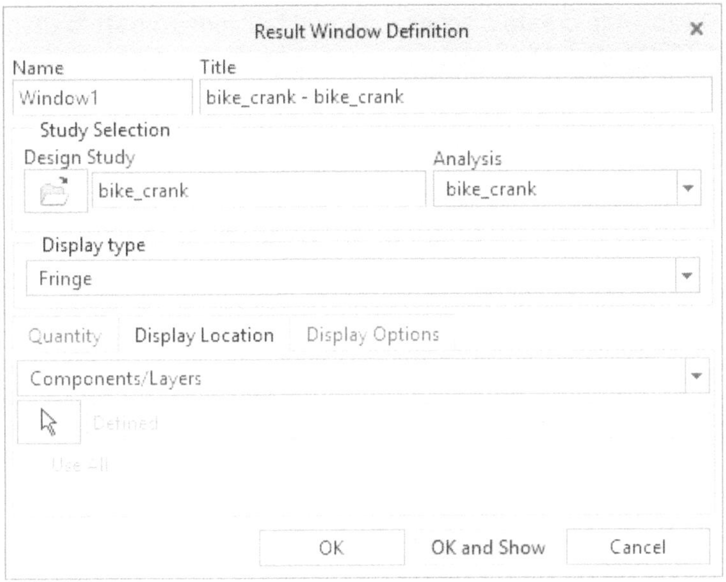

Figure 2–115

12. Rename the window as **fail_index_crank**.

13. Click (Select) to open the *Component and Layer Visibility* dialog box. Set the visibility of the **LHS** component to **Shown** and of the **BOTTOM_BRACKET** and **PEDAL** parts to **Blanked**, as shown in Figure 2–116.

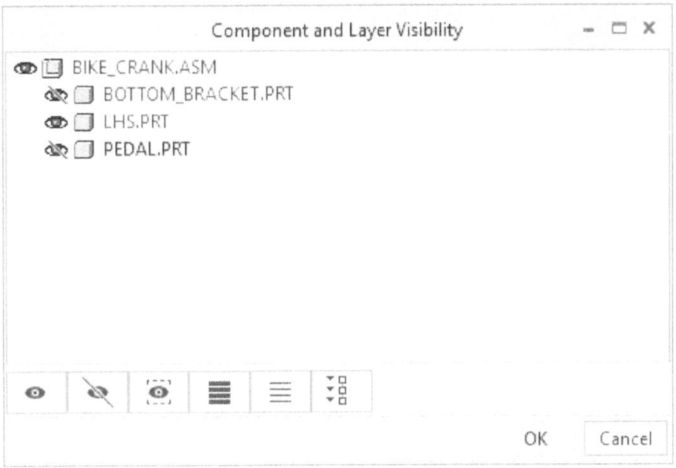

Figure 2–116

14. Click **OK** to close the *Component and Layer Visibility* dialog box and then click **OK** again to close the *Result Window Definition* dialog box and save the result definition without displaying.

15. Repeat Steps 11 to 14 to create a window named **fail_index_shaft** to display the failure index in the **BOTTOM_BRACKET** part.

16. In the *View* tab, click (Show) to open the *Display Result Window* dialog box. Highlight the **fail_index_crank** line, and clear all of the others, as shown in Figure 2–117.

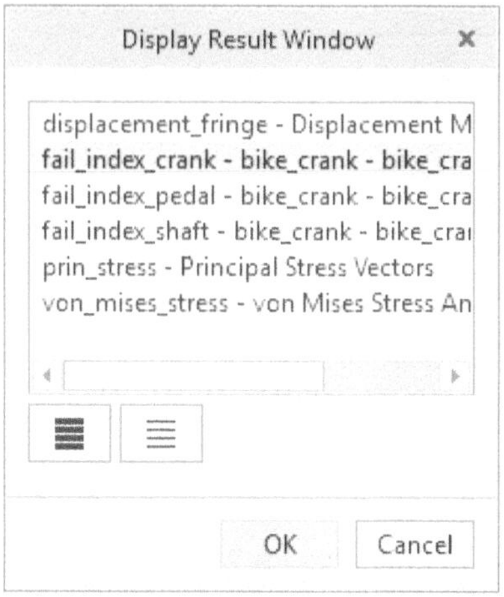

Figure 2–117

17. Click **OK**. The failure index result for the crank part displays as shown in Figure 2–118.

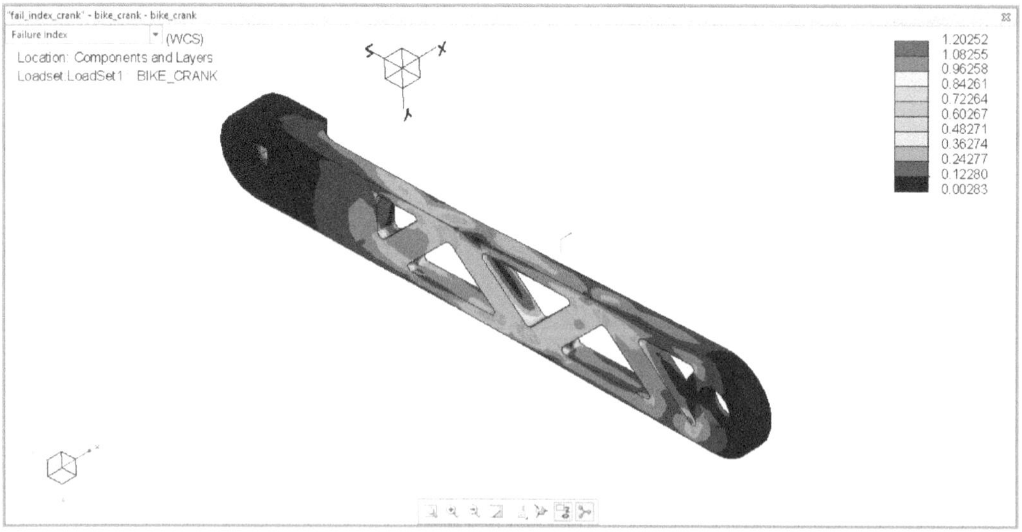

Figure 2–118

18. Right-click and select **Model Max** to locate the maximum failure index in the crank, as shown in Figure 2–119.

Note that the failure index in one of the fillets in the left pocket is approximately 1.203. The stress in this area is 20% over the material's yield stress, which means the material in the fillet is predicted to substantially yield.

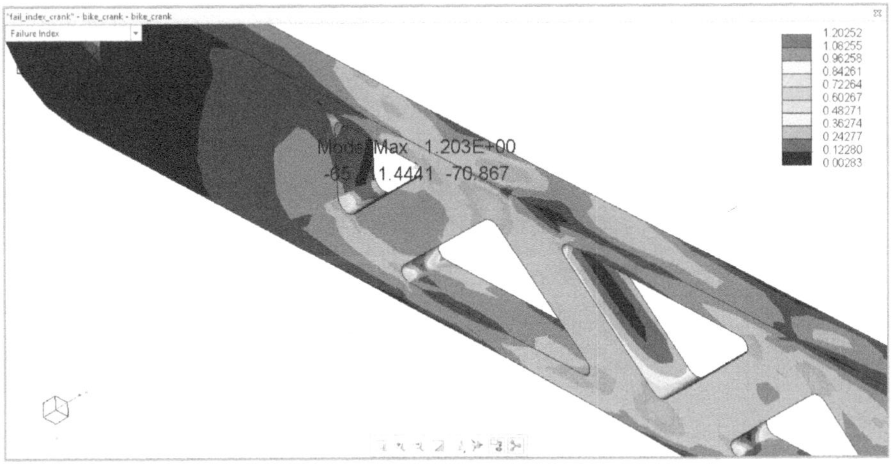

Figure 2–119

19. In the *View* tab, click (Show). Highlight the **fail_index_shaft** line and clear all of the others, as shown in Figure 2–120.

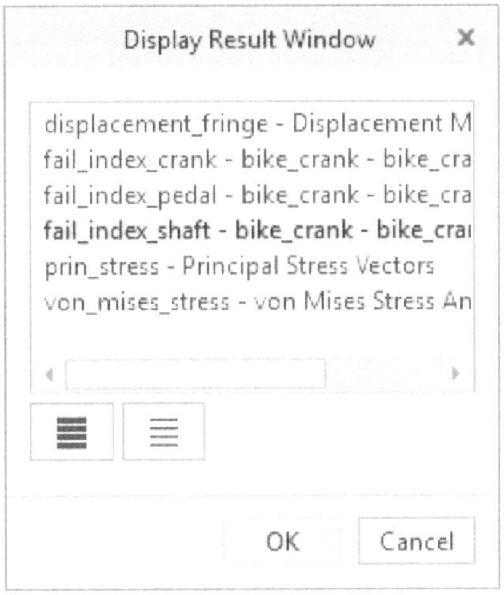

Figure 2–120

20. Click **OK**. The failure index result for the shaft part displays as shown in Figure 2–121.

    Note that the maximum failure index in the shaft is approximately 0.712. Therefore, this part is safe under the given loading.

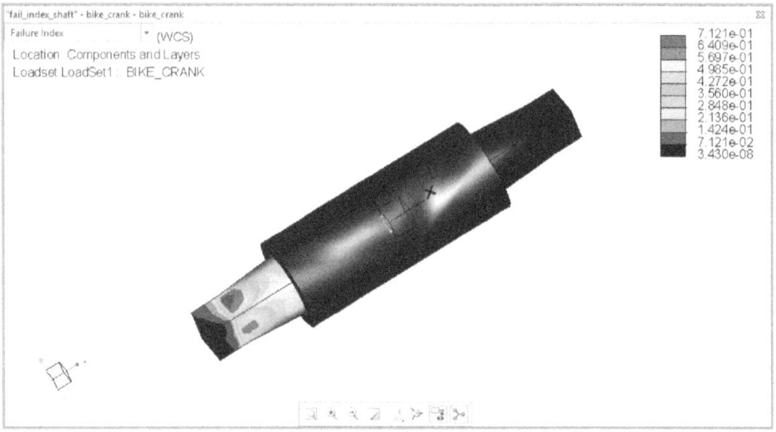

Figure 2–121

Report Tasks

In the following tasks, you will annotate the analysis results and prepare and export a report.

Task 13: Annotate the results.

1. In the *Home* tab, click (Edit). The *Result Window Definition* dialog box opens, as shown in Figure 2–122.

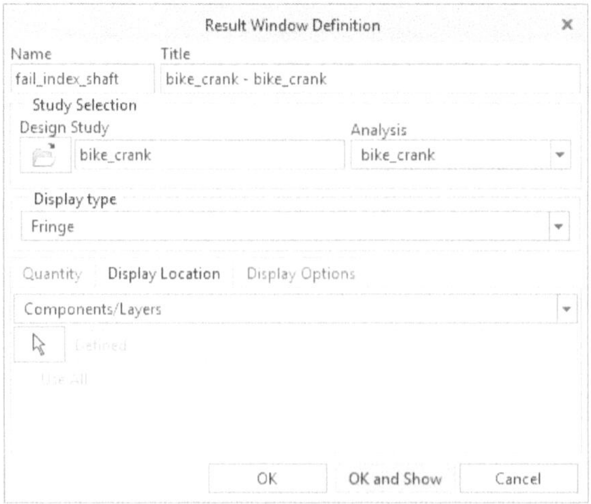

Figure 2–122

2. Expand the *Display Location* drop-down list, select **All**, and click **OK and Show**. The result window displays as shown in Figure 2–123.

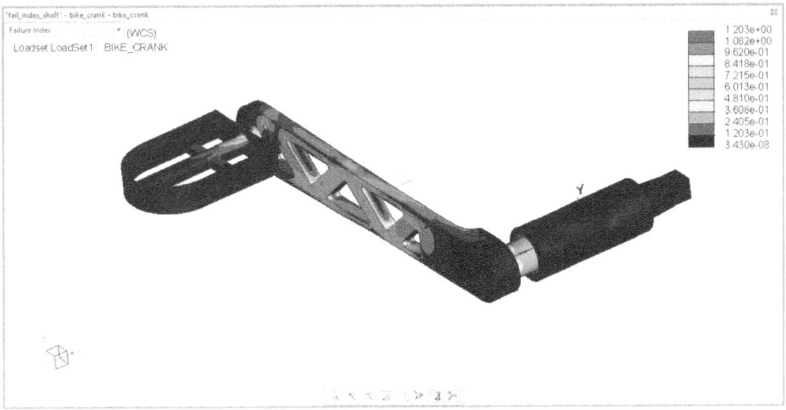

Figure 2–123

3. In the *Annotation* section of the *Format* tab, click (New). The *Note* dialog box opens, as shown in Figure 2–124.

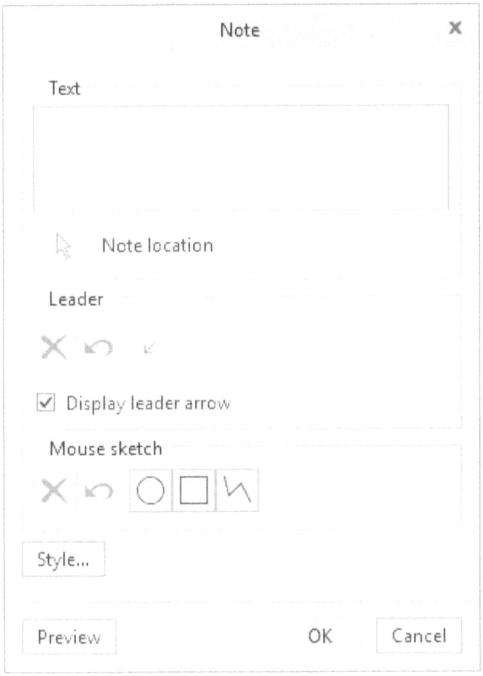

Figure 2–124

4. In the *Text* field, enter "**Unsafe area. Consider increasing the fillet radius and/or using stronger material**", as shown in Figure 2–125.

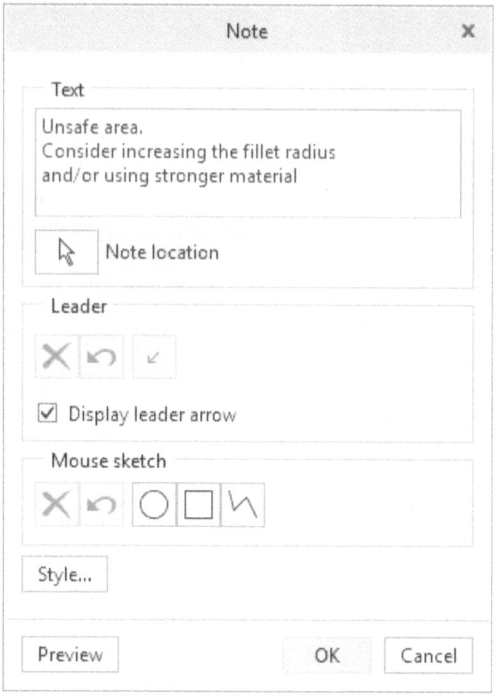

Figure 2–125

5. Click (Select) and select a location in the result window where you want to locate the top left corner of the annotation, as shown in Figure 2–126.

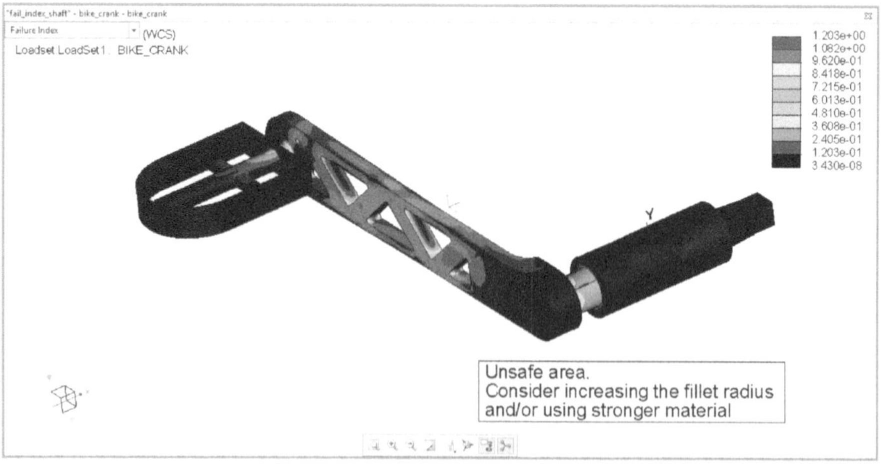

Figure 2–126

6. Click ↙ in the *Note* dialog box, and select the corner of the pocket with the maximum stress. The leader displays as shown in Figure 2–127.

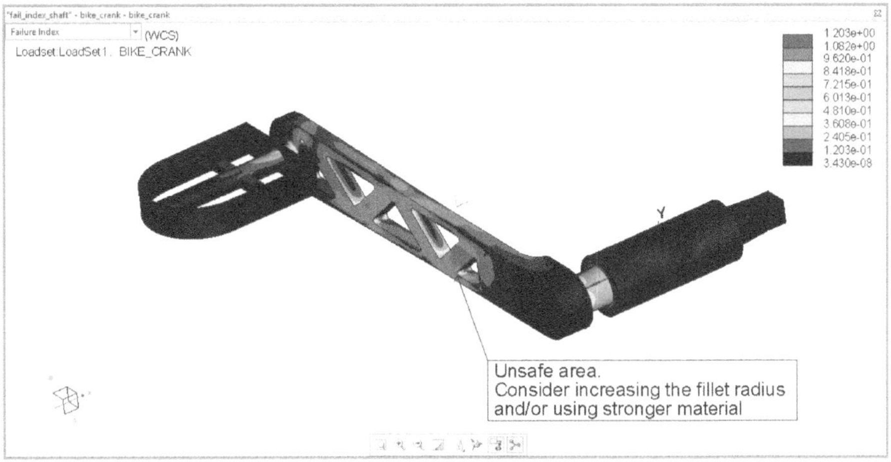

Figure 2–127

7. Repeat Step 6 to add another leader as shown in Figure 2–128.

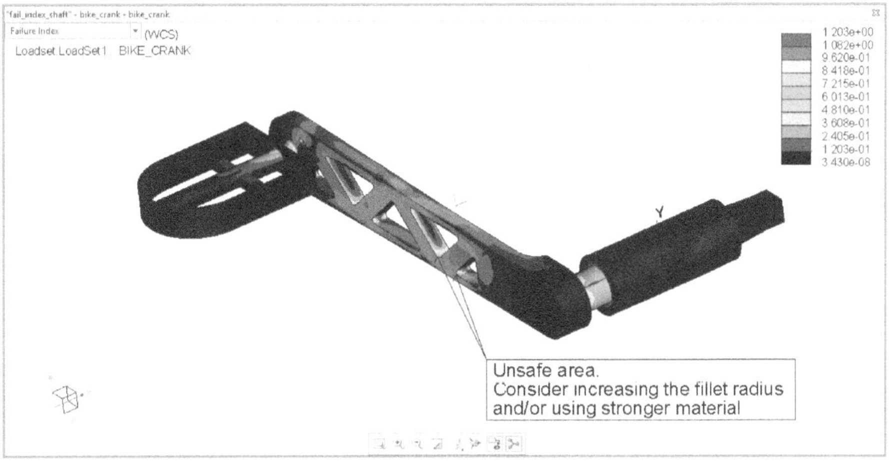

Figure 2–128

8. Click **OK** to finish creating the annotation.

Task 14: Create a report.

1. In the top-level menu, select **File>Save As>Save a Backup**. In the dialog box that opens, select **Web Page (*.html)** in the *Type* drop-down list, and enter **Bike_Crank_Preliminary_Analysis** as the file name, as shown in Figure 2–129.

Figure 2–129

2. Click **Save**. The *HTML Report* dialog box opens, as shown in Figure 2–130.

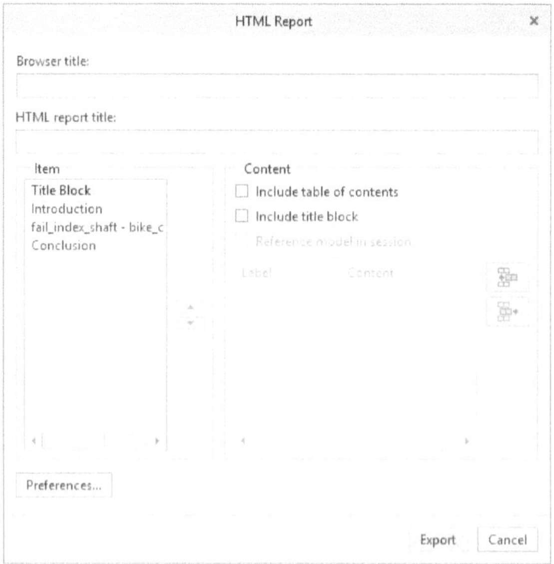

Figure 2–130

3. Rename the report as **Bike_Crank_Preliminary_Analysis**.
4. In the *Item* list, highlight **fail_index_shaft** and select the **Include modeling info** option, as shown in Figure 2–131.

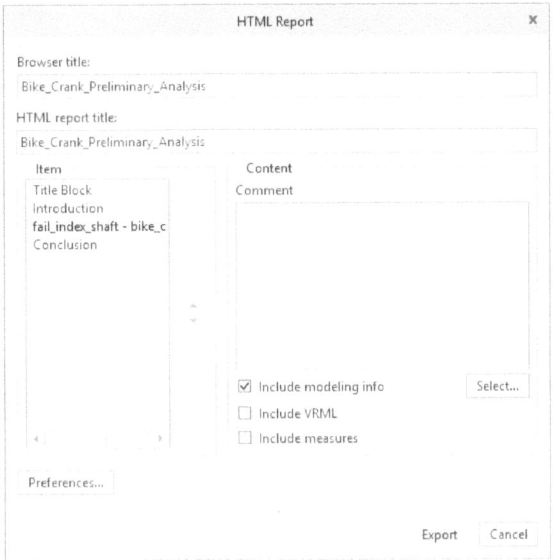

Figure 2–131

5. In the *Item* list, select **Conclusion** and enter "**Bike crank predicted to fail at given loading conditions. Design modification is required**", as shown in Figure 2–132.

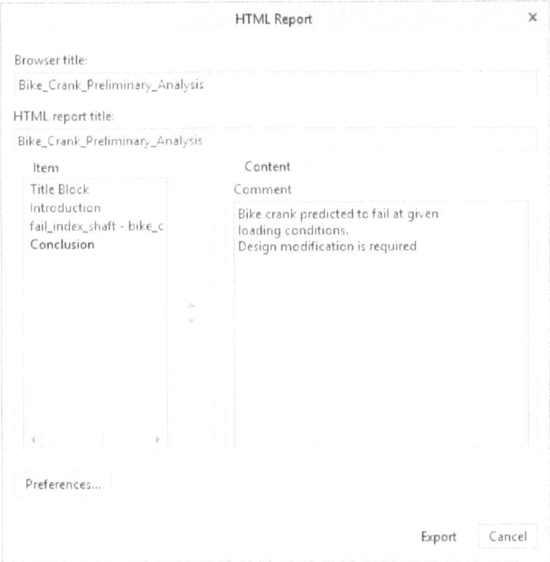

Figure 2–132

6. Click **Export**. The report is exported to the Creo working directory.
7. Open the *Bike_Crank_Preliminary_Analysis* directory in the Creo working directory and open **Bike_Crank_Preliminary_Analysis.html** in a Web browser (such as Internet Explorer), for review. The report displays as shown in Figure 2–133.

Bike_Crank_Preliminary_Analysis

fail_index_shaft - bike_crank - bike_crank

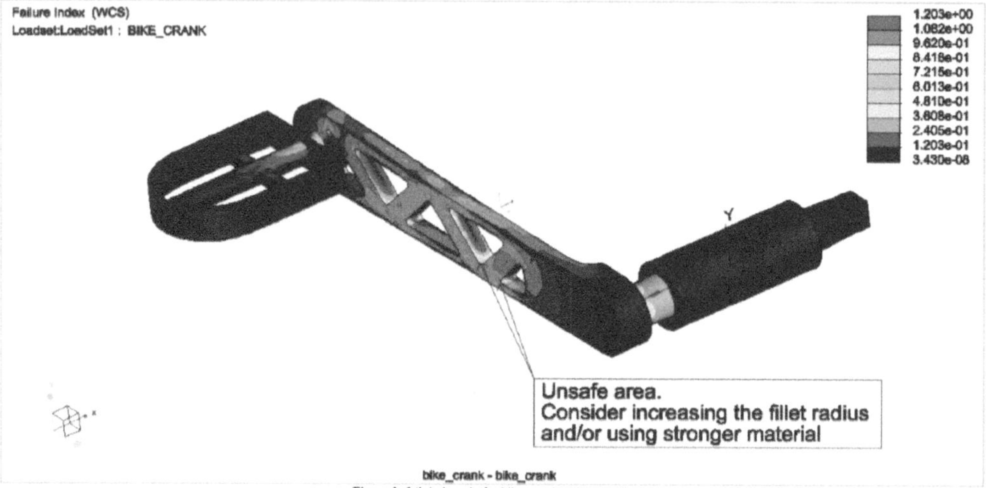

Figure 1. fail_index_shaft - bike_crank - bike_crank

Links

- Show Analysis Report File

BIKE_CRANK.ASM

Material Assignments

Material Assignment "MaterialAssign1"	
References	Model (LHS.PRT) Model (PEDAL.PRT)
Material	AL6061 T4

Material Assignment "MaterialAssign2"	
References	Model (BOTTOM_BRACKET.PRT)
Material	STEEL AISI 304

Figure 2–133

8. Close the report.
9. Exit the Results environment. Save and close the model.

End of practice

Practice 2c
Static Stress Analysis of a Cast Part

Practice Objectives

- Apply loads, constraints, and material properties.
- Mesh the model.
- Set up and run a Multi-Pass Adaptive analysis.
- Display the results.
- Determine the failure index and the safety factor for the part.
- Create the report.

In this practice, you will perform a static stress analysis on the cast part shown in Figure 2–134, with minimum instruction.

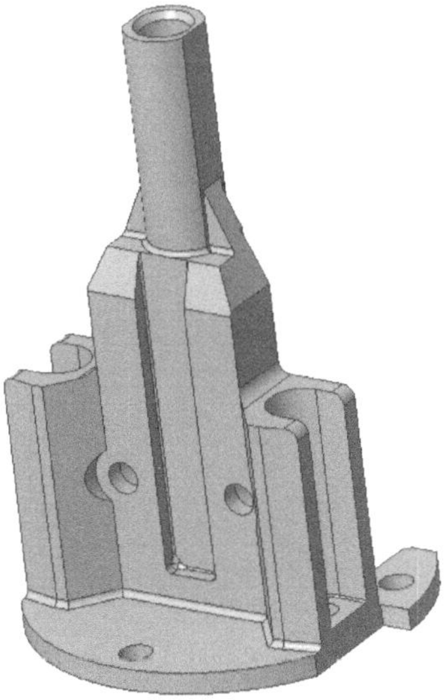

Figure 2–134

Task 1: Prepare the model for analysis.

1. Set the working directory to **Chapter02**, if required.
2. Open **guide.prt** and launch Creo Simulate.

3. Set the model display as follows:
   - *(Datum Display Filters)*: All Off
   - *(Spin Center)*: Off
   - *(Display Style)*: (Shading With Edges)
4. Apply the material:
   - *Material:* **Aluminum casting alloy AA208-T4**
   - *Poisson's ratio:* **0.33**
   - *Young's modulus:* **71000 MPa**
   - *Coefficient of thermal expansion:* **2.23e-5 /C**
   - *Density:* **2.8e-9 tonne/mm^3**
   - *Tensile Yield Stress:* **103 MPa**
   - *Failure Criterion:* **Distortion Energy (von Mises)**

   Note: *To create a new material that is not in the library, copy an existing material from the library into the model, then change the material's name and properties.*
5. Fully constrain the five holes on the bottom flange of the part, as shown in Figure 2–135.

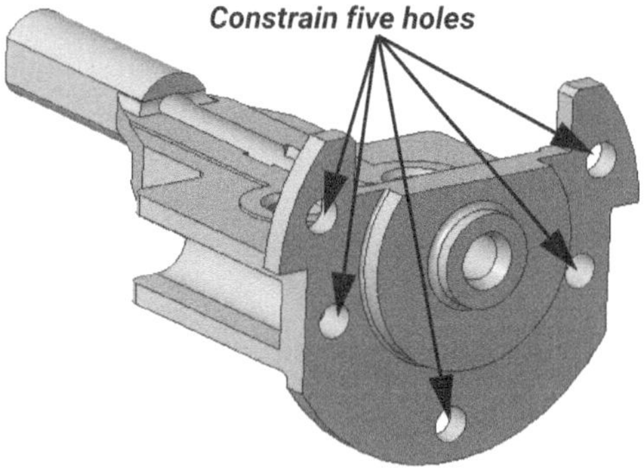

Figure 2–135

6. Apply 100N load in the positive Y-direction to the bore surface, as shown in Figure 2–136.

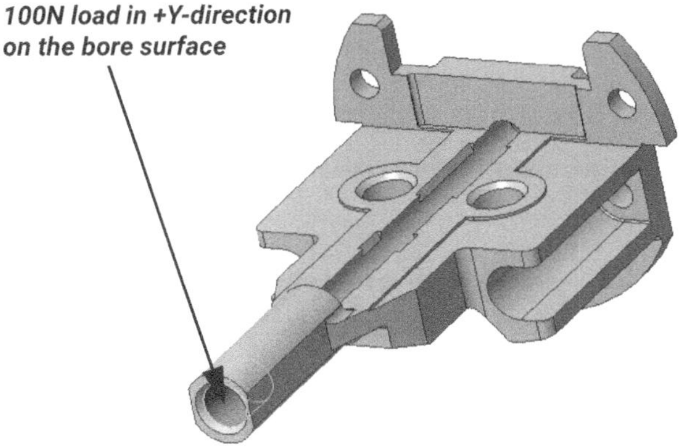

Figure 2–136

7. Mesh the model using the **All with Properties** option. Examine and save the mesh.

Task 2: Set up and run the analysis.

1. Create a new static analysis with the following parameters:
   - *Analysis name:* **guide**
   - *Convergence method:* **Multi-Pass Adaptive**
   - *Maximum Polynomial Order:* **9**
   - *Percent Convergence:* **6**
2. Run the analysis and wait until it completes.
3. Display the *Status* window. Check whether the analysis has converged, and note the RMS Stress Error value.

Task 3: Visualize and examine the analysis results.

1. Visualize and examine the **strain_energy** and **max_stress_vm** convergence graphs.
2. Visualize the **P-Level** fringe plot. Determine the value and the locations of the maximum P-level.
3. Visualize and animate the **Displacement Magnitude** fringe plot. Does the part deform according to the applied loads?
4. Display the **von Mises Stress** fringe plot. Find the location of the maximum stress.
5. Display the **Failure Index** fringe plot. Is the part predicted to fail?

6. Calculate the value of the factor of safety for the part. Can you think of design changes that would lead to improving the factor of safety in this part?

   Note: *Factor of Safety value is the inverse of the Failure Index value.*

7. Annotate the **von Mises Stress** plot, showing the location of the maximum stress.
8. Create and export the analysis report to HTML.
9. Save and close the model.

End of practice

Chapter 3

Loads and Constraints

Loads and constraints are the boundary conditions that the model experiences in its working environment. Selecting the correct boundary conditions for your FEA model is a critical aspect of developing an accurate simulation. Therefore, when you are analyzing a model, the loads and constraints placed on it must realistically represent the operating conditions of your product.

Learning Objectives

- Understand the use of constraints, rigid body motions, and constraint sets.
- Create a displacement constraint.
- Create planar, pin, or ball constraints.
- Create symmetry constraints.
- Understand types of loads and load sets.
- Create a force or moment load.
- Create pressure, bearing, gravity, centrifugal, and temperature loads.
- Create a preload.
- Divide surfaces into regions.
- Understand how to handle models with stress singularities.

3.1 Constraints

In Creo Simulate, a constraint is a form of boundary condition in which a *prescribed displacement* is assigned to one or more geometrical entities in the model. Prescribed displacement means that the displacement of the geometrical entity to which it is applied is enforced throughout the simulation. A prescribed displacement (i.e., constraint) can be of a zero value, which is typically used to simulate all kinds of supports in the analysis model, or of a non-zero value, which is typically used to enforce a specific motion in the model.

Constraints are commonly used to model a true support, such as where a structure is fixed to a rigid foundation or adjoining structure. Another common use is to simulate various symmetry conditions, such as mirror symmetry, cyclic symmetry, or anti-symmetry.

Although constraints are essential for structural analyses, it is usually preferable to limit the use of constraints as much as possible. Since the essence of structural FEA is to calculate displacements (along with the corresponding strains and stresses), the prescribed displacements effectively force an assumed solution onto some of the geometrical entities in the model. Therefore, too many constraints might unnaturally stiffen the model, and, consequently, the stresses might typically err on the low side.

Rigid Body Motions

In static analysis, it is necessary to provide sufficient supports to prevent rigid body motions (RBM), which are the movements of parts of the structure that do not produce strain. An example of a simply supported beam is shown in Figure 3–1.

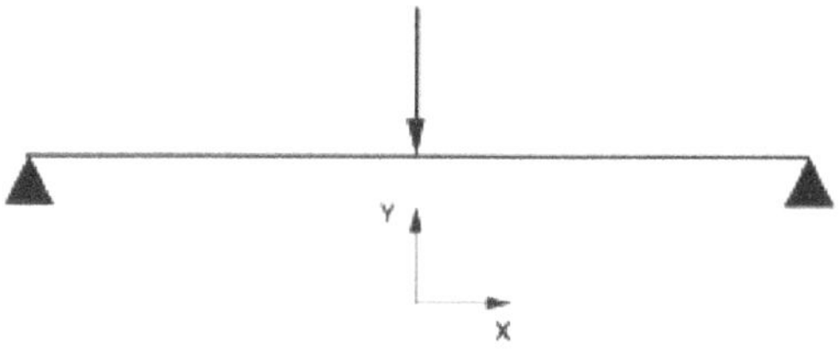

Figure 3–1

When using handbook formulas to calculate stresses, the only supports required for the simply supported beam are those in the Y-direction. Since no loads are applied in the X-direction, a support in that direction is not necessary. However, in FEA the lack of support in X-direction results in a fatal error or inaccurate results. This is because a small load in the X-direction occurs during the FEA solution process, because of rounding errors.

The number of possible RBMs varies from one model to another. For a single part in 3D, there are six possible RBMs: three translations and three rotations. For an assembly, the number could be much greater, since each part now has six possible RBMs that have to be eliminated by applying constraints and connections between the parts.

> ***Note:*** *If possible RBMs are detected, Creo Simulate displays the error message:* ***The model is insufficiently constrained for the analysis****.*

Constraint Sets

Every constraint in Creo Simulate belongs to a constraint set. A constraint set is a collection of constraints that act together on your model.

Constraint sets provide the means of organizing your modeling entities in a logical way, to have the additional flexibility of treating your constraints separately when setting up various analysis scenarios and load cases. A carefully considered approach to constraint sets simplifies the analyses definition.

To manage your constraint sets, select **Constraints>Constraint Sets** drop-down list in the *Home* tab to open the *Constraint Sets* dialog box, as shown in Figure 3–2.

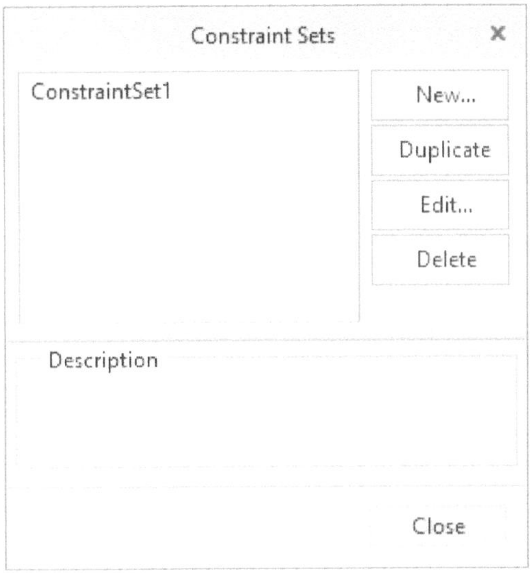

Figure 3–2

Constraint sets can be created, duplicated, edited, or deleted.

Displacement Constraint

The displacement constraint is the most commonly used tool in Creo Simulate that is used to apply constraints. To apply a displacement constraint, click (Displacement) in the *Home* tab, or select the references and click (Displacement) in the mini-toolbar. The *Constraint* dialog box opens, as shown in Figure 3–3.

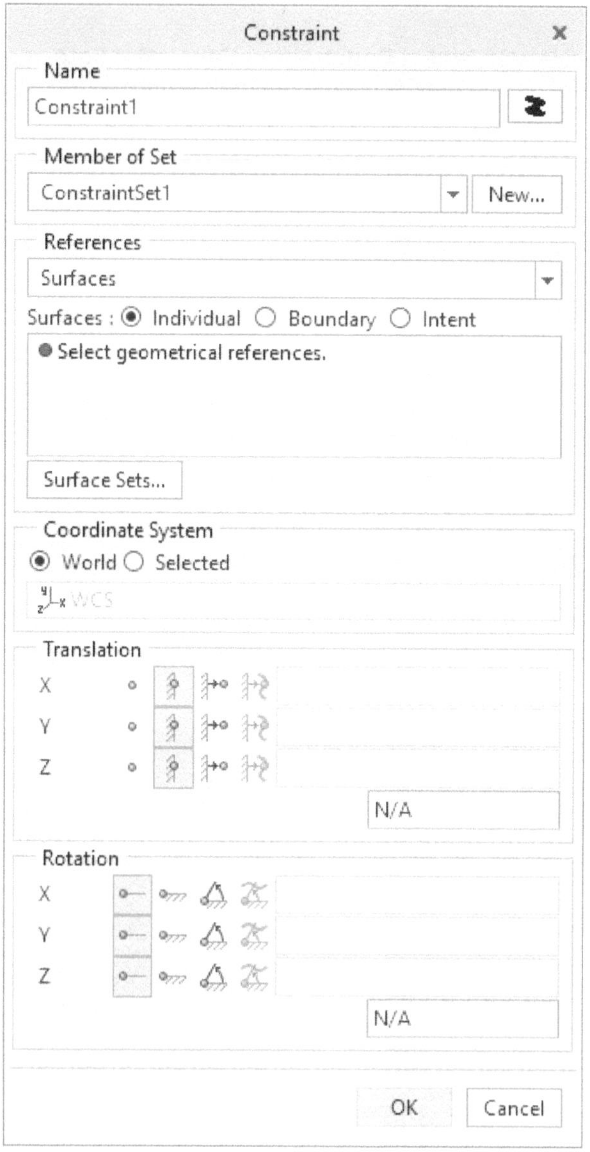

Figure 3–3

The options in the *Constraint* dialog box are as follows:

Section	Option	Description
Name	**N/A**	Assigns a name to the constraint.
Member of Set	**Constraint sets in the model**	Selects a constraint set.
References	**Surfaces**	Assigns the constraint to surfaces.
	Edges/Curves	Assigns the constraint to edges or curves.
	Points	Assigns the constraint to vertices or points.
Coordinate System	**World**	The constraint directions are defined in WCS.
	Selected	Enables you to select another coordinate system to define constraint directions. The coordinate system can be cartesian, cylindrical, or spherical.
Translation		Enables mesh nodes on the selected geometry to move in a direction.
		Constrains mesh nodes on the selected geometry in a direction.
		Forces mesh nodes on the selected geometry to move along a direction by a non-zero prescribed displacement value.
Rotation		Enables mesh nodes on the selected geometry to rotate about a direction. Not applicable to solid elements, which do not carry rotational degrees of freedom at their nodal points.
		Constrains mesh nodes on the selected geometry against rotations about a direction. Not applicable to solid elements, which do not carry rotational degrees of freedom at their nodal points.
		Forces the nodes on the selected geometry into rotation about a direction by a non-zero prescribed angle. Not applicable to solid elements, which do not carry rotational degrees of freedom at their nodal points.

Planar, Pin, and Ball Constraints

A planar constraint enables you to create a constraint that permits full planar movement, but constrains the off-plane displacement. Only planar surfaces can be selected.

To apply a planar constraint, click (Planar) in the *Home* tab or select the references and click (Planar) in the mini-toolbar. The *Planar Constraint* dialog box opens, as shown in Figure 3–4.

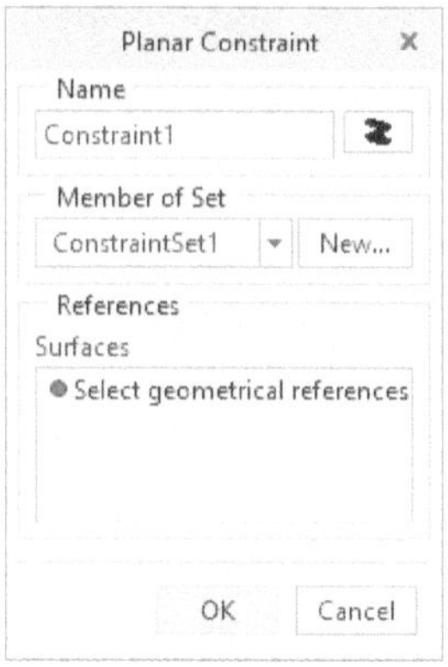

Figure 3–4

A pin constraint enables you to control the translation or rotation about the axis of a cylindrical surface. Only cylindrical surfaces can be selected.

To apply a pin constraint, click (Pin) in the *Home* tab or select the references and click (Pin) in the mini-toolbar. Use the options to control rotation about the cylinder's axis and translation along its axis, as shown in Figure 3–5.

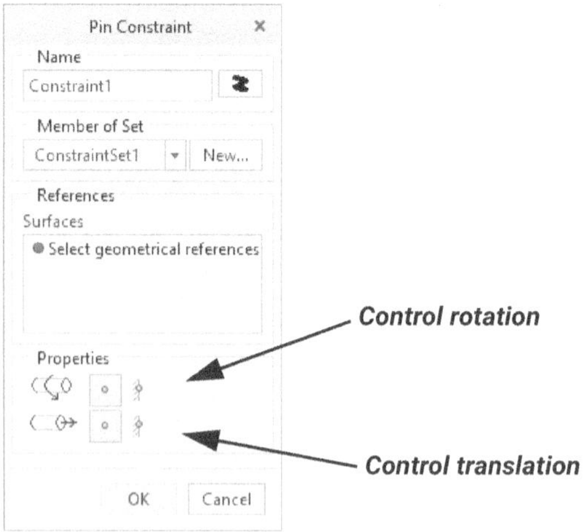

Figure 3–5

A ball constraint simulates a ball support in which all of the translations are fixed while all of the rotations are free. Only spherical surfaces can be selected for this type of constraint.

To apply a ball constraint, click (Ball) in the *Home* tab. The *Ball Constraint* dialog box opens, as shown in Figure 3–6.

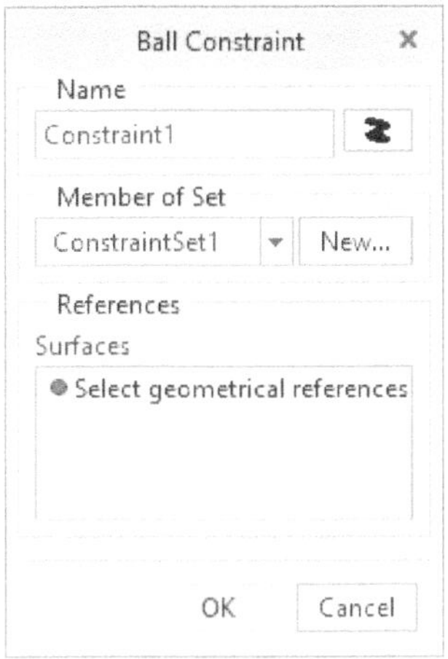

Figure 3–6

Symmetry Constraints

There are two types of symmetry constraints in Creo Simulate:

- Mirror Symmetry
- Cyclic Symmetry

Using symmetry constraints, you can take advantage of the model's symmetry to reduce meshing and analysis time. In essence, symmetry constraints enable you to analyze a segment of the model and project the result onto the entire model.

Mirror Symmetry

The mirror symmetry constraint requires that the model exhibits a *reflective* symmetry about a plane. The geometry and modeling entities on one side of the plane must mirror the geometry and modeling entities on the other side of the plane.

Use the following steps to apply a mirror symmetry constraint:

1. Cut your model in half along the plane of symmetry. The result is 1/2 of the geometry (it could be 1/4 or even 1/8 of the geometry if your analysis model exhibits more than one plane of symmetry).
2. In the *Home* tab, select **Constraints>Symmetry**. The *Symmetry Constraint* dialog box opens.

3. Expand the *Type* drop-down list and select **Mirror**. The *Symmetry Constraint* dialog box displays as shown in Figure 3–7.

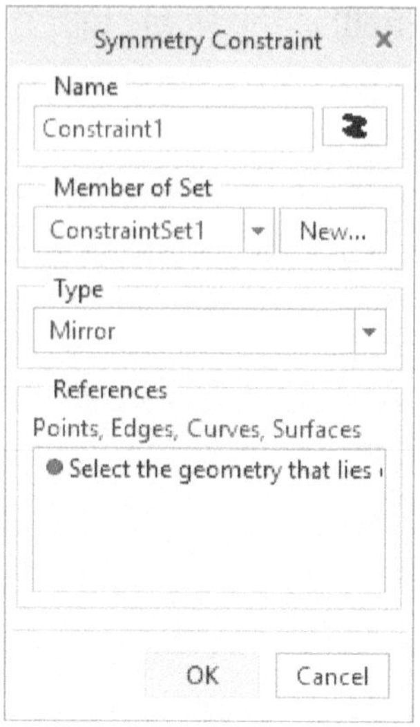

Figure 3–7

4. Select the surfaces, edges, curves, or points located on the symmetry plane.
5. Click **OK** to finish.

Cyclic Symmetry

In a model with cyclic symmetry, a 3D geometric shape is repeated a number of times around the axis of rotation. The geometry is not continuous, but rather cyclic. For example, the fan shown in Figure 3–8 is an example of a cyclically symmetric geometry.

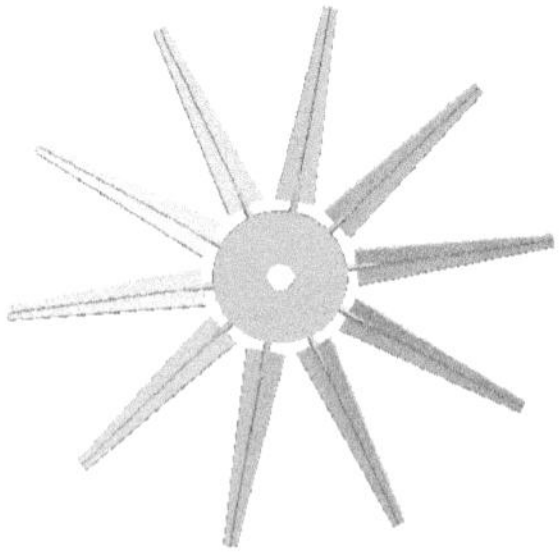

Figure 3–8

If loads, constraints, materials, etc., are cyclic as well, you can analyze a single blade, as shown in Figure 3–9, by correctly isolating it and applying constraints that capture the cyclic symmetry.

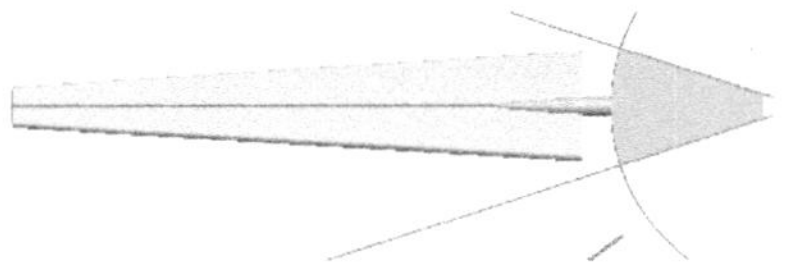

Figure 3–9

Use the following steps to apply a cyclic symmetry constraint:

1. Isolate the cyclic geometry by cutting it out of your model. The cutout surfaces do not have to be planar. The only requirement is that the cross-sections on the cutout surfaces must be identical.
2. In the *Home* tab, select **Constraints>Symmetry**. The *Symmetry Constraint* dialog box opens.
3. Expand the *Type* drop-down list and select **Cyclic**. The *Symmetry Constraint* dialog box displays as shown in Figure 3–10.

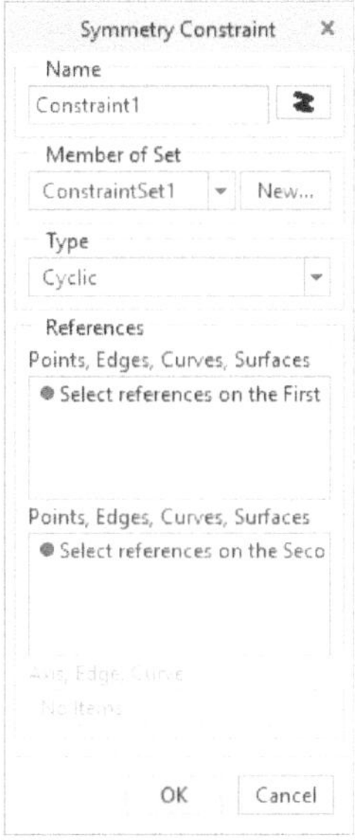

Figure 3–10

4. Select the geometry on the first cutout boundary.
5. Select the geometry on the second cutout boundary.
6. Depending on the selected geometry, Creo Simulate might or might not be able to automatically determine the axis of symmetry. If not, you need to select the axis of symmetry.
7. Click **OK** to finish.

Note that both the geometry and boundary conditions must meet the criteria of cyclic symmetry. If the constraints or loading is not repeated about the axis of rotation by the same number of repetitions as the geometry, the results are invalid.

3.2 Loads

Unsatisfactory representation of the loading is a common cause of inaccurate analysis results. Therefore, gathering adequate information about the magnitude of the loads is a critical aspect of developing an accurate simulation. It should be noted that in a linear analysis the stresses and deformations are directly proportional to the magnitude of the loading. For example, a possible error in loading of 20% leads to a minimum 20% error in stresses and deflections.

There are two main types of loading in structural FEA:

- **Mechanical loads:** Consisting of concentrated or distributed forces or moments and body forces. The mechanical loads are typically related to a coordinate system, and consist of magnitude and orientation. The spatial distribution and time dependence of the load can also be defined. The following types of mechanical loads are available in Creo Simulate:
  - Force/moment load
  - Pressure load
  - Bearing load
  - Gravity load
  - Centrifugal load
- **Initial strains:** Caused by thermal expansion, press-fit, or pre-stress. The following types of initial strain loads are available in Creo Simulate:
  - Temperature load
  - Preload

Load Sets

Every load in Creo Simulate belongs to a load set. A load set is a collection of loads that act together on your model.

Load sets provide a means of organizing your modeling entities in a logical way, to have the additional flexibility of treating your loads separately when setting up various analysis scenarios and load cases. A carefully considered approach to load sets simplifies the analyses definition.

To manage your load sets, select **Loads>Load Sets** in the *Home* tab to open the *Load Sets* dialog box as shown in Figure 3–11.

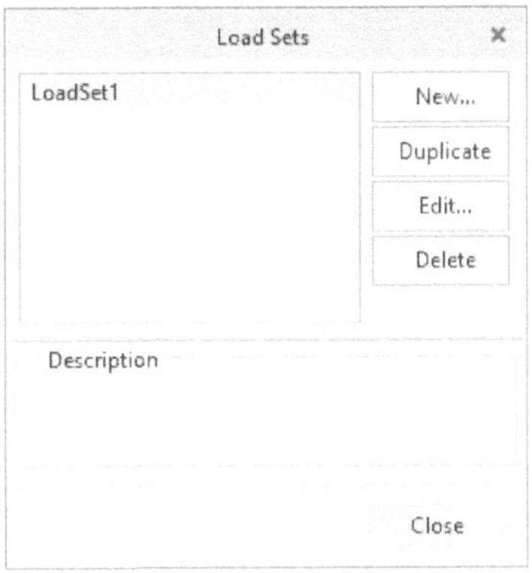

Figure 3–11

Load sets can be created, duplicated, edited, or deleted.

Force/Moment Load

To apply a force/moment load, click (Force/Moment) in the *Home* tab or select the references and click (Force/Moment) in the mini-toolbar. The *Force/Moment Load* dialog box opens, as shown in Figure 3–12.

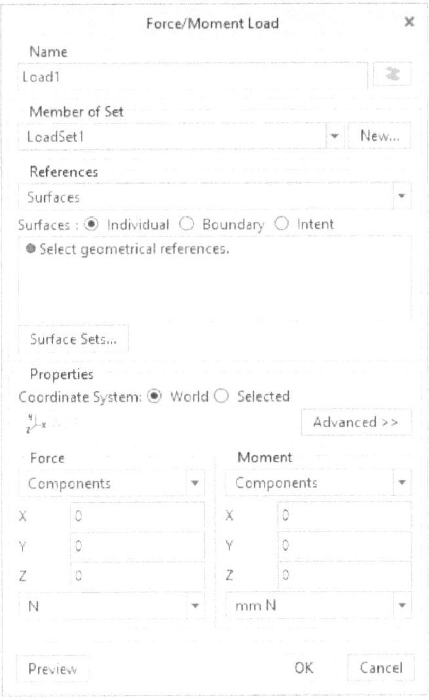

Figure 3–12

The options available in the *Force/Moment Load* dialog box are as follows:

Section	Option	Description
Name	**N/A**	Assigns a name to the load.
Member of Set	**Load sets in the model**	Selects a load set.
References	**Surfaces**	Applies the load to surfaces.
	Edges/Curves	Applies the load to edges or curves.
	Points	Applies the load to vertices or points.
Coordinate System	**World**	The load is related to the WCS.
	Selected	Enables you to select another coordinate system to define the load directions. The coordinate system can be cartesian, cylindrical, or spherical.
Distribution	**Total Load**	Applies a distributed load along the length or area of the entity, so that the sum of the distributed load equals the entered load value.
	Force Per Unit Area / Force Per Unit Length	The entered load value is interpreted as the load density (i.e., force per unit area or length) over the entity.
	Total Load At Point	Applies a distributed load (over the entity) that is statically equivalent to a load applied to a single point.
	Total Bearing Load At Point	Applies a distributed load (on a cylindrical surface) that represents the force and moment that one cylindrically shaped part exerts on another (e.g., a pin and a hole). The distributed load is made statically equivalent to the load applied at a point.
Spatial Variation	**Uniform**	Applies a uniform load over the entity. The load does not have a spatial variation.
	Function of Coordinates	The load's spatial variation is defined as a function of a coordinate system. Cartesian, Cylindrical, or Spherical coordinate systems can be used.
	Interpolated Over Entity	Applies a spatial variation that is either linear, quadratic, or cubic along the entity.

Pressure Load

A pressure load is a distributed load that acts in normal to the part surface direction, even if the surface is curved. The positive direction is toward the part body.

To apply a pressure load, click (Pressure) in the *Home* tab or select the references and click (Pressure) in the mini-toolbar. The *Pressure Load* dialog box opens, as shown in Figure 3–13.

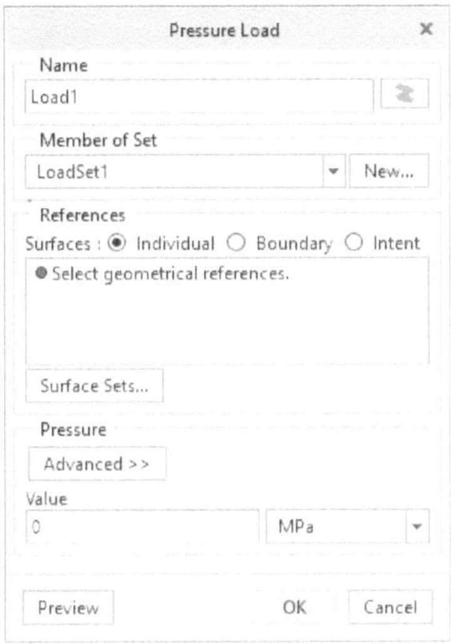

Figure 3–13

The options available in the *Pressure Load* dialog box are as follows:

Section	Option	Description
Name	**N/A**	Assigns a name to the load.
Member of Set	**Load sets in the model**	Selects a load set.
Spatial Variation	**Uniform**	Applies a uniform load over the entity. The load does not have a spatial variation.
	Function of Coordinates	The load's spatial variation is defined as a function of a coordinate system. Cartesian, Cylindrical, or Spherical coordinate systems can be used.
	Interpolated Over Entity	Applies a spatial variation that is either linear, quadratic, or cubic along the entity.
	External Coefficients Field	Imports a file containing the coefficients that specify the spatial variation of the load. The coefficients are automatically mapped onto the model surfaces.

Bearing Load

Bearing loads approximate the pressure applied on a cylindrical hole by a rigid pin or shaft passing through that hole.

To apply a bearing load, click (Bearing) in the *Home* tab. The *Bearing Load* dialog box opens, as shown in Figure 3–14.

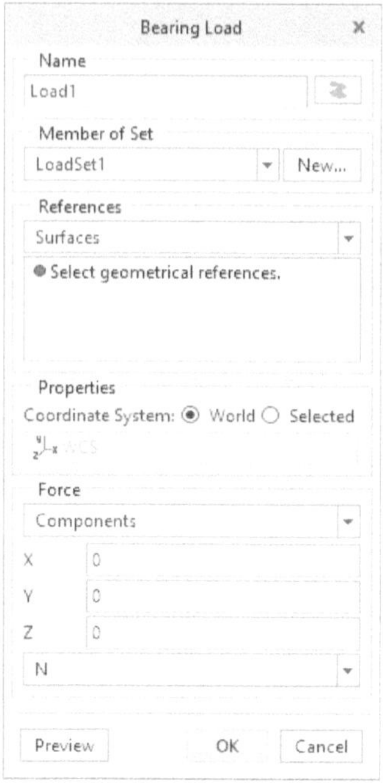

Figure 3–14

The options available in the *Bearing Load* dialog box are as follows:

Section	Option	Description
Name	**N/A**	Assigns a name to the load.
Member of Set	**Load sets in the model**	Selects a load set.
References	**Surfaces**	Applies the load to surfaces. Only cylindrical surfaces are permitted.
	Edges/ Curves	Applies the load to edges or curves in 2D models.
Coordinate System	**World**	The load is related to the WCS.
	Selected	Enables you to select another coordinate system to define the load direction. The coordinate system can be only Cartesian.
Force	**Components**	Load direction and magnitude is determined by the entered force components.
	Dir Vector & Mag	Load direction is defined by a 3D vector.
	Dir Points & Mag	Load direction is defined by selecting two points.

Gravity Load

A gravity load simulates the body force created by the acceleration or deceleration of your model.

To apply a gravity load, click (Gravity) in the *Home* tab. The *Gravity Load* dialog box opens, as shown in Figure 3–15.

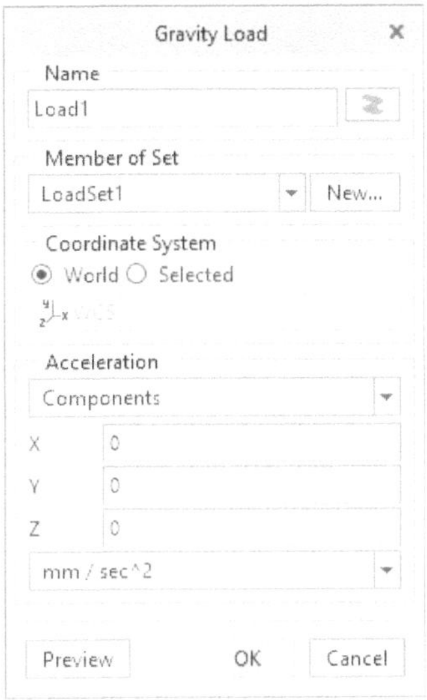

Figure 3–15

The options available in the *Gravity Load* dialog box are as follows:

Section	Option	Description
Name	**N/A**	Assigns a name to the load.
Member of Set	**Load sets in the model**	Selects a load set.
Coordinate System	**World**	The load is related to the WCS.
	Selected	Enables you to select another coordinate system to define the load direction. The coordinate system can be only Cartesian.
Force	**Components**	Load direction and magnitude is determined by the entered acceleration components.
	Dir Vector & Mag	Load direction is defined by a 3D vector.
	Dir Points & Mag	Load direction is defined by selecting two points.

Centrifugal Load

A centrifugal load applies a body force that is created by the rotation of your model. Both angular velocity and acceleration can be applied.

To apply a centrifugal load, click (Centrifugal) in the *Home* tab. The *Centrifugal Load* dialog box opens, as shown in Figure 3–16.

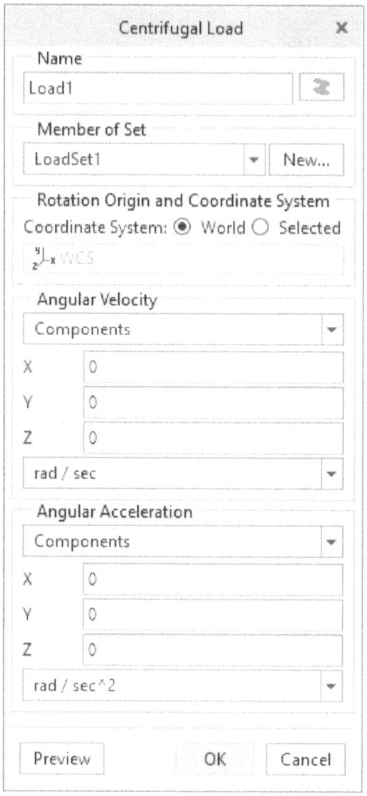

Figure 3–16

The options available in the *Centrifugal Load* dialog box are as follows:

Section	Option	Description
Name	**N/A**	Assigns a name to the load.
Member of Set	**Load sets in the model**	Selects a load set.
Coordinate System	**World**	The load is related to the WCS.
	Selected	Enables you to select another coordinate system to define the load direction. The coordinate system can be only Cartesian.

Section	Option	Description
Angular Velocity	**Components**	Axis of rotation and velocity magnitude are determined by the entered components.
	Dir Vector & Mag	Axis of rotation is defined by a 3D vector.
	Dir Points & Mag	Axis of rotation is defined by selecting two points.
Angular Acceleration	**Components**	Axis of rotation and acceleration magnitude are determined by the entered components.
	Dir Vector & Mag	Axis of rotation is defined by a 3D vector.
	Dir Points & Mag	Axis of rotation is defined by selecting two points.

Temperature Load

The temperature load applies an initial strain to your model exerted by a change in the temperature of the selected geometric entities.

To apply a temperature load, click (Temperature) in the *Home* tab or select the references and click (Temperature) in the mini-toolbar. The *Structural Temperature Load* dialog box opens, as shown in Figure 3–17.

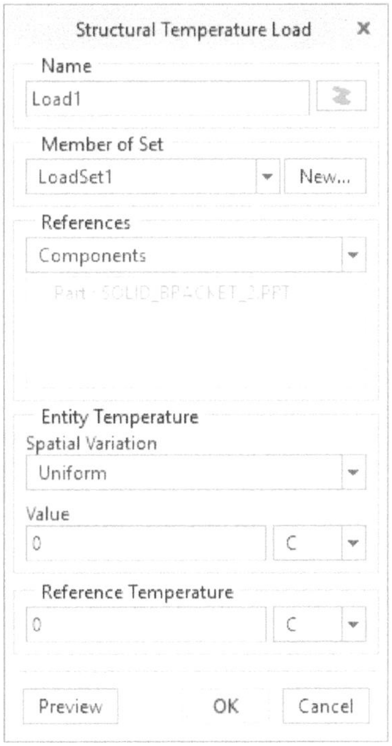

Figure 3–17

The options available in the *Structural Temperature Load* dialog box are as follows:

Section	Option	Description
Name	**N/A**	Assigns a name to the load.
Member of Set	**Load sets in the model**	Selects a load set.
References	**Components**	Applies the temperature change to assembly components.
	Volumes	Applies the temperature change to solid volumes.
	Surfaces	Applies the temperature change to surfaces.
	Edges/Curves	Applies the temperature change to edges or curves on Shells or Beams.
Entity Temperature> Spatial Variation	**Uniform**	The temperature change is distributed uniformly over the entity.
	Function of Coordinates	The temperature change is defined as a function of a coordinate system.
	External Field	Imports the temperature field from a file.
Reference Temperature	**N/A**	Defines the zero strain temperature.

Preload

The preload load simulates a bolt preload on a volume or a component. The preload shortens the volume or component in the axial direction. Note that this functionality requires the Advanced Creo Simulate license.

To apply a preload, click (Preload) in the *Home* tab. The *Preload* dialog box opens, as shown in Figure 3–18.

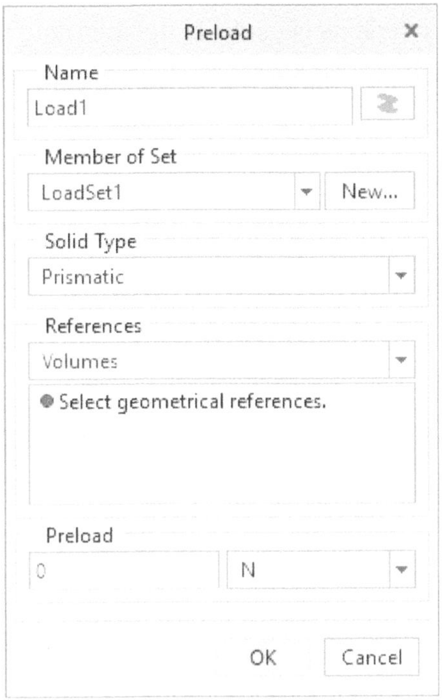

Figure 3–18

The options available in the *Preload* dialog box are as follows:

Section	Option	Description
Name	**N/A**	Assigns a name to the load.
Member of Set	**Load sets in the model**	Selects a load set.
Solid Type	**Prismatic**	Requires the solid to be a prism. It should have two planar bases and all side edges normal to the two bases.
	General	Applies to any solid component or volume. Requires selecting the preload direction.
References	**Volumes**	Applies the preload to solid volumes.
	Components	Applies the preload to assembly components.

3.3 Divide Surface

The **Divide Surface** tool in Creo Simulate enables you to apply modeling entities to a region of a surface. Dividing a surface into regions is useful in the following situations:

- Loads or constraints need to be applied to specific areas of the model.
- Specific contact regions between the faces or surfaces of a model must be analyzed.
- Refinement of the mesh is required in a specific area of the model.

For example, dividing a surface into regions is required for the model shown in Figure 3–19 because the loads and constraints are only applied over small portions of the part's surface.

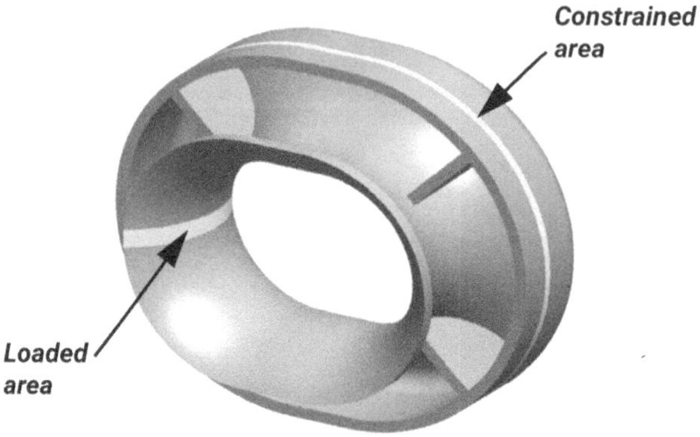

Figure 3–19

Dividing a surface is a two-step process:

1. Define the boundary of the region. It can be created in Creo Parametric or Creo Simulate as a sketch or chain of datum curves. The datum curves must lie exactly on the part's surface, otherwise the surface division fails.
2. Define the parent surfaces. The parent surfaces are then divided by the boundary, separating the region from the parent surface.

It is recommended that you divide surfaces before you apply modeling entities, such as materials, loads, constraints, mesh controls, etc., to the model.

3.4 Singularities

A singularity is the location on a model in which theoretically infinite stress and/or displacement occurs. A simple example of a singularity is a force applied at a point. The stress as calculated by the force over area formula is infinite because the area under a point is zero.

Physically, displacement and stress cannot be infinite. Mathematically, Creo Simulate tries to solve the model exactly as defined, which results in unrealistically high stresses or displacements at the singularities. Additionally, singularities disrupt and slow down the convergence process by requiring very high P-levels, and often causing the model to not converge.

Types of Singularities

Two types of singularities occur in Creo Simulate Structural: those due to loading and constraint conditions and those due to model geometry. Combinations of loads or constraints for types of elements that result in theoretically infinite stresses or displacements for 3D models are shown as follows:

Load or Constraint	Beam	Shell	Solid
Points	Displacement: **OK**	Displacement: **OK**	Displacement: Infinite
	Stress: **OK**	Stress: Infinite	Stress: Infinite
Edges and Curves	Displacement: **OK**	Displacement: **OK**	Displacement: Infinite
	Stress: **OK**	Stress: **OK**	Stress: Infinite
Faces and Surfaces	N/A	Displacement: **OK**	Displacement: **OK**
	N/A	Stress: **OK**	Stress: Infinite

Along with loads and constraints, sharp reentrant corners or other abrupt changes in geometry can cause singularities. It is recommended that you smooth out the discontinuous geometry to improve convergence.

Excluded Elements

If a singularity cannot be avoided, the following technique can be used to improve convergence:

1. Mesh the close vicinity of the singularity with small elements, which can be done using the Isolate for Exclusion AutoGEM control.
2. When setting up the analysis, request that those elements be excluded from the convergence process.

Collectively, this technique is called *excluding the elements*.

Use the following steps to exclude elements from convergence:

1. Once the loads and constraints have been set up, expand (Control) and click (Isolate for Exclusion) in the *AutoGEM* area of the *Refine Model* tab to open the *Isolate for Exclusion Control* dialog box, as shown in Figure 3–20.

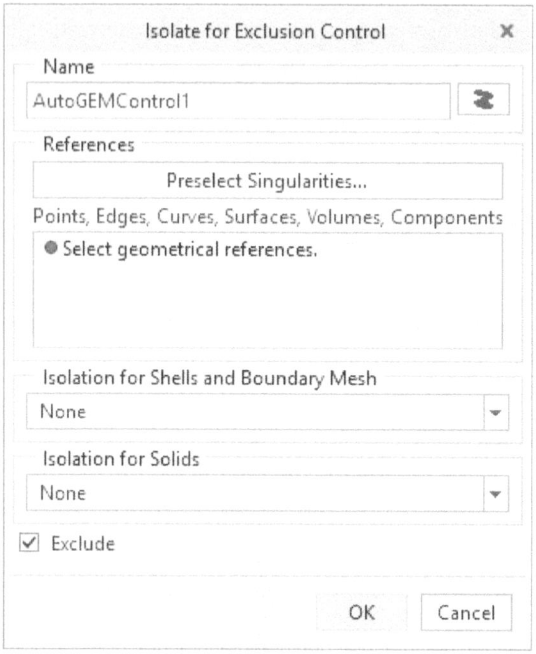

Figure 3–20

2. Manually select the singularities or click **Preselect Singularities** to have Creo Simulate detect the potential singularities automatically.

3. Based on the dimensions of your model, enter the *Maximum Element Size* for the isolation. The *Isolate for Exclusion Control* dialog box should display similar to the one shown in Figure 3–21. Close the dialog box.

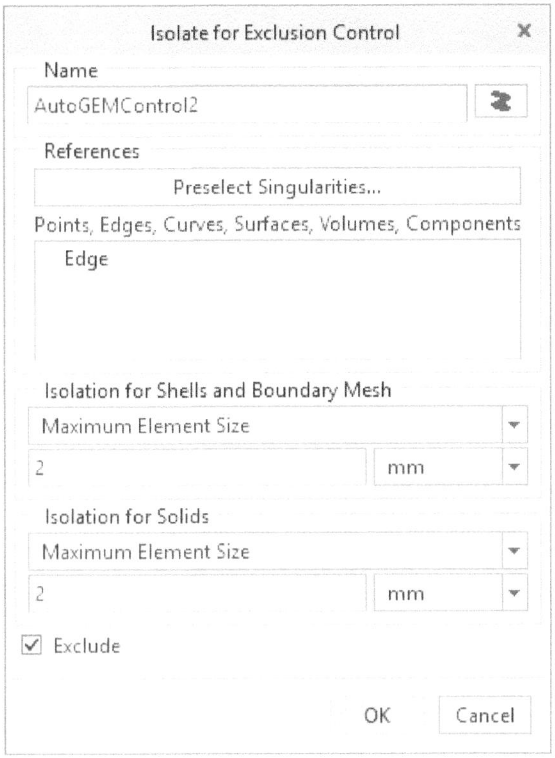

Figure 3–21

4. To highlight the isolating elements in red when meshing the model (as shown in Figure 3–22), select **Info>Isolating Elements** in the *AutoGEM* dialog box.

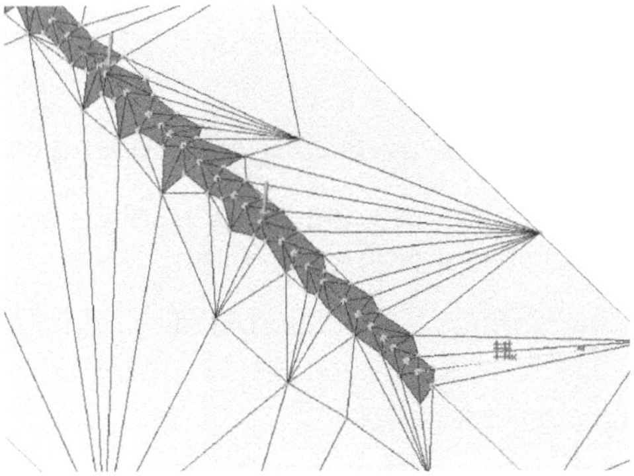

Figure 3–22

5. When setting up the analysis, in the *Excluded Elements* tab, select **Exclude Elements** as shown in Figure 3–23, and select other options as required.

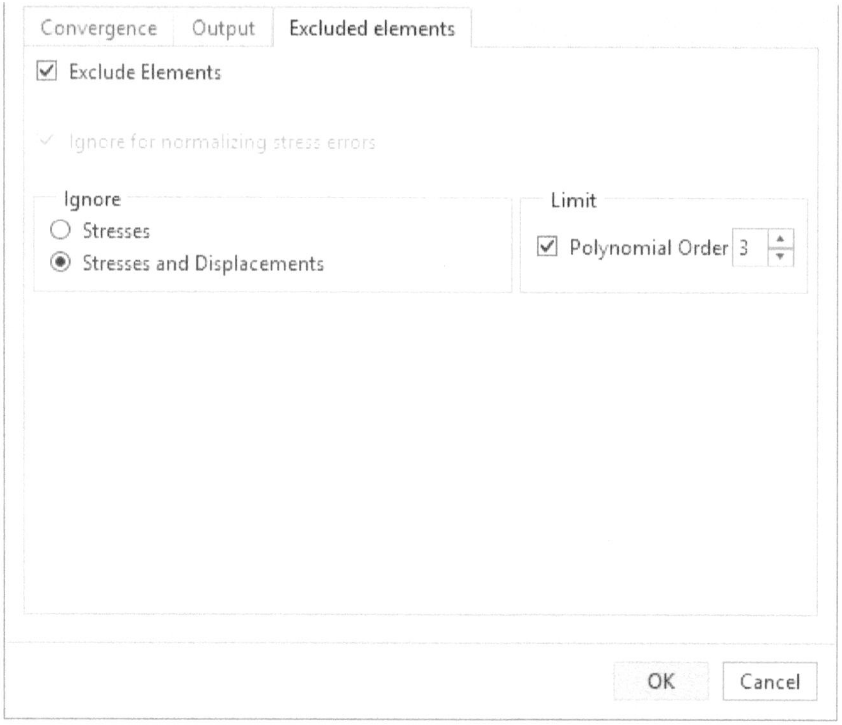

Figure 3–23

Guidelines

The general guidelines for improving convergence and obtaining more reliable analysis results are as follows:

- Spread the load or constraint over a larger area. Avoid using point or line loads and constraints in solid models.
- Prefer the use of soft and flexible supports over rigid constraints.
- If possible, alter the geometry to smooth sharp reentrant corners or other geometrical discontinuities. It is recommended that you use fillets.
- In models that still have singularities, use excluded elements in the analysis.

Practice 3a
Stress Analysis of a Crank

Practice Objectives

- Create multiple load sets.
- Apply pin constraints.
- Apply a bearing load.
- Apply a moment load using the **Total Load at Point** option.

In this practice, you will analyze the crank part shown in Figure 3–24 for two load cases:

- **Bending load case:** A force of 500N is applied to the hole in the upper boss, acting in-plane of the crank.
- **Torsional load case:** A twisting moment of 10,000 Nmm is applied to the upper boss.

The part is constrained by a pin support in the lower boss and by two bushing supports at the ends of the lower rod, as shown in Figure 3–24. This way, the lower beam of the part is not constrained against rotation at its bends, similar to a simply supported beam.

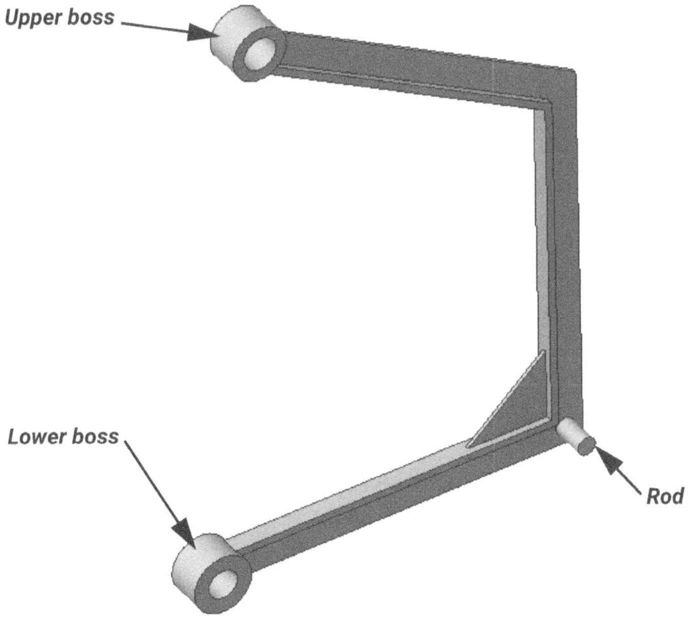

Figure 3–24

Modeling Tasks

Task 1: Open the model.

1. Set the working directory to **Chapter03**.
2. Open **crank.prt**.
3. Set the model display as follows:
   - *(Datum Display Filters)*: (Point Display) Only
   - *(Spin Center)*: Off
   - *(Display Style)*: (Shading With Edges)

   The part displays as shown in Figure 3–25.

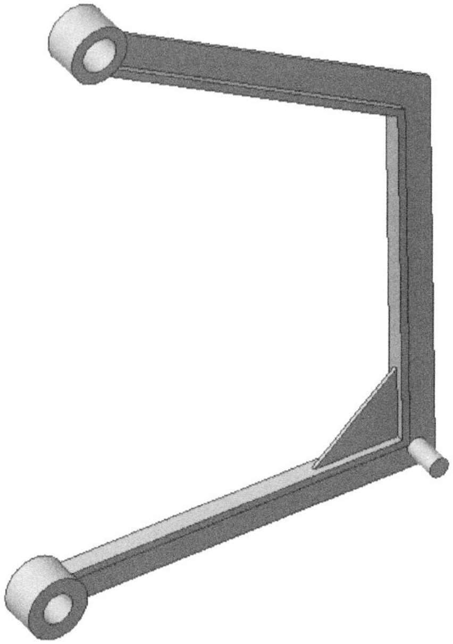

Figure 3–25

4. Ensure that the unit system is set to **mmNs**.
5. Switch to the Creo Simulate environment.

Task 2: Apply the material.

In this task, you will select the material for the part.

1. In the *Home* tab, click (Materials). The *Materials* dialog box opens, as shown in Figure 3–26.

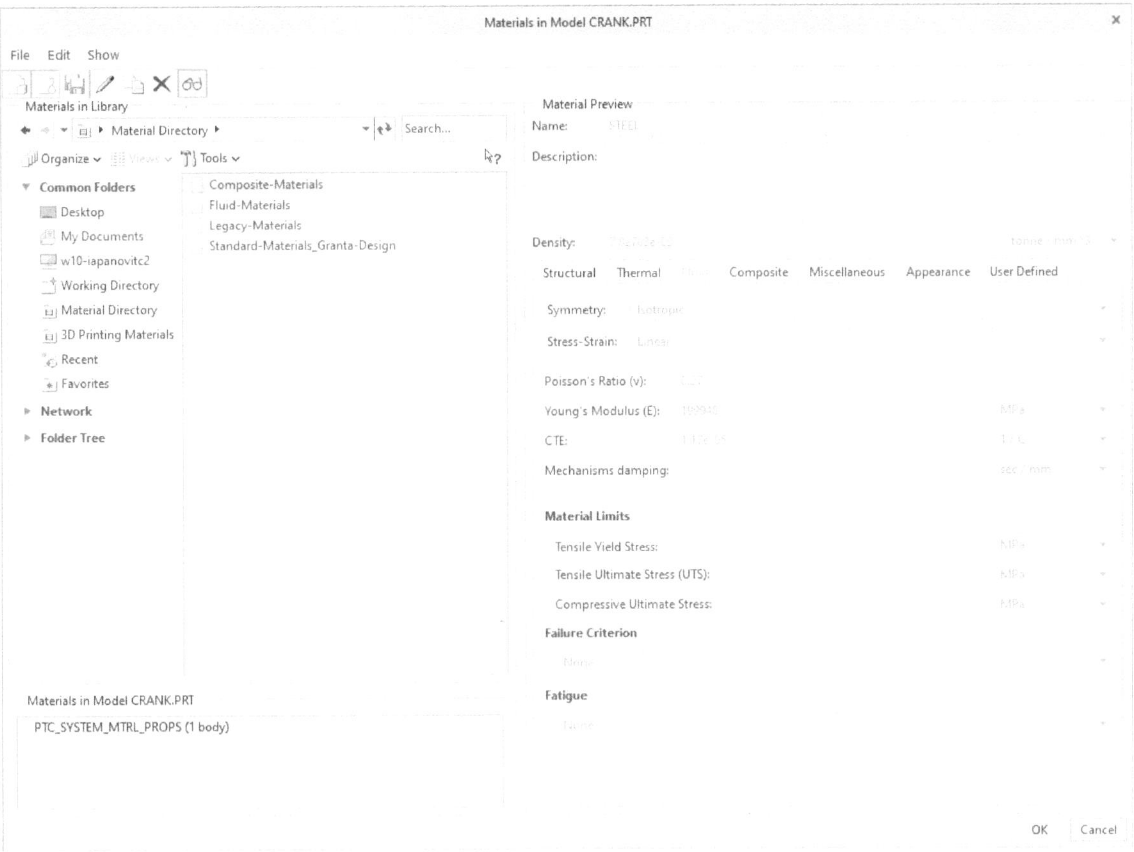

Figure 3–26

2. In the *Materials in Library* area, double-click on **Legacy-Materials** to expand the folder, then double-click on **steel.mtl** to transfer **STEEL** to the *Materials in Model* area.

3. In the *Material Preview* area of the *Materials* dialog box, note that **HS-low-alloy steel** has the following default material properties:

   - *Poisson's ratio:* **0.27**
   - *Young's modulus:* **199948 MPa**
   - *Coeff of thermal expansion:* **1.17e-5 /C**
   - *Density:* **7.82708e-9 tonne/mm^3**

4. Click **OK** to close the *Materials* dialog box.
5. In the *Home* tab, click (Material Assignment). The *Material Assignment* dialog box opens, as shown in Figure 3–27.

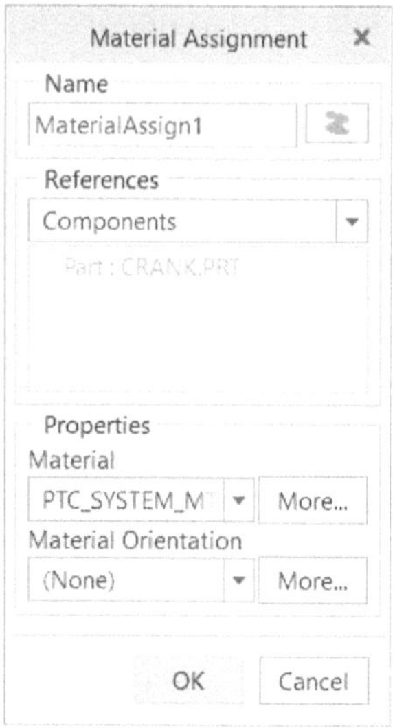

Figure 3–27

6. In the *Material* drop-down list, select **STEEL**.
7. Click **OK** to close the *Material Assignment* dialog box.

Task 3: Mesh the model.

1. In the *Refine Model* tab, click (AutoGEM). The *AutoGEM* dialog box opens, as shown in Figure 3–28.

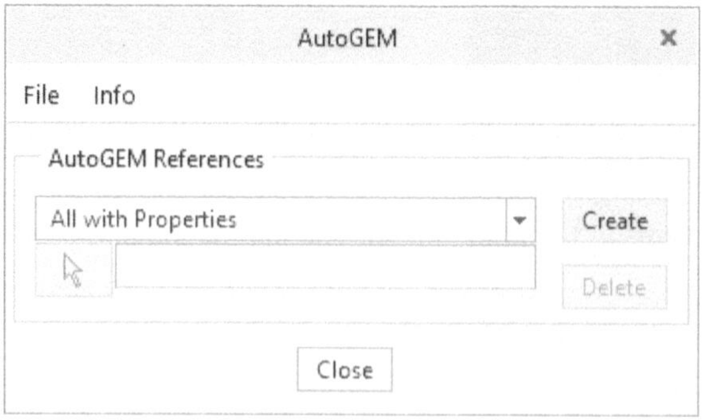

Figure 3–28

2. Expand the *AutoGEM References* drop-down list and select **All with Properties**, if required.

   Note: The ***All with Properties*** *option will automatically mesh all of the solid volumes in the model to which a material has been assigned.*

3. Click **Create**.
4. Creo Simulate meshes the model and displays the *AutoGEM Summary* and *Diagnostics* dialog boxes. Note that AutoGEM created approximately 1023 tetra elements.
5. Close both the *AutoGEM Summary and Diagnostics* dialog boxes, but do not close the *AutoGEM* dialog box. The model displays as shown in Figure 3–29.

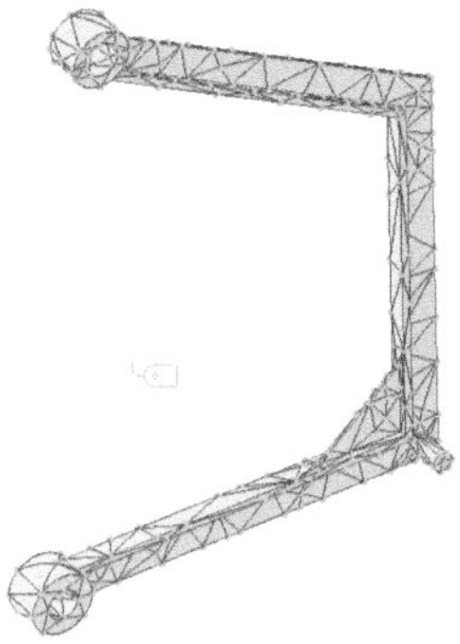

Figure 3–29

6. Click (Simulation Display) in the In-graphics toolbar. The *Simulation Display* dialog box opens.
7. Select the *Modeling Entities* tab and clear the **Material Assignments** option to hide the material assignment icon.

8. Select the *Mesh* tab and clear the **Mesh Points** option in the *Mesh Entities* area, as shown in Figure 3–30.

Figure 3–30

9. Click **OK** to close the *Simulation Display* dialog box. The model displays as shown in Figure 3–31. Rotate the model and review the elements in various areas of the model.

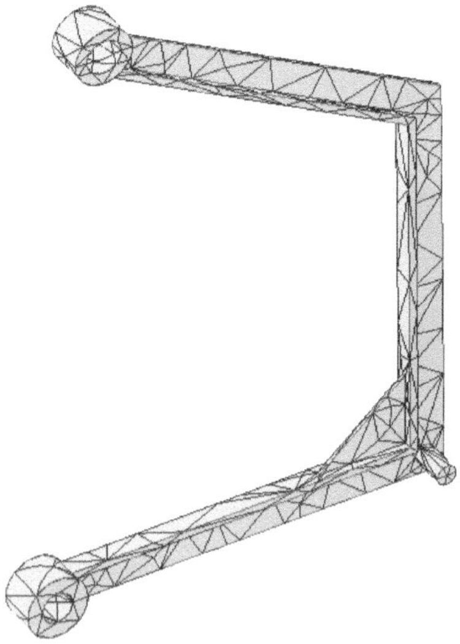

Figure 3–31

10. Close the *AutoGEM* dialog box and save the mesh.

Task 4: Create load sets.

In this task, you will create two load sets for the two load cases in this analysis.

1. In the *Home* tab, expand the *Loads* panel, as shown in Figure 3–32.

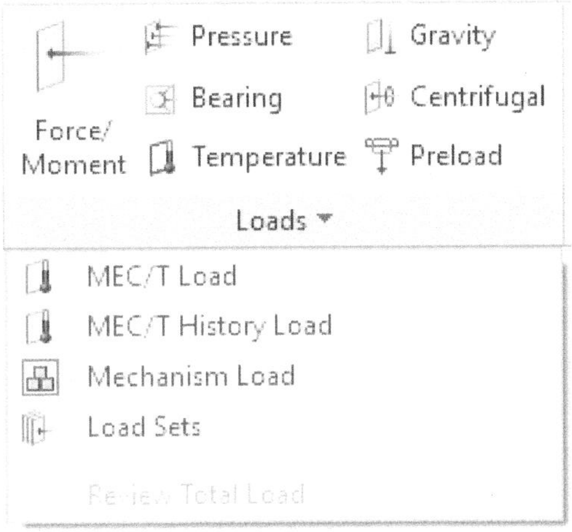

Figure 3–32

2. Select **Load Sets**. The *Load Sets* dialog box opens, as shown in Figure 3–33.

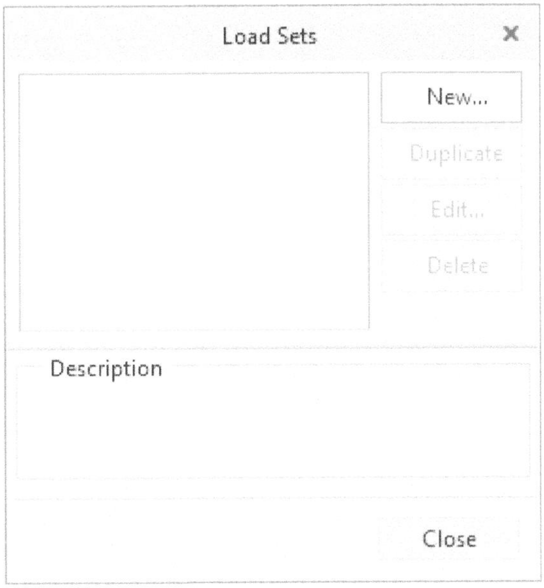

Figure 3–33

3. Click **New**. The *Load Set Definition* dialog box opens, as shown in Figure 3–34.

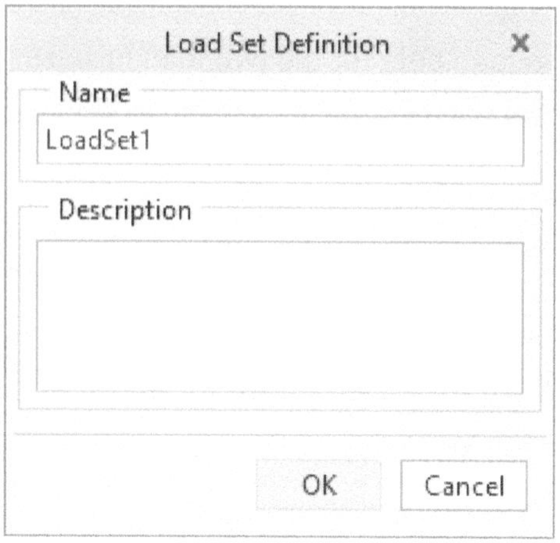

Figure 3–34

4. In the *Name* field, enter **bending** and click **OK**.
5. Repeat Steps 3 and 4 and create another load set named **torsion**.
6. Click **Close** to close the *Load Sets* dialog box.

Task 5: Apply a bending load.

In this task, you will apply a bearing load on the hole in the upper boss, acting in-plane of the part. The bearing load has a resultant force in a specified direction. The bearing load is applied normal to the surface in a non-uniform distribution, such as if a shaft placed in the hole would exert on the hole surface.

1. In the *Refine Model* tab, select (Sketch) and sketch two datum points with datum plane FRONT as the sketching plane and datum plane RIGHT as the reference plane. Sketch the first point at the center of the arm hole (add the edge of the hole as a reference to enable automatic snapping to the center) and the second point at the dimensions shown in Figure 3–35. These points define the bearing load direction.

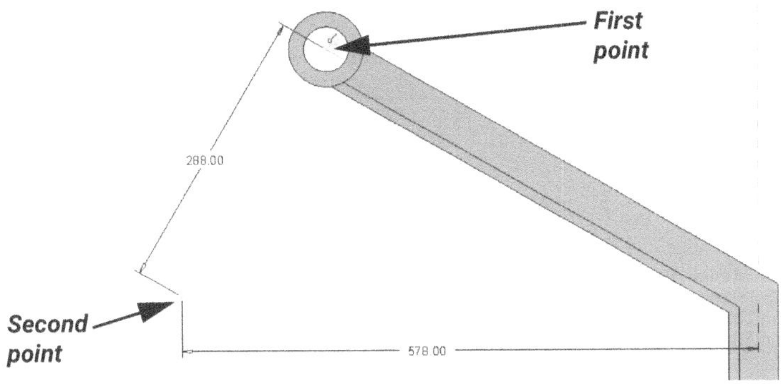

Figure 3–35

Note: *Ensure that the sketched points are datum points, not construction points.*

2. Complete the sketch. In the **FRONT** view, the model displays as shown in Figure 3–36.

Figure 3–36

3. In the *Home* tab, click (Bearing). The *Bearing Load* dialog box opens, as shown in Figure 3–37.

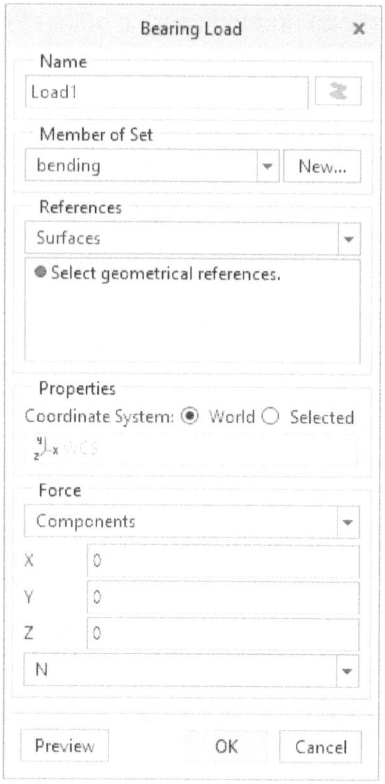

Figure 3–37

4. In the *Name* field, enter **bend_load**.
5. In the *Member of Set* field, select **bending**.
6. Select the hole shown in Figure 3–38.

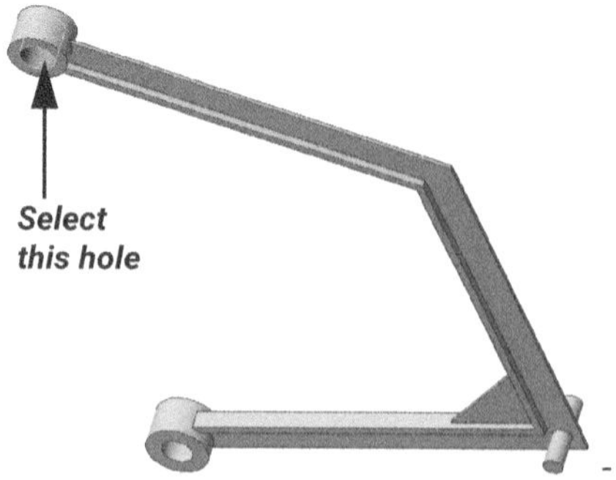

Figure 3–38

7. Expand the *Force* drop-down list and select **Dir Points & Mag**. The *Bearing Load* dialog box opens, as shown in Figure 3–39.

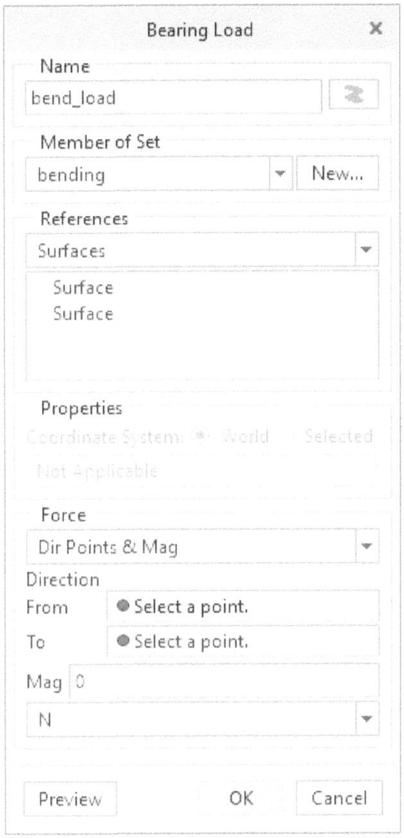

Figure 3–39

8. In the *Direction* area, for *From*, select the point at the hole's center. For *To*, select the second point to define direction for the bearing load.
9. In the *Mag* field, enter **500**.
10. Click **Preview** to display the bearing load distribution, as shown in Figure 3–40.

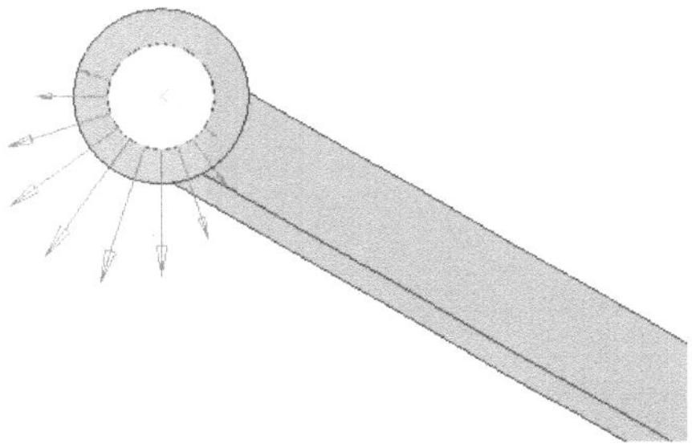

Figure 3–40

11. Click **OK**. The model displays as shown in Figure 3–41.

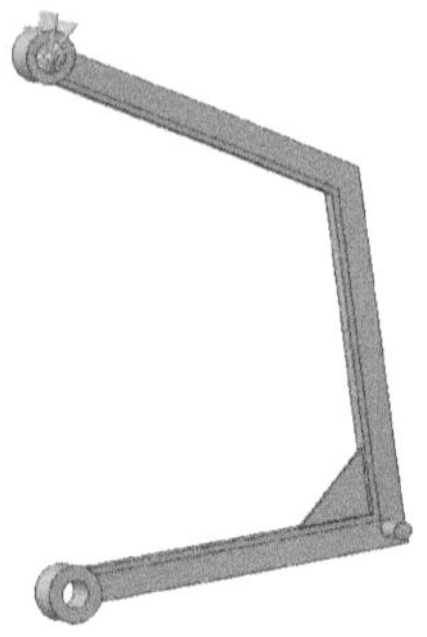

Figure 3–41

12. Use the *Simulation Display* dialog box to hide the bending load set.

Task 6: Apply a torsional load.

In this task, you will apply a twisting moment on the hole in the upper boss. The moment simulates the load exerted by a shaft placed in the hole and torqued about the X-axis of the WCS.

1. Select the hole in the upper boss (the same hole that you selected when applying a bearing load) and select (Force/Moment) in the mini-toolbar. The *Force/Moment Load* dialog box opens, as shown in Figure 3–42.

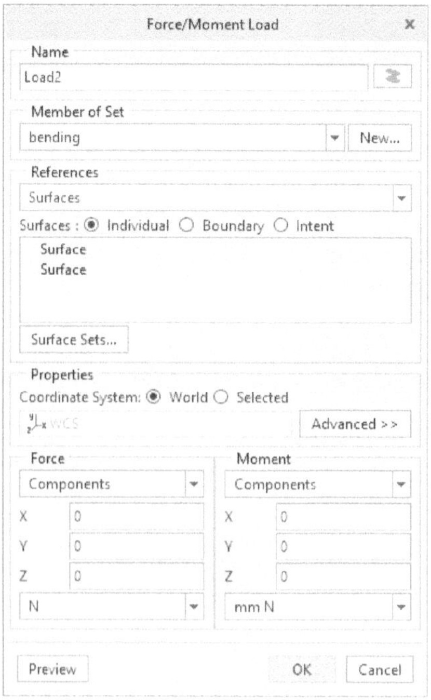

Figure 3–42

2. In the *Name* field, enter **twist_load**.
3. In the *Member of Set* field, select **torsion**. The *Force/Moment* dialog box displays as shown in Figure 3–43.

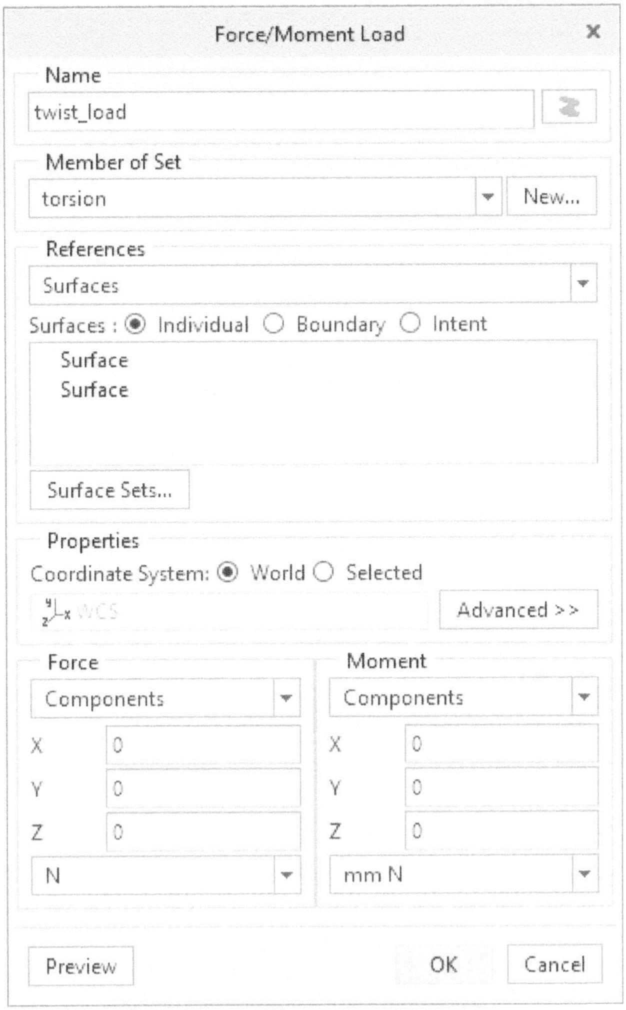

Figure 3–43

Note that a moment in a solid model must be applied as a collection of translational forces that are statically equivalent (i.e., exert the same effect) to the concentrated moment at a point. In Creo Simulate, this can be done using the **Total Load at Point** option.

4. Click **Advanced**.

5. Expand the *Distribution* drop-down list and select **Total Load at Point**. The *Force/Moment* dialog box opens, as shown in Figure 3–44.

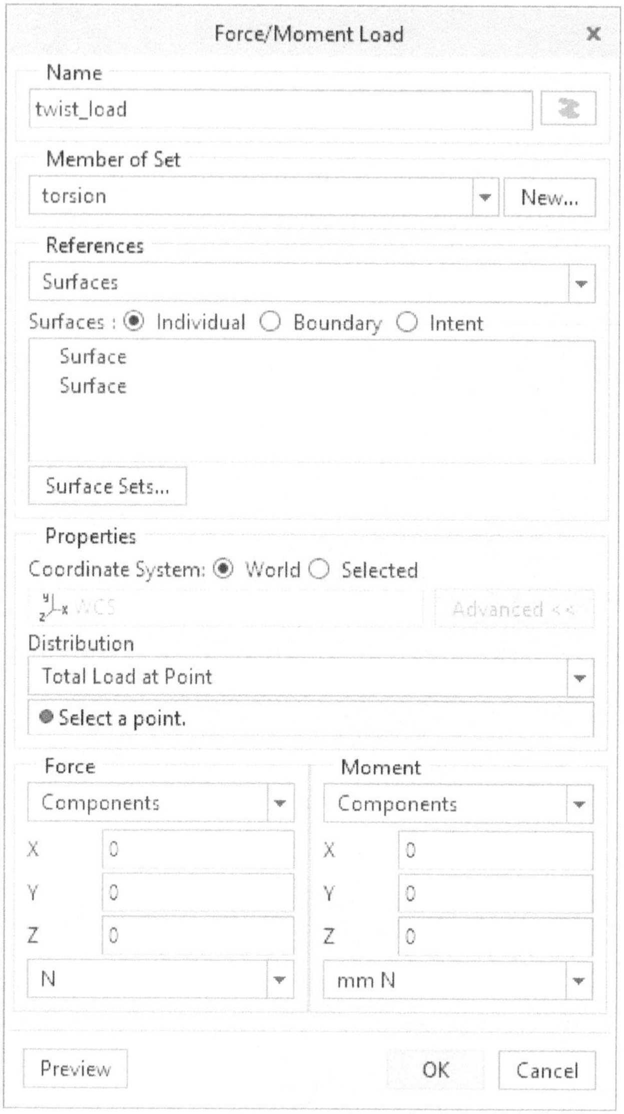

Figure 3–44

6. Select the point at the center of the hole.
7. In the *Moment* area, in the *X* field, enter **10000**.

8. Click **Preview** to display the load distribution, as shown in Figure 3–45.

   Note: The load distribution is statically equivalent to the 10000 mmN moment applied at the point at the center of the hole.

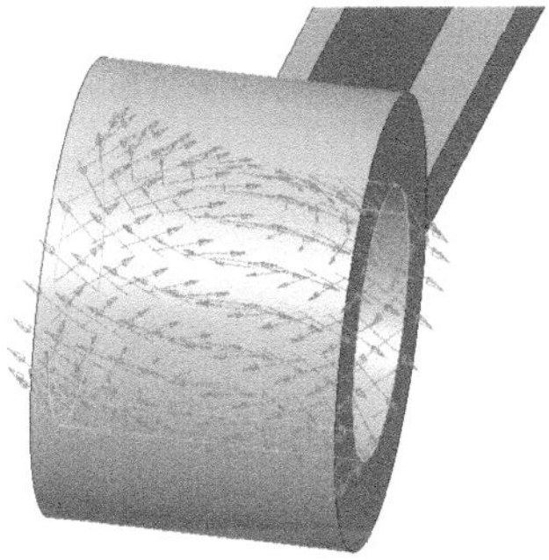

Figure 3–45

9. Click **OK**. The model displays as shown in Figure 3–46.

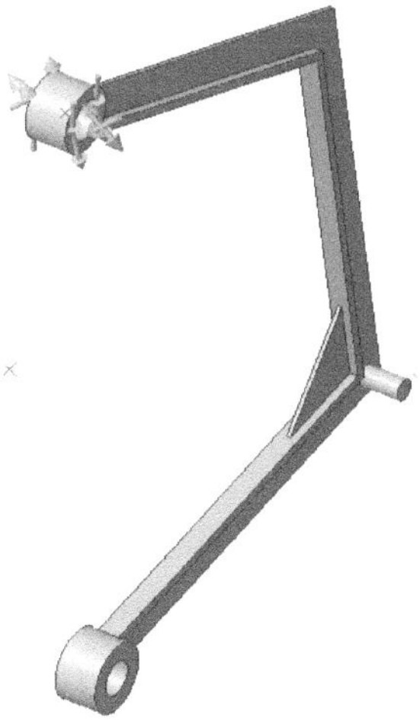

Figure 3–46

10. Use the *Simulation Display* dialog box to hide the torsion load set.

Task 7: Apply the constraints.

In this task, you will constrain the movement of the lower boss and of the rod, as shown in Figure 3–47.

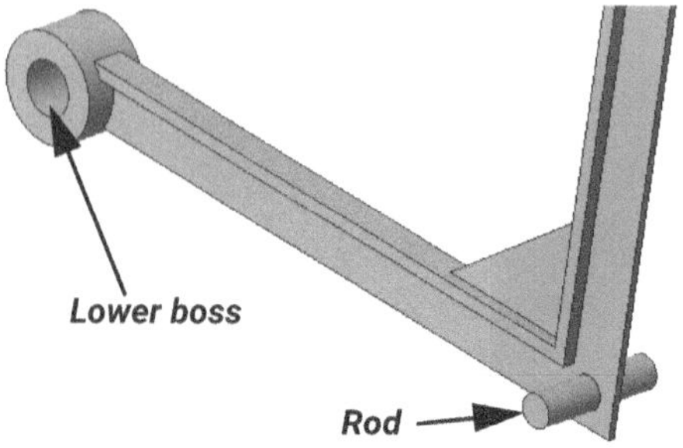

Figure 3–47

The boss is supported by a shaft and the rod is supported by two bushings. Both supports constrain translational motions, but permit rotation of the cylindrical surfaces about their respective axes. This type of support can be modeled using the Pin type of constraint.

1. Select the cylindrical surface of the rod shown in Figure 3–47 and click (Pin) from the mini-toolbar. The *Pin Constraint* dialog box opens.
2. In the *Name* field, enter **rod**.
3. Constrain the axial translation, and leave the rotation free, as shown in Figure 3–48.

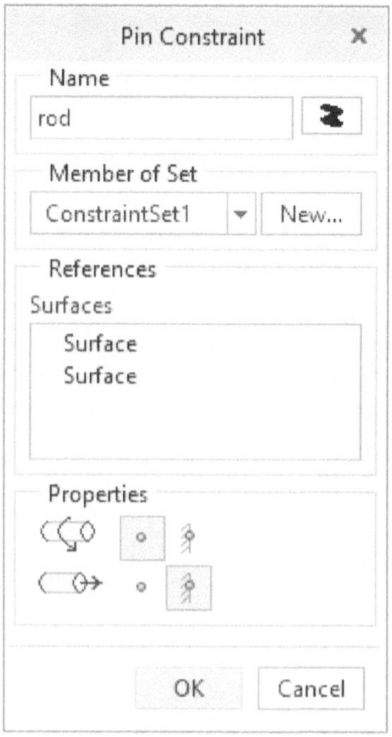

Figure 3–48

4. Click **OK**. The pin constraint displays as shown in Figure 3–49.

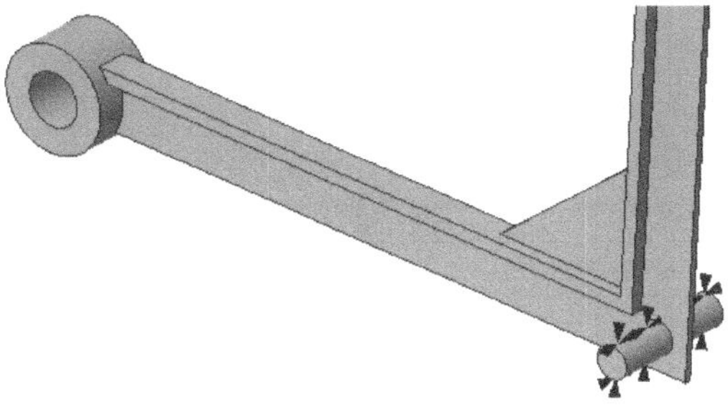

Figure 3–49

5. Select the cylindrical surface of the lower boss shown previously in Figure 3–47 and click (Pin) from the mini-toolbar.
6. In the *Name* field, enter **boss**. Constrain the axial translation and leave the rotation free, as shown in Figure 3–50.

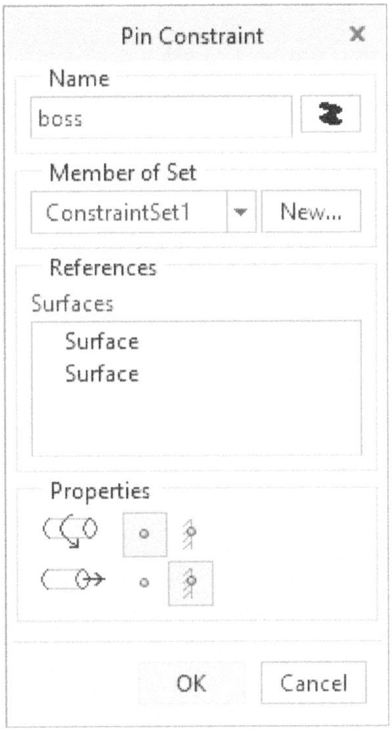

Figure 3–50

7. Click **OK**. The model displays as shown in Figure 3–51.

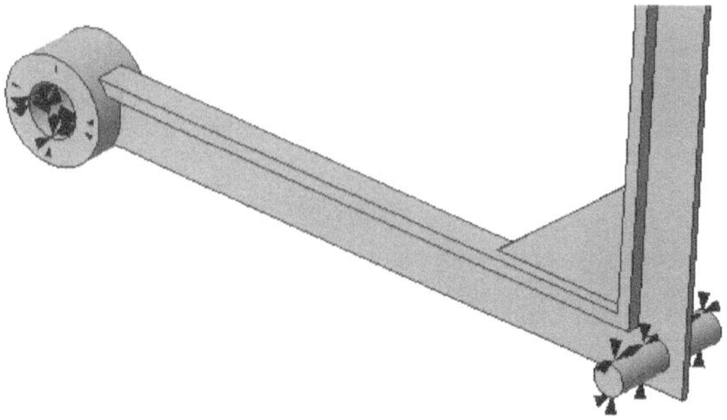

Figure 3–51

Analysis Tasks

Task 8: Set up and run a Multi-Pass Adaptive analysis.

1. Create a new static analysis and name it **crank**.
2. Select both the **bending/CRANK** and **torsion/CRANK** load sets in the *Load Set / Component* area.

3. For the *Percent Convergence*, enter **10**. In the *Maximum Polynomial Order* field, enter **9**. The *Static Analysis Definition* dialog box displays as shown in Figure 3–52.

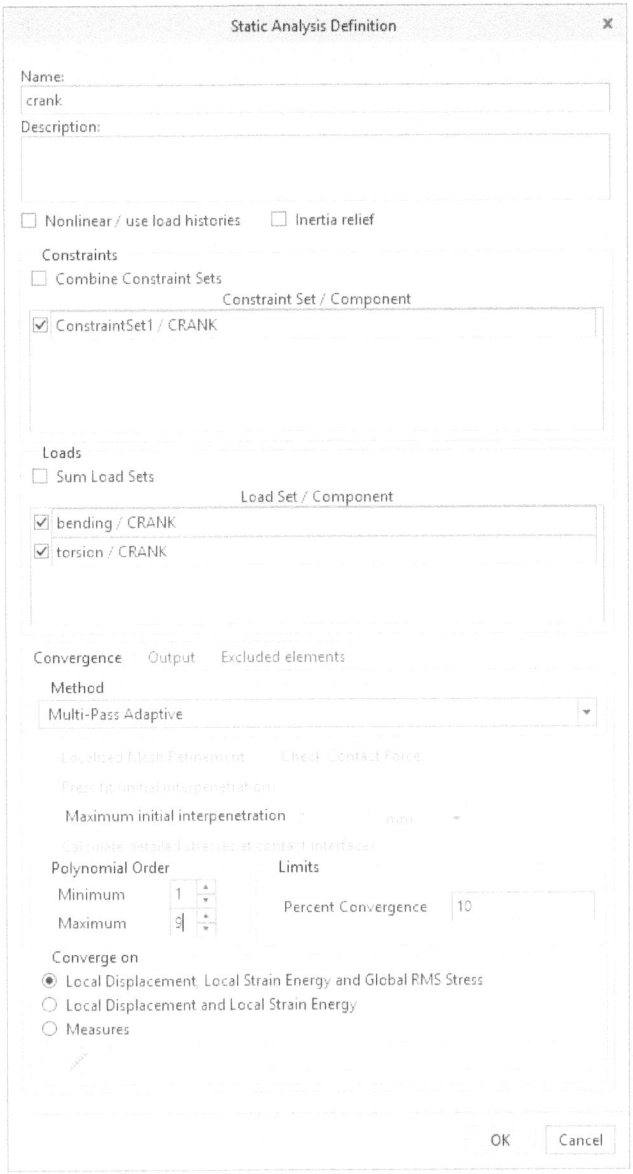

Figure 3–52

4. Verify that the run settings are set so that the elements will be used from the existing mesh file. In the *Memory Allocation* field, enter **512**.

Note: *You created and saved the mesh for the part in Task 3 of the Modeling Tasks.*

5. Run the analysis. Note the warning in the expanded *Run Status* dialog box that states "Convergence was not obtained because the maximum polynomial order of 9 was reached". Also note the second warning in the *Diagnostics* box regarding the local reaction data. The warning displays because Creo Simulate uses the Cylindrical coordinate system on pin constraints and the reaction forces could not be computed.

In the following tasks, you will explore the elements that have not converged.

Task 9: Display the non-converged elements.

1. In the *Analyses and Design Studies* dialog box, click  (Review Results).
2. In the *Result Window Definition* dialog box, check both **bending** and **torsion** load sets, then expand the *Quantity* drop-down list and select **P-Level**, as shown in Figure 3–53.

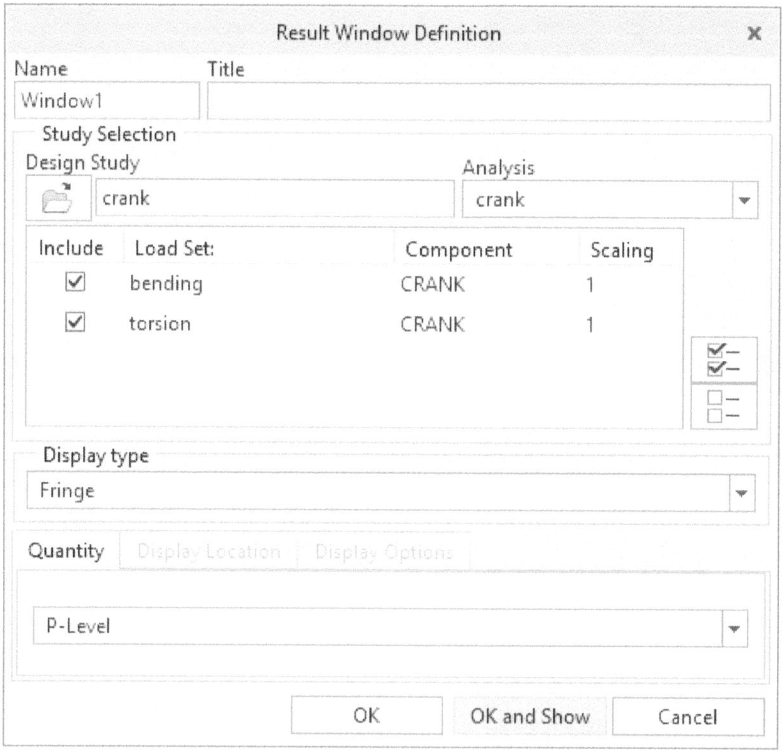

Figure 3–53

3. Click **OK and Show**. The P-Level plot displays as shown in Figure 3–54.

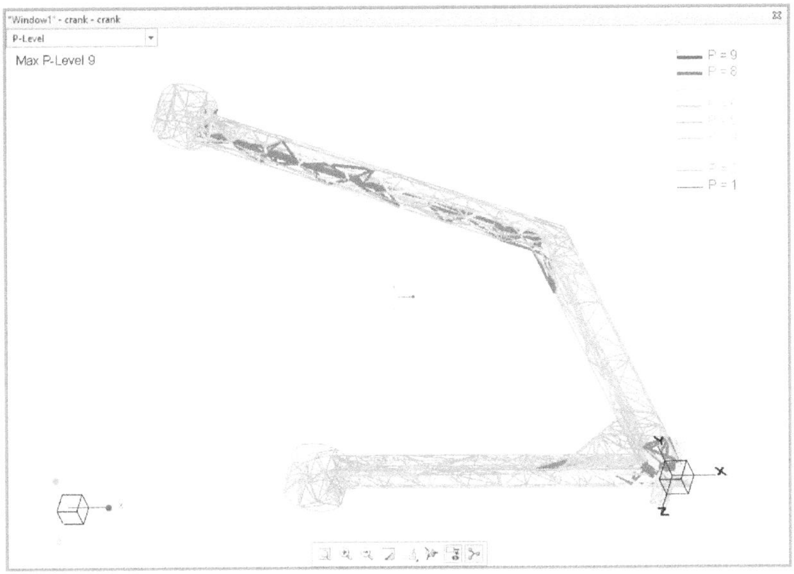

Figure 3–54

Examine the P-Level plot, specifically elements with their edges colored red (P-Level 9) and orange (P-Level 8). These are the elements that are most likely to have not converged. Note that red and orange elements are not concentrated over one or a few small areas in the model, which would be the visual cue that non-convergence might have been due to stress singularities. Rather, the red and orange elements are spread over large areas in the upper arm of the crank, and near the rod.

Therefore, the non-convergence might be attributed to the elements being too large or too distorted. In the next task, you will refine the mesh to obtain convergence.

> ***Note:*** *Generally, convergence is more difficult to obtain for a model with several load cases, since the optimal P-Level map for one load case might not be optimal for another load case, and vice versa.*

4. Exit the Results environment and close the *Analyses and Design Studies* dialog box.

Mesh Refinement Tasks

Creo Simulate has a variety of tools that enable you to control the mesh in your model. These tools are the AutoGEM controls, and are located in the *AutoGEM* section of the *Refine Model* tab, as shown in Figure 3-55.

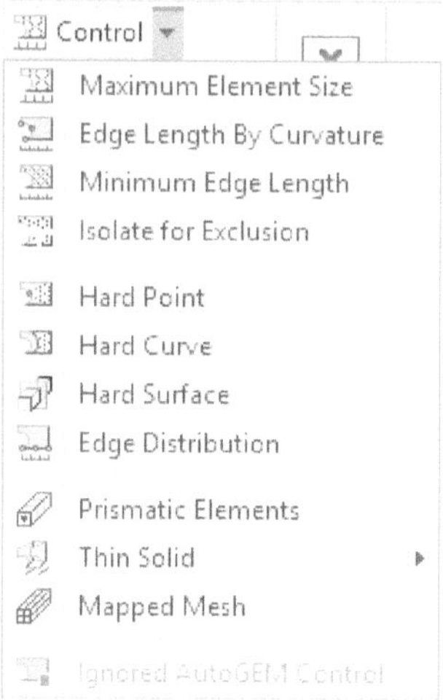

Figure 3–55

The AutoGEM controls, however, are designed for fine-tuning your mesh in local areas, and might not be convenient to use if mesh needs to be changed throughout the entire model.

In this task, you will refine the mesh through the entire model, by adjusting the geometrical limits on the element size and shape.

Task 10: Adjust the AutoGEM Settings.

1. In the *Refine Model* tab, expand the *AutoGEM* drop-down list and select **Settings**, as shown in Figure 3–56.

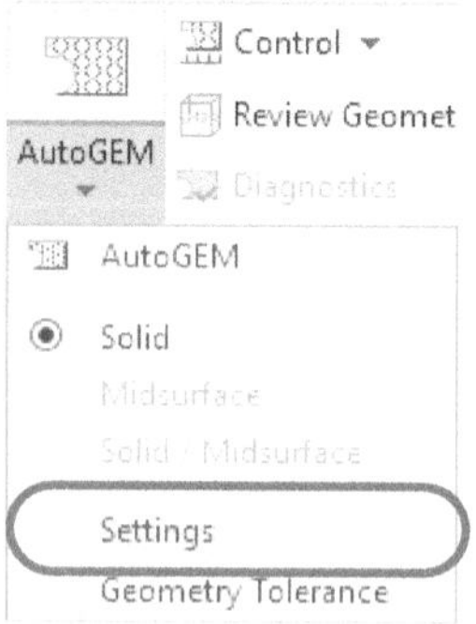

Figure 3–56

2. The *AutoGEM Settings* dialog box opens. Select the *Limits* tab and change **Edge max** and **Face max** angles to **165**, and **Edge min** and **Face min** angles to **15**, as shown in Figure 3–57.

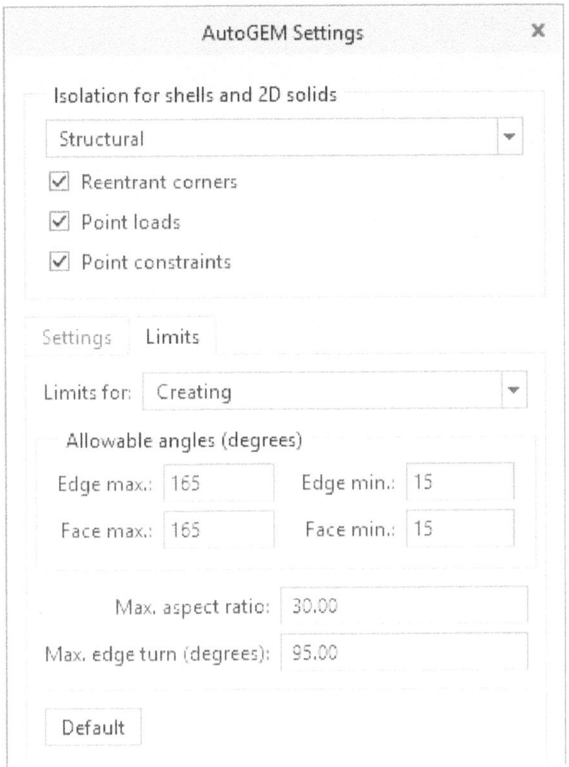

Figure 3–57

3. Click **OK** to finish.

Task 11: Re-mesh the model.

1. Click (AutoGEM). The *Question* dialog box displays, as shown in Figure 3–58.

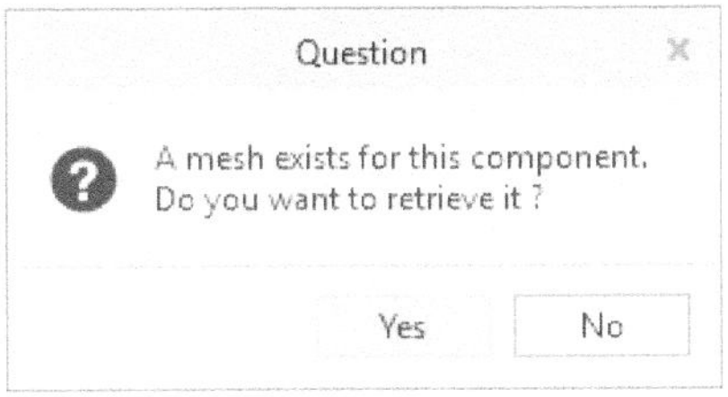

Figure 3–58

2. Click **No**. The *AutoGEM* dialog box opens, as shown in Figure 3–59.

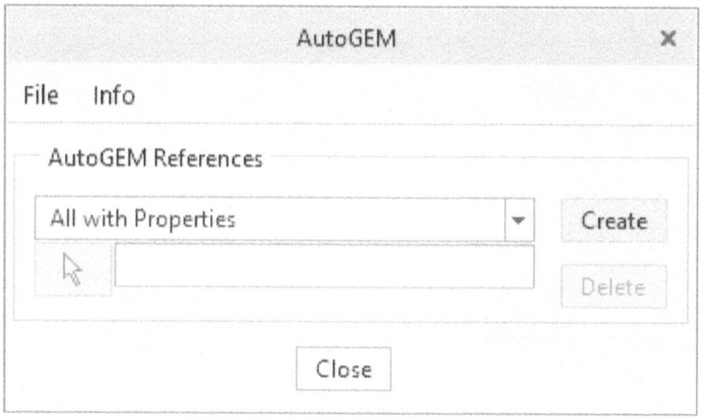

Figure 3–59

3. Click **Create**. Once meshing is finished, note that AutoGEM creates approximately 1994 tetra elements – almost twice as many as with the default meshing settings.

   Note: *The mesh originally created in Task 3 contained approximately 1023 elements.*

4. Close the *AutoGEM Summary and Diagnostics* dialog boxes. The model displays with loads hidden, as shown in Figure 3–60.

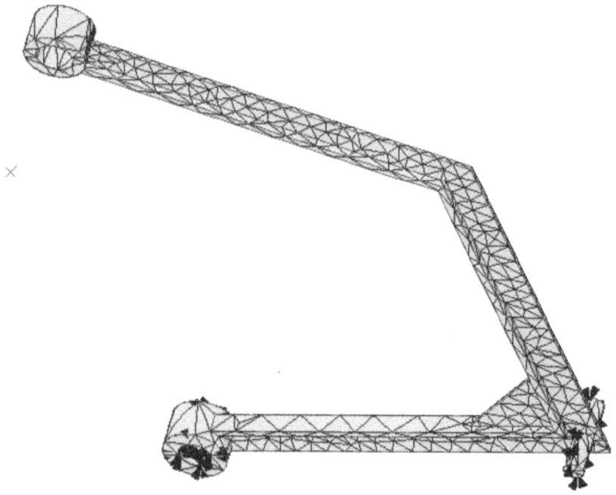

Figure 3–60

5. Click **Close** to close the *AutoGEM* dialog box and save the mesh.

Task 12: Re-run the analysis.

1. Run the **crank** analysis again and wait until it completes.
2. Expand the *Run Status* dialog box and scroll down and note that the analysis has converged, as shown in Figure 3–61.

```
RMS Stress Error Estimates:

Load Set           Stress Error   % of Max Prin Str
----------------   ------------   -----------------
bending             6.05e-01        0.3% of  2.37e+02
torsion             6.03e-01        0.9% of  7.05e+01

Resource Check                                (11:08:17)
   Elapsed Time      (sec):       98.73
   CPU Time          (sec):       93.36
   Memory Usage       (kb):      839951
   Wrk Dir Dsk Usage  (kb):     1333882

The analysis converged to within 10% on
edge displacement, element strain energy,
and global RMS stress.
```

Figure 3–61

3. Close the *Run Status* window.

Results Tasks

Task 13: Animate the deformation for the bending load case.

1. Click (Review Results) in the *Analyses and Design Studies* dialog box. The *Result Window Definition* dialog box opens.
2. In the *Name* field, enter **deform_bending**.
3. Clear the **torsion** load set option.

4. Expand the *Quantity* tab drop-down list and select **Displacement**. The *Result Window Definition* dialog box displays, as shown in Figure 3–62.

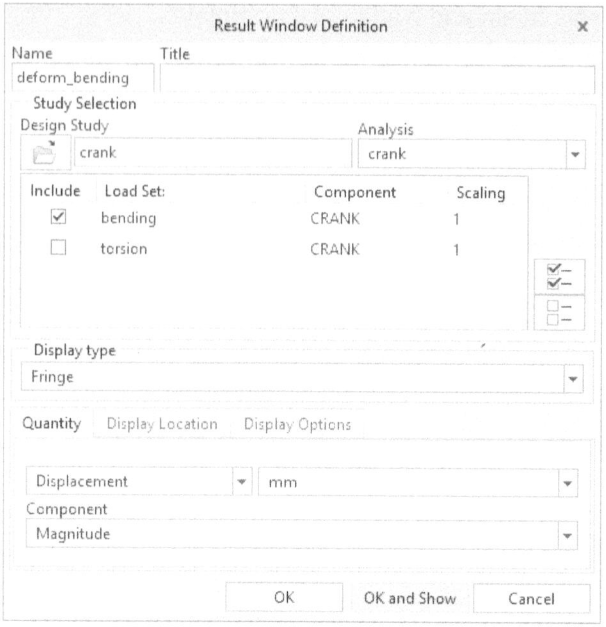

Figure 3–62

5. Select the *Display Options* tab. Select the **Deformed**, **Overlay Undeformed**, **Show Element Edges**, and **Animate** options. In the *Scaling* field, enter **20**, as shown in Figure 3–63.

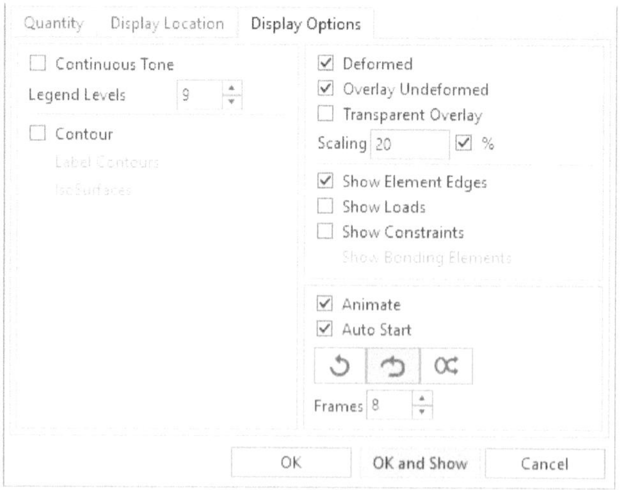

Figure 3–63

6. Click **OK and Show**. The Displacement Magnitude result plot is displayed and animated.

7. Zoom in on the rod. Note that the rod's rotation is not restricted, as if it was supported by sleeve bearings or bushings. This results from applying the Pin constraint to the rod's surface.
8. Stop the animation at Frame 5. The result plot displays as shown in Figure 3–64.

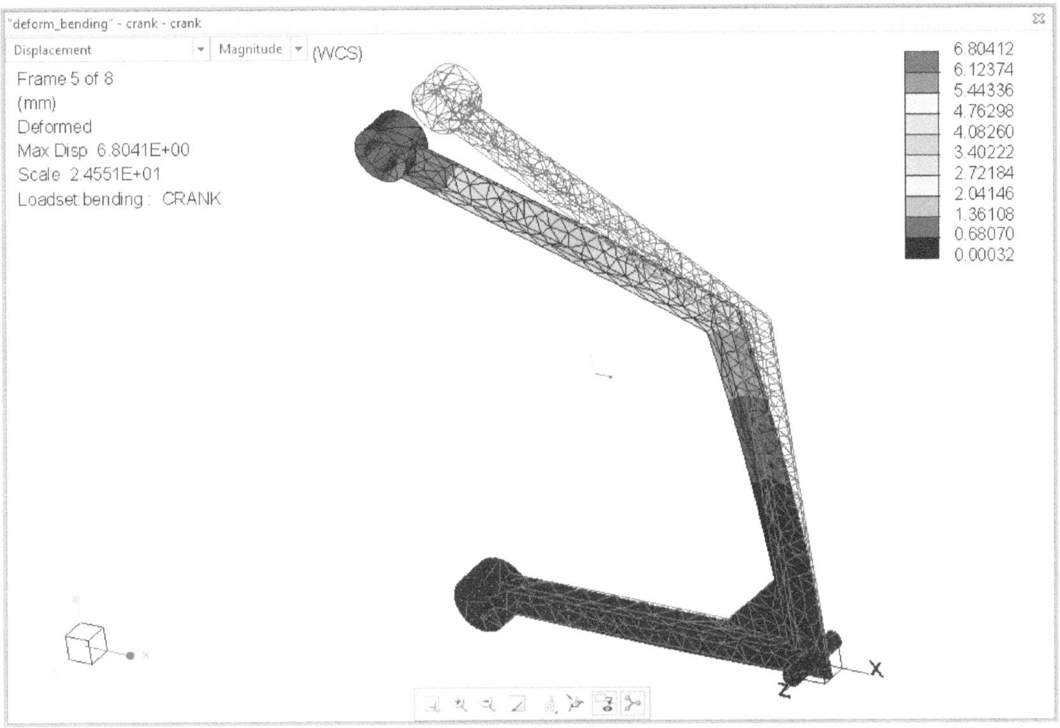

Figure 3–64

Task 14: Animate the deformation for the torsional load case.

1. In the *Home* tab, click (Copy). The *Result Window Definition* dialog box opens.
2. In the *Name* field, enter **deform_torsion**.

3. Clear the **bending** load set and select the **torsion** load set. The *Result Window Definition* dialog box opens, as shown in Figure 3–65.

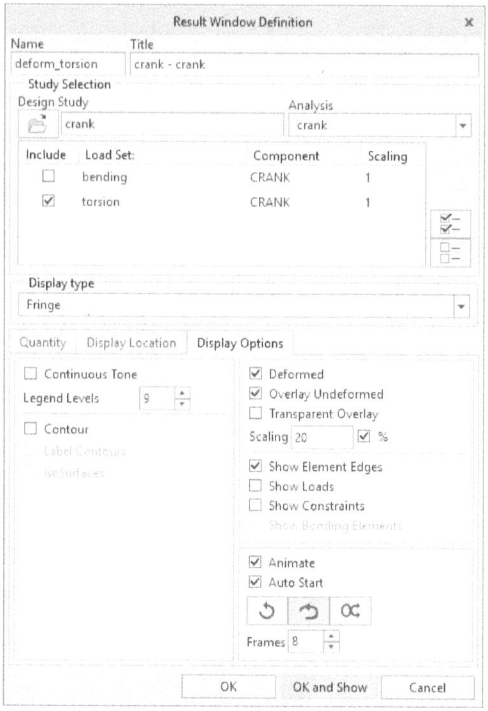

Figure 3–65

4. Click **OK**.
5. In the *View* tab, click (Show). In the *Display Result Window* dialog box, clear **deform_bending** and select **deform_torsion**, as shown in Figure 3–66.

Figure 3–66

6. Click **OK**. The deformation plot for the torsional load case is displayed and animated.

Note: *Did the deformation display as you expected?*

Task 15: Create result windows for the von Mises stress.

1. In the *Home* tab, click (Open). Select the **crank** design study in the *Open Result Windows* dialog box that opens and click **Open**. The *Result Window Definition* dialog box opens, as shown in Figure 3–67.

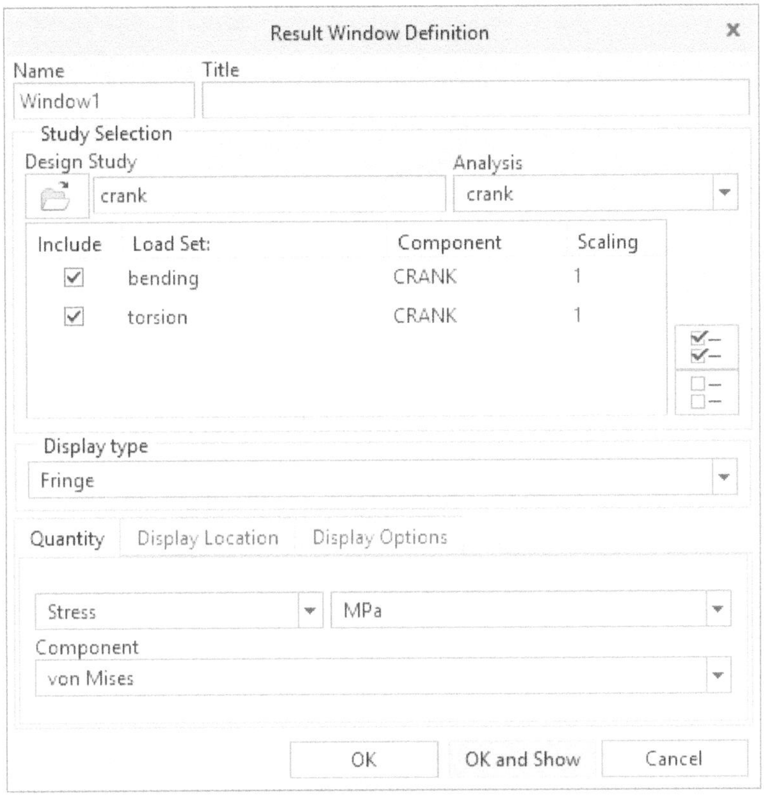

Figure 3–67

2. In the *Name* field, enter **stress_bending**.
3. Leave the **bending** load set selected and clear the **torsion** load set.
4. Select the *Display Options* tab. Select the **Deformed** and **Overlay Undeformed** options.
5. Click **OK**.
6. Repeat Steps 1 through 5, naming the window **stress_torsion** and selecting the **torsion** load set instead of the bending load set.

Task 16: Display the stress results.

1. In the *View* tab, click (Show). In the *Display Result Window* dialog box that opens, select **stress_bending** and clear all of the other windows.
2. Click **OK**. The von Mises stress plot for the bending load case displays as shown in Figure 3–68.

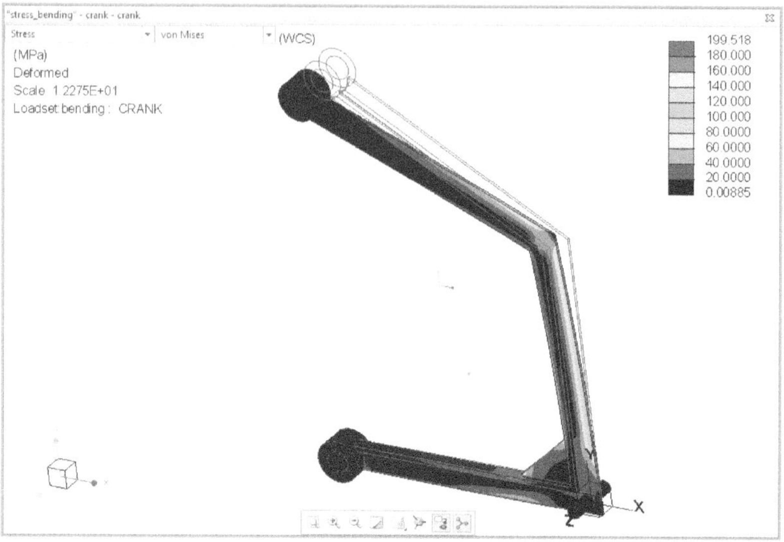

Figure 3–68

3. Locate the area of the maximum stress, as shown in Figure 3–69.

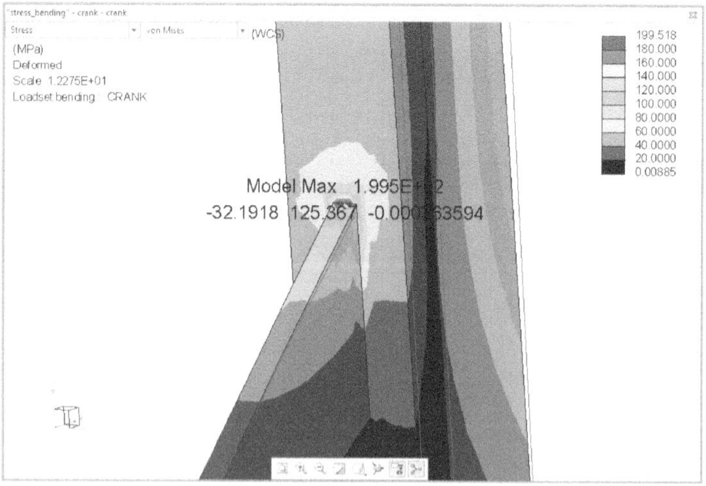

Figure 3–69

4. In the *View* tab, click (Show). In the *Display Result Window* dialog box, select **stress_torsion** and clear all of the other windows.
5. Click **OK**. The von Mises stress plot for the torsional load case displays as shown in Figure 3–70.

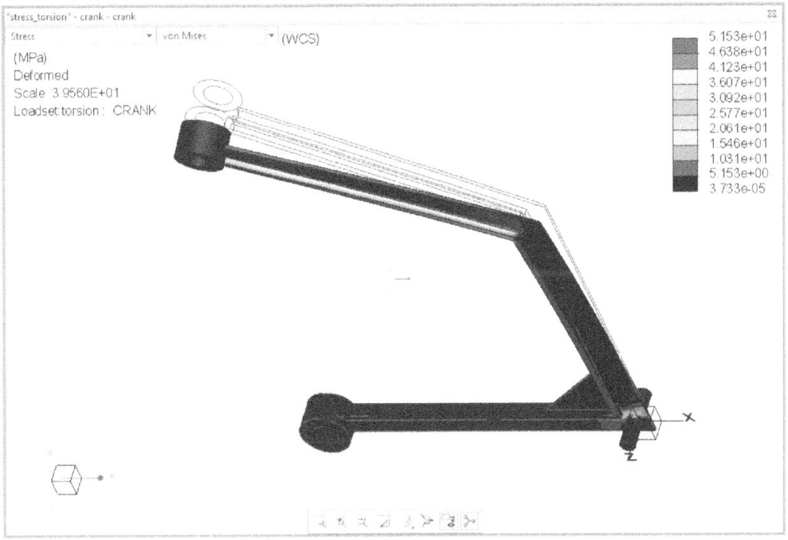

Figure 3–70

6. Locate the area of the maximum stress, as shown in Figure 3–71.

Figure 3–71

Note that the maximum stress in the torsional load case displays at a different location than in the bending load case.

Task 17: Display the stress results for the combined load case.

In this task, you will create and display a von Mises stress result plot for the combined load case, in which both the bending and twisting loads act together.

1. In the *Home* tab, click (Copy). The *Result Window Definition* dialog box opens.
2. In the *Name* field, enter **stress_combined**.
3. Select both the **bending** and **torsion** load sets. The *Result Window Definition* dialog box opens, as shown in Figure 3–72.

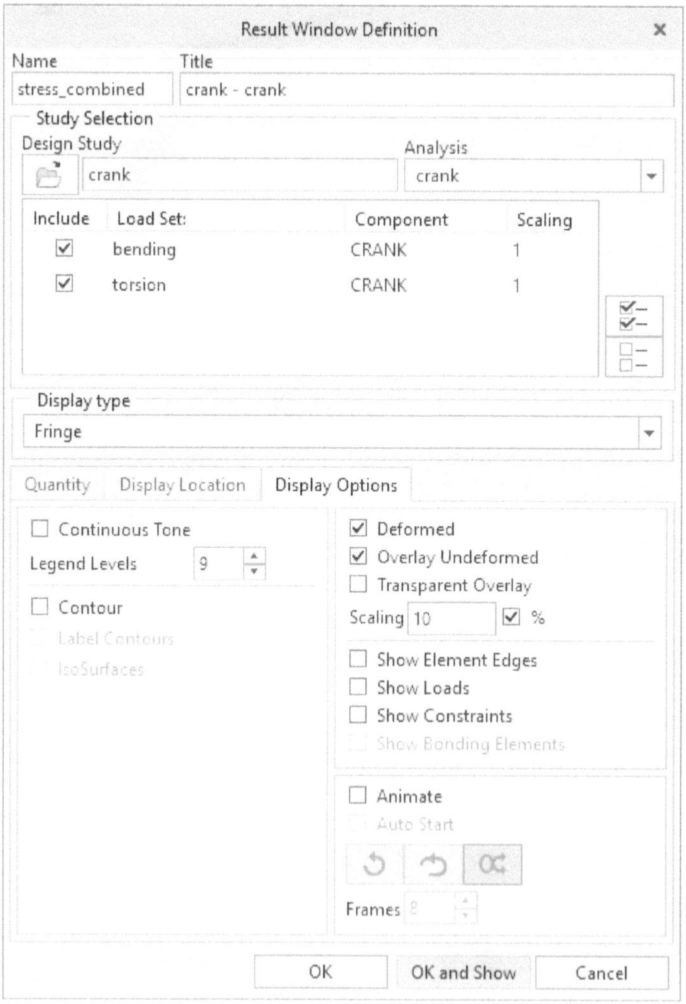

Figure 3–72

4. Click **OK**.

5. In the *View* tab, click (Show). In the *Display Result Window* dialog box that opens, select **stress_combined** and clear all of the other windows.

6. Click **OK**. The von Mises stress plot for the combined load case displays as shown in Figure 3–73.

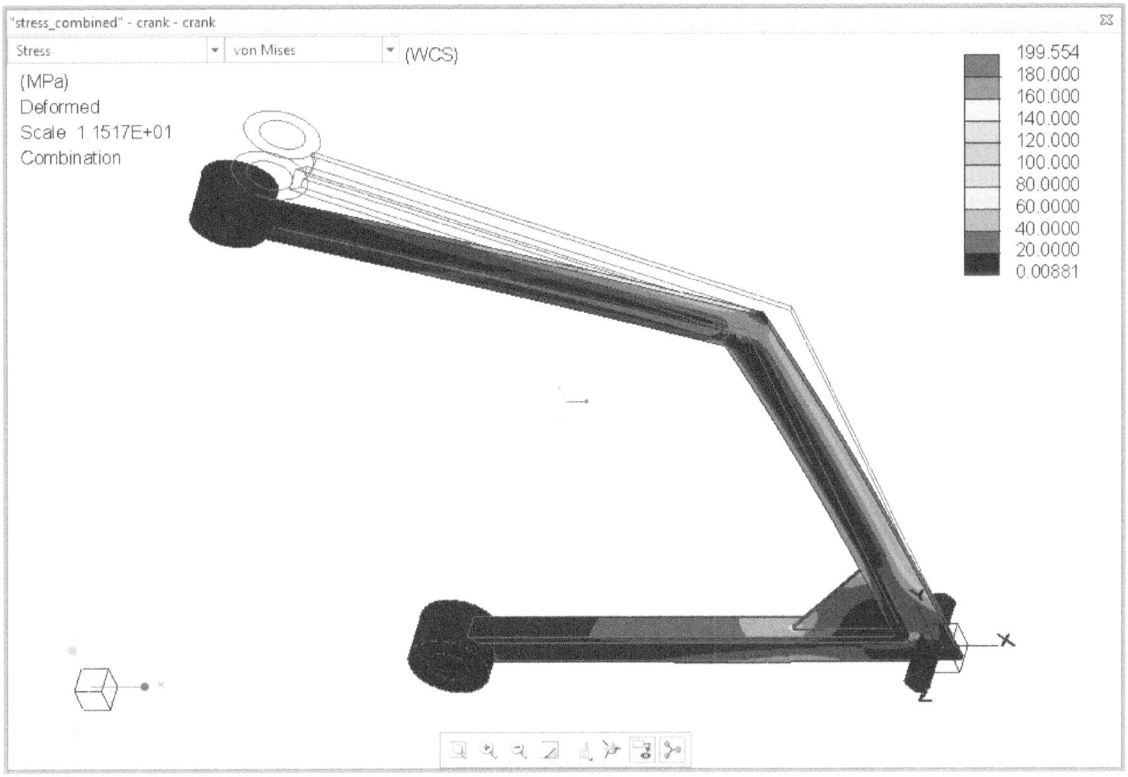

Figure 3–73

7. Examine the stress results. Locate the area of maximum stress.

8. Exit the Results environment. Save and close the model in Creo Parametric.

End of practice

Practice 3b
Cyclic Symmetry Constraints

Practice Objectives

- Apply cyclic constraints to a model.
- Analyze a model using cyclic constraints.

In this practice, you will use cyclic symmetry constraints to set up, run, and analyze the fan shown in Figure 3–74. The fan is rotating at 300rpm (5 rev/sec), and the fan blades are subjected to air pressure that varies linearly along the blade length, from 0.0008psi at the tip to 0psi at the center of the fan.

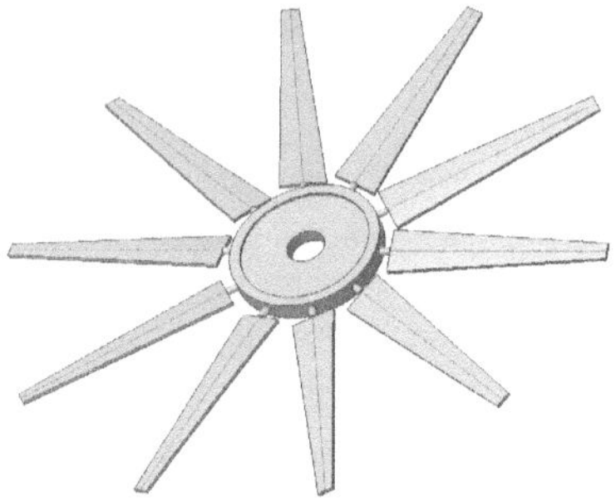

Figure 3–74

Note: You can only use cyclic symmetry constraints with solid and shell elements.

The intent of the cyclic symmetry constraint is to reduce the amount of geometry being analyzed, thus reducing the amount of time required to solve the analysis.

A model with cyclic constraints should be cyclically symmetric so that the entire model can be reproduced by rotating the symmetric section about an axis. The angle between cuts must equal 360° divided by the number of instances (the fan example is divided by ten). You will analyze the cyclic instance of the fan shown in Figure 3–75.

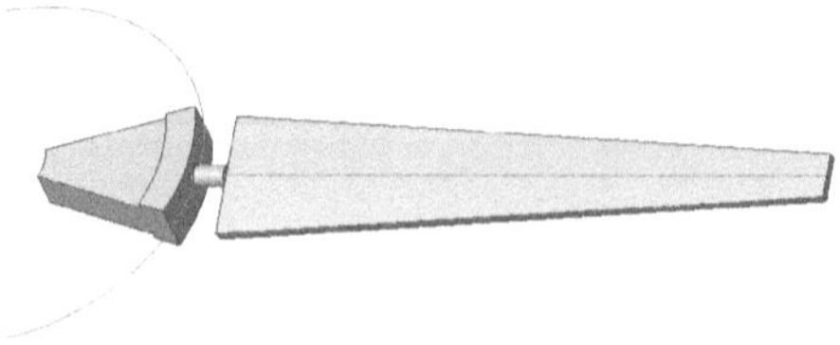

Figure 3–75

Note that both the geometry and boundary conditions must meet the criteria of cyclic symmetry. If the constraints or loading are not repeated about the axis of rotation by the same number of repetitions as the geometry, the results will be invalid.

Modeling Tasks

Task 1: Open the model.

1. Set the working directory to **Chapter03**, if required.
2. Open **fan.asm**.
3. Set the model display as follows:
   - *(Datum Display Filters)*: All Off
   - *(Spin Center)*: Off
   - *(Display Style)*: (Shading With Edges)

   The model displays as shown in Figure 3–76.

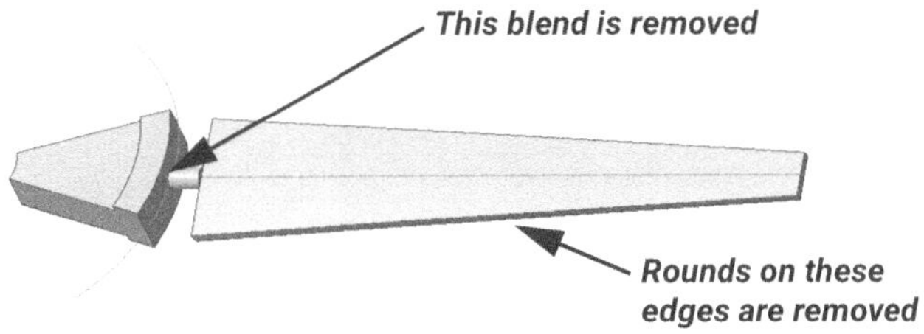

Figure 3–76

4. Ensure that the unit system is set to **IPS**.

   Note: *For this practice, the FEA model has been de-featured (e.g., various rounds have been removed).*

5. Switch to the Creo Simulate environment.

Task 2: Apply the material.

1. Assign **AL6061** to both parts.

   The following values are the default material properties for the AL6061 aluminum alloy:
   - *Poisson's ratio:* **0.3**
   - *Young's modulus:* **1e+07 psi**
   - *Density:* **0.0002536 lbf sec^2/in^4**

   Note: *The material properties should be as stated.*

2. Using the Simulation Display functionality, hide the **Material Assignments** icons.

Task 3: Apply a centrifugal load.

The fan is rotating at a high speed (5 rev/sec equals 31.4 rad/sec) about the Y-axis. In this task, you will apply a centrifugal load to the model to simulate this rotational loading.

1. In the *Home* tab, in the *Loads* group, click (Centrifugal). The *Centrifugal Load* dialog box opens, as shown in Figure 3–77.

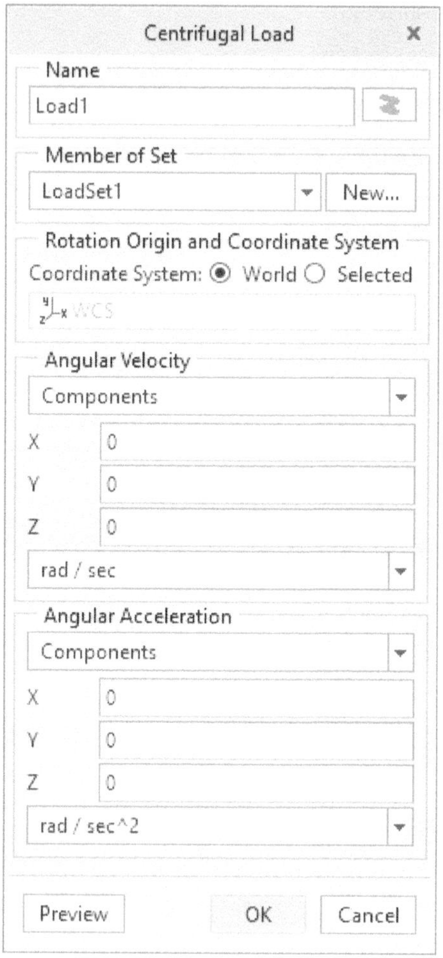

Figure 3–77

2. In the *Name* field, enter **c_force**.
3. For *Member of Set*, accept the default **LoadSet1** option.
4. In the *Angular Velocity* area, in the *Y* field, enter **31.4**.

   Note: *31.4rad/sec = 5 rev/sec*

5. Click **OK**. The applied load in the model is represented as a vector at the origin (0,0,0), as shown in Figure 3–78.

Figure 3–78

Task 4: Create a cylindrical coordinate system.

In this task, you will create a cylindrical coordinate system. The radial direction of this coordinate system will be used later to define the air pressure variation along the length of the fan blade.

1. In the In-graphics toolbar, enable (Plane Display) and (Csys Display).
2. In the *Refine Model* tab, click (Coordinate System).
3. In the *Select a Component* dialog box that opens, click **OK**.
4. The *Coordinate System* dialog box opens, as shown in Figure 3–79.

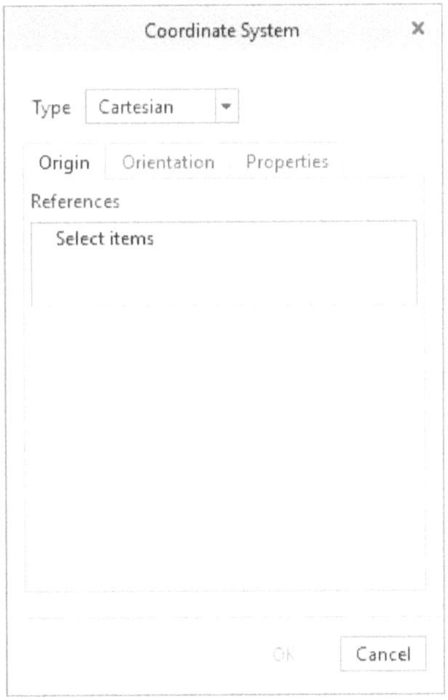

Figure 3–79

5. Expand the *Type* drop-down list and select **Cylindrical**.

6. Select the datum planes **ASM_RIGHT**, **ASM_TOP**, and **ASM_FRONT** (press and hold <Ctrl> to select multiples) to place the origin of the coordinate system at the intersection of the three planes.The *Coordinate System* dialog box opens, as shown in Figure 3–80.

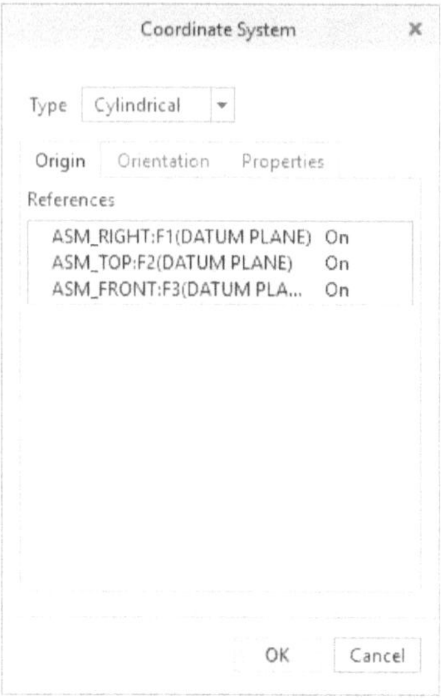

Figure 3–80

7. Select the *Orientation* tab. Use the **ASM_TOP** plane to orient the Z-axis of the new coordinate system and **ASM_FRONT** plane to orient the T = 0 axis. The *Coordinate System* dialog box displays as shown in Figure 3–81.

Figure 3–81

8. Click **OK** to finish.
9. In the In-graphics toolbar, disable (Plane Display).
10. The new coordinate system ACS0 displays at the WCS origin, as shown in Figure 3–82.

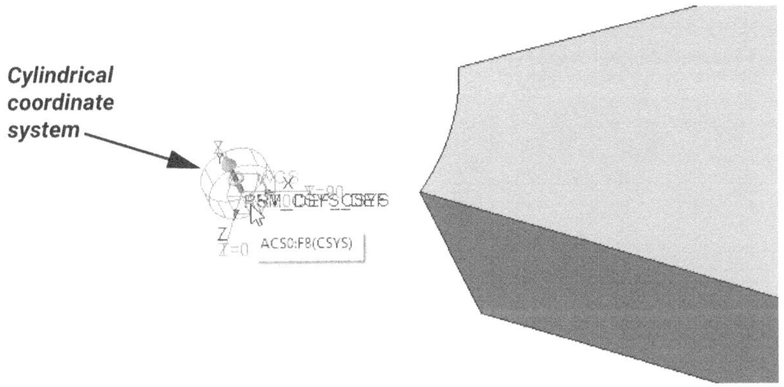

Figure 3–82

Task 5: Apply pressure load.

The fan blade is loaded with the air pressure that varies linearly along the length of the blade. In this task, you will apply a non-uniform pressure load to simulate the air pressure.

1. Select the blade surface that is opposite to the Y-axis side, as shown in Figure 3–83, and select (Pressure) from the In-graphics toolbar.

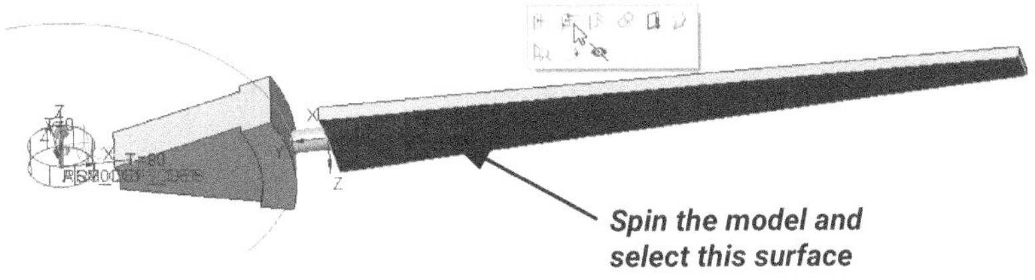

Figure 3–83

2. The *Pressure Load* dialog box opens, as shown in Figure 3–84.

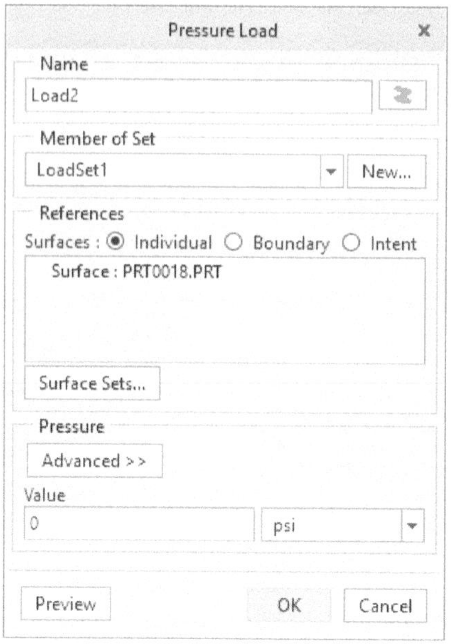

Figure 3–84

3. In the *Name* field, enter **pressure**.
4. For *Member of Set*, accept the default **LoadSet1** option.
5. Click **Advanced**.
6. Expand the *Spatial Variation* drop-down list and select **Function of Coordinates**.
7. Click f(x) (List Available Functions). The *Functions* dialog box opens, as shown in Figure 3–85.

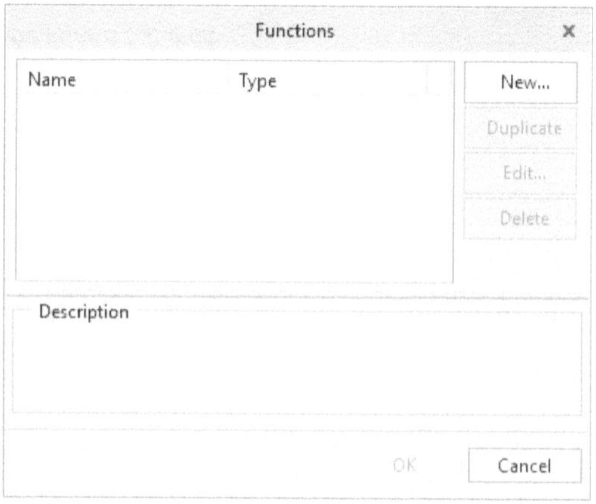

Figure 3–85

8. Click **New**. The *Function Definition* dialog box opens, as shown in Figure 3–86.

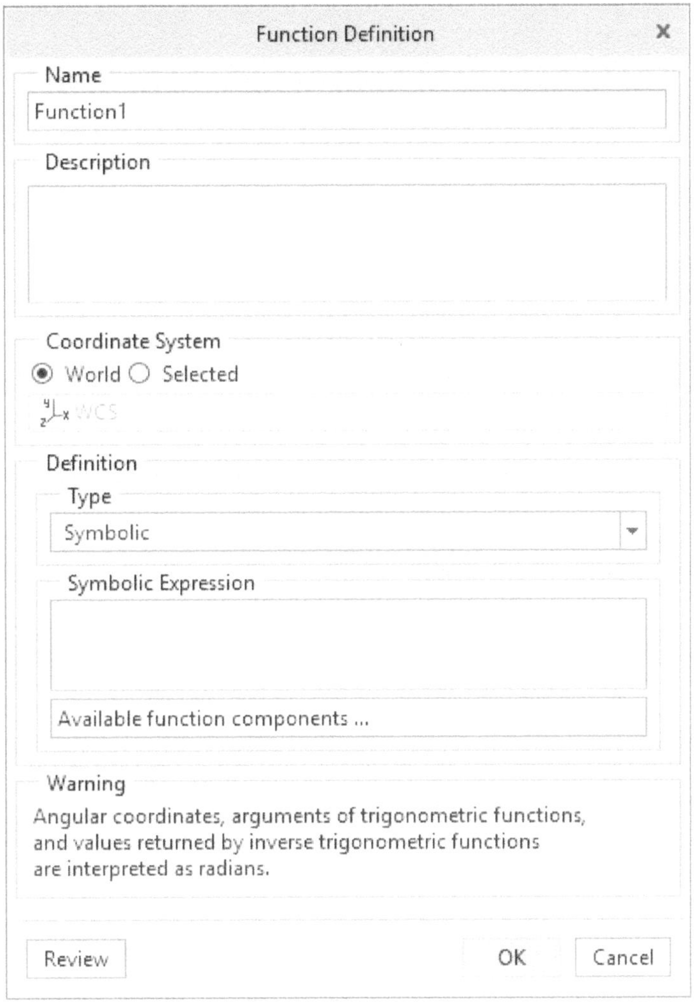

Figure 3–86

9. In the *Name* field, enter **linear**.
10. In the *Coordinate System* area, select the **Selected** option and select the **ACS0** coordinate system.
11. Expand the *Type* drop-down list and select **Symbolic**.

12. Click **Available function components**. The *Symbolic Options* dialog box opens, as shown in Figure 3–87.

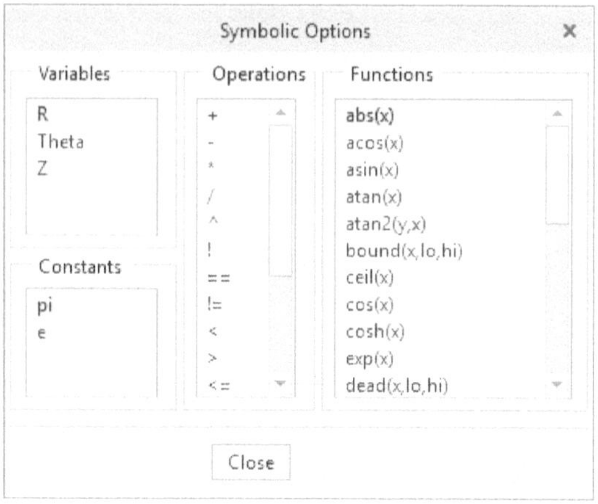

Figure 3–87

13. In the *Variables* area, double-click on the R and click **Close**. The *Function Definition* dialog box opens, as shown in Figure 3–88.

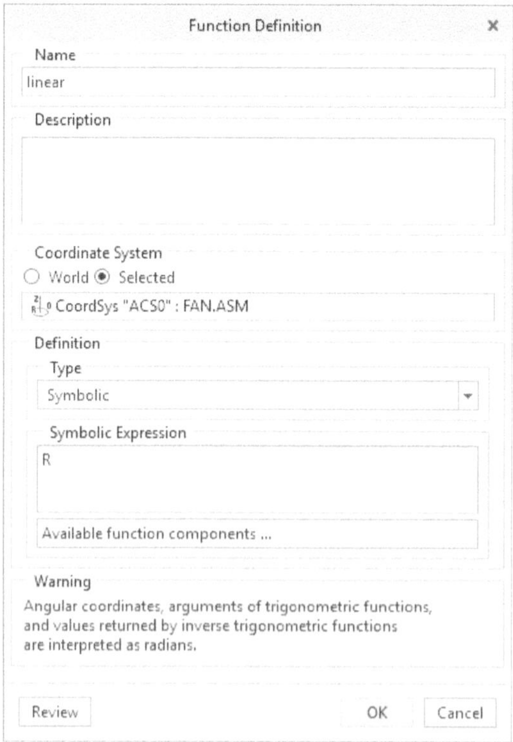

Figure 3–88

14. Click **Review**. The warning message displays as shown in Figure 3–89.

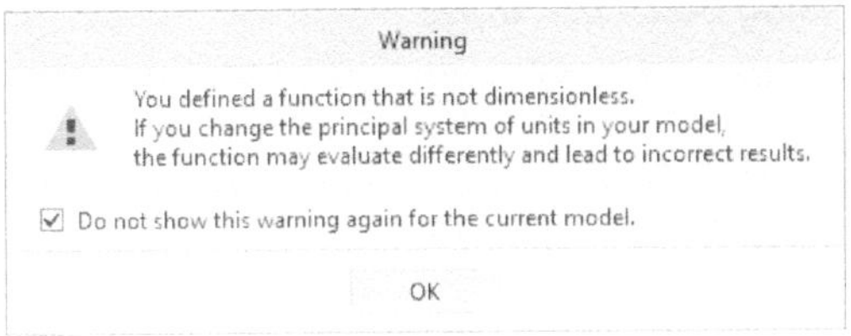

Figure 3–89

15. Click **OK** to close the message box. The *Graph Function* dialog box opens, as shown in Figure 3–90.

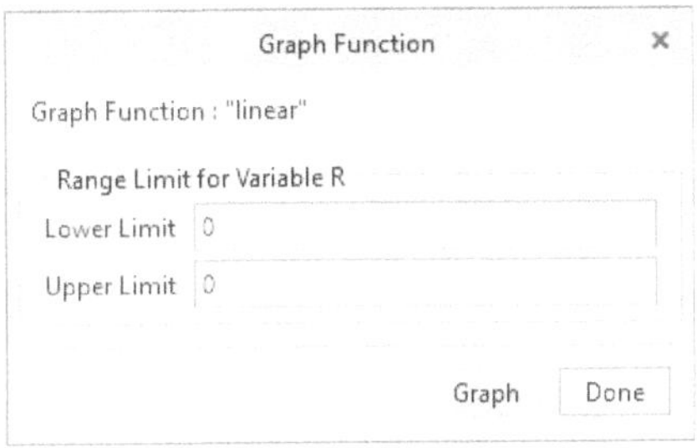

Figure 3–90

16. For the *Upper Limit*, enter **100**, and click **Graph**. The *Function Graph* window displays as shown in Figure 3–91.

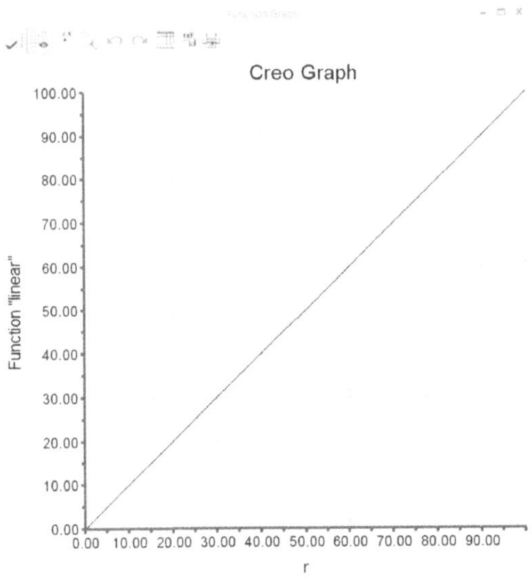

Figure 3–91

17. Verify that the function is linear and close the *Function Graph* window.
18. In the *Graph Function* dialog box, click **Done**.
19. In the *Function Definition* dialog box, click **OK**.
20. In the *Functions* dialog box, click **OK**.
21. In the *Value* field, enter **0.00003846**. The *Pressure Load* dialog box displays as shown in Figure 3–92.

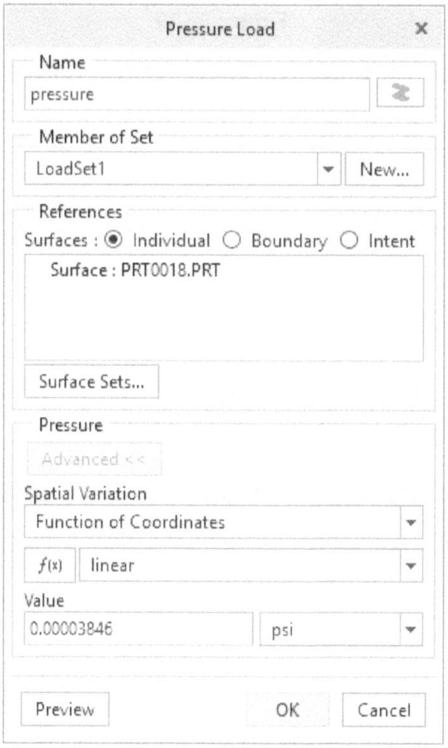

Figure 3–92

Note: *The fan radius is 20.76in and the air pressure at the tip of the blade is 0.0008psi. Given the linear R function, the value to be entered is* ***0.0008/20.76 = 0.00003846****.*

22. Click **Preview**. The model displays as shown in Figure 3–93.

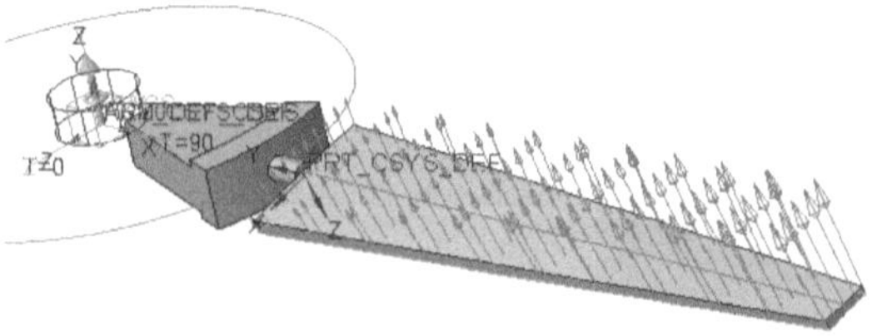

Figure 3–93

Note that the pressure increases linearly with the length of the blade.

23. Click **OK**. The model displays as shown in Figure 3–94.

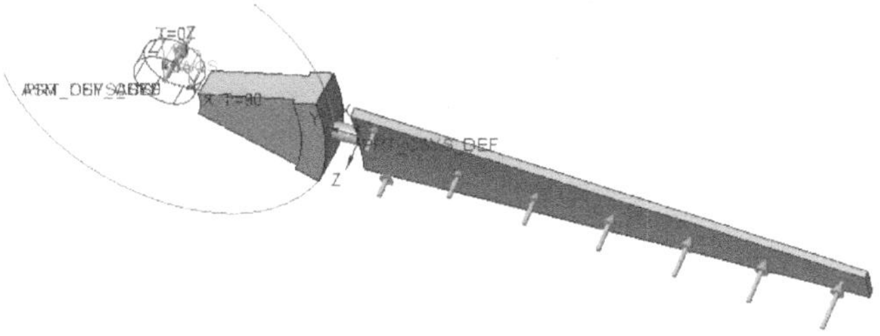

Figure 3–94

Task 6: Apply the constraints.

Apply cyclic constraints to the cut faces of the fan and fully constrain the fan hole surface.

1. In the *Home* tab, expand the *Constraints* group and select (Symmetry). The *Symmetry Constraint* dialog box opens, as shown in Figure 3–95.

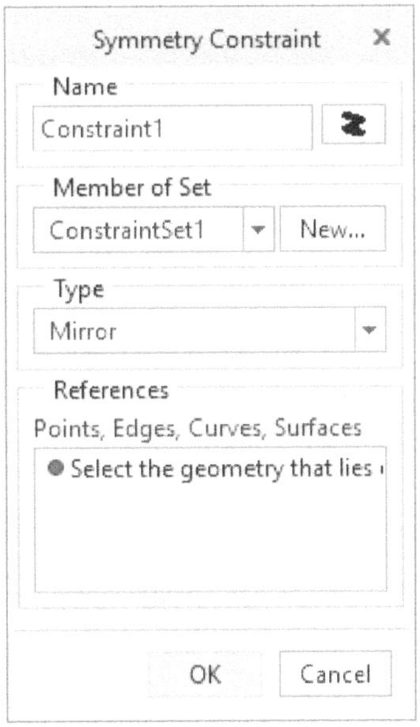

Figure 3–95

2. For the *Name*, enter **cyclic_const**.
3. Expand the *Type* drop-down list and select **Cyclic**.

4. Select the fan's first side cut surface, as shown in Figure 3–96.
5. Select the fan's second side cut surface, as shown in Figure 3–96.

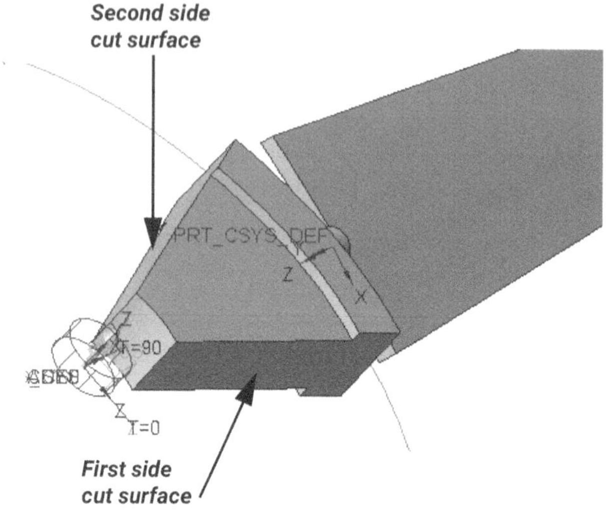

Figure 3–96

Note: For the first or second side, you can select either side of the fan's cut surfaces.

6. Click **OK** to finish. The model displays as shown in Figure 3–97.

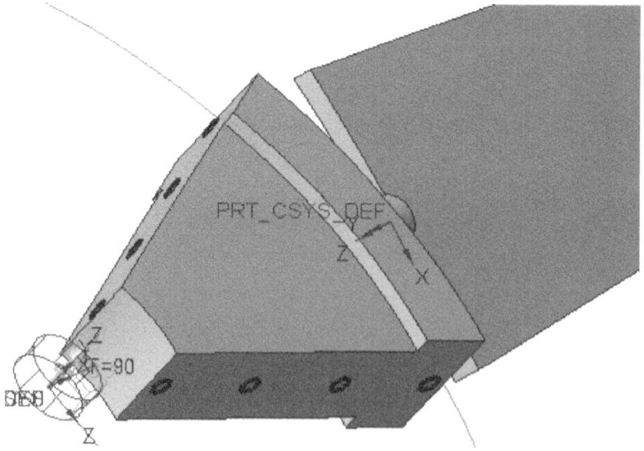

Figure 3–97

7. Select the surface shown in Figure 3–98 and click (Displacement). Constrain the fan's hole surface (all of the translations).

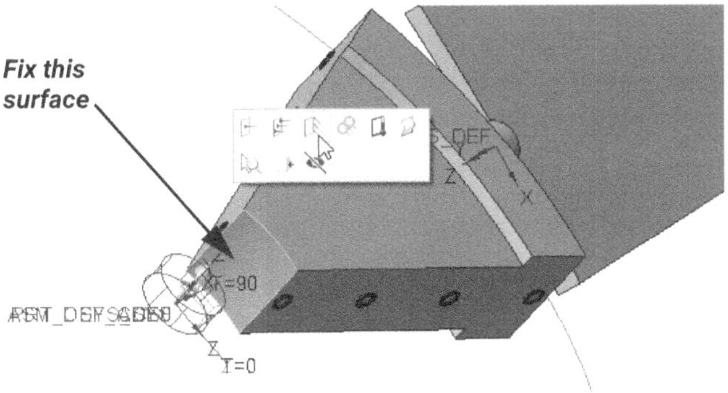

Figure 3–98

Analysis Tasks

Task 7: Solve the model using the Single-Pass Adaptive convergence option.

1. Set up a Single-Pass Adaptive analysis. For *Name*, type **fan**.
2. Run the analysis.
3. Expand the *Run Status dialog* box and note the RMS Stress Error Estimates, as shown in Figure 3–99.

RMS Stress Error Estimates:

Load Set	Stress Error	% of Max Prin Str
LoadSet1	8.91e+00	1.2% of 7.72e+02

Figure 3–99

Results Tasks

Task 8: Display the results.

In this task, you will create and display color plots for von Mises stress and the deflection. Animate these plots to display the effect of the loading on the model.

1. Create and display a color plot for the von Mises stress. The von Mises fringe plot displays as shown in Figure 3–100.

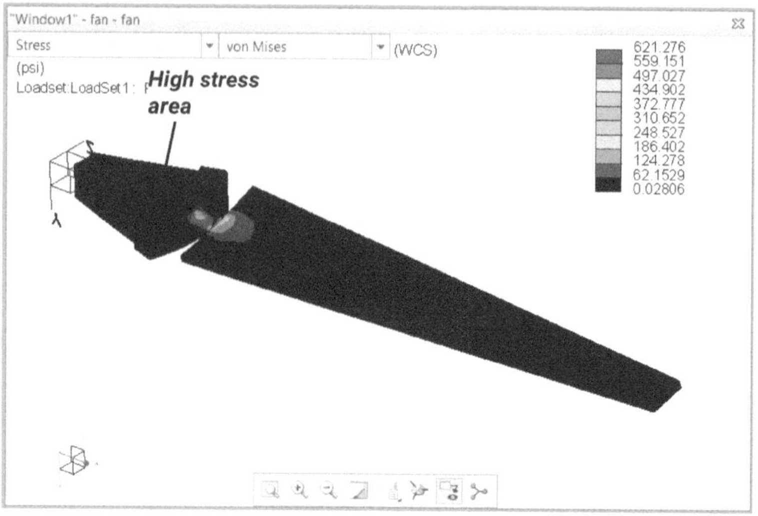

Figure 3–100

Locate the maximum von Mises stress. Note that the maximum stress displays at the junction of the blade and shaft, which is a re-entrant corner. This is expected, considering the load type and the removal of the blend feature. Examine the stress in other parts of your model. Create sections of the model in high stress areas.

2. Animate the von Mises stress window and play the animation frames. Frame 5 is shown in Figure 3–101.

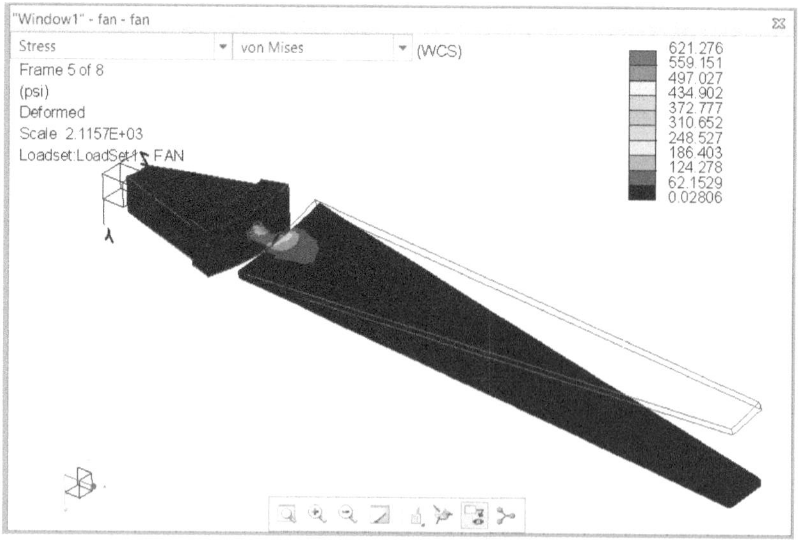

Figure 3–101

Task 9: Create deflection windows.

1. Create and examine a Displacement Magnitude deflection window.
2. Create deflection windows for the X-, Y-, and Z-displacement components and animate the windows.
3. Note the value of deflection for each component.
4. Exit the Results environment. Save and close the model in Creo Parametric.

End of practice

Practice 3c
Divide Surfaces

Practice Objective

- Use the **Divide Surface** tool to apply loads and constraints.

In this practice, you will analyze a mooring chock that is used for fastening ships to piers, etc. The model is shown in Figure 3–102. The chock is welded into the hull of the ship over an area 1" wide going around the outside surface, and loaded by a mooring line over a 2" area, as shown in Figure 3–102.

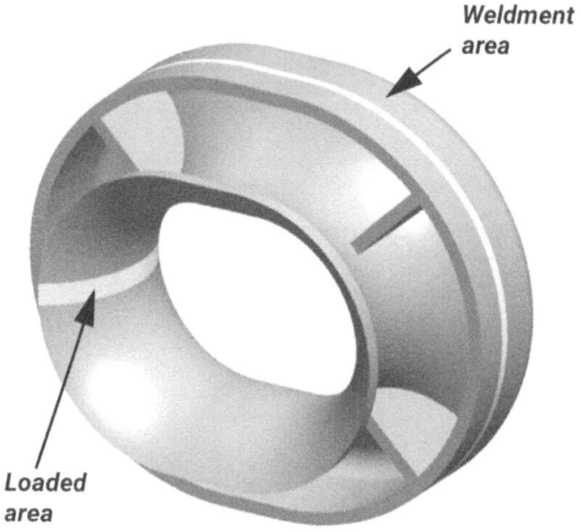

Figure 3–102

You will divide part surfaces to apply the loads and constraints over the areas shown in Figure 3–102.

Modeling Tasks

Task 1: Open the model.

1. Set the working directory to **Chapter03**, if required.
2. Open **chock.prt**.
3. Set the model display as follows:
   - *(Datum Display Filters)*: (Plane Display) Only
   - *(Spin Center)*: Off
   - *(Display Style)*: (Shading With Edges)

The part displays as shown in Figure 3–103.

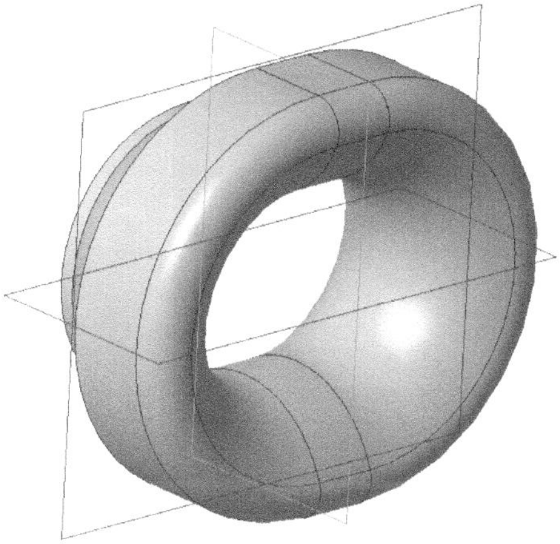

Figure 3–103

4. Ensure that the unit system is set to **IPS**.
5. Switch to Creo Simulate.

Task 2: Create boundary curves for the weldment region.

1. In the *Refine Model* tab, click ▱ (Plane) and create a DTM4 plane parallel to datum plane DTM3 at a distance of **3.5**, as shown in Figure 3–104.

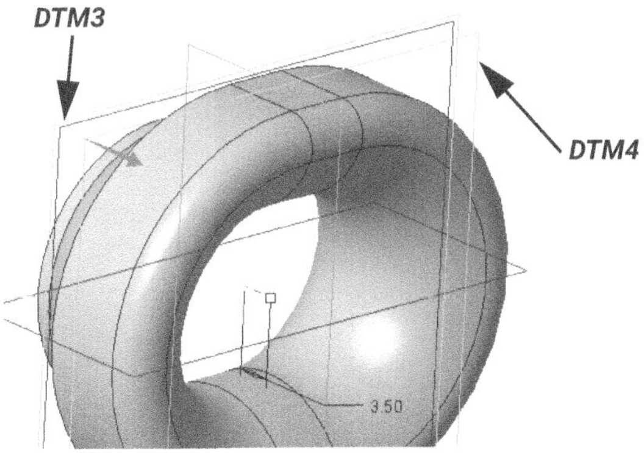

Figure 3–104

2. Click (Plane) again and create DTM5 plane parallel to datum plane DTM4 at a distance of **1**, as shown in Figure 3–105.

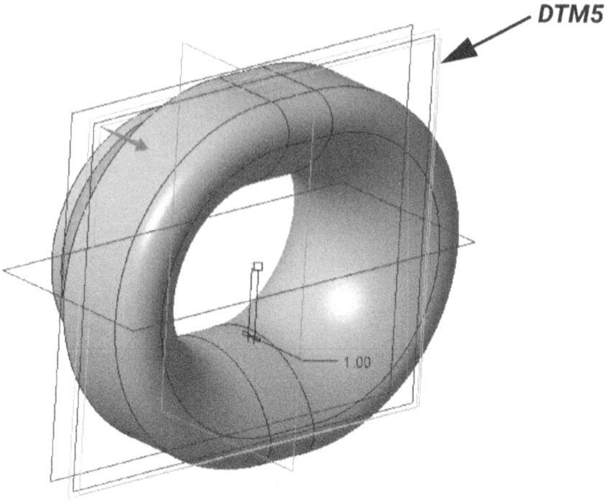

Figure 3–105

3. Select the DTM4 plane and click (Intersect) in the *Editing* group of the *Refine Model* tab. The *Surface Intersection* dashboard opens.
4. Hold <Ctrl> and select four surfaces on the outside of the chock, as shown in Figure 3–106.

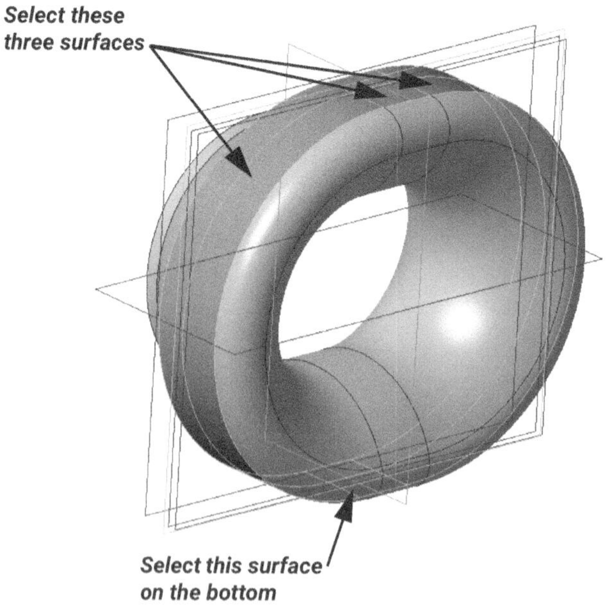

Figure 3–106

5. Click ✓ (OK) to finish. The new datum curve **Intersect 1** displays in the model, as shown in Figure 3–107.

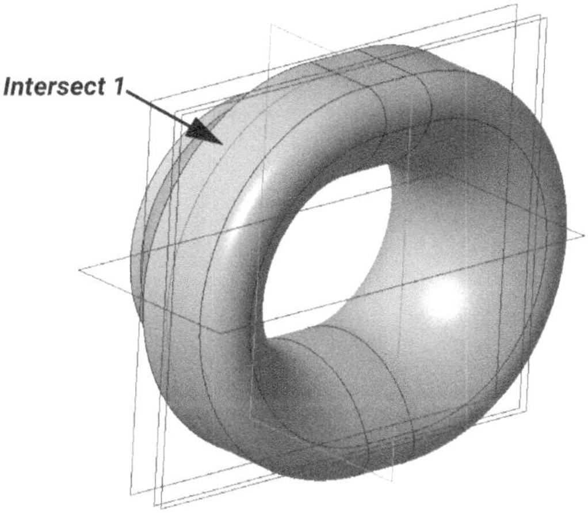

Figure 3–107

6. Repeat Steps 3 to 5, now using the DTM5 plane. The model displays as shown in Figure 3–108.

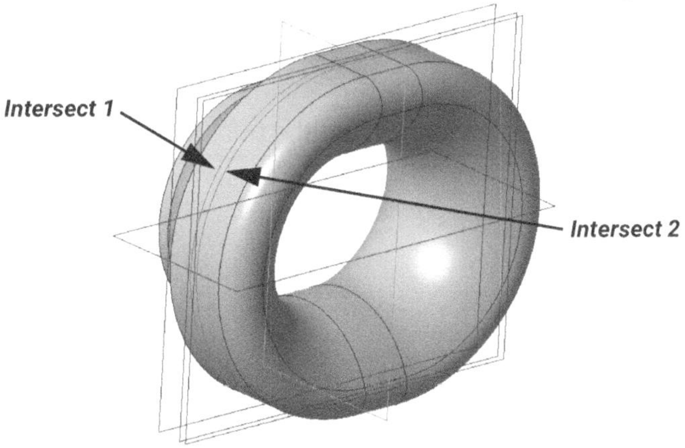

Figure 3–108

Task 3: Create boundary curves for the loaded region.

1. In the *Refine Model* tab, click (Sketch). Select the DTM1 plane as the sketch plane and the DTM2 plane as the reference plane for the Top orientation. Click **Flip** in the *Sketch orientation* dialog box to ensure that the sketch viewing direction is toward the positive X-direction.

2. Sketch the profile shown in Figure 3–109.

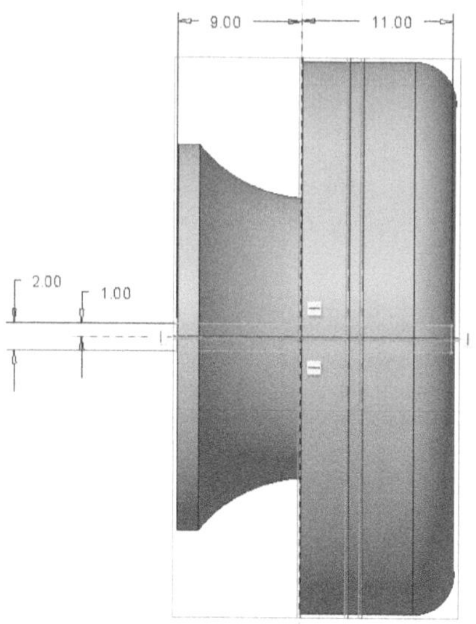

Figure 3–109

3. In the In-graphics toolbar, disable (Plane Display).
4. Select the sketch and click (Project) in the *Editing* group. The *Projected Curve* dashboard displays.
5. Select the inside surface of the chock, toward the positive X-direction, as shown in Figure 3–110.

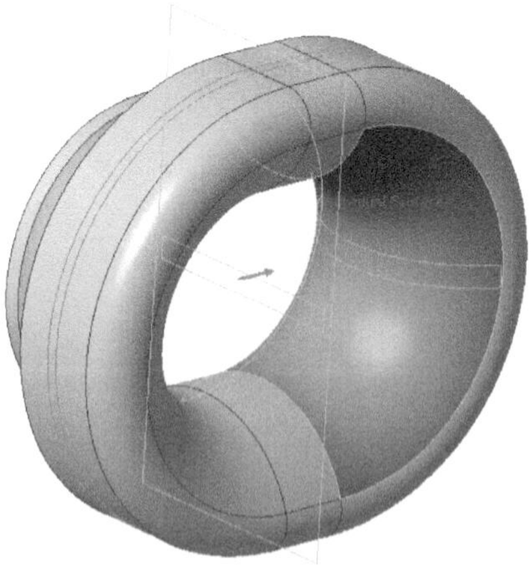

Figure 3–110

6. Click (OK) to finish.

7. The new datum curve **Project 1** displays in the model, as shown in Figure 3–111.

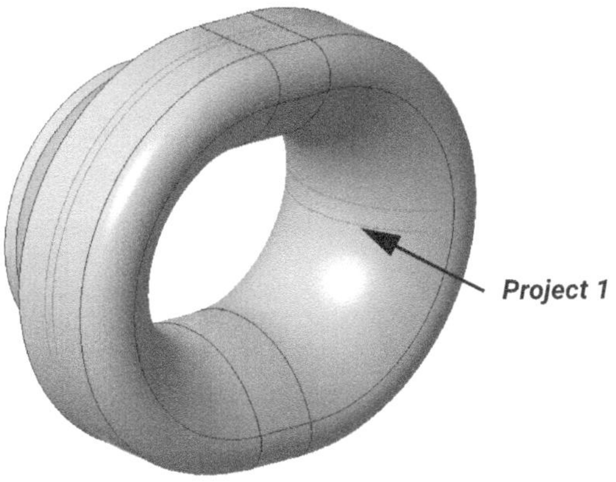

Figure 3–111

Task 4: Divide the surface for the weldment constraint.

1. In the *Refine Model* tab, click (Divide Surface). The *Divide Surface* dashboard opens, as shown in Figure 3–112.

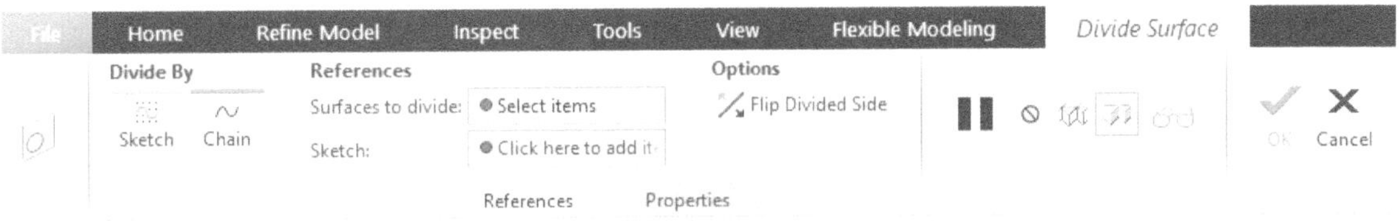

Figure 3–112

2. Select the *Surfaces to divide* field. Hold <Ctrl> and select four surfaces on the outside of the chock, as shown in Figure 3–113.

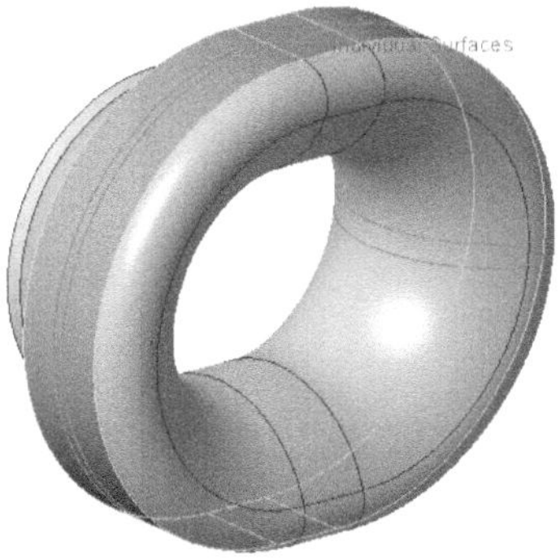

Figure 3–113

3. Click (Chain) in the dashboard.
4. Select the *Chains* field, and select the **Intersect 1** curve. The model displays as shown in Figure 3–114. Select **Flip Divided Side**, if required.

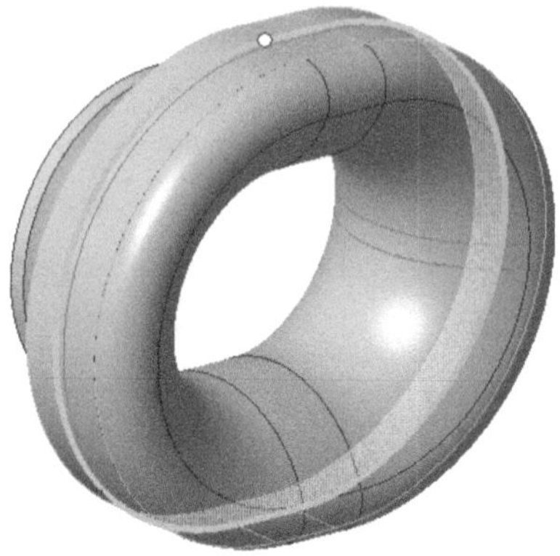

Figure 3–114

5. Click (OK) to finish. The new feature **Divide Surface 1** is created and added to the *Model Tree*.
6. Repeat Steps 2 to 6 using the curve **Intersect 2**. Two **Divide Surface** features display in the *Model Tree*, as shown in Figure 3–115. Click the features in the *Model Tree* to check how they highlight in the model.

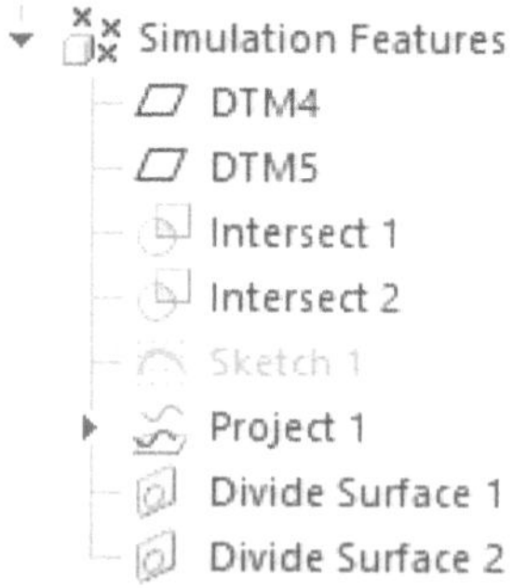

Figure 3–115

Task 5: Divide the surface for the load.

1. Using Task 4 as a guideline, create another Divide Surface feature, now using **Project 1** and the surface shown in Figure 3–116.

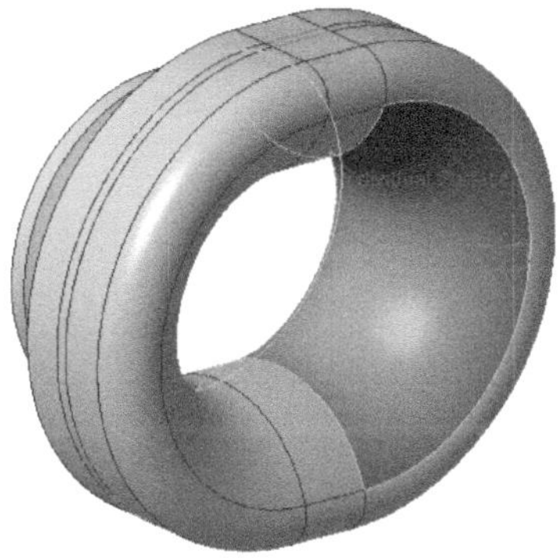

Figure 3–116

Task 6: Apply the material.

1. Assign **STEEL** to the part. The following values are the default material properties for the STEEL:

   - *Poisson's ratio:* **0.27**
   - *Young's modulus:* **2.9e+07 psi**
   - *Density:* **0.0007324 lbf sec^2/in^4**

   Note: *The material properties should be as stated.*

2. Using the Simulation Display functionality, hide the **Material Assignment** icon.

Task 7: Mesh the model.

1. In the *Refine Model* tab, click (AutoGEM). The *AutoGEM* dialog box opens, as shown in Figure 3–117.

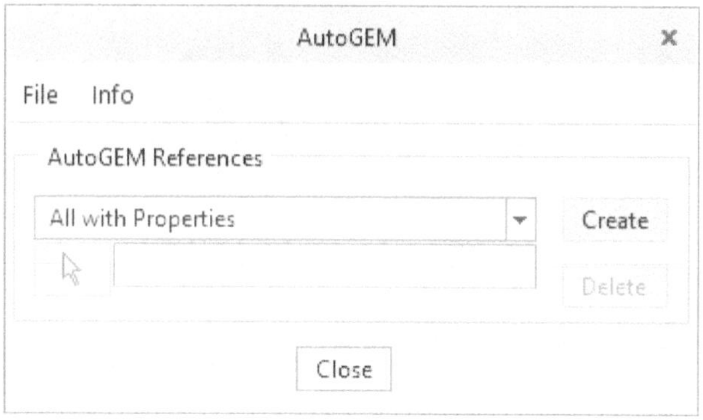

Figure 3–117

2. Leave *AutoGEM References* set to **All with Properties**.
3. Click **Create**.
4. Creo Simulate meshes the model and displays the *AutoGEM Summary and Diagnostics* dialog boxes.
5. Close both the *AutoGEM Summary and Diagnostics* dialog boxes, but do not close the *AutoGEM* dialog box. The model displays as shown in Figure 3–118.

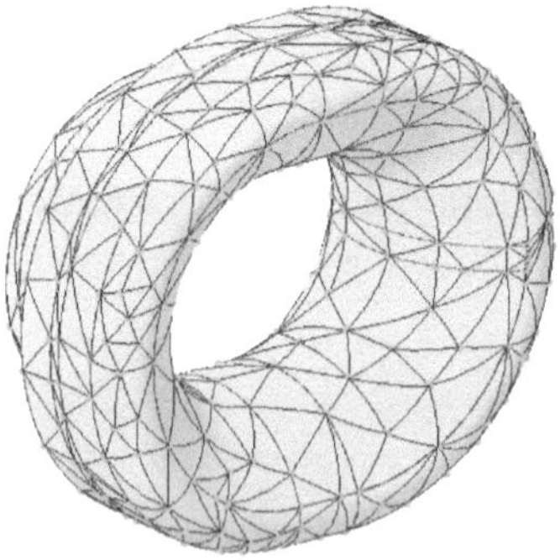

Figure 3–118

6. Review the mesh. Close the *AutoGEM* dialog box and save the mesh.

Task 8: Apply the constraints.

1. Fully constrain the weldment region (in all of the translations), as shown in Figure 3–119.

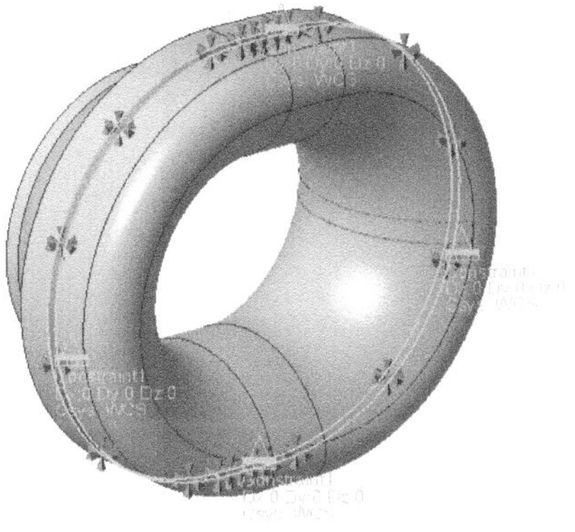

Figure 3–119

Task 9: Apply the load.

The force exerted by the mooring line onto the chock is 100,000lbs. The force is distributed accordingly to the half-sine law. The load is maximum in the middle of the loaded region, and zero at the ends of the loaded region.

1. Select the region for the load, as shown in Figure 3–120, and click (Force/Moment) from the mini-toolbar.

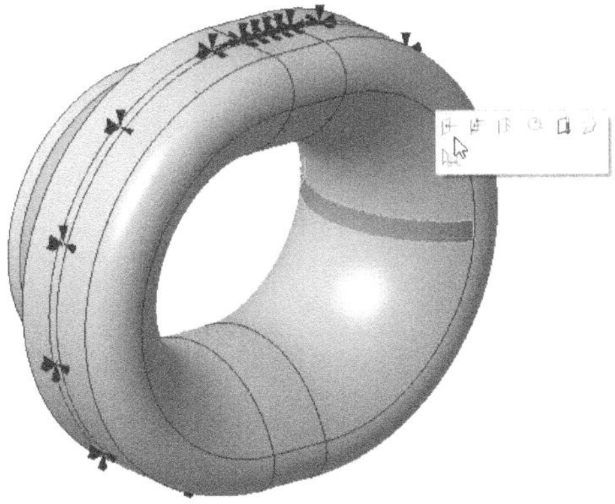

Figure 3–120

2. In the *Name* field, enter **line_load**.

3. Click **Advanced**. The *Force/Moment* dialog box displays as shown in Figure 3–121.

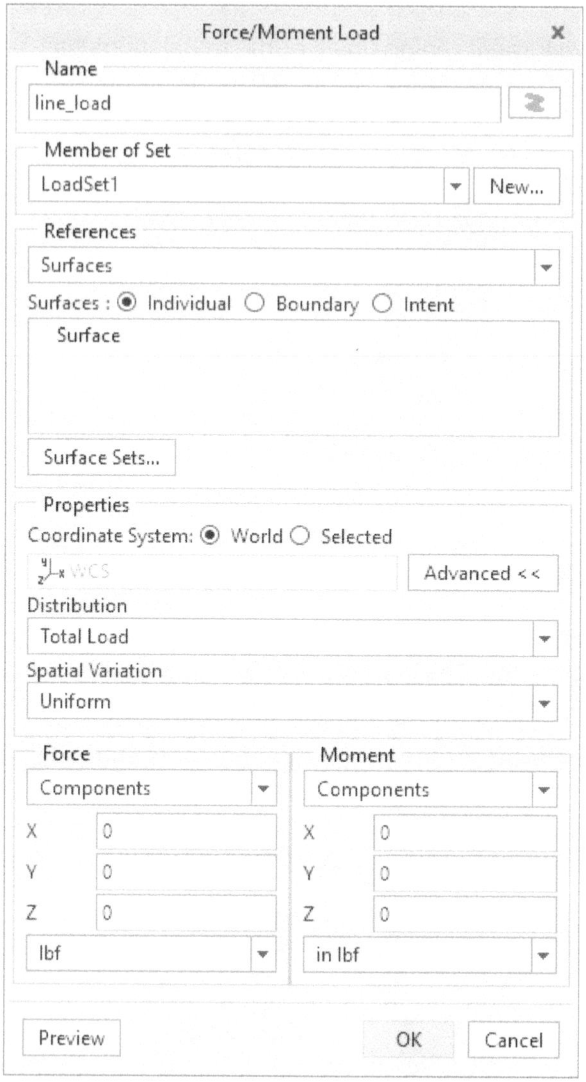

Figure 3–121

4. Expand the *Spatial Variation* drop-down list and select **Function of Coordinates**.
5. Click  (List Available Functions). The *Functions* dialog box opens.
6. Click **New**.
7. In the *Name* field, enter **halfsine**.
8. Expand the *Type* drop-down list and select **Table**.
9. In the *Row* field, select **Z**.

10. In the *Table* area, enter the tabular function as shown in Figure 3–122.

Figure 3–122

11. Click **Review** and close the warning box that opens. Click **Graph**. The *Function Graph* window displays as shown in Figure 3–123.

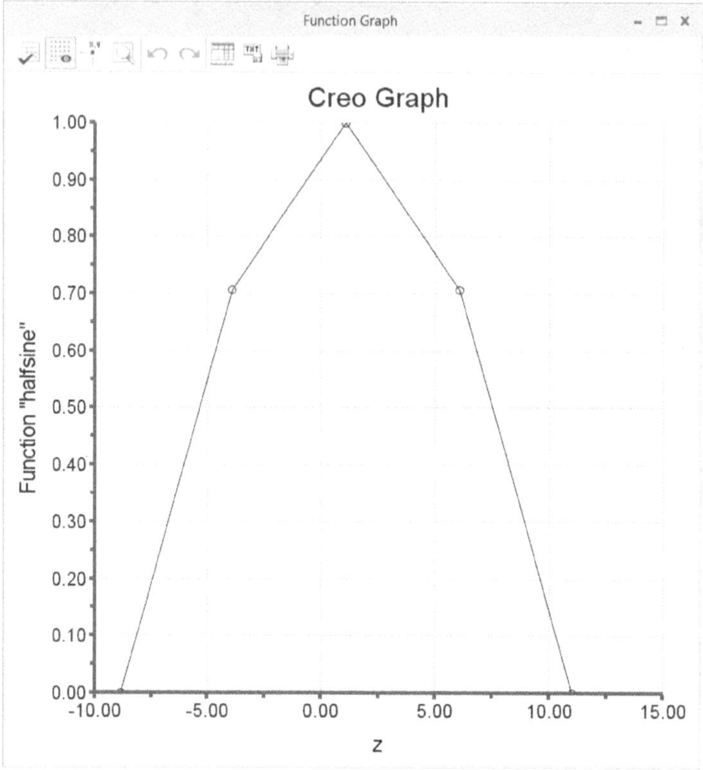

Figure 3–123

12. Verify the function and close the *Function Graph* window.

13. In the *Graph Function* dialog box, click **Done**.

14. In the *Function Definition* dialog box, click **OK**.

15. In the *Functions* dialog box, click **OK**.

16. In the *X* field, enter **100000**. The *Force/Moment Load* dialog box displays as shown in Figure 3–124.

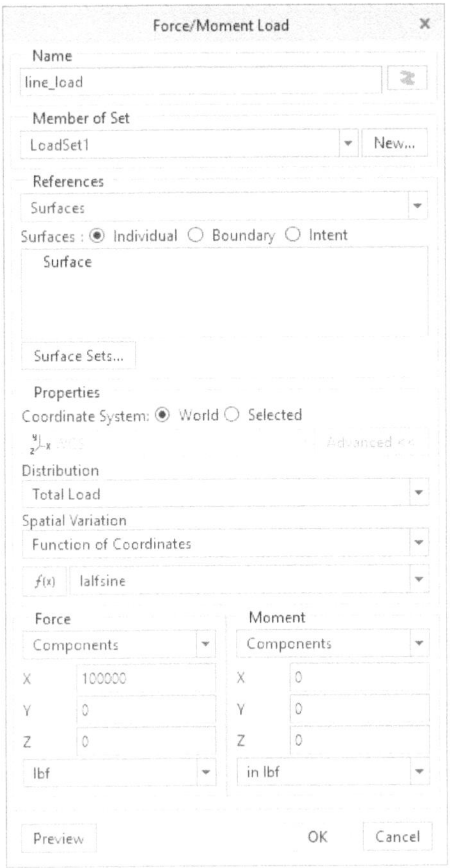

Figure 3–124

17. Click **OK**. The model displays as shown in Figure 3–125.

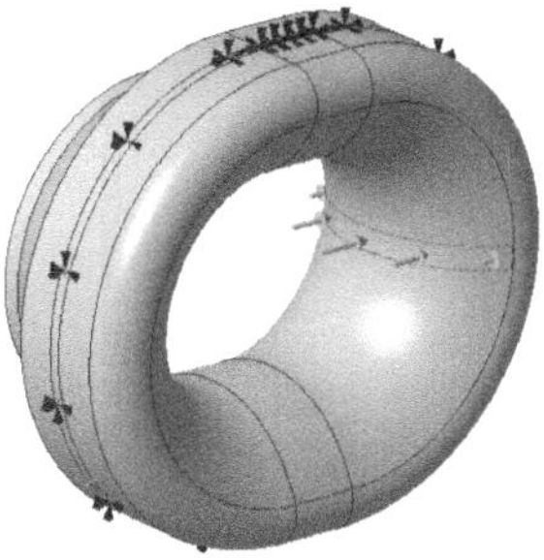

Figure 3–125

Task 10: Verify the load.

Since the load distribution you applied is non-uniform, in this task you will verify that total amount of load applied to the model is 100,000lbs as required.

1. Expand the *Loads* area in the *Home* tab and select **Review Total Load**. The *Load Resultant* dialog box opens, as shown in Figure 3–126.

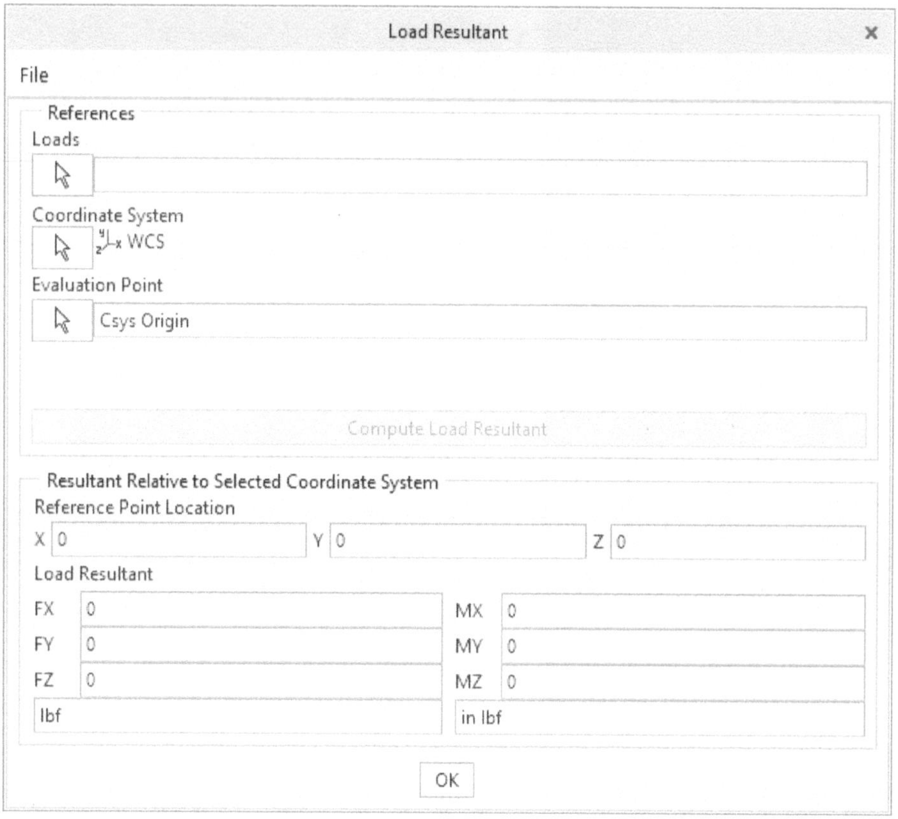

Figure 3–126

2. Click (Select) and select the **line_load** load in the model. Click the middle mouse button to complete the selection.

3. Click **Compute Load Resultant**. The *Load Resultant* dialog box displays as shown in Figure 3–127.

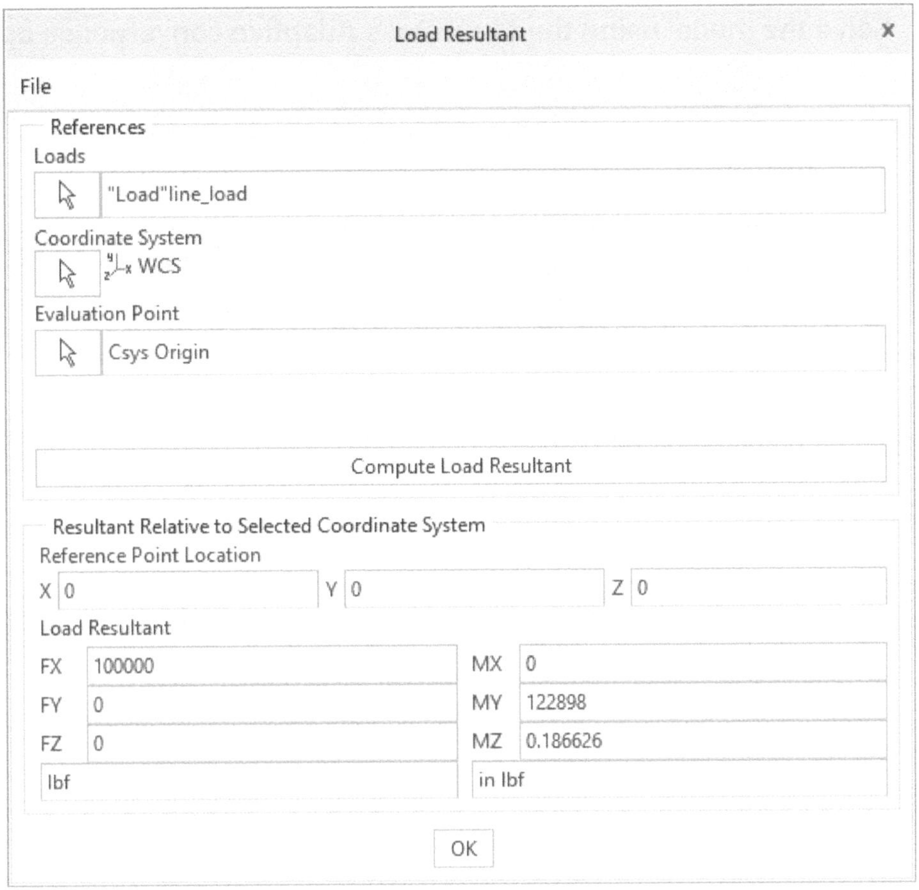

Figure 3–127

Note that the *FX* field might not read exactly **100000** as specified, but the value should be within 0.01% of that specified.

4. Click **OK** to finish.

Analysis Tasks

Task 11: Solve the model using the Multi-Pass Adaptive convergence option.

1. Set up a Multi-Pass Adaptive analysis. For the *Name*, enter **chock**. For the *Maximum Polynomial Order*, enter **9** and in the *Percent Convergence* field, enter **10**.
2. Run the analysis.
3. Expand the *Run Status* window. Extract the following information:
    - Number of solid elements in the model.
    - Number of passes to convergence.
    - Maximum P-Level on the last pass.
    - Number of equations on the last pass.
    - RMS Stress Error estimates.

Results Tasks

Task 12: Display the deformation.

1. Create the displacement magnitude animation plot, as shown in Figure 3–128.
2. Start the animation. Check whether the applied boundary conditions behave correctly.

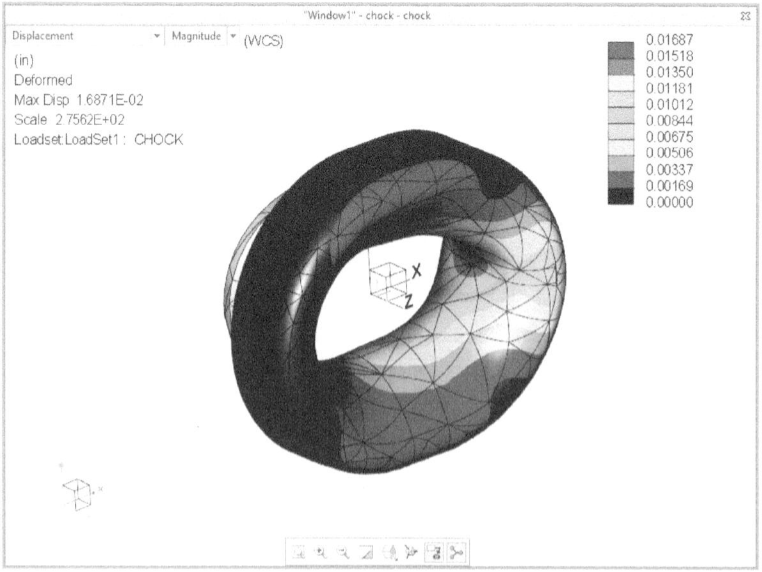

Figure 3–128

Task 13: Display the von Mises stress.

1. Create the von Mises stress undeformed plot, as shown in Figure 3–129.

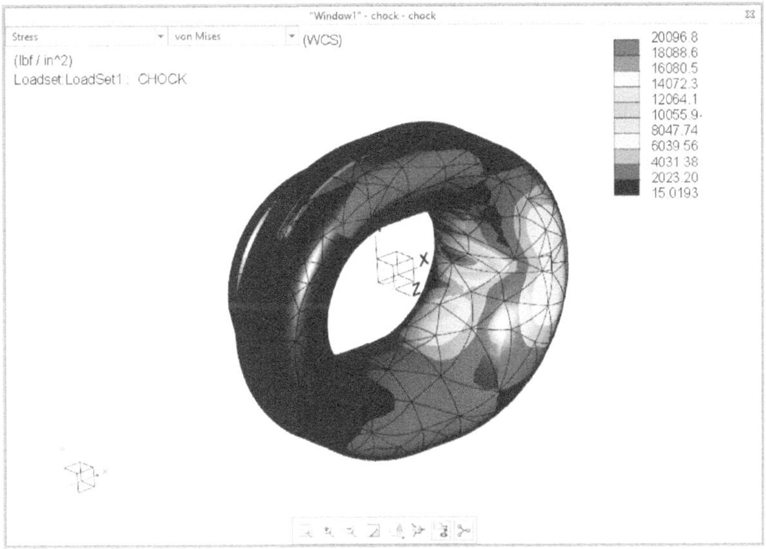

Figure 3–129

2. Using (Model Max), locate the area of maximum stress in the part, as shown in Figure 3–130.

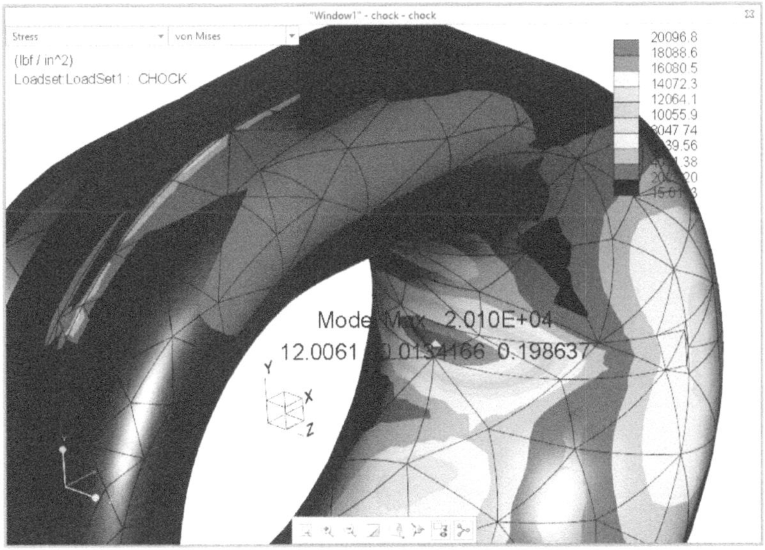

Figure 3–130

3. Select (New) in the *Capping & Cutting Surfs* group in the *View* tab. In the *Results Surface Definition* dialog box, in the *Plane* area, select **XZ**, as shown in Figure 3–131.

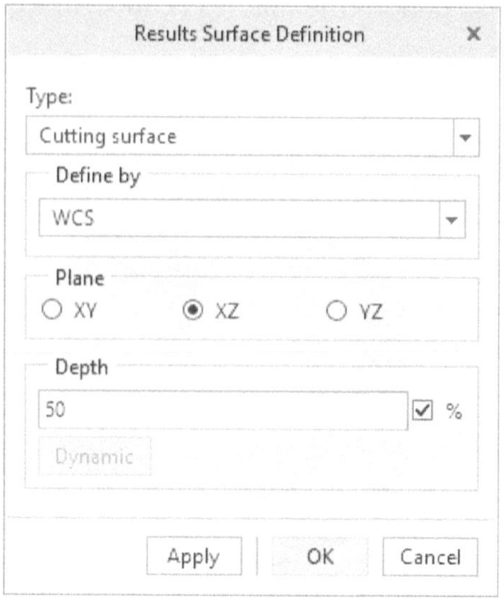

Figure 3–131

4. Click **Apply**. Zoom in on the cross-section. The model displays as shown in Figure 3–132.

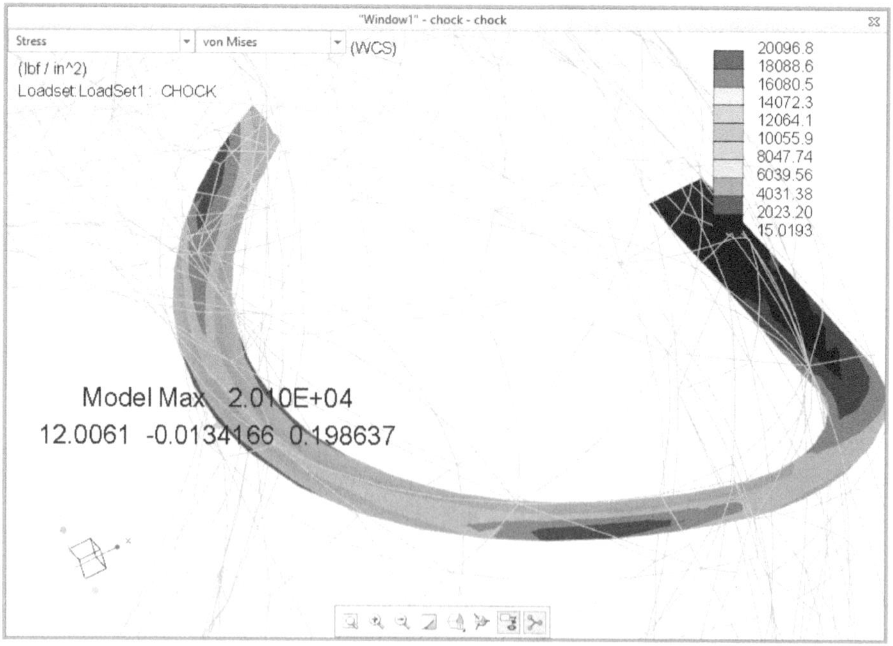

Figure 3–132

Note the characteristic bending pattern of stress through the thickness, with little stress on the neutral fiber and maximum stress on the outermost fibers.

5. Click **Cancel** to close the *Results Surface Definition* dialog box.
6. Exit the Results environment. Save and close the model in Creo Parametric.

End of practice

Practice 3d
Excluded Elements

Practice Objective

- Use excluded elements to improve convergence.

Modeling Tasks

Task 1: Open the model.

1. Set the working directory to **Chapter03**, if required.
2. Open **solid_bracket_2.prt**.
3. Set the model display as follows:
   - *(Datum Display Filters)*: All Off
   - *(Spin Center)*: Off
   - *(Display Style)*: (Shading With Edges)

   The part displays as shown in Figure 3–133.

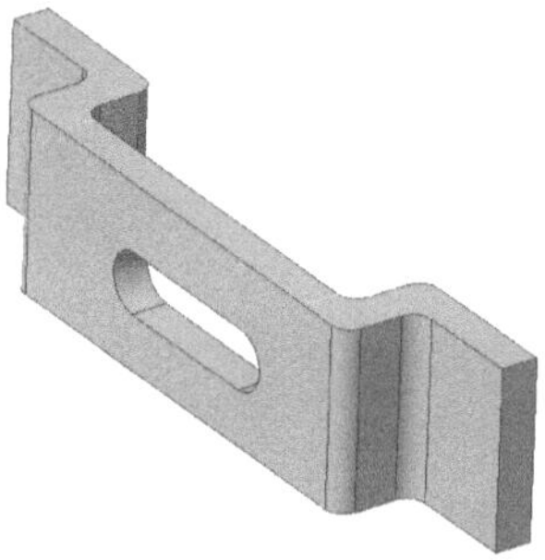

Figure 3–133

4. Switch to the Creo Simulate environment.

Task 2: Apply the material.

1. Assign **STEEL** to the part.

   The following values are the default material properties for the STEEL material:
   - *Poisson's ratio:* **0.27**
   - *Young's modulus:* **199948 MPa**

Task 3: Apply the constraints.

1. Constrain the two surfaces shown in Figure 3–134 in all translations.

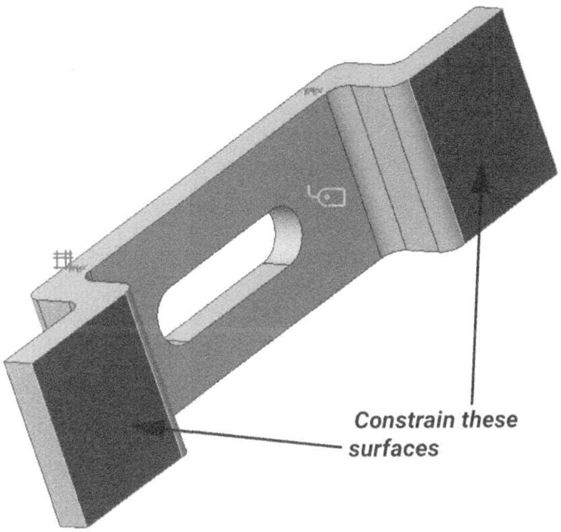

Figure 3–134

Task 4: Apply the load.

1. Apply a 500 N load in the Z-direction on the edge shown in Figure 3–135.

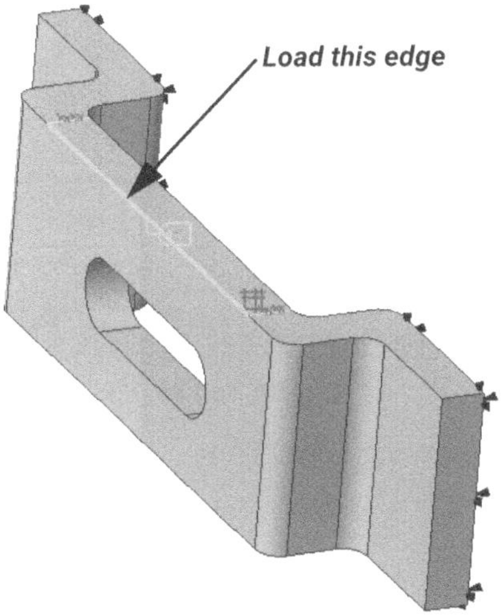

Figure 3–135

Analysis Tasks

Task 5: Solve the model using the Multi-Pass Adaptive convergence option.

1. Set up a Multi-Pass Adaptive analysis. For the *Name*, enter **excluded**. For the *Maximum Polynomial Order*, enter **9** and for the *Percent Convergence* field, enter **10**.
2. Run the analysis.
3. The analysis does not converge. Note that the warning message in the *Diagnostics* window prompts you that *Convergence was not obtained because the maximum polynomial order of 9 was reached.*

Results Tasks

Task 6: Display convergence graphs.

1. Display convergence graphs for the **strain_energy** and **max_stress_vm** measures, as shown in Figure 3–136.

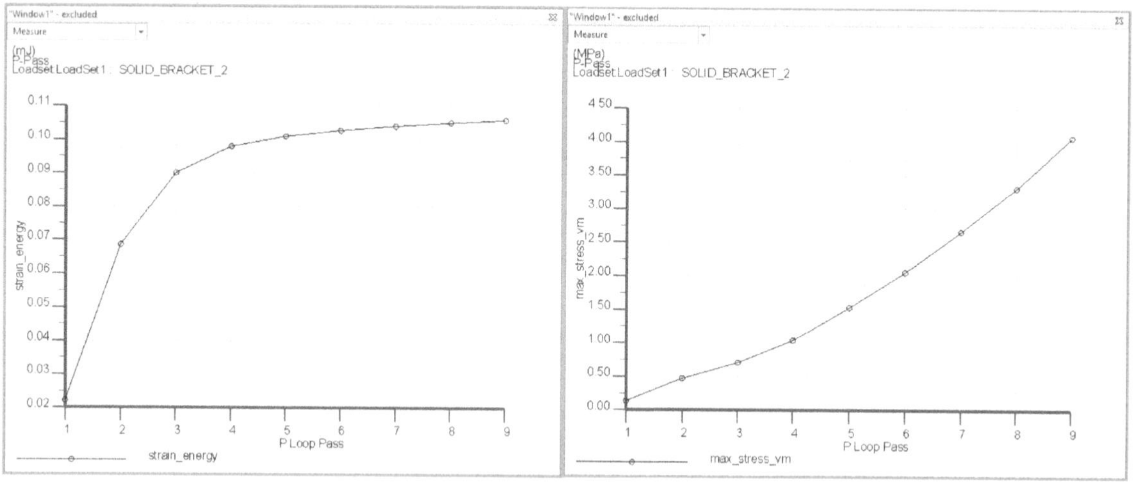

Figure 3–136

Note that the maximum stress does not exhibit any convergence. This is due to the singularity caused by the edge load in the model.

2. Exit the Results environment.

Modeling Tasks

In the following tasks, you will use the excluded elements to improve convergence.

Task 7: Isolate elements for exclusion.

1. In the *Refine Model* tab, in the *AutoGEM* group, expand (Control) and click (Isolate for Exclusion). The *Isolate for Exclusion Control* dialog box opens, as shown in Figure 3–137.

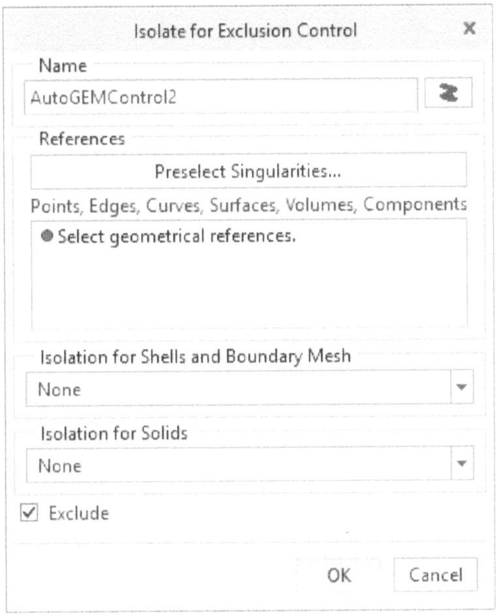

Figure 3–137

2. Click **Preselect Singularities**. In the *Preselect Singularities* dialog box, select the **Edge Loads** option, as shown in Figure 3–138.

Figure 3–138

3. Click **Select** and Creo Simulate automatically selects the area of singularity.

4. Expand the *Isolation for Solids* drop-down list and select **Maximum Element Size**. In the *Isolation for Solids* area, enter **5**, as shown in Figure 3–139.

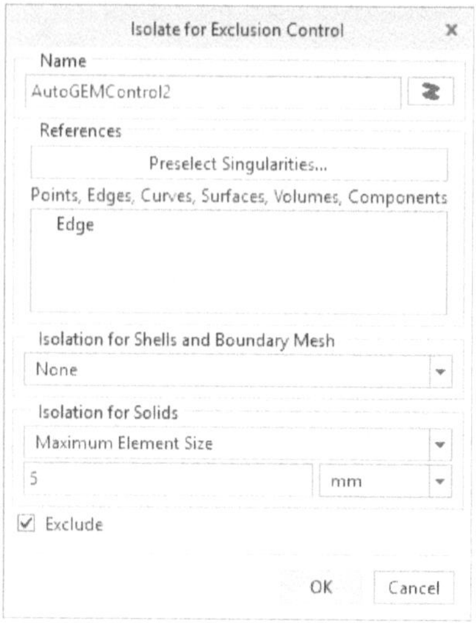

Figure 3–139

5. Click **OK**.

Task 8: Mesh the model.

1. Use the **All with Properties** option to mesh the model.
2. Use the **Simulation Display** tool to hide the mesh points.
3. In the *AutoGEM* dialog box, select **Info>Isolating Elements**.
4. Click **OK** in the *Information* dialog box, then zoom in on the loaded edge. Note that AutoGEM has isolated the edge with small elements, as shown in Figure 3–140.

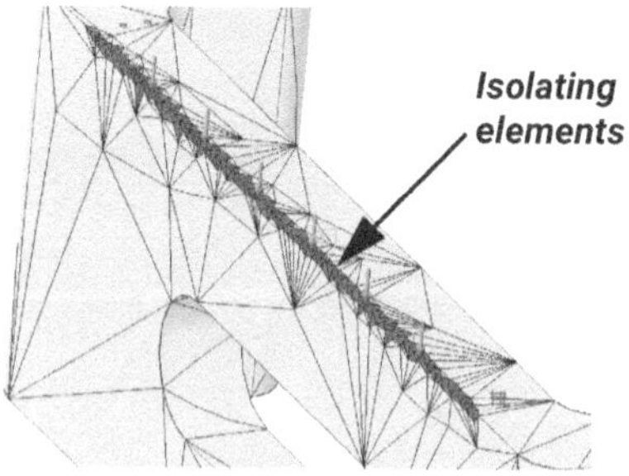

Figure 3–140

5. Close the AutoGEM without saving the mesh.

Analysis Tasks

Task 9: Re-run the analysis.

1. Edit the **excluded** analysis study. In the *Excluded Elements* tab, select **Exclude Elements**. In the *Ignore* area, select **Stresses and Displacements**. In the *Polynomial Order* field, enter **3**, as shown in Figure 3–141.

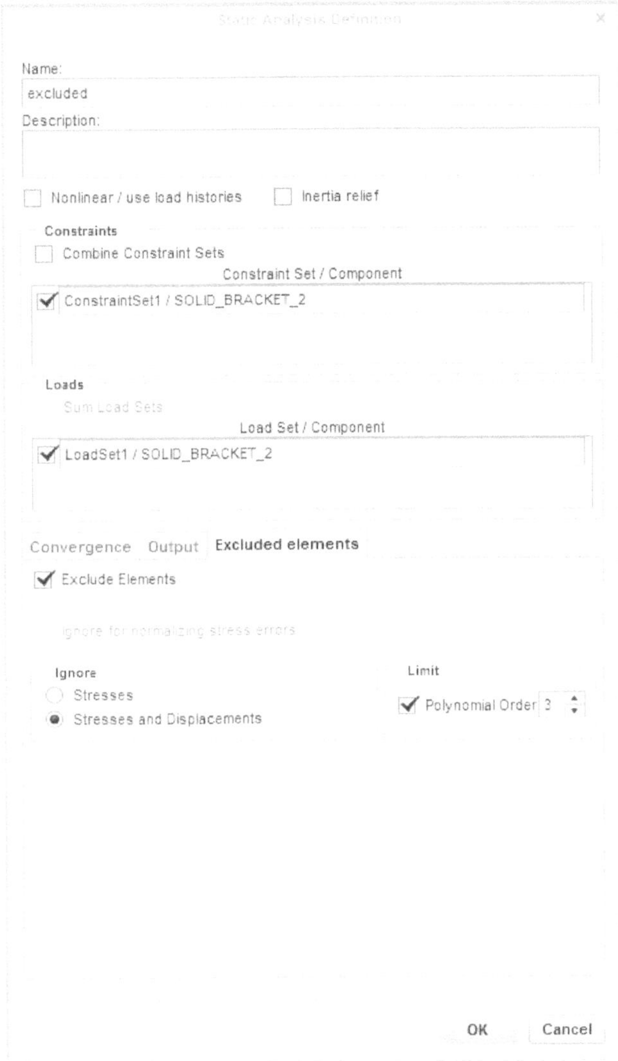

Figure 3–141

2. Re-run the analysis with interactive diagnostics.

3. In the *Run Status* dialog box, click **»** (Show Summary Information) to expand it. Verify that the analysis has now converged on pass 5, as shown in Figure 3–142.

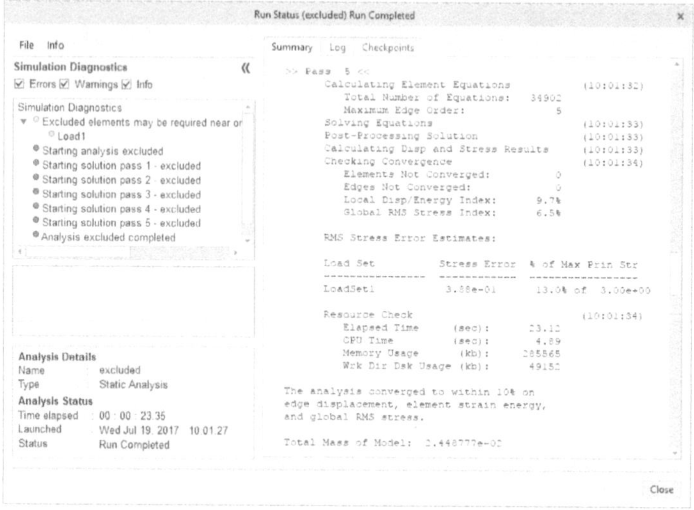

Figure 3–142

Results Tasks

Task 10: Display the convergence graphs.

1. Display convergence graphs for the **strain_energy** and **max_stress_vm** measures, as shown in Figure 3–143.

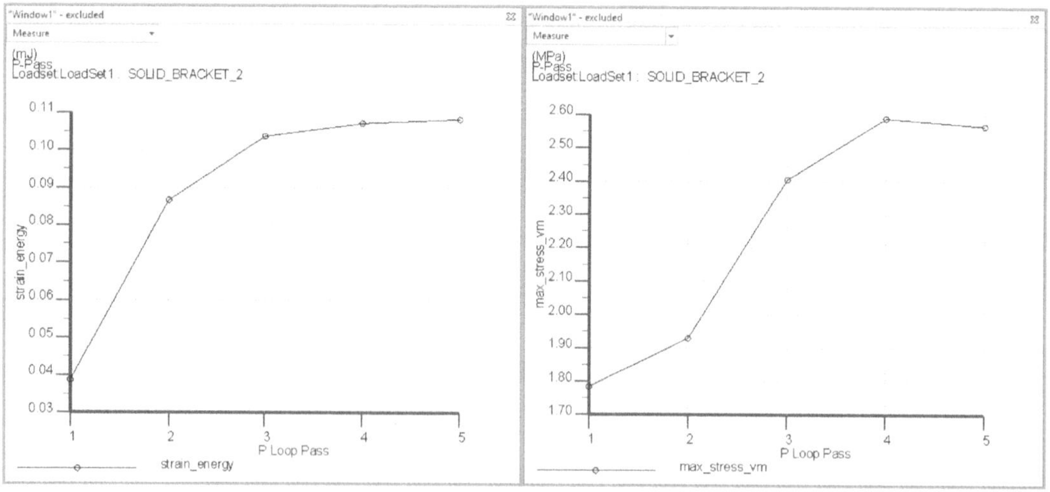

Figure 3–143

Note that the solution now displays perfect convergence on the strain energy and a reasonable convergence on stress.

Task 11: Display the stress results.

1. Display the von Mises Stress fringe plot, as shown in Figure 3–144.

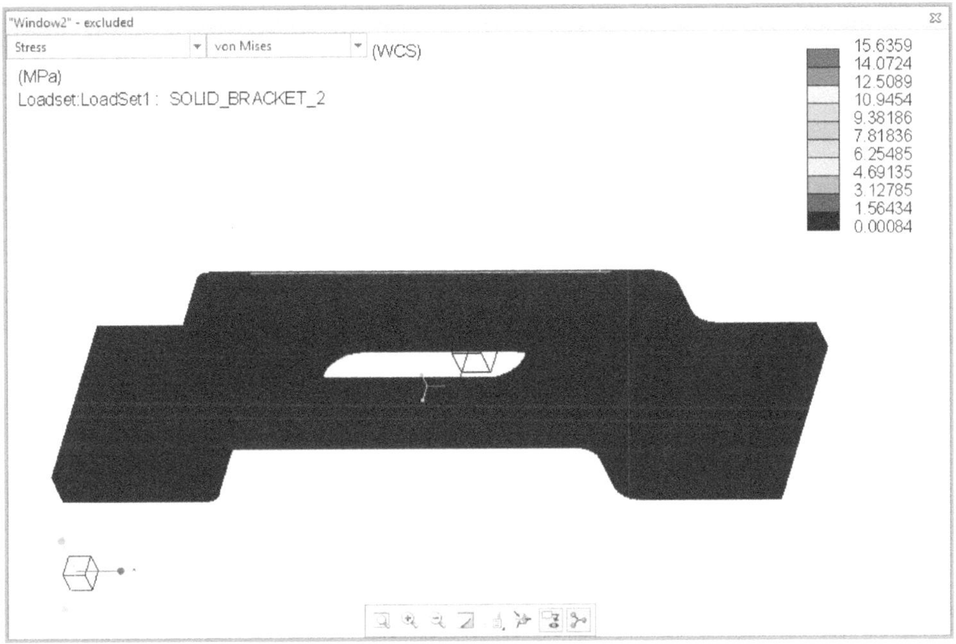

Figure 3–144

Note that the maximum stress is concentrated along the loaded edge. This is an area of singularity and the stress results are not realistic.

2. In the *Format* tab, select (Edit) to edit the result legend. Change the *legend minimum* to **0** and *maximum* to **0.5**. The result plot displays as shown in Figure 3–145.

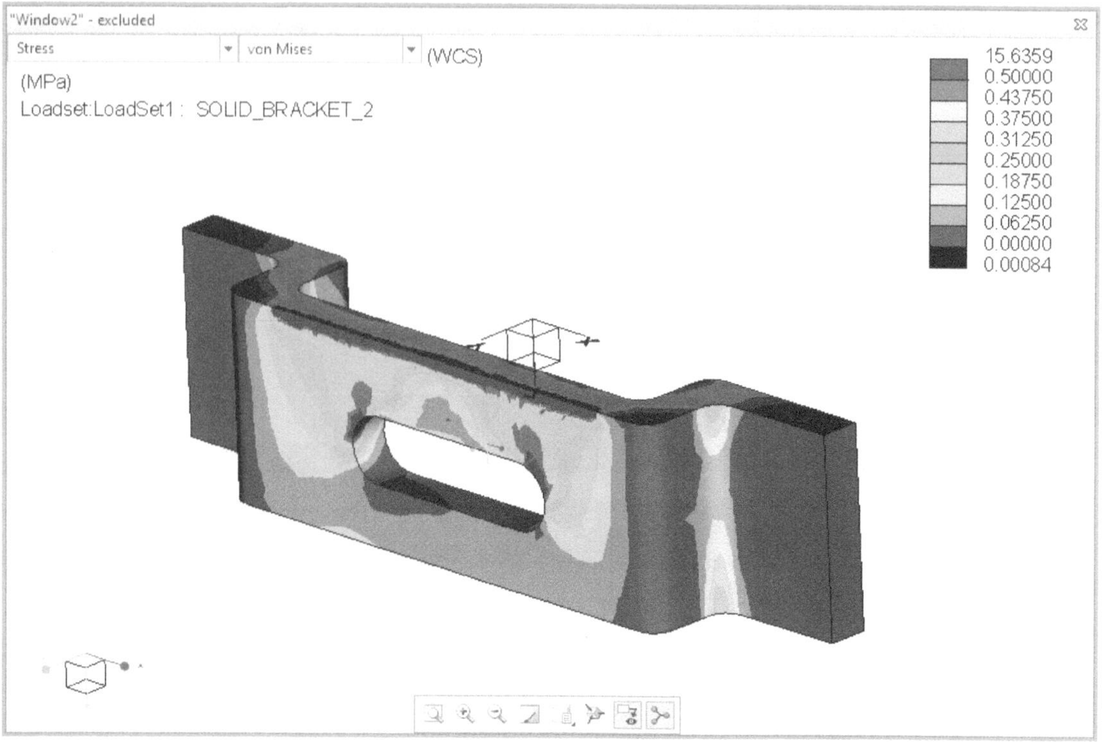

Figure 3–145

The stresses away from the loaded edge are now displayed. These values are not affected by the singularity and can be trusted.

3. Exit the Results environment. Save and close the model in Creo Parametric.

End of practice

Practice 3e
Static Stress Analysis of a Shaft

Practice Objectives

- Create a divided surface.
- Apply loads, constraints, and material properties.
- Set up and run a Single-Pass Adaptive analysis.
- Display the results.

In this practice, you will perform a static stress analysis on the shaft shown in Figure 3–146, with minimum instruction.

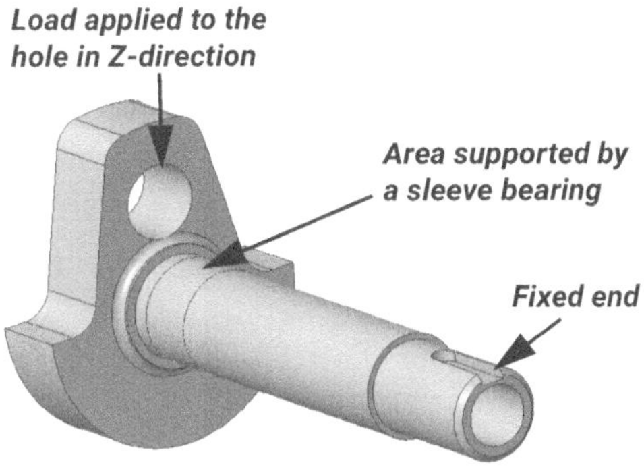

Figure 3–146

Task 1: Create a divided surface for the sleeve bearing support.

1. Set the working directory to **Chapter03**, if required.
2. Open **shaft.prt** and launch Creo Simulate.
3. Set the model display as follows:
   - *(Datum Display Filters)*: (Plane Display) Only
   - *(Spin Center)*: Off
   - *(Display Style)*: (Shading With Edges)
4. Create the two boundaries for the divided surface.
   - The first boundary curve is **5mm** from plane **DTM10**.
   - The second boundary curve is **15mm** from plane **DTM10**.

   Note: *Create two datum planes, then use intersections between the planes and the shaft surface to create the boundaries.*

5. Divide the surface and create a region between the two boundary curves.
6. In the In-graphics toolbar, disable (Plane Display).

Task 2: Apply material, loads, and constraints.

1. Apply the AL6061 material.
2. Fully constrain the cylindrical surface on the key end of the part, as shown in Figure 3–147.
3. Apply a pin constraint on the divided surface, as shown in Figure 3–147. Leave both rotational and translational directions free.

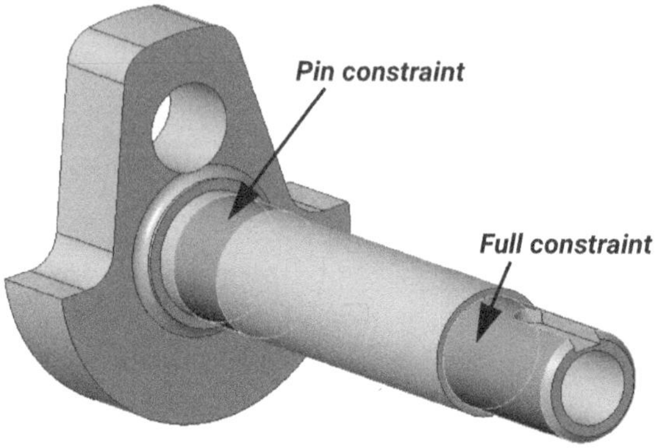

Figure 3–147

4. Apply **150N** load in the positive Z-direction to the hole, as shown in Figure 3–148.

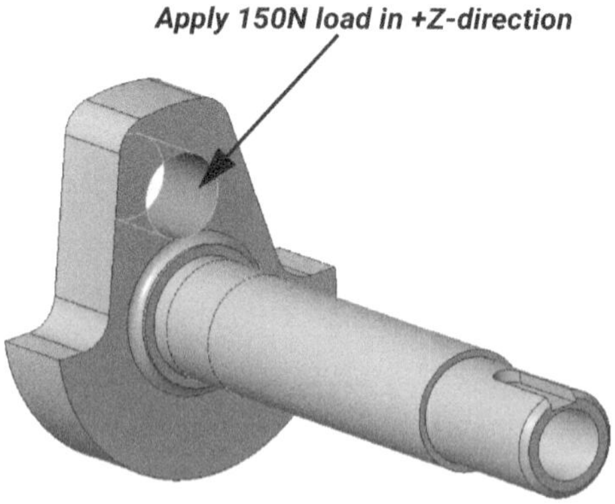

Figure 3–148

Task 3: Set up and run the analysis.

1. Create a new static analysis with the following parameters:
   - *Analysis name:* **shaft**
   - *Convergence method*: **Single-Pass Adaptive**
2. Run the analysis.
3. Display the *Status* window. Determine the RMS Stress Error value.

Task 4: Visualize the analysis results.

1. Visualize and animate the **Displacement Magnitude** fringe plot. Does the part deform according to the applied loads and constraints?
2. Display the **von Mises Stress** fringe plot. Find the location of the maximum stress.

End of practice

Chapter 4

Shell Idealizations

Idealizations are used to simplify a finite element model, resulting in faster analysis runtime. You will first learn how to use shell idealizations.

Learning Objectives

- Understand shell idealization concepts.
- Create shell models from solid Creo Parametric models.
- Create shell pairs manually.
- Automatically detect shell pairs.
- Compress shell pairs to midsurface.
- Create shell models from surface Creo Parametric models.
- Apply loads and constraints to shell models.

4.1 Shell Idealizations

Idealizations are tools that simplify a finite element model, resulting in faster analysis runtime. Creo Simulate has the following idealization options: **Beams**, **Masses**, **Shells**, and **Springs**.

The most common type of idealization is shell idealization. Shell idealizations are used to simplify a thin-walled solid model. Shell models are less CPU-intensive and can be analyzed faster than solid models.

Shell elements are 3D, surface-like elements that are used to represent features that are thin in comparison to the length and width of the surface in your part. The rule of thumb is to use shell elements when the thickness dimension is less than 1/10 of the length and width of the feature. Shell elements in Creo Simulate must be placed on the midsurface of the part, which is a surface that is equidistant from the side surfaces.

An example of a solid model that could be simplified using a shell idealization is shown in Figure 4–1. Portions of the solid model are composed of thin-walled features. The number of solid elements required to represent these features could be large. Therefore, the thin-walled features could be idealized as 3D shell elements represented by pairs of parallel surfaces.

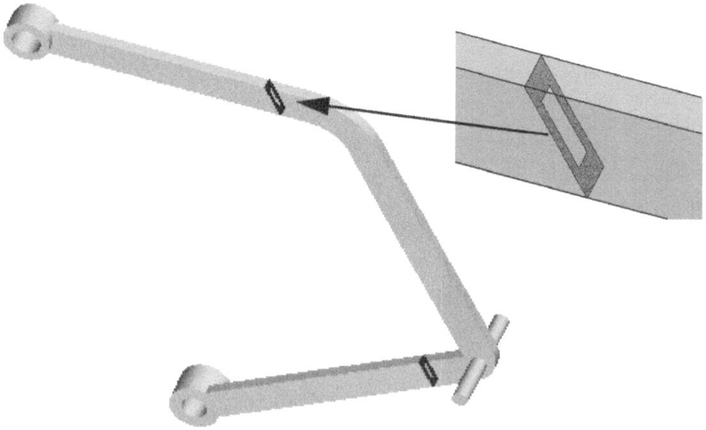

Figure 4–1

There are two types of shells in Creo Simulate:

- **Midsurface Shells:** The opposing faces of the solid model are paired and then compressed to form the midsurfaces for the shell element placement. Shell thickness is automatically imported from the solid model.
- **Standard Shells:** A solid model of the part is not required. Modeling the part geometry with datum surfaces is sufficient. You select surfaces that are assumed to be the midsurfaces for the shell element placement. You must assign shell properties, such as thickness. This option also enables you to define a shell as a laminate consisting of several layers of materials.

4.2 Midsurface Shells

For midsurface shells, Creo Simulate pairs opposing surfaces of a thin-walled feature and compresses them to a midsurface, on which shell elements are placed.

The shell thickness is read directly from the Creo model. The paired surfaces can be parallel planar or non-planar surfaces, and the shell elements can be flat or curved as long as the pairing surfaces are parallel.

Use the following steps to create shell elements in Creo Simulate:

1. Pair two parallel surfaces. Two surfaces that can be paired are shown in Figure 4–2.

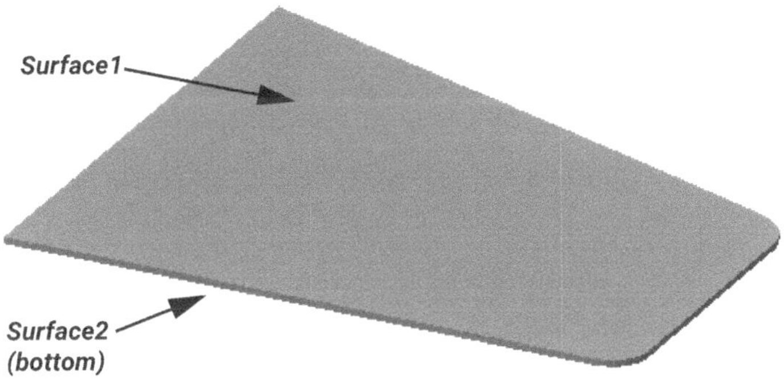

Figure 4–2

Note: *Surface1 is parallel to Surface2.*

2. Compress the paired surfaces to a midsurface, as shown in Figure 4–3.

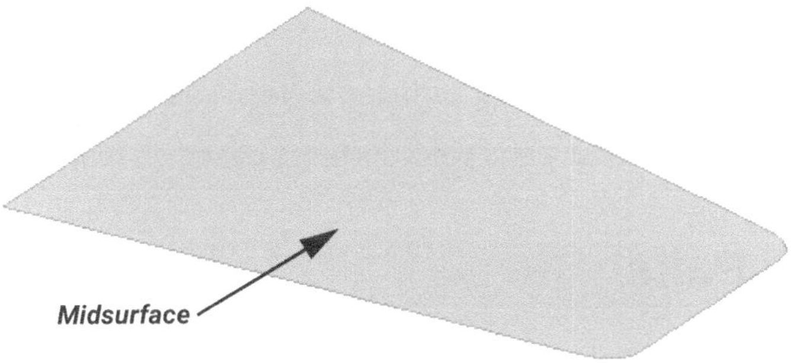

Figure 4–3

3. Create shell elements on the midsurface, as shown in Figure 4–4.

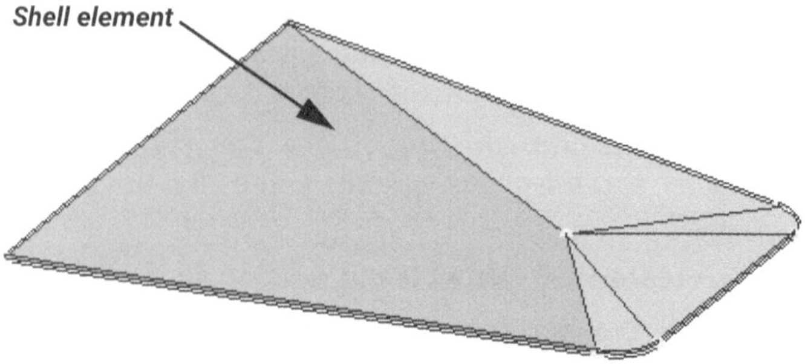

Figure 4–4

Shell Pair Creation

Shell pair creation tools are located in the *Refine Model* tab, as shown in Figure 4–5.

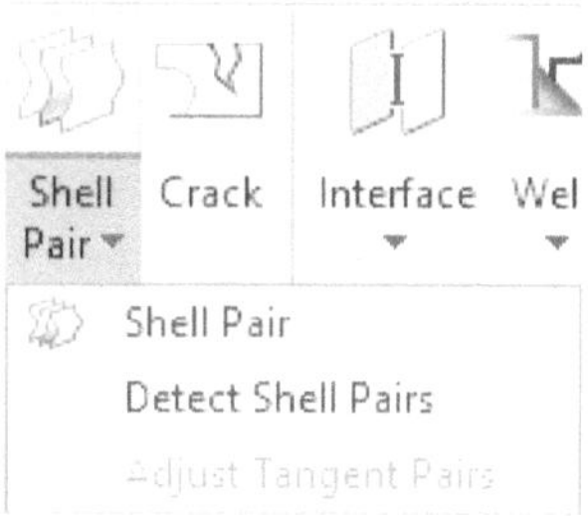

Figure 4–5

There are two options for creating shell pairs:

- **Manual:** You manually select opposing surfaces to be paired.
- **Automatic:** Creo Simulate detects and pairs surfaces based on feature types or feature thicknesses.

Manual Shell Pairs

Manual shell pairing requires you to select opposing surfaces in the part. To create a manual shell pair, click (Shell Pair) to open the *Shell Pair Definition* dialog box, as shown in Figure 4–6.

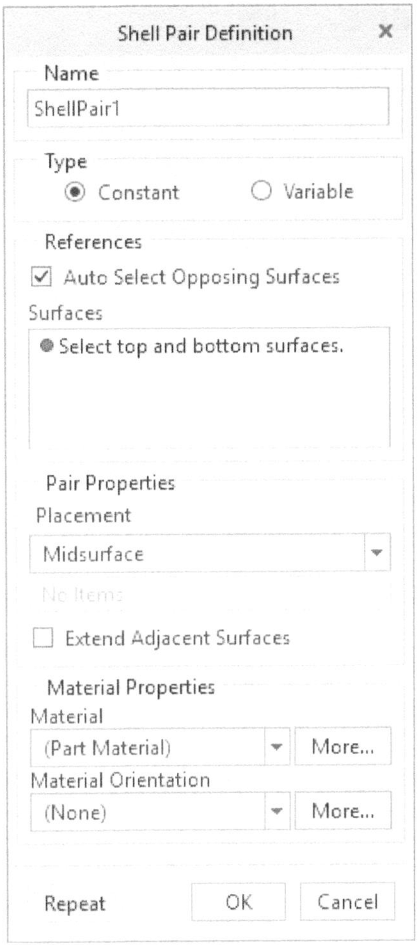

Figure 4–6

The *Shell Pair Definition* dialog box options are as follows:

Option	Description
Constant/Variable	Thickness type of shell pair.
Surfaces	Selection collector for surfaces to be paired.
Placement	Enables you to change shell element placement for the pair. The default is **Midsurface**. Other options are: **Top**, **Bottom**, or **Selected Surface**.
Material	Enables you to apply materials to your shell model. By default, the part material is applied.
Material Orientation	Enables you to create and assign new material orientations in your shell model. Applies to non-isotropic materials only.

Automatic Shell Pairs

Creo Simulate can automatically pair surfaces using the **Detect Shell Pairs** option. In the *Refine Model* tab, expand the *Shell Pair* group and select **Detect Shell Pairs** to open the *Auto Detect Shell Pairs* dialog box, as shown in Figure 4–7.

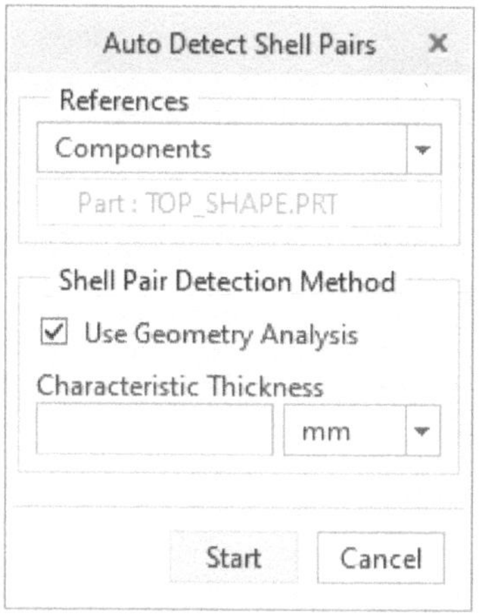

Figure 4–7

Two shell pair detection methods are available:

- **Use Geometry Analysis is enabled:** Creo Simulate searches for all shell pairs with a thickness of equal to or less than the *Characteristic Thickness*.
- **Use Geometry Analysis is disabled:** Creo Simulate detects shell pairs based only on feature type. The following feature types are detected: shells, ribs, thin protrusions, ears, sheet metal, and plastic ribs.

When you click **Start**, Creo Simulate runs the detection algorithm, and displays all of the created shell pairs in the *Model Tree*. When you select the shell pairs in the *Model Tree*, they are highlighted in the model, one side in green and the other in cyan. These surfaces are compressed to create a midsurface.

Shell Pair Compression

After you have defined the shell pairs, you need to check the compressed to midsurface geometry. Click (Review Geometry) in the *AutoGEM* area in the *Refine Model* tab to open the *Simulation Geometry* dialog box. Select the required options, as shown in Figure 4–8.

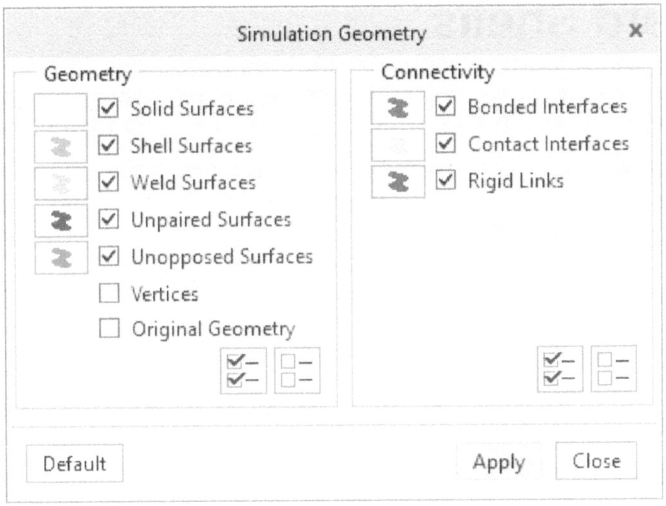

Figure 4–8

Click **Apply**. The midsurfaces are shaded in green, as shown in Figure 4–9.

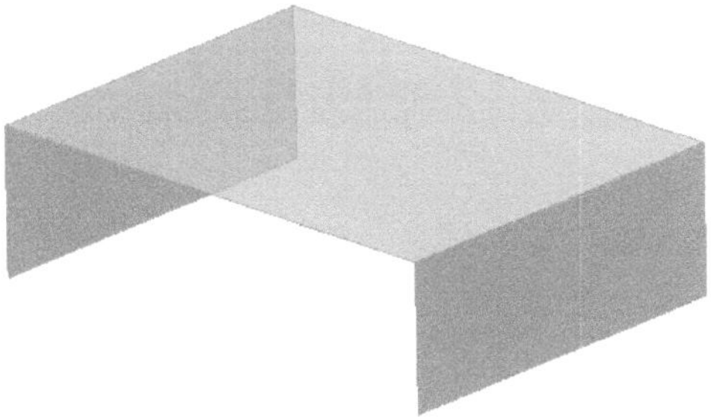

Figure 4–9

Alternatively, you can select **Original Geometry** to display the original solid geometry (wireframe) over the compressed geometry (shaded), as shown in Figure 4–10.

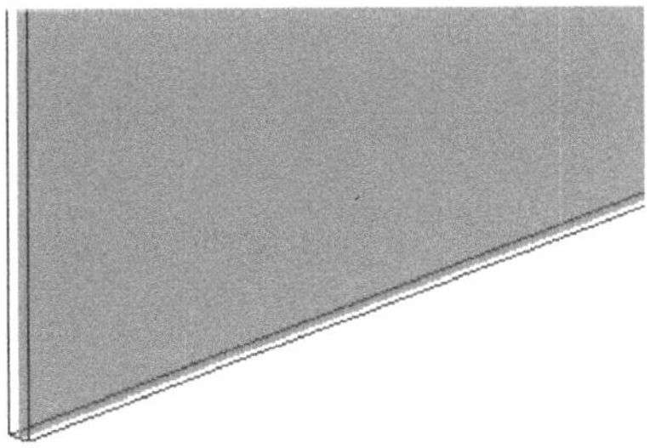

Figure 4–10

4.3 Standard Shells

For standard shells, having a solid model of the part is not necessary. You select datum surfaces that are assumed to be the midsurfaces for the shell element placement. You must assign shell properties, such as thickness.

Standard shells are useful in parts for which datum surfaces rather than solids are typically used to model part geometry, such as thin stampings, car body panels, aircraft skins, etc. An example of this type of model is shown in Figure 4–11.

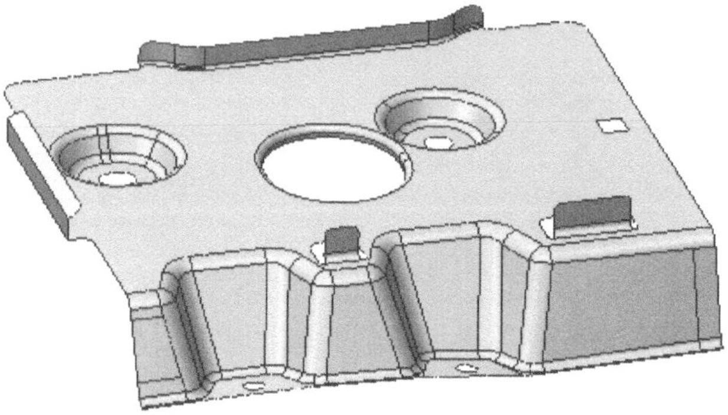

Figure 4–11

Standard Shell Creation

To create a standard shell, click (Shell). The *Shell Definition* dialog box opens, as shown in Figure 4–12.

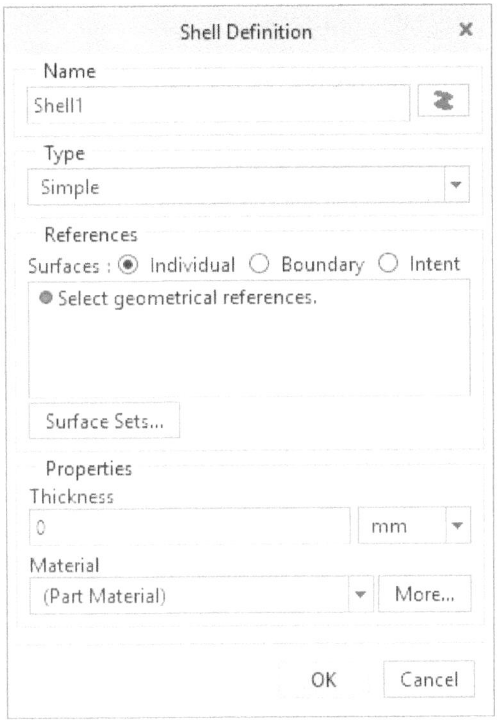

Figure 4–12

Expand the *Type* drop-down list and select one of the following:

- **Simple:** Only *Thickness* and *Material* are required to define the shell properties.
- **Advanced:** Can be used to define shell properties for laminates.This functionality requires the Advanced Creo Simulate license.

Select surfaces for the shell, enter the shell properties as required, and click **OK** to finish.

4.4 Applying Loads and Constraints to Shell Models

Creo Simulate supports the same loads and constraints for both solid and shell models. However, because model geometry is automatically redefined during midsurface compression, you need to use caution when placing loads and constraints in shell models.

In general, loads and constraints applied to either side of the uncompressed model are automatically transferred by Creo Simulate to the midsurface. If you apply a load on both sides of the uncompressed model, the amount of load on the midsurface doubles. However, if you apply a constraint on both sides, Creo Simulate detects a conflict and aborts the analysis, because constraints in this case are effectively applied twice on the same midsurface.

The same applies to the edges. In the example shown in Figure 4–13, a load is applied to an edge on one side of the shell pair. After the midsurface compression, the load is transferred to the corresponding edge on the midsurface.

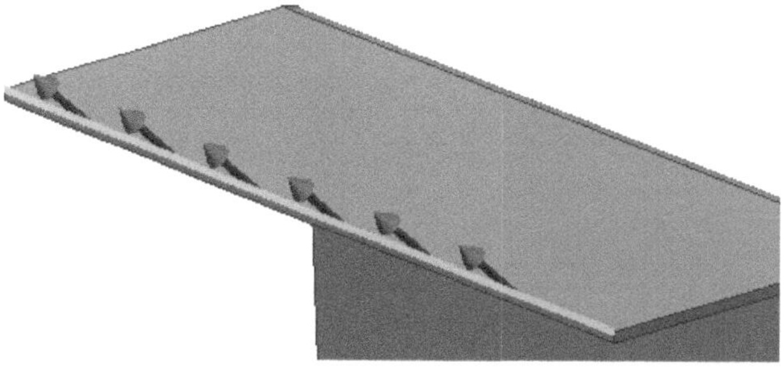

Figure 4–13

However, in the example shown in Figure 4–14, the same load is applied to the edges on both sides of the shell pair. After the midsurface compression, two loads are transferred and summed on the midsurface edge, which doubles the load in the analysis.

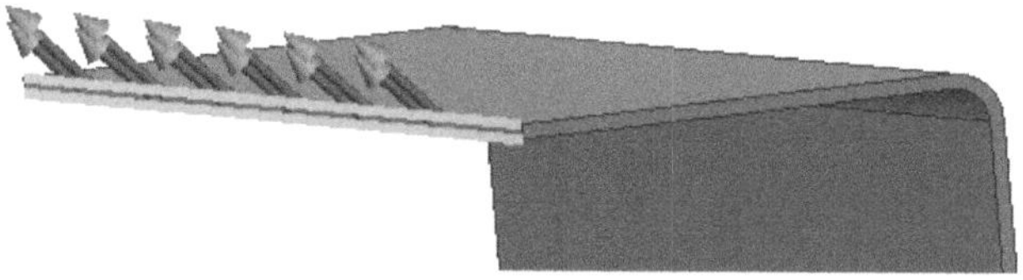

Figure 4–14

Practice 4a
Automatic Shell Creation

Practice Objectives

- Understand how to create shell element models.
- Set up loads, constraints, and material properties.
- Run and analyze a part.

In this practice, you will use shell element idealizations to set up and analyze the thin-walled pressure relief tank shown in Figure 4–15. You will use the **Detect Shell Pairs** option to create shell elements. The tank is created in Creo Parametric using surface features, and then the **Thicken** option is used to create a wall thickness of 0.5mm.

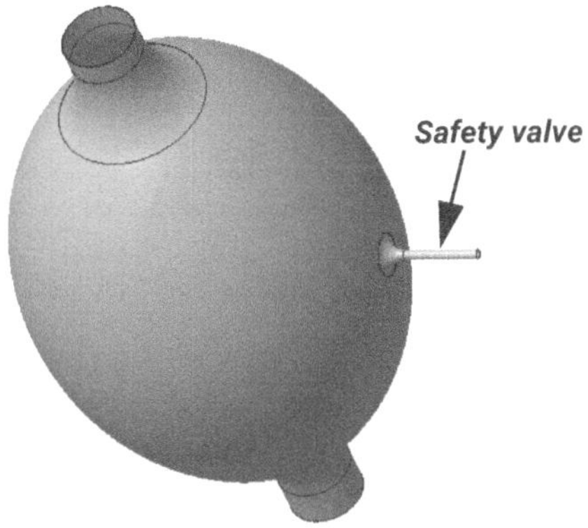

Figure 4–15

The existing symmetry is used to create a vertical cut through the tank to remove the front half of the tank. You will analyze 1/2 of the tank part shown in Figure 4–16, applying the Mirror Symmetry constraint on the cutting surface.

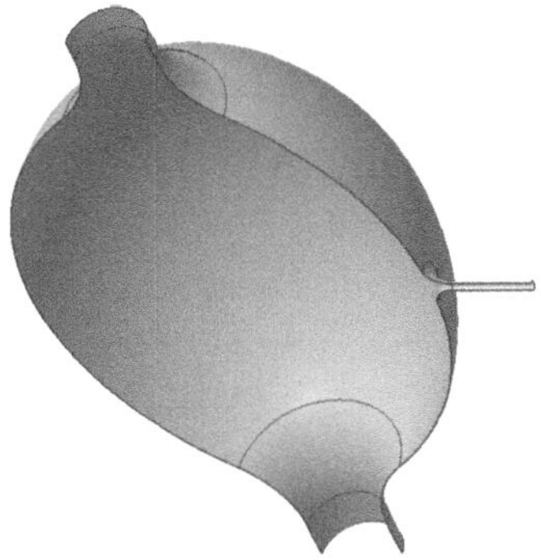

Figure 4–16

Modeling Tasks

Task 1: Open the auto_p_t_02 part in Creo Parametric.

1. Set the working directory to **Chapter04**.
2. Open **auto_p_t_02.prt**.
3. Set the model display as follows:
   - (*Datum Display Filters*): All Off
   - (*Spin Center*): Off
   - (*Display Style*): (Shading With Edges)

   The part displays as shown in Figure 4–17.

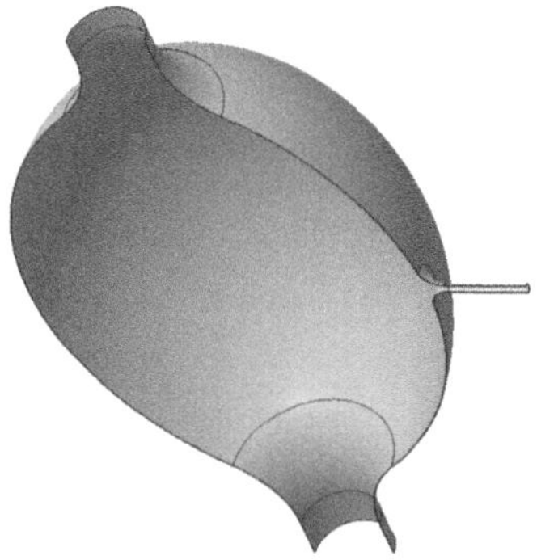

Figure 4–17

4. Ensure that the unit system is set to **mmNs**.

Task 2: Launch Creo Simulate.

1. Select **Applications>Simulate**.
2. Ensure that **Structure** mode is active.

Task 3: Define the shell elements.

1. In the *Refine Model* tab, in the *Idealizations* area, expand (Shell Pair) and select **Detect Shell Pairs**. The *Auto Detect Shell Pairs* dialog box opens, as shown in Figure 4–18.

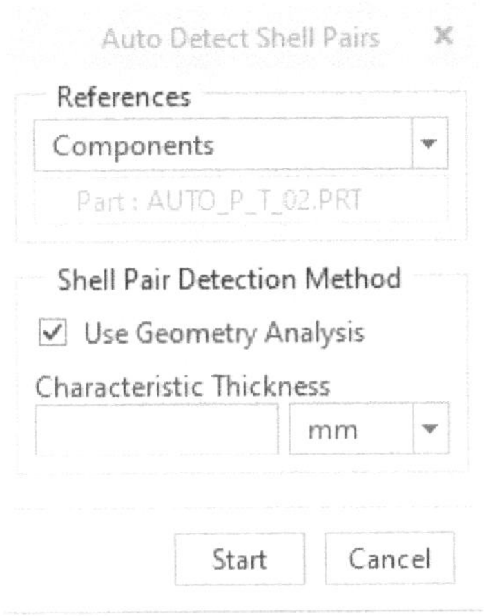

Figure 4–18

2. Clear the **Use Geometry Analysis** option and click **Start**. Creo Simulate creates six shell pairs that display in the *Model Tree*.

   Note: *When* ***Use Geometry Analysis*** *is cleared, shell pair detection is based on feature types - thin protrusions, etc.*

3. In the *Refine Model* tab, in the *AutoGEM* area, click (Review Geometry) to open the *Simulation Geometry* dialog box. Select the required options, as shown in Figure 4–19.

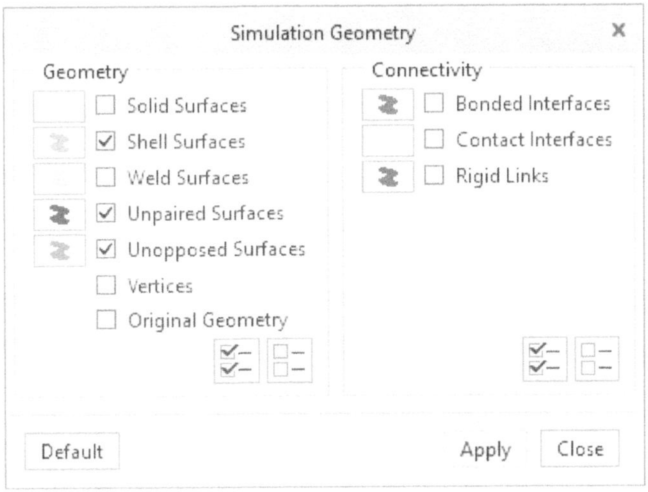

Figure 4–19

Note: *Shells can be either flat or curved.*

4. Click **Apply**. The model displays as shown in Figure 4–20.

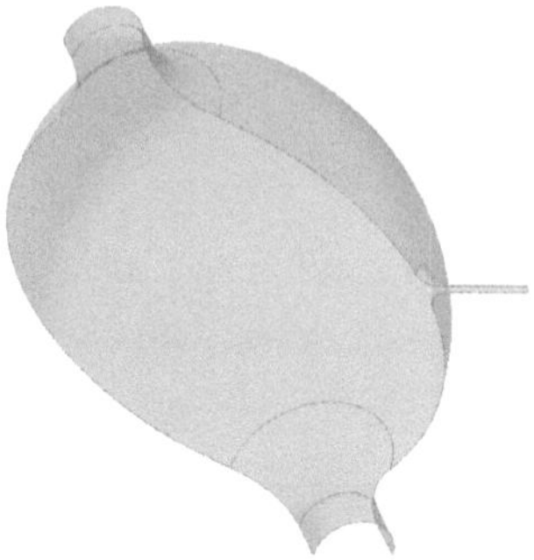

Figure 4–20

5. Select the **Original Geometry** option and click **Apply**. The midsurface is now shaded in green, while the solid edges display as a black wireframe. Zoom in to display these edges more clearly, as shown in Figure 4–21.

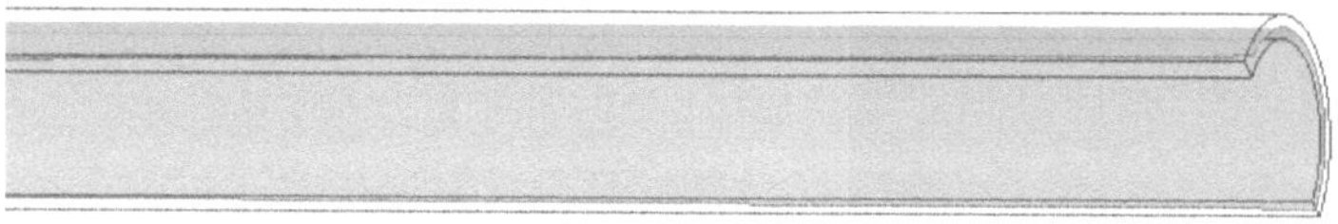

Figure 4–21

6. Click **Close** to finish.

Task 4: Mesh the model.

1. Expand the *AutoGEM* drop-down list and select **Midsurface**, as shown in Figure 4–22.

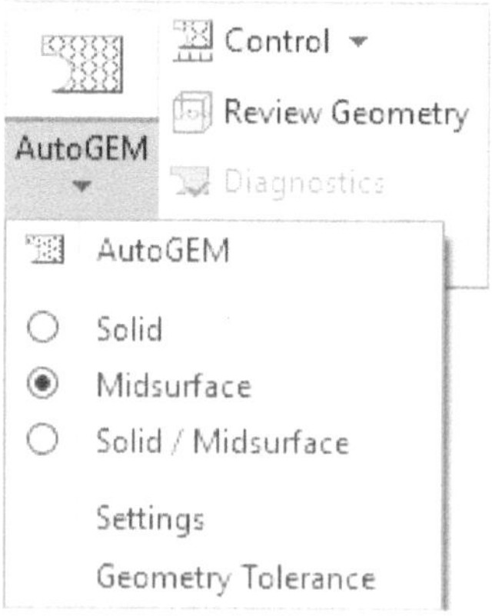

Figure 4–22

*Note: The **Midsurface** option will only create shell elements on paired surfaces.*

2. Click (AutoGEM). The *AutoGEM* dialog box opens, as shown in Figure 4–23.

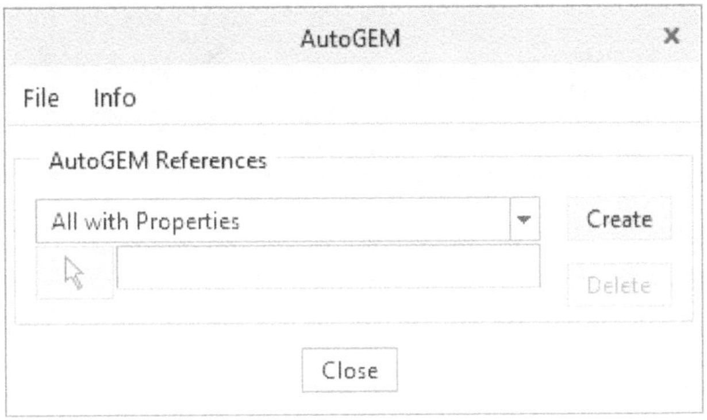

Figure 4–23

3. Expand the *AutoGEM References* drop-down list and select **Surface**.
4. Click (Select). The Surface Selection box opens, as shown in Figure 4–24.

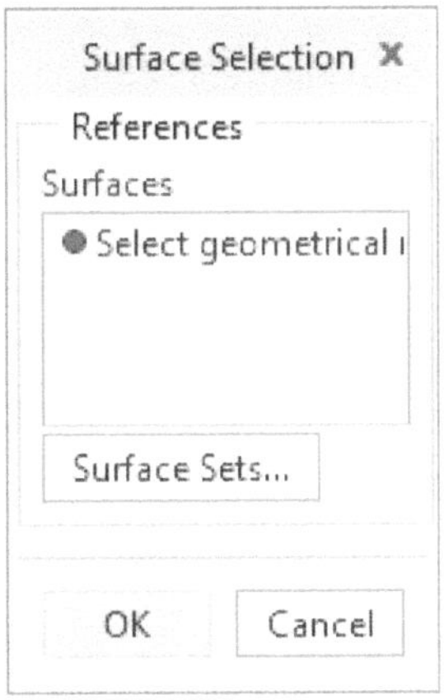

Figure 4–24

5. Draw a box around the model to select all of the surfaces.
6. In the *Surface Selection* dialog box, click **OK** or click the middle mouse button.

7. Click **Create**. The *AutoGEM Summary* and *Diagnostics* dialog boxes open, as shown in Figure 4–25.

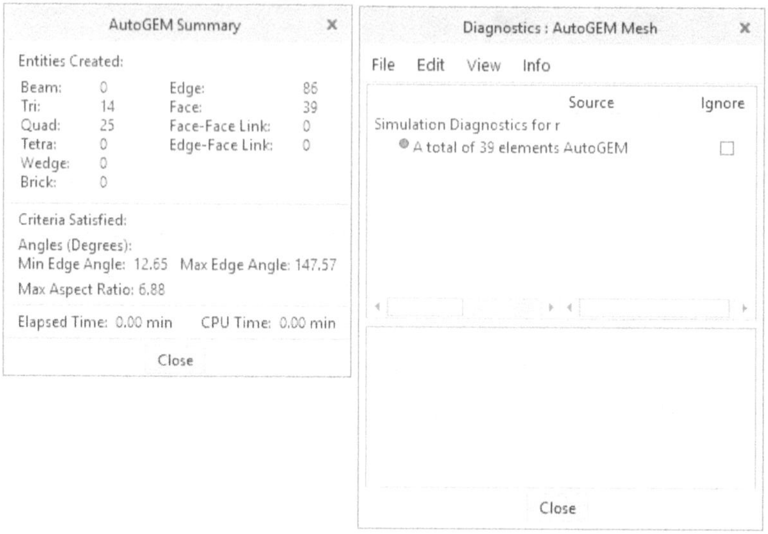

Figure 4–25

Note the information displayed in this dialog box, such as the number of Tri and Quad shell elements.

8. Close both the *AutoGEM Summary* and *Diagnostics* boxes, but do not close the *AutoGEM* dialog box yet. Rotate the model to review it until it displays as shown in Figure 4–26.

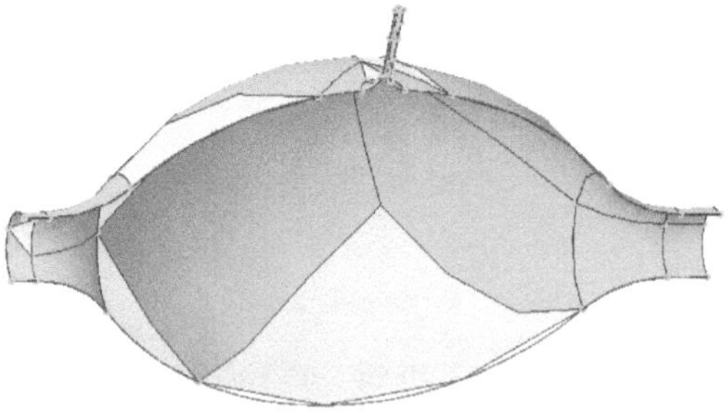

Figure 4–26

9. In the In-graphics toolbar, click (Simulation Display). The *Simulation Display* dialog box opens.

   Note: *The* ***Shrink Elements*** *option does not affect the analysis. It is only a visualization tool that helps to display the mesh more clearly.*

10. Select the *Mesh* tab. In the *Mesh Display* area, select **Shrink Elements** and increase the shrinkage value to 20%.

11. Click **OK**. The model displays as shown in Figure 4–27.

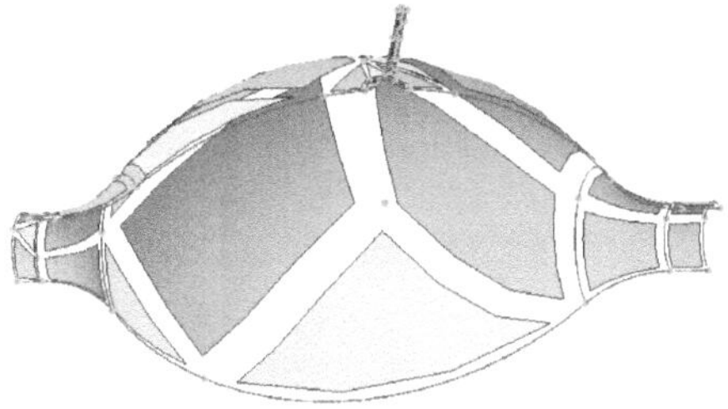

Figure 4–27

12. Click **Close** to close the *AutoGEM* dialog box and save the mesh.

    Note: *The mesh is saved with model name and extension .MMP (**auto_p_t.mmp**).*

Task 5: Apply a load to the model.

In this task, you will apply a pressure load to the interior surfaces of the model. This load represents the pressure exerted on the inside walls of the tank when the tank is pressurized.

1. In the *Loads* group of the *Home* tab, click (Pressure). The *Pressure Load* dialog box opens, as shown in Figure 4–28.

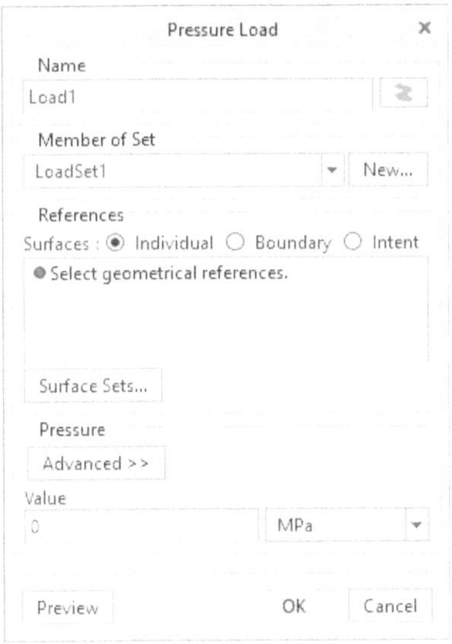

Figure 4–28

Note: *Load and constraint sets provide a logical means of organizing your modeling entities so that you can define the analyses clearly and effectively. A load set is a set of loads that act together on the model.*

2. In the *Name* field, enter **preload**.
3. For *Member of Set*, accept the default **LoadSet1** option.
4. Select the **Intent** option and select any interior surface of the tank. (This effectively selects all of the interior surfaces).
5. Click **Advanced**. Expand the *Spatial Variation* drop-down list and select **Uniform** (the other options are **Function Of Coordinates** and **External Coefficients Field**).
6. In the *Value* field for the pressure magnitude, enter **1**.
7. Click **Preview** to review the load.
8. Click **OK** to finish applying the load. The model displays as shown in Figure 4–29.

Figure 4–29

Task 6: Control load settings and visibilities.

1. In the In-graphics toolbar, click (Simulation Display).
2. Select the *Settings* tab and the *Simulation Display* dialog box displays as shown in Figure 4–30.

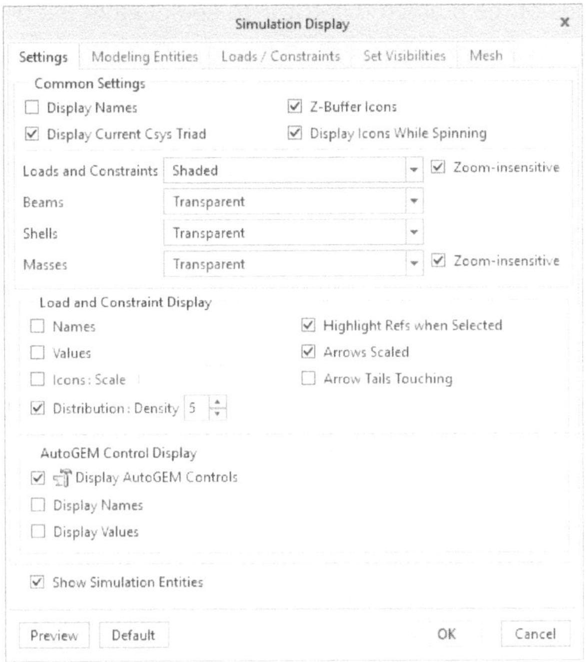

Figure 4–30

Examine the settings and visibilities in the *Simulation Display* dialog box. Note that in the *Settings* tab, the load arrows can be set to **Arrow Tails Touching** to help visualize your loads. Additionally, you can remove the pressure load from the display (e.g., to see other constraints or loads more clearly).

3. Select the *Set Visibilities* tab.
4. Clear the **LoadSet1** row to toggle off the display of the pressure load.
5. Click **Preview** to display the model without the pressure load.
6. Click **OK** to close the *Simulation Display* dialog box.

Task 7: Apply constraints to the model.

In this task, you will constrain the edges at the top of the inlet/outlet pipes and the side of the safety valve pipe.

1. In the *Constraints* panel, click (Displacement).

   Note: *Shell elements have six degrees of freedom per node (three translations and three rotations).*

2. In the *Constraint* dialog box, in the *Name* field, enter **sidepipe**. For *Member of Set*, accept the default **ConstraintSet1** option.
3. Expand the *References* drop-down list and select **Edges/Curves**.

4. Select the outer edges of the pipes (hold <Ctrl> to select all of the outer edges of the pipes).
5. Constrain all of the *Translation* and *Rotation* directions. The *Constraint* dialog box displays as shown in Figure 4–31.

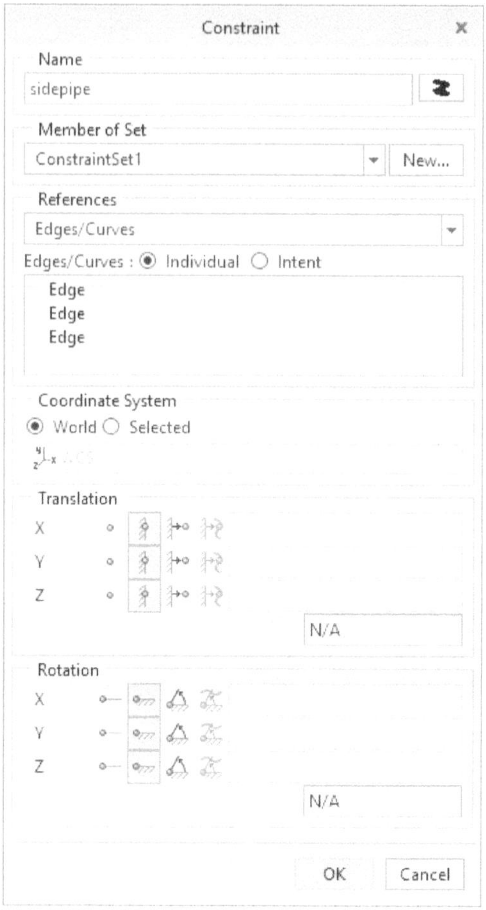

Figure 4–31

6. Click **OK**. The constraints display as shown in Figure 4–32.

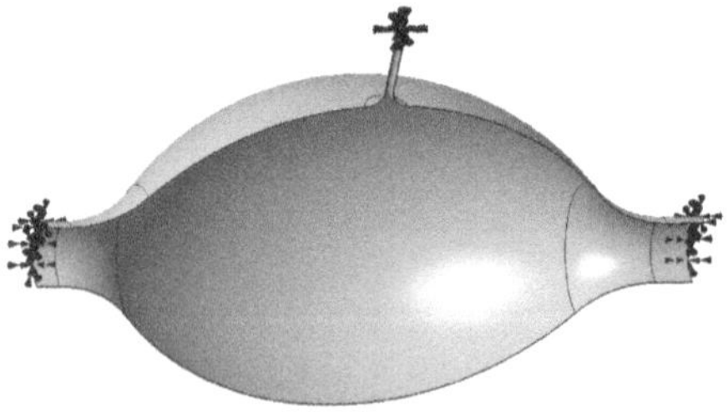

Figure 4–32

Task 8: Apply symmetry constraints.

In this task, you will apply a Mirror Symmetry constraint to the edges in the plane of symmetry to use the model's symmetry.

1. In the *Home* tab, expand the *Constraints* panel, and click (Symmetry). The *Symmetry Constraint* dialog box opens, as shown in Figure 4–33.

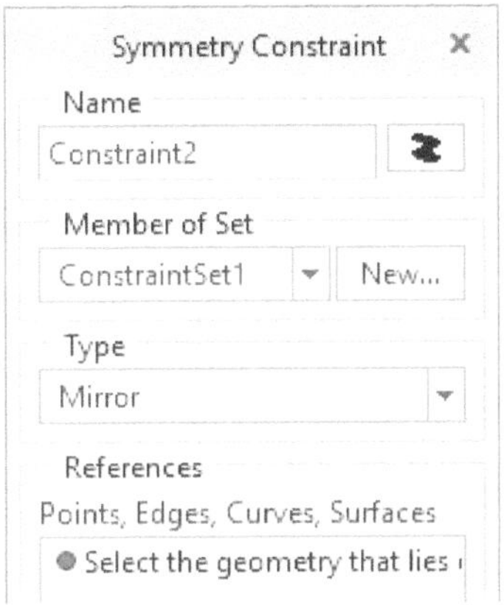

Figure 4–33

Note: To edit and delete your constraint sets, right-click and select the required option.

2. In the *Name* field, enter **sym_edges**. For *Member of Set,* select **ConstraintSet1**.
3. For the *Type*, select **Mirror**.
4. Select all of the outside edges of the model that are on the symmetry plane (do not select the interior edges). (Hold <Ctrl> to select all of the edges.)
5. Click **OK**. The model displays as shown in Figure 4–34.

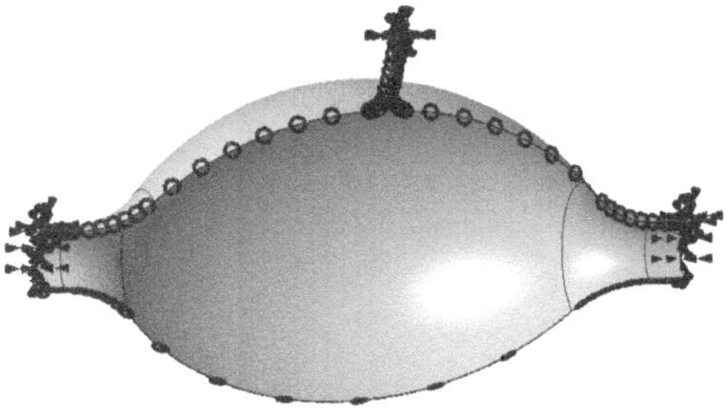

Figure 4–34

6. Click (Simulation Display). The *Simulation Display* dialog box opens.

7. In the *Setting* tab, select **Icons** and clear **Distribution**, as shown in Figure 4–35.

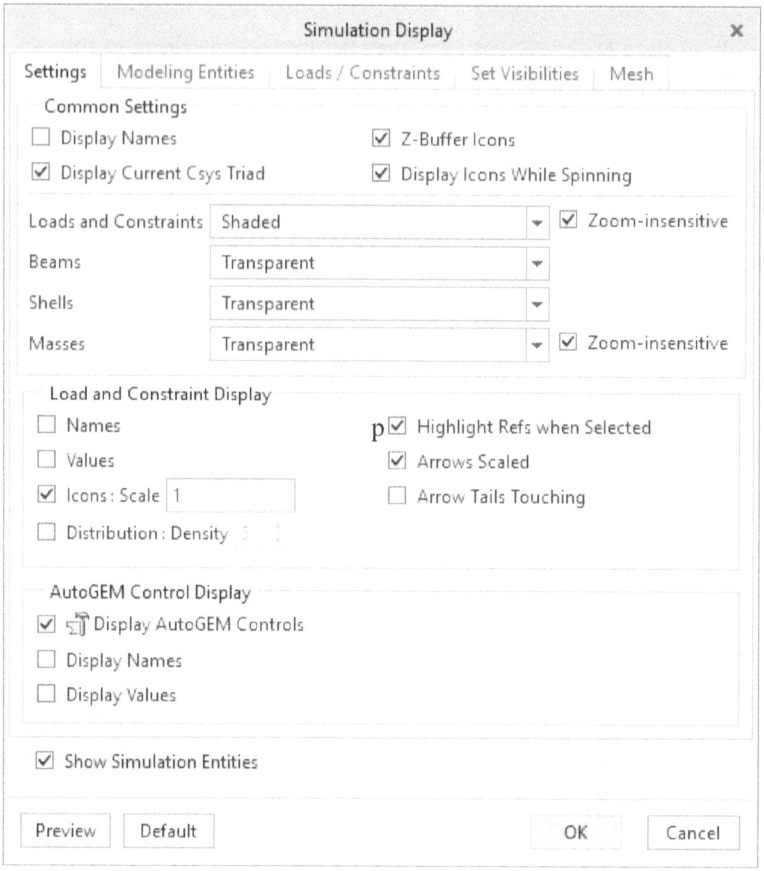

Figure 4–35

8. Click **OK** to close the *Simulation Display* dialog box. The constraints display as shown in Figure 4–36.

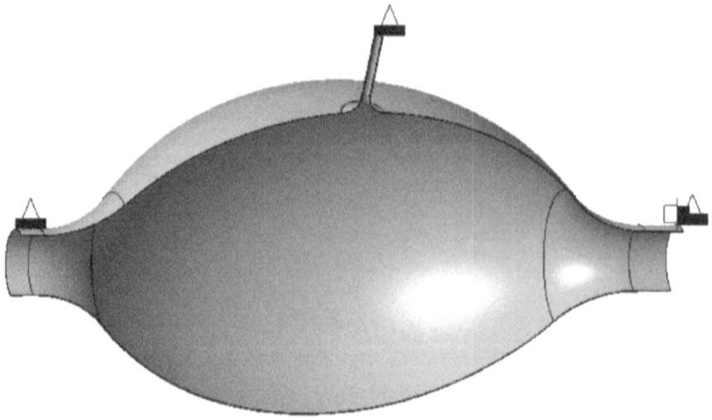

Figure 4–36

Task 9: Apply the material for the pressure tank.

1. Click (Materials). The *Materials* dialog box opens.
2. In the *Materials in Library* area, double-click on **Legacy-Materials**, then double-click on **ss.mtl** (stainless steel) to transfer **SS** to the *Materials in Model* area.
3. Review the material properties in the *Material Preview* area of the dialog box.

   The following values are the default material properties for stainless steel (SS):

   - *Poisson's Ratio:* **0.3**
   - *Young's modulus:* **193053 MPa**
   - *Density:* **7.74372e-9 tonne/mm3**
4. Click **OK** to close the *Materials* dialog box.
5. Click (Material Assignment) to assign the SS material to the part. Click **OK** to close the *Material Assignment* dialog box.
6. In the *Simulation Display* dialog box, in the *Set Visibilities* tab, toggle on the loads display.

Analysis Tasks

Task 10: Set up and run the analysis.

1. In the *Home* tab, click (Analyses and Studies). The *Analyses and Design Studies* dialog box opens, as shown in Figure 4–37.

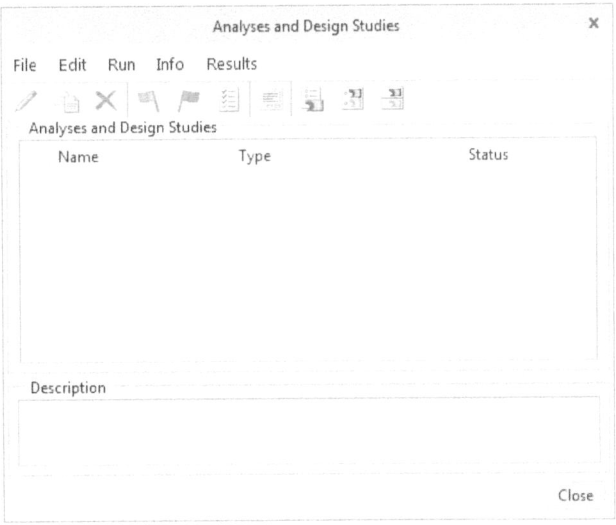

Figure 4–37

2. Select **File>New Static**. The *Static Analysis Definition* dialog box opens, as shown in Figure 4–38.

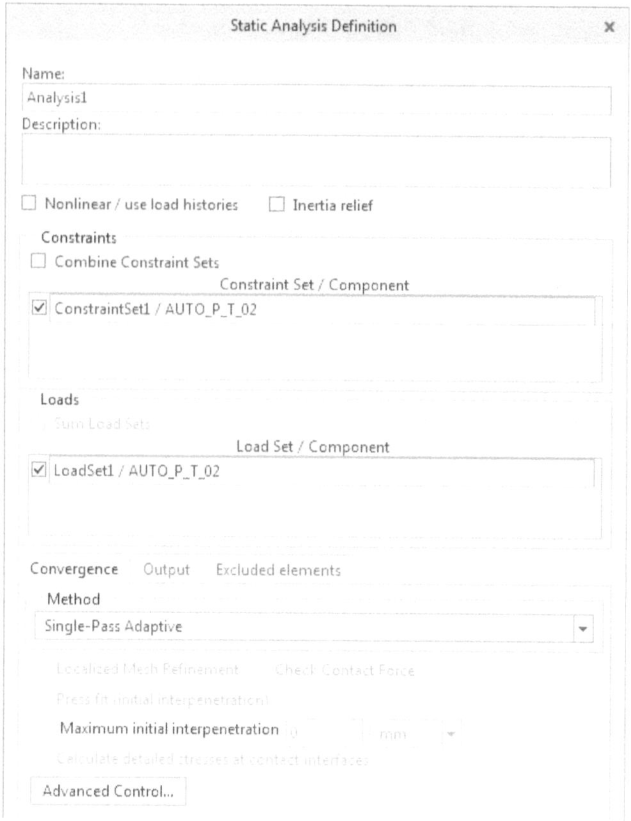

Figure 4–38

3. In the *Name* field, enter **tank**. (Tank becomes the name of a sub-directory containing all of your results files.)
4. (Optional) In the *Description* field, enter **static analysis of a relieve pressure tank**. This help to identify your analysis.
5. For a static stress analysis, you need to specify or select the constraint and load sets, which have already been created. In this case, they are **ConstraintSet1** and **LoadSet1**. Ensure that these sets are highlighted.
6. To define the type of convergence, expand the *Method* drop-down list and select **Multi-Pass Adaptive**.
7. In the *Limits* area, in the *Percent Convergence* field, enter **5** percent convergence.
8. In the *Polynomial Order* area, set the *Maximum polynomial order* to **9**.
9. Select the *Output* tab and set the *Plotting Grid* to **9**. The *Static Analysis Definition* dialog box displays as shown in Figure 4–39.

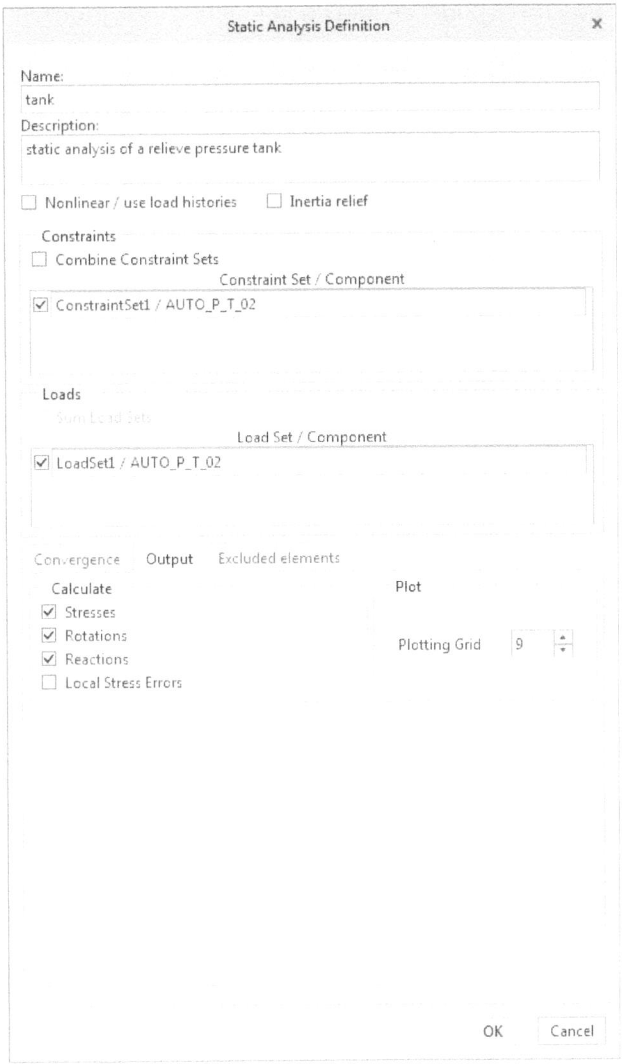

Figure 4–39

Note: *The Plotting Grid is a grid of points that Creo Simulate uses to display results within the elements. A higher density plotting grid is recommended to obtain smoother looking result plots.*

10. In the *Static Analysis Definition* dialog box, click **OK**.
11. Expand the **Info** menu and select **Check Model**. This command checks the validity of the simulation model.

Note: *The **Check Model** option highlights any modeling errors (e.g., load-constraint conflicts or unassigned material properties) and errors from modeling edits.*

12. The *Information* dialog box opens, as shown in Figure 4–40, prompting you that there are no errors.

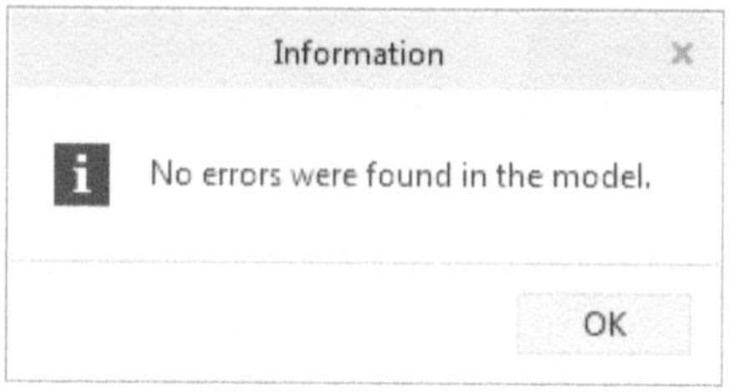

Figure 4–40

13. Click **OK** to finish checking the validity of the model.

14. Click (Start) in the *Analyses and Design Studies* dialog box to start your analysis. The *Question* dialog box opens, as shown in Figure 4–41.

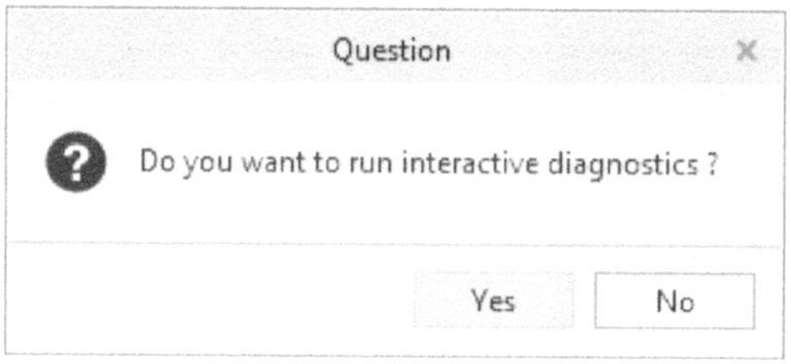

Figure 4–41

15. In the *Question* dialog box, click **Yes**. The prompt *The design study has started* displays in the message window.

16. The *Run Status* dialog box opens, displaying information about the analysis progress. Wait until the last line in the box says *Run completed*, as shown in Figure 4–42.

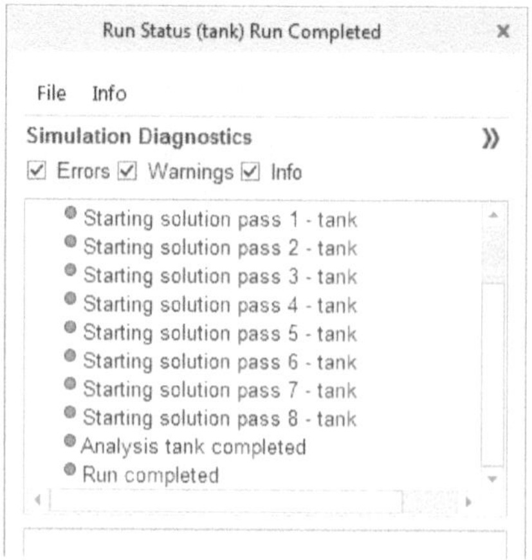

Figure 4–42

Task 11: Review the Run Status results.

1. Expand the *Run Status* dialog box to display the *Summary* tab.
2. Extract the following information from the dialog box:
   - Number of shell elements
   - Number of elements not converged at pass 4
   - Number of edges not converged at pass 7
   - RMS stress error estimates

   Did the solution converge at 5% (you set the convergence percentage in Step 7 of Task 1)?
3. Close the *Run Status* dialog box.

Results Tasks

Task 12: Display the results.

In this task, you will create and display von Mises stress and Displacement color plots.

1. In the *Analyses and Design Studies* dialog box, click (Review Results). The *Result Window Definition* dialog box opens, as shown in Figure 4–43.

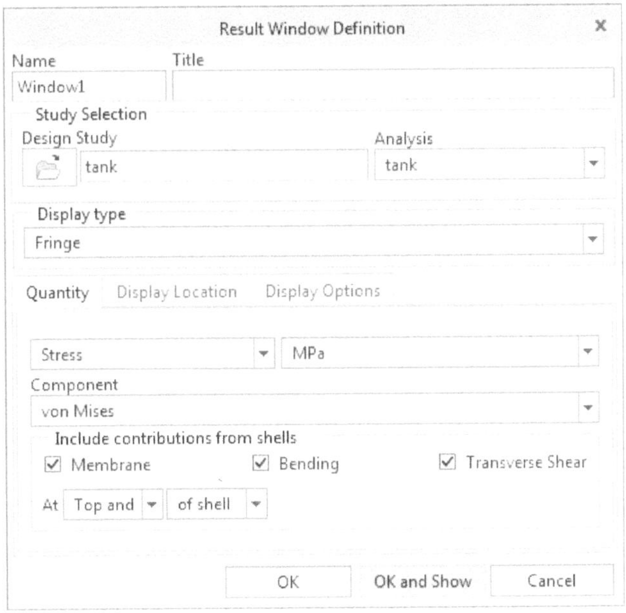

Figure 4–43

2. In the *Name* field, accept the default of **Window1**.

3. In the *Title* field, enter **VM_PLOT**.
4. Select the *Display Options* tab and clear the **Show Element Edges**, **Show Loads**, and **Show Constraints** options, if required.
5. Click **OK and Show**. The Creo Simulate Results environment displays, with the Von Mises Stress fringe plot displayed, as shown in Figure 4–44.

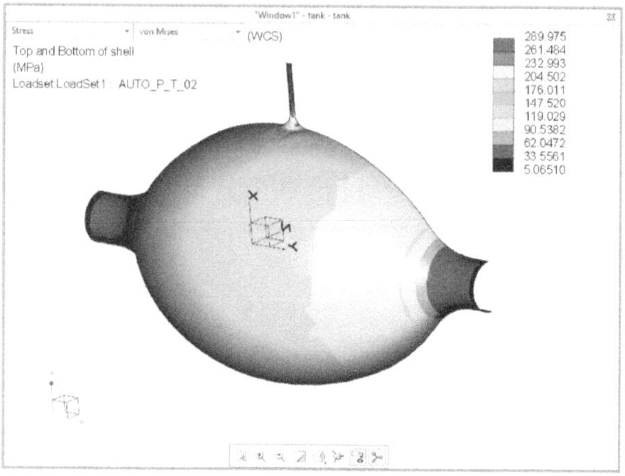

Figure 4–44

6. In the *Home* tab, click (Copy). The *Result Window Definition* dialog box opens.
7. In the *Name* field, enter **deformation**.
8. In the *Title* field, enter **DEF_PLOT**.
9. Expand the *Quantity* drop-down list and select **Displacement**.
10. In the *Display Options* tab, select **Deformed** and **Animate**.
11. Clear the **Auto Start** option and click **OK**.
12. In the *View* tab, click (Show). In the *Display Result Window* dialog box, clear **Window1** and select **deformation**, as shown in Figure 4–45.

Figure 4–45

13. Click **OK**. The deformation plot displays.

    Note: Did the deformation display correctly?

14. In the *View* tab, click ▶ (Start) to start the animation. Click ▶| (Step Forward) or |◀ (Step Back) to step through the animation frames.

15. Click ■ (Stop) to stop the animation at Frame 5 of the animation, as shown in Figure 4–46.

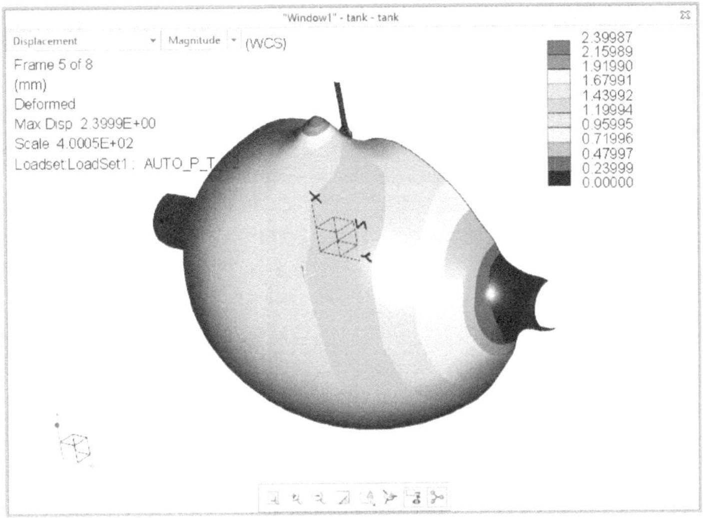

Figure 4–46

Note: Use animations to check for errors and verify your results.

Note that the area around the small pipe seems to have excessive deformation. This is only a visual effect, due to Creo Simulate magnifying the amount of displayed deformation, for better clarity. Note the Scale value (shown in the top left corner in Figure 4–46), which is approximately 400, this is the deformation magnification factor. Therefore, the displayed deformation is 400 times the actual deformation (which is actually approximately 2.4mm).

16. In the *Home* tab, click ✎ (Edit).

17. In the *Display Options* tab, select **Overlay Undeformed** and **Transparent Overlay**.

    Note: If % is selected, the magnification factor is automatically set by Creo Simulation, based on the size of the model.

18. Near the *Scaling* field, clear the **%** option. In the *Scaling* field, enter **50**. This is the magnification factor that is used to display deformation in the model.

19. In the *Display Options* tab, clear the **Animate** option. The *Result Window Definition* dialog box displays as shown in Figure 4–47.

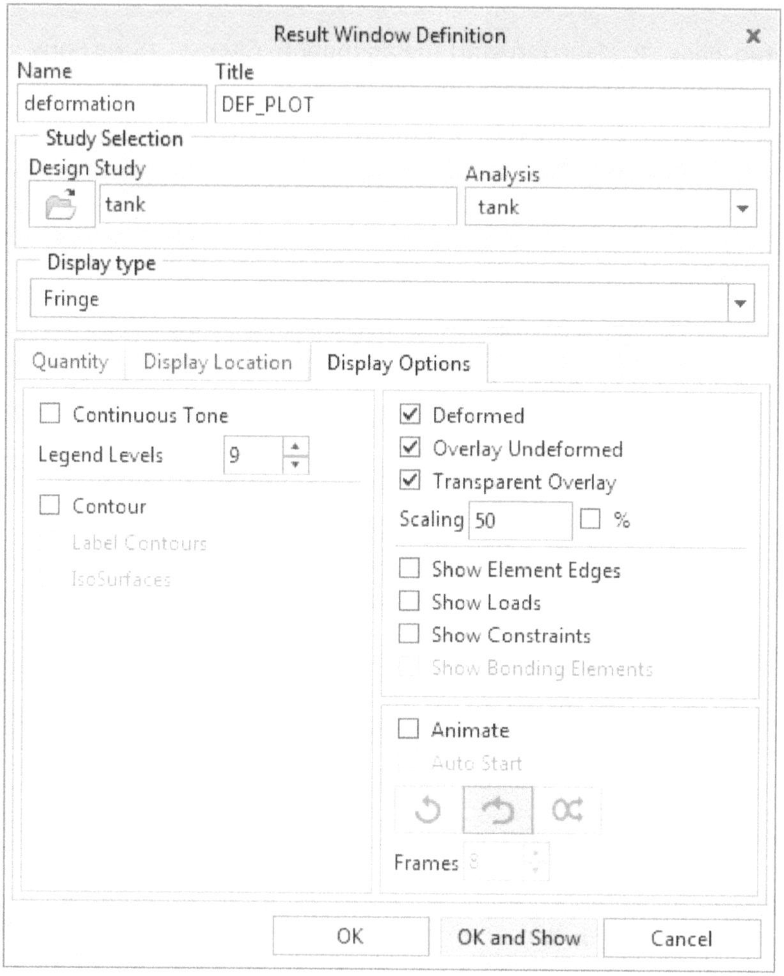

Figure 4–47

20. Click **OK and Show**. The **DEF_PLOT** displays, as shown in Figure 4–48. Note that the deformation around the small pipe is not now excessive (although it is still magnified by the factor of 50).

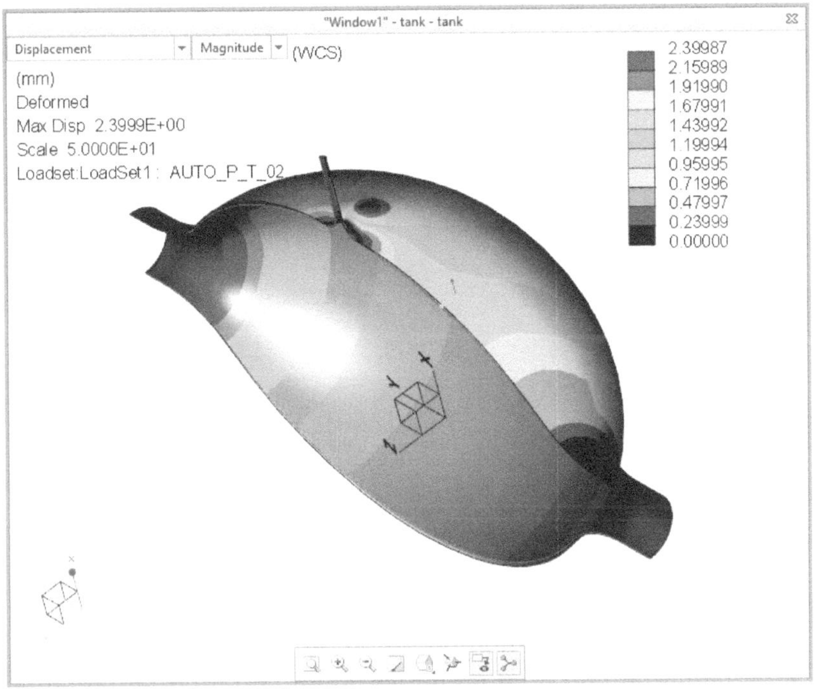

Figure 4–48

Task 13: Use predefined measures to study the convergence.

1. In the *Home* tab, click (Open) to create a new results window. The *Open Result Windows Definition* dialog box opens.
2. Select the **tank** study and click **Open**. The *Result Window Definition* dialog box opens.
3. In the *Name* field, enter **strain_energy**.
4. Expand the *Display type* drop-down list and select **Graph**.
5. Expand the first *Graph Ordinate (Vertical) Axis* drop-down list and select **Measure**.

6. Click (Measure). Highlight **strain_energy** (near the bottom of the list) and the *Measures* dialog box displays as shown in Figure 4–49.

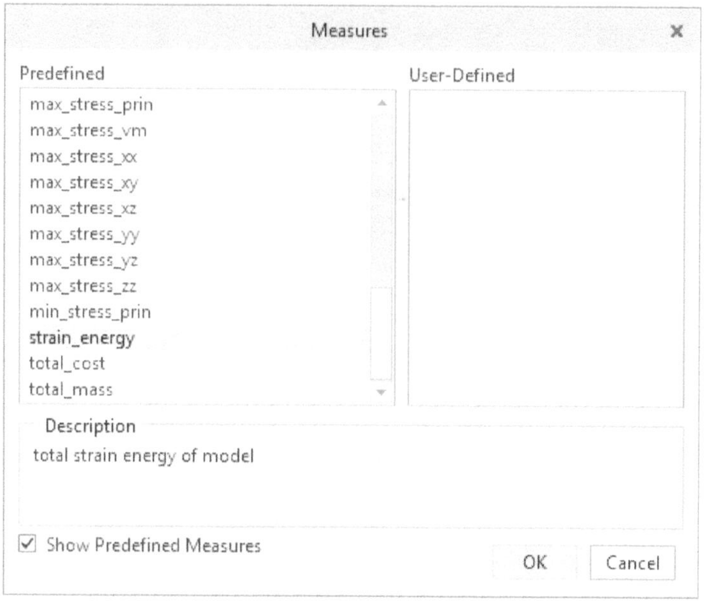

Figure 4–49

7. Click **OK**. The *Result Window Definition* dialog box opens.
8. Click **OK and Show**.
9. In the *View* tab, click (Show). The *Display Result Window* dialog box opens, as shown in Figure 4–50.

Figure 4–50

10. In the *Display Result Window* dialog box, select only **strain_energy** and click **OK**. The convergence plot displays as shown in Figure 4–51.

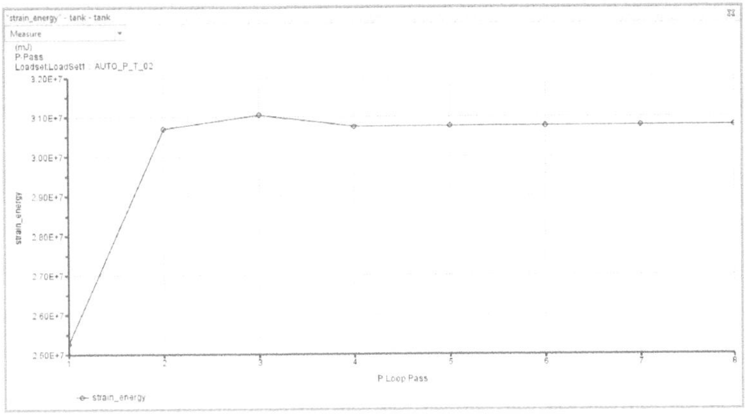

Figure 4–51

Note that the strain energy converges after pass 4.

11. Repeat the first eight steps of this task to create a convergence graph for the **max_disp_mag** measure.

12. Click (Show) in the *View* tab. The *Display Result Window* dialog box opens.

13. In the dialog box, highlight only **max_disp_mag** and then click **OK**. The convergence plot displays as shown in Figure 4–52.

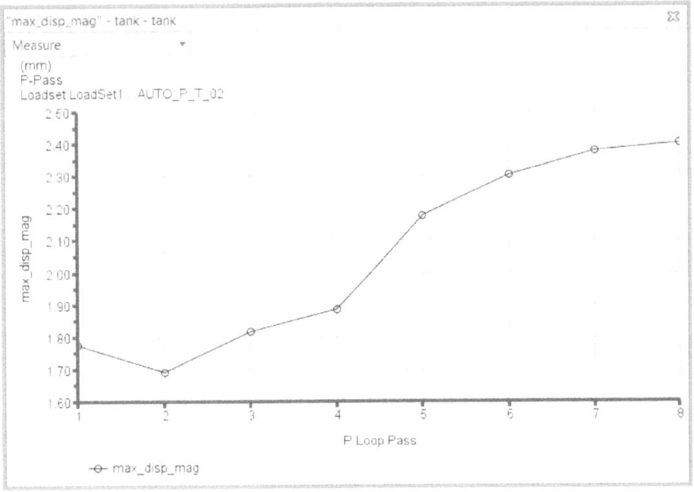

Figure 4–52

Note that the displacement curve converges after pass 7.

Task 14: Explore the Query options.

In this task, you will use the options in the *Query* section of the *Home* tab. You will also locate the point and value of the maximum stress.

1. Click (Show) in the *View* tab. In the *Display Result Window* dialog box, highlight only **Window1** and then click **OK**.
2. Select (Model Max). The location and value of maximum von Mises stress displays as shown in Figure 4–53. Rotate and/or zoom in on the model to display the location more clearly.

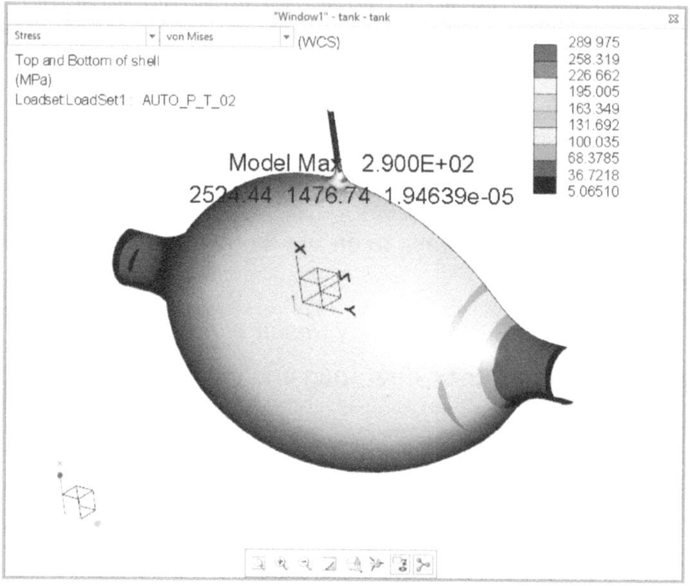

Figure 4–53

3. Investigate the other options in the *Query* section. For example, the **Dynamic Query** tool displays the result values dynamically in the *Query* dialog box, as you move the mouse cursor along the model.

Task 15: Save and close the model.

1. Select **File>Close** or click (Close) to exit the Results environment. Click **Don't Save** in the *Confirm Exit* window.
2. Close the *Analyses and Design Studies* dialog box.
3. Exit Creo Simulate. Save and close the model in Creo Parametric.

End of practice

Practice 4b
Manual Shell Creation

Practice Objective

- Set up and run an analysis on an assembly using shell element idealizations.

In this practice, you will use shell element idealizations to set up, run, and analyze a thin-walled assembly (a miniature model of a diving stand). The assembly consists of two cross members with a bend part, diving board, and supporting wedge. The assembly is shown in Figure 4–54.

In assemblies, shell pairs can be defined on component level or assembly level. In this practice, you will use both methods.

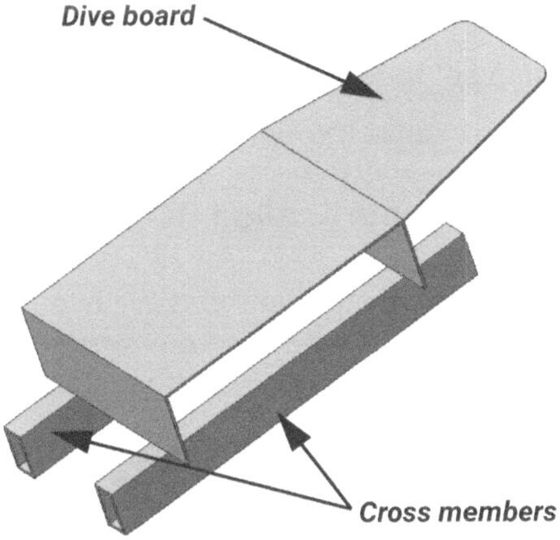

Figure 4–54

Note: *All parts in the assembly must use the same unit system.*

Modeling Tasks

Task 1: Open the assembly.

1. Set the working directory to **Chapter04**, if required.
2. Open **dive_board.asm**.
3. Set the model display as follows:
   - *(Datum Display Filters)*: All Off
   - *(Spin Center)*: Off
   - *(Display Style)*: (Shading With Edges)

The assembly displays as shown in Figure 4–55.

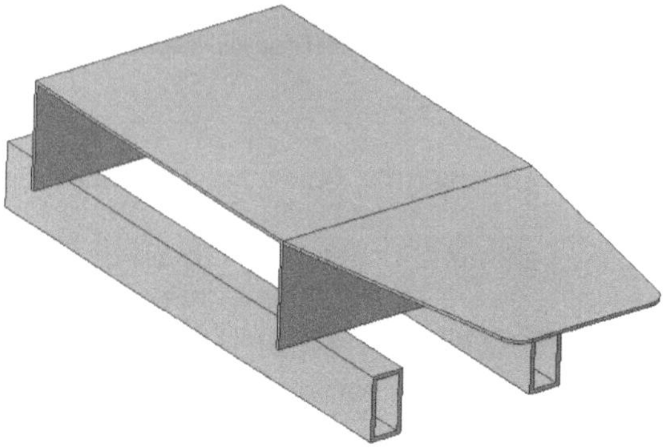

Figure 4–55

4. Ensure that the unit system is set to **mmNs**.
5. Select **Applications>Simulate** to enter the Creo Simulate environment.

Task 2: Define shell pairs for the part called BOX.prt.

Examine the structure of the assembly. Note that there are two instances of the part called **BOX.prt**. Therefore, it is more efficient to create shell pairs for this part on the component level, which will automatically apply the shell pairs to all of the instances of the part in the assembly.

1. In the *Model Tree*, select **box.prt** and click (Open) in the mini-toolbar. The part opens in a new window, as shown in Figure 4–56.

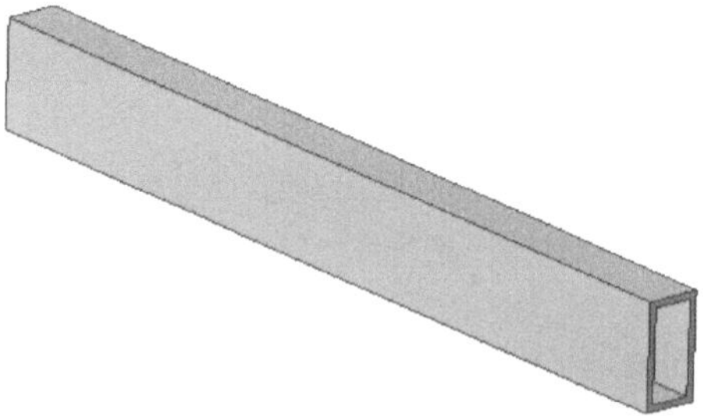

Figure 4–56

2. Select **Applications>Simulate** to enter the Creo Simulate environment.
3. In the *Refine Model* tab, click (Shell Pair). The *Shell Pair Definition* dialog box opens, as shown in Figure 4–57. Ensure that the **Auto Select Opposing Surfaces** option is selected.

   ***Note:** Although it would be more efficient to use the automatic shell pair detection tool in this part, in this case, you will use manual shell pair creation.*

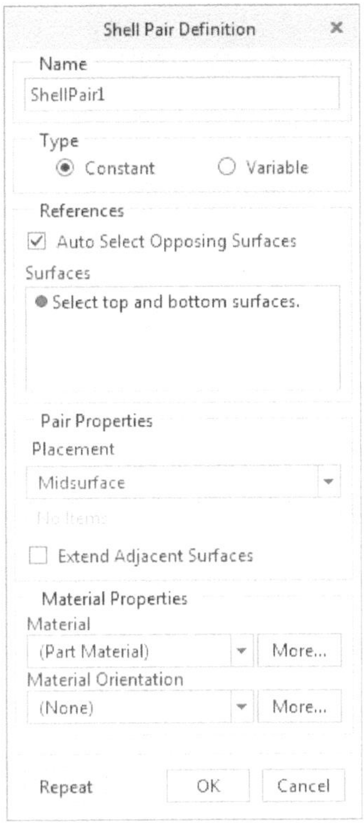

Figure 4–57

4. Select the outer surface of the top flange, as shown in Figure 4–58. Note that the inner surface of the top flange gets selected automatically. Click **Repeat** to complete the shell pair and reopen the *Shell Pair Definition* dialog box.

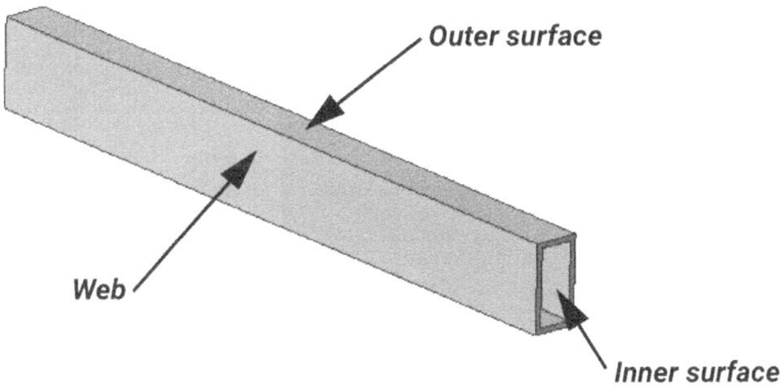

Figure 4–58

5. Repeat the previous Step for all other outer surfaces of the part. When selecting the last outer surface, click **OK** to close the *Shell Pair Definition* dialog box.
6. Four shell pairs should now be displayed in the *Model Tree*.

7. Click (Review Geometry) in the AutoGEM area and click **Apply**. The compressed model displays as shown in Figure 4–59.

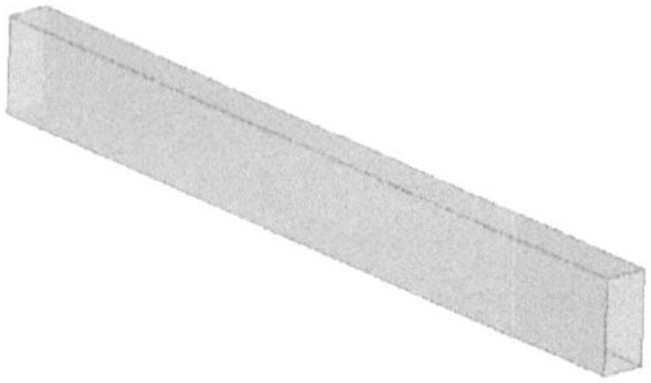

Figure 4–59

8. Close the *Simulation Geometry* dialog box.
9. Exit Creo Simulate.
10. Save and close the part to return to the assembly window.

Task 3: Define shell pairs for all of the other parts.

Shell pairs for all of the other parts in the assembly will be defined on the assembly level. You will use the **Detect Shell Pairs** tool to automatically create the shell pairs.

1. In the *Refine Model* tab, expand the (Shell Pair) drop-down list and select **Detect Shell Pairs**. The *Auto Detect Shell Pairs* dialog box opens, as shown in Figure 4–60.

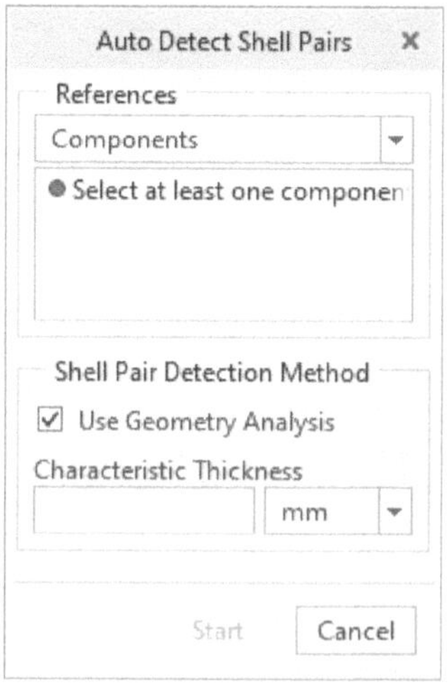

Figure 4–60

2. In the assembly, select the **TOP_SHAPE.PRT**, **PLATE.PRT**, and **WEDGE.PRT** parts (hold <Ctrl> to multi-select).
3. Ensure that **Use Geometry Analysis** is selected. In the *Characteristic Thickness* field, enter **0.4**. This means that shell pairs will be detected for all parts that are 0.4mm or thinner. The *Auto Detect Shell Pairs* dialog box displays as shown in Figure 4–61.

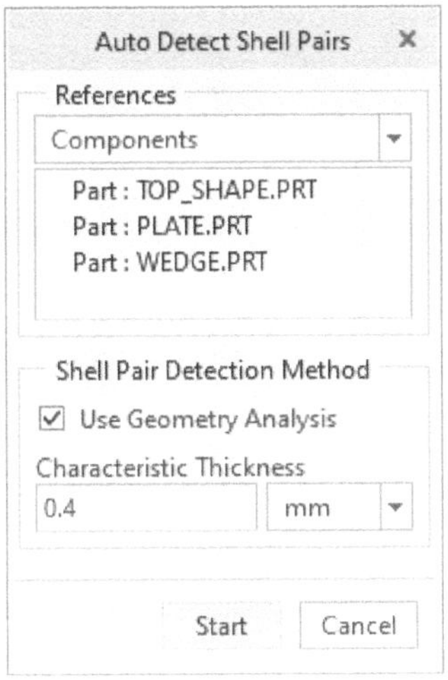

Figure 4–61

Note: *The thickness of the parts in this assembly is 0.3mm.*

4. Click **Start**. Creo Simulate runs the automatic detection algorithm and closes the *Auto Detect Shell Pairs* dialog box.
5. Five shell pairs should now be displayed in the *Model Tree* on the assembly level.

Task 4: Test the midsurface compression.

1. In the *Refine Model* tab, in the *AutoGEM* group, click (Review Geometry) to open the *Simulation Geometry* dialog box. Select the required options as shown in Figure 4–62.

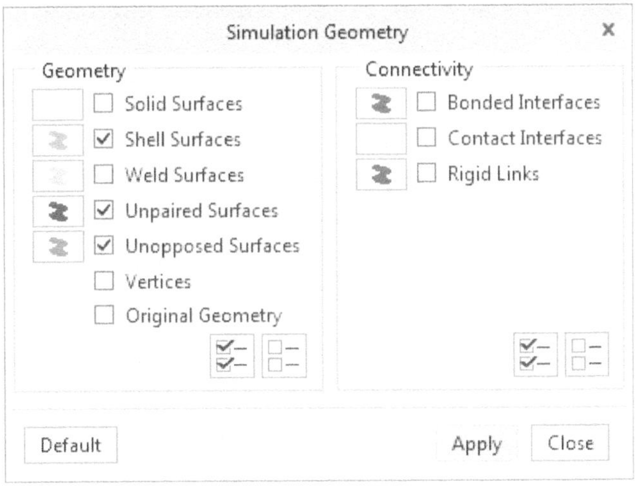

Figure 4–62

2. Click **Apply**. The model displays as shown in Figure 4–63. Ensure that there are no unpaired surfaces (displayed in red) or unopposed surfaces (displayed in orange) in the model.

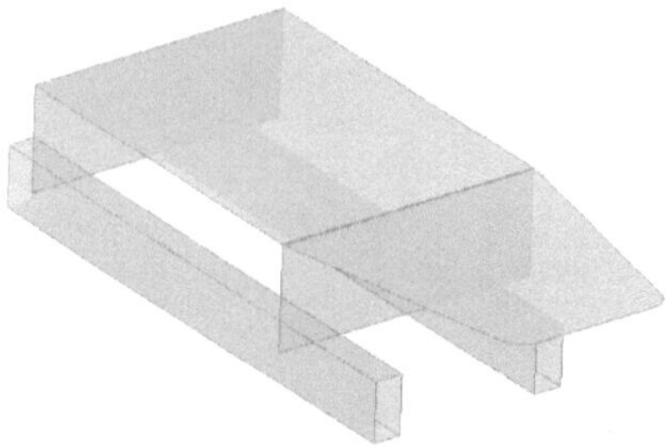

Figure 4–63

3. Zoom in on the areas where the parts join, and note that there are gaps between the midsurface, as shown in Figure 4–64. This is because the midsurfaces are obtained by offsetting the part surfaces by a half thickness. Therefore, although the part surfaces being mated in the assembly, the midsurfaces are not mated.

Figure 4–64

4. In the *Simulation Geometry* dialog box, select the **Bonded Interface** option, as shown in Figure 4–65.

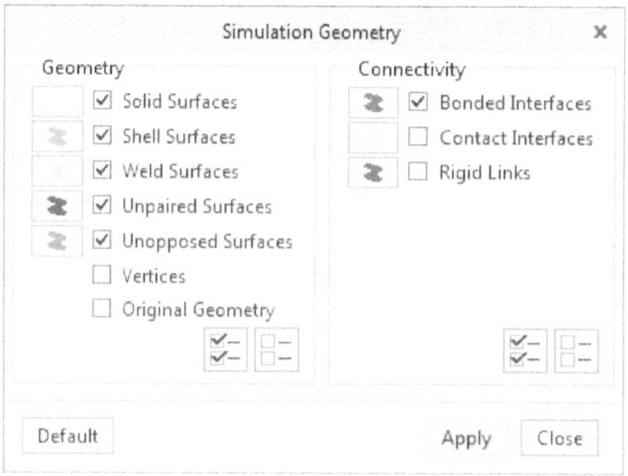

Figure 4–65

5. Click **Apply**. The model displays as shown in Figure 4–66.

Note that the areas of contact between the parts are now highlighted in magenta. Creo Simulate detects the mated in assembly surfaces, and assumes that the parts in those areas should be bonded during the analysis.

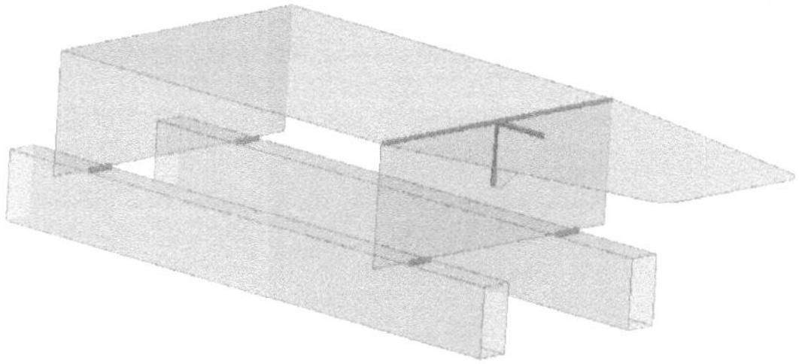

Figure 4–66

6. Click **Close** to finish.

Task 5: Apply material to parts in the assembly.

1. In the *Home* tab, click (Materials). The *Materials* dialog box opens.
2. In the *Materials in Library* area, double-click on **Legacy-Materials**, then double-click on **steel.mtl** to transfer **STEEL** to the *Materials in Model* area.
3. Review the material properties in the *Material Preview* area of the dialog box.

   The following values are the default material properties for HS-low-alloy steel (STEEL):

   - *Poisson:* **0.27**
   - *Young's modulus:* **199948 MPa**
   - *Density:* **7.82708e-9 tonne/mm3**

   Note: *The model's material properties should be as stated.*

4. Click **OK** to close the *Materials* dialog box.
5. Click (Material Assignment) to assign the material to the parts.

6. Select all of the parts in the assembly (hold <Ctrl> to multi-select). The *Material Assignment* dialog box should be as shown in Figure 4–67.

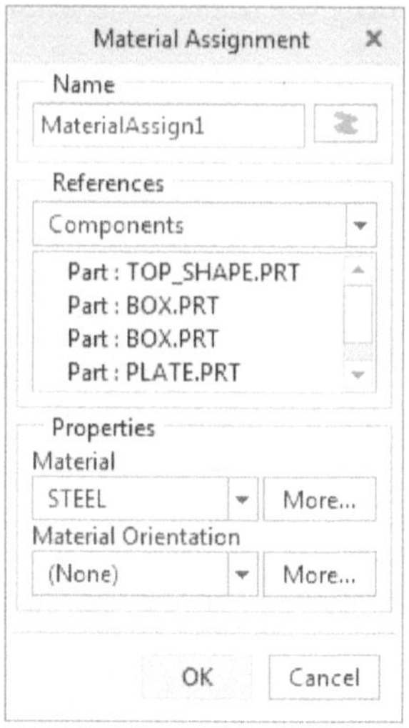

Figure 4–67

7. Click **OK** to close the *Material Assignment* dialog box.
8. Click (Simulation Display) in the In-graphics toolbar. The *Simulation Display* dialog box opens.
9. In the *Modeling Entities* tab, clear the **Material Assignments** option.
10. Click **OK** to close the *Simulation Display* dialog box.

Task 6: Mesh the model.

1. Expand the *AutoGEM* drop-down list and select **Midsurface**, as shown in Figure 4–68.

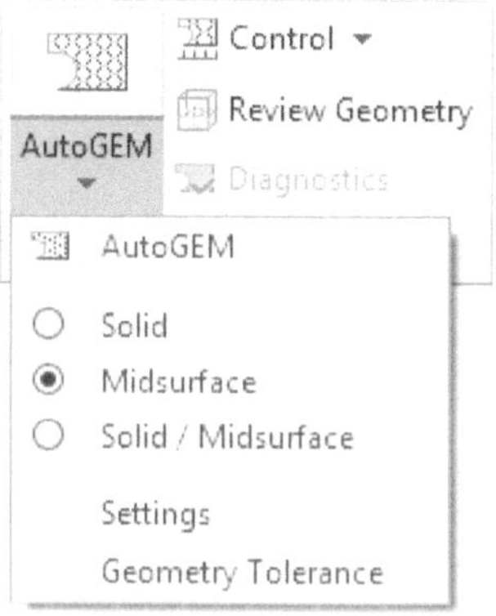

Figure 4–68

2. Click (AutoGEM). The *AutoGEM* dialog box opens, as shown in Figure 4–69.

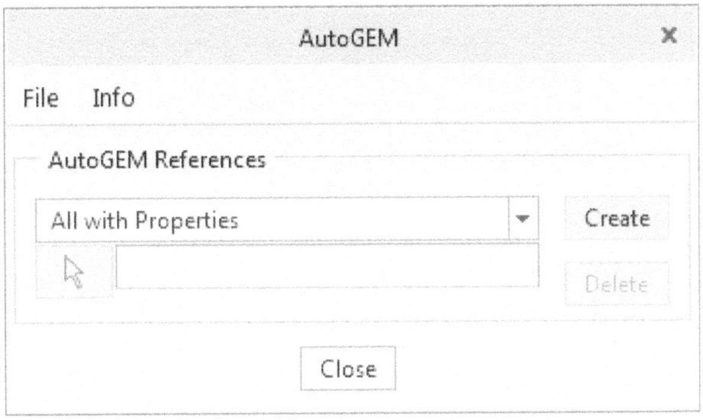

Figure 4–69

3. Expand the *AutoGEM References* drop-down list, select **All with Properties**, and click **Create**. The *AutoGEM Summary* and *Diagnostics* dialog boxes open, as shown in Figure 4–70.

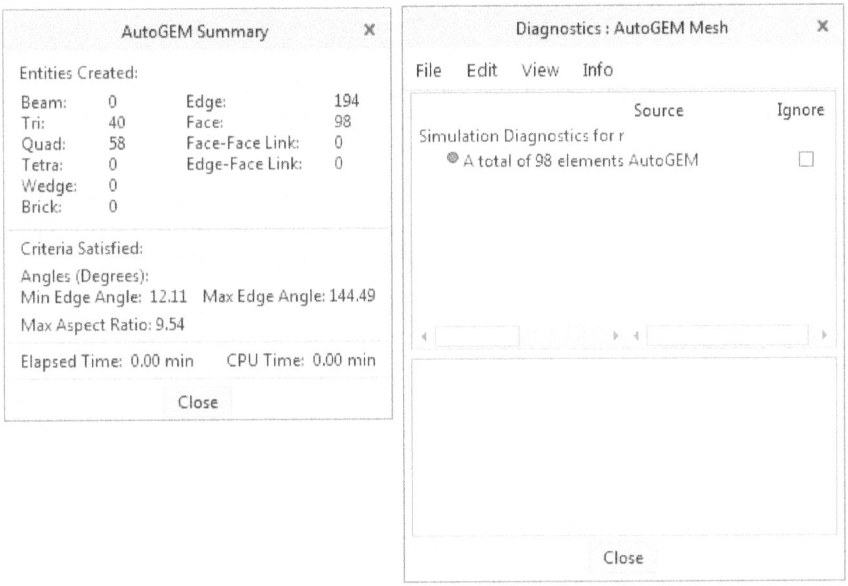

Figure 4–70

***Note:** The **All with Properties** option requires that materials be applied before meshing.*

4. Close both of the *AutoGEM Summary* and *Diagnostics* dialog boxes, but do not close the *AutoGEM* dialog box yet. The model displays as shown in Figure 4–71.

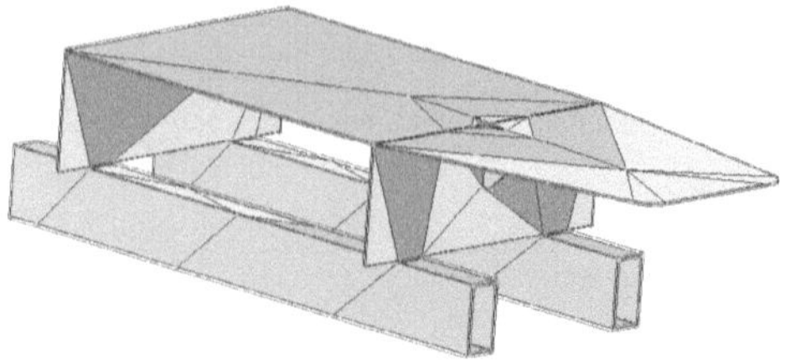

Figure 4–71

5. Zoom in on the model and examine the areas where the parts join, as shown in Figure 4–72.

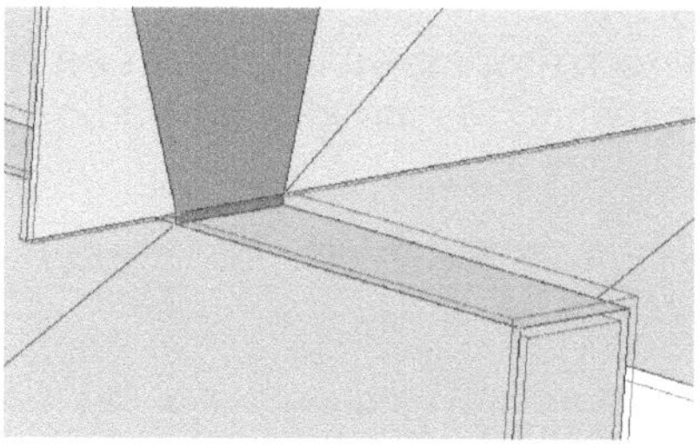

Figure 4–72

Note that the shell elements (displayed in green) in those areas are connected using blue-colored elements, which are the Bonding elements. Bonding elements in Creo Simulate are specifically designed to connect compressed parts in shell assemblies.

6. Click **Close** to close the *AutoGEM* dialog box and save the mesh.

Task 7: Apply a load to the model.

In this task, you will apply a load of 15N to the top surface of **plate.prt** (dive board).

1. In the *Home* tab, click (Force/Moment). Select the top surface of the plate, and enter the information in the *Force/Moment* dialog box, as shown in Figure 4–73.

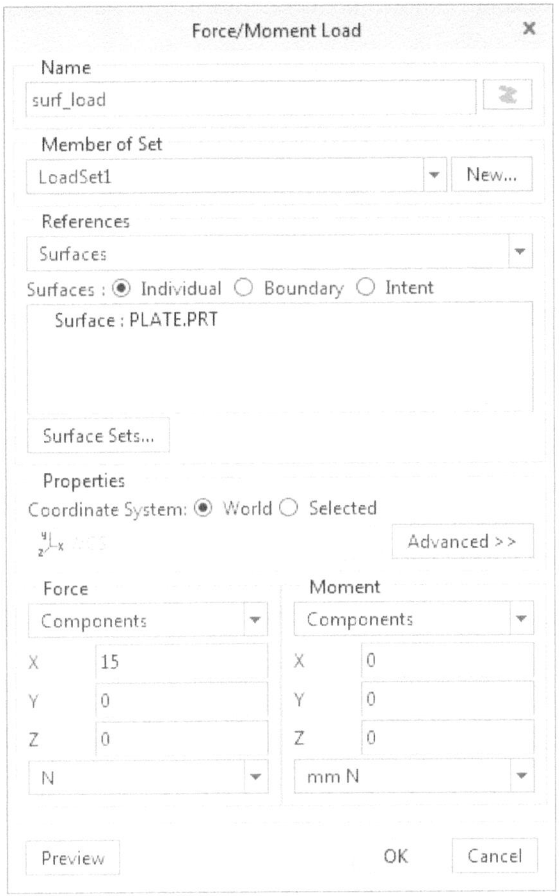

Figure 4–73

2. Click **OK** to finish. The assembly displays as shown in Figure 4–74.

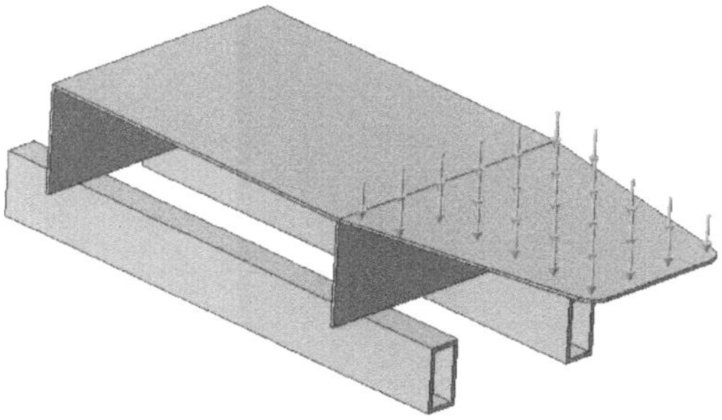

Figure 4–74

Task 8: Apply constraints to the model.

In this task, you will apply constraints to the ends of the beams shown in Figure 4–75.

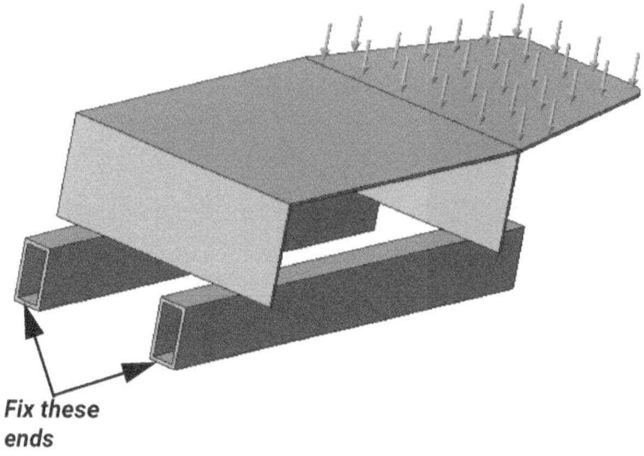

Figure 4–75

1. Click (Displacement). The *Constraint* dialog box opens.
2. In the *Name* field, enter **asm_const**. For *Member of Set*, accept the default **ConstraintSet1**.
3. Expand the *References* drop-down list and select **Edges/Curves**.
4. Select eight outer edges on the end faces, as shown in Figure 4–76. (Hold <Ctrl> to multi-select.)

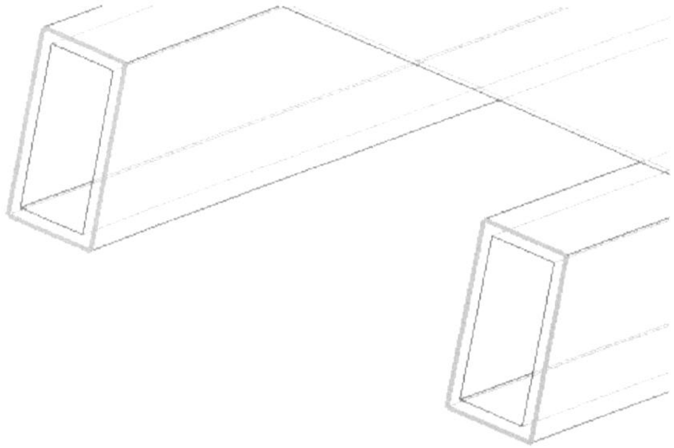

Figure 4–76

Note: *Display set to* ***Hidden Line*** *for clarity.*

5. Fix all of the *Translations* and *Rotations*, as shown in Figure 4–77.

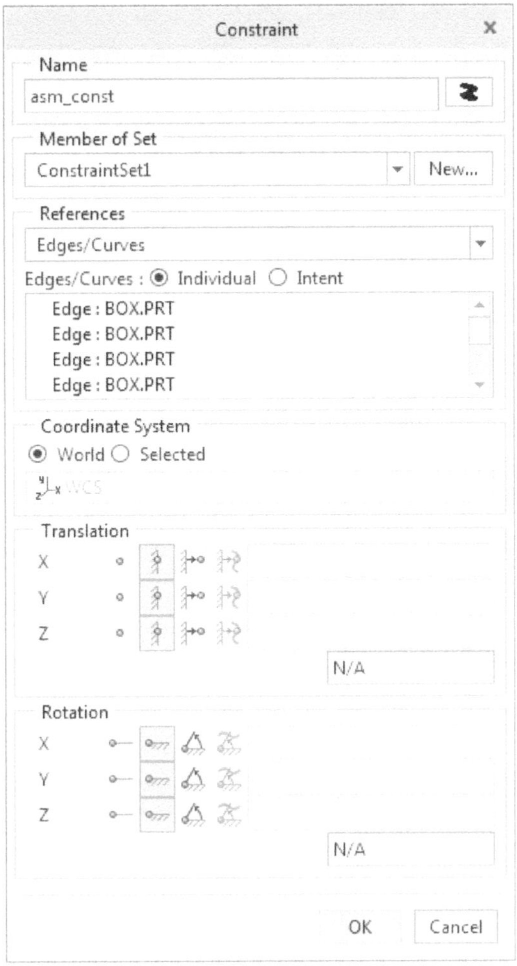

Figure 4–77

6. Click **OK**. The constraints display as shown in Figure 4–78.

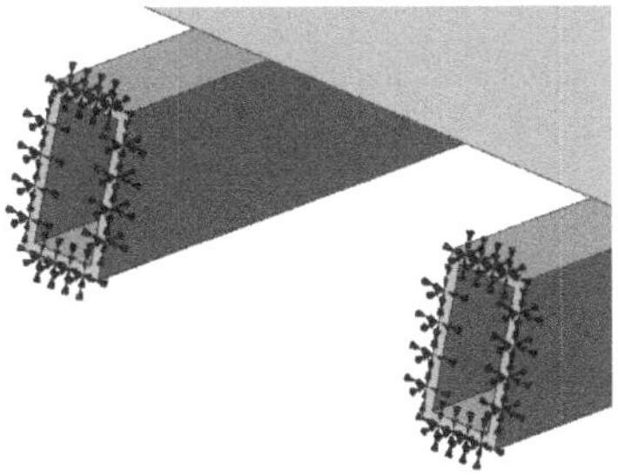

Figure 4–78

Analysis Tasks

Task 9: Set up the analysis.

1. Set up a Quick Check static analysis. For the name of the analysis, enter **dive_asm**.
2. In the *Analyses and Design Studies* dialog box, run **Info>Check Model** to check the validity of the model.
3. Run the Quick Check analysis to check for errors in loads or constraints.

Task 10: Solve the assembly using the Multi-Pass Adaptive convergence option.

1. Change *Quick Check* to the **Multi-Pass Adaptive convergence** method.
2. In the *Polynomial Order* field, enter **9** maximum and in the *Limits* area, in the *Percent Convergence* field, enter **10** percent convergence.
3. In the *Output* tab, increase the *Plotting Grid* value to **10**.
4. Start the analysis run and wait until it completes.
5. Expand the *Run Status* dialog box to display the information about the analysis, as shown in Figure 4–79.

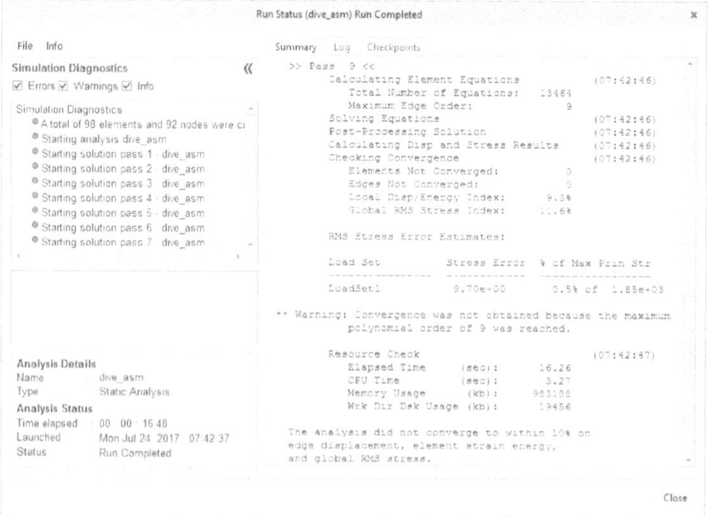

Figure 4–79

Note that the analysis did not converge on the Global RMS Stress to the required 10% because the maximum polynomial order 9 was not sufficient to obtain the convergence. In the following tasks, you will explore the elements that have not converged.

6. Close the *Run Status* window.

Task 11: Display the non-converged elements.

1. In the *Analyses and Design Studies* dialog box, click (Review Results). In the *Result Window Definition* dialog box, expand the *Quantity* drop-down list and select **P-Level**, as shown in Figure 4–80.

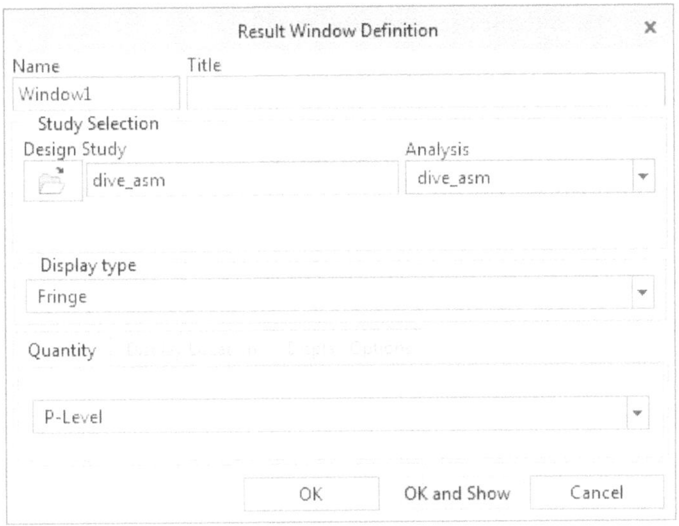

Figure 4–80

2. Click **OK and Show**. The P-Level plot displays as shown in Figure 4–81.

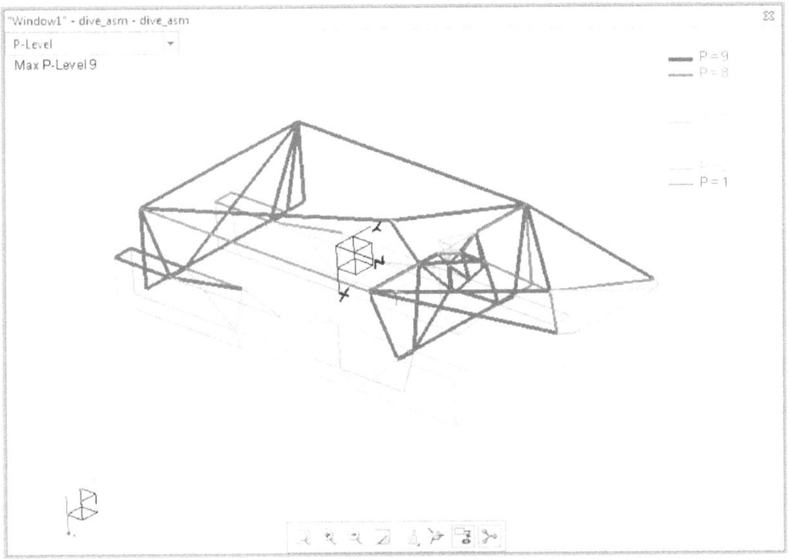

Figure 4–81

Examine the P-Levels and note that majority of the elements, in all but the beam parts, have their edges displayed in red, which corresponds to P-Level 9. These are the elements that are most likely to have not converged.

Note that the elements in the model are very large. Therefore, the non-convergence might be attributed to the elements being too large. In the following task, you will refine the mesh to obtain convergence.

3. Select **File>Close** and exit without saving the result window.
4. Close the *Analyses and Design Studies* dialog box.

Mesh Refinement Tasks

Task 12: Set up the AutoGEM Controls.

1. In the *Refine Model* tab, in the *AutoGEM* group, expand the *Control* drop-down list and select **Maximum Element Size**, as shown in Figure 4–82.

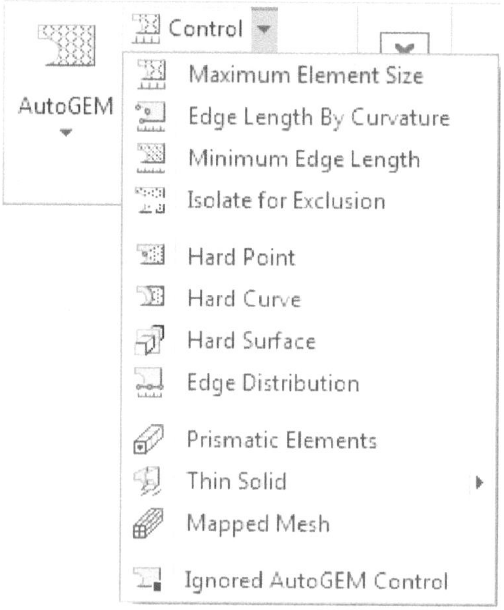

Figure 4–82

2. The *Maximum Element Size Control* dialog box opens. Expand the *References* drop-down list and select **Components**. Select all of the parts in the assembly (hold <Ctrl> to multi-select), and in the *Element Size* field, enter **8**, as shown in Figure 4–83.

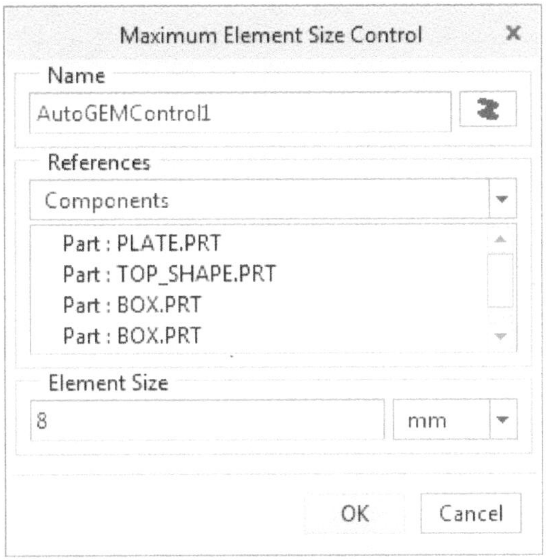

Figure 4–83

3. Click **OK** to finish. Note that AutoGEM Control icons display in the model and in the *Model Tree*.

Task 13: Re-mesh the model.

1. Click (AutoGEM). The *Question* dialog box displays, as shown in Figure 4–84.

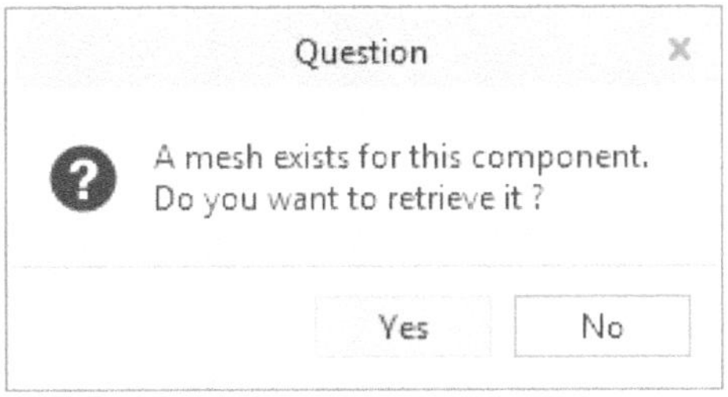

Figure 4–84

2. Click **No**. The *AutoGEM* dialog box opens, as shown in Figure 4–85.

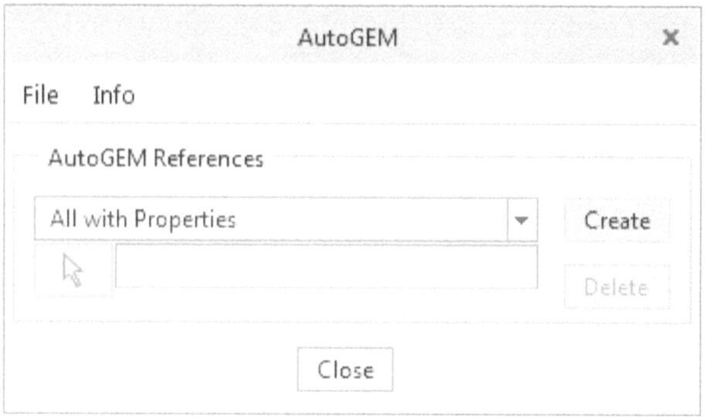

Figure 4–85

3. Click **Create**. Once meshing is finished, close both the *AutoGEM Summary* and *Diagnostics* dialog boxes. The model displays (with loads and constraints hidden) as shown in Figure 4–86.

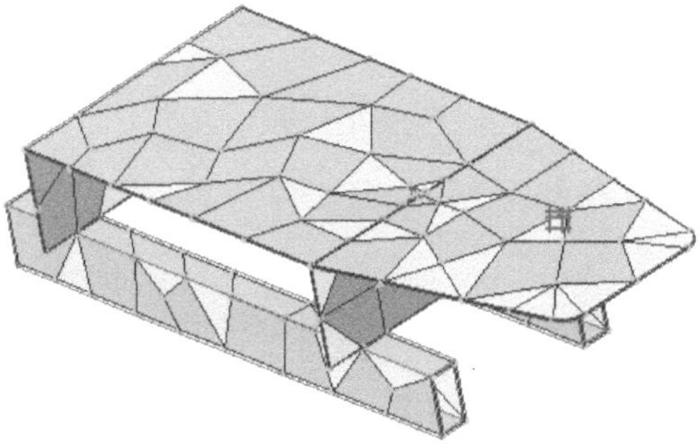

Figure 4–86

Note that AutoGEM now creates a much finer mesh, according to the element size that you specified in an earlier task.

4. Click **Close** to close the *AutoGEM* dialog box and save the mesh.

Task 14: Re-run the analysis.

1. Run the **dive_asm** analysis again. When prompted, click **Yes** to delete the existing results, then wait until the analysis completes.
2. Expand the *Run Status* window and check whether the analysis has converged, as shown in Figure 4–87.

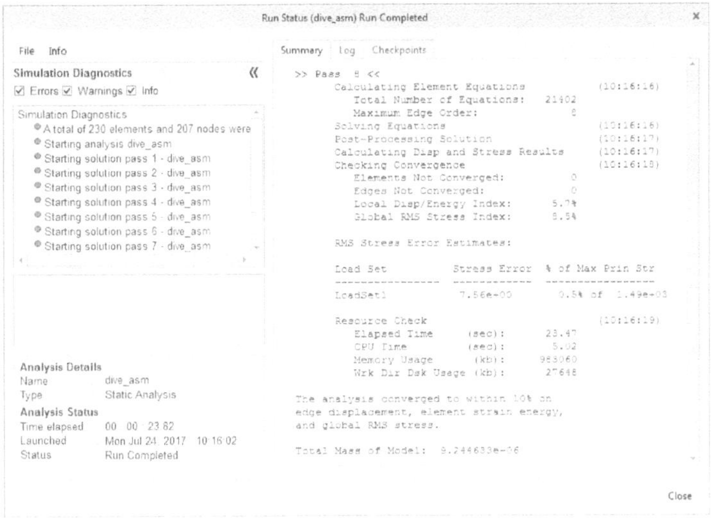

Figure 4–87

Note that the analysis now converges on Pass 8, with the maximum P-level 8 (**Maximum Edge Order** in the *Run Status* window).

3. Click **Close** to close the *Run Status* window.

Results Tasks

Task 15: Display the stress results.

1. Create and display a color plot of the von Mises stress. It should display as shown in Figure 4–88.

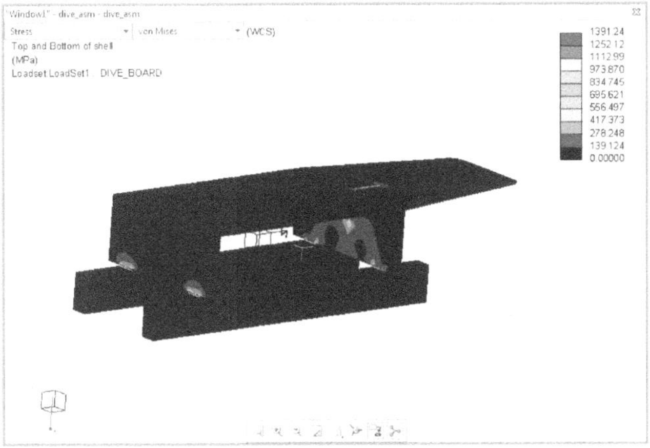

Figure 4–88

The stress values that you obtain once you run the analysis might be slightly different than those that have been provided. This is because each build of Creo Simulate has a slightly different solver, which will produce variations in the creation of the mesh and the solution of the analysis.

2. In the *Format* tab, click (Edit). The *Edit Legend* dialog box opens, as shown in Figure 4–89. Explore the options in the box.

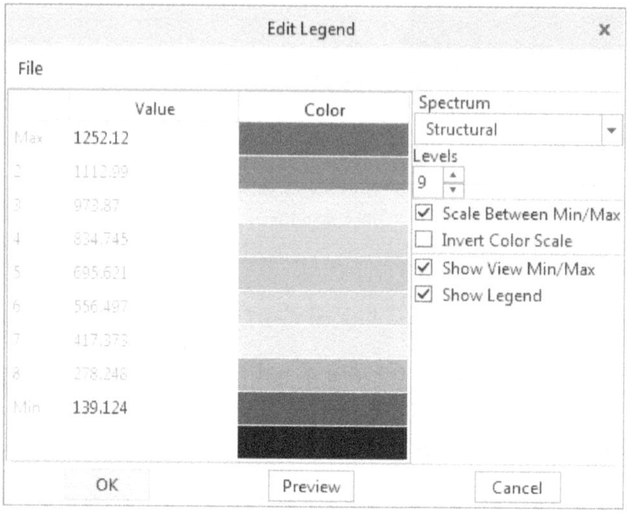

Figure 4–89

3. Clear the **Show View Min/Max** option and change the *Max* value to **500**, as shown in Figure 4–90.

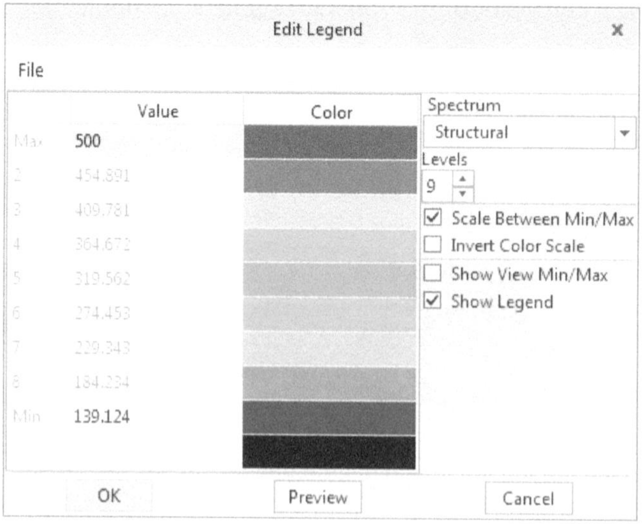

Figure 4–90

4. Click **OK**. The model displays as shown in Figure 4–91. Note that the changed legend enables the stress distribution in the model to be displayed more clearly.

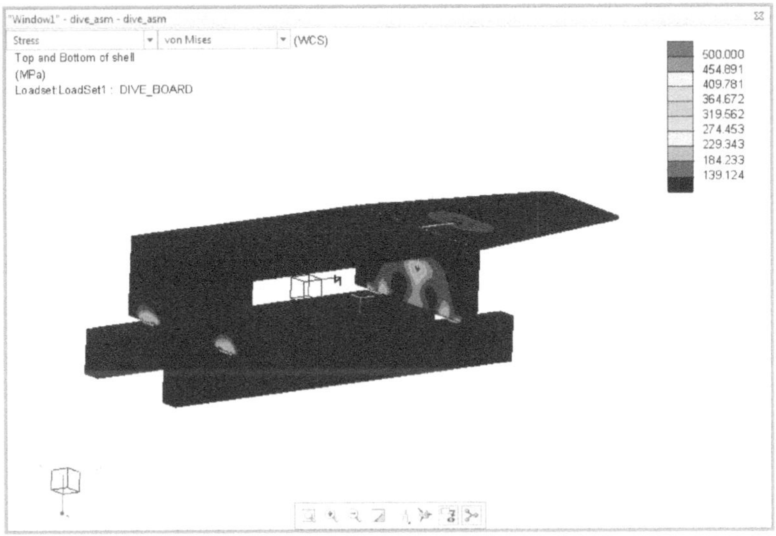

Figure 4–91

Task 16: Examine areas of high stress.

1. Select (Model Max). The result plot displays as shown in Figure 4–92. Zoom in on the location of the maximum stress.

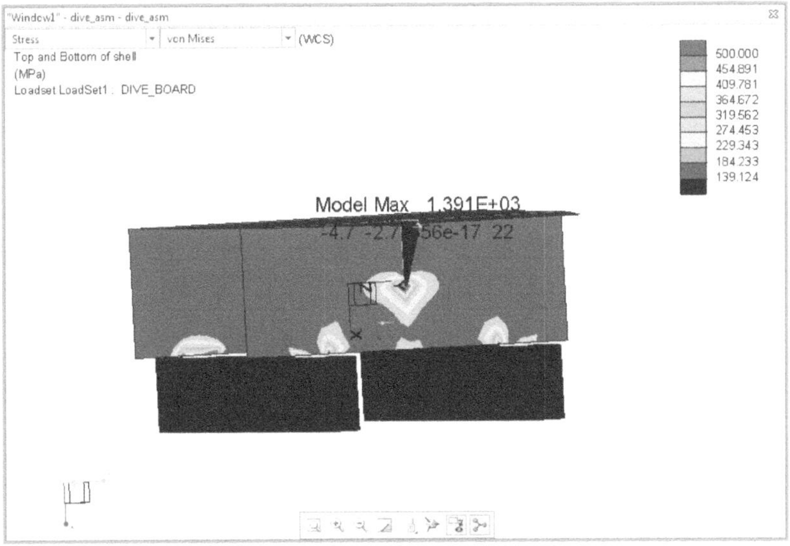

Figure 4–92

2. Zoom in on the area in which the top C-shape is attached to the left beam, and select (View Max). Creo Simulate now only displays the location of the maximum stress within the viewing area, as shown in Figure 4–93.

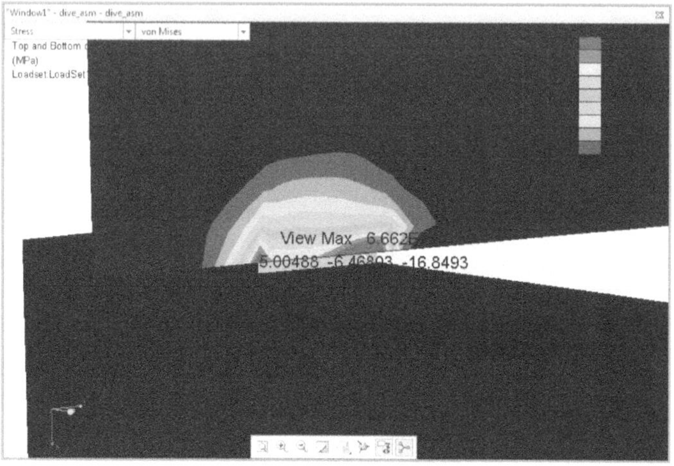

Figure 4–93

Note: *The values you see will vary slightly from those shown, depending on your model's exact orientation.*

3. Click (Dynamic Query) and explore the stresses in the area by moving the cursor over the model, as shown in Figure 4–94. Note that the *Query* dialog box displays the coordinates of the queried point as well.

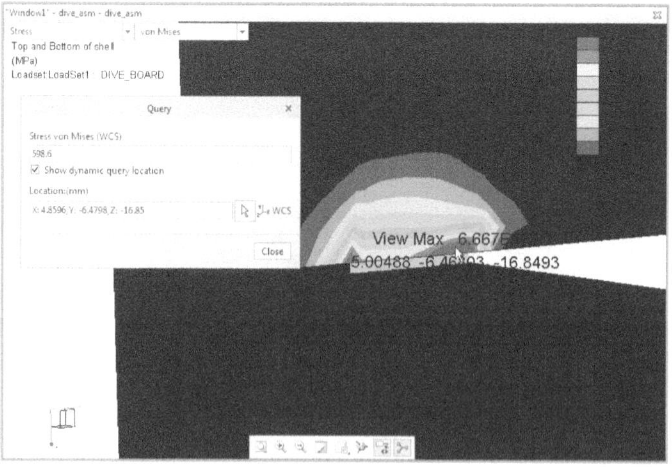

Figure 4–94

4. Click **Close** in the *Query* dialog box to finish.

Task 17: Display the displacement results.

1. In the *Home* tab, click (Copy). The *Result Window Definition* dialog box opens.
2. In the *Name* field, enter **deformation**.
3. In the *Title* field, enter **DEF_PLOT**.
4. Expand the *Quantity* drop-down list and select **Displacement**.
5. In the *Display Options* tab, select the **Deformed**, **Overlay Undeformed**, **Transparent Overlay**, and **Animate** options.
6. Clear the **Auto Start** option.
7. Click **OK**.
8. In the *View* tab, click (Show). In the *Display Result Window* dialog box, highlight the **deformation**, as shown in Figure 4–95.

Figure 4–95

Note: Ensure that only ***deformation*** *is highlighted in the Display Result Window.*

9. Click **OK**. The deformation plot displays.

   Note: Did the deformation display correctly?

10. In the *View* tab, click (Start) to start the animation. Click (Stop) to stop the animation.
11. Click (Step Forward) or (Step Back) to step through the animation frames.

12. Review Frame 5, as shown in Figure 4–96.

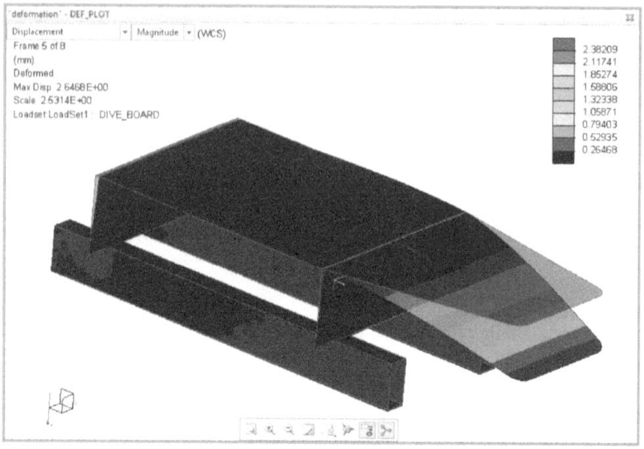

Figure 4–96

Note: Use animations to check for errors and verify your results.

Task 18: Use predefined measures to study the convergence.

1. Create convergence graphs (i.e., against the P-loop pass) for the following predefined measures:
   - **max_stress_vm**
   - **strain_energy**
   - **max_disp_mag**

   The convergence plot for **max_stress_vm** displays as shown in Figure 4–97.

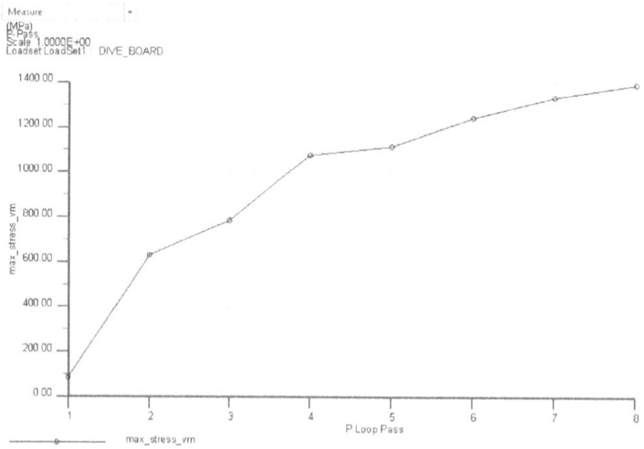

Figure 4–97

2. The convergence plot for **strain_energy** displays as shown in Figure 4–98.

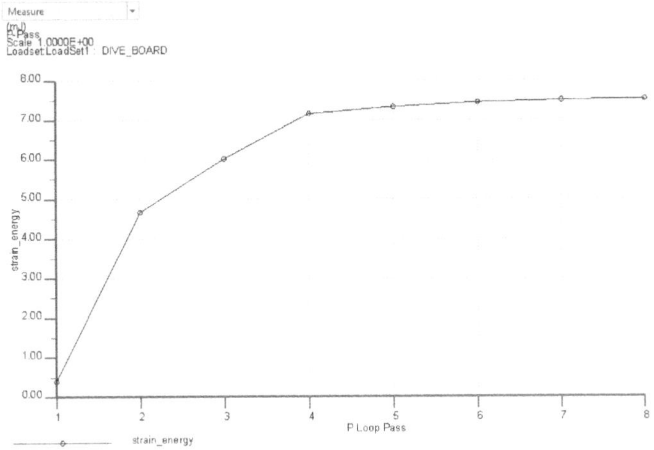

Figure 4–98

3. The convergence plot for the **max_disp_mag** displays as shown in Figure 4–99.

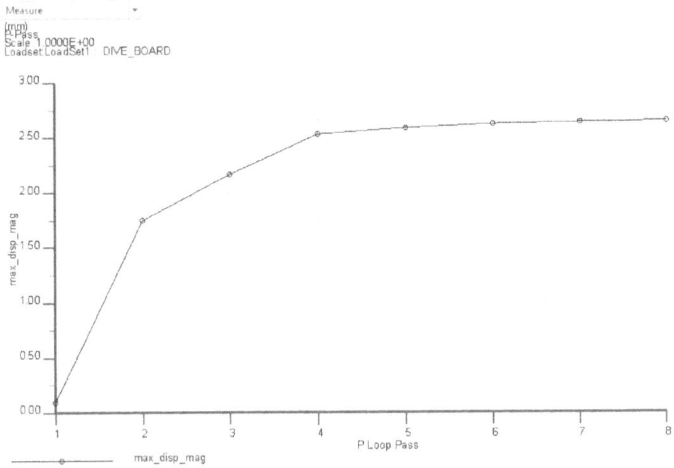

Figure 4–99

These plots indicate that the solution converges after eight passes.

Task 19: Use the graph *Options* dialog box.

1. In the *Format* tab, click (Edit). The *Options* dialog box opens, as shown in Figure 4–100.

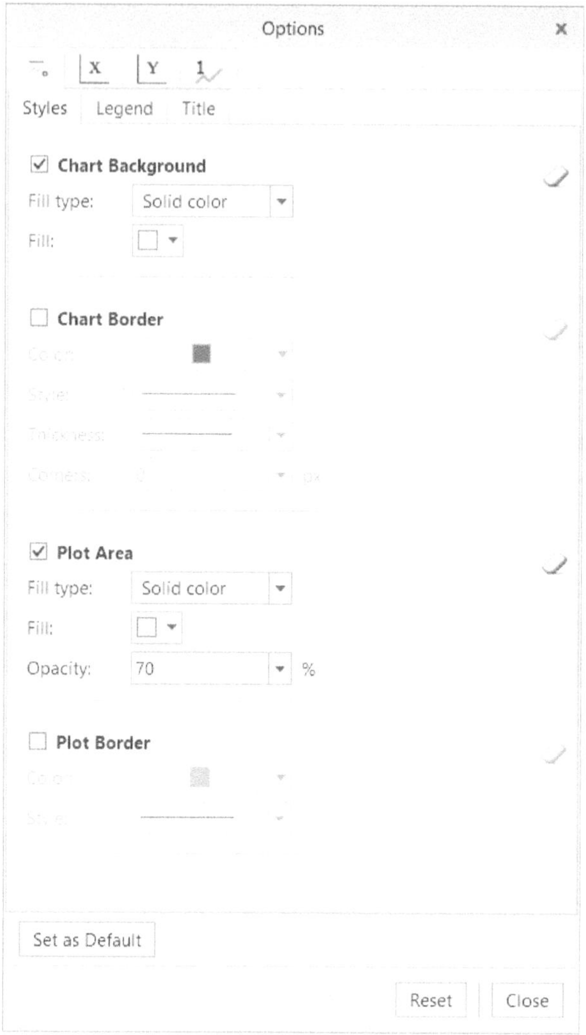

Figure 4–100

2. Select the *Format Trace 1* tab. In the *Symbols* area, change *Shape* to **Square** and *Weight* to **10px**, as shown in Figure 4–101.

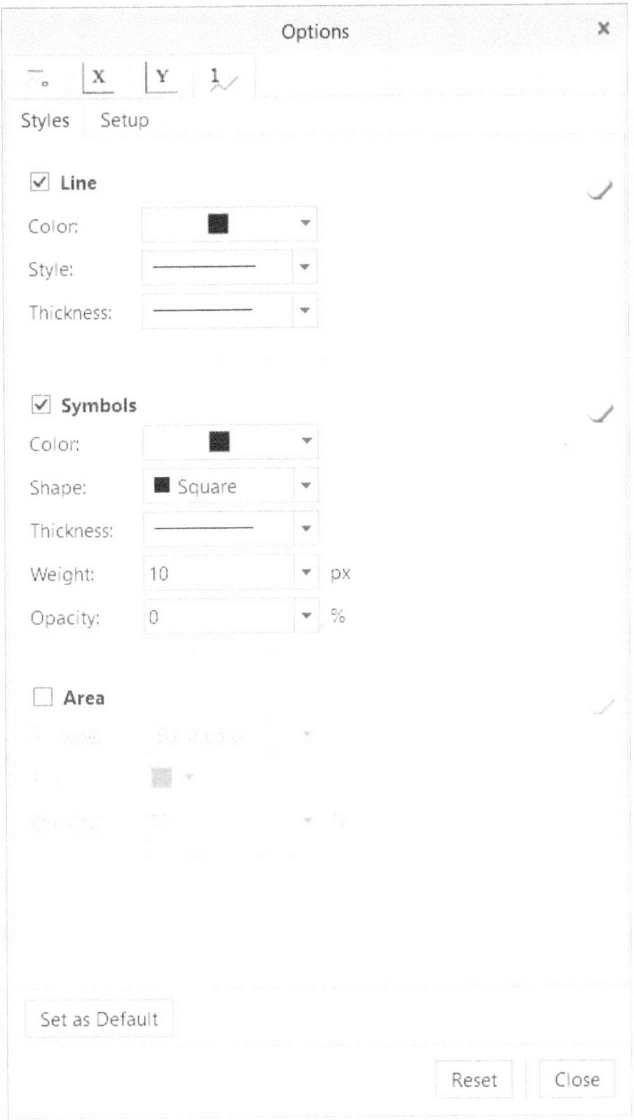

Figure 4–101

3. Click **Close** to finish. The graph displays as shown in Figure 4–102.

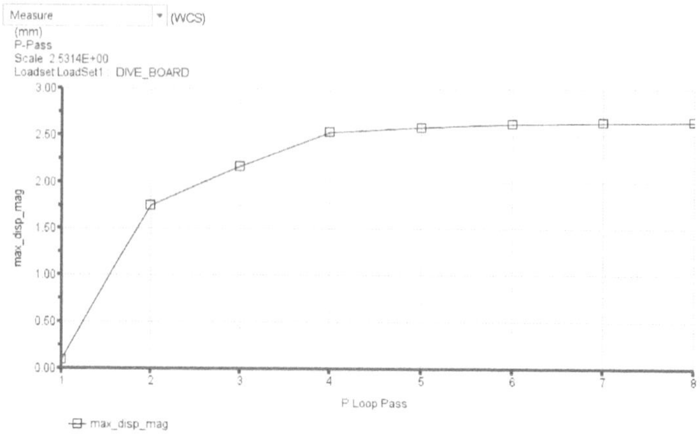

Figure 4–102

4. Point your mouse to any square symbol in the graph at P Loop Pass to obtain the **max_disp_mag** value in that analysis pass, as shown in Figure 4–103.

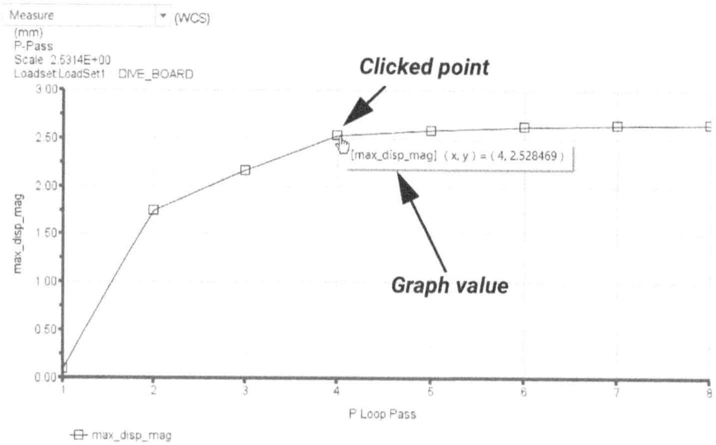

Figure 4–103

Task 20: Save and close the model.

1. Select **File>Close**. Click **Don't Save** when prompted to save the results.
2. Close the *Analyses and Design Studies* dialog box.
3. Exit Creo Simulate. Save and close the model in Creo Parametric.

End of practice

Practice 4c
Shells from Surfaces

Practice Objectives

- Create shell elements from surface models.
- Set up loads, constraints, and material properties.
- Run and analyze a part.

In this practice, you will use shell element idealizations to set up and analyze the bent tube with flanges shown in Figure 4–104. The tube is created in Creo Parametric using surface features only (i.e., there are no solid volumes in the model). The tube is about 13in long and just over 3in in diameter. The tube wall thickness is 0.15in and flange thickness 0.4in.

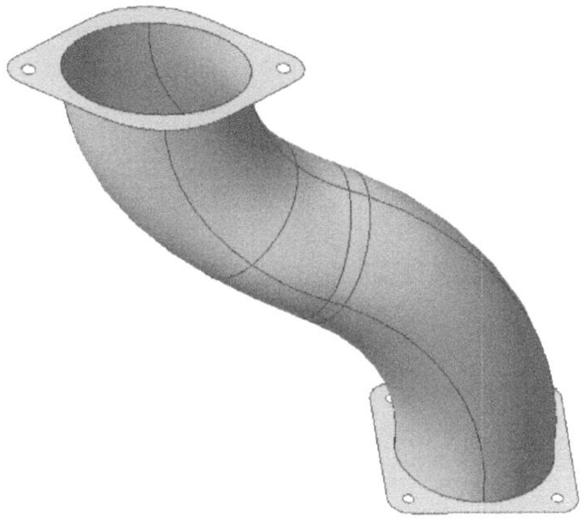

Figure 4–104

Modeling Tasks

Task 1: Open the tube_quilt part.

1. Set the working directory to **Chapter04**, if required.
2. Open **tube_quilt.prt**.
3. Set the model display as follows:
   - *(Datum Display Filters)*: All Off
   - *(Spin Center)*: Off
   - *(Display Style)*: (Shading With Edges)

The part displays as shown in Figure 4–105.

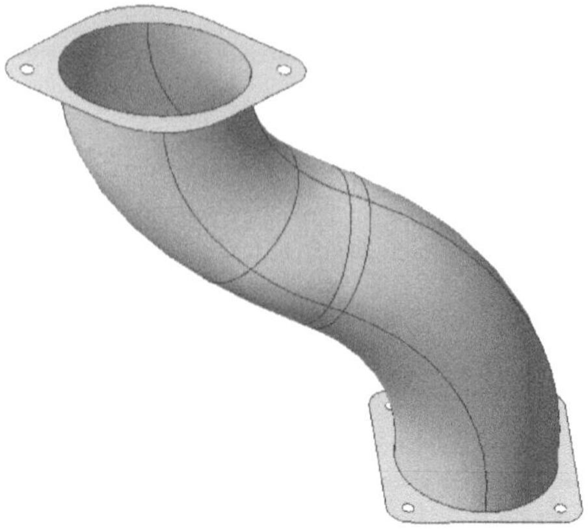

Figure 4–105

4. Select **Applications>Simulate** to switch to the Creo Simulate environment. Ensure that the **Structure** mode is active.

Task 2: Apply material.

1. Click (Materials) and transfer **STEEL** to the *Materials in Model* area.
2. Review the material properties in the *Material Preview* area of the dialog box.

   The following values are the default material properties for HS-low-alloy steel (STEEL):

   - *Poisson's ratio:* **0.27**
   - *Young's modulus:* **2.9e+7 psi**
   - *Density:* **0.0007324 lbf sec2/in4**

   Note: *The model's material properties should be as stated.*

3. Click **OK** to close the *Materials* dialog box.
4. Click (Material Assignment) to assign **STEEL** to the part.

Task 3: Define the shells.

Since this part is not a solid model, the compression from solid to midsurface does not apply. In this task, you will use the standard **Shell** option to define the shell elements.

1. In the *Refine Model* tab, in the *Idealizations* area, click (Shell). The *Shell Definition* dialog box opens, as shown in Figure 4–106.

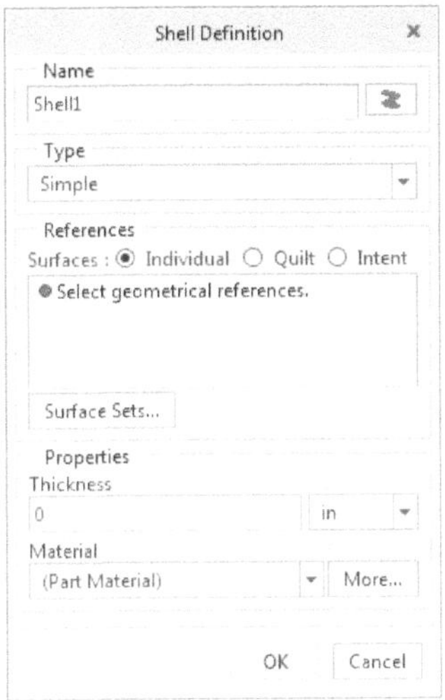

Figure 4–106

2. Select the **Quilt** option and select any surface in the tube portion of the part. This selects all of the individual surfaces that comprise the tube surface.
3. In the *Thickness* field, enter **0.15**. The dialog box displays as shown in Figure 4–107.

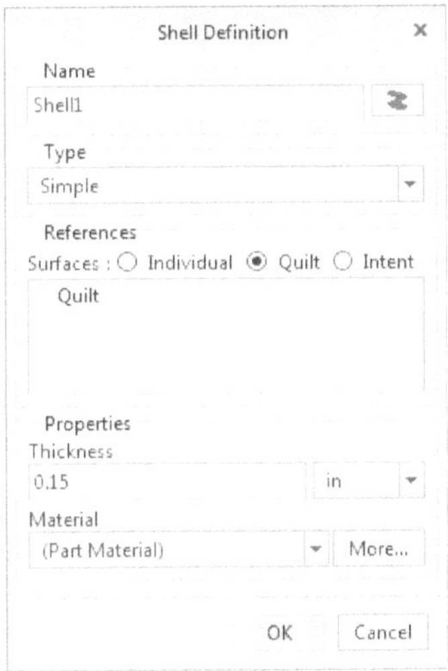

Figure 4–107

Note: *Creo Simulate assumes the selected surface is the midsurface through the thickness of the part. The tube material in the analysis is extended by 0.075in to the inside and outside of the surface.*

4. Click **OK** to finish.
5. Click (Shell) again.

6. Select **Individual** and then multi-select both flange surfaces.
7. In the *Thickness* field, enter **0.4**. The dialog box displays as shown in Figure 4–108.

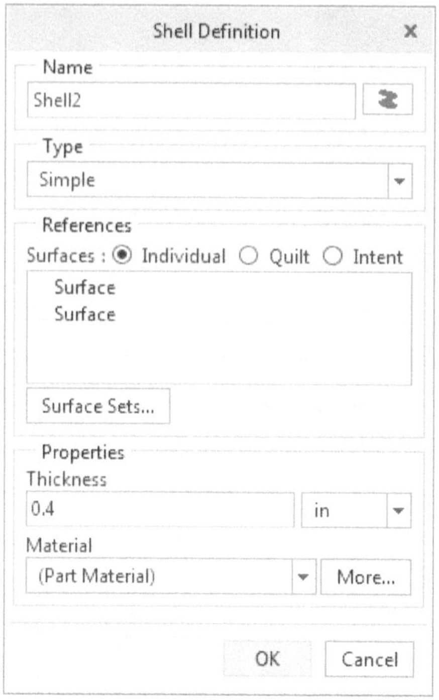

Figure 4–108

Note: Creo Simulate assumes the selected surfaces to be the midsurfaces of the part. The flange material is extended by 0.2in in either direction.

8. Click **OK** to finish.
9. The model displays as shown in Figure 4–109. Note that Creo Simulate visually thickens the created shells, according to their actual thicknesses, and shows them as transparent solids.

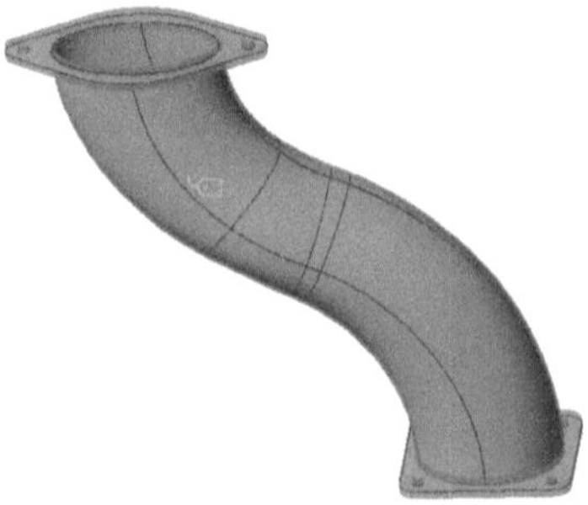

Figure 4–109

10. Click (Simulation Display) in the In-graphics toolbar. The *Simulation Display* dialog box opens, as shown in Figure 4–110.

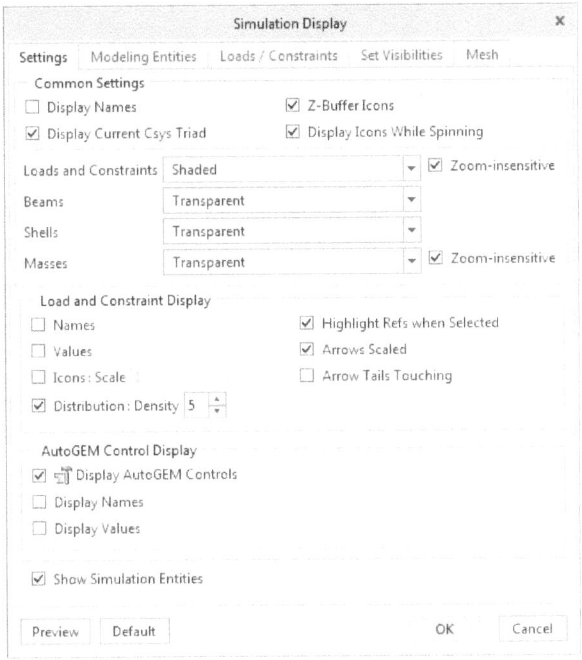

Figure 4–110

11. Explore the *Shells* drop-down list by selecting various options (e.g., **Outline**, **Wireframe**, **Shaded**, **Transparent**) and clicking **Preview**.

12. Select the *Modeling Entities* tab and clear the **Shells** and **Material Assignments** options, as shown in Figure 4–111.

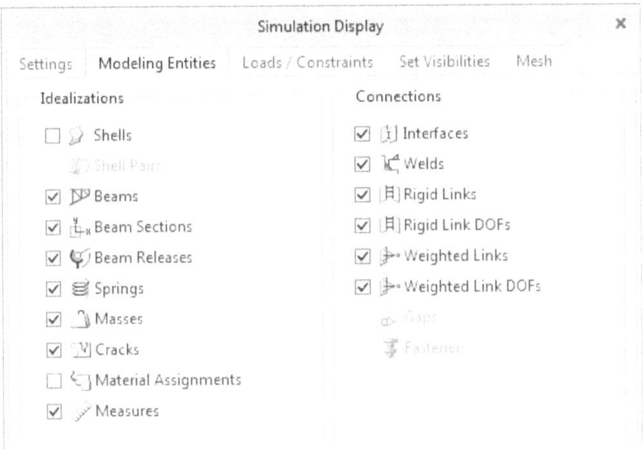

Figure 4–111

13. Click **OK**. The model displays as shown in Figure 4–112.

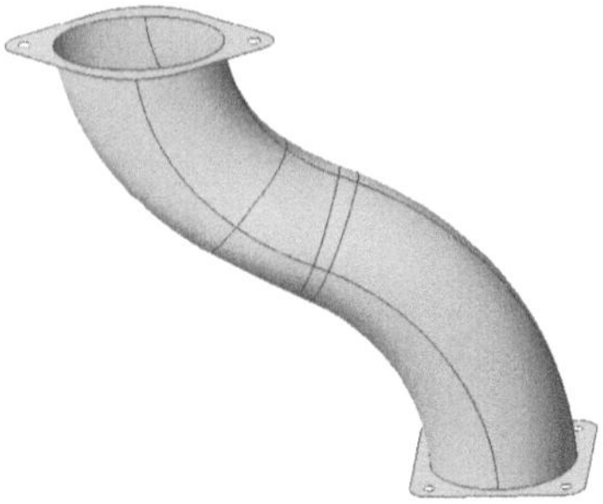

Figure 4–112

14. In the *Refine Model* tab, in the *AutoGEM* group, click (Review Geometry) to open the *Simulation Geometry* dialog box and then click **Apply**. The model displays as shown in Figure 4–113. Check whether all of the surfaces are highlighted in green – these are the shell surfaces.

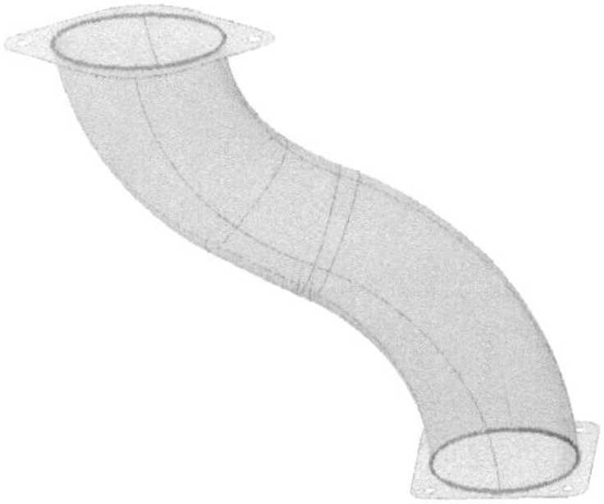

Figure 4–113

15. Click **Close**.

Task 4: Mesh the model.

1. In the *Refine Model* tab, in the *AutoGEM* area, expand the *Control* drop-down list and select **Edge Length By Curvature**, as shown in Figure 4–114.

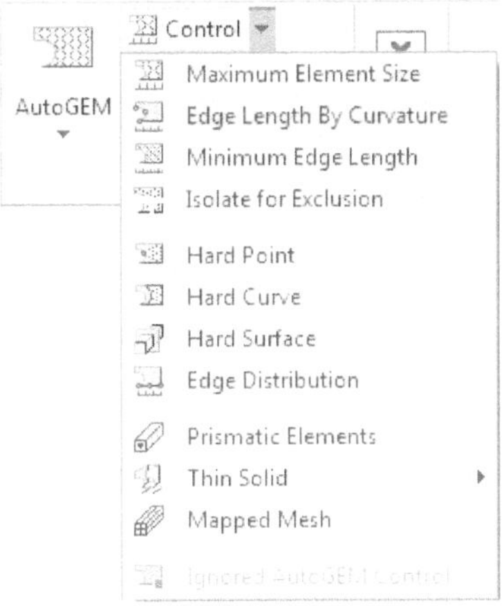

Figure 4–114

2. In the *Edge Length By Curvature Control* dialog box that opens, note that **Components** is the default selection in the *References* drop-down list. This automatically selects the part. In the *Edge Length / Radius of Curvature ratio* field, enter **1** as shown in Figure 4–115.

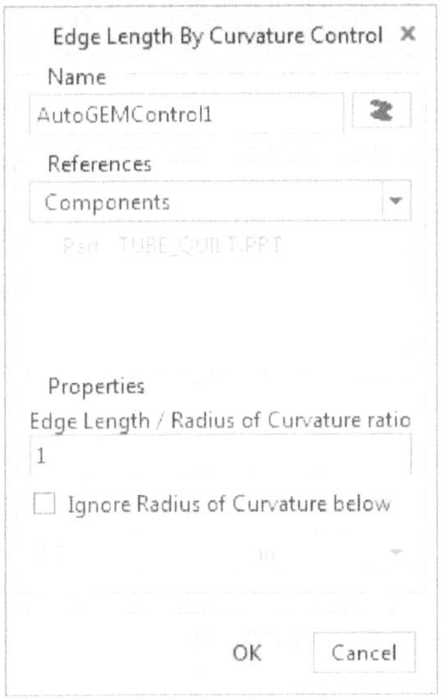

Figure 4–115

Note: The ***Edge Length By Curvature*** *option is useful for accurate meshing of curved surfaces. Ratio 1.0 means that the mesh size will be made roughly equal to the radius of curvature of the surface.*

3. Click **OK** to finish.
4. Click (AutoGEM). The *AutoGEM* dialog box opens. Click **Create**.

5. Once the meshing has finished, close both the *AutoGEM Summary* and *Diagnostics* dialog boxes. The model displays as shown in Figure 4–116. Note that quad elements are displayed in the darker green color, and triangular elements are displayed in lighter green.

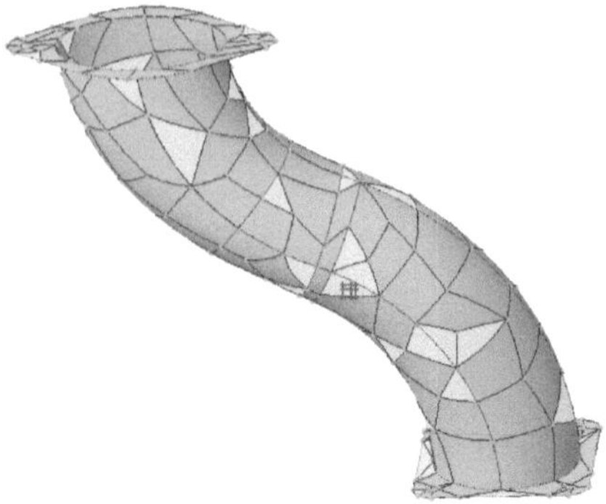

Figure 4–116

6. Click (Simulation Display) in the In-graphics toolbar. The *Simulation Display* dialog box opens.
7. Select the *Mesh* tab and clear the **Display Shells with Zero Thickness** option, as shown in Figure 4–117.

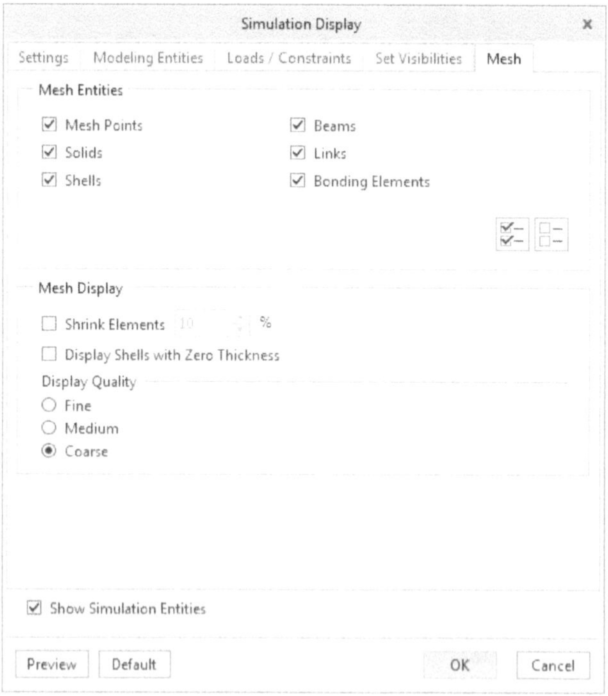

Figure 4–117

8. Click **OK**. The model displays as shown in Figure 4–118.

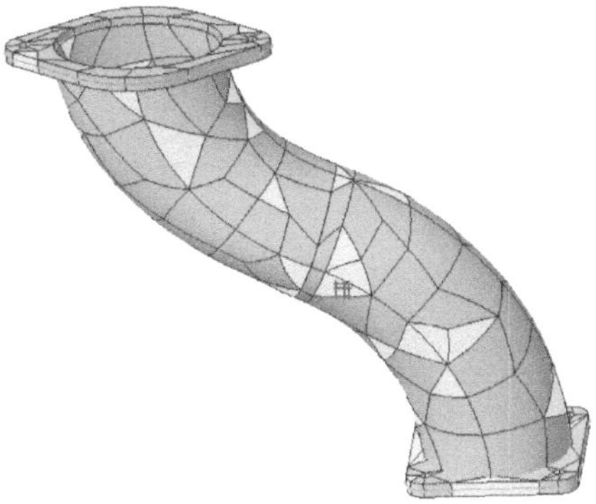

Figure 4–118

Note that the elements have now been thickened, using the thicknesses that you applied when creating the shells.

9. Click **Close** to close the *AutoGEM* dialog box and save the mesh.

Task 5: Apply a load to the model.

In this task, you will apply a load of 1000lbs to the holes in the oval flange.

1. In the *Home* tab, click (Force/Moment). The *Force/Moment* dialog box opens.
2. Expand the *References* drop-down list, select **Edges/Curves**, and then multi-select the edges of the two holes in the oval flange, as shown in Figure 4–119.

Figure 4–119

Note: *Display set to* ***Hidden Line*** *for clarity.*

3. In the *Force/Moment* dialog box, enter the other required information as shown in Figure 4–120.

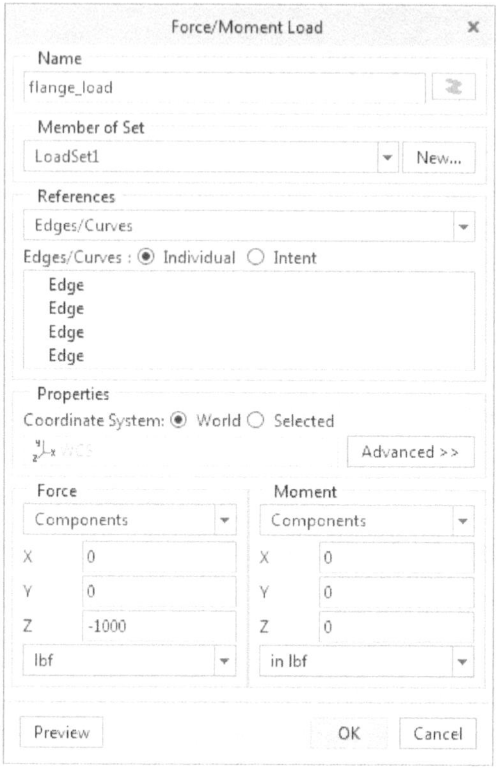

Figure 4–120

4. Click **OK**. The model displays as shown in Figure 4–121.

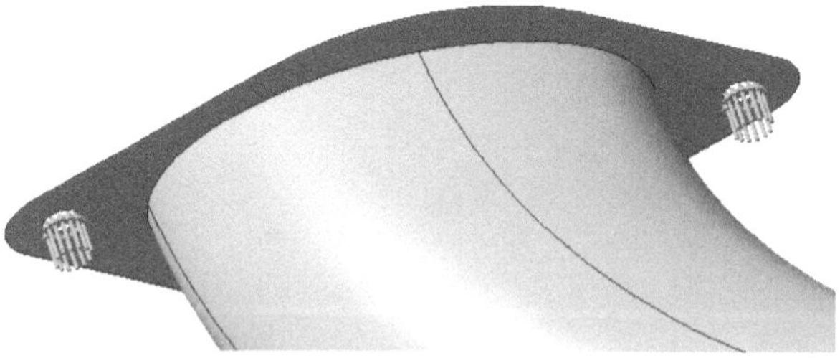

Figure 4–121

Task 6: Apply constraints to the model.

In this task, you will constrain the four holes in the square flange.

1. Click (Displacement). The *Constraint* dialog box opens.

2. Expand the *References* drop-down list, select **Edges/Curves**, and then multi-select the edges of the four holes in the square flange, as shown in Figure 4–122.

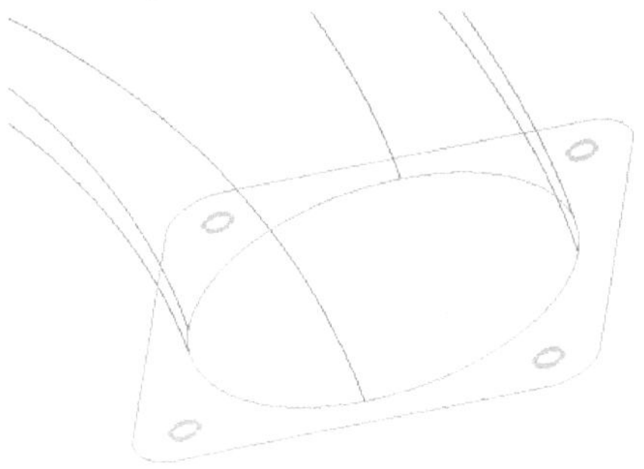

Figure 4–122

Note: *Display set to* ***Hidden Line*** *for clarity.*

3. For the constraint, for the *Name*, enter **fixed**. Fix all of the *Translations* and *Rotations*, as shown in Figure 4–123.

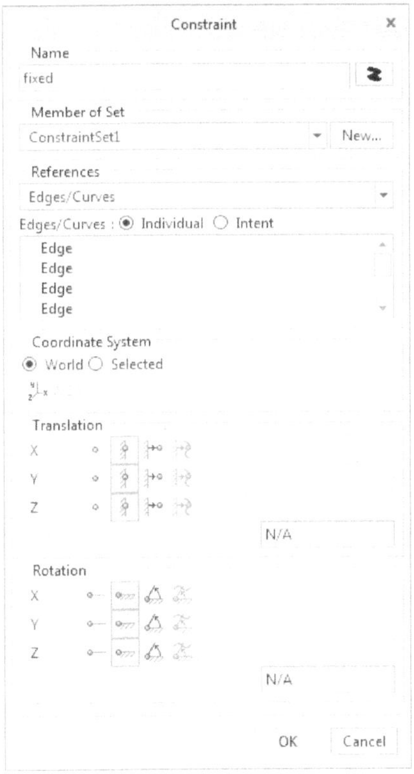

Figure 4–123

4. Click **OK**. The model displays as shown in Figure 4–124.

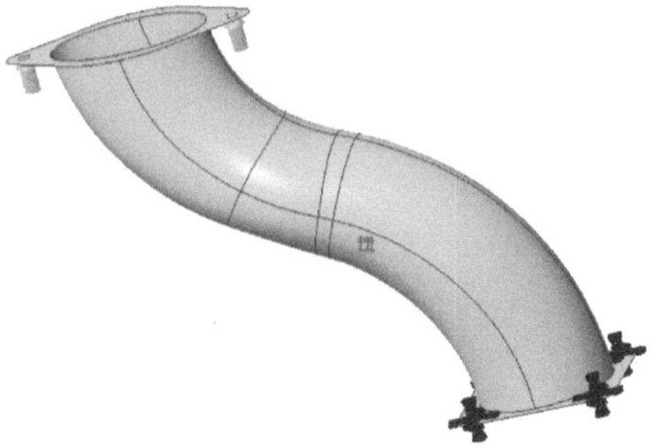

Figure 4–124

Analysis Tasks

Task 7: Solve the model using the Multi-Pass Adaptive convergence option.

1. Create a *Static Analysis* named **tube_shell**.
2. Select the **Multi-Pass Adaptive** convergence method.
3. In the *Polynomial Order* field, enter **9** for *Maximum* and in the *Limits* area, in the *Percent Convergence* field, enter **5** percent convergence, as shown in Figure 4–125.

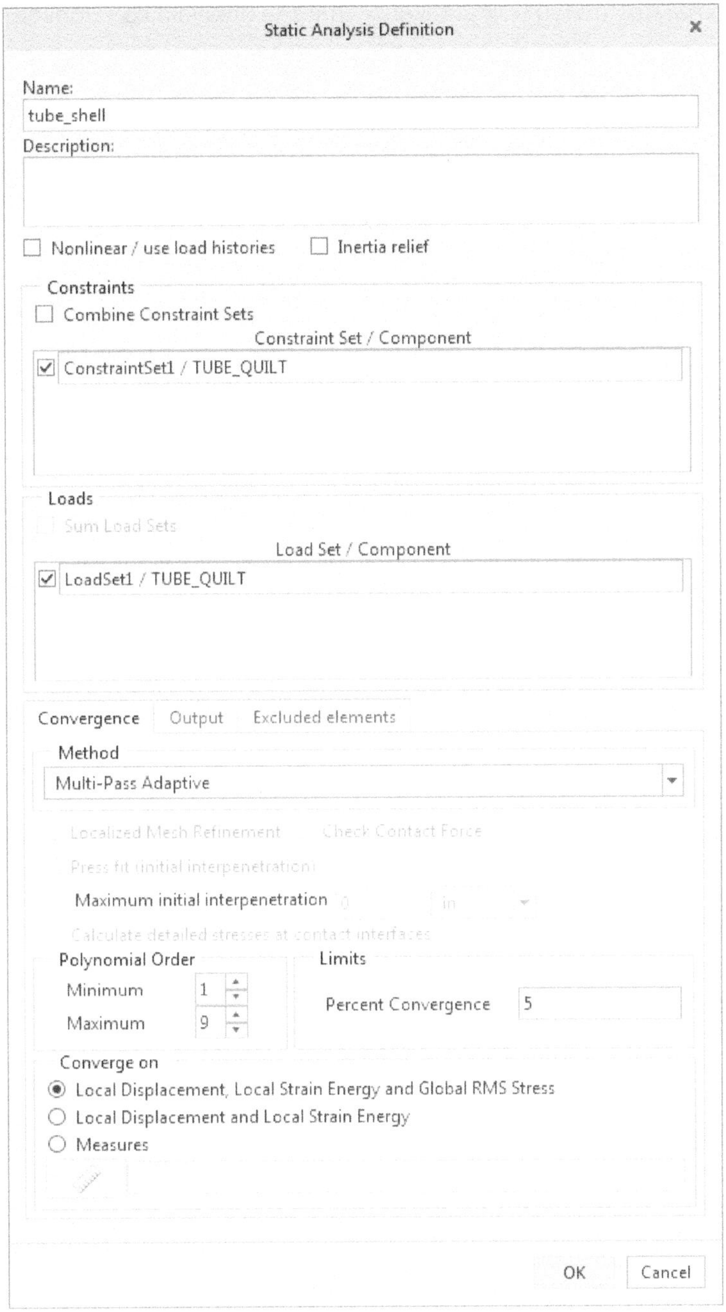

Figure 4–125

4. Start the analysis run and wait until it finishes.

5. Expand the *Run Status* dialog box and verify that the analysis has converged, as shown in Figure 4–126.

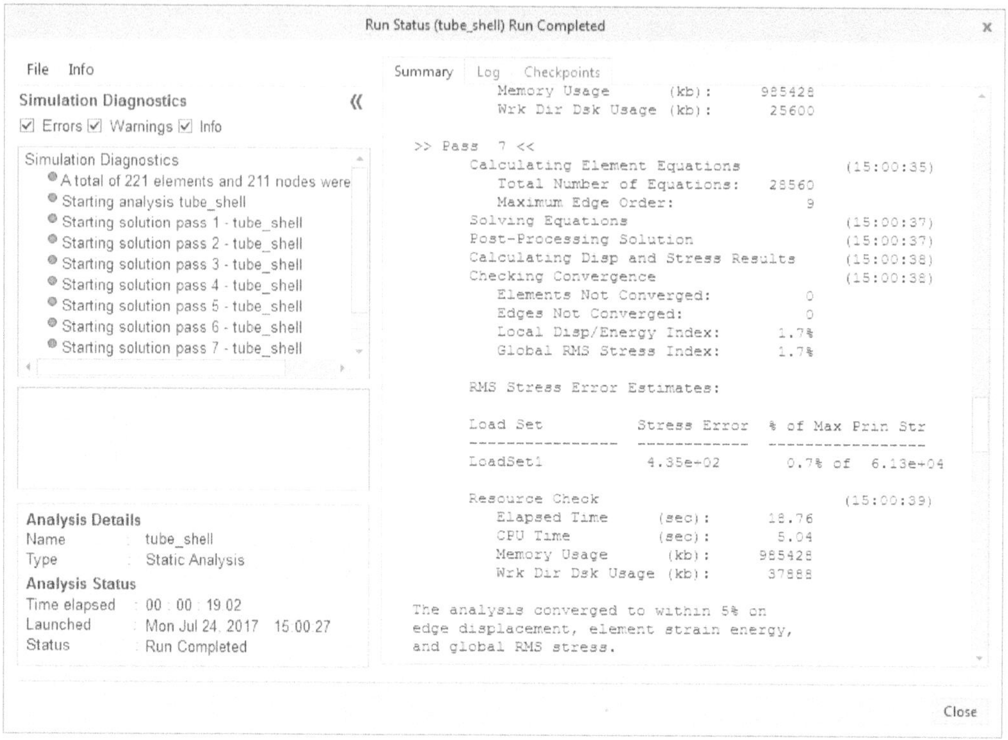

Figure 4–126

Results Tasks

Task 8: Display the displacement results.

1. Create and display an animated fringe plot of the Displacement Magnitude. Use the animation controls to start, stop, and step through the frames of the animation. Frame 5 of the animation should display as shown in Figure 4–127.

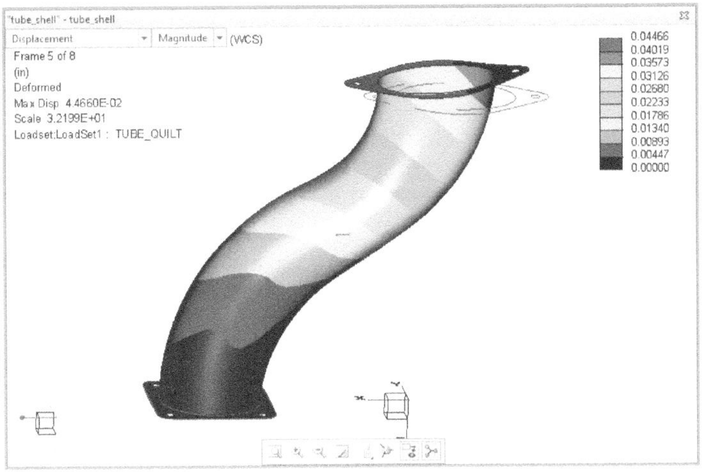

Figure 4–127

Note that the maximum displacement in the model is approximately 0.0447 inches.

2. Create and display an undeformed fringe plot of the von Mises Stress. It should display as shown in Figure 4–128.

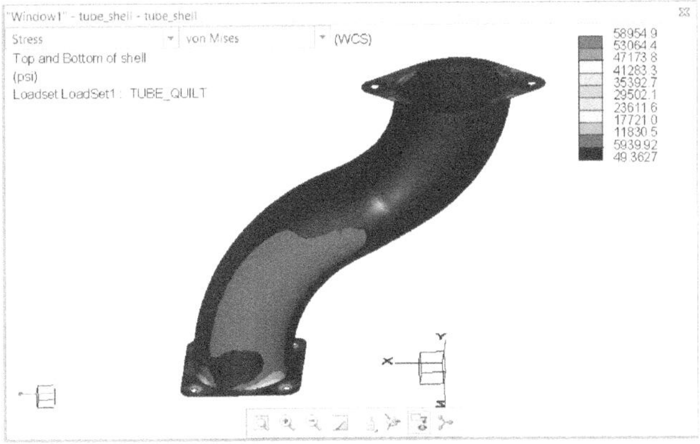

Figure 4–128

Note that the maximum stress is approximately 59ksi, and that it occurs at one of the holes in the square flange. Use (Model Max) to find the exact location if required.

3. Click (Edit) to edit the von Mises Stress plot. In the *Result Window Definition* dialog box, in the *Quantity* tab, clear the **Bending** and **Transverse Shear** options, as shown in Figure 4–129.

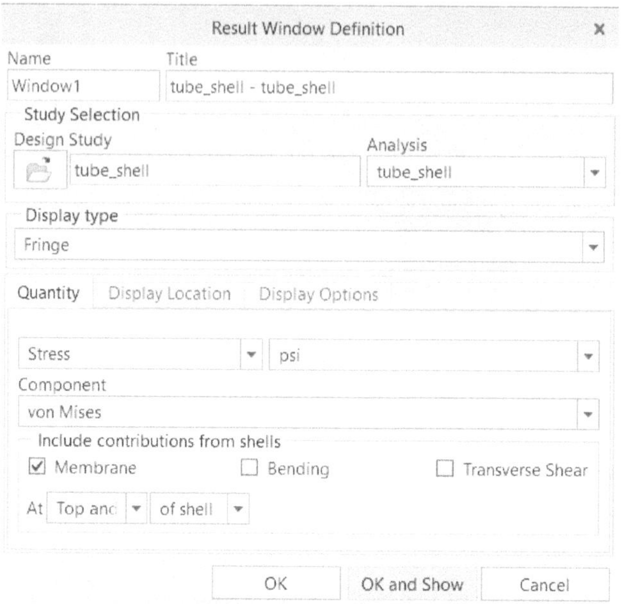

Figure 4–129

4. Click **OK and Show**. Now the result plot displays only the membrane component of stress in the part, as shown in Figure 4–130.

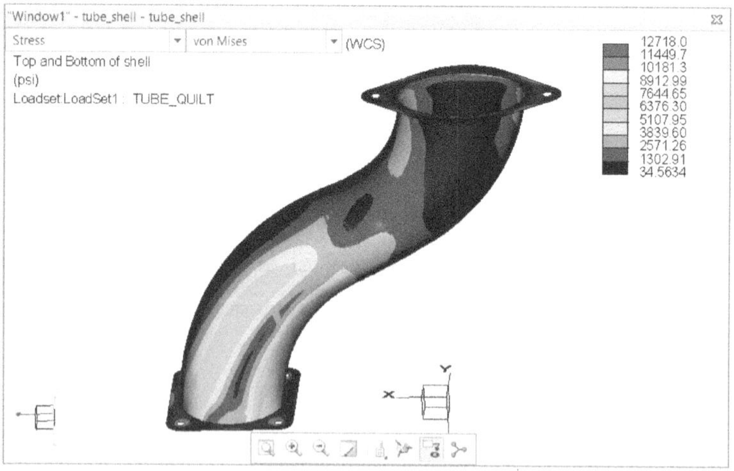

Figure 4–130

Note: *The membrane component of the stress is constant through the shell thickness, and is due to loads acting in-plane of the midsurface.*

Note that the maximum membrane stress occurs in the tube walls near the square flange.

5. Click (Edit) again. In the *Result Window Definition* dialog box, in the *Quantity* tab, clear the **Membrane** and **Transverse Shear** options, and select the **Bending** option, as shown in Figure 4–131.

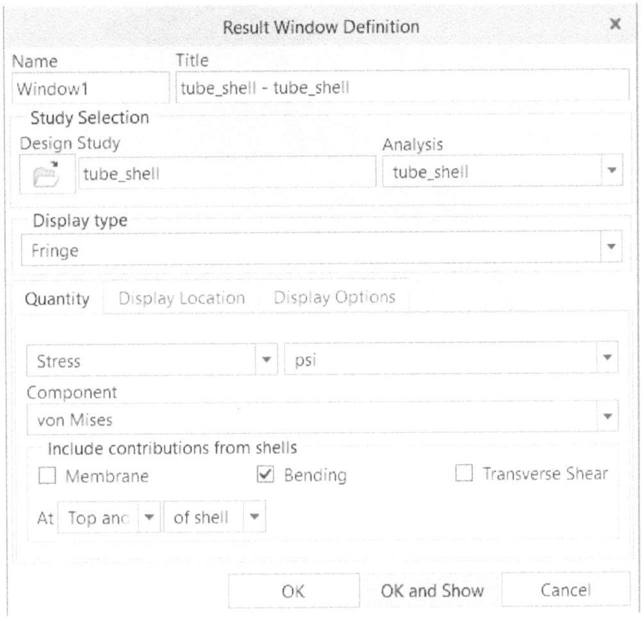

Figure 4–131

6. Click **OK and Show**. Now the result plot only displays the bending component of stress in the part, as shown in Figure 4–132.

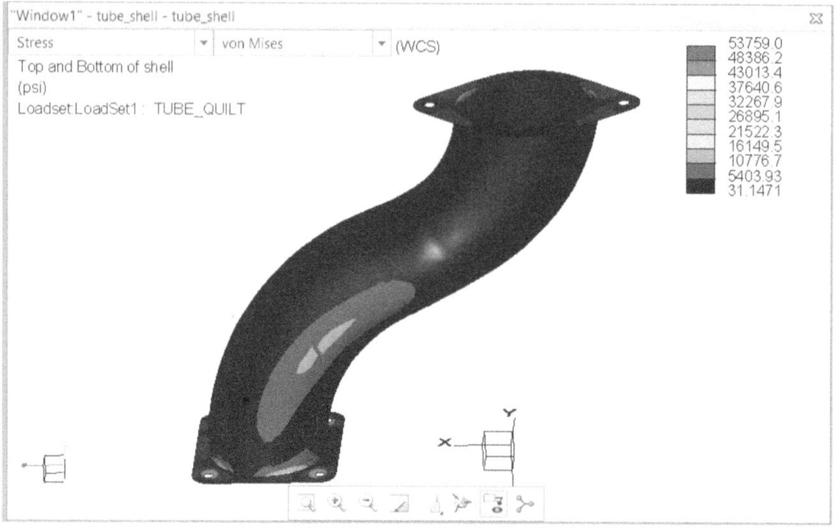

Figure 4–132

> ***Note:*** *The bending component of stress is anti-symmetric through the thickness, (i.e., it is tensile on one side and compressive on the other side). It is caused by the out-of-plane bending loads.*

Note that the bending stress is most pronounced in the square flange of the part.

Task 9: Save and close the model.

1. Select **File>Close**. Click **Don't Save** when prompted to save the results.
2. Close the *Analyses and Design Studies* dialog box.
3. Exit Creo Simulate. Save and close the model in Creo Parametric.

End of practice

Practice 4d
Shell and Solid Combination

Practice Objective

- Set up and run an analysis on a part using a combination of solid and shell elements.

Shell elements can drastically reduce the number of elements in the model and computation time to obtain a solution.

In this practice, you will use the shell element idealizations to set up and analyze a crank part, as shown in Figure 4–133. The crank arms are thin-walls. The part could be analyzed using solid elements. However, it is more efficient to idealize any thin-walled features using shell elements.

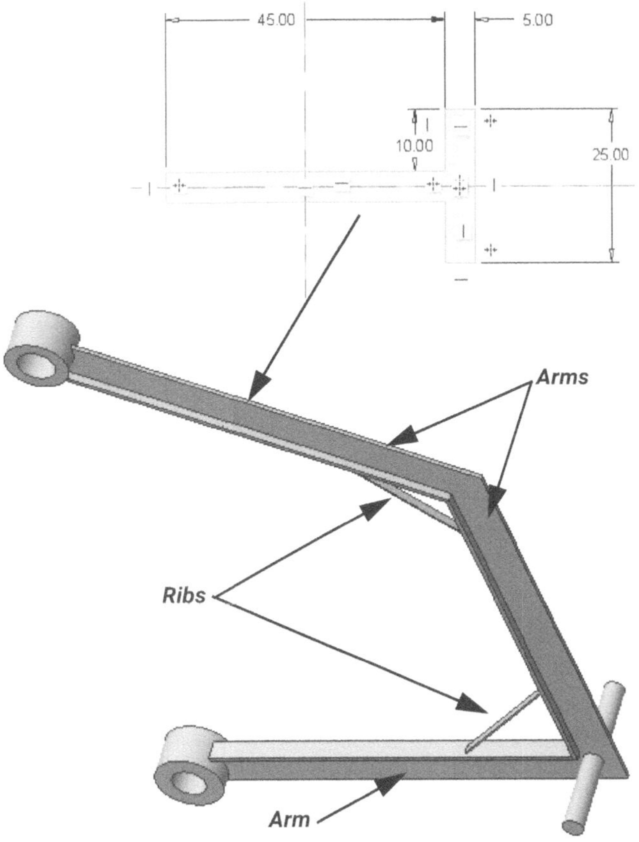

Figure 4–133

Modeling Tasks

Task 1: Open the part.

1. Set the working directory to **Chapter04**, if required.
2. Open **solid_shell.prt**.
3. Set the model display as follows:
    - *(Datum Display Filters)*: All Off
    - *(Spin Center)*: Off
    - *(Display Style)*: (Shading With Edges)

    The part displays as shown in Figure 4–134.

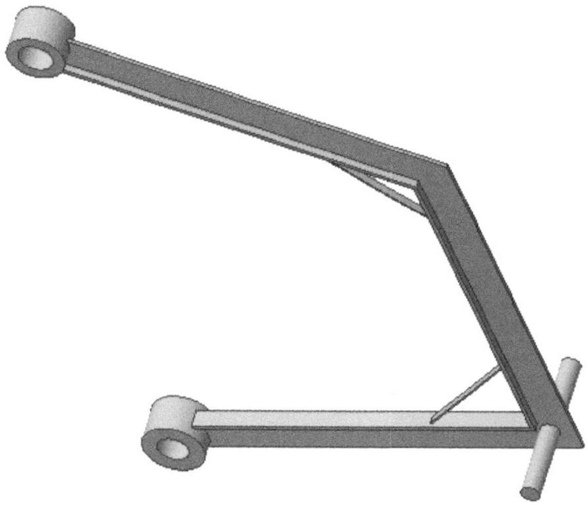

Figure 4–134

4. Ensure that the unit system is set to **mmNs**.
5. Switch to Creo Simulate environment.

Task 2: Apply the material.

1. Click (Materials). The *Materials* dialog box opens.
2. In the *Materials in Library* area, double-click on **Legacy-Materials**, then double-click on **ss.mtl** (stainless steel) to transfer **SS** to the *Materials in Model* area.

3. Review the material properties in the *Material Preview* area of the dialog box.

   The following values are the default material properties for stainless steel (SS):

   - *Poisson:* **0.3**
   - *Young's modulus:* **193053 MPa**
   - *Density:* **7.74372e-9 tonne/mm3**

4. Click **OK** to close the *Materials* dialog box.
5. Click (Material Assignment) to assign stainless steel to the part.
6. Using the *Simulation Display* dialog box, toggle off the Material Assignment visualization.

Task 3: Define the shell elements.

The intent of this analysis is to use shell elements to model the arms of the crank, while using solid elements to model the end bosses and the pin. The wall and flange thickness in the arms of the crank is 5mm. You will use the **Detect Shell Pairs** tool to automatically create the shell pairs in those areas.

1. In the *Refine Model* tab, expand the *Shell Pair* drop-down list and select **Detect Shell Pairs**. The *Auto Detect Shell Pairs* dialog box opens, as shown in Figure 4–135.

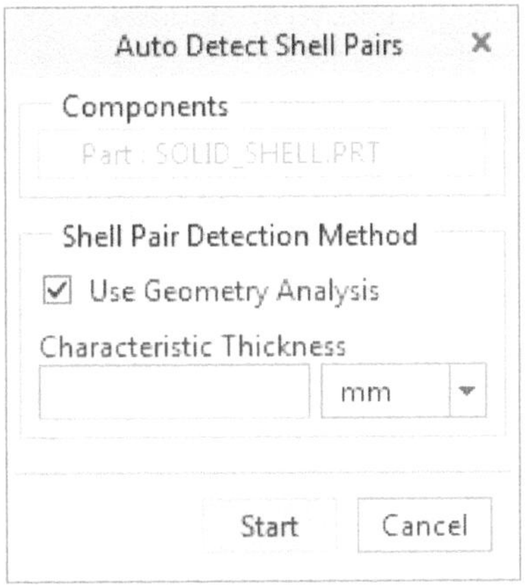

Figure 4–135

2. In the *Characteristic Thickness* field, enter **6** and click **Start**. Creo Simulate runs the automatic detection algorithm and closes the *Auto Detect Shell Pairs* dialog box.

   Note: *Creo Simulate will pair all of the parallel surfaces in the model that are closer than 6mm.*

3. Check the *Model Tree*. Six shell pairs should be displayed in the *Model Tree*, in the **Idealizations>Shell Pairs** branch.

4. In the *Refine Model* tab, in the *AutoGEM* area, click (Review Geometry) to open the *Simulation Geometry* dialog box. Select the required options, as shown in Figure 4–136.

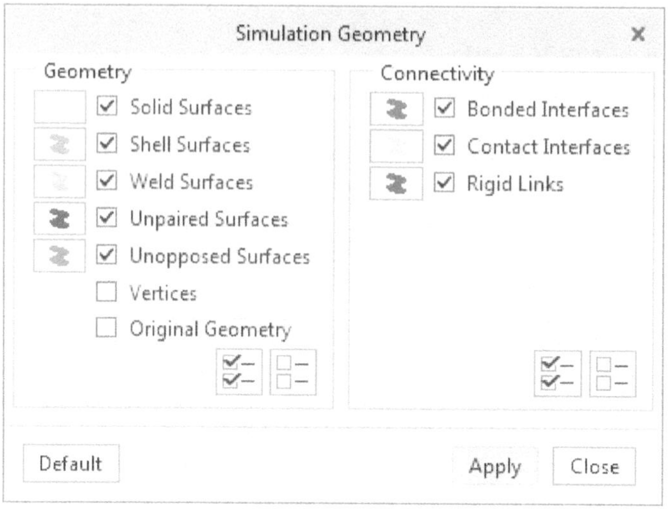

Figure 4–136

5. Click **Apply**. The model displays as shown in Figure 4–137.

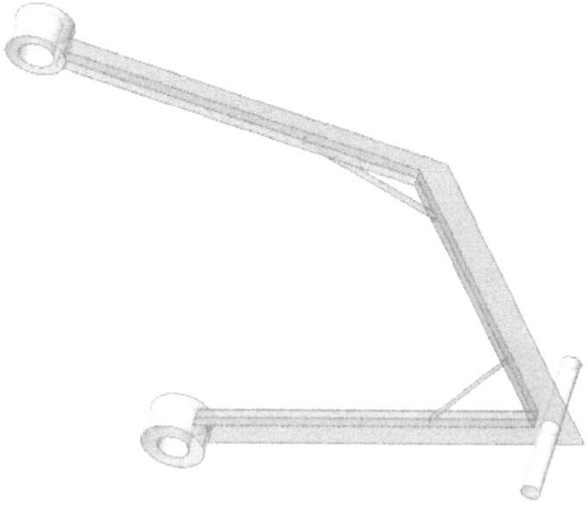

Figure 4–137

Verify that the end bosses and pin display in gray (these are the uncompressed areas), and that the thin-walled arms display in green (these are the shell pairs compressed to a midsurface).

6. In the *Simulation Geometry* dialog box, click **Close**.

Task 4: Mesh the model.

1. Expand the *AutoGEM* drop-down list and verify that the **Solid/Midsurface** option is enabled, as shown in Figure 4–138.

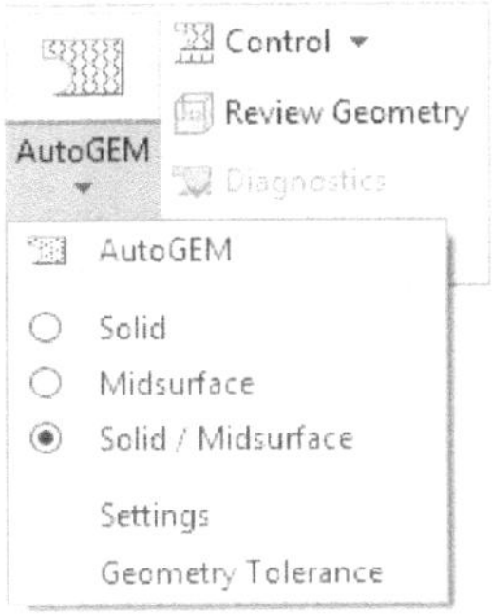

Figure 4–138

Note: *The* ***Solid/Midsurface*** *option will create shell elements in the compressed areas, while creating solid elements in the rest of the model.*

2. Expand the *AutoGEM* drop-down list and select **Settings**. The *AutoGEM Settings* dialog box opens. Clear the **Create Links Where Needed** option, as shown in Figure 4–139.

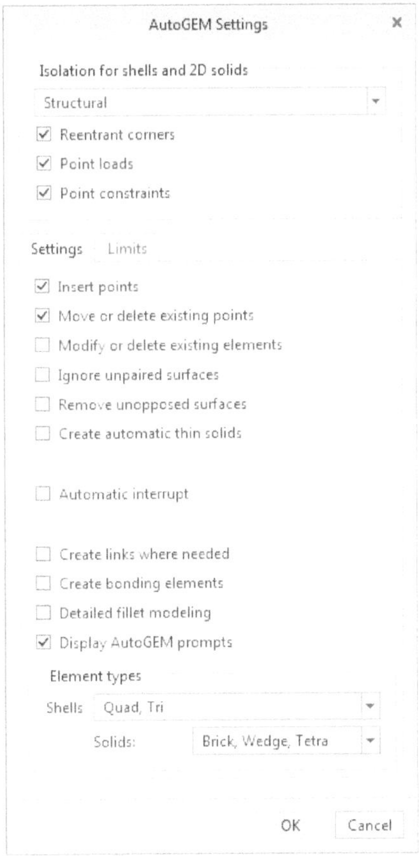

Figure 4–139

The Links in Creo Simulate are used to ensure the connectivity of the shell and solid elements along rotational degrees of freedom, so the shells attached to solids do not rotate like on a hinge. The Links can significantly increase the analysis runtime.

Links are only required if you have a shell in your model that is connected to a solid along a straight line. In the crank model, shells are connected to solids along T-shaped lines. Therefore, Links are not required.

3. Click **OK**.
4. Click (AutoGEM). The *AutoGEM* dialog box opens, as shown in Figure 4–140.

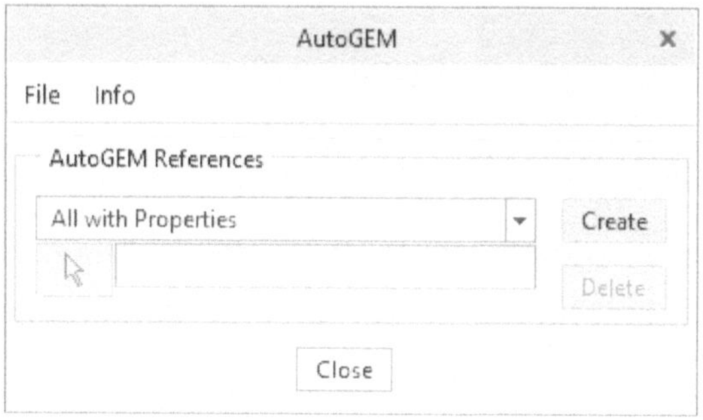

Figure 4–140

5. Expand the *AutoGEM References* drop-down list, select **All with Properties**, and click **Create**.

   Note: *The* ***All with Properties*** *option requires that materials be applied before meshing.*

6. The *AutoGEM Summary* and *Diagnostics* dialog boxes open, as shown in Figure 4–141.

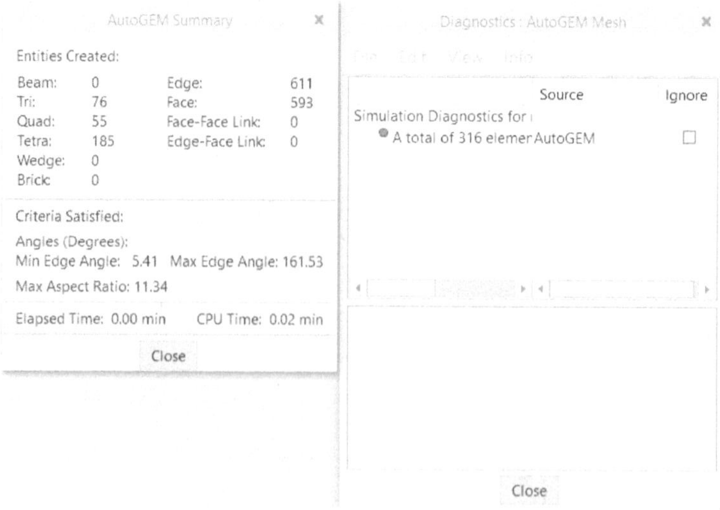

Figure 4–141

In the *AutoGEM Summary* dialog box, note that the AutoGEM has now created both the solid elements (approximately 185 Tetra) and shell elements (76 Tri and 55 Quad).

7. Close both the *AutoGEM Summary* and *Diagnostics* boxes, but do not close the *AutoGEM* dialog box yet. The model displays as shown in Figure 4–142.

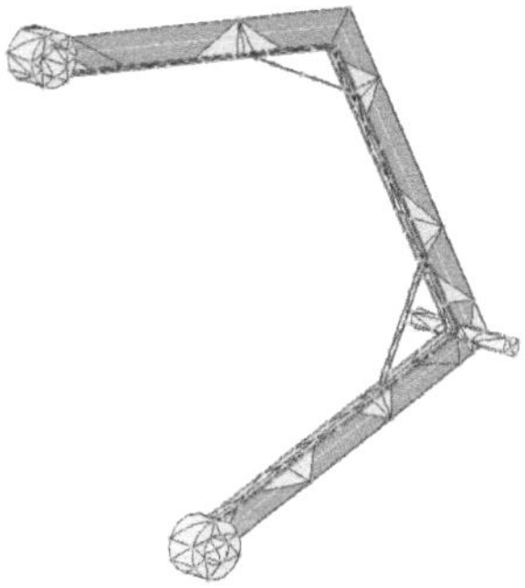

Figure 4–142

Note that two end bosses and the pin have been meshed onto solid elements (displayed in blue), while the arms have been meshed onto shell elements (displayed in green).

8. Click **Close** to close the *AutoGEM* dialog box and save the mesh.

Task 5: Apply loads to the model.

In this task, you will apply a bearing load on the hole in the boss shown in Figure 4–143. The bearing load has a resultant force in a specified direction (in this case, the negative Y-direction in the WCS). The bearing load is applied normal to the bearing surface in a non-uniform distribution. The bearing load simulates a lateral load that is exerted on a hole by a shaft placed in the hole.

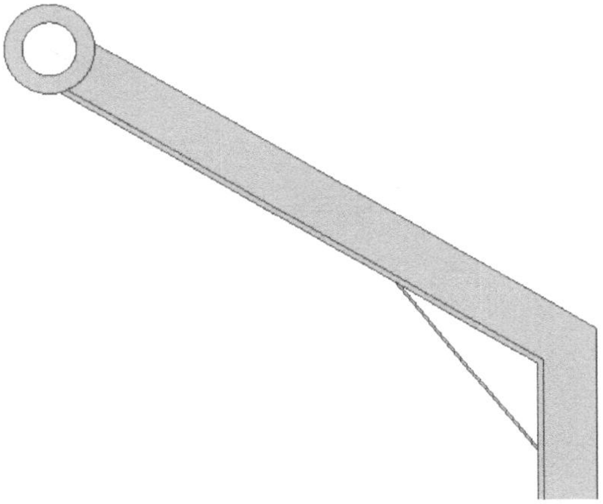

Figure 4–143

1. In the *Loads* area of the *Home* tab, click (Bearing). The *Bearing Load* dialog box opens, as shown in Figure 4–144.

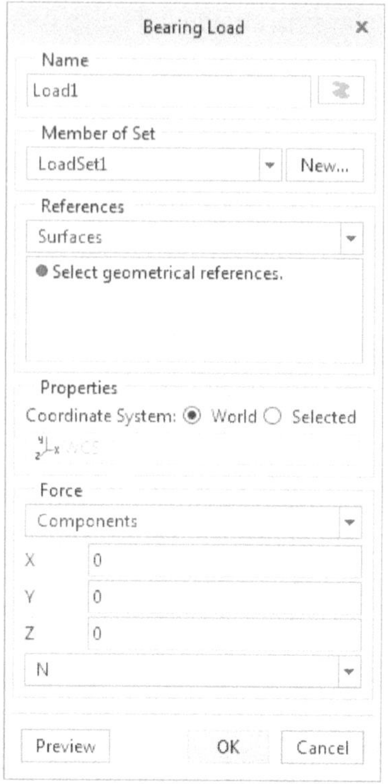

Figure 4–144

2. In the *Name* field, enter **b_load**.
3. Select the surface of the arm hole shown in Figure 4–145.

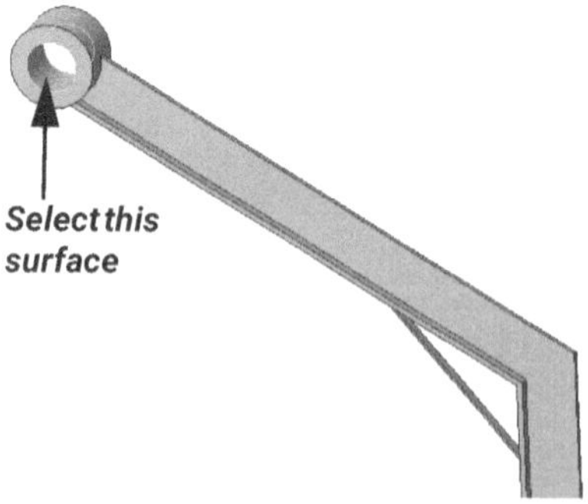

Figure 4–145

4. In the *Y* field, enter **-500**.

5. Click **Preview** to display the bearing load distribution, as shown in Figure 4–146.

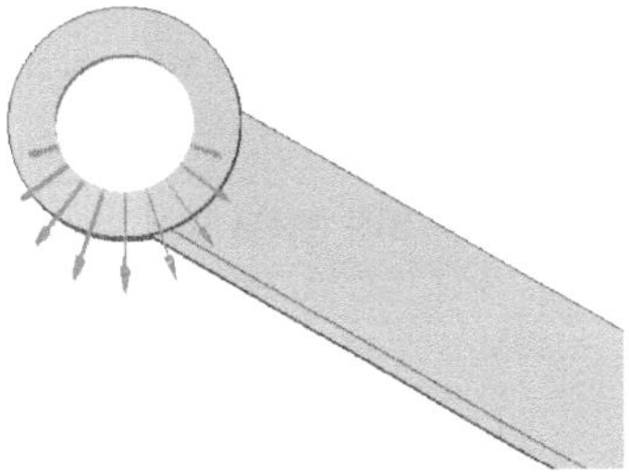

Figure 4–146

6. Click **OK**. The bearing load displays as shown in Figure 4–147.

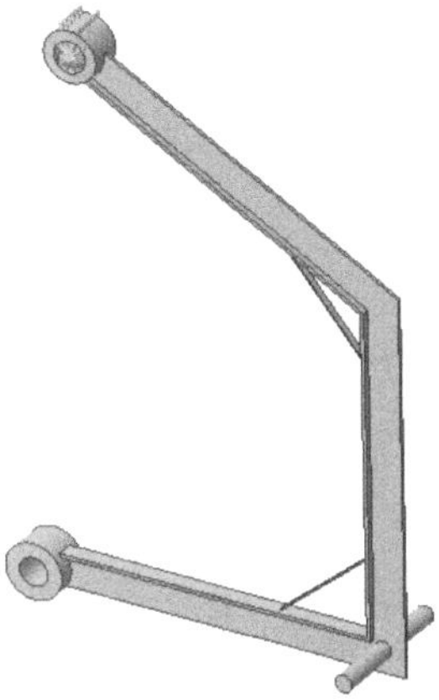

Figure 4–147

Task 6: Apply constraints.

In this task, you will constrain the movement of the central rod and the end boss of the crank arms, as shown in Figure 4–148.

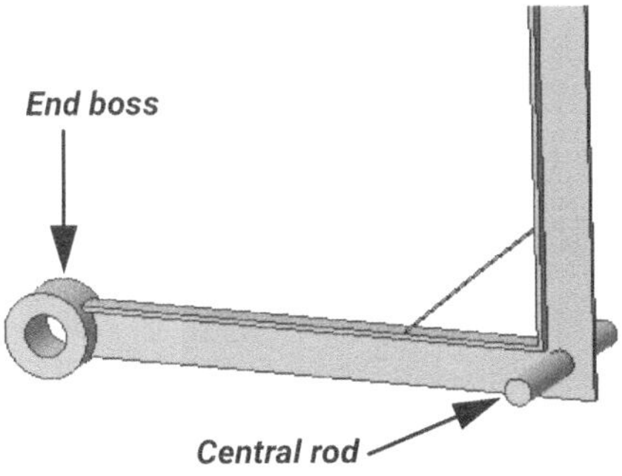

Figure 4–148

You will constrain each cylindrical surface against radial and axial motion, but enable rotation around their axes. This can be done using **Pin** constraint.

1. Select the cylindrical surface of the central rod (shown in Figure 4–148).
2. In the mini-toolbar, click (Pin). The *Pin Constraint* dialog box opens.
3. In the *Name* field, enter **rod**. Constrain the axial translation and leave the rotation free, as shown in Figure 4–149.

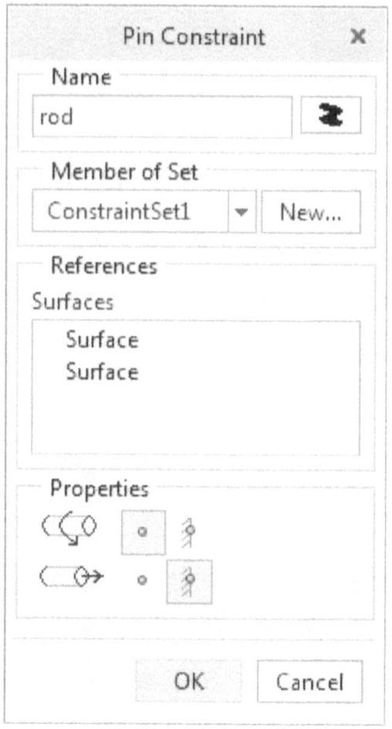

Figure 4–149

> **Note:** *Fixing the axial direction and freeing the rotation simulates the rod being supported by a sleeve bearing or bushing.*

4. Click **OK**. The pin constraint displays as shown in Figure 4–150.

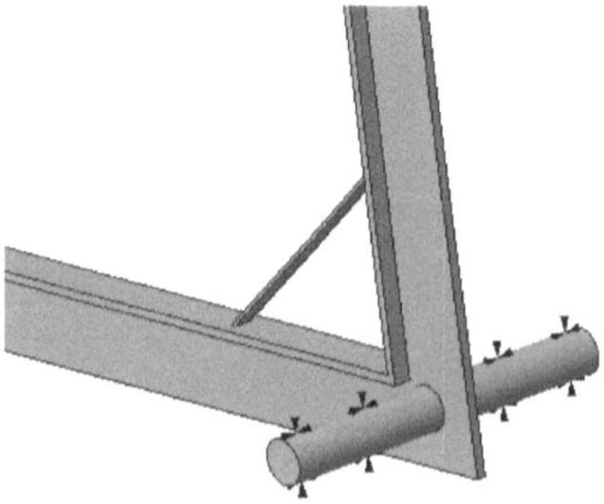

Figure 4–150

5. Select the hole surface in the end boss (shown previously in Figure 4–148).

   Note: *Fixing the axial direction and freeing the rotation simulates the end boss being supported by a pin.*

6. In the mini-toolbar, click (Pin).
7. In the *Name* field, enter **end_boss**. Constrain the axial translation and leave the rotation free, as shown in Figure 4–151.

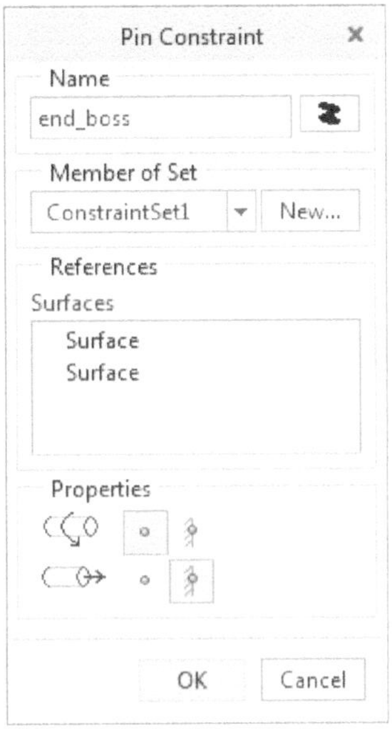

Figure 4–151

8. Click **OK**. The pin constraint displays as shown in Figure 4–152.

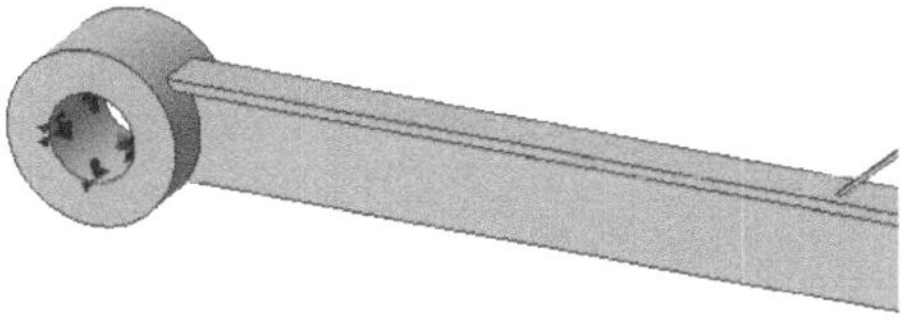

Figure 4–152

Analysis Tasks

Task 7: Solve the model using the Single-Pass Adaptive convergence option.

1. Create a *Static Analysis* named **crank_shell**.
2. Select the **Single-Pass Adaptive** convergence method.

3. In the *Output* tab, increase the *Plotting Grid* value to **10**.

   Note: *The Plotting Grid is a grid of points that Creo Simulate uses to display results within the elements. A higher density plotting grid is recommended to obtain smoother looking result plots.*

4. Start the analysis run and wait until it finishes.

5. Expand the *Run Status* window and scroll up or down to the *RMS Stress Error Estimates* area and note that the analysis converged to approximately 6.5% RMS Stress Error, as shown in Figure 4–153.

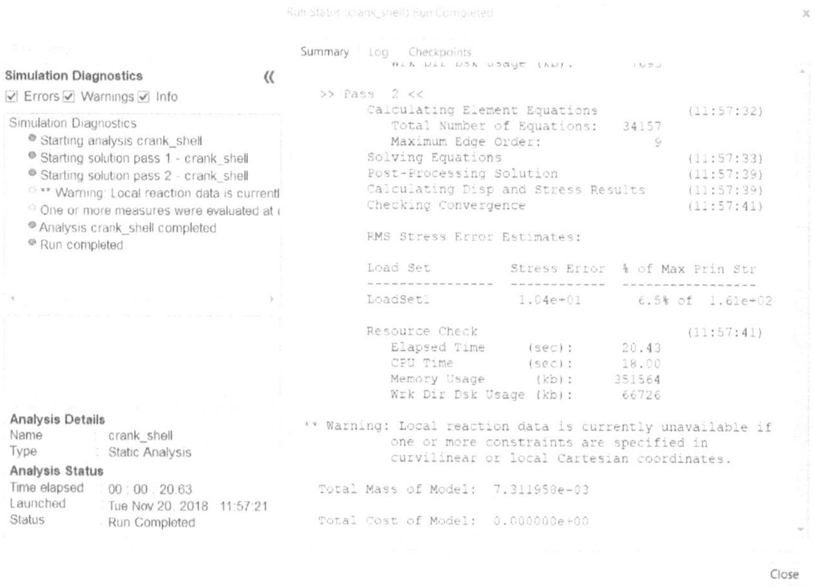

Figure 4–153

Ignore the warning in the *Simulation Diagnostics* area regarding the local reaction data. This is just a notification that force reactions are not available on pin constraints.

6. Close the *Run Status* window.

Results Tasks

Task 8: Display and animate the displacement results.

1. In the *Analyses and Design Studies* dialog box, click (Review Results). The *Result Window Definition* dialog box opens.
2. In the *Name* field, enter **deformation**.
3. Expand the *Quantity* tab drop-down list and select **Displacement**.

4. In the *Display Options* tab, select the **Deformed**, **Overlay Undeformed**, **Show Element Edges**, and **Animate** options.
5. Click **OK and Show**. The Displacement Magnitude result plot is displayed and animated.
6. Zoom in on the rod. Note that the rod's rotation is not restricted, as if the rod was supported by sleeve bearings or bushings. This is because you applied the pin constraint in a previous task.
7. Stop the animation at Frame 5. The result plot displays as shown in Figure 4–154.

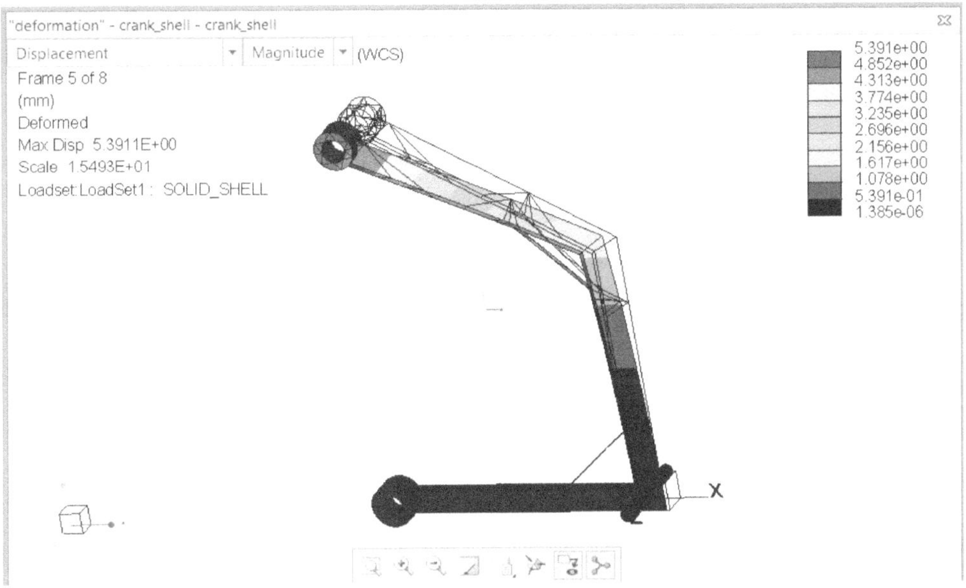

Figure 4–154

Note that the maximum displacement magnitude under the given loading is approximately 5.4mm.

Task 9: Display the stress results.

1. In the *Home* tab, click (Copy). The *Result Window Definition* dialog box opens.
2. In the *Name* field, enter **von_mises**.
3. In the *Display options* tab, clear the **Deformed**, **Overlay Undeformed**, **Show Element Edges**, and **Animate** options.
4. Select the *Quantity* tab and select **Stress** from the *Quantity* drop-down list.
5. Click **OK and Show**. The Stress von Mises result plot displays along with the Displacement Magnitude result plot.

6. In the *View* tab, click (Show). In the *Display Result Window* dialog box, clear **deformation**, as shown in Figure 4–155.

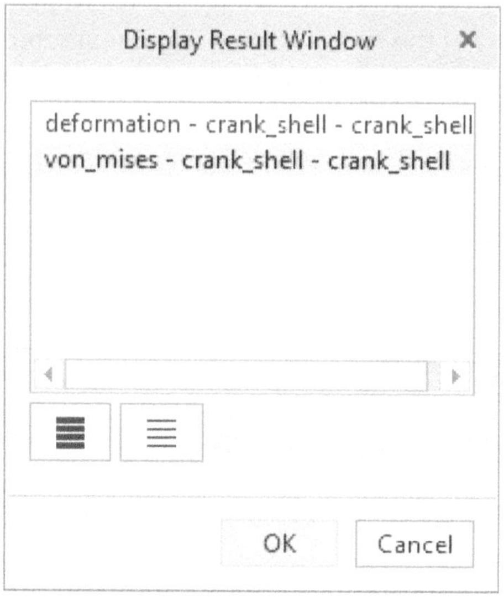

Figure 4–155

7. Click **OK**. The von Mises stress plot displays as shown in Figure 4–156.

Figure 4–156

8. In the *View* tab, expand the *Appearance* group and select **Visibilities**. In the *Visibilities* window, clear the **Labels** and **Coordinate Systems** options, as shown in Figure 4–157. Click **Close** when finished.

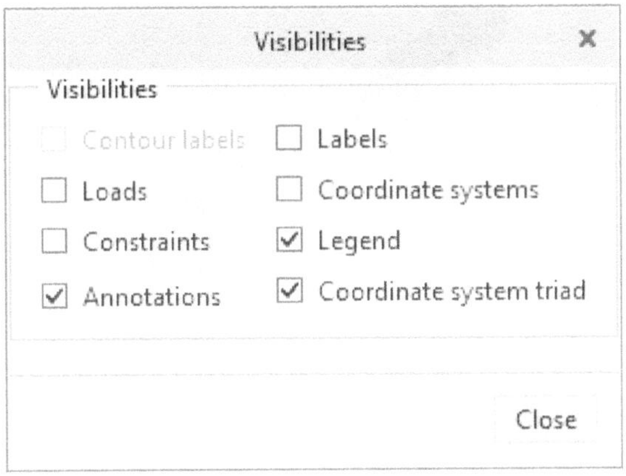

Figure 4–157

9. In the *Format* tab, select (Edit). In the *Edit Legend* dialog box, change the *Max value* to **80**, as shown in Figure 4–158.

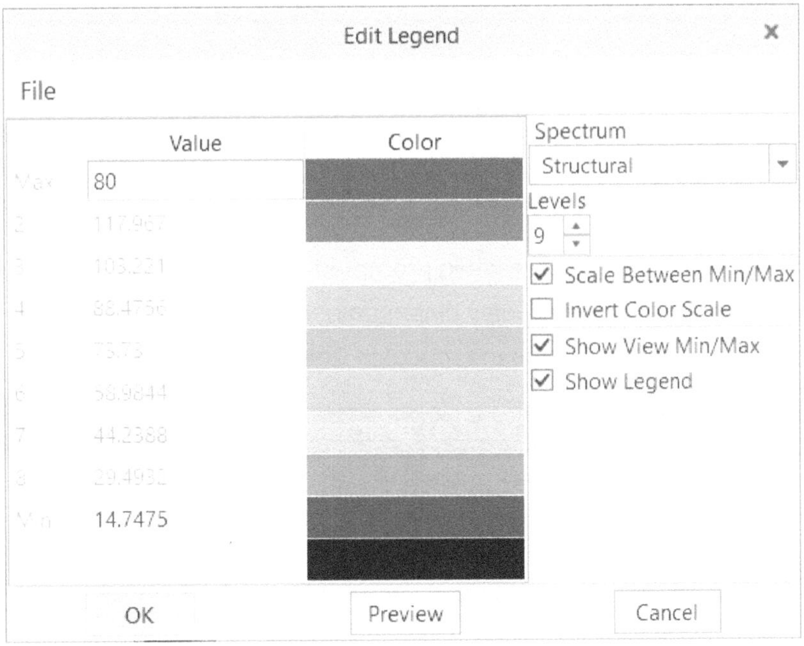

Figure 4–158

10. Click **OK**. The von Mises stress result plot displays as shown in Figure 4–159.

Figure 4–159

Note that the result window is now less cluttered and that it is easier to examine the results.

Task 10: Save and close the model.

1. Select **File>Close**. Click **Don't Save** when prompted to save the results.
2. Close the *Analyses and Design Studies* dialog box.
3. Exit Creo Simulate. Save and close the model in Creo Parametric.

End of practice

Practice 4e
Analysis of a Sheet Metal Bracket

Practice Objectives

- Create shell pairs.
- Apply loads, constraints, and material properties.
- Set up and run a Multi-Pass Adaptive analysis.
- Display the results.

In this practice, you will perform a static stress analysis on the sheet metal bracket shown in Figure 4–160, with minimum instruction.

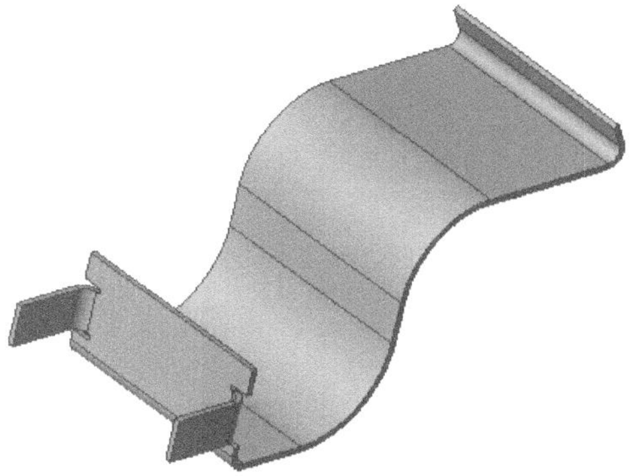

Figure 4–160

Task 1: Create shell pairs.

1. Set the working directory to **Chapter04**, if required.
2. Open **sm_bracket.prt** and launch Creo Simulate.
3. Set the model display as follows:
   - *(Datum Display Filters)*: All Off
   - *(Spin Center)*: Off
   - *(Display Style)*: (Shading With Edges)
4. Using the **Detect Shell Pairs** tool, create shell pairs.

   Note: *The part is sheet metal, therefore there is no need to use the* ***Use Geometry Analysis*** *option.*

Task 2: Apply material, loads, and constraints.

1. Apply the SS material:
    - *Tensile Yield Stress:* **50 ksi**
    - *Failure Criterion:* **Distortion Energy (von Mises)**
2. Fully constrain both tabs and the back surface of the bracket, as shown in Figure 4–161.

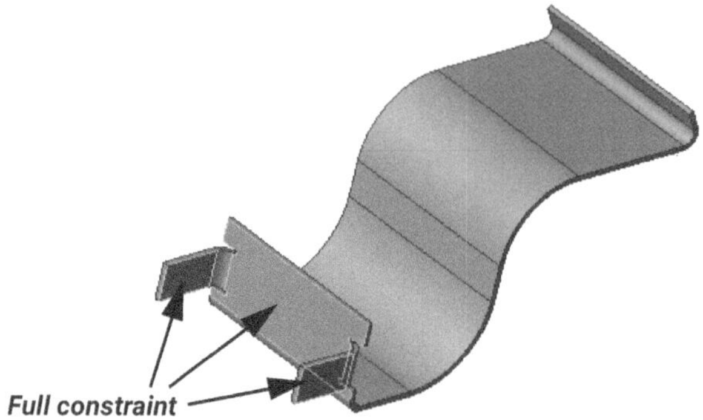

Figure 4–161

3. Apply **100lbf** load in the positive Y-direction to the edge shown in Figure 4–162.

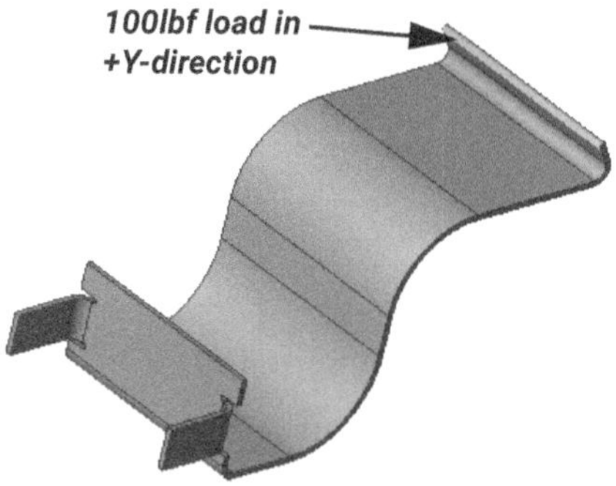

Figure 4–162

Task 3: Set up and run the analysis.

1. Create a new static analysis with the following parameters:
    - *Analysis name:* **sm_bracket**
    - *Convergence method:* **Multi-Pass Adaptive**
    - *Maximum Polynomial Order:* **9**
    - *Percent Convergence:* **5**
    - *Plotting Grid:* **10**
2. Run the analysis.
3. Display the *Status* window. Note the RMS Stress Error value.

Task 4: Visualize the analysis results.

1. Visualize and animate the **Displacement Magnitude** fringe plot.
    - Does the part deform according to the applied loads and constraints?
2. Visualize the **Displacement Y** fringe plot.
    - What is the maximum deflection of the part in the direction of the load?
3. Display the **von Mises Stress** fringe plot. Find the location of the maximum stress.
4. Does the maximum stress exceed the yield strength of the material?

End of practice

Chapter 5

Beams and Frames

Beam elements in FEA are one-dimensional idealizations of 3D parts that are long compared to the size of their cross-section. Beam idealizations can be used to model 3D beams and frames.

Learning Objectives

- Understand the beam idealization assumptions.
- Create beam model geometry.
- Define beam attributes.
- Create beam sections.
- Understand beam coordinate systems.
- Understand beam releases.
- Understand beam analysis results.

5.1 Beam Idealization

One of the common types of FEA idealization is beam idealization. Beam idealizations are used to simplify structures consisting of slender parts, such as frames and trusses. Beam models are less computationally intensive and can be solved much faster than solid models.

Beam elements are 1D, wireframe-like elements used to represent parts that are long in comparison to the size of their cross-section. While there are no absolutes regarding permissible ratio between the length of the part and the cross-section size (also called slenderness ratio), the rule of thumb typically recommended in the literature is to use beam idealization for the parts with slenderness ratio of 10 or greater.

In Creo Simulate, beam elements are based on the Timoshenko beam theory, which includes transversal shear effects in addition to bending. The deformation of the beam is defined by three translational displacements and three rotational angles on the beam's centroid line, and the stress distribution in the beam's cross-section is defined by the normal force P, two shear forces Vy and Vz, two bending moments My and Mz, and torsional moment Mx, as shown in Figure 5–1.

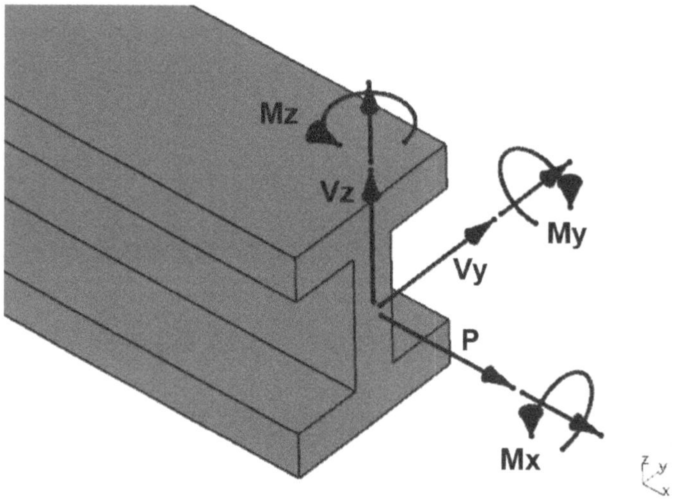

Figure 5–1

An example of a solid model that could be simplified using a beam idealization is shown in Figure 5–2.

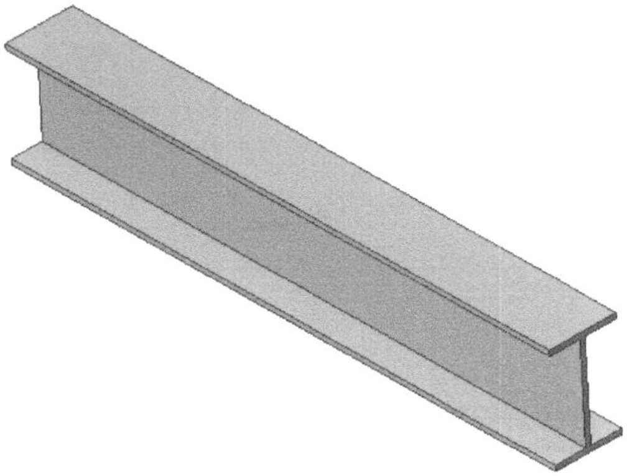

Figure 5–2

Geometrically, a beam model in FEA is represented by a wireframe line or a curve with a cross-section assigned to it. Therefore, the beam idealization for the part shown in Figure 5–2 would look as shown in Figure 5–3.

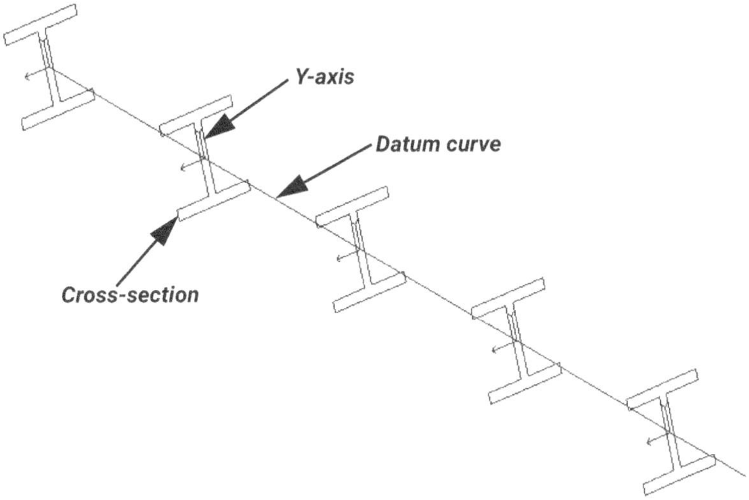

Figure 5–3

Different beam section shapes can be used for different purposes. In the example shown in Figure 5–4, a hollow circle section is used for a frame.

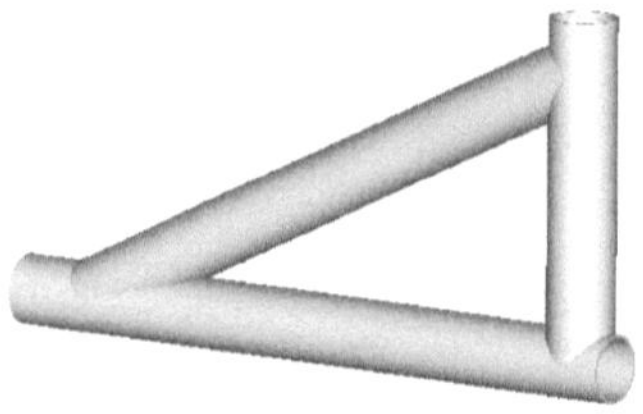

Figure 5–4

The idealized model of the frame shown in Figure 5–4 is represented by a network of datum curves with a hollow circle cross-section assigned to the curves, as shown in Figure 5–5. The beam elements are then automatically placed on the datum curves.

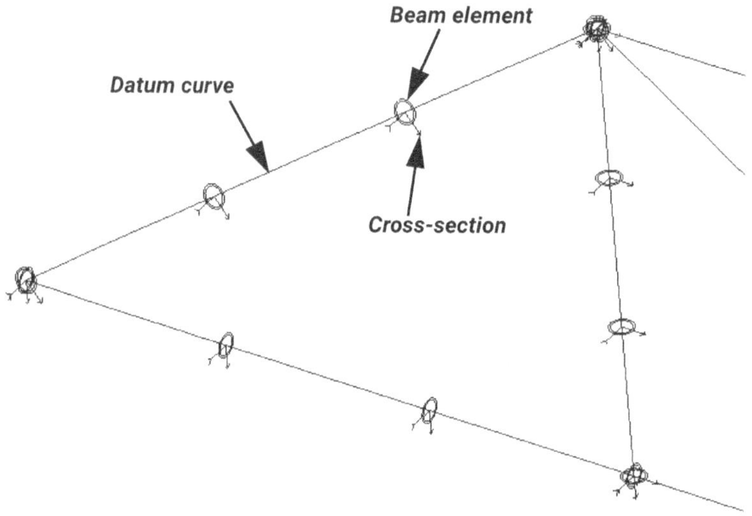

Figure 5–5

Creo Simulate does not have the tools to automatically convert the beam or frame solid model into a network of centroid curves, which is what is required for the beam FEA idealization. The centroid curves must be created manually by the user, using either datum curves or datum points.

Once the wireframe geometry for the beam idealization is created, you must also define the attributes of the beam elements, such as material and cross-section dimensions and orientation, before running the analysis.

5.2 Beam Definitions

Use the following steps to define the attributes (e.g., material, beam cross-section, etc.) of the beam:

1. In the *Refine Model* tab, click (Beam). The *Beam Definition* dialog box opens, as shown in Figure 5–6.

Figure 5–6

2. In the *Name* field, enter a name for the beam.

3. Define the geometry references. References define the underlying curve. The following types of geometry references are available:
    - Edge(s)/Curve(s)
    - Point-Point
    - Point-Surface (Projection)
    - Point-Edge (Projection)
    - Chain
    - Point-Point Pairs
4. Expand the *Material* drop-down list and select an option to define the material of the beam.
5. Define the direction of the Beam Action Coordinate System (BACS) Y-axis by selecting a point, axis, or vector in WCS.
6. Define the type and dimensions of the beam section.
7. Define the orientation of the beam cross-section relative to BACS.
8. Define the degrees of freedom to release at the beam's ends.
9. Click **OK** to complete the beam definition.

5.3 Beam Sections

Creo Simulate has 11 standard types of beams that you can use for your analysis. These beams are shown in Figure 5–7.

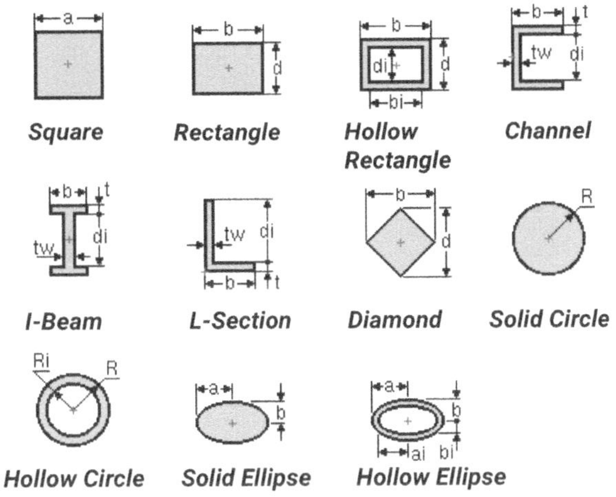

Figure 5–7

The cross-sectional properties, such as area, moments of inertia, etc., can be previewed in Creo Simulate, as shown in Figure 5–8.

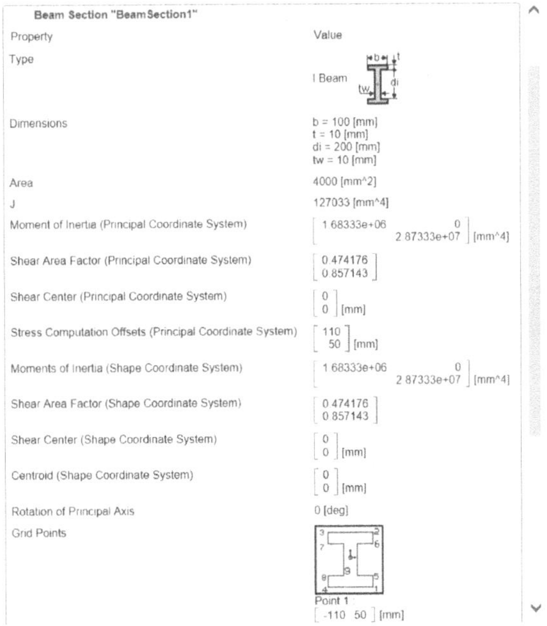

Beam Section "BeamSection1"

Property	Value
Type	I Beam
Dimensions	b = 100 [mm] t = 10 [mm] di = 200 [mm] tw = 10 [mm]
Area	4000 [mm^2]
J	127033 [mm^4]
Moment of Inertia (Principal Coordinate System)	[1.68333e+06 0; 2.87333e+07] [mm^4]
Shear Area Factor (Principal Coordinate System)	[0.474176; 0.857143]
Shear Center (Principal Coordinate System)	[0; 0] [mm]
Stress Computation Offsets (Principal Coordinate System)	[110; 50] [mm]
Moments of Inertia (Shape Coordinate System)	[1.68333e+06 0; 2.87333e+07] [mm^4]
Shear Area Factor (Shape Coordinate System)	[0.474176; 0.857143]
Shear Center (Shape Coordinate System)	[0; 0] [mm]
Centroid (Shape Coordinate System)	[0; 0] [mm]
Rotation of Principal Axis	0 [deg]
Grid Points	Point 1: [-110 50] [mm]

Figure 5–8

The *Grid Points* (also called *stress recovery points*) are the locations in the section for which Creo Simulate calculates and displays the stress results.

For the custom beam sections, you can use a Creo sketch. Two options are available here:

- **Sketched Solid:** Creates a closed solid section.
- **Sketched Thin:** Creates an open or closed section with thickness.

An example of a Sketched Solid section is shown in Figure 5–9. Note that the grid points must be created in the sketch as construction points.

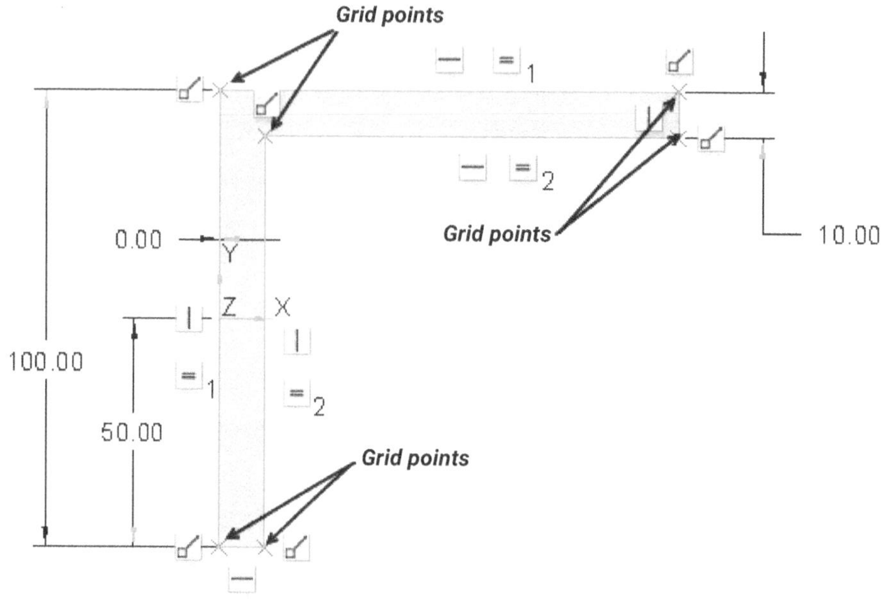

Figure 5–9

5.4 Beam Coordinate Systems

The beam orientation in 3D space, such as the direction of the beam's axis and the rotation of the cross-section about the beam's axis, affects the stiffness and strength properties of the beam, hence affects the analysis results. Therefore, with beam elements it is necessary to set their orientations relative to the World Coordinate System (WCS).

In Creo Simulate, the beam's orientation in 3D is defined using two auxiliary coordinate systems:

- Beam Action Coordinate System (BACS)
- Beam Shape Coordinate System (BSCS)

Beam Action Coordinate System

The beam resultant forces and moments, shown previously in Figure 5–1, are calculated and reported by the software in the Beam Action Coordinate System (BACS), shown in Figure 5–10. Also, Beam Releases are defined in the BACS.

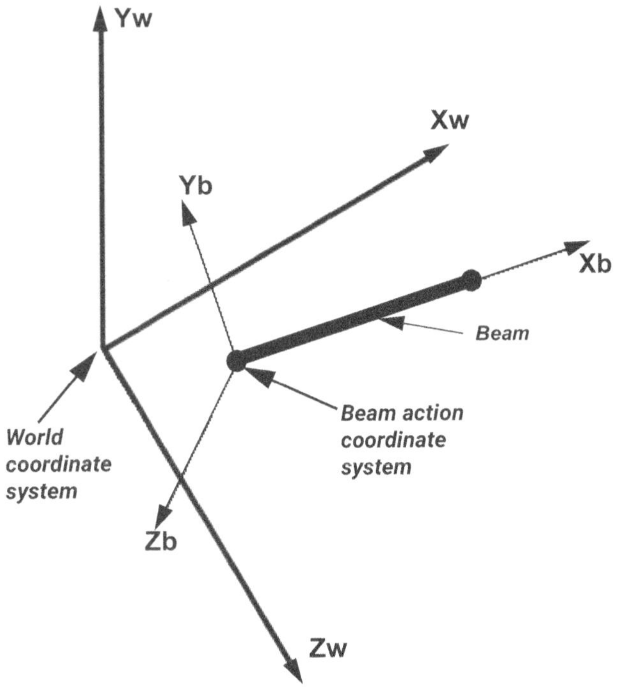

Figure 5–10

The BACS **Xb**, **Yb**, **Zb** is a local coordinate system associated with every beam element, as shown in Figure 5–10.

- The origin is located on the axis of the beam.

- The **Xb** axis is parallel to the datum curve used to create the beam element.
- The **Yb** and **Zb** axes are perpendicular to the beam and lie in the plane of the beam's cross-section.
- The **Yb** direction is controlled by the user and must be specified in the *Beam Definition* dialog box relatively to the World Coordinate System (WCS) **Xw, Yw, Zw**.
- The **Zb** direction is calculated by the software as a cross-product of **Xb** and **Yb**.

The following options are available for specifying the Yb direction:

- Vector in WCS
- Point
- Axis

Essentially, all the orientation options boil down to defining the **XbYb** plane passing through the beam and a vector or a point, as shown in Figure 5–11. The **Yb** axis is then drawn in the **XbYb** plane, perpendicular to the **Xb** axis. The **Zb** axis is then obtained as a cross-product of **Xb** and **Yb**.

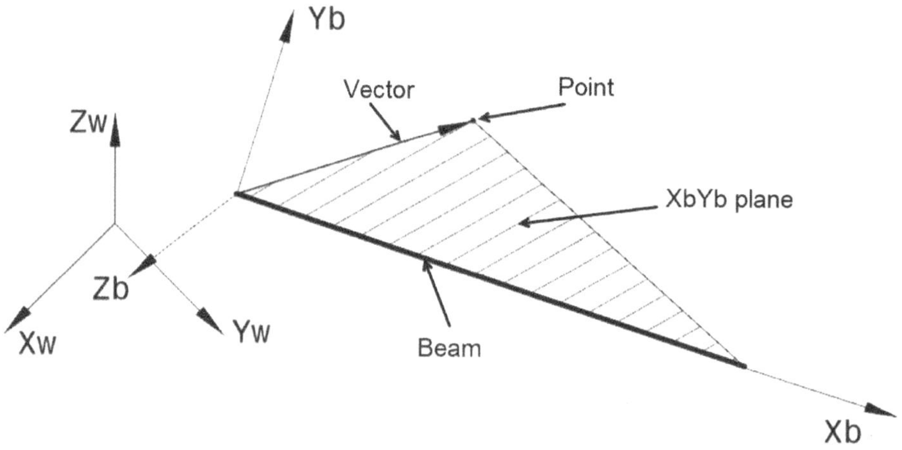

Figure 5–11

Some examples of the specification of the BACS Y-axis using vector components are shown in Figure 5–12.

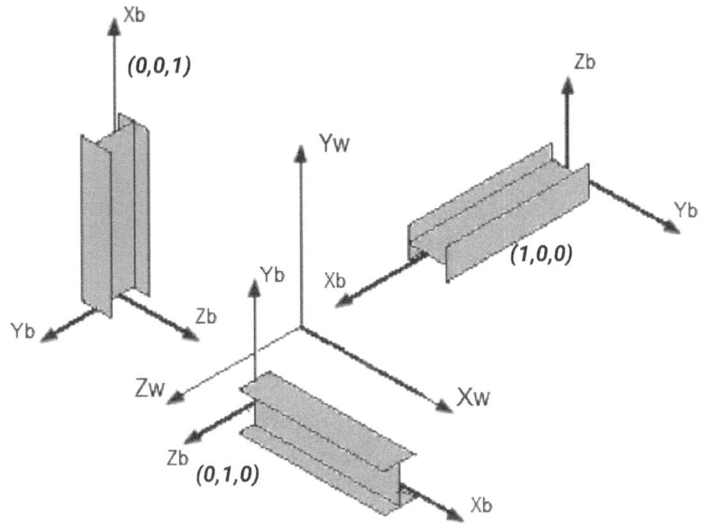

Figure 5–12

For curved beams (which must lie in a plane), the BACS X-axis lies along the length of the beam, tangent to the beam. The BACS Y-axis lies in the plane of the curved beam. The BACS Z-axis is perpendicular to the plane of the curved beam. The BACS Y-axis changes direction as the beam curves. Figure 5–13 shows an example of a curved beam.

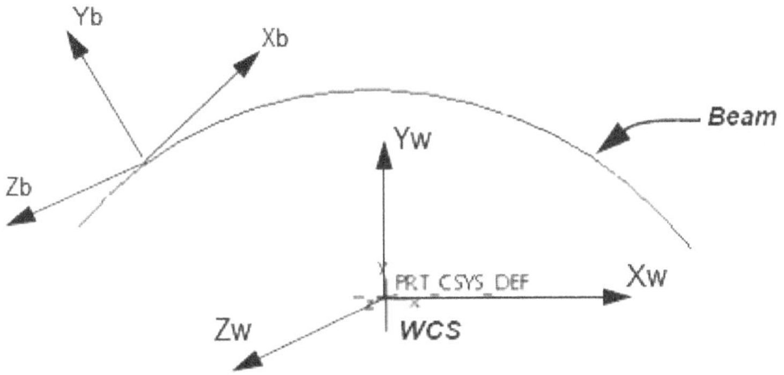

Figure 5–13

Beam Shape Coordinate System

Creo Simulate defines the beam cross-section shape and dimensions relative to the Beam Shape Coordinate System (BSCS) **Xs**, **Ys**, **Zs**, as shown in Figure 5–14. The **Xs** axis is along the length of the beam and is parallel to the BACS **Xb** axis. The **Ys** axis is always vertical and the **Zs** axis is always horizontal, the same as the Y- and X-axes in the sketcher.

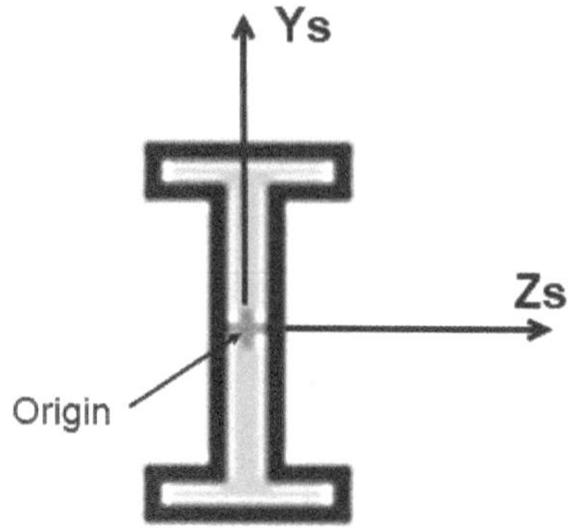

Figure 5–14

When Creo Simulate displays the beam section outline as part of the beam icon in the model window, it also draws the BSCS, with a Y-shape at the tip for the **Ys** axis and an arrow at the tip for the **Zs** axis, as shown in Figure 5–15.

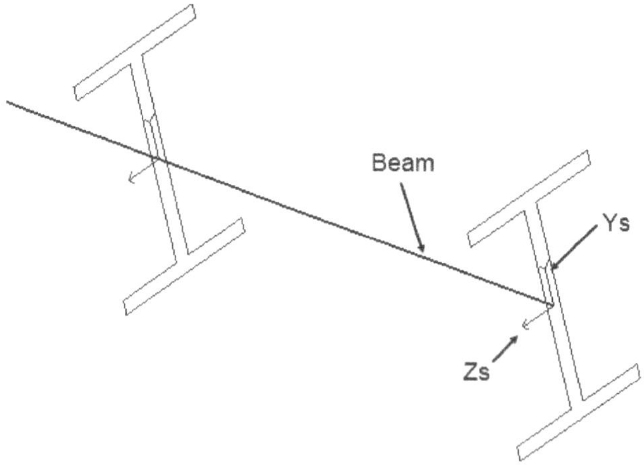

Figure 5–15

By default, the BSCS is coincident with the BACS. Optionally, you can offset the origin of the BSCS from the BACS using the values **Dy** and **Dz** and rotate the **Ys** and **Zs** axes about the axis of the beam using orientation angle **A**, as shown in Figure 5–16.

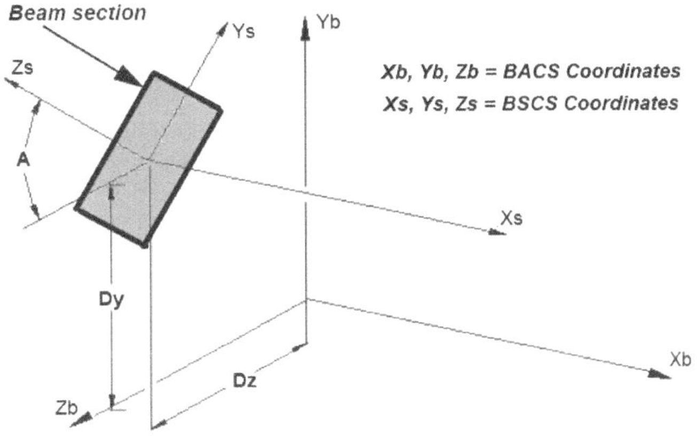

Figure 5–16

Offsetting or rotating the BSCS is optional and might only be needed in some specific cases. Consider the example of two square beams welded together, as shown in Figure 5–17.

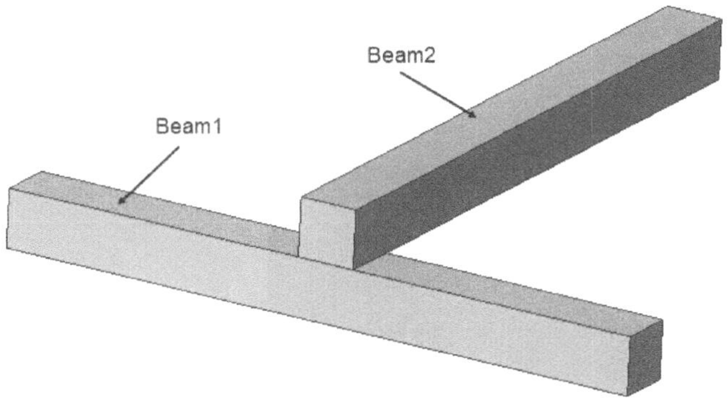

Figure 5–17

The centerlines of the beams do not intersect, as shown in Figure 5–18. This is a problem, because the datum curves in the beam FEA model must intersect in order to have the beams connected in the analysis.

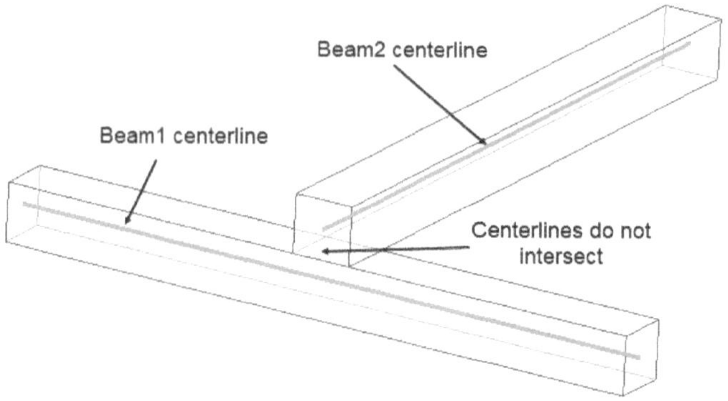

Figure 5–18

The solution is to use the intersecting datum curves as the reference geometry for the beams, while offsetting the section of the second beam off its datum curve by the half-height of the cross-section, as shown in Figure 5–19.

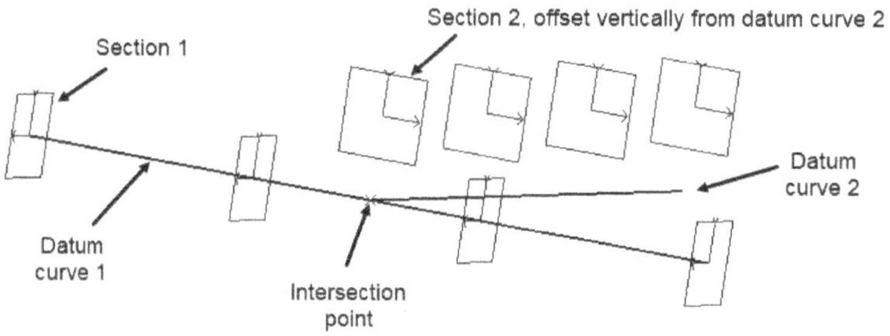

Figure 5–19

The shaded beam model in Creo Simulate is shown in Figure 5–20.

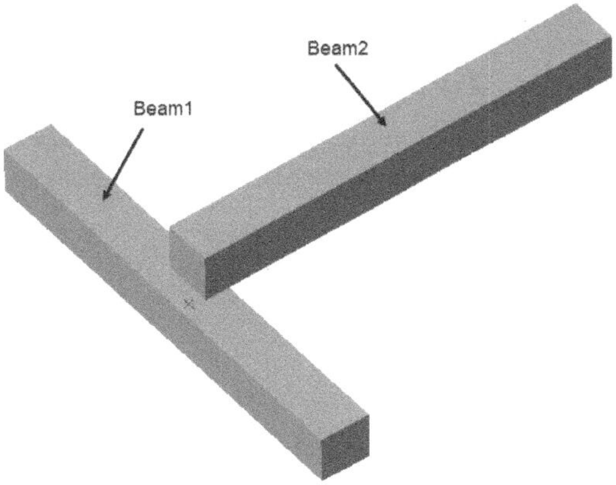

Figure 5–20

Use the following steps to position the origin of the BSCS relative to the BACS:

1. In the *Beam Definition* dialog box, click **More** next to the *Beam Orientation* field and click **New** to define a new beam orientation.
2. The *Beam Orientation Definition* dialog box opens, as shown in Figure 5–21.

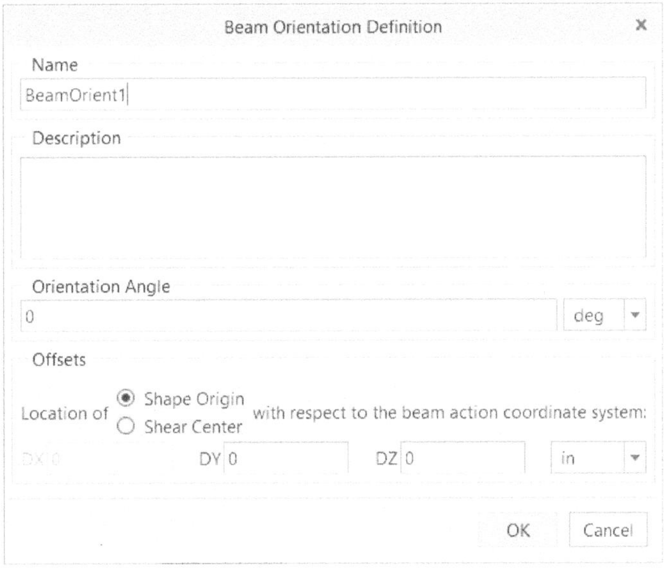

Figure 5–21

3. In the *Name* field, enter a name for the beam orientation.

   Note: *Shear Center is the point where a shear force can act without producing any twist in the beam's section. For symmetrical sections, the shear center coincides with the centroid point.*

4. Specify the beam section's rotation angle about the BACS X-axis.
5. Select the **Shape Origin** or **Shear Center** option to define how the software should interpret the offset values.
6. Define the values for each offset in the BACS Y- and Z-directions.
7. Click **OK** to complete the beam orientation definition.

5.5 Beam Releases

A beam release can be used to change the type of connection between adjacent beam elements.

The default (unreleased) connection models a rigid join type of connection between the beams. In a rigid join, all six components of force and moment at the end of one element are carried through the connection to the next element. This results in continuity of these internal forces and moments between the beam elements (except at constraints or point loads).

Consider an example of two beams welded to one another, as shown in Figure 5–22. The all-around weld creates a rigid join type of connection between **Beam1** and **Beam2**. The vertical force on the free end of **Beam2** creates a vertical bending moment at the join. This bending moment is then fully transferred, through the rigid join, to **Beam1**, which will cause **Beam1** to bend as well, and which is correct.

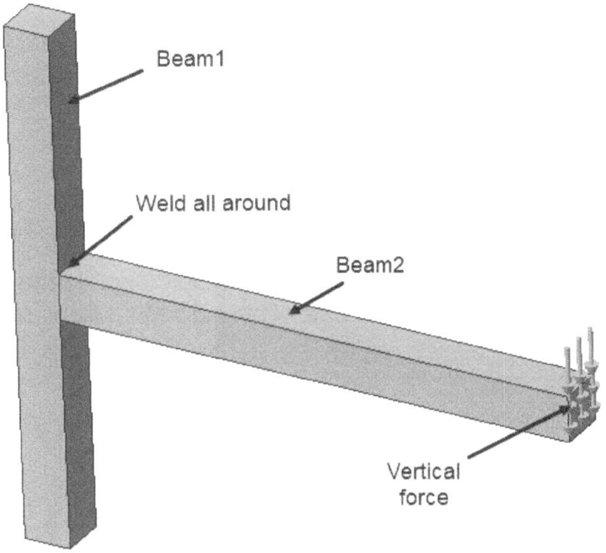

Figure 5–22

Consider a different example, in which the beams are connected through a pin, as shown in Figure 5–23. Since the pin connection will not transfer the vertical moment from **Beam2** to **Beam1**, **Beam1** will not bend under the vertical load on **Beam2**. Rather, **Beam2** will freely rotate around the axis of the pin. In such a case, the use of the default (unreleased) rigid join connection would be incorrect.

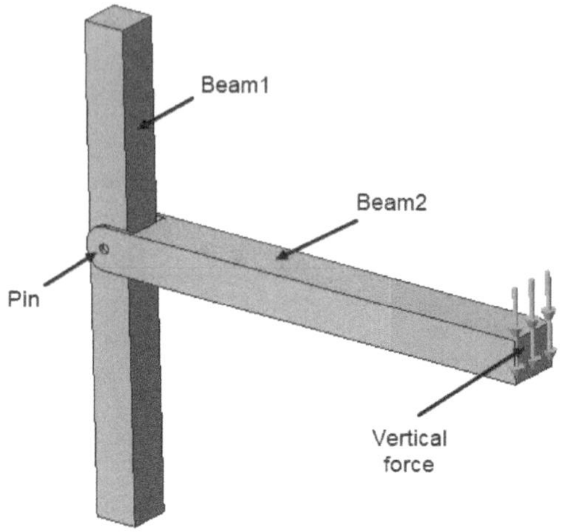

Figure 5–23

To model the pinned connection shown above in Figure 5–23, the rotational degree of freedom on the pinned end of **Beam2** must be released, which would disable the moment load transfer from **Beam2** to **Beam1** through the joint. The resulting Creo Simulate model is shown in Figure 5–24.

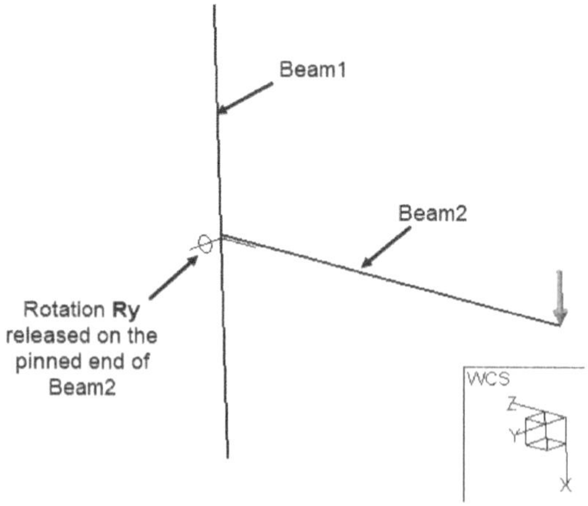

Figure 5–24

Use the following steps to release degrees of freedom on a beam:

1. In the *Beam Definition* dialog box, select either the *Start* or the *End* tab at the bottom of the dialog box, depending on which end of the beam you want to release the degrees of freedom.
2. Click **More** next to the *Beam Release* field and click **New** to define a new beam release.
3. The *Beam Release* dialog box opens, as shown in Figure 5–25.

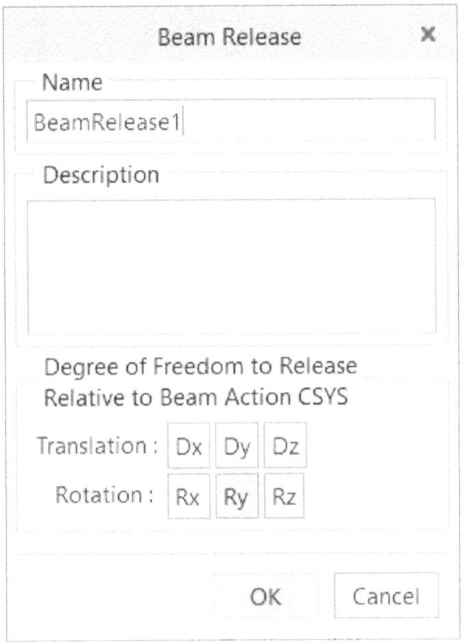

Figure 5–25

4. In the *Name* field, enter a name for the beam release.
5. Select the degrees of freedom to release. **Dx**, **Dy**, and **Dz** are translations, while **Rx**, **Ry**, and **Rz** are rotations.

   Note: *The released degrees of freedom are defined in the beam's BACS.*

6. Click **OK** to complete the beam release definition.

5.6 Beam Analysis Results

The beam analysis results are displayed on the wireframe model, as shown in Figure 5–26.

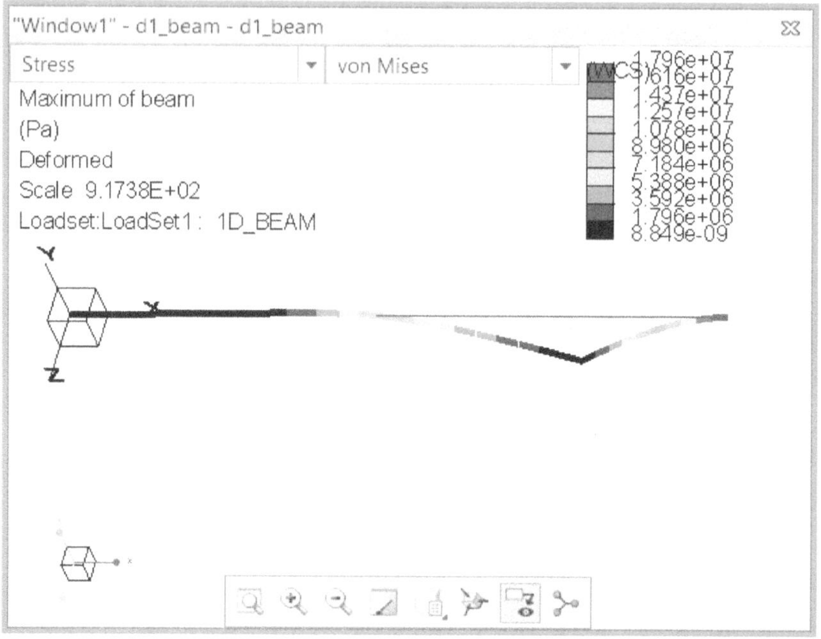

Figure 5–26

When displaying stress results, Creo Simulate calculates stresses at several characteristic locations on the beam cross-section (called grid points or stress recovery points) and displays the maximum value among all the recovery points. For example, the grid points for a channel section are shown in Figure 5–27.

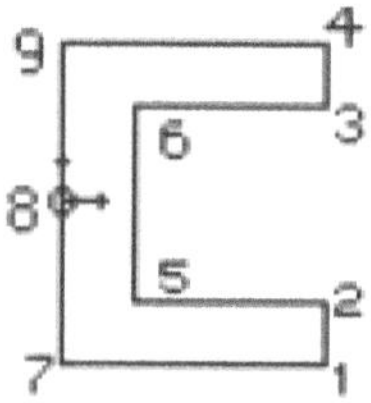

Figure 5–27

You can also select to visualize tensile stresses, bending stresses, and torsional stresses either separately or all summed up, as shown in Figure 5–28.

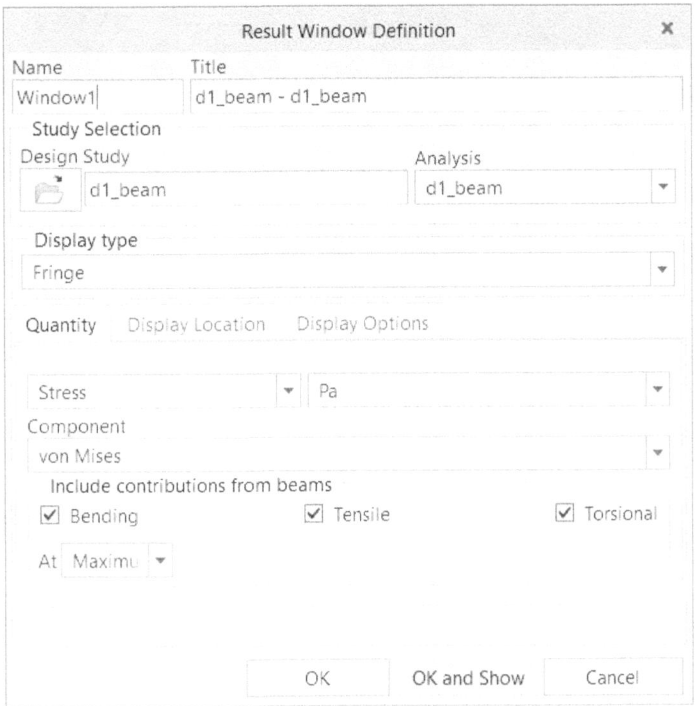

Figure 5–28

In addition to displacements and stresses, you can also display graphs of the internal forces and moments in the beams, as shown in Figure 5–29.

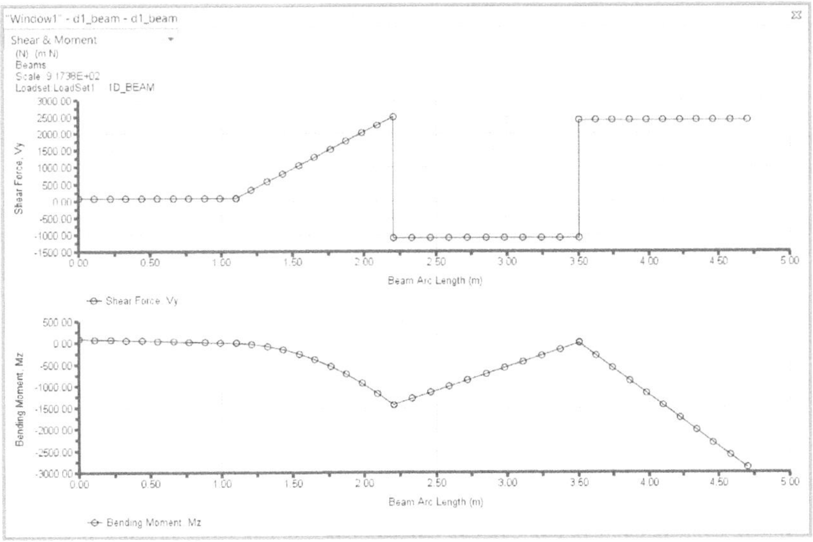

Figure 5–29

Practice 5a
Beam Analysis

Practice Objectives

- Set up a beam model.
- Set up beam releases.
- Run a beam model.
- Analyze a beam model.

The aspect ratio of the beam element should be greater than 10:1 (the ratio of its length to its largest section dimension).

In this practice, you will use beam element idealizations to set up, run, and analyze a beam model. The beam model is shown in Figure 5–30. The beam cross-section is an I-beam. The beam's ends are fixed and the middle support is a roller.

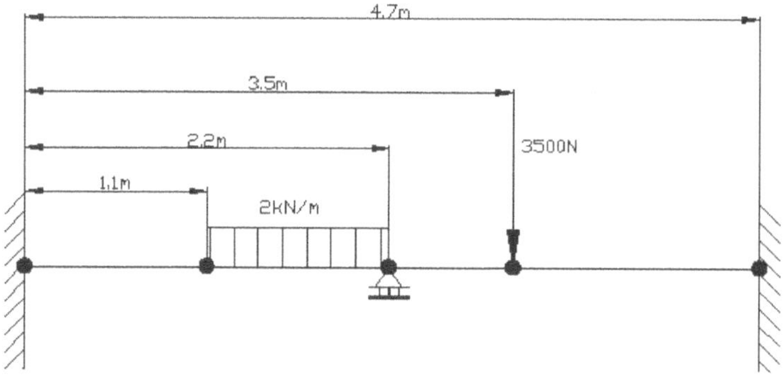

Figure 5–30

You will apply linear distributed loads to a section of the model and a point load 3.5m from the left side of the beam, as shown in Figure 5–31.

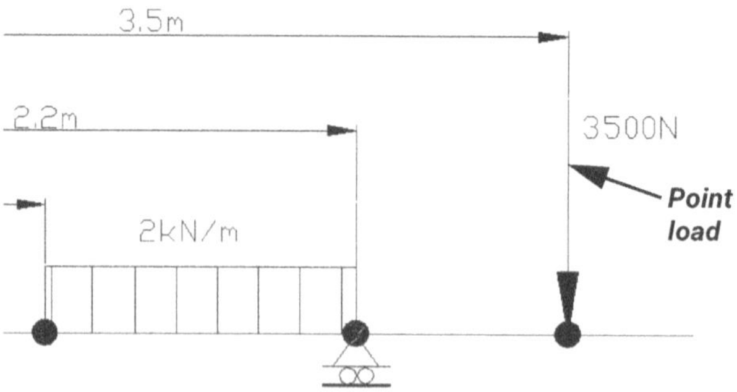

Figure 5–31

Modeling Tasks

Task 1: Open 1d_beam.prt and start Creo Simulate.

1. Set the working directory to **Chapter05**.
2. Open **1d_beam.prt**.
3. Set the model display as follows:
   - *(Datum Display Filters)*: (Point Display), (Plane Display)
   - *(Spin Center)*: Off
   - *(Display Style)*: (Shading With Edges)

   The part displays as shown in Figure 5–32.

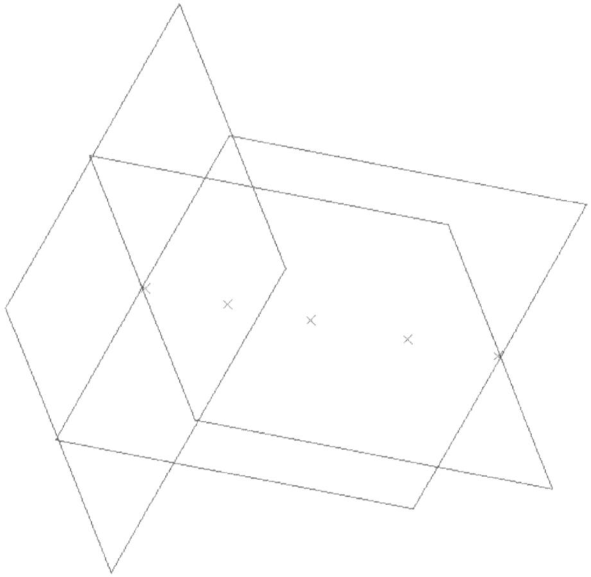

Figure 5–32

4. Ensure that the unit systems are **MKS**.
5. Switch to the Creo Simulate environment.

6. In the *View* tab, in the *Show* area, click (Point Tag Display) to display the datum point tags. The model displays as shown in Figure 5–33.

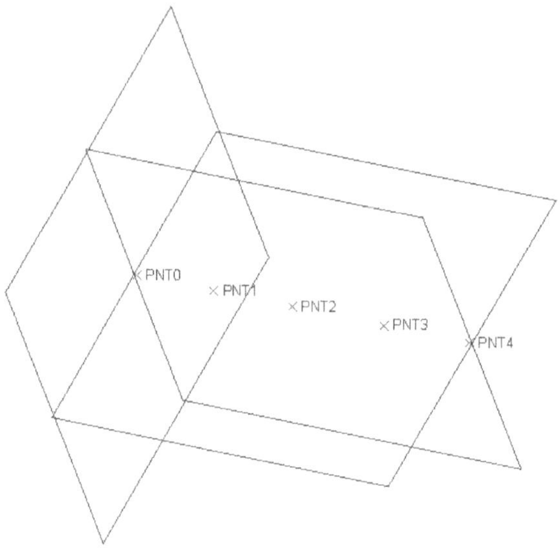

Figure 5–33

Task 2: Create a datum curve as a simulation feature.

In beam models, distributed loads can only be defined on datum curves. The load is transferred to the beam elements created on the curve.

1. In the *Refine Model* tab, expand the *Datum* group and click **Curve>Curve through Points**, as shown in Figure 5–34.

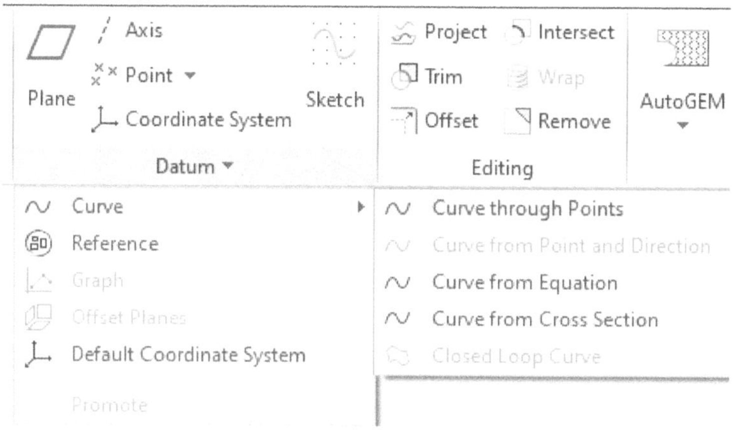

Figure 5–34

2. Select **PNT1** and **PNT2** to create a datum curve between them, as shown in Figure 5–35.

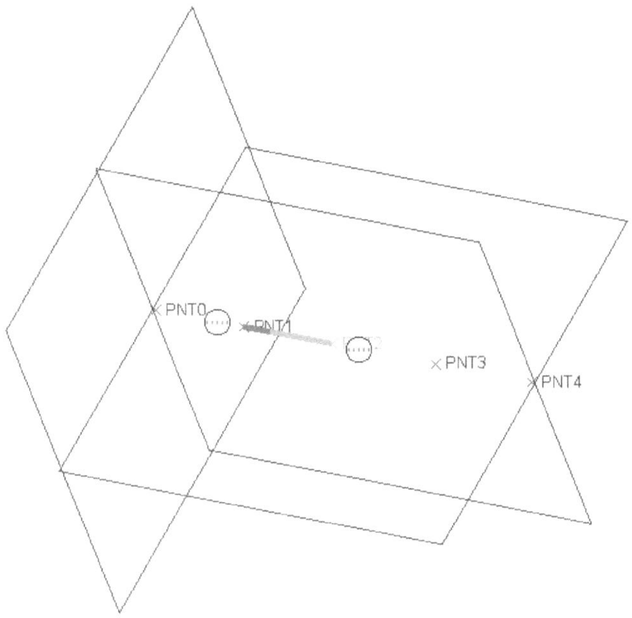

Figure 5–35

3. Click ✓ (OK).

Task 3: Create a beam element between PNT0 and PNT1.

1. In the *Refine Model* tab, click (Beam). The *Beam Definition* dialog box opens, as shown in Figure 5–36.

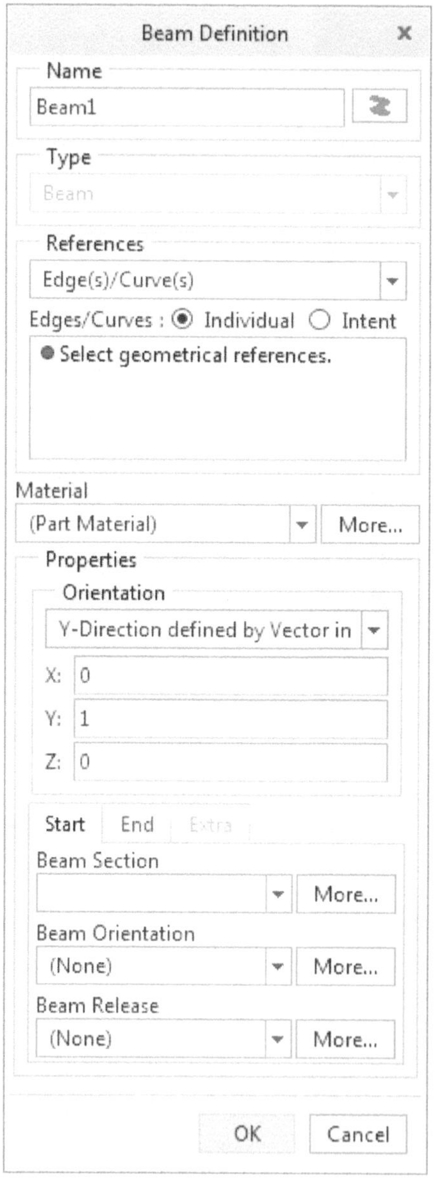

Figure 5–36

2. In the *Name* field, enter **beam_1**.

3. Expand the *References* drop-down list and select **Point-Point**.
4. Select **PNT0** and **PNT1**.
5. In the *Material* area, click **More**. The *Materials* dialog box opens.
6. In the *Materials in Library* area, double-click on **Legacy-Materials**, then double-click on **steel.mtl** to transfer STEEL to the *Materials in Model* area.
7. Review the material properties. The following values are the default material properties for HS-low-alloy steel (STEEL):
   - *Poisson:* **0.27**
   - *Young's modulus:* **1.99948 e11 Pa**
   - *Density:* **7827.08 Kg/m^3**

   Note: *The model's material properties should be as stated.*

8. Click **Select** in the *Materials* dialog box. **STEEL** displays in the *Material* field in the *Beam Definition* dialog box.
9. In the *Orientation* area, accept the default X-, Y-, and Z-values.
10. Next to the *Beam Section* drop-down list, click **More**. The *Beam Sections* dialog box opens, as shown in Figure 5–37.

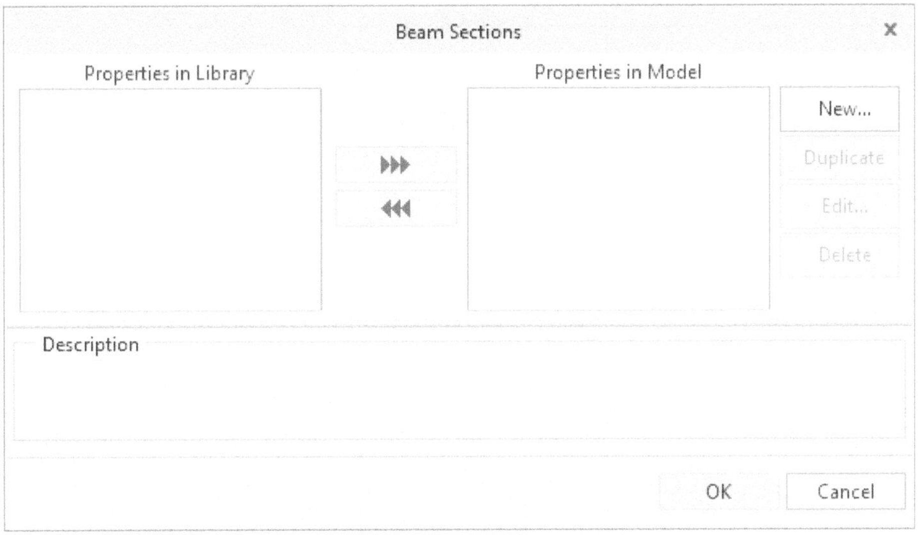

Figure 5–37

11. Click **New**. The *Beam Section Definition* dialog box opens, as shown in Figure 5–38.

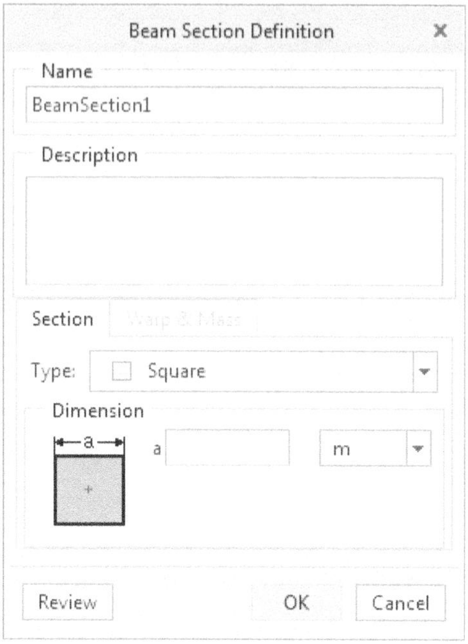

Figure 5–38

12. In the *Name* field, enter **I_beam_section**.

13. Expand the *Type* drop-down list and select **I-Beam**, as shown in Figure 5–39.

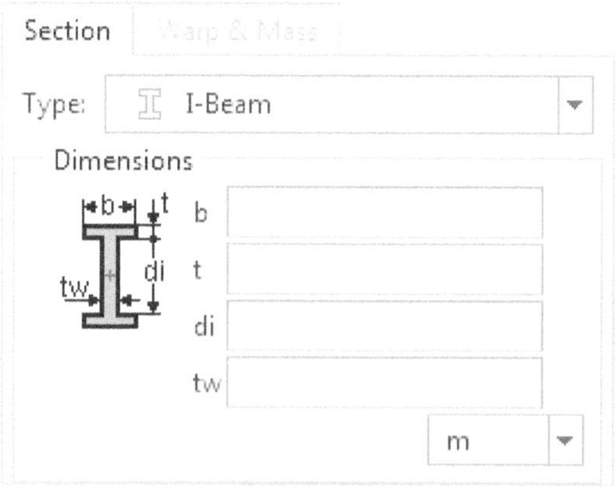

Figure 5–39

Note: *If the section is not listed in the Type drop-down list, you can sketch it using the* ***Sketched Solid*** *and* ***Sketched Thin*** *sketch options in the Type drop-down list. These options open Sketcher in Creo Parametric.*

14. Set the following:

- In the *b* field, enter **0.092**.
- In the *t* field, enter **0.009**.
- In the *di* field, enter **0.164**.
- In the *tw* field, enter **0.006**.

15. Click **Review**. The *Simulation Information* window displays. The window contains the section properties shown in Figure 5–40.

Figure 5–40

16. Close the *Simulation Information* window.

17. Click **OK** to close the *Beam Section Definition* dialog box.

18. Click **OK** to close the *Beam Sections* dialog box.

19. Click **OK** to close the *Beam Definition* dialog box. The model displays as shown in Figure 5–41.

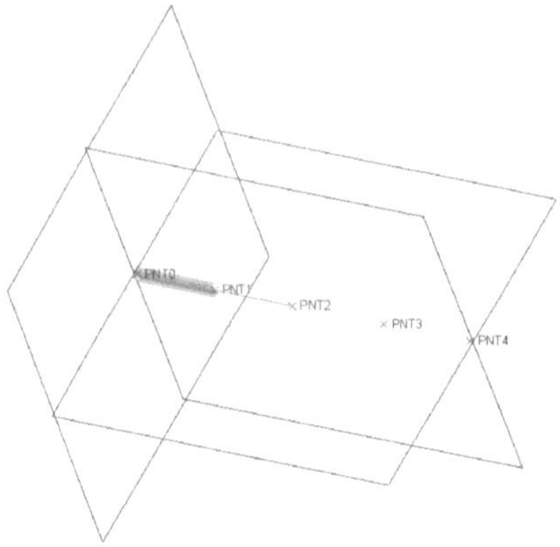

Figure 5–41

Task 4: Create a beam element between PNT1 and PNT2.

1. Click (Beam). The *Beam Definition* dialog box opens.
2. In the *Name* field, enter **beam_2**.
3. Expand the *References* drop-down list and select **Edge/Curve**.
4. Select the curve between **PNT1** and **PNT2**.
5. Expand the *Material* drop-down list and select **STEEL**.
6. In the *Orientation* area, in the *X*, *Y*, and *Z* fields, accept the default values.
7. Click **OK** to close the *Beam Definition* dialog box. The model displays as shown in Figure 5–42.

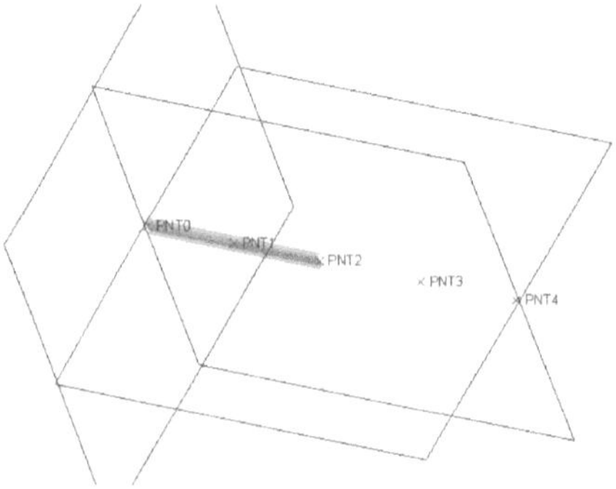

Figure 5–42

Note: The section property of the beam is the ***I_beam_section*** *that you created in the previous task.*

Task 5: Create a beam element between PNT2 and PNT3.

1. Click (Beam). The *Beam Definition* dialog box opens.
2. In the *Name* field, enter **beam_3**.
3. Expand the *References* drop-down list and select **Point-Point**.
4. Select **PNT2** and **PNT3**.
5. Expand the *Material* drop-down list and select **STEEL**.
6. In the *Beam Definition* dialog box, accept the other defaults.
7. Click **OK** to close the *Beam Definition* dialog box. The model displays as shown in Figure 5–43.

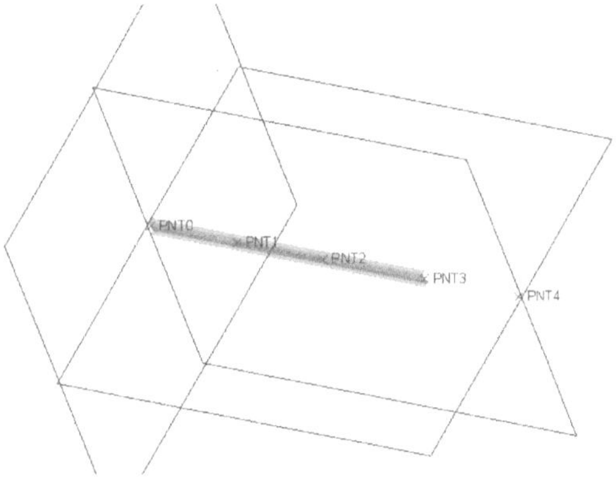

Figure 5–43

Note: *To display the section icons, use the zoom function.*

Task 6: Create a beam element between PNT3 and PNT4.

1. Click (Beam). The *Beam Definition* dialog box opens.
2. In the *Name* field, enter **beam_4**.
3. Expand the *References* drop-down list and select **Point-Point**.
4. Select **PNT3** and **PNT4**.
5. Expand the *Material* drop-down list and select **STEEL**.
6. In the *Beam Definition* dialog box, accept the other defaults.

7. Click **OK** to close the *Beam Definition* dialog box. The model displays as shown in Figure 5–44.

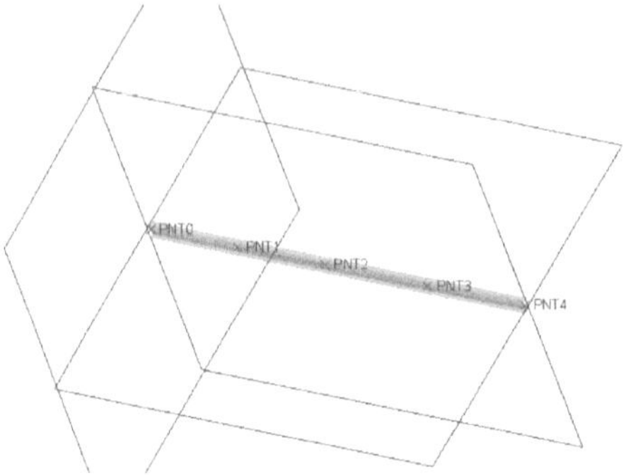

Figure 5–44

8. In the In-graphics toolbar, disable (Plane Display).

Task 7: Explore Beam visualization options.

1. In the In-graphics toolbar, click (Simulation Display). The *Simulation Display* dialog box opens, as shown in Figure 5–45.

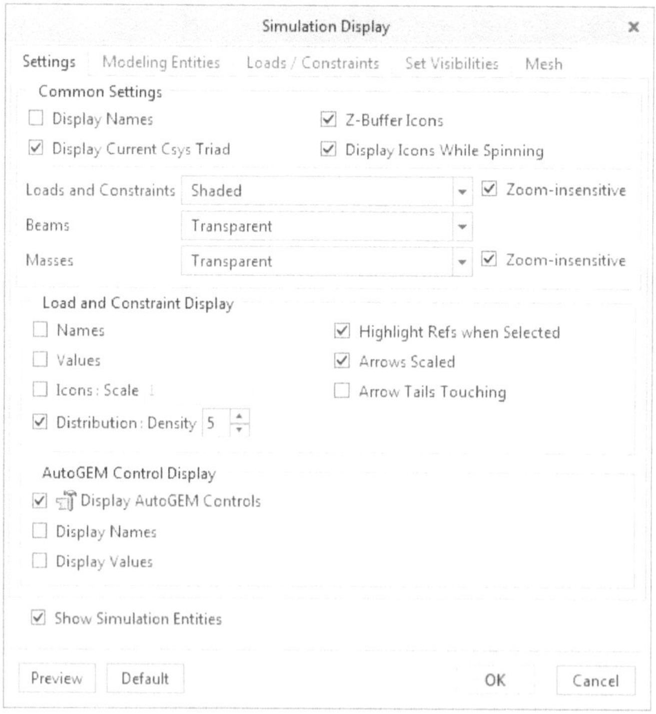

Figure 5–45

2. Select the **Wireframe** option in the *Beams* drop-down list and click **Preview**. The model displays as shown in Figure 5–46.

Figure 5–46

3. Select the *Modeling Entities* tab and clear the **Beam Sections** option.
4. Click **OK** to close the *Simulation Display* dialog box. The model displays as shown in Figure 5–47.

Figure 5–47

Task 8: Apply the loads.

The loading is uniformly distributed on the section between **PNT1** and **PNT2** of the model, and a point load is also applied at **PNT3**. In this task, you will apply the distributed load to the curve between **PNT1** and **PNT2**.

1. In the *Home* tab, click (Force/Moment). The *Force/Moment Load* dialog box opens, as shown in Figure 5–48.

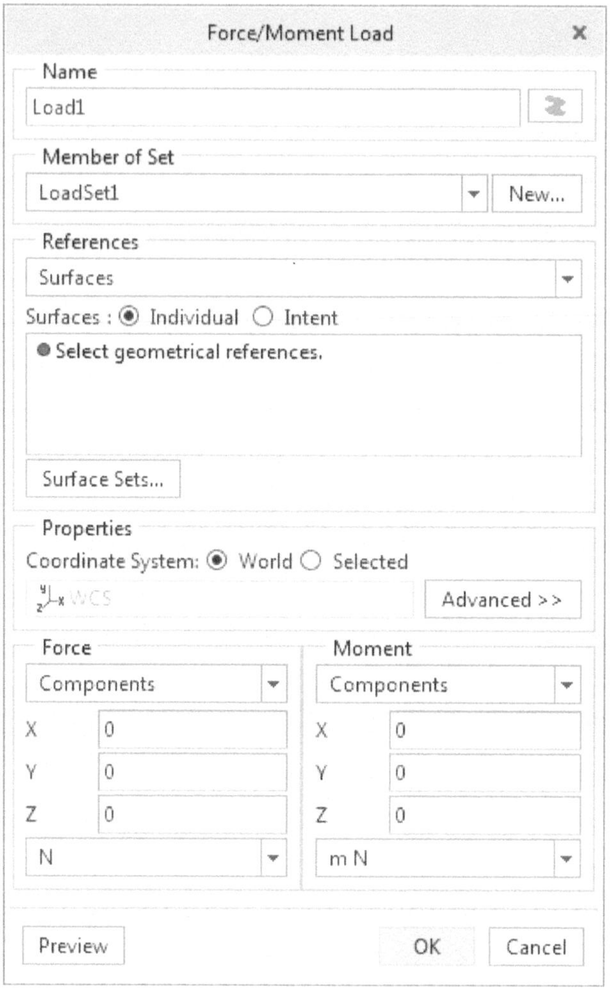

Figure 5–48

2. In the *Name* field, enter **uniform_load**.
3. For *Member of Set*, accept the default **LoadSet1** option.
4. Expand the *References* drop-down list and select **Edges/Curves**.

5. Select the curve between **PNT1** and **PNT2**, as shown in Figure 5–49.

Figure 5–49

Note: The load is related to the WCS.

6. Click **Advanced**.
7. Expand the *Distribution* drop-down list and select **Force Per Unit Length**.
8. In the *Spatial Variation* area, select the **Uniform** option.
9. In the *Force/Moment Load* dialog box, in the *Force* area, in the *Y* field, enter **-2200**.
10. Click **OK**. The model displays as shown in Figure 5–50.

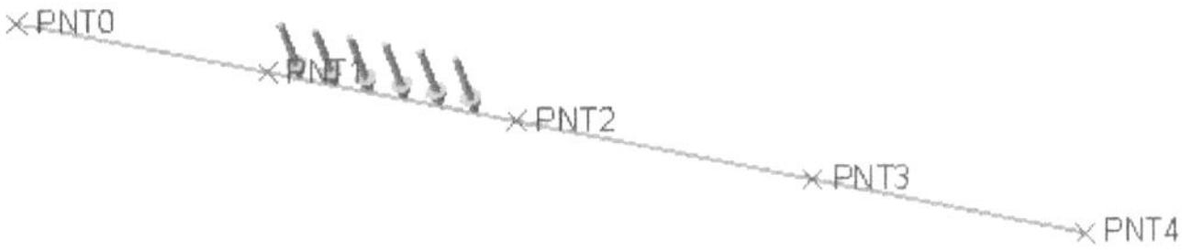

Figure 5–50

Note: You can toggle off the load values in the Simulation Display dialog box.

Task 9: Apply the point load to the PNT3.

1. Select **PNT3** and select (Force/Moment) from the mini-toolbar. *The Force/Moment Load* dialog box opens.
2. In the *Name* field, enter **point_load**.
3. For *Member of Set*, accept the default **LoadSet1** option.
4. Note that since a point was initially selected, the *References* drop-down list is automatically set to **Points**.

   Note: The load is related to the WCS.

5. In the *Force* area, in the *Y* field, enter **-3500**.

6. Click **OK**. The model displays as shown in Figure 5–51 with the default datum planes toggled off.

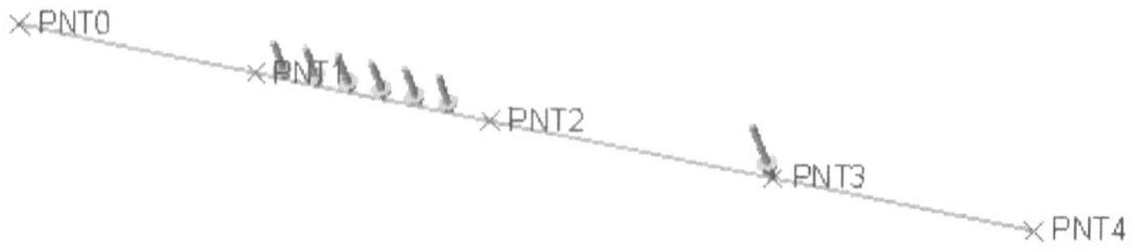

Figure 5–51

Task 10: Apply the constraints.

The beam ends (**PNT0** and **PNT4**) are constrained (fixed) and the middle support (**PNT2**) is a roller (free Z-rotation and free X-translation). In this task, you will constrain the beam ends.

1. Multi-select **PNT0** and **PNT4** and select (Displacement) from the mini-toolbar. The *Constraint* dialog box opens.
2. In the *Name* field, enter **end_constraints**.
3. For *Member of Set*, accept the default **ConstraintSet1** option.
4. Fix all of the translations and rotations.
5. Click **OK**. The model displays as shown in Figure 5–52.

Figure 5–52

Task 11: Apply the constraints to PNT2.

1. Select **PNT2** and select (Displacement) from the mini-toolbar. The *Constraint* dialog box opens.
2. In the *Name* field, enter **roller**.
3. For *Member of Set*, accept the default **ConstraintSet1** option.

4. Free the X-translation and Z-rotation, and fix all of the other degrees of freedom, as shown in Figure 5–53.

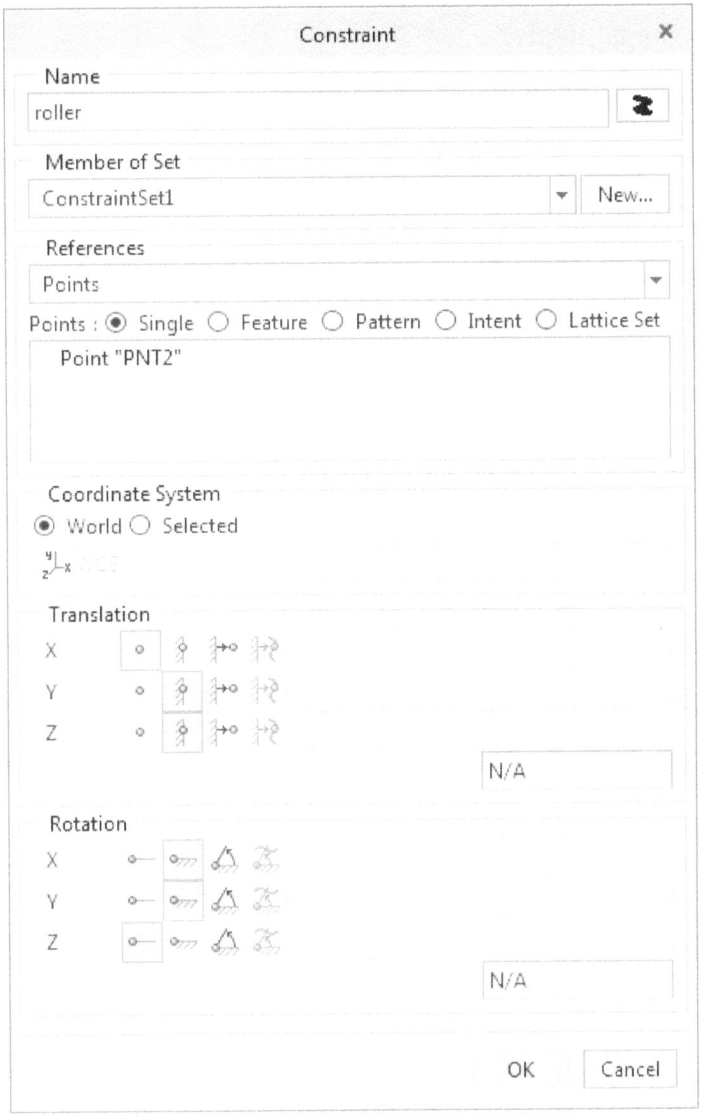

Figure 5–53

5. Click **OK** to close the dialog box. The model displays as shown in Figure 5–54.

Figure 5–54

Analysis Tasks

Task 12: Set up the analysis.

1. Set up a Quick Check analysis to check for errors. For the name of the analysis, enter **beam_q_c**.
2. In the *Output* tab, increase the plotting grid to **10**.
3. In the *Analyses and Design Studies* dialog box, in the **Info** menu, select **Check Model** to check the validity of the model.

   Note: *The* ***Check Model*** *option highlights any modeling errors (e.g., load-constraint conflicts or unassigned material properties) and errors from modeling edits.*

4. Click (Settings) and ensure that the **Create Elements during Run** option is selected in the *Run Settings* dialog box.
5. Click **OK** to close the *Run Settings* dialog box.

Task 13: Run the Quick Check analysis.

1. Click (Start) to start the analysis.
2. Review the status of the run and any errors or warnings.
3. Close the *Run Status* dialog box when the run is complete.

Task 14: Solve the analysis using the Multi-Pass Adaptive convergence option.

1. Change the convergence method to Multi-Pass Adaptive. In the *Maximum Polynomial Order* field, enter **6**. In the *Limits* area, in the *Percent Convergence* field, enter **1**.

   Note: *The Single-Pass Adaptive convergence method is not applicable to beams. It is only applicable to continuum finite elements, such as solids and shells.*

2. Re-run the analysis.

Results Tasks

Task 15: Display the results.

Create and display the color plot for the displacement. Animate the plot to ensure that the boundary conditions are correct.

1. In the *Analyses and Design Studies* dialog box, click (Review Results). The *Result Window Definition* dialog box opens.

2. Create, animate, and display a fringe color plot for the displacement.
3. Stop the animation. In the *View* tab, expand the *Appearance* drop-down list and select **Visibilities**. Select **Loads** and **Constraints** and close the *Visibilities* dialog box.
4. Click (Step Back) and (Step Forward) to step through the animation frames. Frame 5 is shown in Figure 5–55.

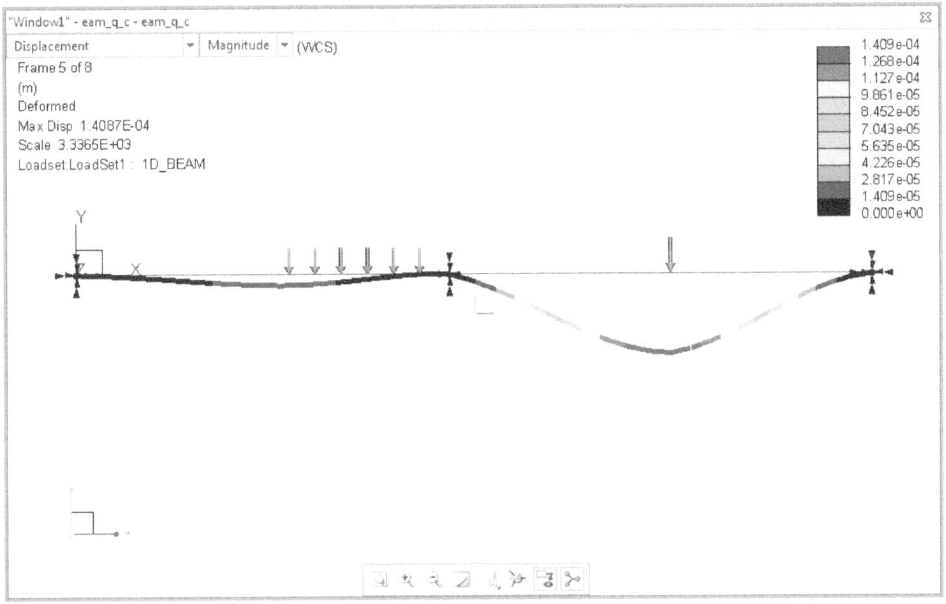

Figure 5–55

Note that the deflection is zero at the beam ends and at the roller support, which is correct.

5. Animate and display the components of displacement (X, Y, and Z). Note that the deflection of the model in the X- and Z-directions is zero because loads have only been applied in the Y-direction.

Task 16: Create a shear and bending moment plot window for beam elements.

1. Click (Copy) in the *Home* tab. The *Result Window Definition* dialog box opens.
2. In the *Name* field, enter **shear_moment_window**.
3. In the *Title* field, enter **shear_moment_graph**.
4. Expand the *Display type* drop-down list and select **Graph**.
5. Expand the *Graph Ordinate (Vertical) Axis* drop-down list and select **Shear & Moment**.
6. In the *Shear and Moment* area, clear all of the options except **Vy** and **Mz** in the *Beam* area.
7. Expand the *Graph Location* drop-down list and select **Beams**.

8. Click (Select) and select all four beam elements from left to right (hold <Ctrl> to multi-select). Click the middle mouse button. The *Information* dialog box opens, as shown in Figure 5–56.

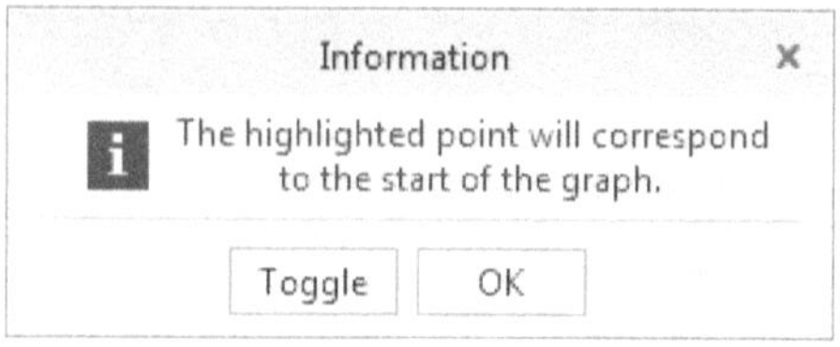

Figure 5–56

9. Read the information and verify that the start of the graph corresponds to the point **PNT0**.
10. In the *Information* dialog box, click **OK**. The *Result Window Definition* dialog box opens, as shown in Figure 5–57.

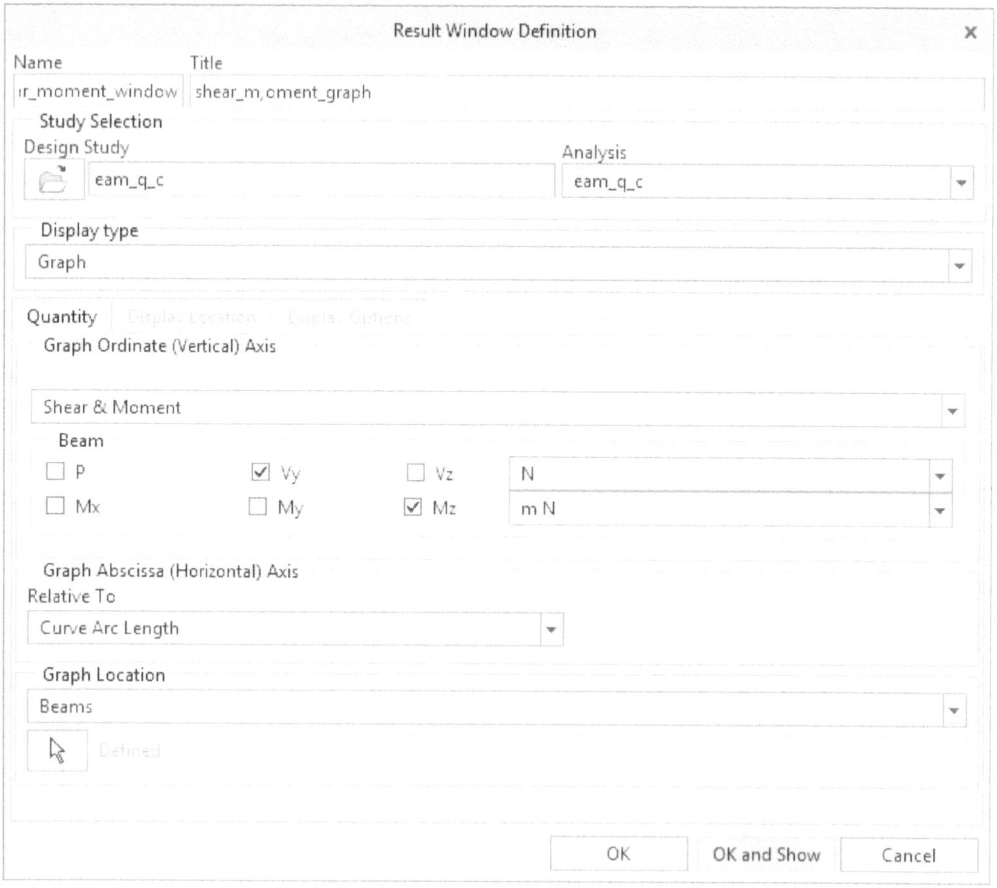

Figure 5–57

11. Click **OK**.
12. In the *View* tab, click (Show). In the *Display Result Window* dialog box, clear **Window1** and select **shear_moment_window**.
13. Click **OK**. The result window displays as shown in Figure 5–58.

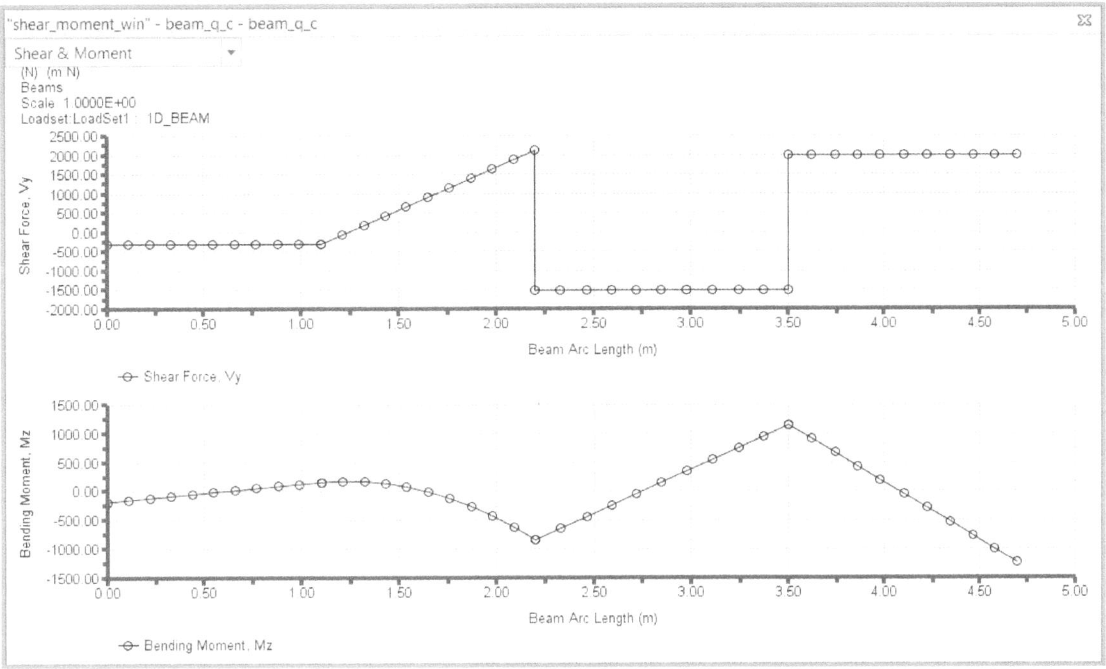

Figure 5–58

The plot shown in Figure 5–58 displays the shear and moment plots along the beam elements in the model. Note the bending moment continuity along the model. Note the shear force discontinuity at the roller support and at the point load.

14. Select **File>Close**. Click **Don't Save** when prompted to save the results.
15. Close the *Analyses and Design Studies* dialog box.

Task 17: Set up the beam releases.

In this task, you will release the **beam_4** start point (free rotation in the Z-direction) to simulate a pinned connection between **beam_3** and **beam_4**.

> **Note:** *Beam release is a term that describes the type of connections (pinned or rigid) between two beam elements.*

1. In the *Model Tree*, expand **Idealizations>Beams**, select **beam_4** (the curve between **PNT3** and **PNT4**), and select (Edit Definition) from the mini-toolbar. The *Beam Definition* dialog box opens, as shown in Figure 5–59.

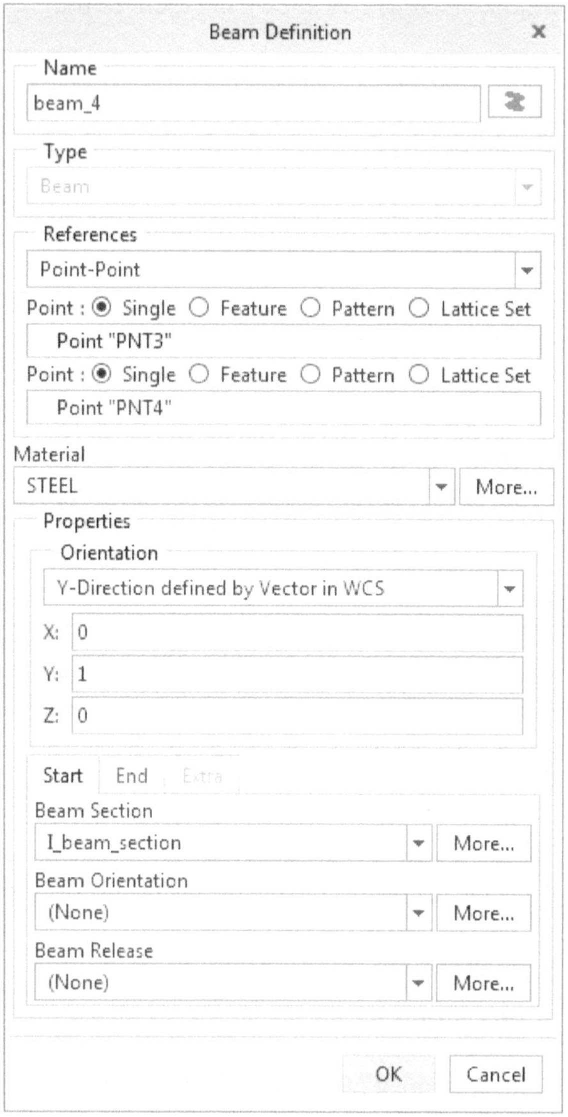

Figure 5–59

Note: *Release can only be applied directly to beam elements.*

2. Next to the *Beam Release* drop-down list, click **More**. The *Beam Releases* dialog box opens, as shown Figure 5–60.

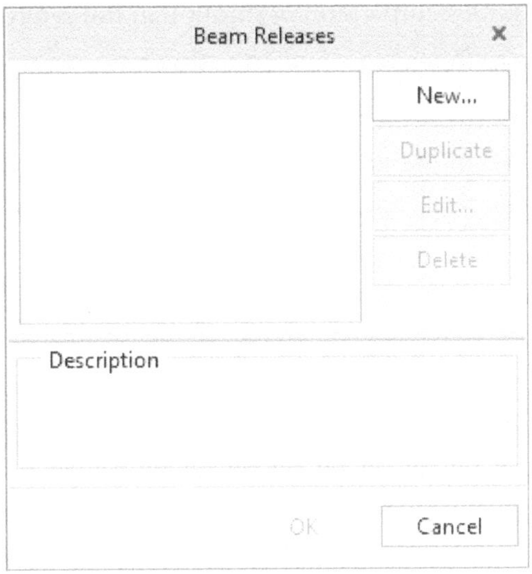

Figure 5–60

Note: *Releases are handy when modeling trusses (because no moment is transmitted through a connection), when modeling an expansion joint (because no axial load is transmitted), or when modeling dovetails (because all of the forces and moments are transmitted except shear in one direction).*

3. In the *Beam Releases* dialog box, click **New**. The *Beam Release* dialog box opens, as shown in Figure 5–61.

Figure 5–61

4. In the *Name* field, enter **beam_4_rz**.

5. Click **Rz** to release (free) the beam element rotation in the Z-direction at **PNT3**.
6. Click **OK** to close the *Beam Release Definition* dialog box.
7. Click **OK** to close the *Beam Releases* dialog box.
8. Click **OK** to close the *Beam Definition* dialog box.
9. Create and run a new Multi-Pass Adaptive analysis **d1_beam** for the modified model.

Note: 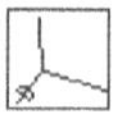 *(Beam Release) indicates the degrees of freedom and the end of the beam on which the release is acting.*

Task 18: Display the results.

1. Create and display a color plot for the displacement. Additionally, animate this plot to ensure that the boundary conditions are correct. The deformed shape is shown in Figure 5–62. Note the changes in the slope at the point of the release.

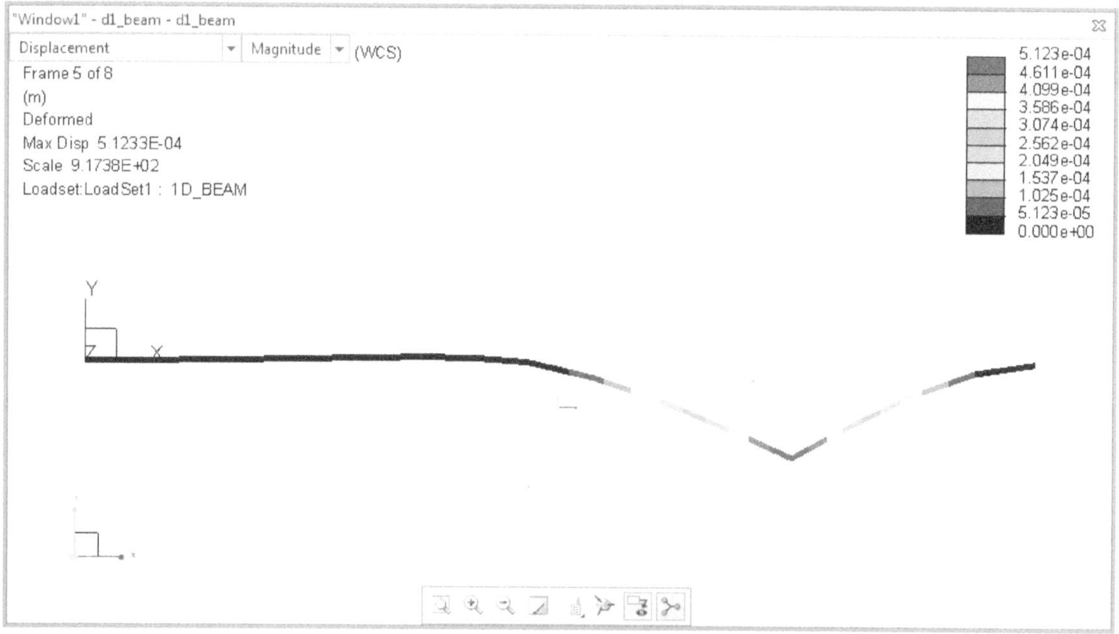

Figure 5–62

2. Create shear and bending moment plot windows for the beam elements (four beam elements), as shown in Figure 5–63. Note that the shear is non-zero and that the bending moment is zero at the pinned connection, which is correct.

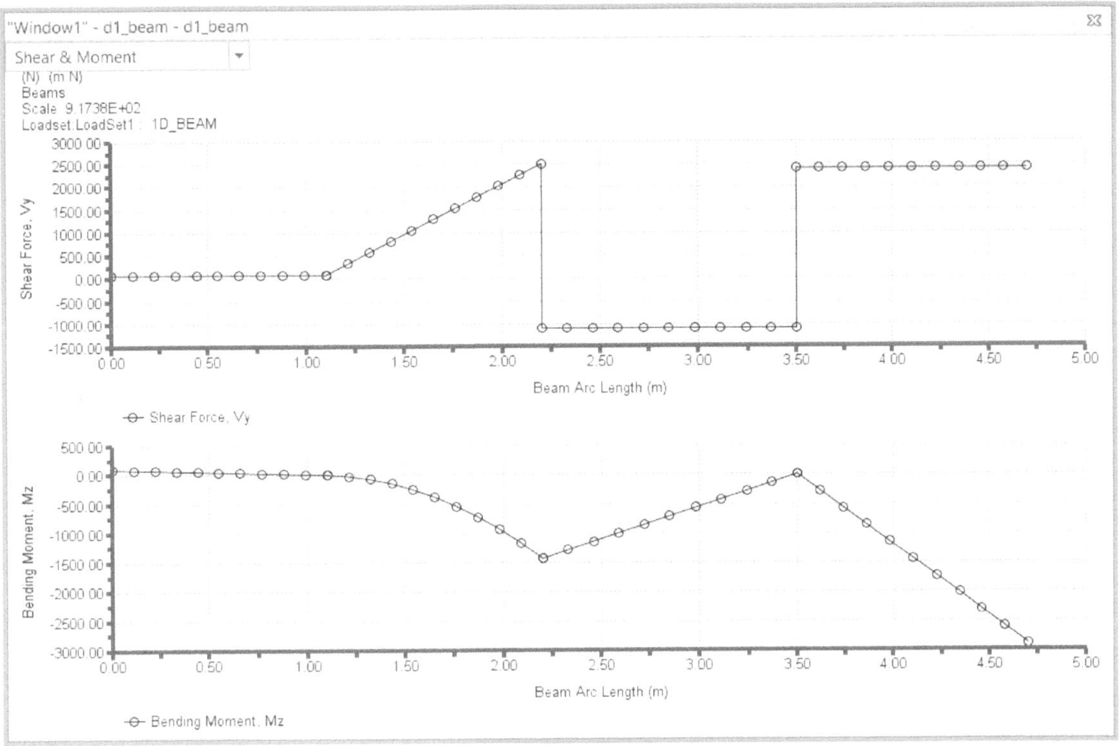

Figure 5–63

Task 19: Save and close the model.

1. Select **File>Close**. Click **Don't Save** when prompted to save the results.
2. Close the *Analyses and Design Studies* dialog box.
3. Exit Creo Simulate. Save and close the model in Creo Parametric.

End of practice

Practice 5b
2D Frame Analysis

Practice Objectives

- Set up a 2D beam model.
- Run a 2D beam model.
- Analyze a 2D beam model.

The aspect ratio of the beam element should be greater than 10:1 (the ratio of its length to its largest section dimension).

In this practice, you will use beam element idealizations to analyze a 2D frame. The frame part is shown in Figure 5–64. The beam section is a hollow circular pipe and the frame ends are fixed. The frame loading is a linearly distributed load in the Y-direction, a uniform total load in the Z-direction, a point load in the X-direction, and a load due to gravity.

Figure 5–64

Modeling Tasks

Task 1: Open the d2_frame.prt.

1. Set the working directory to **Chapter05**, if required.
2. Open **d2_frame.prt**.

3. Set the model display as follows:
   - *(Datum Display Filters)*: (Point Display), (Plane Display), (Csys Display)
   - *(Spin Center)*: Off
   - *(Display Style)*: (Shading With Edges)
4. In the *View* tab, in the *Show* group, click (Point Tag Display) to visualize the datum point tags, if not already displayed. The part displays as shown in Figure 5–65.

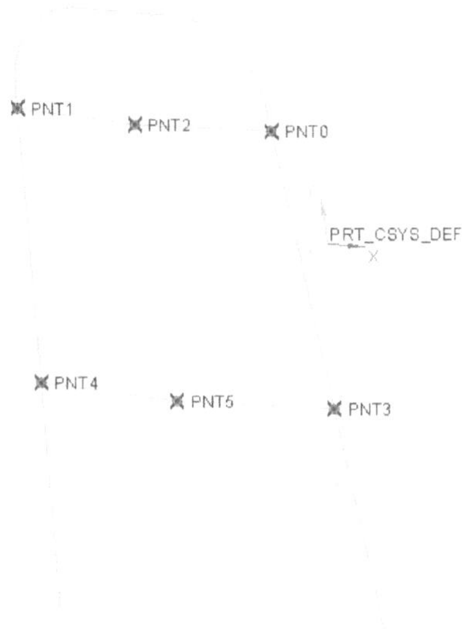

Figure 5–65

5. Ensure that the unit system is **IPS**.
6. Switch to the Creo Simulate environment.
7. Click (Simulation Display). In the *Simulation Display* dialog box, clear the **Display AutoGEM Controls** option.

Task 2: Create a datum point as a simulation feature.

In beam models, Creo Simulate can only define distributed loads on curves. The load is transferred to the beam elements created on the curve. Concentrated loads can be defined on the curve's vertices (i.e., ends) and on datum points within the curve. In this task, you will create a datum point on curve, to which you will later apply a concentrated force.

1. In the In-graphics toolbar, disable (Plane Display).
2. In the *Refine Model* tab, click (Point).

3. Create a datum point at the end of the curve in the location shown in Figure 5–66.

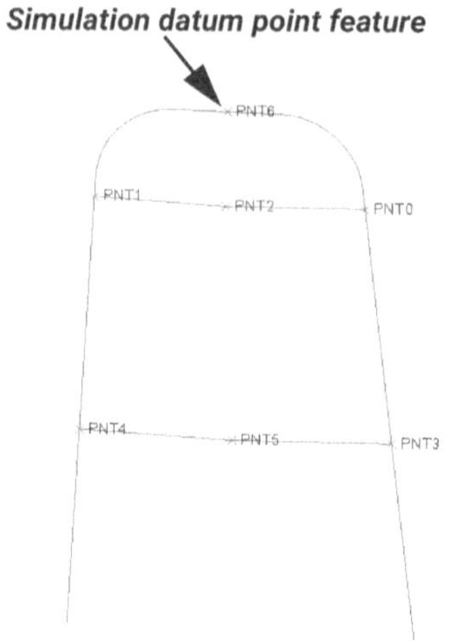

Figure 5–66

Task 3: Create beam elements.

1. Click (Beam). The *Beam Definition* dialog box opens.
2. In the *Name* field, enter **d2_beam_1**.
3. Expand the *References* drop-down list and select **Edge(s)/Curve(s)**, if required.
4. Select the curve shown in Figure 5–67. As you select the curve, a direction arrow displays on the curve (clicking the arrow again changes the direction of the arrow). The direction is shown in Figure 5–67.

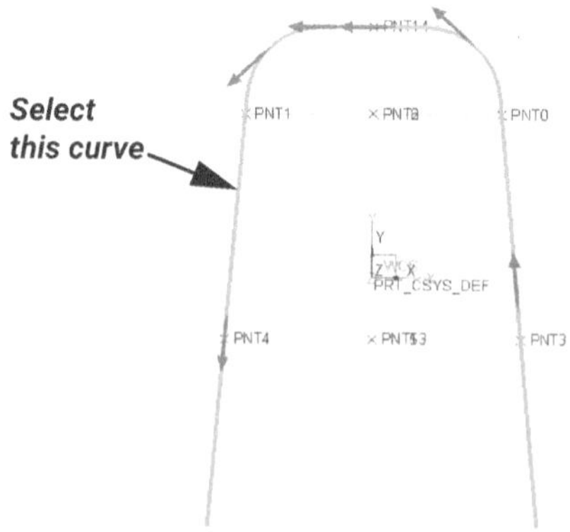

Figure 5–67

5. In the *Material* area, click **More**. The *Materials* dialog box opens.
6. In the *Materials in Library* area, double-click on **Legacy-Materials** and double-click on **al2014.mtl** to transfer AL2014 to the *Materials in Model* area.

7. Review the material properties. The following values are the default material properties for Aluminum alloy 2014-T6:
   - *Poisson*: **0.33**
   - *Young's modulus:* **1.06e+07 psi**
   - *Density:* **0.0002614 lbf sec^2/in^4**
8. Click **Select** in the *Materials* dialog box. AL2014 displays in the *Material* area in the *Beam Definition* dialog box.
9. In the *Orientation* area, in the *X* field, accept the default; in the *Y* field, enter **0**; and in the *Z* field, enter **1**.

   Note: *Since the cross-section is round, the Y-direction of the beam's BACS can be defined as any direction, as long as it does not coincide with the beam's X-axis.*

10. Next to the *Beam Section* drop-down list, click **More**. The *Beam Sections* dialog box opens.
11. Click **New**. The *Beam Section Definition* dialog box opens, as shown in Figure 5–68.

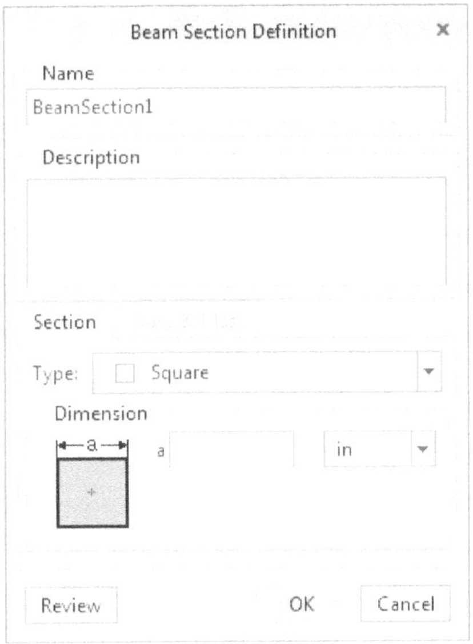

Figure 5–68

12. In the *Name* field, enter **d2_frame_section_1**.
13. Expand the *Type* drop-down list and select **Hollow Circle**.

    Note: *If the section is not in the Type drop-down list, you can sketch the section using the* ***Sketched Solid*** *and* ***Sketched Thin*** *sketch options in the Type drop-down list. These options open Sketcher in Creo Parametric.*

14. In the *R* field, enter **1.50**.

15. In the *Ri* field, enter **1.10**.
16. Click **OK** to close the *Beam Section Definition* dialog box.
17. Click **OK** to close the *Beam Sections* dialog box.
18. Click **OK** to close the *Beam Definition* dialog box. The model displays as shown in Figure 5–69.

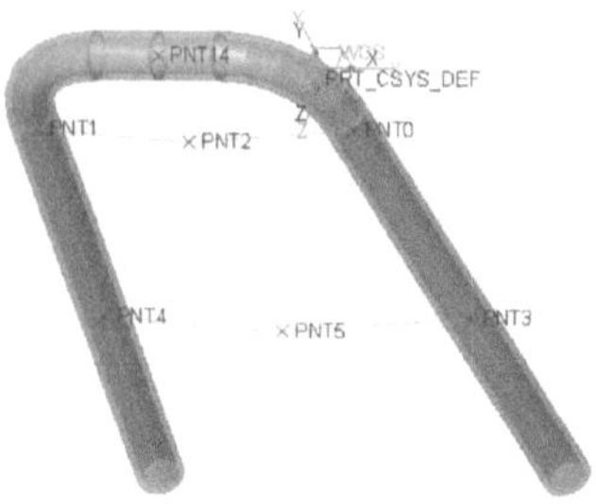

Figure 5–69

19. Click (Beam). The *Beam Definition* dialog box opens.
20. In the *Name* field, enter **d2_beam_2**.
21. Select the curves shown in Figure 5–70. As you select each curve, a direction arrow displays on the curve (selecting the curve again will change the direction of the arrow). The direction is shown in Figure 5–70.

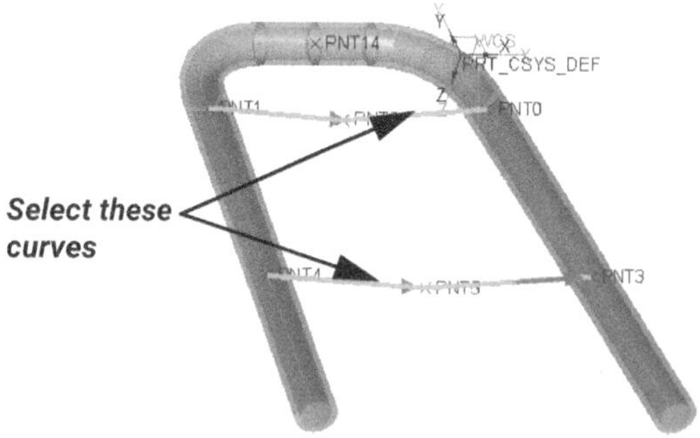

Figure 5–70

22. In the *Material* drop-down list, select **AL2014**.
23. In the *Orientation* area, in the *X* field, accept the default; in the *Y* field, enter **0**; and in the *Z* field, enter **1**.
24. Next to the *Beam Section* drop-down list, click **More**. The *Beam Sections* dialog box opens.
25. Click **New**. The *Beam Section Definition* dialog box opens.
26. In the *Name* field, enter **d2_frame_section_2**.
27. Expand the *Type* drop-down list and select **Hollow Circle**.

28. In the *R* field, enter **1.20**.
29. In the *Ri* field, enter **0.80**.
30. Click **OK** to close the *Beam Section Definition* dialog box.
31. Click **OK** to close the *Beam Sections* dialog box.
32. Click **OK** to close the *Beam Definition* dialog box. The model displays as shown in Figure 5–71.

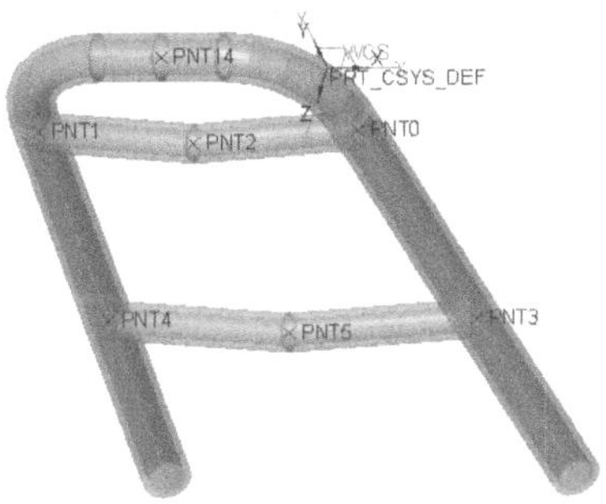

Figure 5–71

33. Click (Simulation Display). The *Simulation Display* dialog box opens.
34. In the *Settings* tab, in the *Beams* drop-down list, select **Wireframe**.
35. Select the *Modeling Entities* tab and clear the **Beam Sections** option.
36. Click **OK** in the *Simulation Display* dialog box.
37. In the In-graphics toolbar, disable (Point Display), and (Csys Display).
38. The model displays as shown in Figure 5–72 with the default datum planes, points, and coordinate systems toggled off.

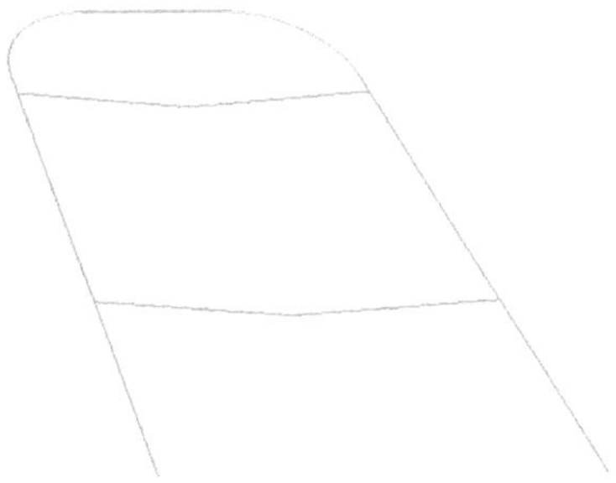

Figure 5–72

Task 4: Apply the loads.

The loading is a linearly distributed load in the Y-direction, a uniform total load in the Z-direction, a point load in the X-direction, and a load due to gravity. In this task, you will apply the linear distributed load to the curve shown in Figure 5–73.

1. In the *Home* tab, click (Force/Moment). The *Force/Moment Load* dialog box opens.
2. In the *Name* field, enter **distributed_load**.
3. For *Member of Set*, accept the default **LoadSet1** option.
4. Expand the *References* drop-down list and select **Edges/Curves**.
5. Select the section of the curve shown in Figure 5–73.

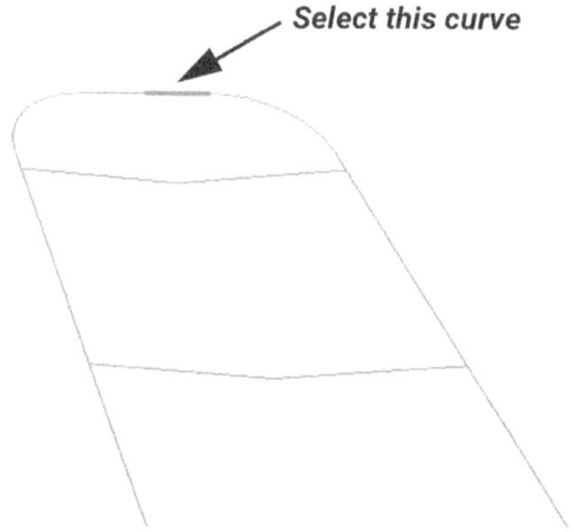

Figure 5–73

Note: The easiest way to select this section of the curve is to hover the cursor over the curve, hold the right mouse button, and select ***Pick From List*** *in the context menu. Toggle through the items in the Pick From List dialog box until the required curve highlights.*

6. Click **Advanced**. Expand the *Distribution* drop-down list and select **Force Per Unit Length**.
7. Expand the *Spatial Variation* drop-down list and select **Interpolated Over Entity**.
8. In the first row of the *Value* column, enter **0.25**.
9. In the second row of the *Value* column, enter **1.00**.

Note: The values (0.25, 1) are scale factors that Creo Simulate applies to the load at the ends of the curve.

10. In the *Force* area, in the *Y* field, enter **-4350**. The *Force/Moment Load* dialog box displays as shown in Figure 5–74.

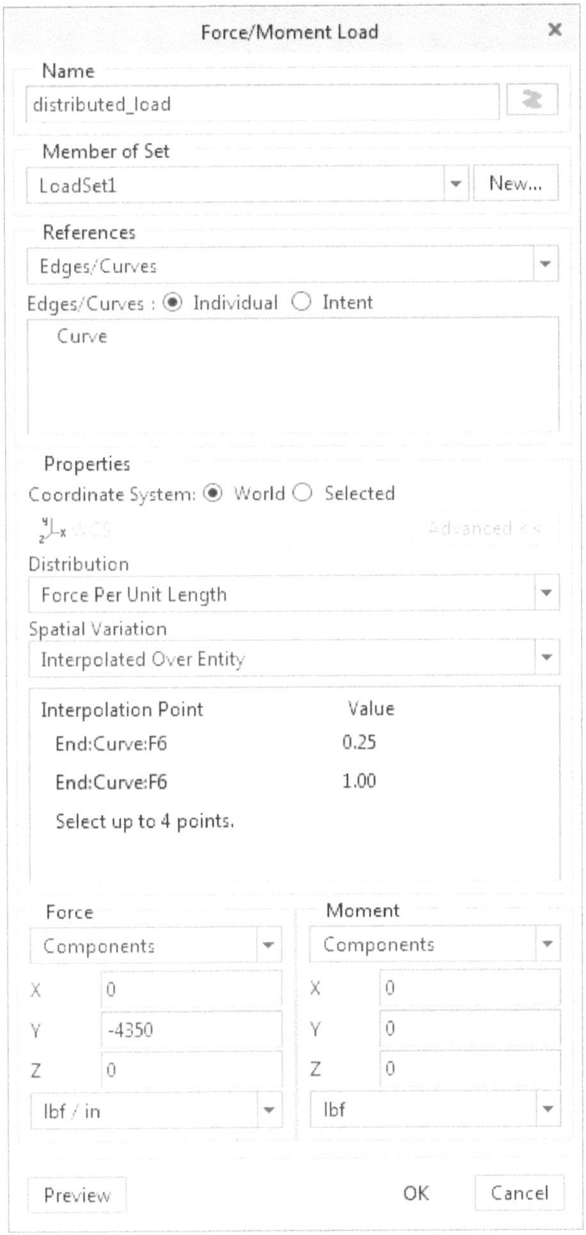

Figure 5–74

11. Click **Preview** to verify that the load distribution is linear, as shown in Figure 5–75.

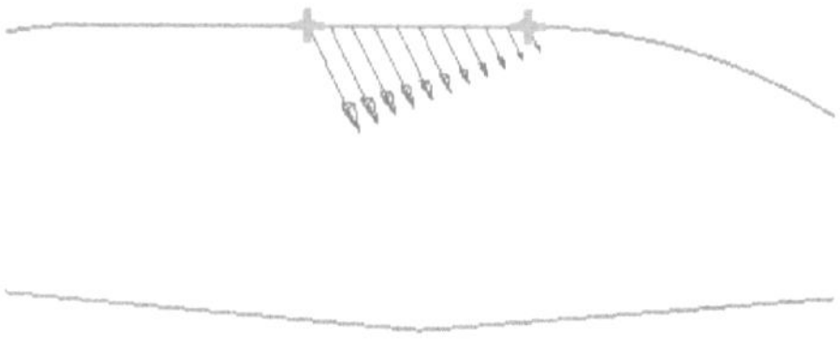

Figure 5–75

Note: *If the load distribution is reversed, swap the **0.25** and **1** values defined in Steps 8 and 9.*

12. Click **OK**. The model displays as shown in Figure 5–76. Default datum planes are toggled off.

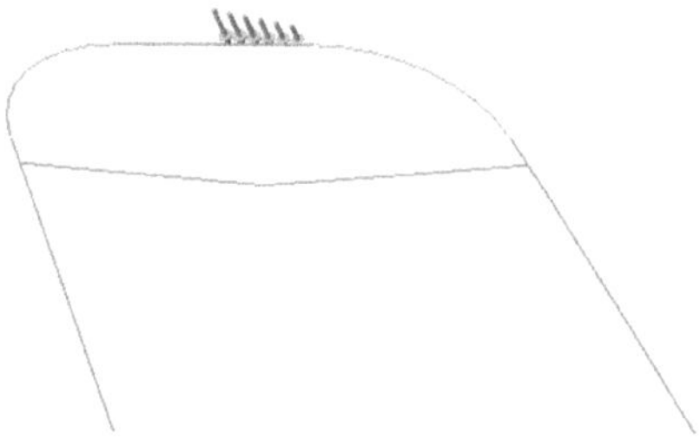

Figure 5–76

Note: *You can toggle the load values off in the Simulation Display dialog box.*

13. Repeat Steps 1 to 7 of this task to apply the load to the curve shown in Figure 5–77.

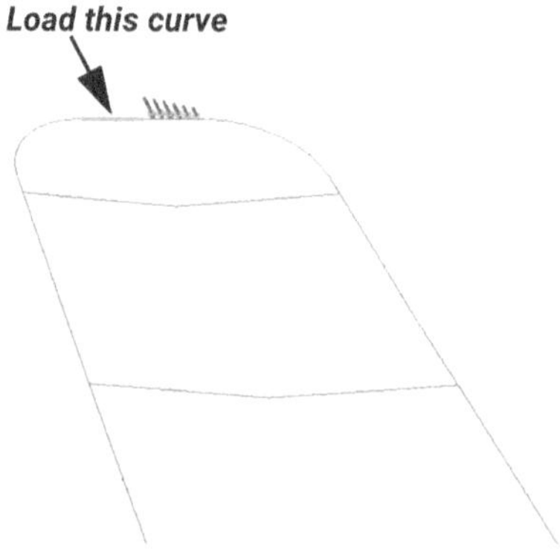

Figure 5–77

Note: *Name the load **distributed_load_1**.*

14. In the first row of the *Value* column, enter **1.00**.

15. In the second row of the *Value* column, enter **0.25**.
16. Repeat Steps 10 to 12 to finish applying the loads. The model displays as shown in Figure 5–78.

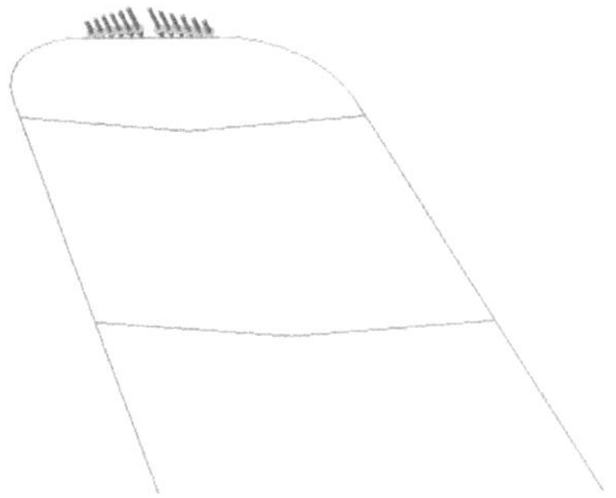

Figure 5–78

Task 5: Apply the point load.

1. In the In-graphics toolbar, enable (Point Display).
2. Click (Force/Moment). The *Force/Moment Load* dialog box opens.
3. In the *Name* field, enter **point_load**.
4. For *Member of Set*, accept the default **LoadSet1** option.
5. Expand the *References* drop-down list and select **Points**.

   Note: *The load is related to the WCS.*

6. Select **PNT6**, as shown in Figure 5–79.

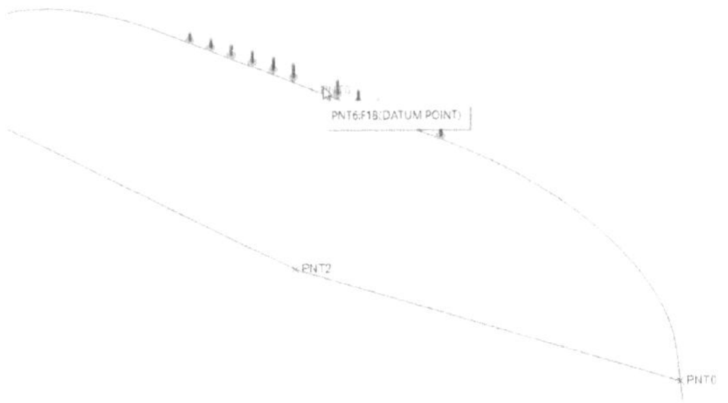

Figure 5–79

7. In the *Force/Moment Load* dialog box, in the *Force* area, in the *X* field, enter **-1930**.
8. Click **OK** to create the load.

Task 6: Apply a uniform total load in the Z-direction.

1. In the *Model Tree*, fully expand the **Loads/Constraints** node, select the three existing loads, and select (Hide) from the mini-toolbar, as shown in Figure 5–80.

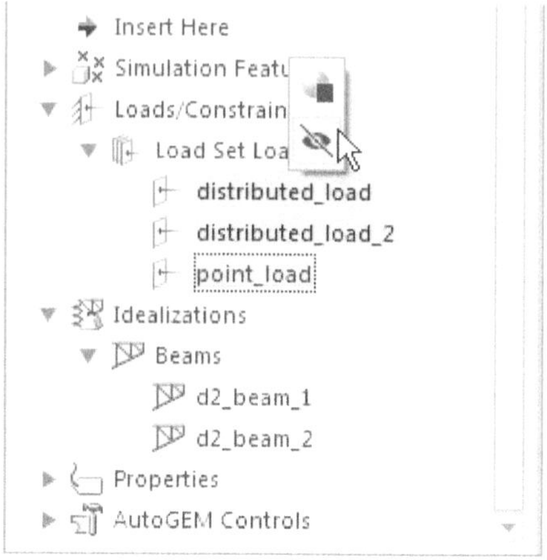

Figure 5–80

Note: This will temporarily remove the loads from display.

2. Click (Force/Moment). The *Force/Moment Load* dialog box opens.
3. In the *Name* field, enter **total_uniform_load**.
4. In *Member of Set*, accept the default **LoadSet1** option.
5. Expand the *References* drop-down list and select **Edges/Curves**. Select the two curves shown in Figure 5–81.

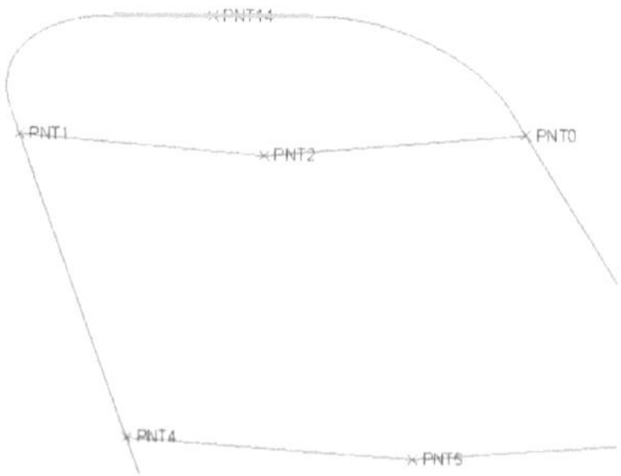

Figure 5–81

Note: The load is related to the WCS.

6. In the *Force/Moment Load* dialog box, in the *Force* area, in the *Z* field, enter **1930**.

7. Click **OK** to finish.
8. In the *Model Tree*, select the hidden loads and click (Show) in the mini-toolbar. The model displays as shown in Figure 5–82.

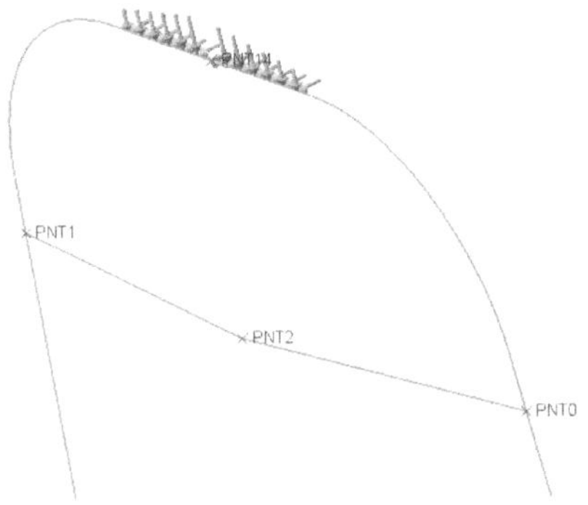

Figure 5–82

Task 7: Apply the gravity load.

1. Click (Gravity). The *Gravity Load* dialog box opens, as shown in Figure 5–83.

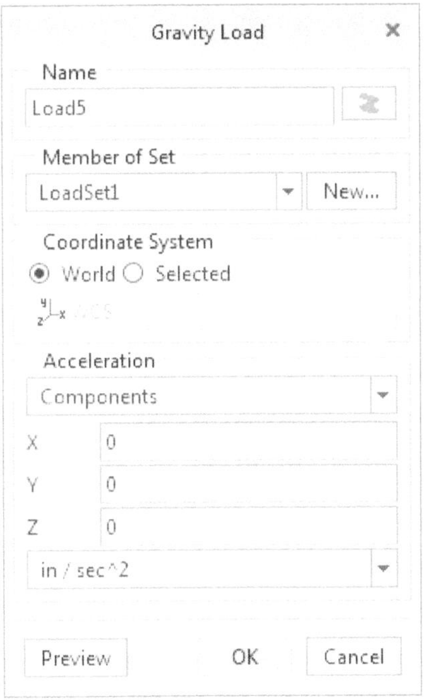

Figure 5–83

2. In the *Name* field, enter **gravity**.

3. Click **New** to define a new load set. The *Load Set Definition* dialog box opens, as shown in Figure 5–84.

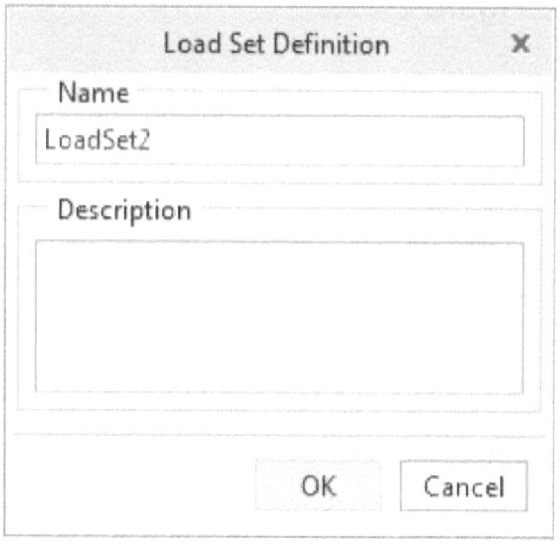

Figure 5–84

4. Accept the default name and click **OK**.
5. In the dialog box, in the *Acceleration* area, in the *Y* field, enter **-386**.

   Note: *386in/sec^2 is the 1G acceleration.*

6. Click **OK** to finish defining the gravity load. The model displays as shown in Figure 5–85.

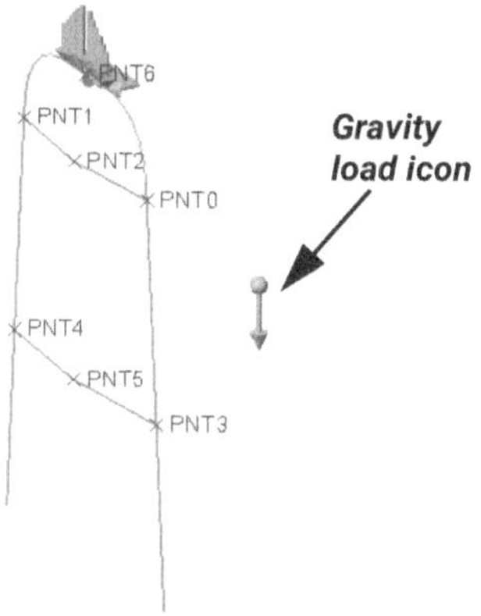

Figure 5–85

Task 8: Apply the constraints.

In this task, you will constrain the ends of the frame model (fix in translation and rotation). To constrain the ends, create two datum points as simulation features at the ends of the frame model.

1. In Creo Simulate, create the two datum points shown in Figure 5–86.

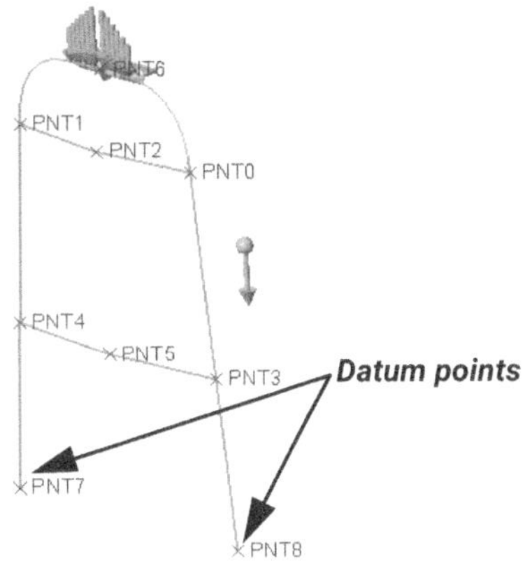

Figure 5–86

Note: A beam end point has six degrees of freedom.

2. In the *Home* tab, click (Displacement). The *Constraint* dialog box opens.
3. In the *Name* field, enter **end_constraints**.
4. Expand the *References* drop-down list and select **Points**.
5. Select the points created in Step 1 of this task.
6. Fix all of the translations and rotations.
7. Click **OK**. The model displays as shown in Figure 5–87.

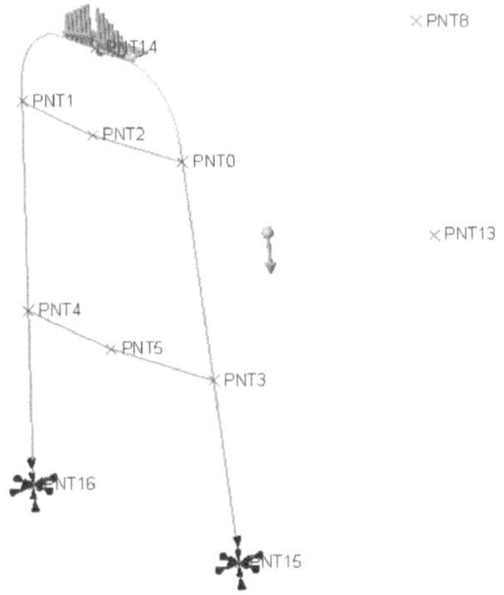

Figure 5–87

Analysis Tasks

Task 9: Set up the analysis.

In this task, you will set up and run a Multi-Pass Adaptive convergence analysis.

1. For the name of the analysis, enter **d2_frame**.
2. Select both load sets.
3. In the *Limits* area, in the *Polynomial Order* field, enter **6** and in the *Percent Convergence* field, enter **1**.
4. In the *Output* tab, increase the *Plotting Grid* to **10**.
5. Run the analysis.

Results Tasks

Task 10: Display the results.

In this task, you will create and display four result windows.

1. In the *Analyses and Design Studies* dialog box, click  (Review Results). The *Result Window Definition* dialog box opens, as shown in Figure 5–88.

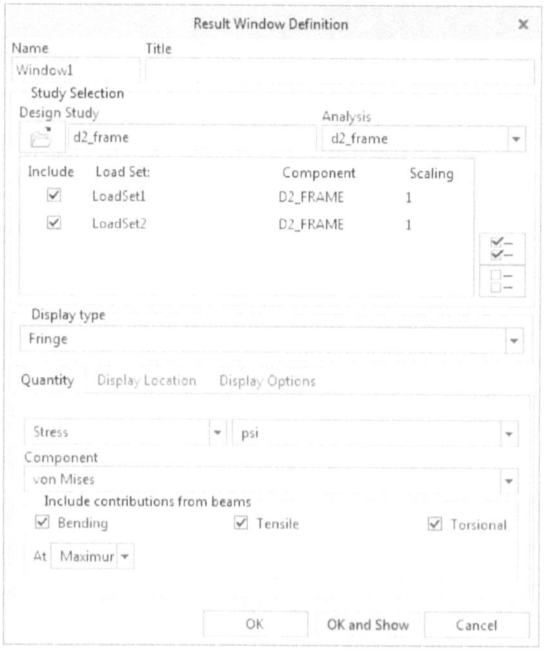

Figure 5–88

Note: *Both load sets are included. You can display results for them individually or combined. The default combination factor is 1. You can change it for a different load combination ratio. Note the* ***Bending***, ***Tensile***, *and* ***Torsional*** *stress options.*

2. Create, display, and animate a displacement result window. Include both load sets. The display type is **Fringe** and the displacement component is **Magnitude**. The window displays as shown in Figure 5–89.

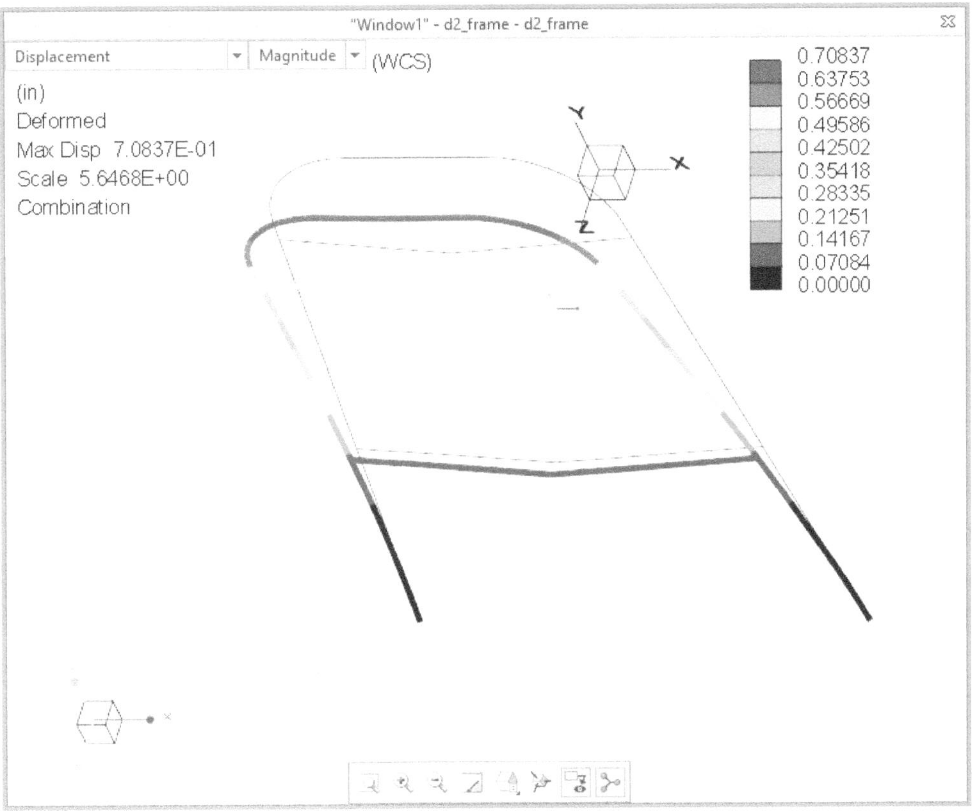

Figure 5–89

Note that the displacements at the end points of the frame are zero, according to the applied constraints.

3. Create and display the beam bending stress plot for the combined load sets. Toggle off the Animation. The plot displays as shown in Figure 5–90. Select (Model Max) to display the maximum beam bending stress.

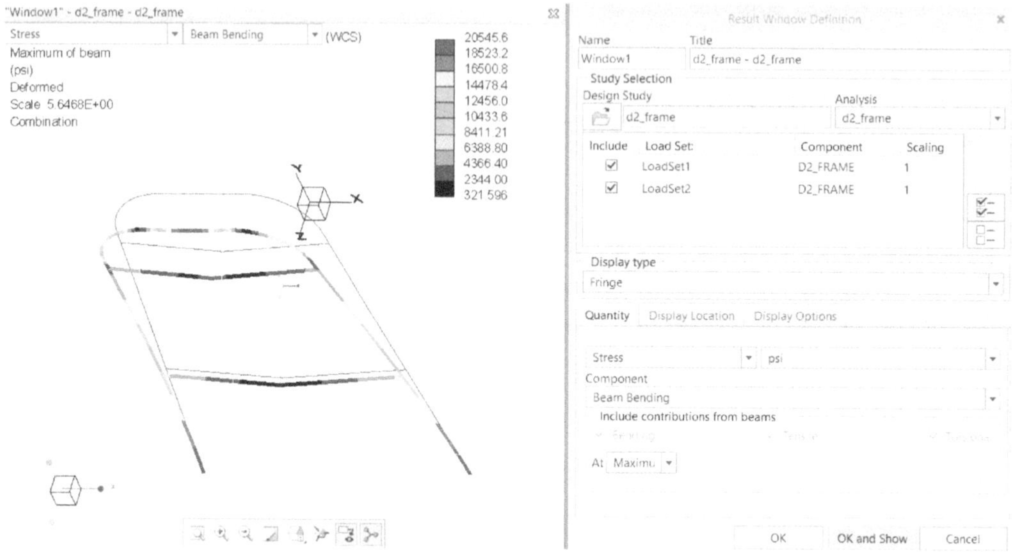

Figure 5–90

Note: *The* ***Model Max*** *option is not available in an animated result window.*

4. Create and display the deformed torsional stress plot for the combined load sets. Display the minimum and maximum torsional stress locations. The plot displays as shown in Figure 5–91.

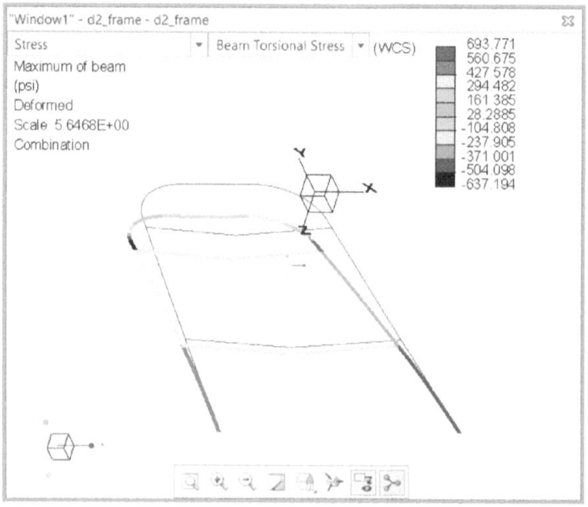

Figure 5–91

5. Create and display the reaction force Y at the point constraints. Enter the information in the *Result Window Definition* dialog box, as shown on the right in Figure 5–92. The plot displays as shown on the left in Figure 5–92.

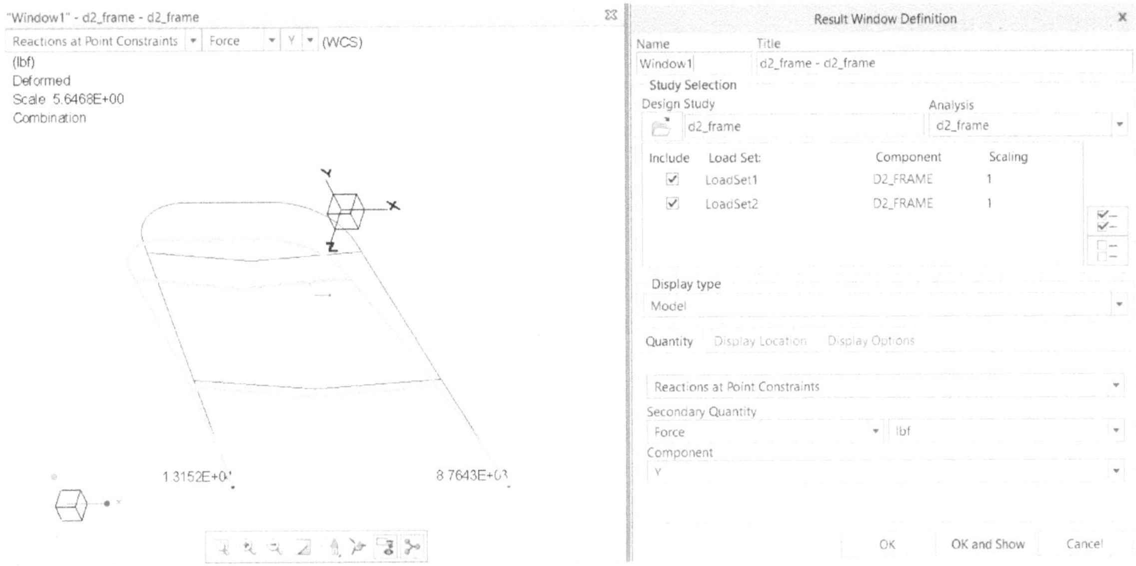

Figure 5–92

Task 11: Save and close the model.

1. Select **File>Close**. Click **Don't Save** when prompted to save the results.
2. Close the *Analyses and Design Studies* dialog box.
3. Exit Creo Simulate. Save and close the model in Creo Parametric.

End of practice

Practice 5c
3D Frame Analysis

Practice Objectives

- Set up a 3D beam model.
- Run a 3D beam model.
- Analyze a 3D beam model.

In this practice, you will use beam element idealizations to set up, run, and analyze a 3D Aluminum walker frame. The frame part is shown in Figure 5–93. The beam section is a hollow circular pipe and the frame ends are fixed. The walker supports a 225lb person.

Figure 5–93

Modeling Tasks

Task 1: Open the d3_frame.prt.

1. Set the working directory to **Chapter05**, if required.
2. Open **d3_frame.prt**.
3. Set the model display as follows:
    - *(Datum Display Filters)*: All Off
    - *(Spin Center)*: Off
    - *(Display Style)*: (Shading With Edges)

The part displays as shown in Figure 5–94.

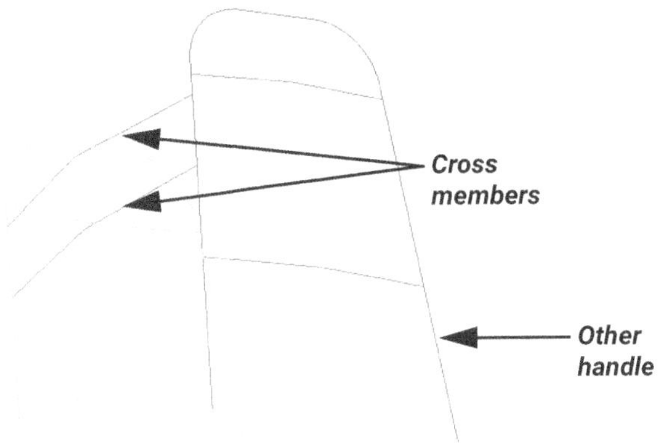

Figure 5–94

4. The unit systems are set to the Creo Parametric default.
5. Switch to the Creo Simulate environment.
6. Click (Simulation Display). In the *Simulation Display* dialog box, select **Wireframe** in the *Beams* drop-down list and clear the **Display AutoGEM Controls** option. Click **OK**.
7. The frame model displays as shown in Figure 5–95.

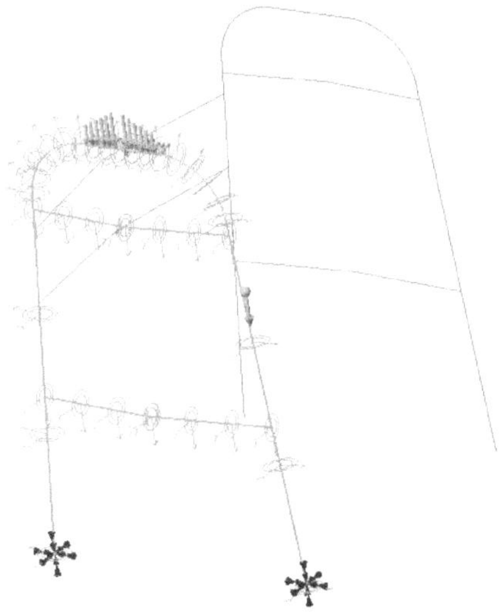

Figure 5–95

Note: *The 2D frame (original curves) in the previous practice was used to create this 3D frame. The 2D frame sections and properties are maintained in this practice.*

Task 2: Create the beam elements for the other walker handle.

1. Double-click on the curve shown in Figure 5–96. The *Beam Definition* dialog box opens.

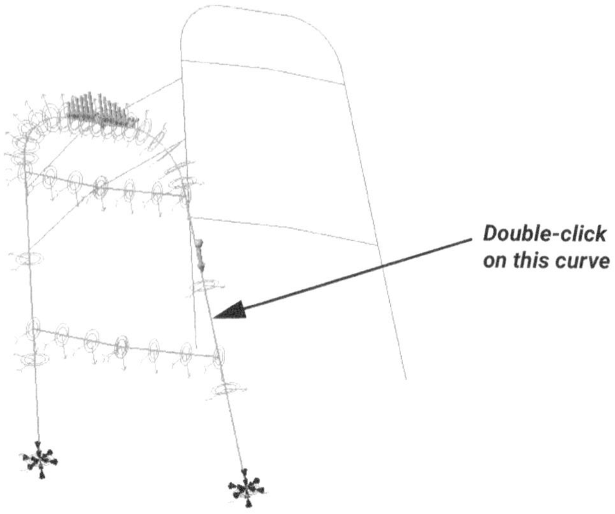

Figure 5–96

2. Hold <Ctrl> and select the other handle curve shown in Figure 5–97.

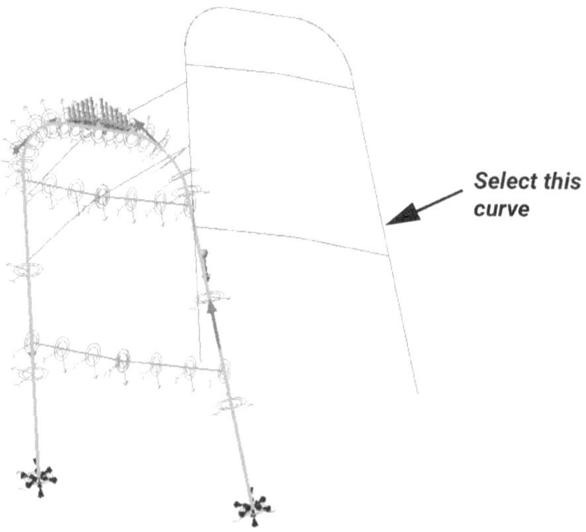

Figure 5–97

3. Click **OK** to close the *Beam Definition* dialog box. The model displays as shown in Figure 5–98.

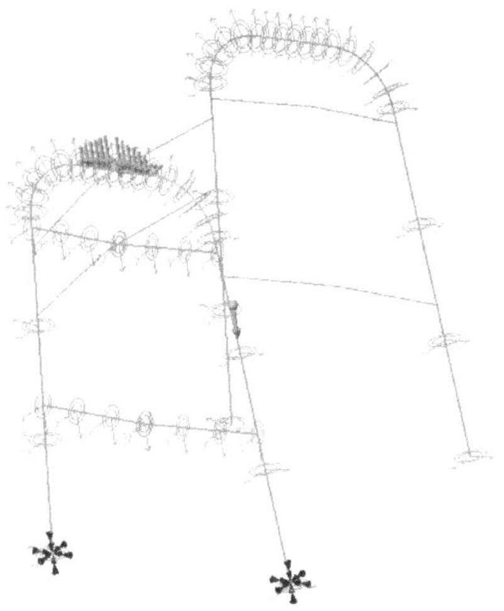

Figure 5–98

Note: *The beam section is **d2_frame_section_1**.*

4. Double-click on the curve shown in Figure 5–99. The *Beam Definition* dialog box opens.

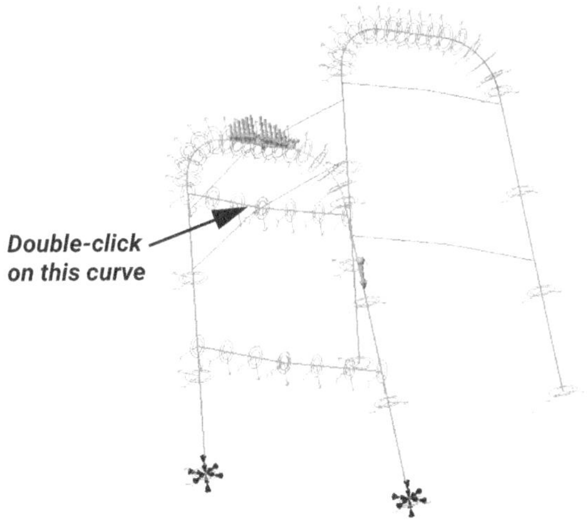

Figure 5–99

5. Hold <Ctrl> and select two cross member curves on the other handle and two cross member curves that connect the left handle to the right handle, as shown in Figure 5–100.

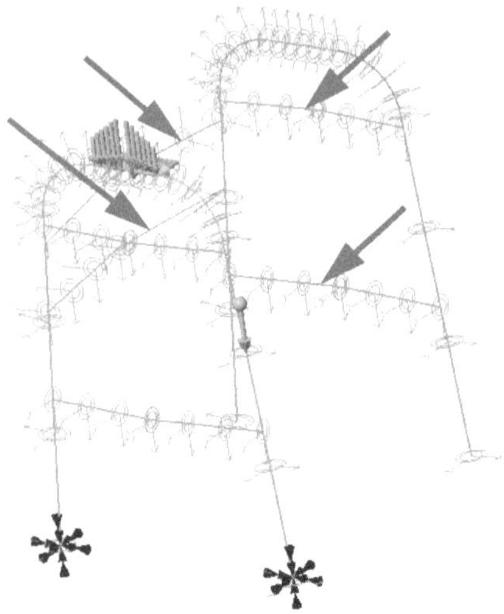

Figure 5–100

6. Click **OK** to close the *Beam Definition* dialog box.
7. Click (Simulation Display). The *Simulation Display* dialog box opens.
8. Select the *Modeling Entities* tab and clear the **Beam Sections** option.

Task 3: Delete the gravity load.

1. Expand the *Model Tree* and locate the **gravity** load, as shown in Figure 5–101.

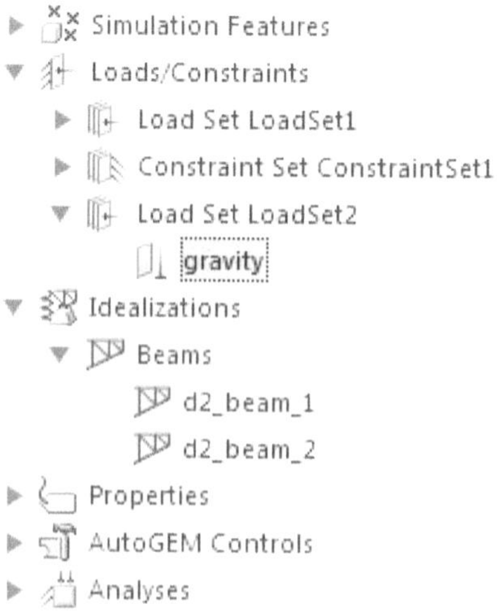

Figure 5–101

2. Right-click on the **gravity** load and select **Delete**. In the *Question* dialog box, click **Yes**.

Task 4: Copy the vertical load to the other handle.

1. In the *Model Tree*, highlight the **distributed_load** load, right-click and select **Copy**.
2. In the *Model Tree*, highlight **Load Set Load Set1**, right-click, and select **Paste**. The *Force/Moment Load* dialog box opens, as shown in Figure 5–102.

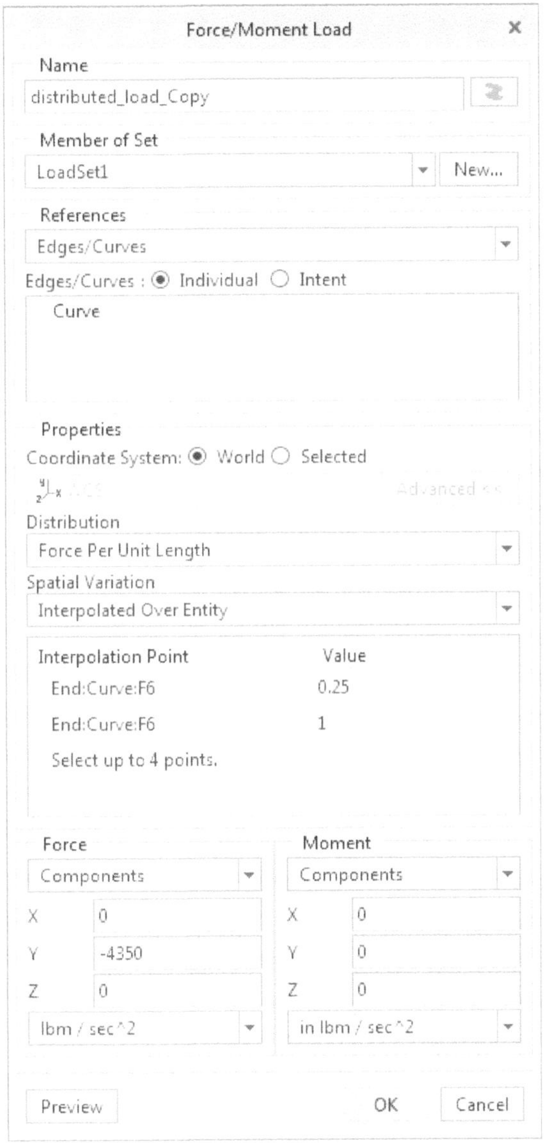

Figure 5–102

Note: *Assign **LoadSet1** to all of the loads.*

3. Right-click in the *Edges/Curves* selection collector and select **Remove** to clear the selection.
4. Select the curve on the other handle, as shown in Figure 5–103.

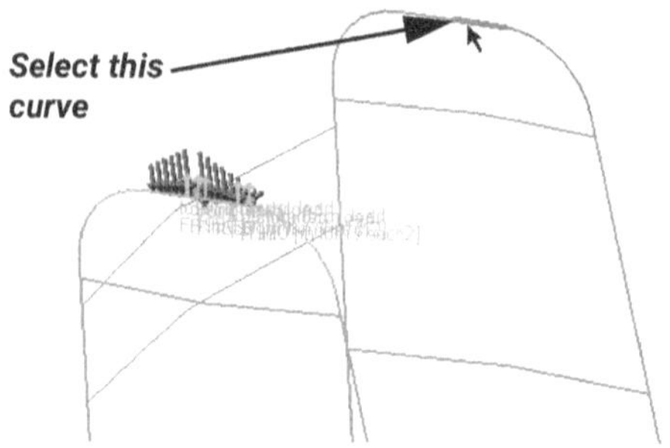

Figure 5–103

5. In the first row of the *Value* column, enter **0.25**, and in the second row of the *Value* column, enter **1.00**. The *Force/Moment Load* dialog box displays as shown in Figure 5–104.

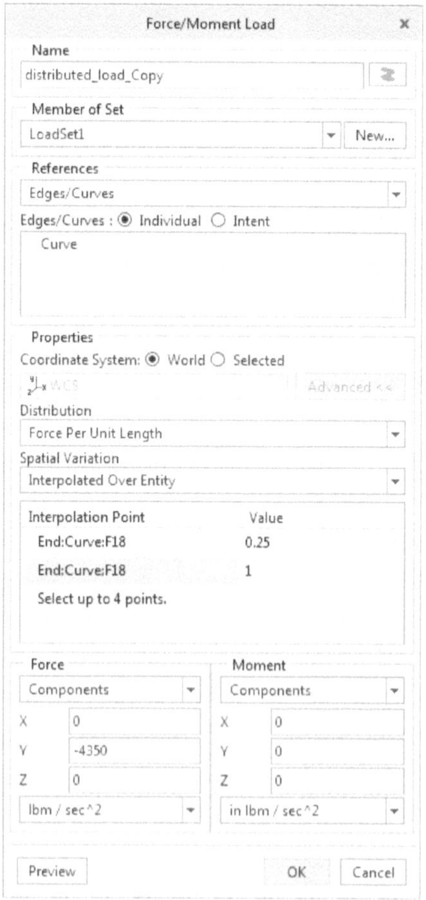

Figure 5–104

6. Click **OK**. The model displays as shown in Figure 5–105.

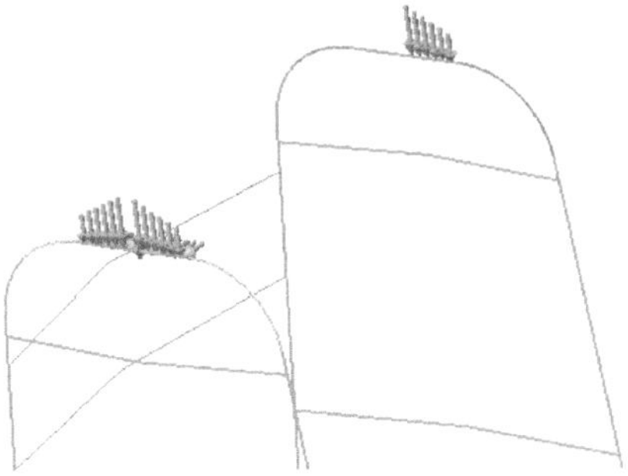

Figure 5–105

7. Follow Steps 1 to 6 to copy **distributed_load_1** to the other handle. If necessary, swap the 0.25 and 1 values at the ends of the curve to obtain correct load variation. The model displays as shown in Figure 5–106.

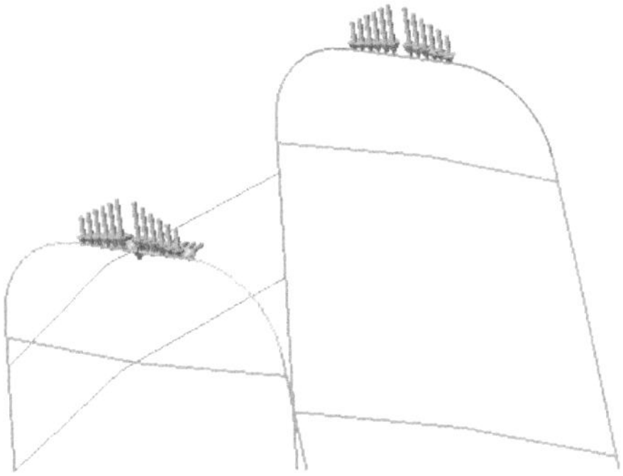

Figure 5–106

Task 5: Copy the side load to the other handle.

1. Follow Steps 1 to 6 in the previous task to copy **total_uniform_load** to the other handle. However, change the sign of the force in the Z-direction from *1930* to **-1930**. The model displays as shown in Figure 5–107.

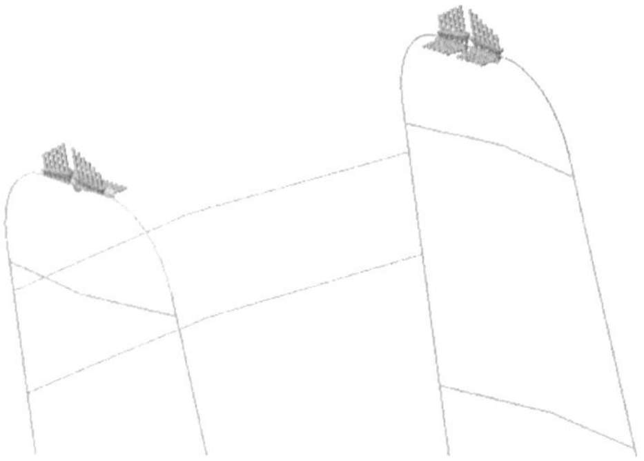

Figure 5–107

Note: *Changing the sign of the force is required to maintain the symmetry of the loading.*

Task 6: Copy the point load to the other handle.

1. In the *Model Tree*, select the existing loads and select (Hide) from the mini-toolbar.
2. In the In-graphics toolbar, enable (Point Display).
3. Create a datum point in the middle of the other handle, as shown in Figure 5–108.

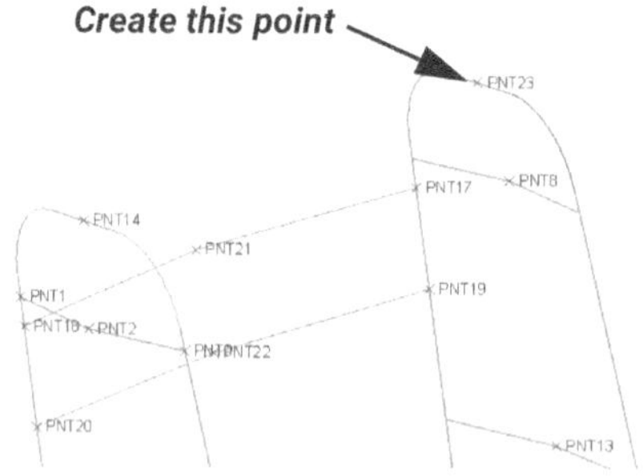

Figure 5–108

4. In the *Model Tree*, select the existing loads and select (Show) from the mini-toolbar.
5. In the *Model Tree*, select the **point_load** load and select (Edit Definition) from the mini-toolbar. The *Force/Moment Load* dialog box opens.
6. Hold <Ctrl> and click the point you created in Step 1. The selection collector displays two points.

7. Verify that the **Load Per Point** option is selected for the *Distribution*. The *Force/Moment Load* dialog box displays as shown in Figure 5–109.

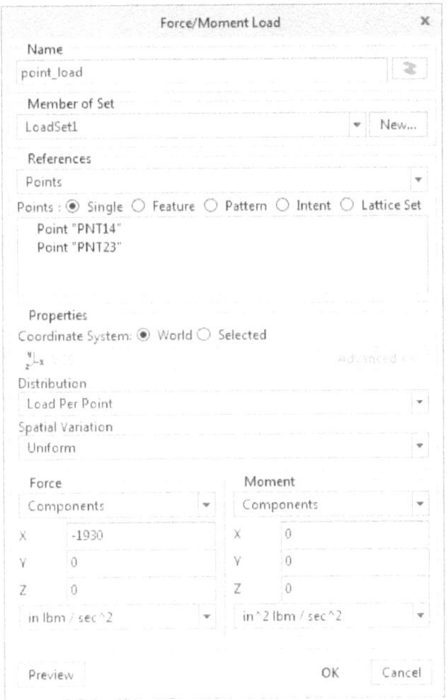

Figure 5–109

*Note: The **Load Per Point** option applies the entered amount of load to each selected point. The other option is **Total Load**, which evenly divides the entered load among all of the points.*

8. Click **OK**.

9. In the In-graphics toolbar, disable (Point Display).The model displays as shown in Figure 5–110.

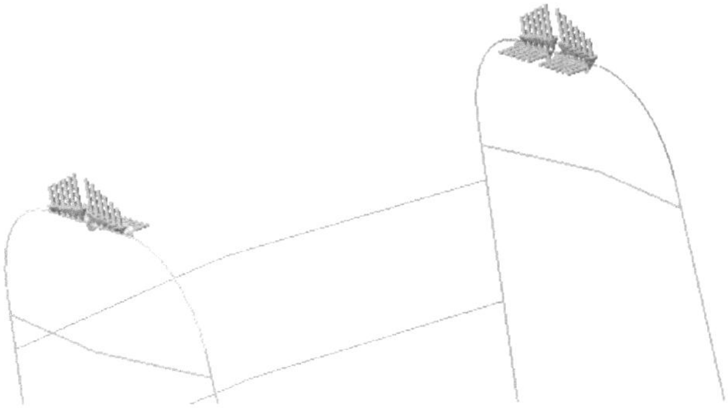

Figure 5–110

Task 7: Constrain the ends of the other handle.

1. In the *Model Tree*, select the **end_constraints** load and select (Edit Definition) from the mini-toolbar. The *Constraint* dialog box opens.
2. Hold <Ctrl> and click the end points (vertices) on the other handle. The selection collector displays the four selected points.
3. Click **OK**. The model displays as shown in Figure 5–111.

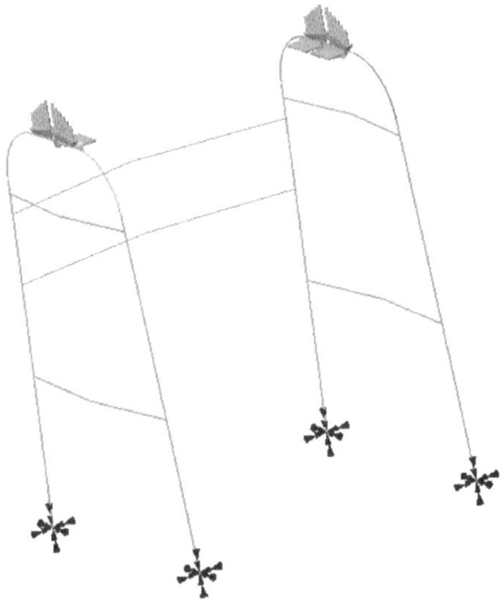

Figure 5–111

Analysis Tasks

Task 8: Set up the analysis.

Set up and run a Multi-Pass Adaptive convergence analysis.

1. For the name of the analysis, enter **d3_frame**.
2. In the *Limits* area, in the *Polynomial Order* field, enter **6**, and in the *Percent Convergence* field, enter **1**.
3. In the *Output* tab, increase the *Plotting Grid* to **10**.
4. Run the analysis. Ignore the warning messages in the *Diagnostics* window.

Task 9: Display the results.

1. Create and display a color plot of the displacement for the frame model. Animate this plot to verify that the boundary conditions are correct and the deformation is symmetrical.
2. Step through the animation. On Frame 5, the result window displays as shown in Figure 5–112.

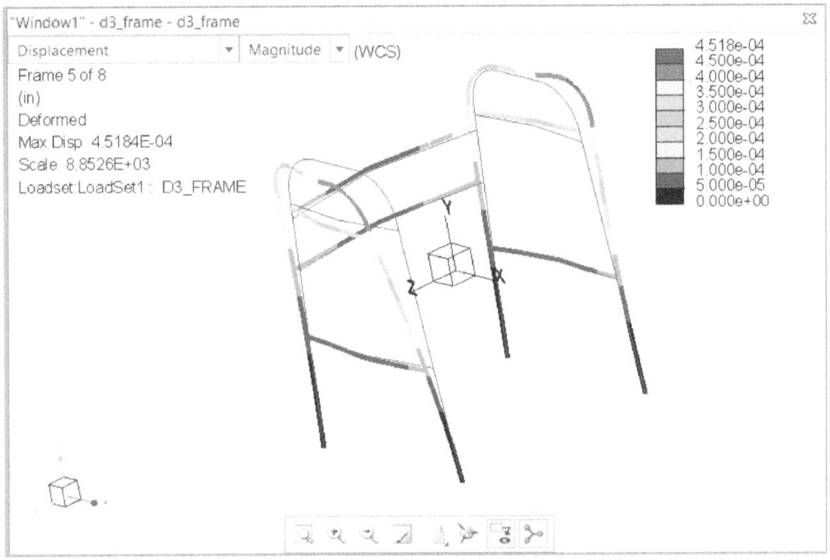

Figure 5–112

3. Start the animation. Note that each beam displays some bending.

Task 10: Modify the constraint on PNT15.

In this task, you will modify the constraint on **PNT15** to simulate a settling foundation for the walker at this corner. This represents a forced displacement in the Y-direction for the constraint at **PNT15**.

1. Select **File>Close**. Click **Don't Save** when prompted to save the results. Close the *Analyses and Design Studies* dialog box.
2. In the *Model Tree*, select the **end_constraints** constraint and select (Edit Definition). The *Constraint* dialog box opens.
3. Right-click on the **PNT15** in the selection collector and select **Remove**.
4. Click **OK** to close the *Constraint* dialog box.
5. Click (Displacement). The *Constraint* dialog box opens.
6. In the *Name* field, enter **forced_constraint**.
7. Expand the *References* drop-down list and select **Points**.

8. Select **PNT15**.
9. Fix *Translations* X and Z and fix all of the *Rotations*.
10. In the *Translation* area, for *Y*, click . In the *Y* field, enter **-0.0625**.

    Note: *The frame at this corner will be forced to move down by 0.0625in (the unit length is inch).*

11. Click **OK** to close the *Constraint* dialog box.
12. Re-run the analysis.

Task 11: Display the results.

1. Create and display a color plot of the displacement for the frame model. Overlay the undeformed model and animate the plot to verify that the boundary conditions are correct.
2. Step through the animation. On Frame 5, the result window displays as shown in Figure 5–113.

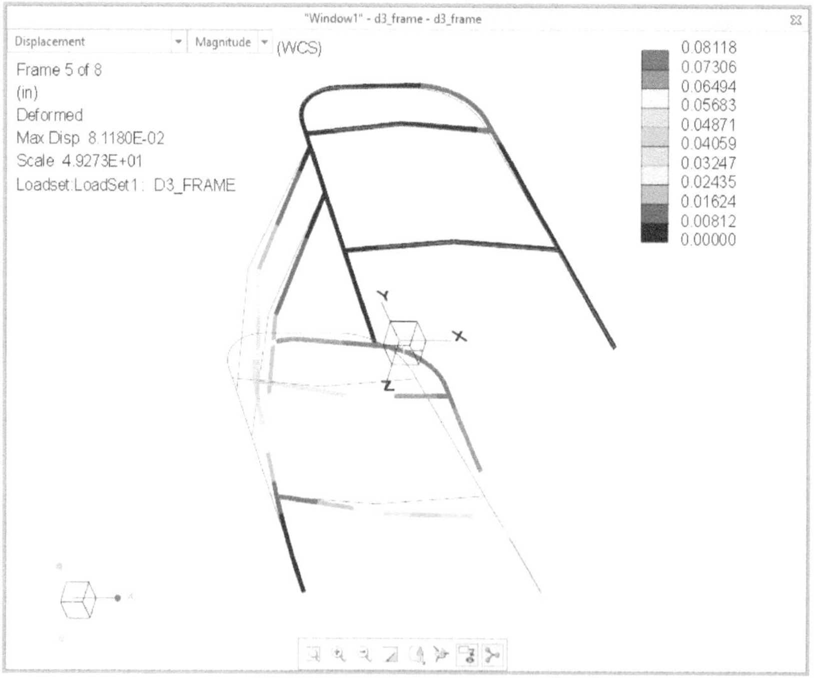

Figure 5–113

- Note that the end of the frame with the enforced displacement constraint is moving down, as required.

3. Exit the Results environment. Save and close the model in Creo Parametric.

End of practice

Practice 5d
Analysis of a Grain Hopper

Practice Objectives

- Create standard shells.
- Create beams.
- Apply loads and constraints.
- Set up and run a Single-Pass Adaptive analysis.
- Display the results.

In this practice, you will perform a static stress analysis on the grain hopper shown in Figure 5–114 with minimum instruction.

The hopper consists of a steel box mounted on a tubular frame.

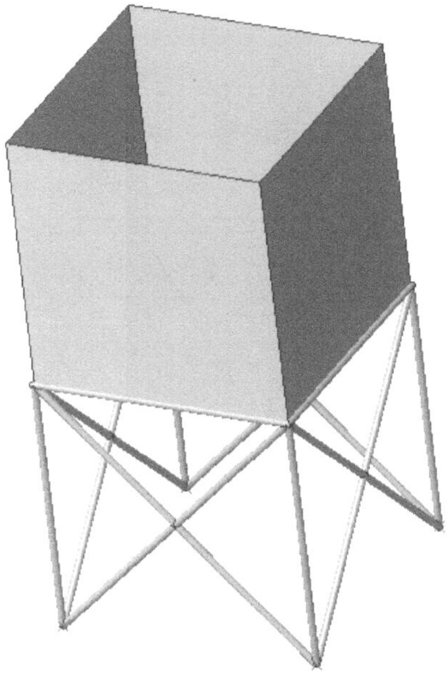

Figure 5–114

Task 1: Create shells.

1. Set the working directory to **Chapter05**, if required.
2. Open **hopper.prt** and launch Creo Simulate.
3. Set the model display as follows:
   - *(Datum Display Filters)*: (Point Display) Only
   - *(Spin Center)*: Off
   - *(Display Style)*: (Shading With Edges)
4. For all datum surfaces comprising the box (five surfaces altogether, as shown on Figure 5–115), create shells with the following properties:
   - *Thickness:* **0.5in**
   - *Material:* **STEEL**

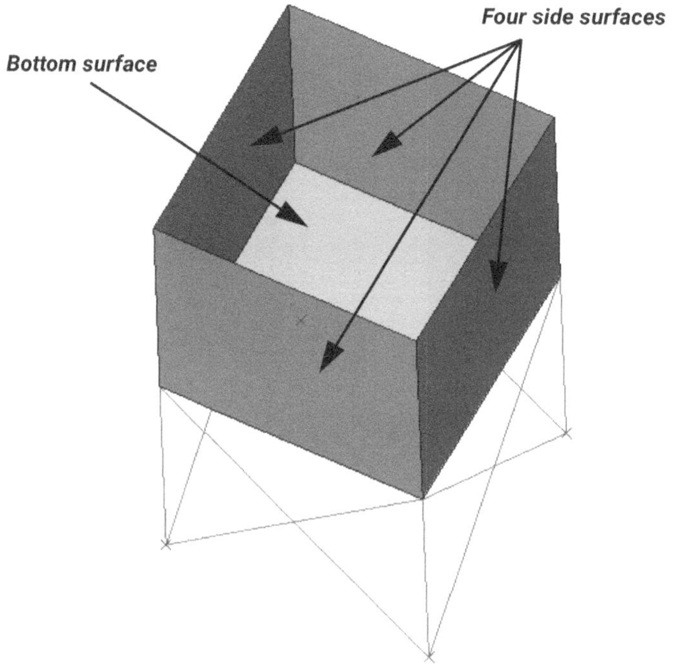

Figure 5–115

Task 2: Create beams.

1. For the twelve datum curves shown in Figure 5–116, create beams with the following properties:
   - *Cross-section:* Hollow tube **2in OD** and **0.1in thick**
   - *Material:* **STEEL**
   - *Orientation:* **WCS Z-direction**

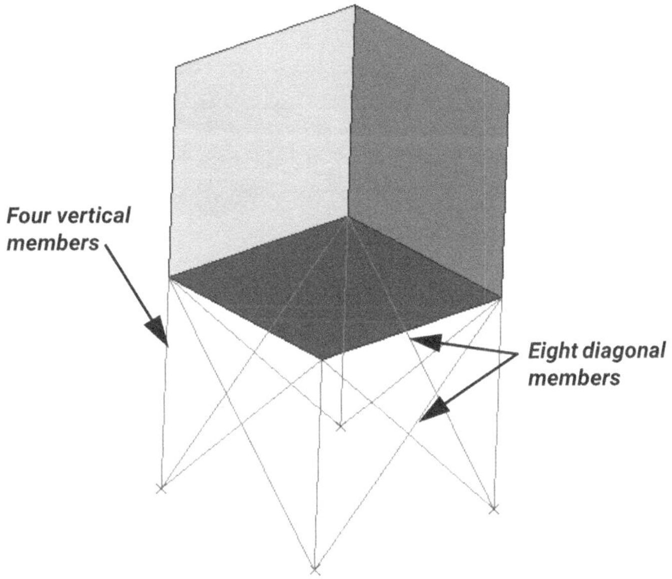

Figure 5–116

Note: *Since each beam cross-section is round, the only requirement for the orientation vector is that it does not coincide with any beam's axis.*

2. For the four edges at the bottom of the box shown in Figure 5–117, create beams with the following properties:
    - *Cross-section* and *Material:* Same as for the vertical and diagonal beams
    - *Orientation:* **WCS Y-direction**

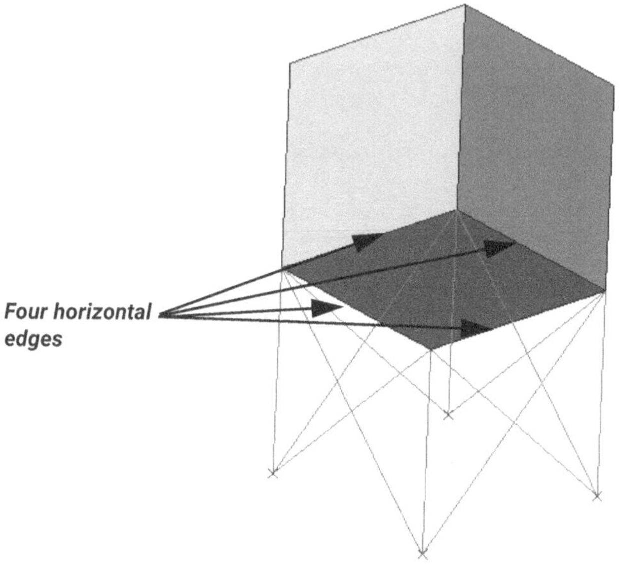

Figure 5–117

Task 3: Apply loads and constraints.

1. Fully constrain (translations and rotations) the four points at the bottom of the frame, as shown in Figure 5–118.

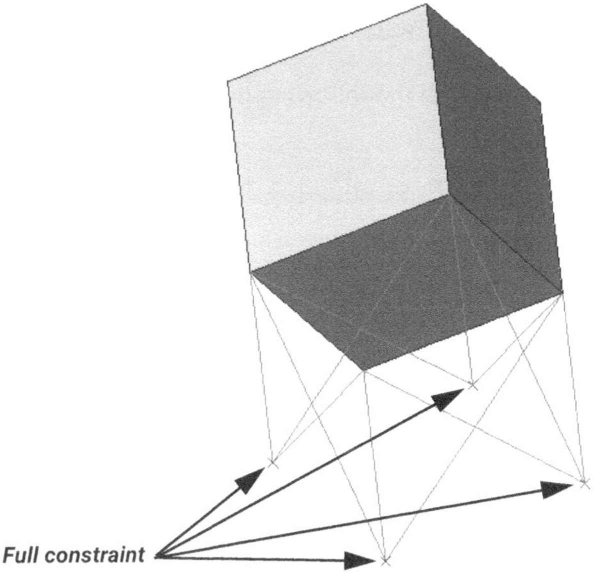

Figure 5–118

2. Apply **100psi** pressure load in the downward direction to the bottom surface of the box, as shown in Figure 5–119.

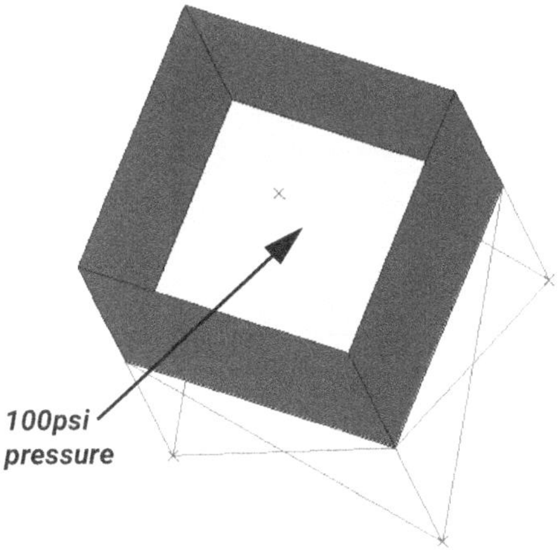

Figure 5–119

Task 4: Set up and run the analysis.

1. Create a new static analysis with the following parameters:
   - *Analysis name:* **hopper**
   - *Convergence method:* **Multi-Pass Adaptive, P-max=9**
   - *Plotting Grid:* **10**
2. Run the analysis.
3. If the analysis does not converge, change the mesh size for the box's surfaces to half the size of the box and then re-run the analysis.

Task 5: Visualize the analysis results.

1. Visualize and animate the **Displacement Magnitude** fringe plot. Does the part deform according to the applied loads and constraints?
2. Display the **von Mises Stress** fringe plot. Does the maximum stress occur in the box or in the frame?
3. Display the **von Mises Stress** fringe plot for the box only. Do you think the bottom of the box might require additional structural support?
4. Display the **von Mises Stress** plot for the beams only. Which beams are loaded the most?

End of practice

Chapter 6

Sensitivity and Optimization Design Studies

Design studies enable you to explore design alternatives and to optimize your model. You can perform three types of design studies in Creo Simulate: standard, sensitivity, and optimization. Standard design studies calculate results for an analysis with different design variable settings. Sensitivity design studies calculate results for several different values of design variables (e.g., dimensions). Optimization design studies adjust a model's parameters to meet a specified goal or to test the feasibility of a design.

Learning Objectives

- Understand the design study objectives and variables.
- Understand the standard, sensitivity, and optimization design studies.
- Set up the variables for a design study.

6.1 Design Considerations

Before you set up a design study, it is recommended that you define your objectives, measures, and design variables. This enables you to organize and provide the correct data to Creo Simulate for the study.

For example, the lift point shown in Figure 6–1 needs to be run through a design study in order to minimize its mass. Before the design study is set up, the objective, design limits, measures, and design variables need to be defined.

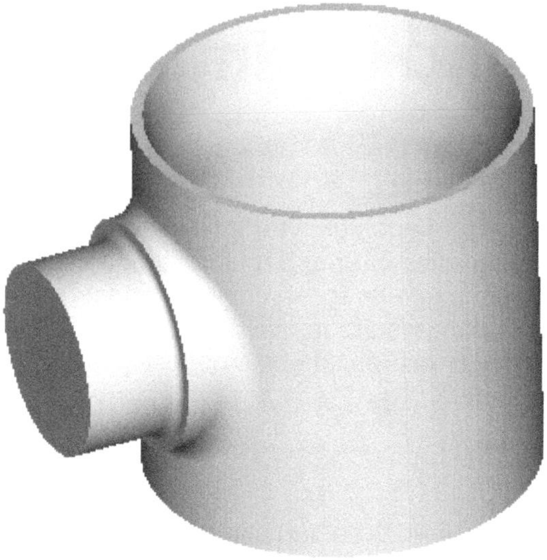

Figure 6–1

- The objective is to minimize the mass of the part.Therefore, we need to have a simulation measure that measures the mass of the part.
- The maximum stress in the part cannot exceed the yield strength of the material. This becomes the design limit, for which we need the second simulation measure, the maximum von Mises stress in the part.
- The design variables are the dimensions that will be varied or adjusted during the design study. For this example, these include the diameter of the trunnion, the diameter of the leg, and the distance from the center of the trunnion to the center of the leg.

Objectives

Objectives are the goals that you want to achieve with a design study (e.g., minimize weight, minimize reaction forces, etc.). You set your objectives during the setup of the optimization design studies. Your objective can be user-defined or system-defined using the options in the *Predefined* area in the *Measures* dialog box, as shown in Figure 6–2. For example, a system-defined objective might be to minimize stress (i.e., the system-defined simulation measure **max_stress_vm**). An example of a user-defined objective would be to ensure that clearance (i.e., a user-defined parameter calculated by subtracting 2D values) is maximized.

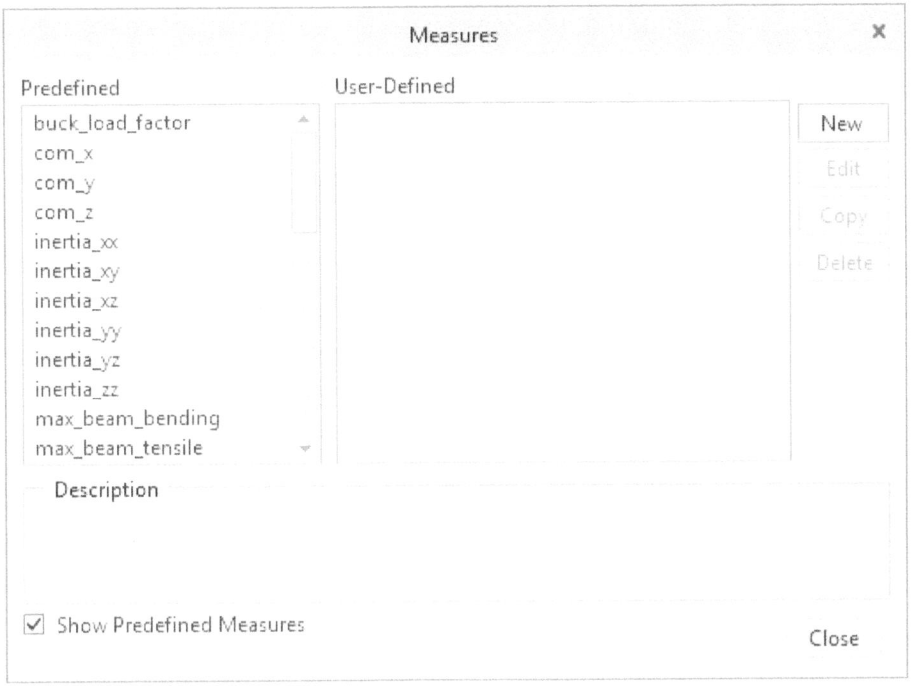

Figure 6–2

Note: *Objectives are only required for optimization design studies.*

Measures

Measures are the scalar quantities of interest that Creo Simulate calculates during analysis (e.g., maximum von Mises stress, maximum principal stress, etc.).

Design Variables

Design variables are the Creo Parametric dimensions or parameters that you set to achieve your objective.

6.2 Types of Design Studies

Standard Studies

Standard design studies evaluate the model for an alternative set of design variables, similarly to running a *what if* scenario.

Sensitivity Studies

Sensitivity studies calculate how the variation in a design variable affects the results in which you are interested (i.e., the maximum stress or deflection). You might want to determine how a particular dimension or model property is going to affect the results of an analysis (i.e., you want to assess the sensitivity of the model to changes in this parameter). You could manually edit the model (i.e., geometry or properties) and perform the analysis many times. However, this method would be time-consuming and potentially error-prone. A Creo Simulate sensitivity study automates this task.

You can perform two types of sensitivity studies: local and global. Local sensitivity studies assess which parameters have the greatest effect on a measure at the current parameter values (within a range of 2%). Local sensitivity studies are useful when you are testing small variations of data. They enable you to test the validity of your parameters and provide data on whether to increase or decrease them to meet your design goal.

Global sensitivity studies vary a parameter over a user-defined range of values (the range is larger than that in a local sensitivity study). They are useful when you have done a local study and want to test a larger range of variables to get the best possible parameter values to achieve your design goal.

Optimization Studies

Optimization studies manipulate parameters and determine an optimal solution to your design goal, within the specified design limits. It is necessary to have a design goal or design limit or both. If you do not have a goal, Creo Simulate searches for the first possible design while conforming to your design limit. This is called feasibility study.

Optimization studies are set up and run using the same procedure as sensitivity studies. The report generated by an optimization study contains the following information:

- Optimized value of each parameter
- Value of the goal and of each design limit measure

Setting Up Design Studies

In Creo Simulate, design studies are recommended to be set up and run in the following order:

1. Run an analysis to ensure that the model converges to a solution.
2. Set up the design parameters for the design studies.
3. Run a local sensitivity study and select the parameters that have an effect on the measures and on the goal.
4. Run a global sensitivity study on the selected parameters and find the parameter values (maximum or minimum) that have the greatest effect on the goal and on the measures.
5. Run an optimization study for the parameters that have the greatest effect on the goal. Select initial values for the parameters based on data from the global sensitivity study.

6.3 Design Variables

Design variables are Creo Parametric dimensions and/or parameters that you want to change during a design study. Design variables are selected in the *Design Study Definition* dialog box, which is opened from the *Analyses and Design Studies* dialog box.

For example, the *Optimization Study Definition* dialog box is shown in Figure 6–3. (Select Dimension) enables the selection of model dimensions to vary and (Select Parameter) enables you to select the model parameters.

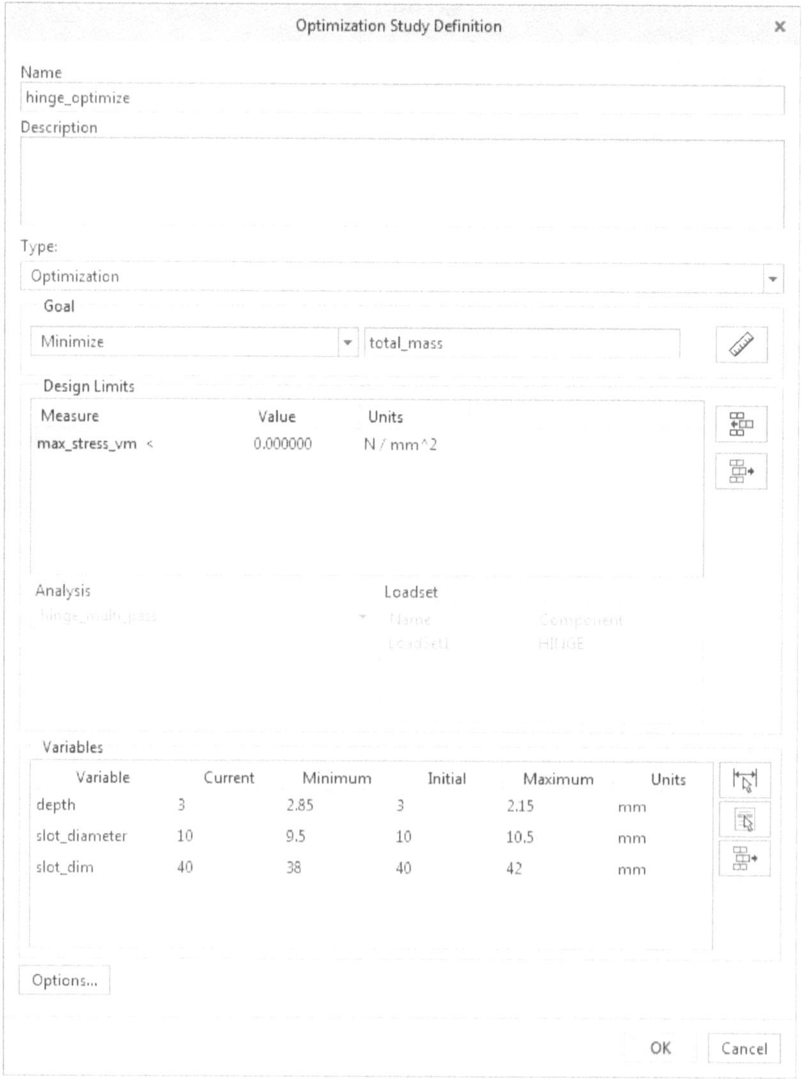

Figure 6–3

Practice 6a
Design Study of a Hinge Plate

Practice Objectives

- Set up and run sensitivity design studies.
- Set up and run an optimization design study.

In this practice, you will use sensitivity and optimization design studies to set up, run, analyze, and optimize a hinge plate part, as shown in Figure 6–4. The part is made of steel.

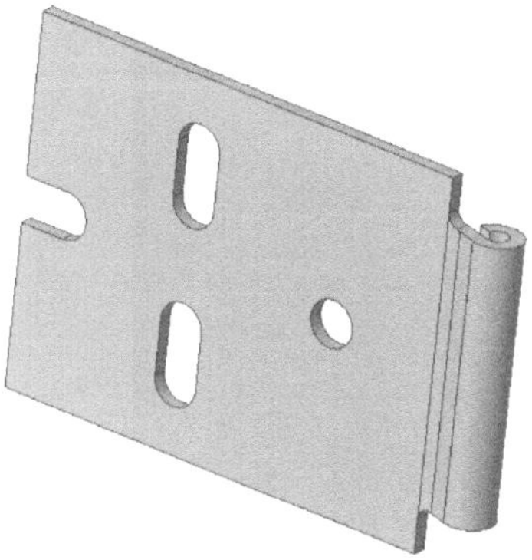

Figure 6–4

> ***Note:*** *Sensitivity and optimization design studies automate some of the repetitive work involved in design.*

When setting up design studies, you need to define the following information:

- The goal for the study.
- The measure to be used to analyze the parameter's effect on the hinge part.
- The design variables (Creo Parametric dimensions).

These requirements are summarized as follows:

Goal	Measure	Design Variables
Minimize the weight of the part.	• Von Mises stress • Total mass	• Dimension from left edge to center of vertical slots (40mm) • Holes and slots diameter (10mm) • Hinge Plate thickness (3mm) • Dimension from left edge to center of right hand side hole (75mm)

Modeling Tasks

Task 1: Open hinge.prt.

1. Set the working directory to **Chapter06**.
2. Open **hinge.prt**.
3. Set the model display as follows:
   - *(Datum Display Filters)*: All Off
   - *(Spin Center)*: Off
   - *(Display Style)*: (Shading With Edges)

   The part displays as shown in Figure 6–5.

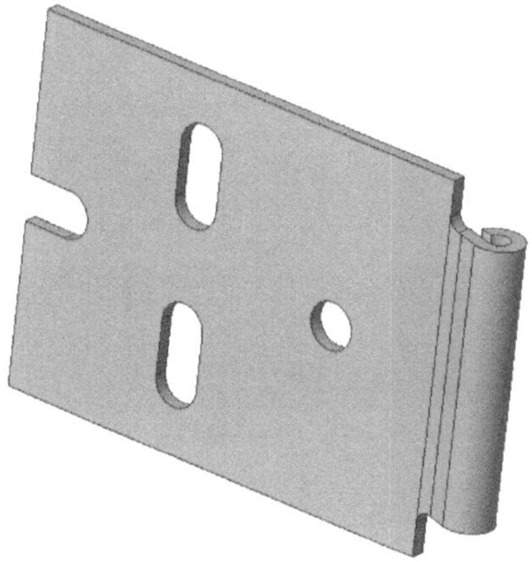

Figure 6–5

4. Ensure that the unit system is set to **mmNs**.

Task 2: Rename the design variables.

In this task, you will rename the Creo Parametric dimensions to make it easier to identify the design variables in Creo Simulate.

1. In the ribbon, in the *Tools* tab, select d= (Relations). The *Relations* dialog box opens. Enter the relation shown in Figure 6–6. It ties the plate thickness to the hole depth.

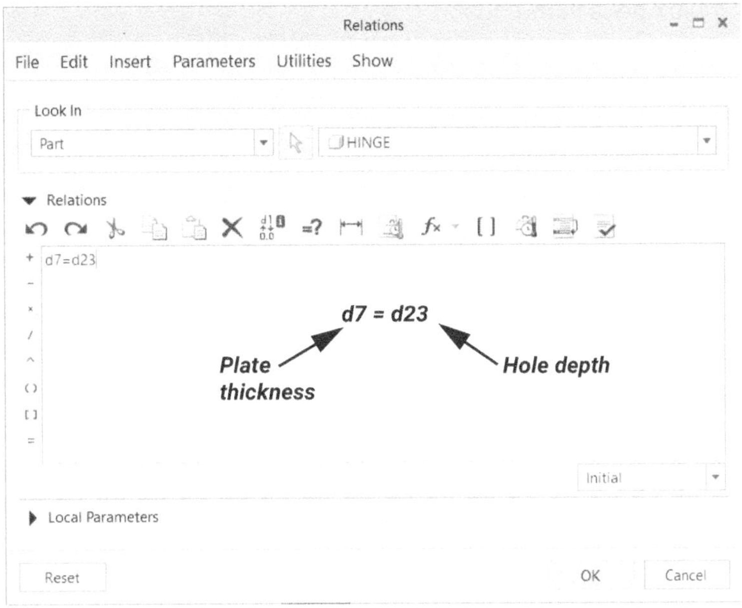

Figure 6–6

Note: *d7 = d23*

2. Click **OK** to close the *Relations* dialog box.
3. In the *Model Tree*, select **Cut id 226** and select (Edit Dimensions) from the mini-toolbar.
4. Select the 40 dimension as shown in Figure 6–7.

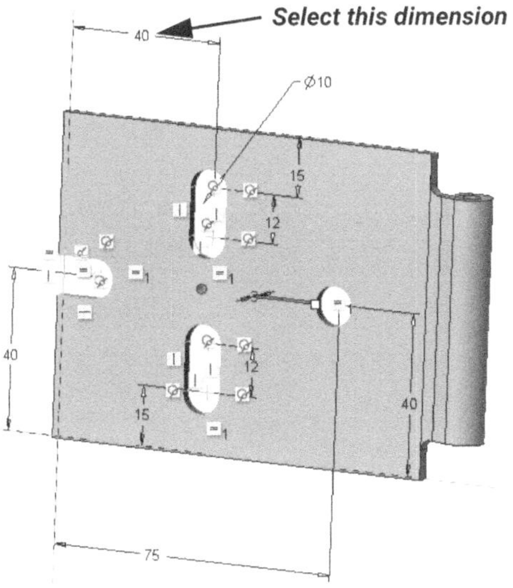

Figure 6–7

5. The *Dimension* tab opens in the ribbon.
6. In the *Value* group in the *Dimension* tab, edit the *name* to **slot_dim**, as shown in Figure 6–8.

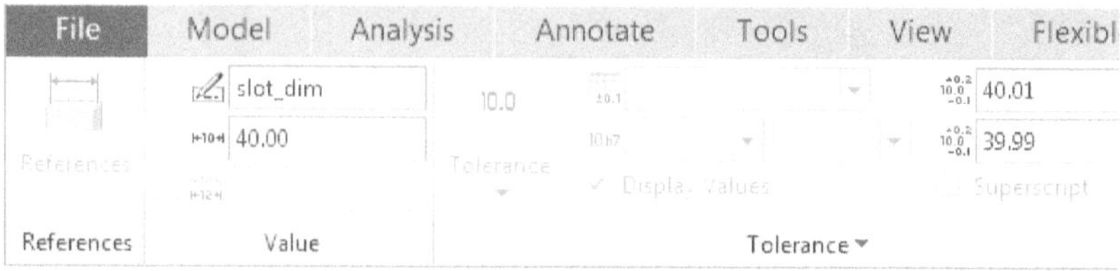

Figure 6–8

7. Repeat Steps 4 to 6 for the 75, Ø10, and 3 dimensions. For the *75* dimension, enter **hole_dim**, for the *Ø10* dimension, enter **slot_diameter**, and for the *3* dimension, enter **depth**.

   Note: *The 3 dimension is the depth of the holes in the plate, which is equal to the plate thickness.*

8. Click anywhere on the screen.
9. In the *Tools* tab, select (Switch Dimensions). The part displays as shown in Figure 6–9.

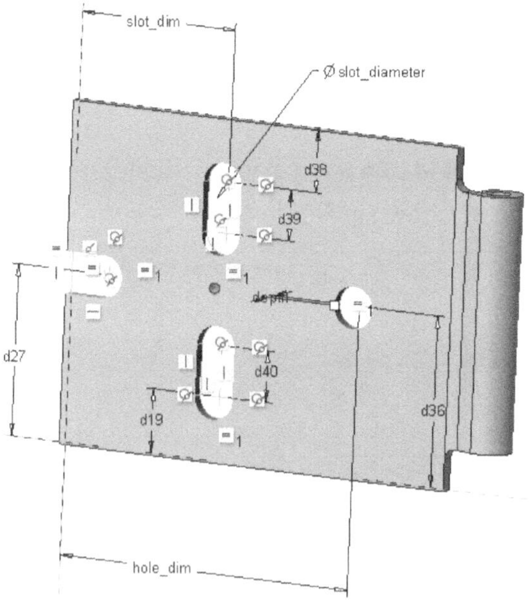

Figure 6–9

10. Click on the screen to clear the dimension display.
11. Save the part.

Task 3: Mesh the part with 3D solid elements.

1. Switch to Creo Simulate.
2. In the *Refine Model* tab, click (AutoGEM).
3. Expand the *AutoGEM References* drop-down list and select **Volume**.
4. Click (Select geometry).Select any surface on the part and click **Create** to create the mesh.
5. The *AutoGEM Summary* and *Diagnostics* dialog boxes open with a summary of the entities created, criteria satisfied, and time elapsed. Close both dialog boxes. The meshed model displays as shown in Figure 6–10.

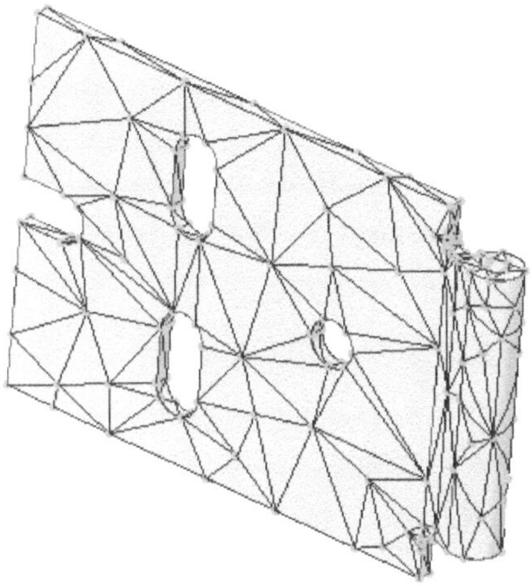

Figure 6–10

6. Close the *AutoGEM* dialog box and save the mesh. The mesh is saved with your model name and the .MMP extension (e.g., **hinge.mmp**) in the part's directory.

Task 4: Apply loads.

The hinge supports a door of 200Kg = 2000N at 10° to the vertical. In this task, you will apply this force in two components.

1. Select the surface shown in Figure 6–11.

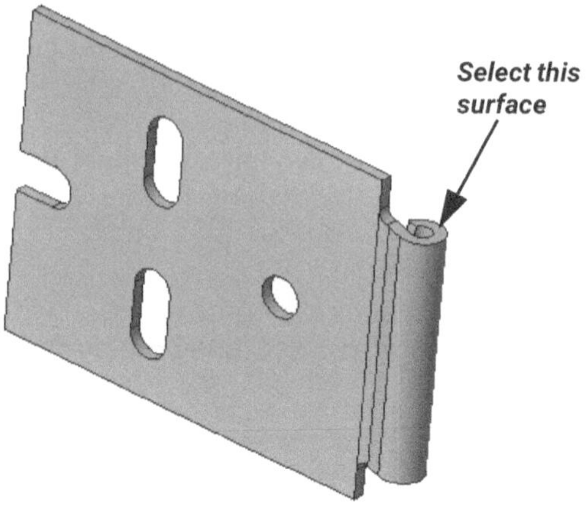

Figure 6–11

2. In the mini-toolbar, click (Force/Moment). The *Force/Moment Load* dialog box opens.
3. In the *Name* field, enter **hinge _force_1**.
4. In the *Force* area, in the *Y* field, enter **-1970**.
5. Click **OK**. The model displays as shown in Figure 6–12.

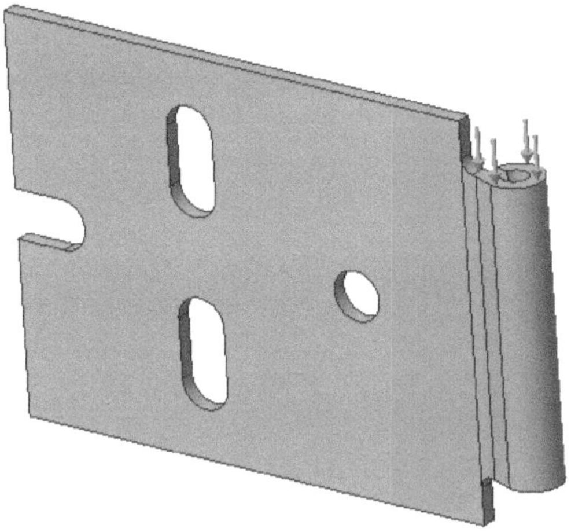

Figure 6–12

Note: *You can use the **Simulation Display** option to place the load vectors as **Tails Touching** and to toggle on the load values.*

6. Select the inside surface of the hinge hook as shown in Figure 6–13.

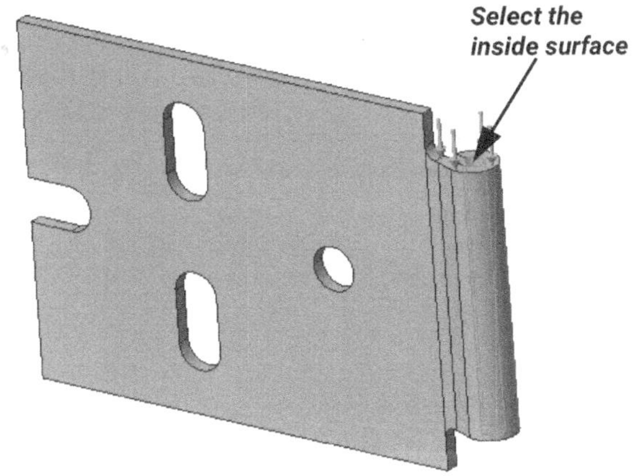

Figure 6–13

Note: *Select the internal surface of the hinge hook.*

7. In the mini-toolbar, select (Force/Moment). The *Force/Moment Load* dialog box opens.
8. In the *Name* field, enter **hinge _force_2.**
9. In the *Force* area, in the *X* field, enter **375**.
10. Click **OK**. The model displays as shown in Figure 6–14.

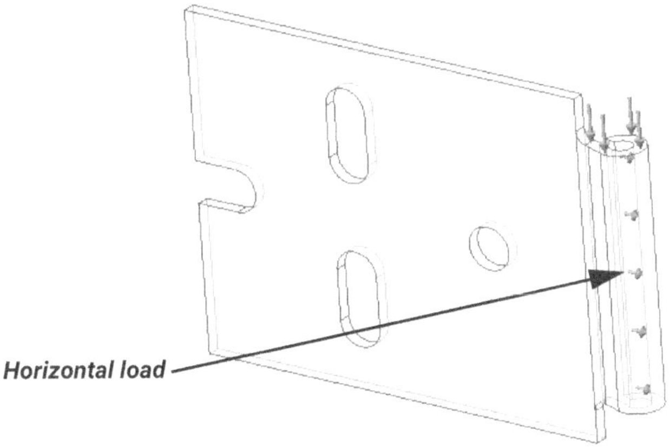

Figure 6–14

Note: *Display set to **Hidden Line** for clarity.*

Note: *You can toggle on the load values in the Simulation Display dialog box.*

Task 5: Constrain the surface of the hinge plate.

1. Select the surface shown in Figure 6–15, and select (Displacement) from the mini-toolbar.

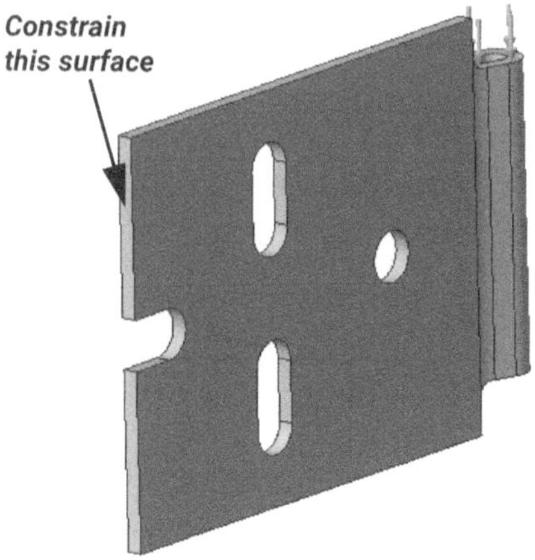

Figure 6–15

2. The *Constraint* dialog box opens.
3. In the *Name* field, enter **hinge_surface_const**.
4. Fix all of the *Translations*.
5. Click **OK**. The model displays as shown in Figure 6–16.

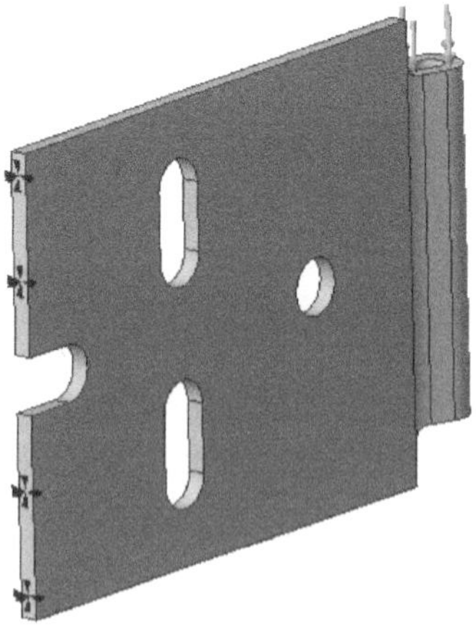

Figure 6–16

Task 6: Apply the material.

1. Assign **STEEL** to the model. The following values are the default material properties for HS-low-alloy steel (STEEL):
   - *Poisson:* **0.27**
   - *Young's modulus:* **199948 MPa**
   - *Coeff of thermal expansion:* **1.17e-5 /C**
   - *Density:* **7.82708e-9 tonne/mm^3**

Analysis Tasks

Task 7: Set up and run the analysis.

1. Set up a Multi-Pass Adaptive analysis with a 5% convergence and a maximum polynomial order of 9. For the name of the analysis, enter **hinge_multi_pass**.
2. Run the analysis. It should converge after 6 passes.

Task 8: Display the results.

1. Create and display a fringe color plot of the von Mises stress for the hinge. It displays as shown in Figure 6–17.

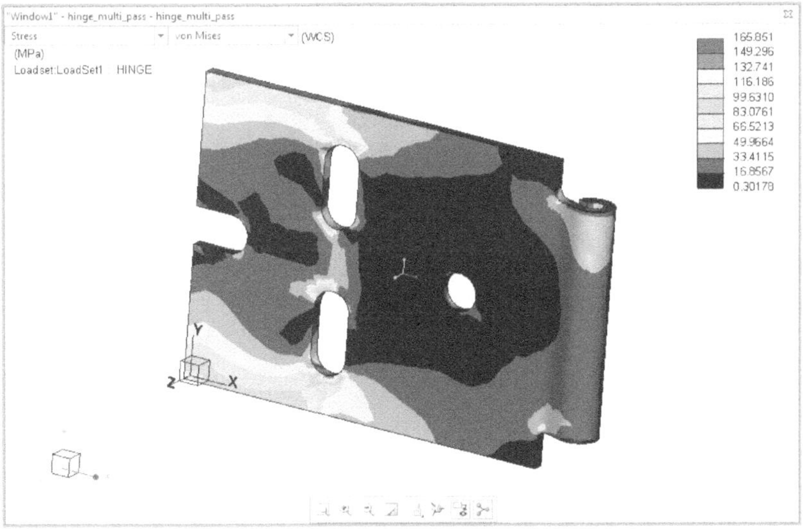

Figure 6–17

2. Exit the Results environment but leave the *Analyses and Design Studies* dialog box open.

Summary

In the previous tasks, you ensured that no errors have occurred in the model and that convergence is achieved. In the following tasks, you will determine the changes in the measure due to small variations in each parameter. This is a local sensitivity study.

> **Note:** *Design variables = Creo dimensions or parameters.*

The maximum von Mises stress is approximately 166 MPa. The yield strength for the hinge material is 230 MPa. The difference (230 - 166 = 64 MPa) leaves a good margin for weight optimization.

Task 9: Run a local sensitivity study.

In this task, you will vary the parameters by a small amount (± 2%) and examine the effect of the small parameter's variation on your measure (von Mises stress).

1. In the *Analyses and Design Studies* dialog box select **File>New Sensitivity Design Study.** The *Sensitivity Study Definition* dialog box opens.
2. In the *Name* field, enter **hinge_local**.
3. Expand the *Type* drop-down list and select **Local Sensitivity**.
4. In the *Analyses* field, highlight **hinge_multi_pass (Static)**.
5. Click (Select Dimension) and select **cut id 226** in the *Model Tree*. In the *Tools* tab, click (Switch Dimensions). The model displays as shown in Figure 6–18.

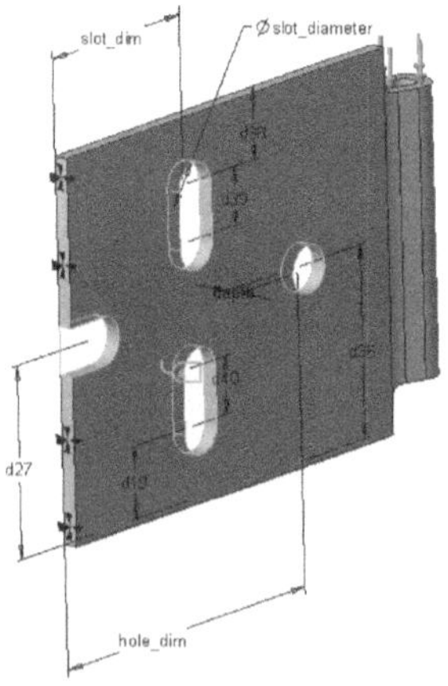

Figure 6–18

6. Select **slot_dim (40mm)**.

> **Note:** *Select the **Cut id 226** in the Model Tree. The dimensions display. Select the dimension symbol named **slot_dim**.*

7. Click (Select Dimension) and select **cut id 226**.
8. Select **hole_dim (75mm)**.
9. Click (Select Dimension) and then select **cut id 226**.
10. Select **depth (3mm)**.
11. Click (Select Dimension) and select **cut id 226**.
12. Select **slot_diameter (10mm)**.
13. The *Sensitivity Study Definition* dialog box displays as shown in Figure 6–19.

Figure 6–19

14. Click **OK** to close the *Sensitivity Study Definition* dialog box.
15. Run the design study.

Results Tasks

Task 10: Display the results.

1. In the *Analyses and Design Studies* dialog box, click (Review Results). The *Result Window Definition* dialog box opens, as shown in Figure 6–20.

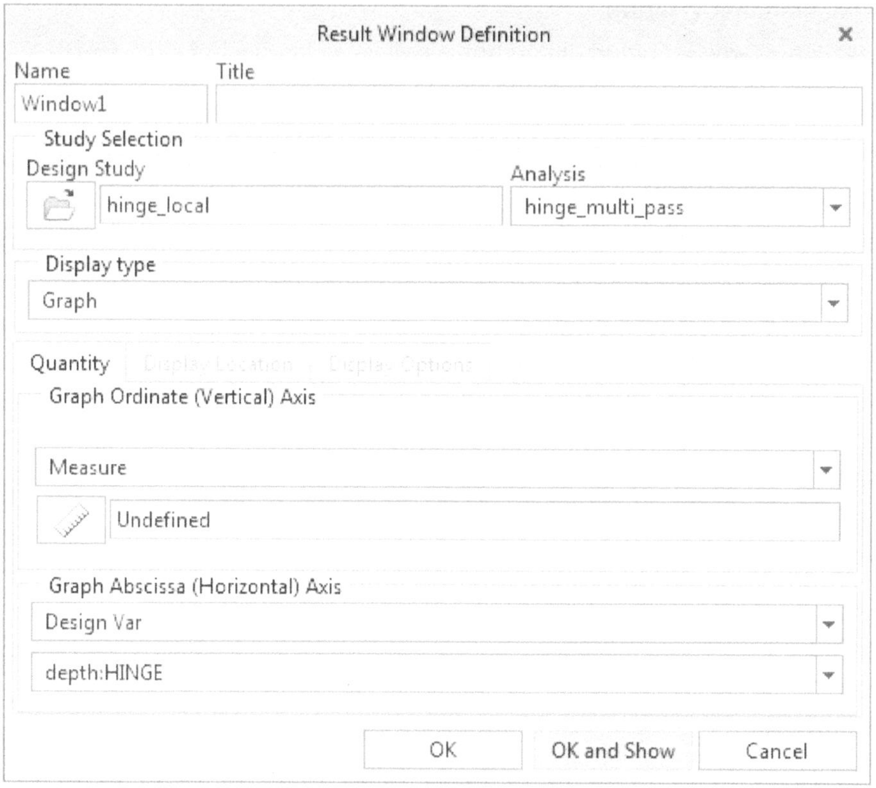

Figure 6–20

2. Edit the *Name* field to **slot_dim**.

3. Click (Measure) and select **max_stress_vm** in the list of predefined measures and click **OK**.

4. Expand the drop-down list at the bottom and select **slot_dim: HINGE**. The dialog box displays as shown in Figure 6–21.

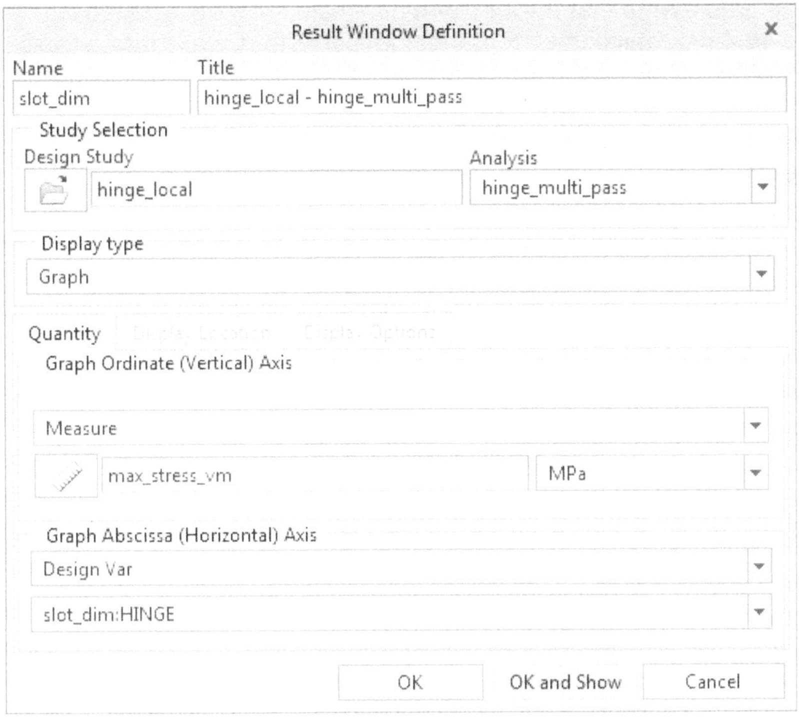

Figure 6–21

5. Click **OK and Show**. The result graph displays as shown in Figure 6–22.

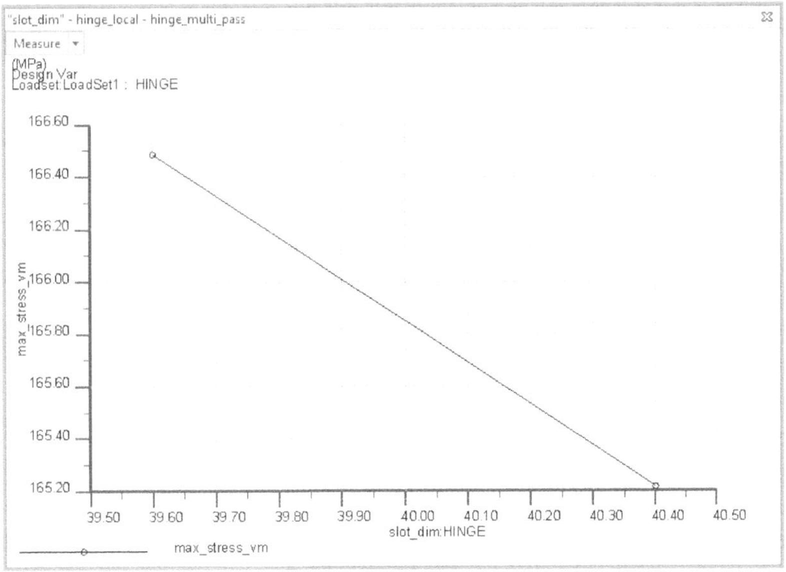

Figure 6–22

Examine the graph. Note that the **slot_dim** dimension has been varied in the study from **39.6mm** to **40.4mm**, which is ± 2% of the nominal **40mm**, while **max_stress_vm** changed from **166.5 MPa** to **165.2 MPa**, which is only ± 0.4% of the average **165.85 MPa** at **40mm**. In other words, for every 1% change in the dimension value, there is a 0.2% change in the stress result.

6. Repeat Steps 1 through 5 to create **max_stress_vm** sensitivity graphs for the **depth**, **hole_dim**, and **slot_diameter** dimensions. The results are shown in Figure 6–23.

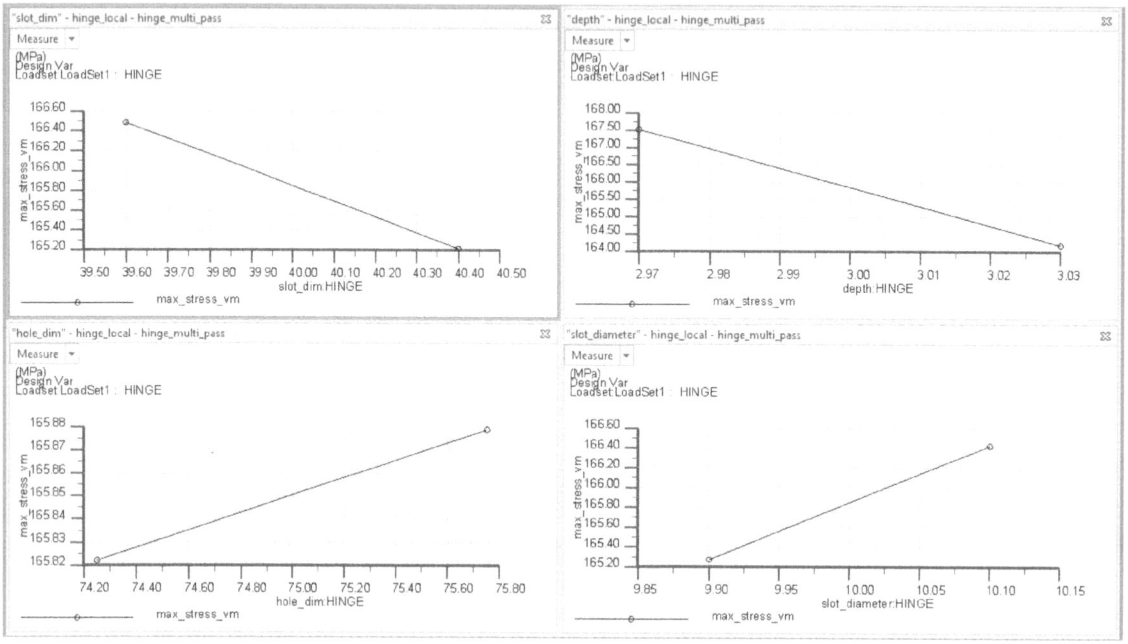

Figure 6–23

You will now determine which dimensions have the greatest effect on the maximum stress in the model.

Note that the largest variation of the **max_stress_vm** (which is approx. between 164 and 168 MPa) is exhibited for the dimension **depth**, which is the graph at the top right corner. You will now display the other three graphs in the same scale, from 164 to 168 MPa.

7. Select the graph for the **slot_dim** dimension (top left corner). In the *Format* tab, click (Edit).

8. In the *Options* dialog box, select the *Format the Y-axis* tab, then in the *Setup* tab, activate the **User-Defined Range** option.

9. Enter **168** in the *Maximum* field and **164** in the *Minimum* field, as shown in Figure 6–24.

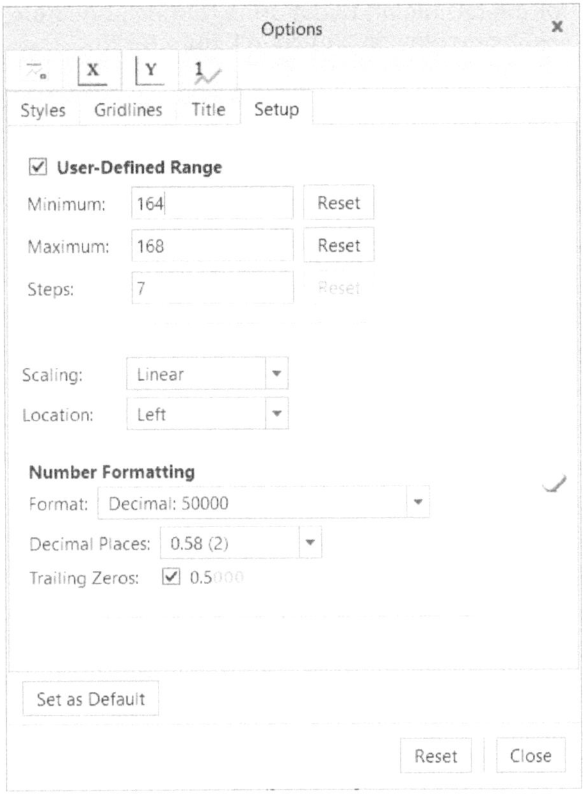

Figure 6–24

10. Click **Close** in the *Options* dialog box. The results display as shown in Figure 6–25.

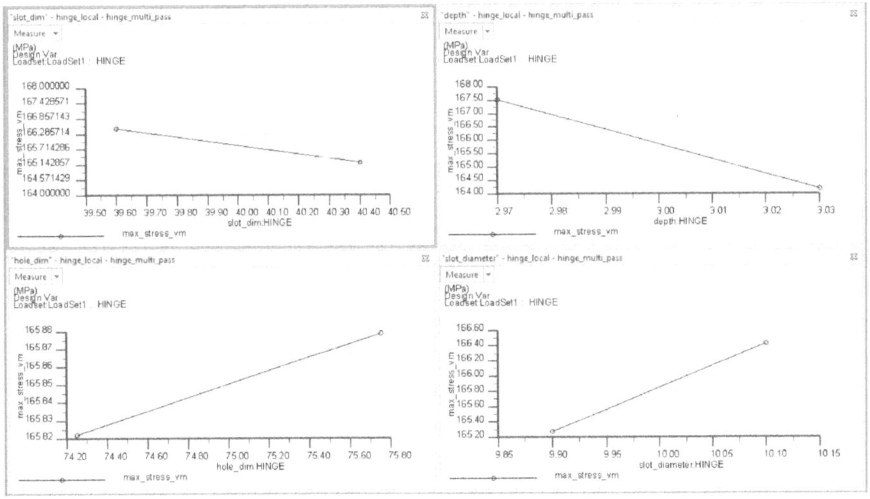

Figure 6–25

11. Repeat Steps 7 to 9 for the remaining two graphs (dimensions **hole_dim** and **slot_diameter**). The results display as shown in Figure 6–26.

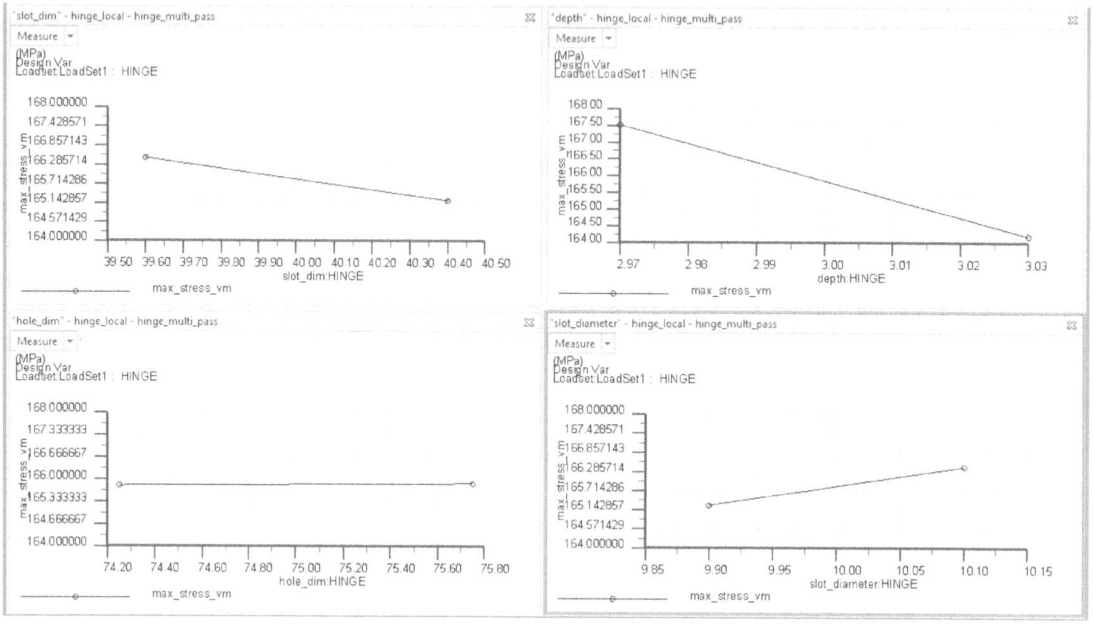

Figure 6–26

Examining the graphs in Figure 6–26 determines that the maximum stress measure is not sensitive to the **hole_dim** parameter. The slope of the sensitivity graph (bottom left corner) is rather shallow, and the difference in measure in the parameter range (4%) is only 165.88 - 165.82 = 0.06 MPa.

The other three dimensions (**slot_dim**, **slot_diameter**, and **depth**) exhibit sensitivity graphs with much steeper slopes, which means that the maximum stress in the model is sensitive to changes in those dimensions.

12. Close the results window.

Summary

At this stage, you have completed the local sensitivity studies and created the result windows. Use local sensitivity studies to determine which parameters have the greatest effect on a measure (such as the maximum von Mises stress) with a small variation in the parameter values. The result windows indicate that the measure is sensitive to the **slot_dim**, **hole_diameter**, and **depth** parameters.

Note: *If the von Mises stress is not sensitive to a specific parameter, the parameter should not be carried over for the next task.*

Those three parameters are now selected for the next task, in which you will run a global sensitivity study and determine the variations of the stress measure over a larger range of dimensions.

Task 11: Create global sensitivity design studies.

In this task, you will examine the variation of the selected three parameters over a range of user-defined values and examine the effect of the parameter's variation on the measure (von Mises stress).

In order to determine the effect of variation in each parameter separately, you will create and run three global sensitivity studies.

1. In the *Analyses and Design Studies* dialog box, select the **hinge_local** study and click (Copy).

2. Select the **Copy_of_hinge_local** study and click (Edit). The *Sensitivity Study Definition* dialog box opens, as shown in Figure 6–27.

Figure 6–27

3. In the *Name* field, enter **hinge_global_slot_dim**.

4. Expand the *Type* drop-down list and select **Global Sensitivity**.
5. Select **hole_dim** from the variables and click (Delete Row) to remove it.
6. Repeat Step 5 to remove the **depth** and **slot_diameter** parameters from the study. When you are finished, the only remaining parameter in the study is **slot_dim**.
7. In the *Variables* section, set the *Start* value as **20** and the *End* value as **60**. Set the *Steps* value to **4**, as shown in Figure 6–28.

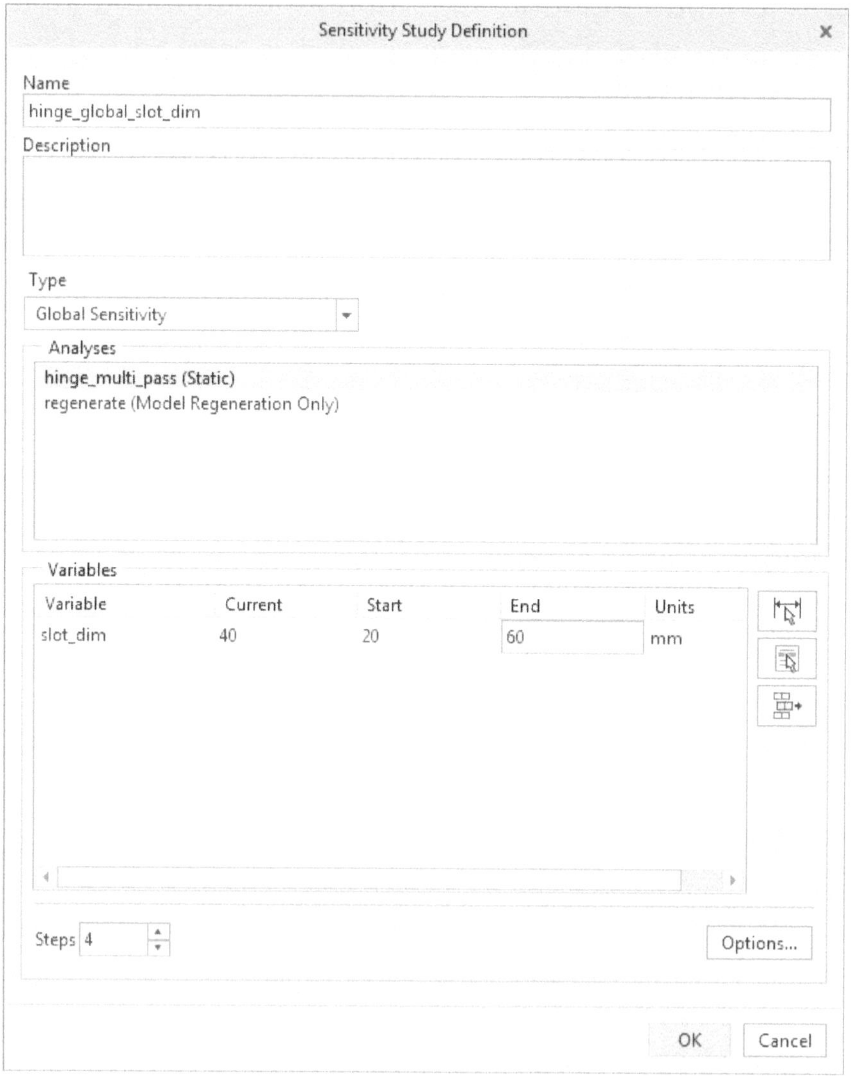

Figure 6–28

Note: *Use the* ***Options*** *button to set the* ***Repeat P-Loop Convergence*** *option when the parameter's range is high and the shape of the model changes considerably.*

8. Click **Options**. The *Design Study Options* dialog box opens, as shown in Figure 6–29.

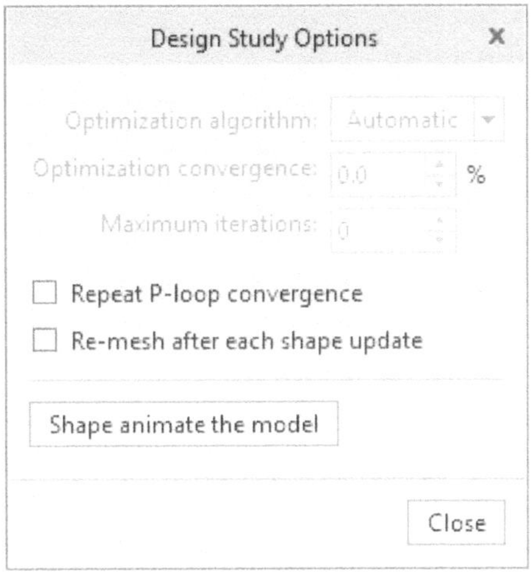

Figure 6–29

9. Click **Shape Animate the Model** and step through the model shape animation to ensure that the model regenerates on each sensitivity study step. When prompted, click **Yes** to restore the model to its original shape.
10. Click **Close** to close the *Design Study Options* dialog box.
11. Click **OK** to close the *Sensitivity Study Definition* dialog box.
12. Run the design study.
13. Repeat Steps 1 to 12 using the following settings:
    - *Name of the study:* **hinge_global_depth**
    - *Parameter to keep:* **depth**
    - *Start value:* **1**
    - *End value:* **5**
    - *Steps:* **4**
14. Repeat Steps 1 to 12 again, using the following settings:
    - *Name of the study:* **hinge_global_slot_diameter**
    - *Parameter to keep:* **slot_diameter**
    - *Start value:* **5**
    - *End value:* **12**
    - *Steps:* **4**
15. Close the *Analyses and Design Studies* dialog box.

Task 12: Display the results.

1. In the *Home* tab, click (Results).
2. Click (Open).
3. In the dialog box that opens, select **hinge_global_slot_dim** study and click **Open**. The *Result Window Definition* dialog box displays, as shown in Figure 6–30.

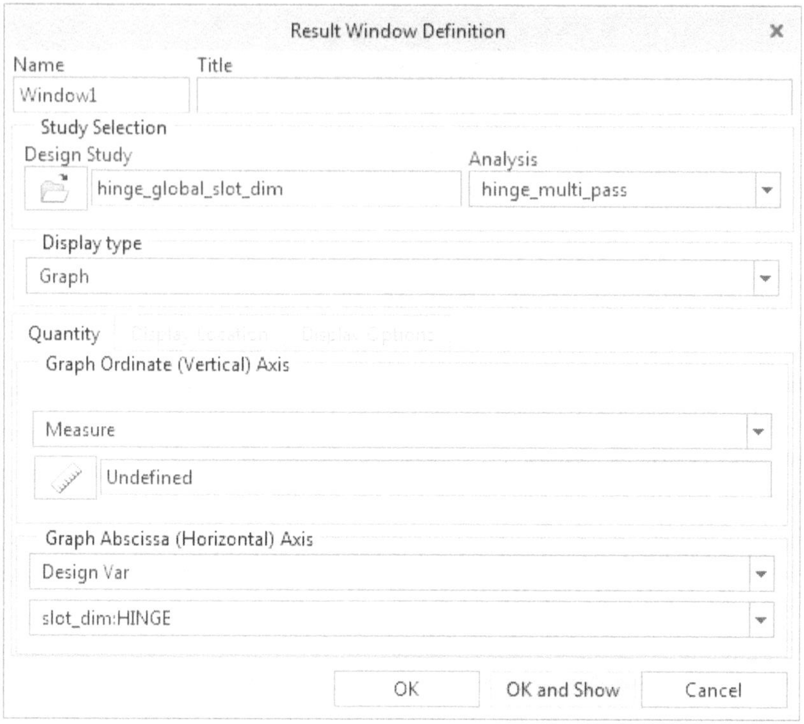

Figure 6–30

4. Click (Measure), select **max_stress_vm** from the list and then click **OK**. In the *Result Window Definition* dialog box, click **OK and Show**. The result window displays as shown in Figure 6–31.

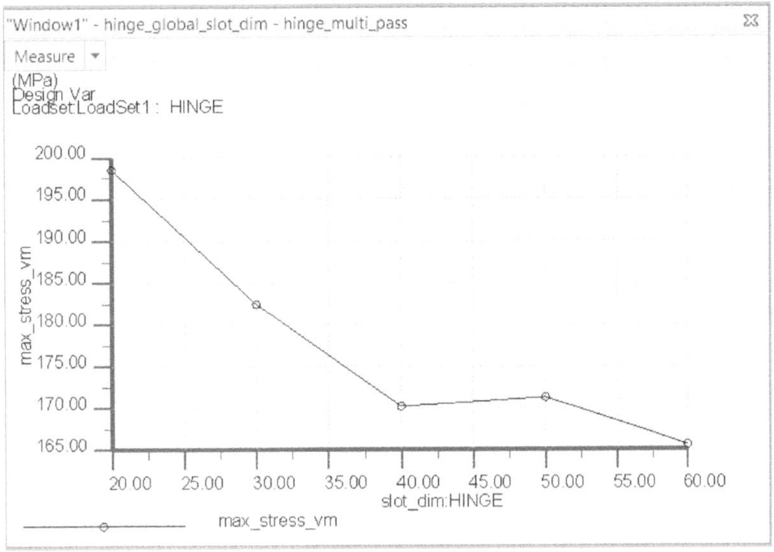

Figure 6–31

5. Repeat Steps 2 to 4 using the **hinge_global_depth** study. The result window for the **depth** dimension displays as shown in Figure 6–32.

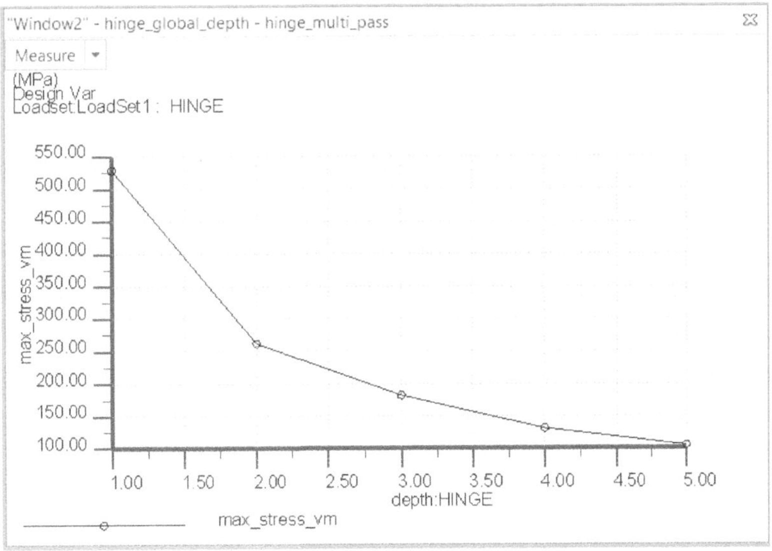

Figure 6–32

6. Repeat Steps 2 to 4 using the **hinge_global_slot_diameter** study. The result window for the **slot_diameter** dimension displays as shown in Figure 6–33.

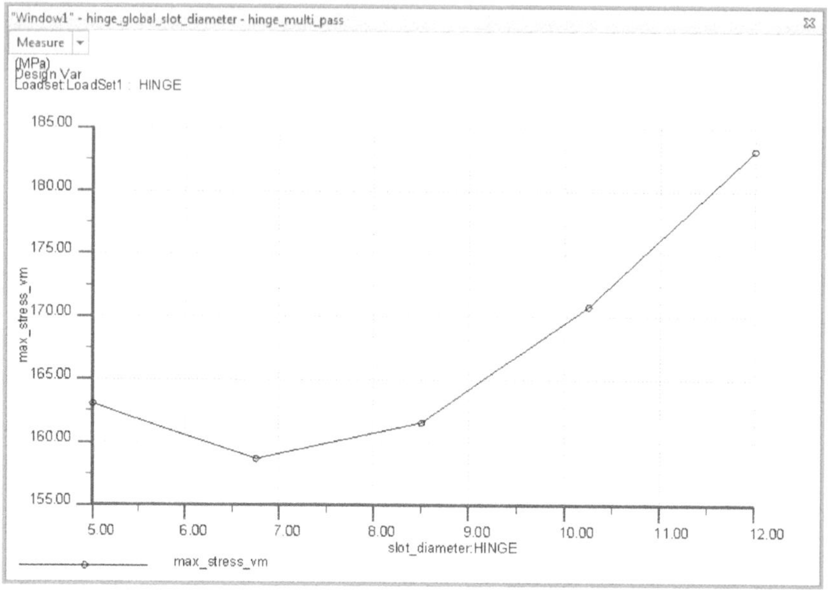

Figure 6–33

7. Note that the greatest variation of the **max_stress_vm** is exhibited for the dimension **depth**, and is approximately between 100 and 550 MPa. The other two design variables (**slot_dim** and **slot_diameter**) have a lesser, but still substantial effect on the stress. Therefore, all three design variables should be carried over into the optimization study.
8. Close the results.

Summary

At this stage, you have completed your global sensitivity study and examined the sensitivity graphs. The sensitivity graphs indicate that the following dimensions could be optimized for minimum von Mises stress:

- depth (plate thickness)
- slot_diameter (holes diameter)
- slot_dim

> **Note:** *You ran this study to determine the parameters that have an effect on the von Mises stress.*

In the next tasks, you will determine the dimension values that result in the minimum weight of the hinge model without exceeding the allowable stress for the material.

Task 13: Create an optimization design study.

In this task, you will create a design study to optimize your model weight.

1. In the *Analyses and Design Studies* dialog box, select **File>New Optimization Design Study**. The *Optimization Study Definition* dialog box opens.
2. In the *Name* field, enter **hinge_optimize**.
3. Configure the *Optimization Design Study Definition* dialog box as shown in Figure 6–34.

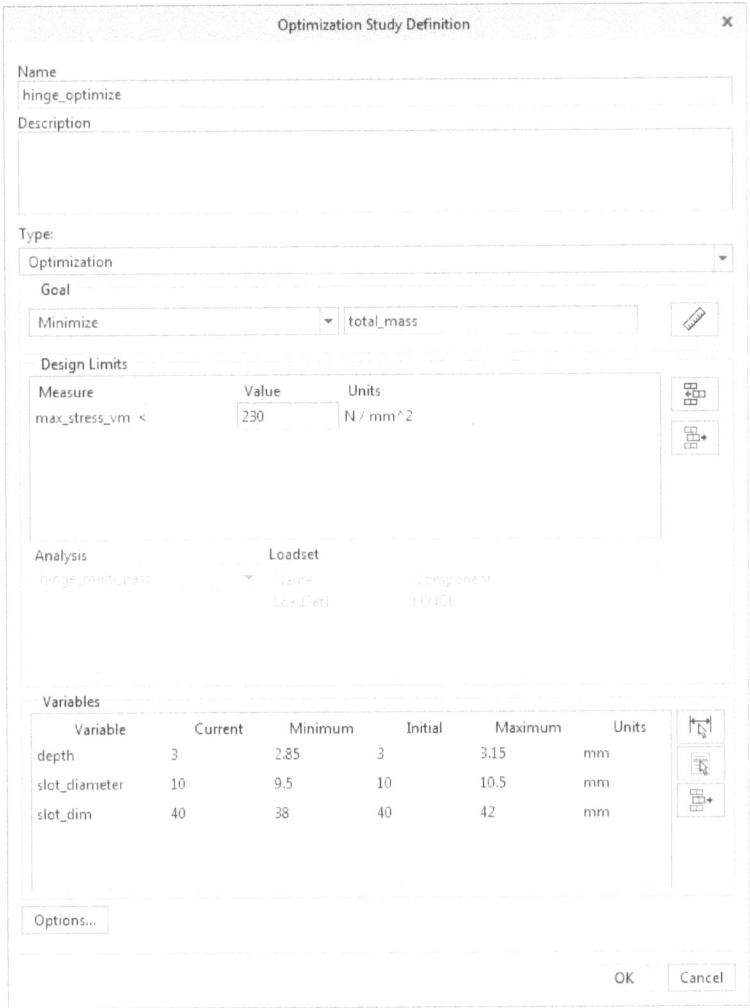

Figure 6–34

4. Click **OK** to close the *Optimization Study Definition* dialog box.
5. Run the design study and click **Yes** when prompted to run Interactive Diagnostics.

Task 14: Display the results.

In this task, you will locate the optimum model mass and dimension values. You will also create two graphs displaying the optimization process for measures: **max_stress_vm** and **total_mass**.

1. Expand the *Run Status* window to display the run details.
2. Locate the optimum model mass and parameter values as shown in Figure 6–35.

```
Begin Optimization Iteration 6                         (11:47:54)
Converged to optimum design.

Best Design Found:
Parameters:
  slot_dim                      40
  slot_diameter                 10.5
  depth                         2.85
Goal:    2.0017e-04

Optimization study statistics:
Number of Base Analyses: 6
Number of Perturbation Analyses: 1
```

Figure 6–35

*Note: Note that the unit mass is **metric tons** and the unit length is **mm**.*

Task 15: Create two graphs for the measures: max_stress_vm and total_mass.

1. Create a graph for the **max_stress_vm** measure versus the **Optimization Pass**. The graph displays as shown in Figure 6–36.

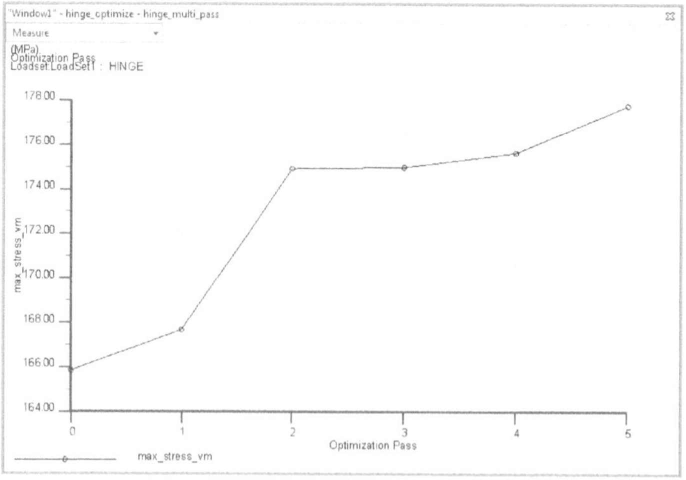

Figure 6–36

2. Create a graph for the **total_mass** measure versus **Optimization Pass**. The graph displays as shown in Figure 6–37.

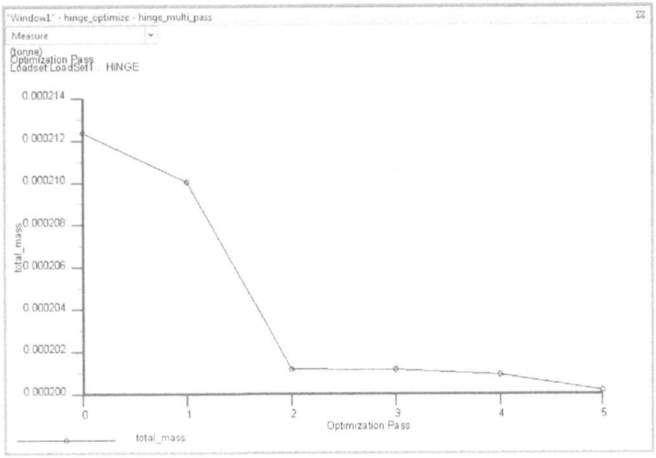

Figure 6–37

Note that the optimization algorithm reduced the weight of the hinge from **0.000212356** tonne to **0.000200172** tonne, which is approximately 5.7% less than the original design.

Task 16: Display the stress plot.

1. Create and display a fringe plot for the von Mises stress in the optimized model. The result plot displays as shown in Figure 6–38.

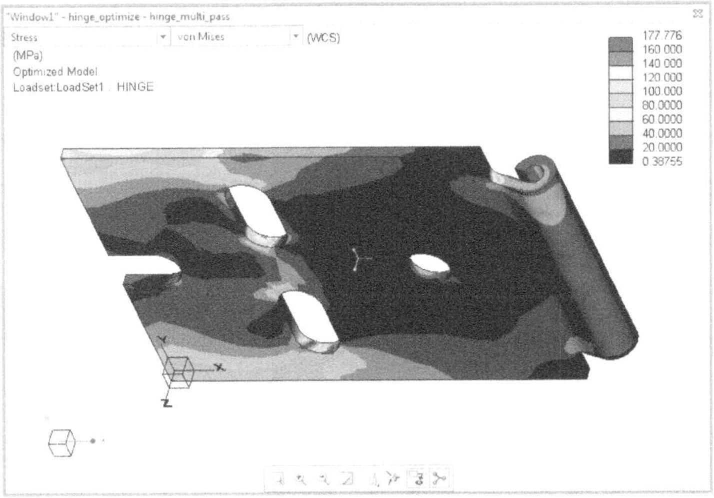

Figure 6–38

2. Close the results and save the model in Creo Parametric.

End of practice

Practice 6b
Design Study of a Hanger

Practice Objectives

- Set up and run a sensitivity design study.
- Set up and run a standard design study.

In this practice, you will use sensitivity and standard design studies to set up, run, analyze, and redesign a hanger part shown in Figure 6–39.

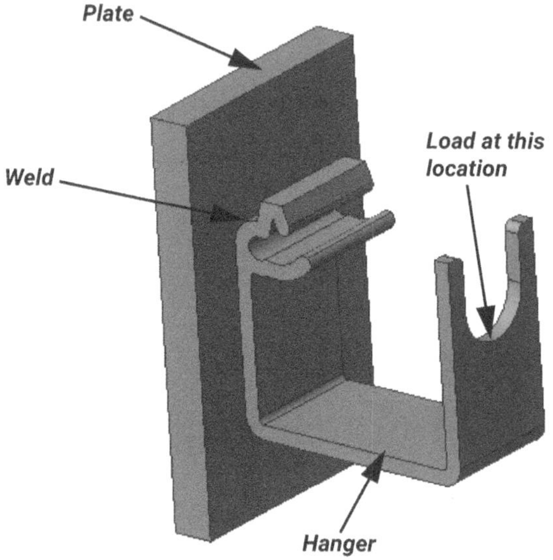

Figure 6–39

Note: *Sensitivity design studies automate some of the repetitive work involved in design.*

The hanger is made of aluminum alloy 6005-T6, which has the following settings:

- *Modulus of elasticity:* **10600ksi**
- *Poisson's ratio:* **0.33**
- *Tensile yield stress:* **36ksi**

The part is welded to the support plate at the top, and is loaded by a downward force of 65lbf at the bottom of the cutout on the other end, as shown above in Figure 6–39.

The design requirement for the part is that the factor of safety against yielding under the given load should be no less than 1.2. The goal of the study is to ensure that this design requirement is met.

Check the Current Design

The goal of the following tasks is to check the current design by setting up and running a static stress analysis.

Task 1: Open gearrack.prt.

1. Set the working directory to **Chapter06**, if required.
2. Open **gearrack.prt**.
3. Set the model display as follows:
   - *(Datum Display Filters)*: All Off
   - *(Spin Center)*: Off
   - *(Display Style)*: (Shading With Edges)

   The part displays as shown in Figure 6–40.

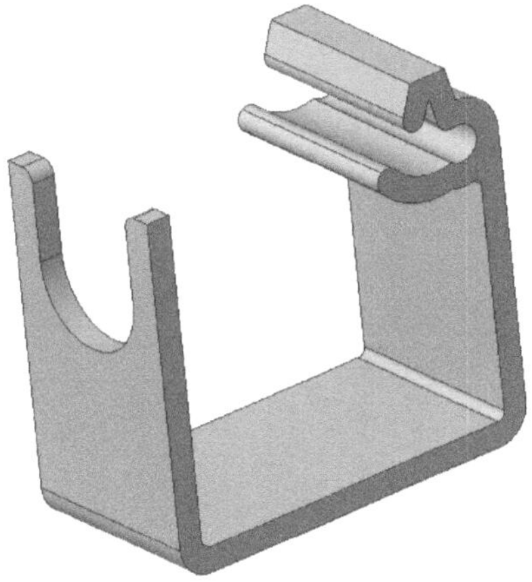

Figure 6–40

4. Ensure that the unit system is set to **IPS**.
5. Switch to Creo Simulate.

Task 2: Apply the material.

1. In the *Home* tab, click (Materials). Add **al2014.mtl** and to the *Materials in Model* area.

2. Select (Edit) and change the following material properties, as shown in Figure 6–41:
   - *Name:* **AL6005-T6**
   - *Poisson's Ratio:* **0.33**
   - *Young's Modulus:* **1.06e+07 psi**

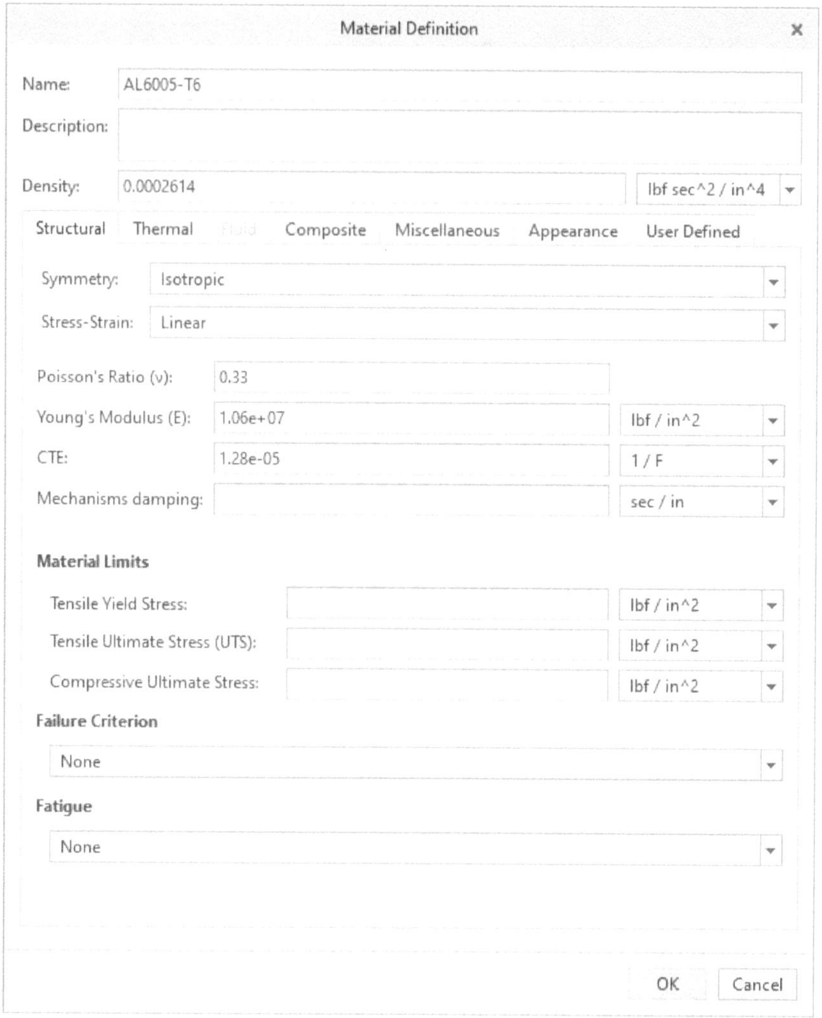

Figure 6–41

3. Click **OK** to close the *Material Definition* dialog box, and click **OK** again to close the *Materials* dialog box.
4. Assign the material **AL6005-T6** to the part.

Task 3: Apply constraints.

1. Using (Displacement), fully constrain (all translations) the two surfaces shown in Figure 6–42.

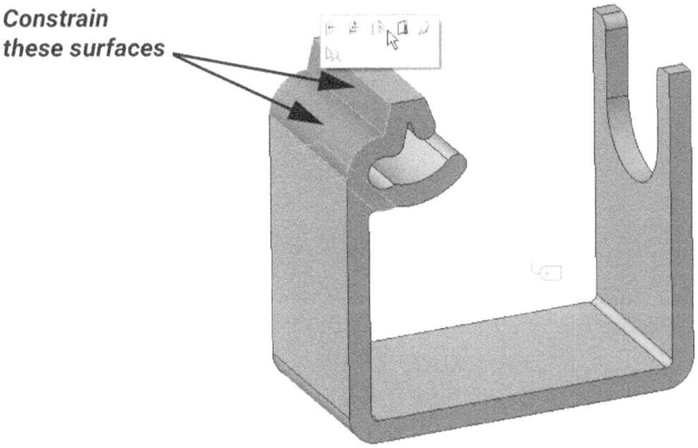

Figure 6–42

Note: This constraint simulates the weldment to the support plate.

2. Click **OK** to close the *Constraint* dialog box.
3. Using (Displacement) again, constrain the edge at the bottom of the hanger (shown in Figure 6–43) in the **X**-direction only.

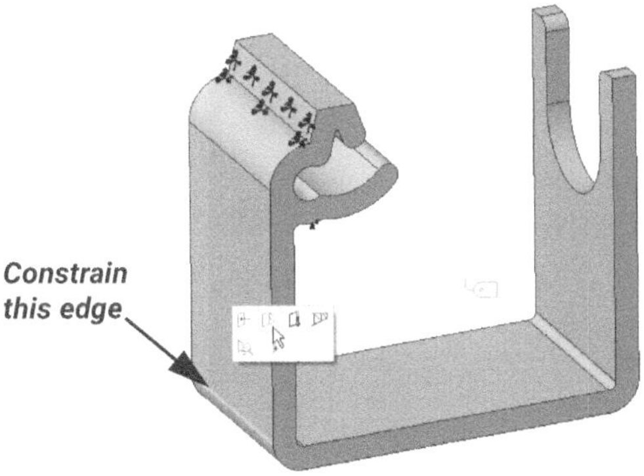

Figure 6–43

Note: The second constraint models the support provided by the plate at the bottom of the hanger, when the load tries to bend the hanger downward.

4. Click **OK** to close the *Constraint* dialog box. The model displays as shown in Figure 6–44.

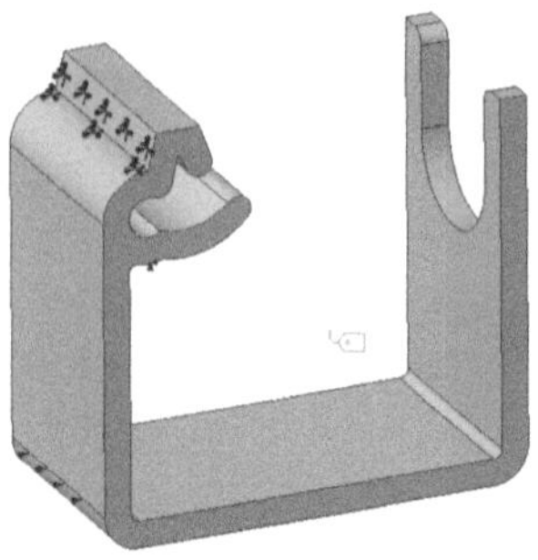

Figure 6–44

Task 4: Apply the load.

1. Using (Force/Moment), apply **65lbf** force in the negative Y-direction to the surface shown in Figure 6–45.

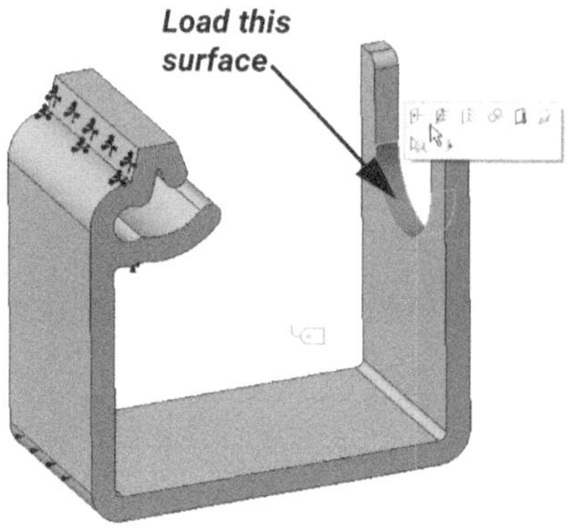

Figure 6–45

2. Click **OK** to close the *Force/Moment Load* dialog box.The model displays as shown in Figure 6–46.

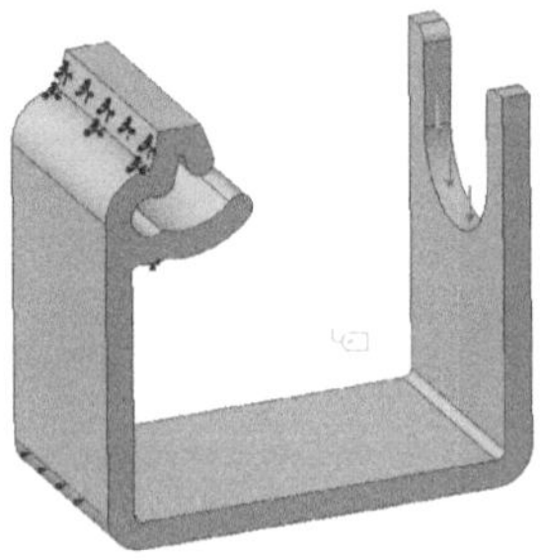

Figure 6–46

Task 5: Set up and run an analysis and display the results.

1. Set up a Single-Pass Adaptive analysis. For the name of the analysis, enter **hanger_anls**.
2. Run the analysis.
3. Create and display a fringe plot of the von Mises stress for the part. It displays as shown in Figure 6–47.

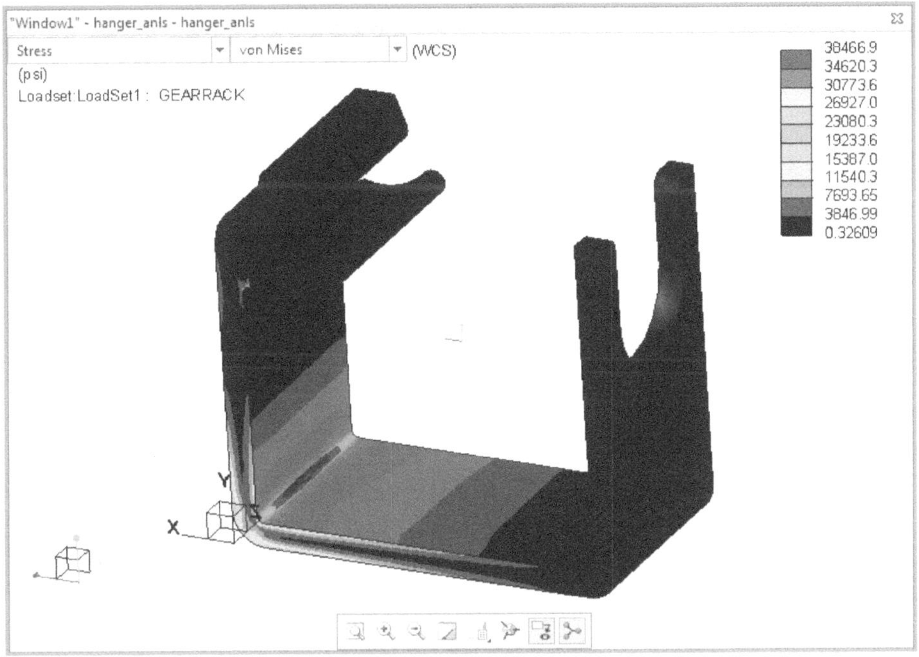

Figure 6–47

- Note that the maximum stress is over 38000psi.
- Note that the yield strength of the material is 36ksi = 36000psi. Given the required factor of safety 1.2, this means that the maximum permitted stress for the part is 36000/1.2 = 30000psi. Therefore, in the current design of the hanger, the factor of safety requirement is not met and the part's design should be modified.
- Note that the maximum stress occurs in the inside fillet at the bottom of the hanger, which is likely due to the stress concentration effect. It is well known that stress concentration around fillets and holes is greatly affected by the fillet radius. Therefore, in the next tasks you will study how sensitive the maximum stress is to the radius of that fillet.

4. Exit the Results environment and close the *Analyses and Design Studies* dialog box.
5. Exit Creo Simulate.

Run a Sensitivity Study

In the following tasks, you will determine if the design requirements could be met by adjusting the fillet radius.

Task 6: Rename the design variables.

In this task, you will rename the Creo Parametric fillet radius to make it easier to identify in the sensitivity study.

1. In the *Model Tree*, select **Round 8** and select (Edit Dimensions) from the mini-toolbar. The part displays. Select the **R.062** dimension, as shown in Figure 6–48.

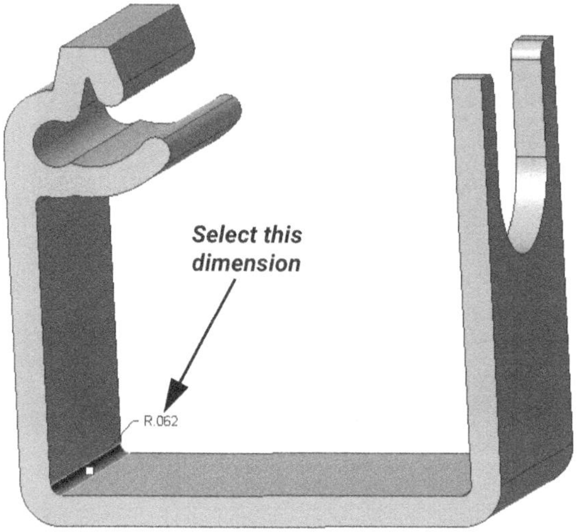

Figure 6–48

2. In the *Value* group of the ribbon, in the *Name* field, enter **round_radius**, as shown in Figure 6–49.

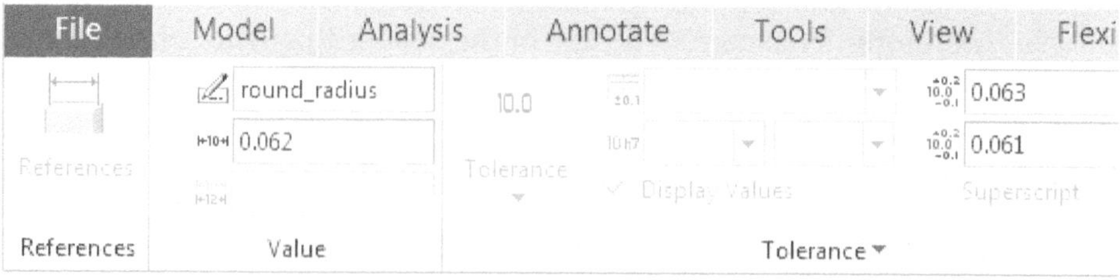

Figure 6–49

3. Click anywhere on the screen.

4. In the *Tools* tab, click (Switch Dimensions). The part displays as shown in Figure 6–50.

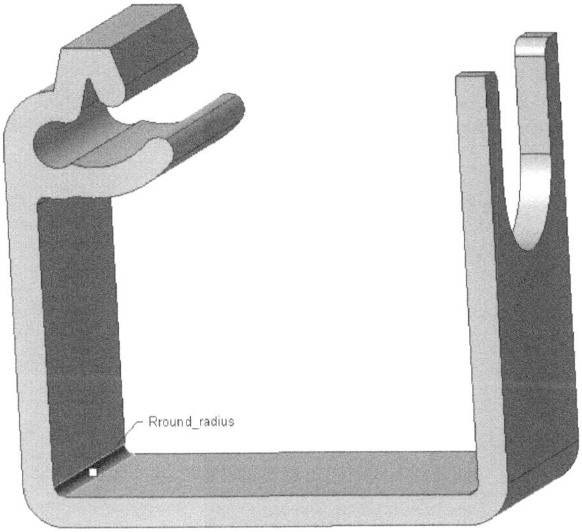

Figure 6–50

5. Save the part.

Task 7: Run a sensitivity study.

In this task, you will vary the fillet radius and examine its effect on the von Mises stress.

1. Switch to Creo Simulate.
2. Open the *Analyses and Design Studies* dialog box and select **File>New Sensitivity Design Study**. The *Sensitivity Study Definition* dialog box opens.
3. In the *Name* field, enter **hanger_sensitivity**.
4. Expand the *Type* drop-down list and select **Global Sensitivity**.
5. In the *Analyses* field, highlight **hanger_anls (Static)**.
6. Click (Select Dimension) and select **Round 8** in the *Model Tree*.
7. Select the radius dimension.

8. In the *Sensitivity Study Definition* dialog box, set the following, as shown in Figure 6–51:
   - Enter **0.062** in the *Start* column.
   - Enter **0.162** in the *End* column.
   - Ensure that **10** is set as the number of *Steps*.

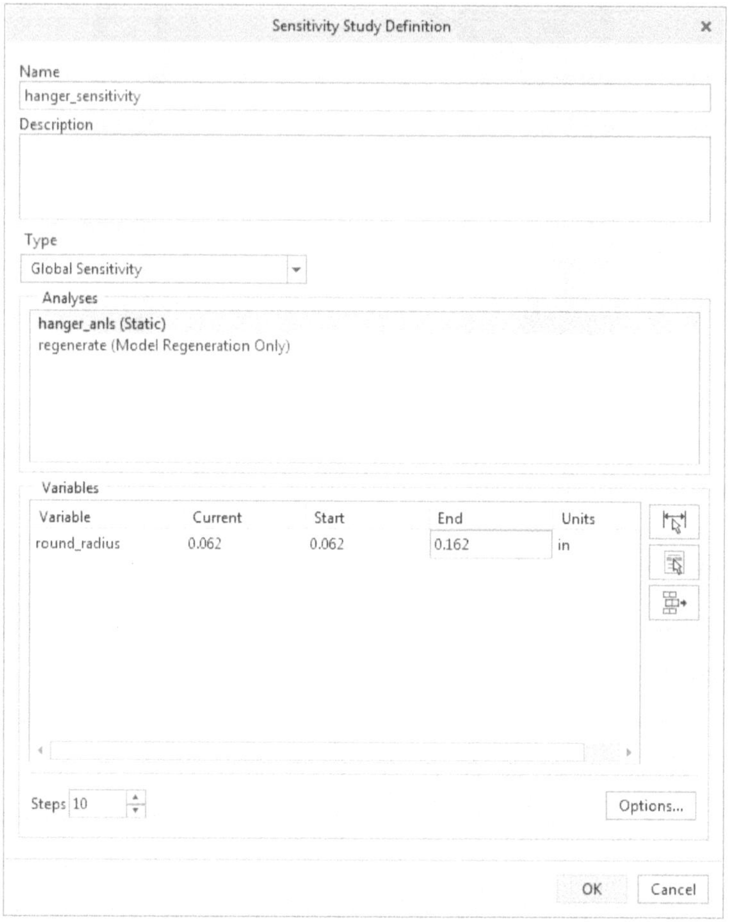

Figure 6–51

9. Click **OK** to close the *Sensitivity Study Definition* dialog box.
10. Run the design study.

Task 8: Display the results.

1. In the *Analyses and Design Studies* dialog box, highlight **hanger_sensitivity** and then click  (Review Results). The *Result Window Definition* dialog box opens, as shown in Figure 6–52.

Figure 6–52

2. Click (Measure), select **max_stress_vm** from the list, and then click **OK**.
3. In the *Result Window Definition* dialog box, click **OK and Show**. The result window displays as shown in Figure 6–53.

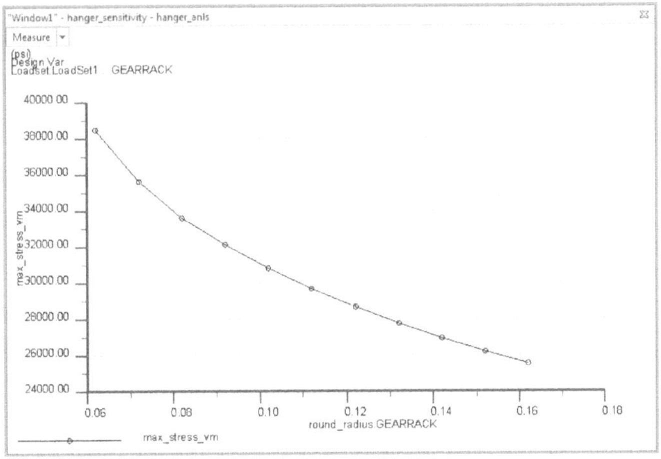

Figure 6–53

The sensitivity graph clearly shows that the maximum stress in the hanger can be brought down to under the permitted stress of 30000psi by increasing the radius of the fillet at the bottom of the hanger. At the sixth step of the sensitivity study, the stress has already dropped under 30000psi, and at the last step of the study (radius 0.162in) the stress is under 26000psi.

Task 9: Calculate the proposed fillet radius.

In this task, you will calculate the new fillet radius using the sensitivity graph.

1. Point the cursor to the point in the graph that corresponds to the fifth step in the study, shown in Figure 6–54. The flyout should read **[max_stress_vm] (x,y) = (0.102, 30815.369141)**.

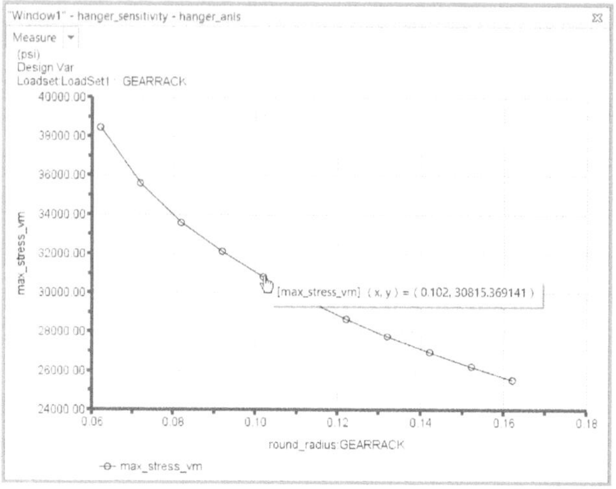

Figure 6–54

2. Point the cursor to the point in the graph that corresponds to the sixth step in the study, shown in Figure 6–55. The flyout should read **[max_stress_vm] (x,y) = (0.112, 29678.089844)**.

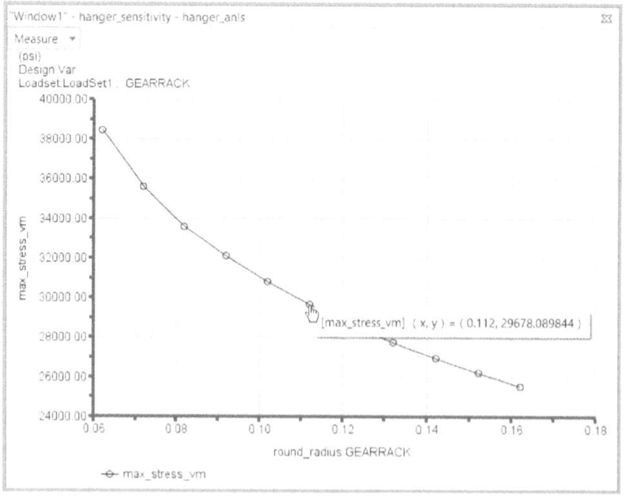

Figure 6–55

3. Using linear interpolation between the graph points, the radius that corresponds to the 30000psi stress is:

$$0.102 + (30000 - 30815.4) \times \frac{0.112 - 0.102}{29678.1 - 30815.4} = 0.1092$$

   Since linear interpolation was used between the points while the sensitivity graph is in reality a curve, to account for the inaccuracy, add a10% margin to the calculated radius:

   0.1092 + 10% = 0.12012

   Rounded to the hundredth of an inch, the proposed fillet radius that corresponds to maximum stress just under 30000psi, becomes 0.12in.

4. Exit the Results environment.

Validate the Design Change

In the following tasks, you will validate the proposed design change of an increase in fillet radius from 0.062in to 0.12in by using a standard design study.

Task 10: Create and run standard design study.

1. Open the *Analyses and Design Studies* dialog box and select **File>New Standard Design Study.** The *Standard Study Definition* dialog box opens.
2. In the *Name* field, enter **hanger_new_design**.
3. In the *Analyses* field, select **hanger_anls (Static)**.
4. Click (Select Dimension) and select **Round 8** in the *Model Tree*. Select the **radius** dimension.

5. Enter **0.12** in the *Setting* column. The *Standard Design Study* dialog box opens, as shown in Figure 6–56.

Figure 6–56

6. Click **OK** to close the dialog box.
7. Run the **hanger_new_design** study.

Task 11: Display the results.

1. In the *Analyses and Design Studies* dialog box, select **hanger_new_design** and click (Review Results).
2. Create a von Mises stress plot. The plot displays as shown in Figure 6–57.

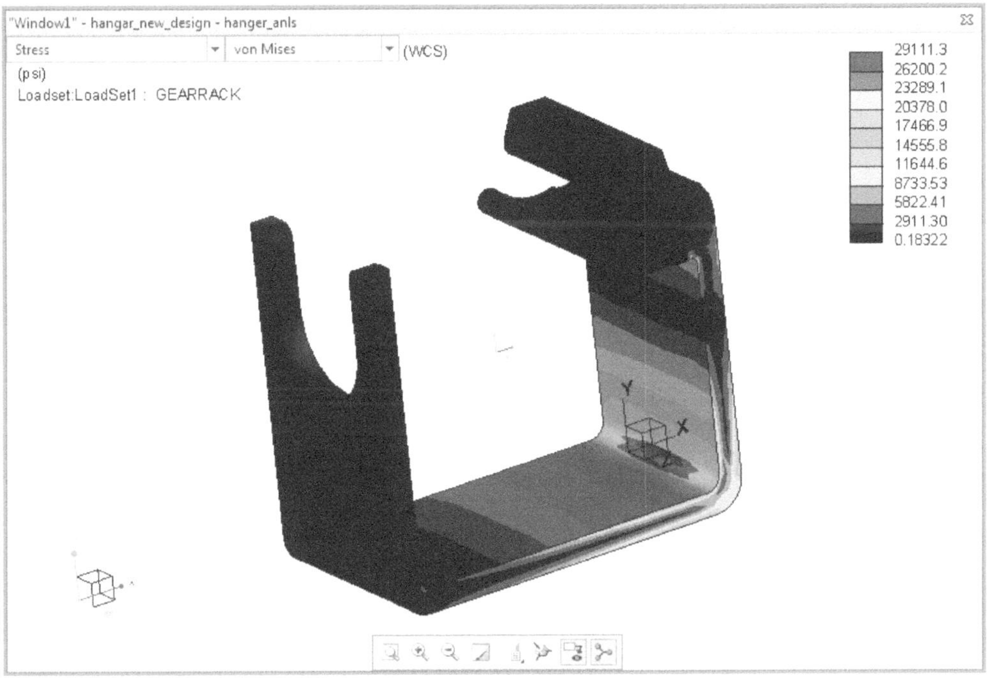

Figure 6–57

Note that the maximum stress is now 29111.3psi.

The factor of safety for the new design is 36000/29111.3 = 1.237, which is greater than the required minimum 1.2.

Therefore, the new design meets the stress requirements.

3. Exit the Results environment.
4. Exit Creo Simulate and save and close the part in Creo Parametric.

End of practice

Chapter 7

Assembly Interfaces

You will learn how to model the interfaces between assembly components and to set up a contact analysis.

Learning Objectives

- Understand the types of part interfaces in Creo Simulate.
- Create bonded and free interfaces.
- Understand the contact interface properties.
- Create contact interfaces manually or automatically.
- Review the interfaces in your model.
- Set up an analysis with contact interfaces.
- Refine the mesh in contact areas.

7.1 Types of Interfaces

Interfaces in Creo Simulate define the treatment of mated or adjacent surfaces in an assembly model.

There are three types of interfaces in Creo Simulate Structural:

- **Bonded:** The interfacing surfaces are essentially *glued* together.
- **Free:** The interfacing surfaces are not connected in any way.
- **Contact:** The interfacing surfaces cannot interpenetrate, but can still separate and/or slide along each other under the applied loading.

Default Interface

By default, Creo Simulate treats all of the mated surfaces in the model according to the option selected in the *Default Interface* drop-down list in the *Model Setup* dialog box, as shown in Figure 7–1.

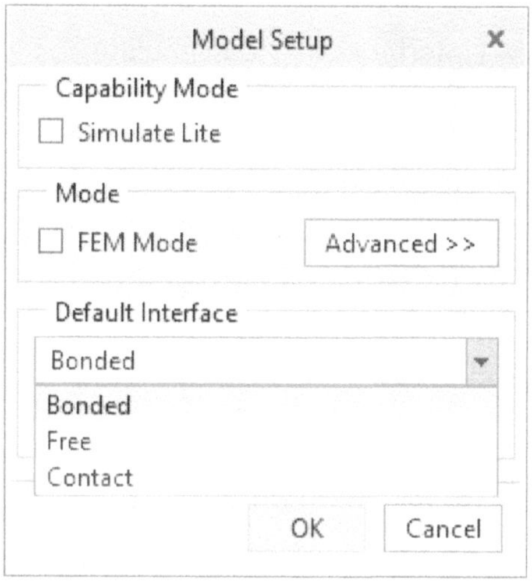

Figure 7–1

7.2 Bonded Interface

A bonded interface is a connection that essentially *glues* two parts together. Displacement continuity between the interfacing surfaces is ensured (i.e., the surfaces remain *attached* to each other during the analysis).

This type of interface is typically used for, but not limited to, bonded, glued, surface-welded, etc., connections between parts in an assembly. The key criterion for the correct use is either no or negligible separation or the sliding of the two surfaces under applied loading.

The applied forces are fully transmitted through the bonded interfaces. Creo Simulate automatically creates a simulation measure to calculate the resultant force over each manually-created bonded interface.

Use the following steps to create a bonded interface:

1. In the *Refine Model* tab, in the *Connections* group, click (Interface) to open the *Interface Definition* dialog box.
2. Expand the *Type* drop-down list and select **Bonded**. The *Interface Definition* dialog box displays as shown in Figure 7–2.

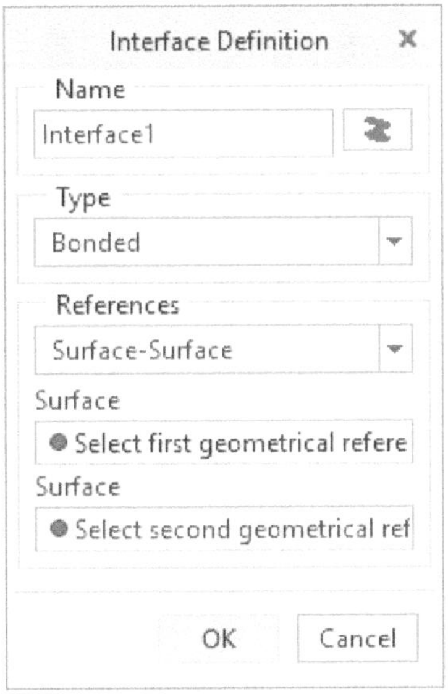

Figure 7–2

3. Select the geometrical references (**Surface-Surface, Body-Body**, or **Component-Component**).
4. Click **OK** to finish.

7.3 Free Interface

A free interface does not connect the two surfaces in any way. The surfaces can freely separate or pass through each other under the applied loading, and no forces are transmitted through the interface. The surfaces ignore each other.

This type of interface should only be used for parts that are expected to separate and never to press against each other under the loading in the model. The analysis results should also be carefully reviewed afterward, to ensure there is no interpenetration of the surfaces in the model, which would otherwise render the analysis as incorrect.

Use the following steps to create a free interface:

1. In the *Refine* tab, in the *Connections* group, click (Interface) to open the *Interface Definition* dialog box.
2. Expand the *Type* drop-down list and select **Free**. The *Interface Definition* dialog box displays as shown in Figure 7–3.

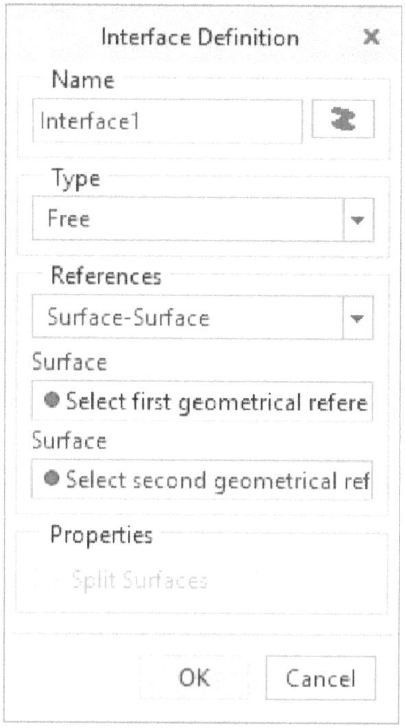

Figure 7–3

3. Select the geometrical references (**Surface-Surface, Body-Body**, or **Component-Component**).
4. Click **OK** to finish.

7.4 Contact Interface

In a contact interface, the two surfaces are free to move apart and/or slide along each other under the applied loading, but they cannot interpenetrate. The surfaces are initially permitted to be at a clearance, but might come into contact during the analysis. Only compressive normal stresses are transmitted through the interface (i.e., the interfacing surfaces cannot *pull* each other).

The contact interface is the most realistic model for simulating parts that must remain separate from each other during the analysis, yet do not interpenetrate. From the FEA standpoint, the contact interface represents a boundary condition that changes during the loading. For example, when a chain roller is pressed against a sprocket, the line contact changes to an area contact.

In the example shown in Figure 7–4, there is a gap between the plate and block initially (configuration 1 in Figure 7–4). Once the load has been applied, the plate bends freely, until it comes into contact with the block, as shown in configuration 2 in Figure 7–4. If the load is further increased, the area of contact shifts from the edge of the plate to the edge of the block (configuration 3 in Figure 7–4). Therefore, the contact area and location change depending on the amount of load applied.

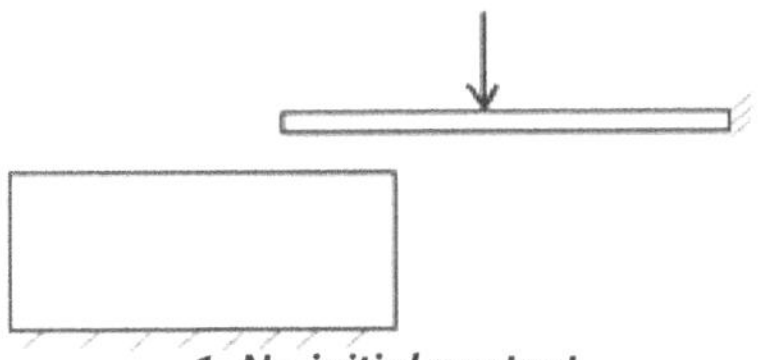

1. No initial contact

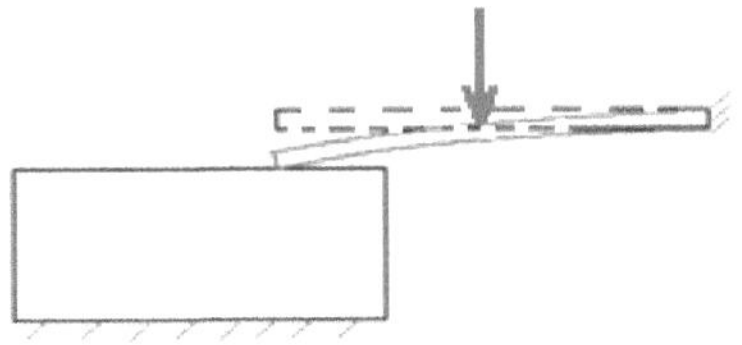

2. Contact along the edge of the plate

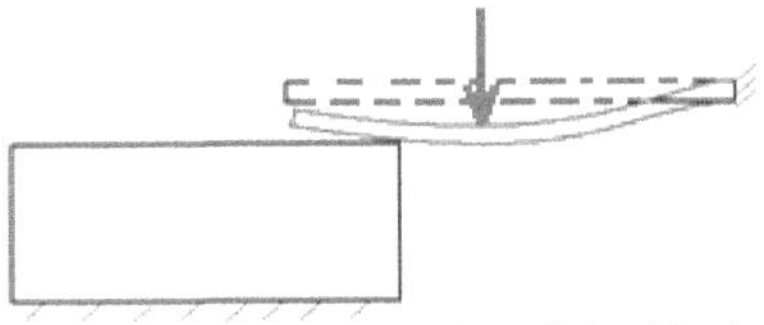

3. Contact along the edge of the block

Figure 7–4

Contact in Creo Simulate can use or ignore friction. The following friction options are available:

- **None:** Creates a frictionless contact. Only compressive forces are transmitted through a frictionless contact interface, and the surfaces will slip relative to each other whenever there is a tangential force between them.
- **Finite:** Creates a contact with friction. The surfaces will slip relative to each other only if tangential force exceeds the friction force. The friction force is the coefficient of friction times the compressive force.
- **Infinite:** The interfacing surfaces are able to come apart in the normal direction, but they cannot slip relative to each other. For a contact with infinite friction, Creo Simulate automatically creates slippage measures. A positive value of a slippage measure indicates that the surfaces in contact might have slid relative to each other. Therefore, the assumption of infinite friction is not accurate.

Creo Simulate automatically creates simulation measures to calculate the contact area and the resultant force over a contact interface.

To create a contact interface, click (Interface) to open the *Interface Definition* dialog box, and select **Contact** option in the *Type* drop-down list, as shown in Figure 7–5.

Figure 7–5

The options in the dialog box are as follows:

Section	Option	Description
References	**Surface-Surface**	User selects the surfaces that are in contact, or might come into contact during the analysis.
	Body-Body or Component-Component	Creo Simulate creates contact interfaces between any two surfaces that satisfy the user-defined **Separation Distance** and **Angle** criteria.
Properties	**Override Model Contact Penetration**	Specifies the extent to which contact surfaces can interpenetrate, as a percentage of the square root of the contact area. The default value is 5 percent.
	Detailed stresses	Overrides the **Calculate detailed stresses at contact interfaces** setting in the *Analysis* dialog box. Detailed stress calculation improves stress accuracy in contacts but requires longer computation time. Only available with finite friction.
Friction	**None**	Creates a frictionless contact.
	Finite	Creates a contact with finite friction.
	Infinite	Creates a contact with infinite friction.
	Create Slippage Indicators	Creates slippage measures. Only available with the **Infinite Friction** option. A positive value of the slippage measure indicates that the surfaces might have slid relatively to each other, therefore, the assumption of infinite friction is inaccurate.
	Static Coefficient of Friction	Specify the friction coefficient at which the sliding occurs.
	Dynamic Coefficient of Friction	Specify the friction coefficient at which the sliding continues once started. Only available with the **Finite Friction** option.

Automatic Contact Detection

Creo Simulate has a tool that enables you to automatically create contact interfaces between parts in the assembly, based on user-specified criteria.

To start the auto detection, expand the *Interface* area in the *Refine Model* tab, as shown in Figure 7–6, and select **Detect Contacts**.

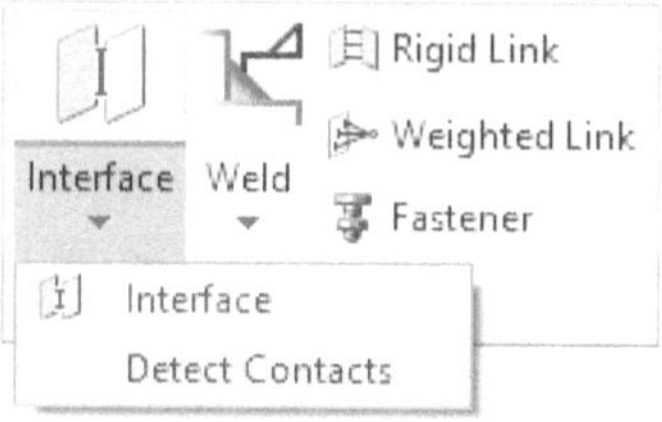

Figure 7–6

The *Auto Detect Contacts* dialog box opens, as shown in Figure 7–7.

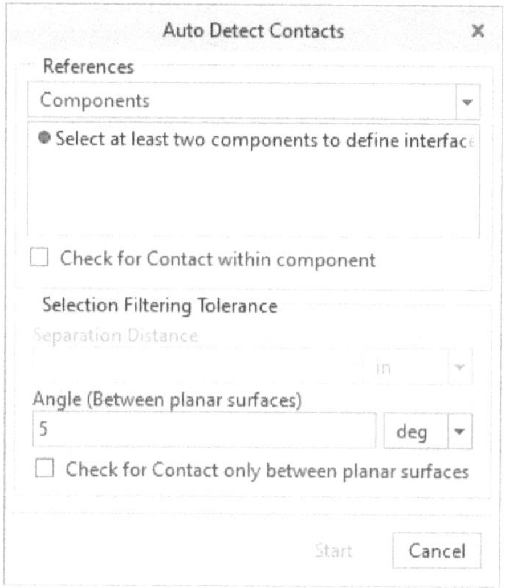

Figure 7–7

The options in the dialog box are as follows:

Option	Description
Separation Distance	Maximum distance between surface pairs on which you want to define a contact.
Angle (between planar surfaces)	Only surfaces that are at an angle less than the specified are considered.
Check for Contact only between planar surfaces	Creates contacts only between planar surfaces.
Check for Contact within components	Activates detection of self-contact within components.

7.5 Reviewing Interfaces

Once created, all of the interfaces display under **Connections>Interfaces** in the *Model Tree*, as shown in Figure 7–8. You can review and delete the interfaces in the model using the *Model Tree*.

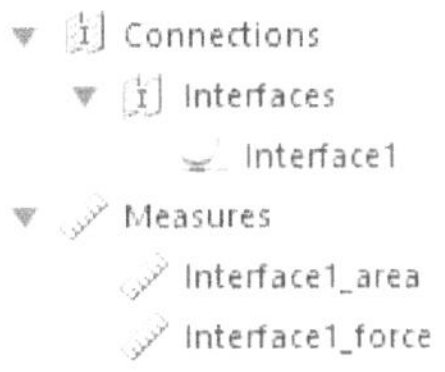

Figure 7–8

You can also visualize the interfaces in your model by clicking (Review Geometry) in the *Refine Model* tab and selecting the *Connectivity* options, as shown in Figure 7–9.

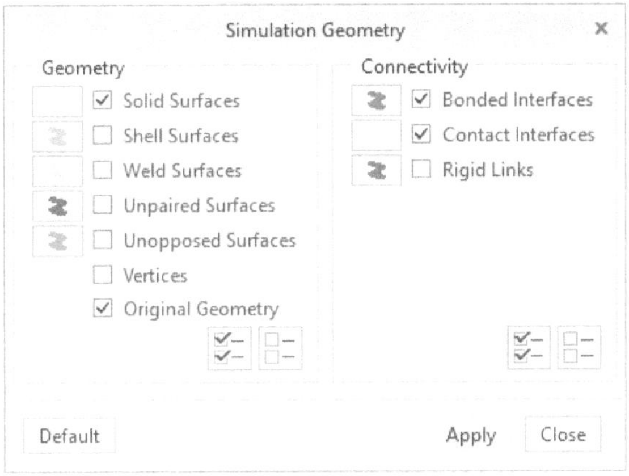

Figure 7–9

Once you click **Apply**, the model displays in semi-transparent mode, with all of the interfaces shaded and color-coded, as shown in Figure 7–10.

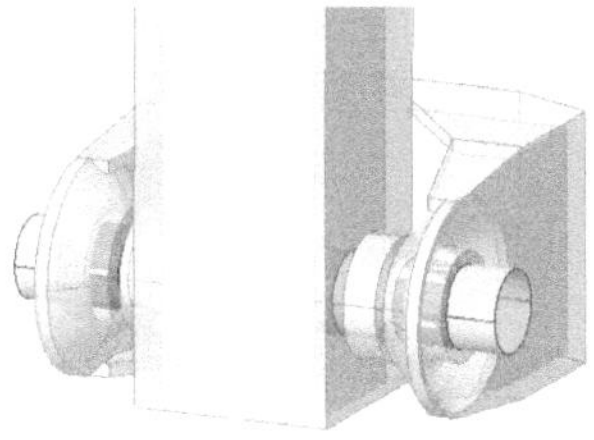

Figure 7–10

7.6 Setting Up Contact Analysis

Structural analysis with contact interfaces is a non-linear FEA analysis. A non-linear analysis is solved in small steps (controlled by the FEA solver), with the applied loads gradually incremented from no load to the full load, and with the equation system solved iteratively on every load increment, until iterations converge to the static equilibrium (Newton-Raphson method). A non-linear FEA takes much longer to solve than a comparable linear analysis. Therefore, use caution when setting up an analysis with many contact interfaces.

The *Static Analysis Definition* dialog box for an analysis with contact interfaces is shown in Figure 7–11.

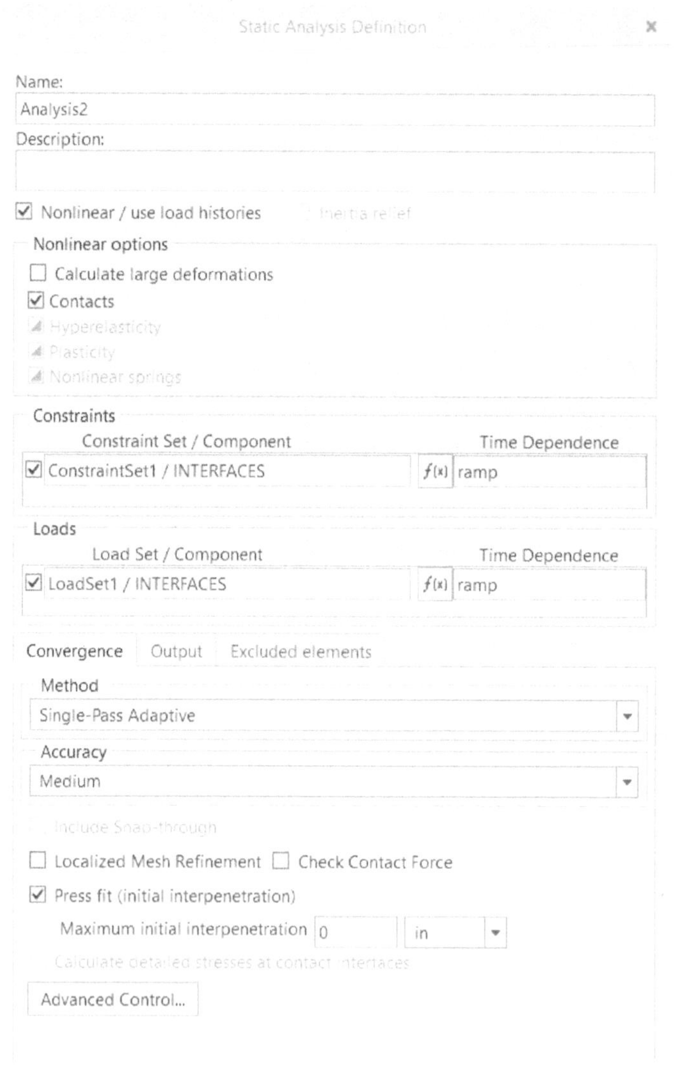

Figure 7–11

The following options must be set to run a non-linear analysis with contact interfaces:

1. Ensure that the **Nonlinear/Use Load Histories** and **Contacts** options are selected.
2. Activate the **Calculate large deformations** option if you anticipate a substantial sliding to occur in some contact regions or if you use contact with Finite friction.

   Note: *The* ***Calculate large deformations*** *option requires the Advanced Simulation license.*

3. In the *Constraints* and the *Loads* areas, use $f(x)$ (Function) to define the time histories for the constraints and loads in your model. The default time history is a simple ramp function with the load linearly increased from zero to the full load.
4. Set the *Convergence* options:
   - **Accuracy:** Controls the equilibrium convergence tolerance. Can be set to **Medium**, or **High**.
   - **Localized Mesh Refinement:** Automatically refines the mesh in the contact regions. Only available with the Single-Pass Adaptive convergence method.
   - **Check Contact Force:** Ensures convergence on contact forces.
   - **Press fit (initial interpenetration):** Activates detection of the press fit conditions in the model (otherwise Creo Simulate ignores initial interpenetrations).
   - **Maximum initial interpenetration:** Specifies the press fit detection value. Any initial interpenetration larger than this value is ignored.
   - **Calculate detailed stresses at contact interfaces:** Improves stress accuracy in contact regions. Requires longer computation time.

5. In the *Output* tab, select the *Output Steps*. This setting defines the load intervals (also called *load percentage factors*) at which Creo Simulate increments the load from no load to the full load, as well as calculates the full results for displaying.

   - **Automatic Steps within Range:** The load intervals are determined by the **Time Dependence** function. For the **ramp** function, results are calculated for the full load only.
   - **User-defined Output Steps:** Enables you to define the load intervals for the load incrementation and for the result calculation, as shown in the example in Figure 7–12.

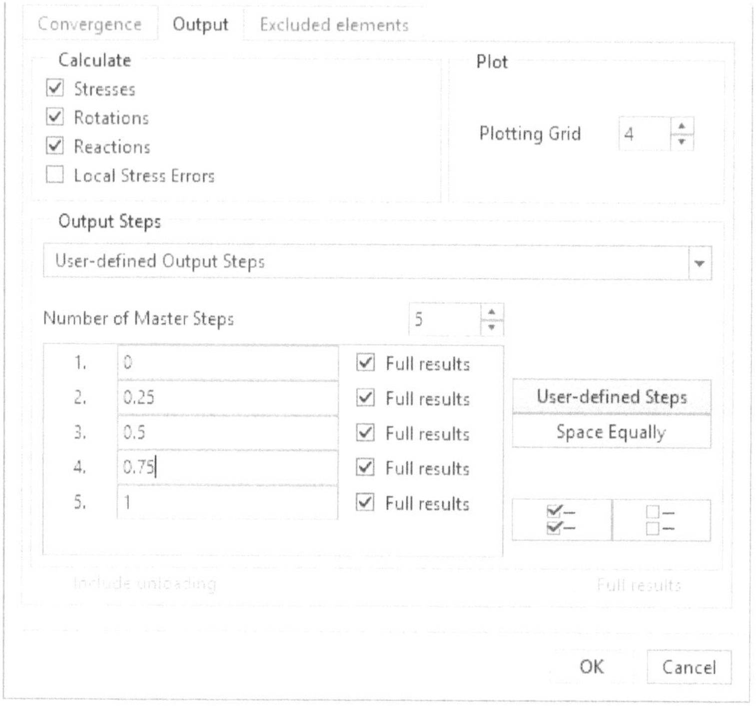

Figure 7–12

7.7 Mesh Refinement

The accuracy of the contact analyses are affected by the mesh density in the contact areas. The element size should be smaller than the contact region.

Use the following guidelines to achieve this condition:

- Enable the **Localized Mesh Refinement** option in the *Analysis* dialog box.
- Create divided surfaces to separate areas of contact from the rest of the part surface.
- Use the **AutoGEM Control, Maximum Element Size** option, as shown in Figure 7–13, to apply a smaller element size in the contact areas.

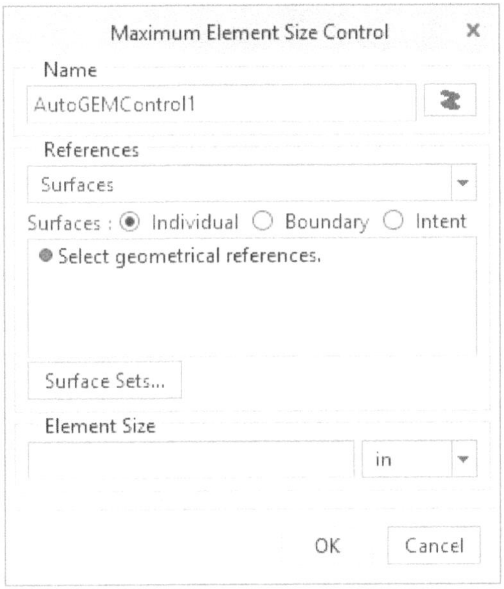

Figure 7–13

- Use 2D models when possible. Doing so improves accuracy, eases setup, and reduces run time.

Practice 7a
Door Handle Assembly

Practice Objectives

- Create free and contact interfaces.
- Set up and run a contact analysis.

In this practice, you will set up a contact analysis on a part of the door handle assembly. The assembly model is shown in Figure 7–14.

Figure 7–14

Note: The model has been defeatured (various rounds and blends have been removed).

The area of interest is only the contact between the sleeve and barrel. The assembly that you analyze consists of a sleeve part, the barrel part, and the door slab part, as shown in Figure 7–15. The model will be solved using one possible simulation scenario.

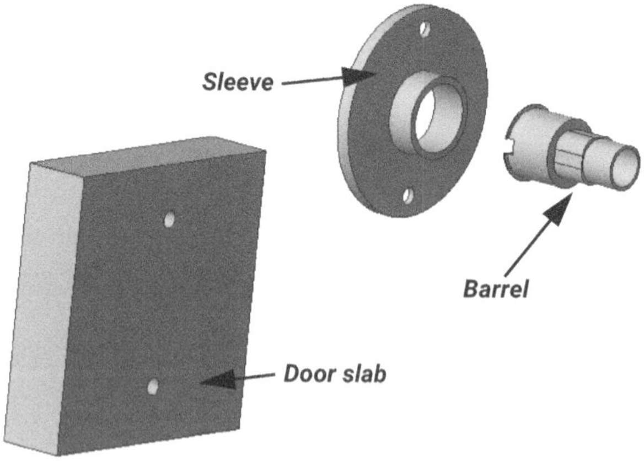

Figure 7–15

Modeling Tasks

Task 1: Open the model and launch Creo Simulate.

1. Set the working directory to **Chapter07**.
2. Open **door_handle.asm**.
3. Set the model display as follows:
   - *(Datum Display Filters)*: All Off
   - *(Spin Center)*: Off
   - *(Display Style)*: (Shading With Edges)

   The assembly displays as shown in Figure 7–16.

Figure 7–16

4. Ensure that the unit system is set to **IPS**.
5. Select **Applications>Simulate** to launch Creo Simulate.

Task 2: Apply the loads.

In this task, you will apply loads to the barrel end surface shown in Figure 7–17.

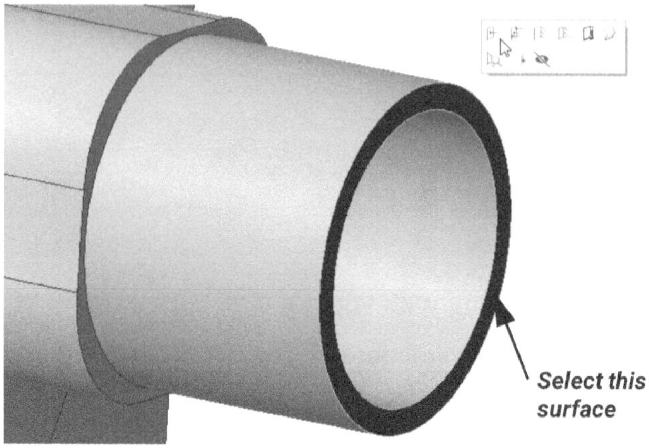

Figure 7–17

1. Apply **100lbs** to the surface in the Z-direction. For the *Name*, enter **handle_load**. The model displays as shown in Figure 7–18.

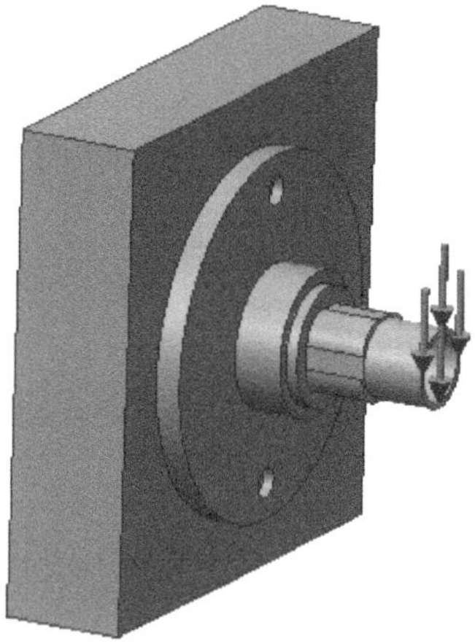

Figure 7–18

Note: *To apply the load, use the* ***Uniform*** *and* ***Total Load*** *options in the Distribution area in the Force/Moment dialog box. Note that the load is applied in the Z-direction.*

Task 3: Apply the constraints.

1. Fully constrain the door slab end surfaces, as shown in Figure 7–19.
2. For the *Name*, enter **door_const**. The model displays as shown in Figure 7–19.

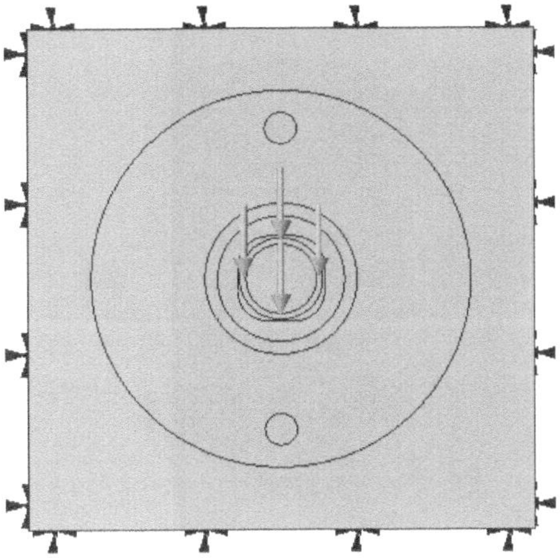

Figure 7–19

3. In the *Model Tree*, click (Tree Filters) and in the *General* area, enable **Features** and click **OK**.
4. In the In-graphics toolbar, enable (Point Display).
5. Select the Force/Moment load arrows and select (Hide) from the mini-toolbar, as shown in Figure 7–20.

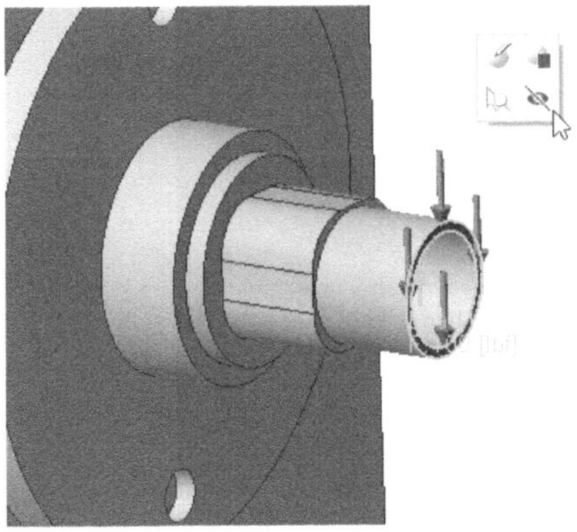

Figure 7–20

Note: *This hides the icons from display to make selection in the next step easier.*

6. Create a datum point in the middle of the barrel edge, as shown in Figure 7–21. Use the main assembly as the **Component for Feature**. Press and hold <Ctrl> and select the barrel edge on the model and **ASM_RIGHT** datum plane from the *Model Tree* as the **References** for the point.

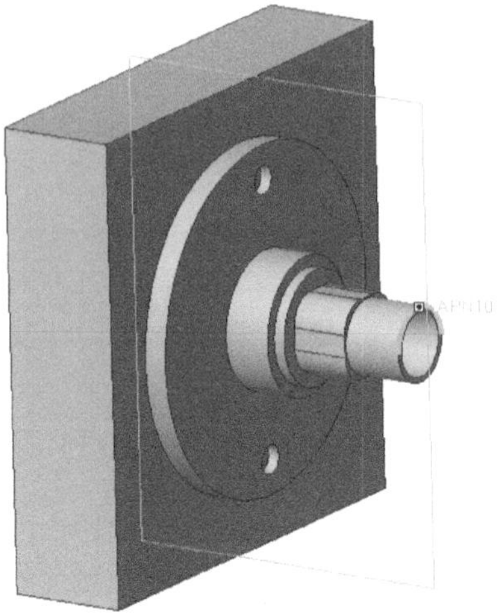

Figure 7–21

7. Constrain the point in the X- and Y-directions to prevent the rotation and slippage of the barrel (you will use a frictionless contact interface in this analysis). Leave the Z-direction free.
8. For the *Name*, enter **barrel_const**. The model displays as shown in Figure 7–22.

Figure 7–22

Task 4: Create a contact interface.

In this task, you will create a contact interface between the sleeve and the barrel.

1. In the *Refine Model* tab, click (Interface). The *Interface Definition* dialog box opens, as shown in Figure 7–23.

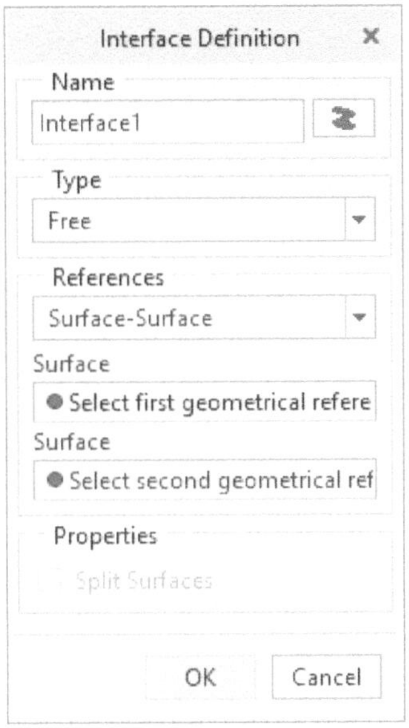

Figure 7–23

2. Expand the *Type* drop-down list and select **Contact**.
3. Expand the *References* drop-down list and select **Component-Component**.
4. Select the **SLEEVE** and **BARREL** parts as the references.

5. The *Interface Definition* dialog box displays as shown in Figure 7–24.

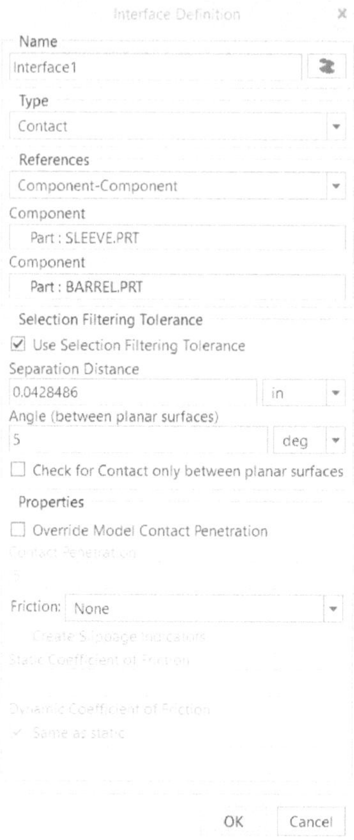

Figure 7–24

6. Accept all of the defaults and click **OK** to finish.
7. In the *Model Tree*, fully expand the **Loads/Constraints** branch, select **handle_load**, and select (Show) from the mini-toolbar. The model displays as shown in Figure 7–25.

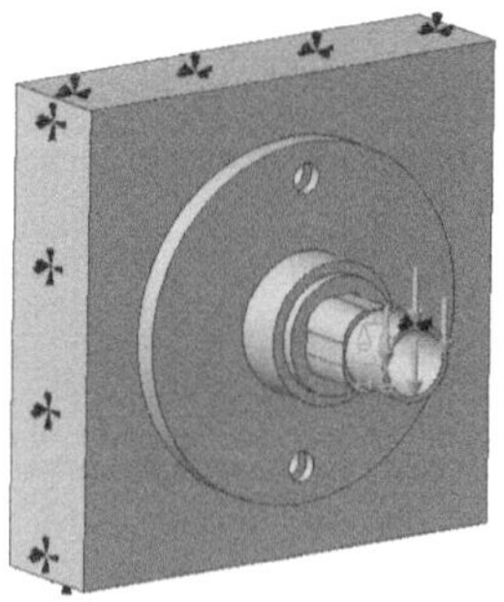

Figure 7–25

Task 5: Create a free interface.

The sleeve and door slab in this analysis are assumed to be only interacting through the screws. In this task, you will create a free interface to ensure that the sleeve is not pressing against the door slab along their surfaces during the analysis.

1. Click (Interface). The *Interface Definition* dialog box opens.
2. Expand the *Type* drop-down list and select **Free**.
3. Expand the *References* drop-down list and select **Component-Component**.
4. Select the **SLEEVE** and **DOOR** parts as the references and accept all of the other default options. The *Interface Definition* dialog box displays as shown in Figure 7–26.

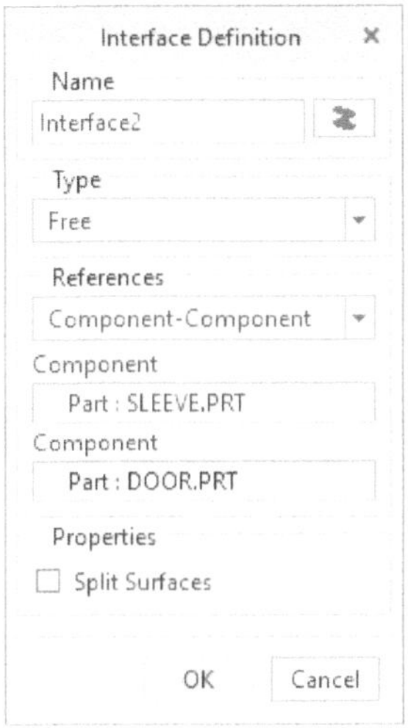

Figure 7–26

5. Accept all of the other defaults and click **OK** to finish.
6. In the In-graphics toolbar, select (Hidden Line) to show internal icons and geometry. The model displays as shown in Figure 7–27.

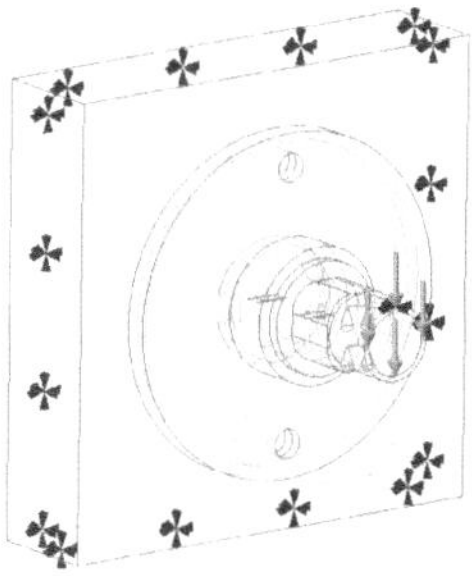

Figure 7–27

Task 6: Create rigid links.

In this task, you will create rigid links to model the screws that attach the sleeve to the door slab.

1. In the *Connections* group, click (Rigid Link). The *Rigid Link Definition* dialog box opens, as shown in Figure 7–28.

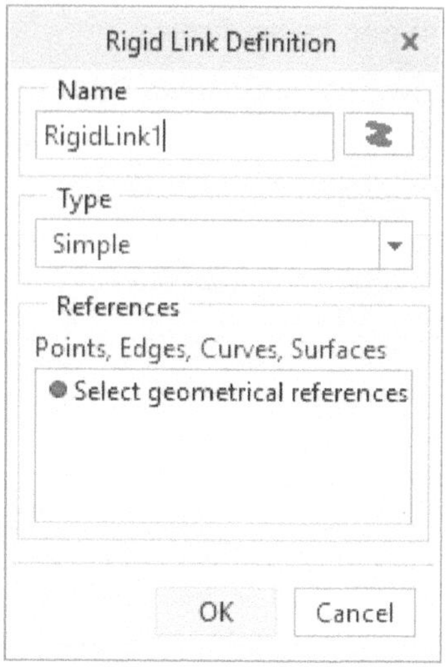

Figure 7–28

2. Select the inside cylindrical surfaces of the top hole in the sleeve and of the top hole in the door slab, as shown in Figure 7–29.

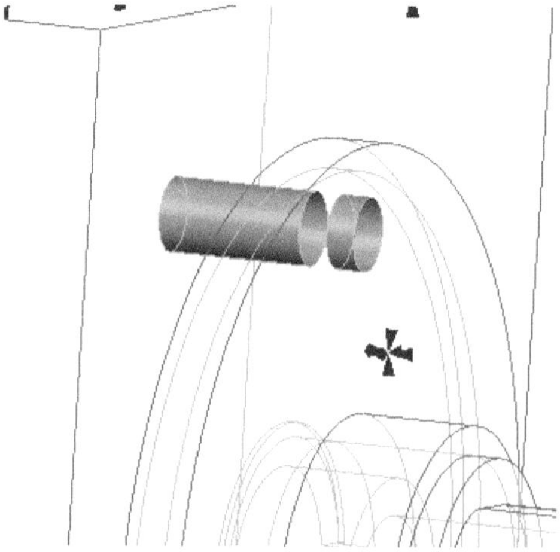

Figure 7–29

3. The *Rigid Link Definition* dialog box displays as shown in Figure 7–30.

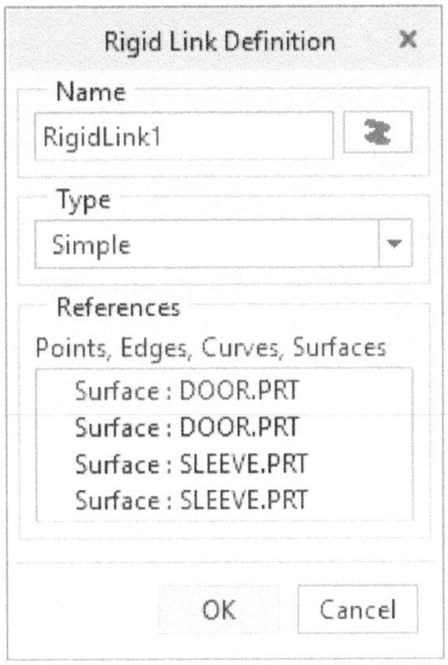

Figure 7–30

4. Click **OK** to finish. The rigid link displays as shown in Figure 7–31.

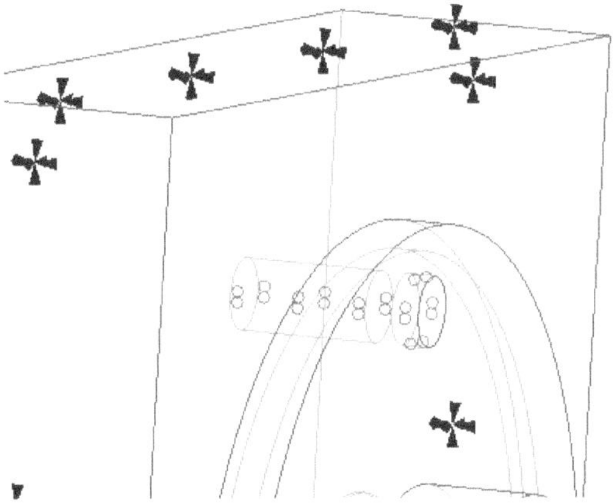

Figure 7–31

5. Repeat Steps 1 to 4 to create a rigid link for the bottom holes.

6. Use the *Simulation Display* dialog box to hide the loads and constraints. The model displays as shown in Figure 7–32.

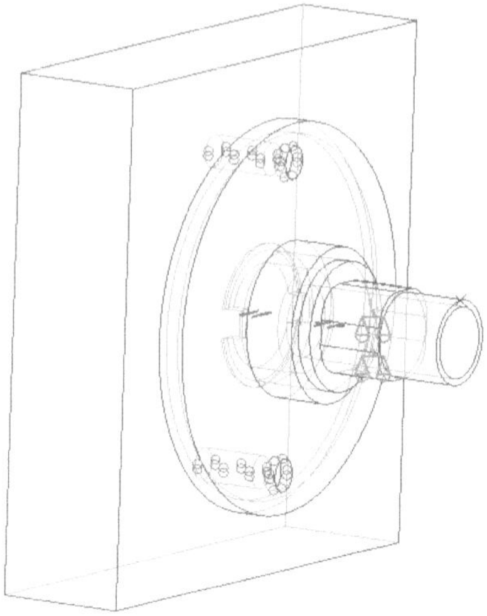

Figure 7–32

Task 7: Review the connections.

1. In the *Refine Model* tab, in the *AutoGEM* group, click (Review Geometry) to open the *Simulation Geometry* dialog box.
2. Select the options shown in Figure 7–33.

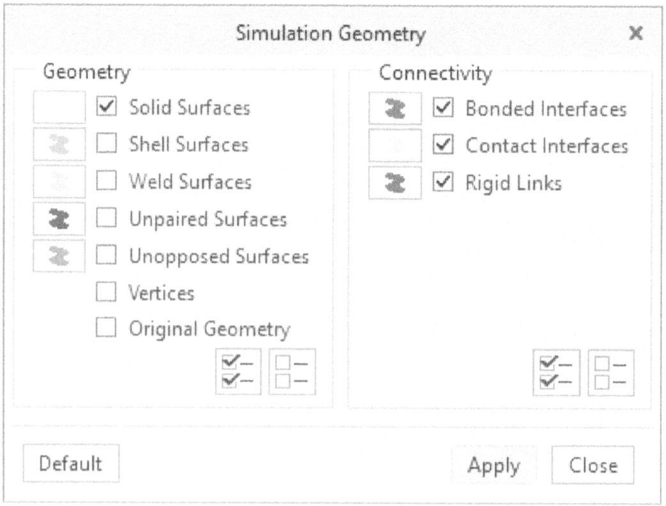

Figure 7–33

3. Click **Apply**. The model displays as shown in Figure 7–34.

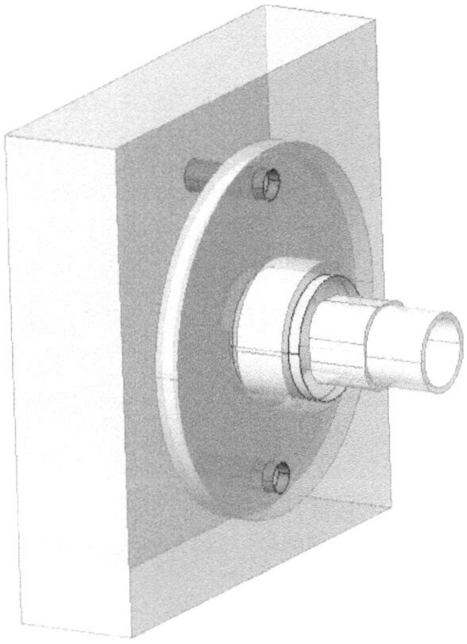

Figure 7–34

Examine the model display. Locate the contact interfaces and the rigid links. Ensure that there are no bonded interfaces in the model.

4. Click **Close** to finish.

Task 8: Apply the material.

1. Assign **AL2014** to all of the assembly parts. The following values are the default material properties for Aluminum, wrought 2014-T6:
   - *Poisson:* **0.33**
   - *Young's modulus:* **1.06e+07 psi**

Analysis Tasks

Task 9: Set up and run the analysis.

1. Set up a Single-Pass Adaptive convergence analysis. For the analysis name, enter **door_handle** and keep all of the other defaults. The *Static Analysis Definition* dialog box opens, as shown in Figure 7–35.

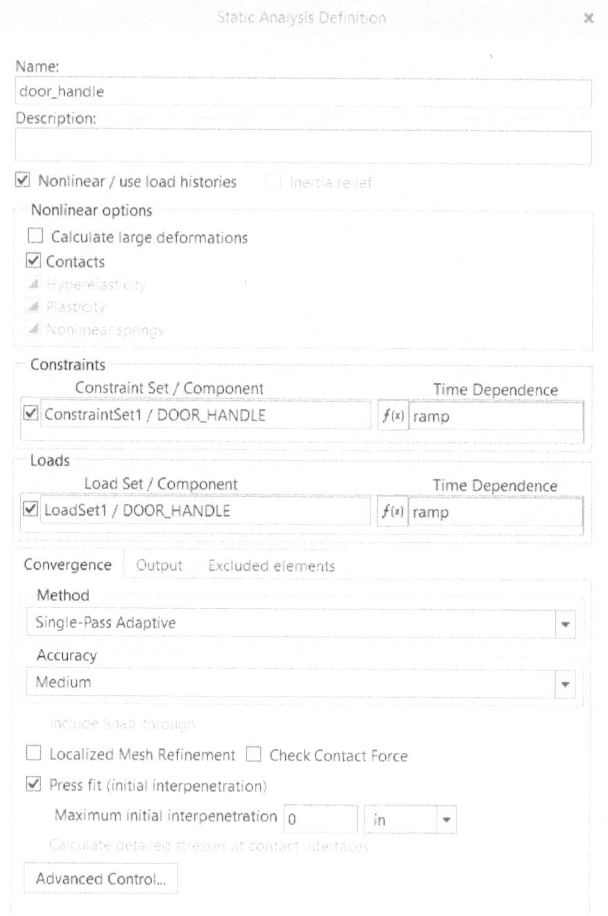

Figure 7–35

2. Select the *Output* tab.
3. Expand the *Output Steps* drop-down list and select **User-defined Output Steps**.
4. For the *Number of Master Steps*, select **5**.
5. Click **User-defined Steps** and **Space Equally**. In the *Static Analysis Definition* dialog box, the *Output* area displays as shown in Figure 7–36.

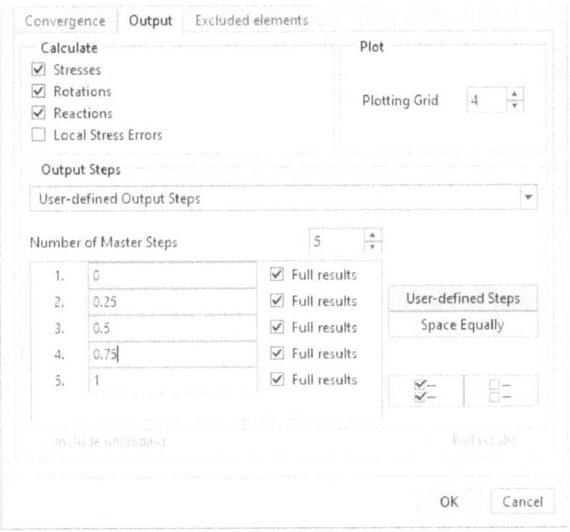

Figure 7–36

6. Click **OK** to close the *Static Analysis Definition* dialog box.
7. In the *Analyses and Design Studies* dialog box, in the **Info** menu, select **Check Model** to check the validity of the model.
8. Run the analysis.

Results Tasks

Task 10: Display the deformation results.

1. In the *Analyses and Design Studies* dialog box, click (Review Results). In the *Result Window Definition* dialog box, in the *Steps* list, highlight the last row as shown in Figure 7–37.

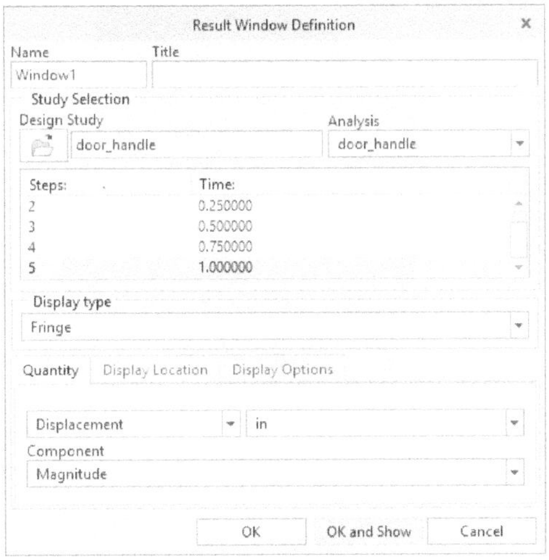

Figure 7–37

2. Select the *Display Options* tab. Select the **Deformed**, **Overlay Undeformed**, and **Animate** options, as shown in Figure 7–38.

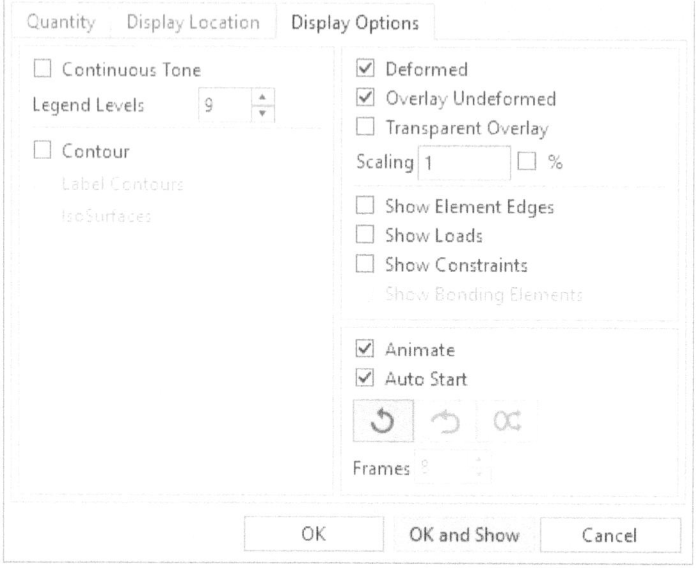

Figure 7–38

3. Click **OK and Show** to display and animate the Displacement Magnitude result.
4. Note that the animation frames correspond to the load factor, from 0 (no load) to 1 (full load). Stop the animation at Step 4. The model displays as shown in Figure 7–39.

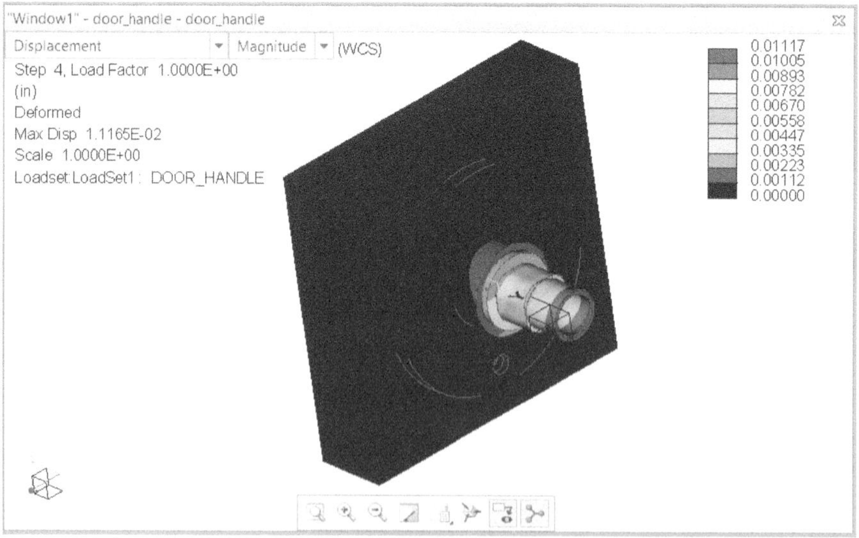

Figure 7–39

Task 11: Display the stress results.

1. In the *Home* tab, click (Edit) to edit the result window. In the *Quantity* area, select **Stress, von Mises**.
2. Select the *Display Location* tab. Expand the drop-down list and select **Components/Layers**. Set the visibility of the **DOOR** component to (Blanked).
3. Select the *Display Options* tab and clear the **Animate** option.
4. Click **OK and Show**. The von Mises stress plot displays as shown in Figure 7–40.

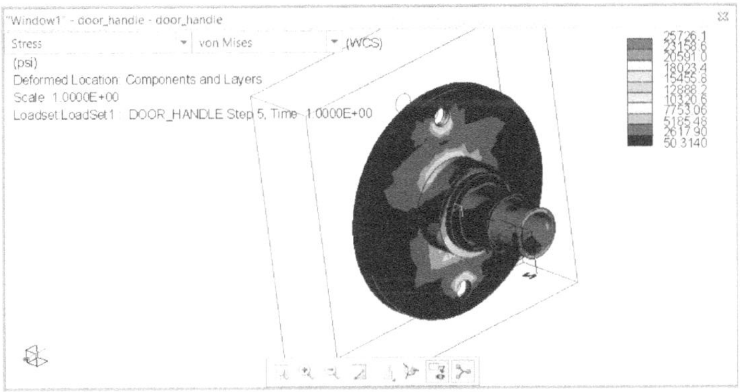

Figure 7–40

Examine the stress plot. Use the tools in the *Query* section of the *Home* tab to locate the area of maximum stress.

Task 12: Display the contact pressure results.

1. Click (Edit) to edit the result window. In the *Steps* area, highlight the last row, and in the *Quantity* area, select **Contact Pressure**.
2. Click **OK and Show**. The Contact Pressure plot displays as shown in Figure 7–41.

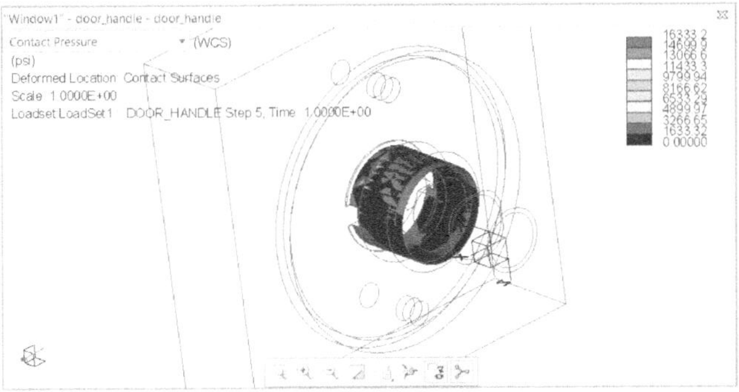

Figure 7–41

3. Select (Model Max) to locate the maximum. Note that the maximum contact pressure occurs at the back of the top of the contact region, as shown in Figure 7–42.

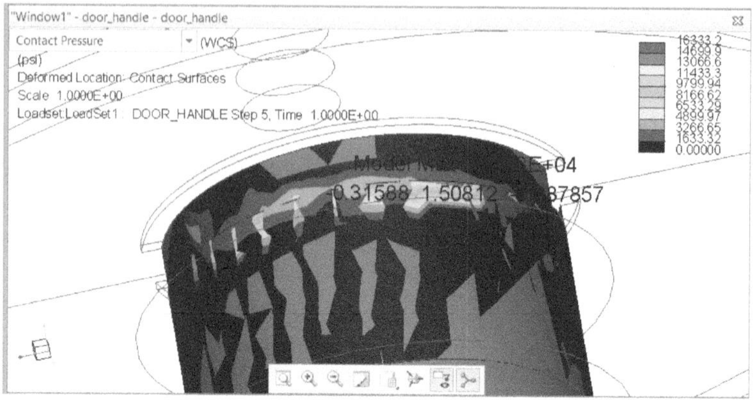

Figure 7–42

Task 13: Display the contact pressure graph.

1. Click (Edit) to edit the result window. In the *Display type* list, select **Graph** and in the *Quantity* area, select **Measure**. The *Result Window Definition* dialog box displays as shown in Figure 7–43.

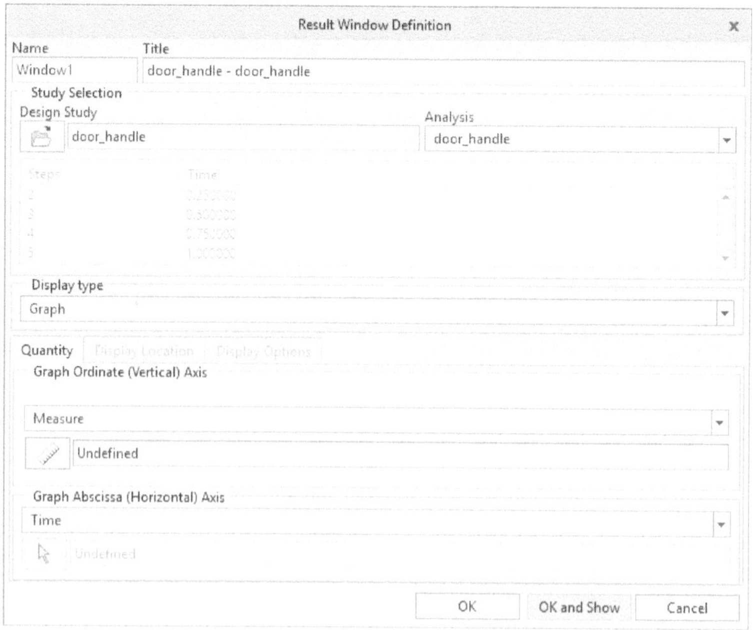

Figure 7–43

2. Click (Measure). In the list of predefined measures, select **contact_max_pres**. Click **OK** to complete.
3. Click **OK and Show**. The **contact_max_pres** graph displays as shown in Figure 7–44.

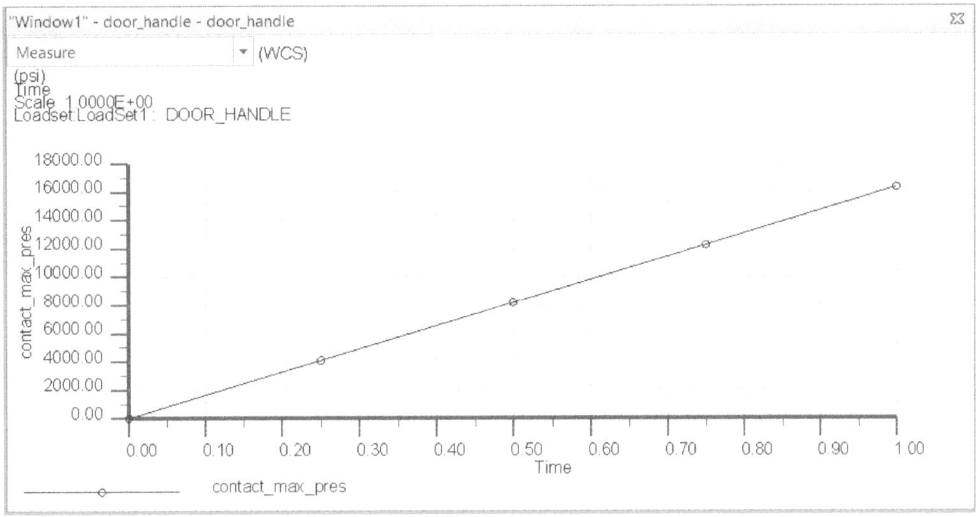

Figure 7–44

Note how the maximum contact pressure is increasing with the load, from no load to the full load. Although the horizontal axis in the graph displays *Time*, this is not a physical time because a static analysis was solved. Rather, it is a load factor (i.e., the 0.50 value on the horizontal axis corresponds to the 50% load applied, etc.).

4. Exit the Results environment and save and close the model.

End of practice

Practice 7b
Pin-Jointed Assembly

Practice Objectives

- Create divided surfaces.
- Create contact interfaces.
- Refine mesh in contact regions.
- Run a contact analysis.

In this practice, you will set up a contact analysis on a pin-jointed assembly model. The assembly model is part of a hydraulic boom mechanism, as shown in Figure 7–45.

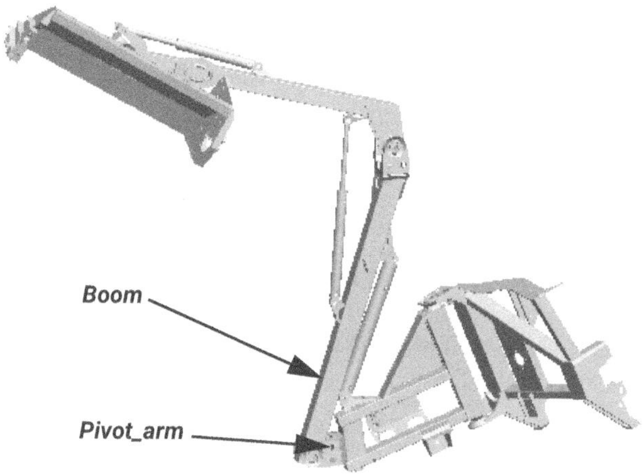

Figure 7–45

The contact analysis takes a long time and the area of interest is only the contact between the pin, boom, and pivot arm. The assembly that you will analyze consists of these parts, as shown in Figure 7–46. The model will be solved with one possible simulation scenario.

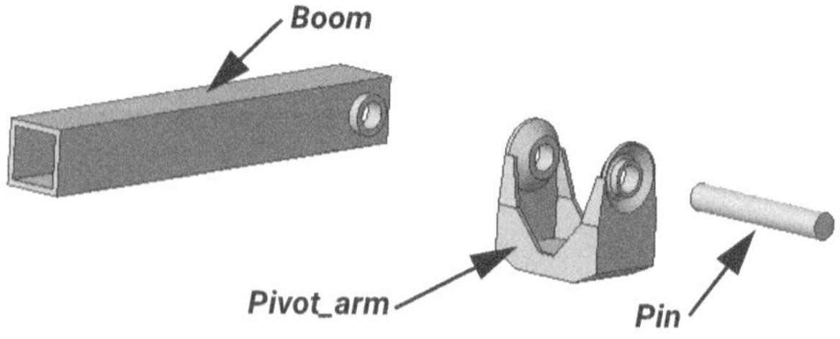

Figure 7–46

The pin is press-fit into the pivot arm holes. Therefore, the pin is fully fixed to the pivot arm. However, the boom is assembled on the pin with a small clearance, to be able to rotate around the pin when the mechanism (shown previously in Figure 7–45) is moving.

Modeling Tasks

Task 1: Open the assembly.

1. Set the working directory to **Chapter07**, if required.
2. Open **hydraulic.asm**.
3. Set the model display as follows:
   - *(Datum Display Filters)*: All Off
   - *(Spin Center)*: Off
   - *(Display Style)*: (Shading With Edges)

   The assembly displays as shown in Figure 7–47.

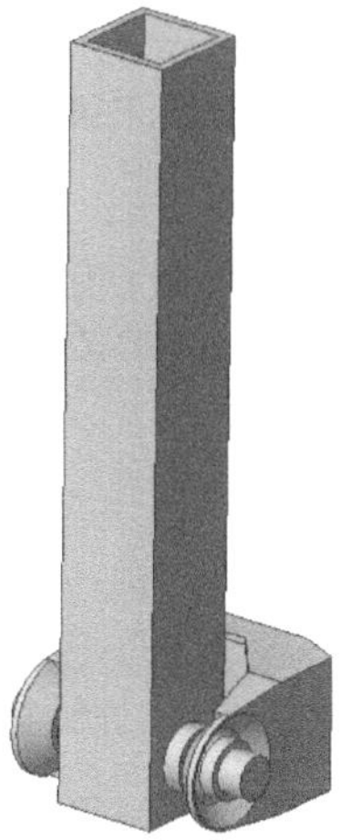

Figure 7–47

4. Ensure that the unit system is set to **mmNs**.

   Note: *All parts in the assembly must use the same system of units.*

5. Do not launch Creo Simulate yet.

Task 2: Create the contact regions.

In this task, you will define the surface areas that are used later to create contact interfaces between the pin and boom.

1. Select **pin_1.prt** in the *Model Tree* and select (Open) in the mini-toolbar.
2. In the In-graphics toolbar, enable (Plane Display). The pin displays as shown in Figure 7–48.

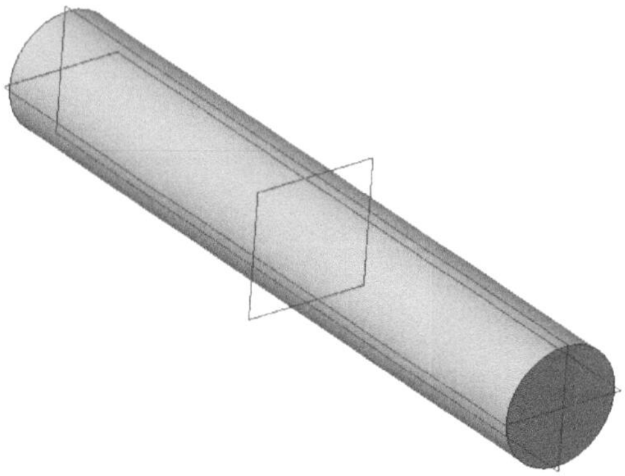

Figure 7–48

3. Switch to Creo Simulate.
4. In the *Refine Model* tab, click (Plane) and create **DTM1** plane parallel to datum plane **RIGHT** at a distance of **80**, as shown in Figure 7–49.

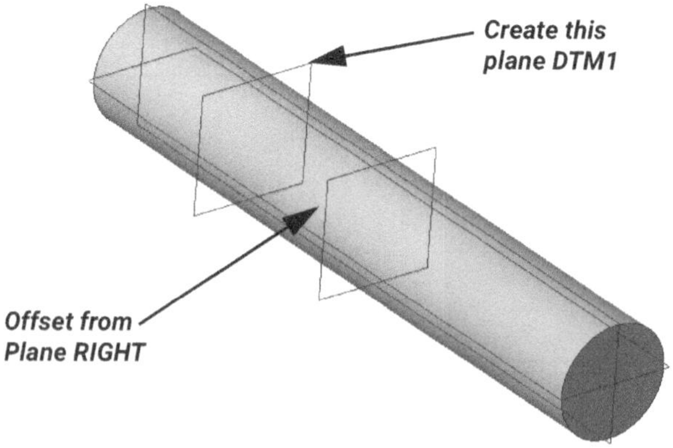

Figure 7–49

Note: *The plane is created on the left side of datum plane RIGHT, using the pin orientation shown in Figure 7–49.*

5. Create another plane (**DTM2**) on the same side of datum plane RIGHT, now at a distance of **48**, as shown in Figure 7–50.

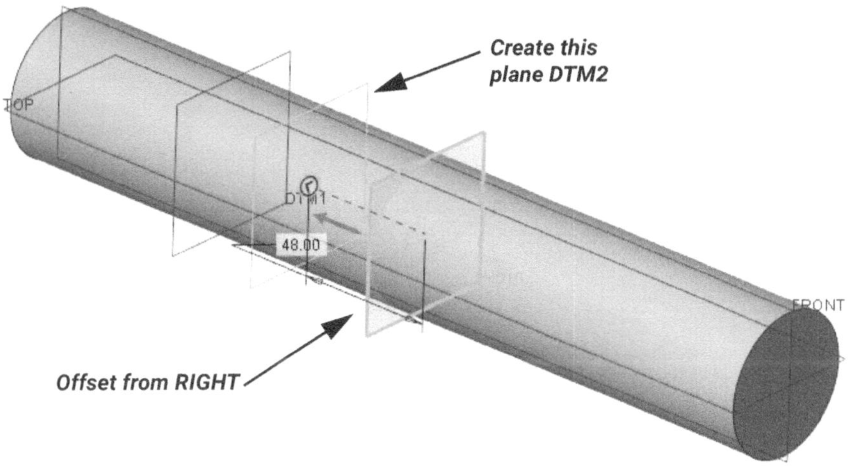

Figure 7–50

6. Create two more datum planes on the right side of datum plane RIGHT, as follows:
   - **DTM3:** 48mm offset from the **RIGHT** datum plane
   - **DTM4:** 80mm offset from the **RIGHT** datum plane

   The model displays as shown in Figure 7–51.

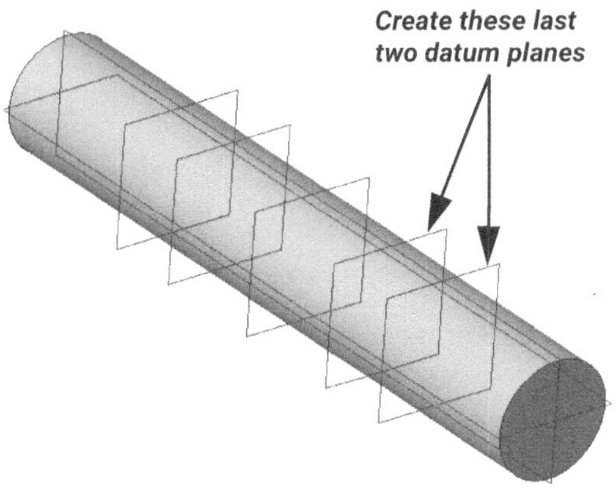

Figure 7–51

The datum planes you created have been placed at the ends of the boom holes, where the pin contacts the boom. The planes are symmetrical about the middle of the pin.

7. Select the **DTM1** plane and click (Intersect). The *Intersect* dashboard opens.

8. Hold <Ctrl> and select both halves of the cylindrical surface of the pin, as shown in Figure 7–52.

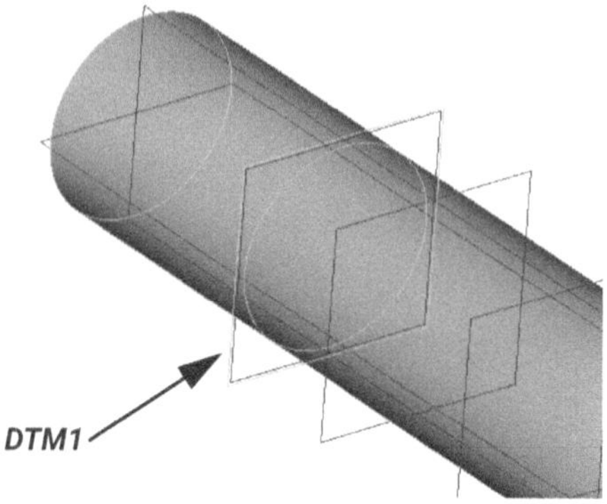

Figure 7–52

9. Click ✓ (OK) to finish. The new datum curve **Intersect_1** displays in the model, as shown in Figure 7–53.

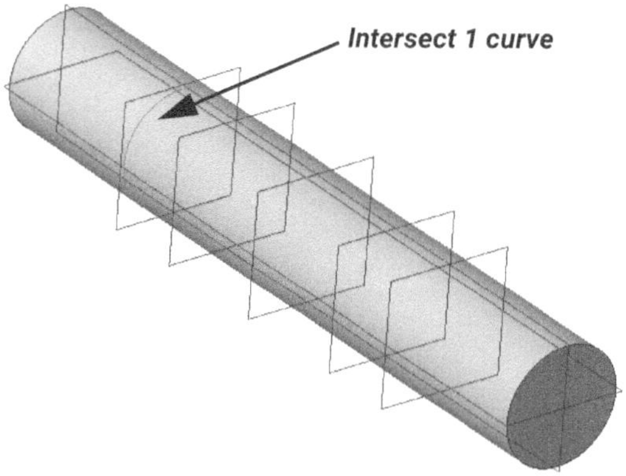

Figure 7–53

10. Repeat Steps 6 to 7 to create intersection curves between the pin surface and the planes **DTM2**, **DTM3**, and **DTM4**.

11. In the In-graphics toolbar, disable (Plane Display). The model displays as shown in Figure 7–54.

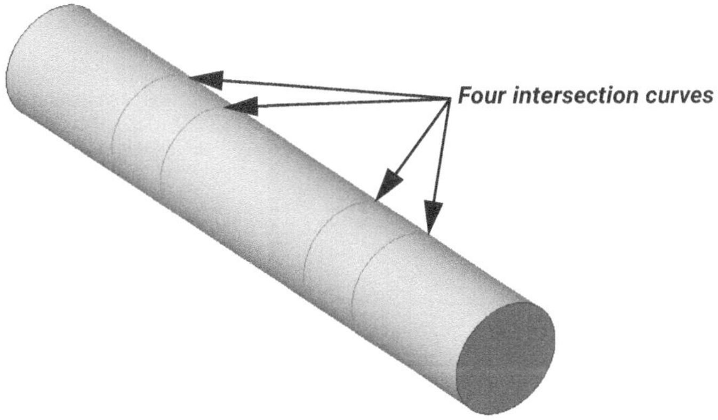

Figure 7–54

12. In the *Refine Model* tab, click (Divide Surface). The *Divide Surface* dashboard opens, as shown in Figure 7–55.

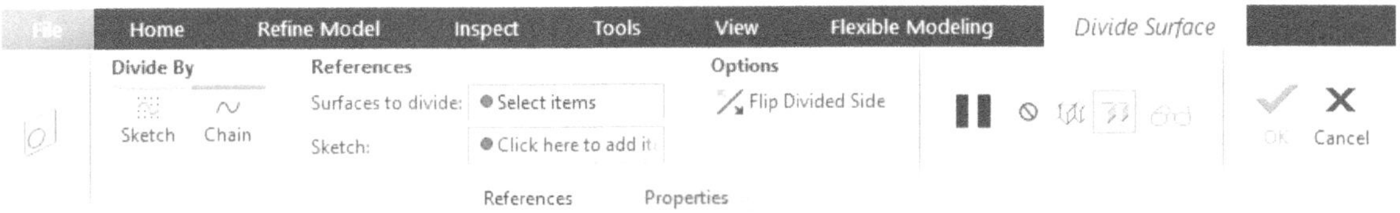

Figure 7–55

13. Select the *Surfaces to divide* field and select both halves of the cylindrical surface of the pin, as shown in Figure 7–56.

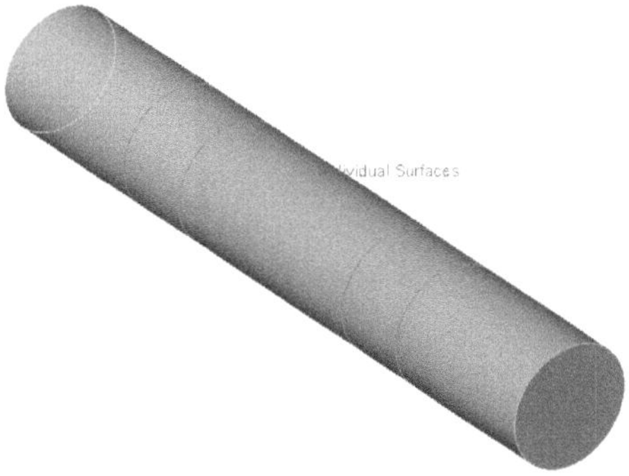

Figure 7–56

14. Click (Chain).

15. Select the *Chains* field and select the **Intersect 1** curve. The model displays as shown in Figure 7–57.

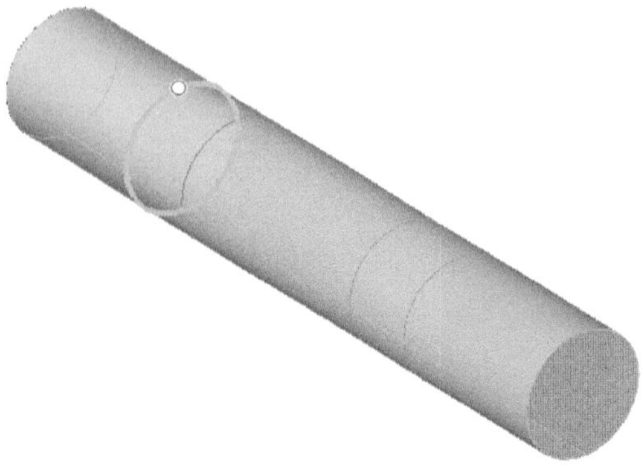

Figure 7–57

16. Click (OK) to finish.
17. Repeat Steps 10 to 14 to divide the surface of the pin using the curves **Intersect 2**, **Intersect 3**, and **Intersect 4**. The surface divisions display in the *Model Tree*, as shown in Figure 7–58. Select the surface divisions in the *Model Tree* and note how they highlight in the model.

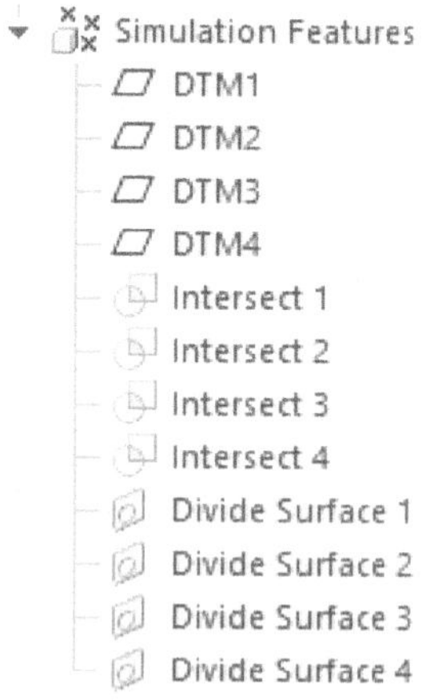

Figure 7–58

Task 3: Refine the mesh on the pin.

1. In the *AutoGEM* group in the ribbon, expand (Control) and click (Maximum Element Size). The *Maximum Element Size Control* dialog box opens, as shown in Figure 7–59.

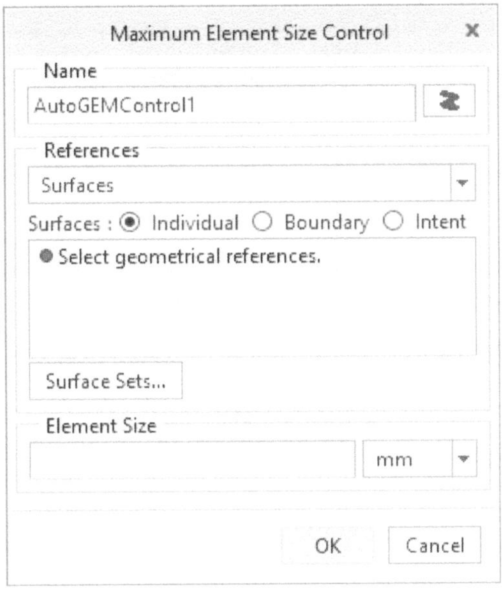

Figure 7–59

Note: *Refining the mesh in the contact areas improves the accuracy of the contact analysis.*

2. Select the two divided surfaces between the curves (these are the contact areas between the pin and the boom), as shown in Figure 7–60.

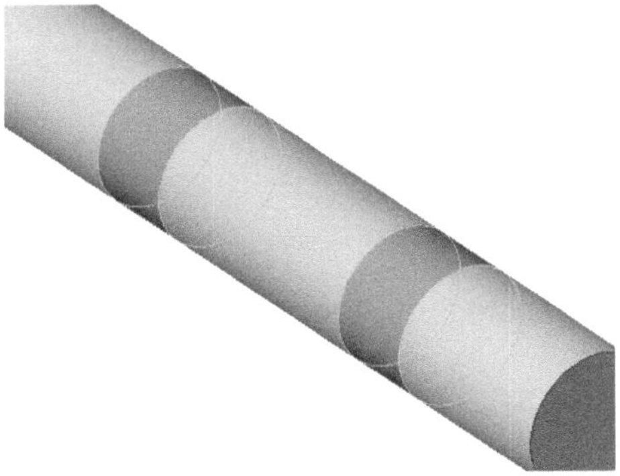

Figure 7–60

Note: *The pin diameter is 50mm.*

3. In the *Element Size* field, enter **15** and click **OK** to finish.
4. Use the **Volume** option to mesh the pin. The mesh displays as shown in Figure 7–61.

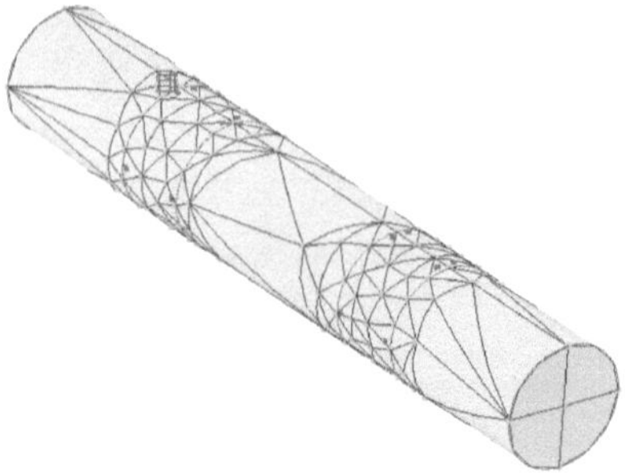

Figure 7–61

Note the finer mesh that has been created on the contact areas.

5. Exit AutoGEM without saving the mesh.
6. Save and close the **pin_1** part in Creo Parametric.

Task 4: Open the assembly.

1. Ensure that **hydraulic.asm** is open in the current window and switch to the Creo Simulate environment.
2. Expand the *Model Tree* and note that the simulation features and AutoGEM controls created on the part level in Tasks 2 and 3 have been propagated into the assembly analysis model.
3. Use the *Simulation Display* dialog box to toggle off display of the AutoGEM controls.

Task 5: Apply the material.

1. Assign **STEEL** to all of the parts in the assembly. The following values are the default material properties for HS low-alloy steel:
   - *Poisson:* **0.27**
   - *Young's modulus:* **199948 MPa**
   - *Density:* **7.82708e-9 tonne/mm^3**
2. Using the *Simulation Display* dialog box, toggle off the display of the **Material Assignments**.

Task 6: Create the interfaces.

In this task, you will create bonded interfaces between the pivot arm and the pin, and contact interfaces between the pin and the boom.

> **Note:** *The pin is press-fit into the pivot arm holes, while the boom is assembled on the pin with a clearance.*

1. Click (Model Setup) in the *Home* tab. Expand the *Default Interface* drop-down list and verify that **Bonded** is selected, as shown in Figure 7–62.

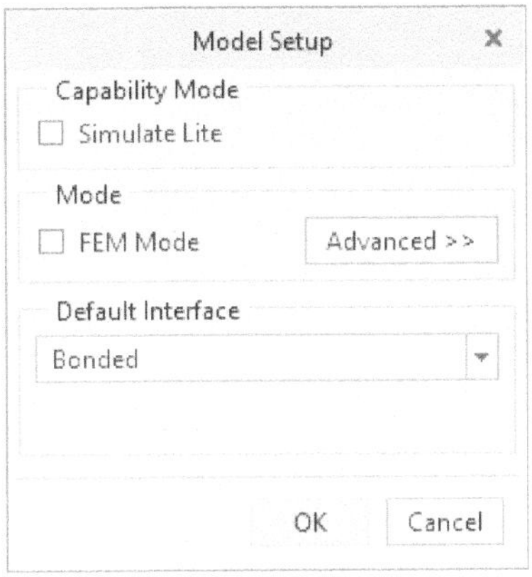

Figure 7–62

The default bonded interface will apply to the mated areas between the pin and the pivot arm.

2. Click **OK**.
3. In the *Refine Model* tab, click (Interface). The *Interface Definition* dialog box opens, as shown in Figure 7–63.

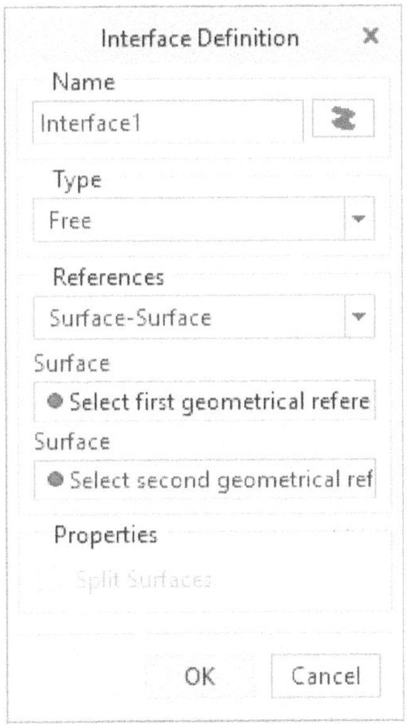

Figure 7–63

4. Expand the *Type* drop-down list and select **Contact**.
5. Expand the *References* drop-down list and select **Component-Component**.

6. Select the **PIN_1** and **BOOM_1** parts as the references.
7. The *Interface Definition* dialog box displays as shown in Figure 7–64.

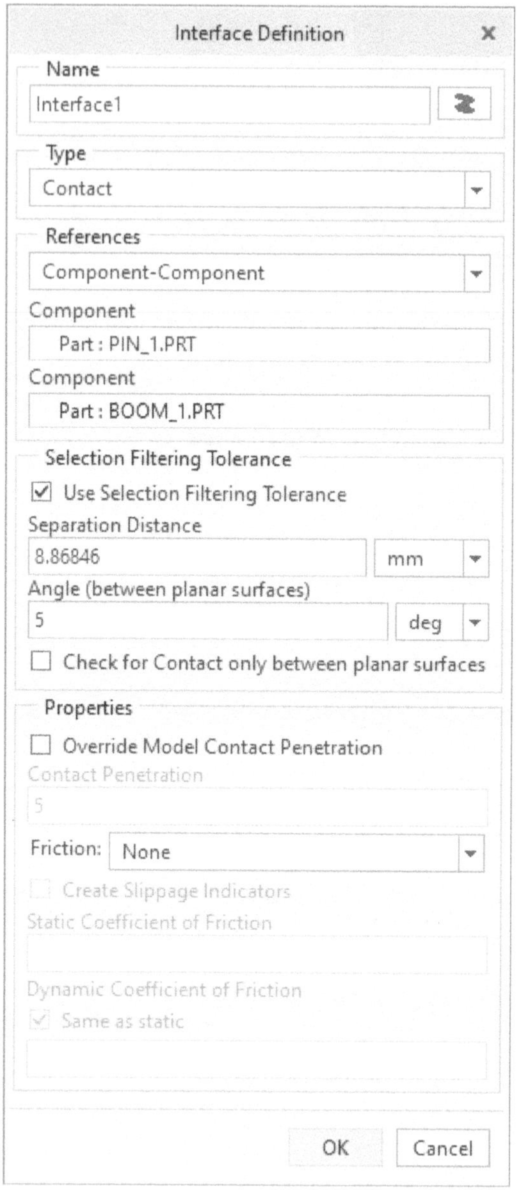

Figure 7–64

8. Accept all of the other defaults and click **OK** to finish. The model displays as shown in Figure 7–65.

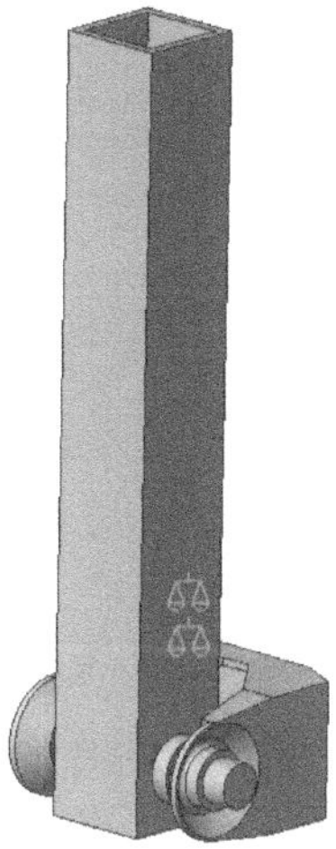

Figure 7–65

9. In the *Refine Model* tab, in the *AutoGEM* area, click (Review Geometry) to open the *Simulation Geometry* dialog box.

10. Select the options shown in Figure 7–66.

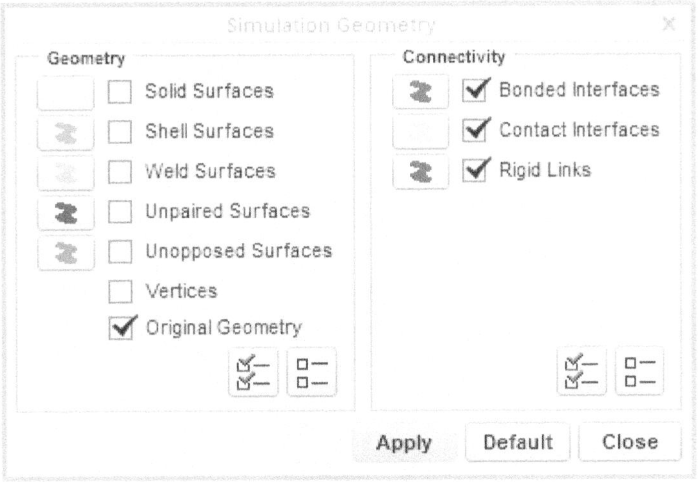

Figure 7–66

11. Click **Apply**. The model displays as shown in Figure 7–67.

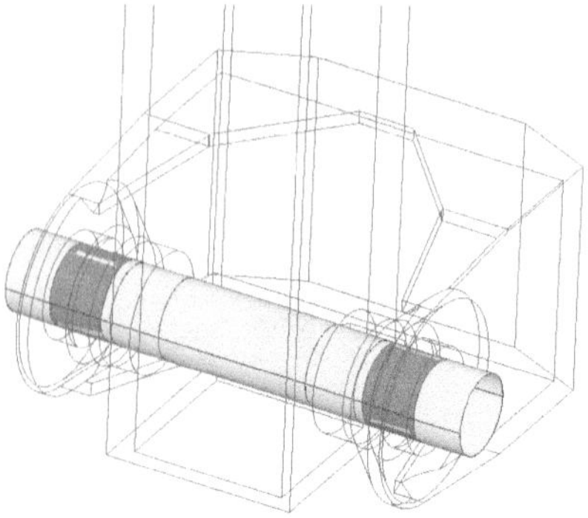

Figure 7–67

Compare the interface colors (shown as shaded in Figure 7–67) to the color scheme in the *Simulation Geometry* dialog box. Ensure that the bonded interfaces are shown between the pin and the pivot arm, and that the contact interfaces are shown between the pin and the boom.

12. Click **Close** to finish.
13. Using the *Simulation Display* dialog box, toggle off the visibilities of the **Measures** and of the **Interfaces**.

Task 7: Apply loads.

In this task, you will apply loads to the top surface of the boom part.

1. In the *Name* field, enter **boom_load**.
2. In Y-direction, apply **10,000N** to the top surface of the boom. The model displays as shown in Figure 7–68. WCS is the default coordinate system.

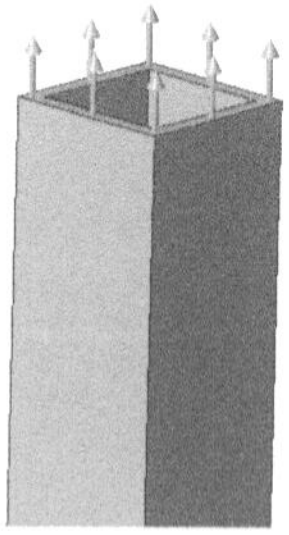

Figure 7–68

*Note: To apply the load, use the **Uniform** and **Total Load** options in the Distribution area in the Force/Moment Load dialog box.*

3. Using the *Simulation Display* dialog box, hide the loads.

Task 8: Apply the constraints.

1. Fully constrain the surface of the **pivot_arm** shown in Figure 7–69. Enter **pivot_const** as the constraint name.

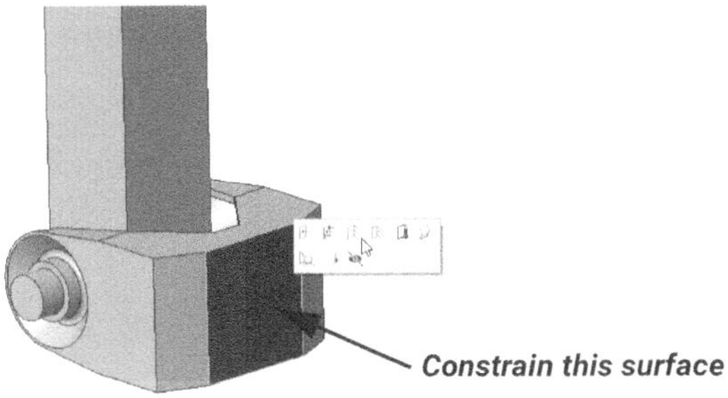

Figure 7–69

Note: *Ensure that the two named constraints are members of ConstraintSet1.*

The model displays as shown in Figure 7–70.

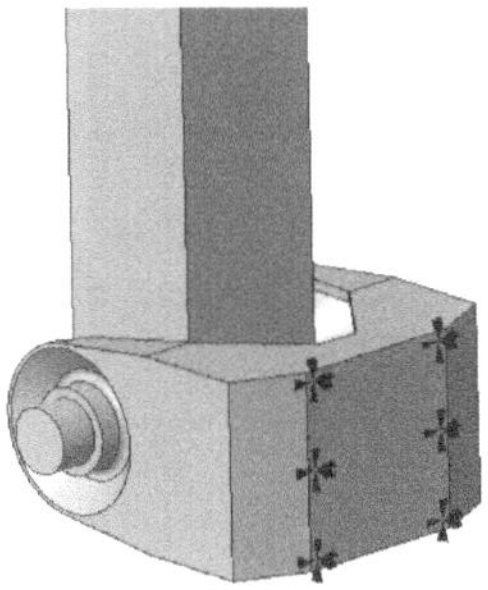

Figure 7–70

2. Constrain the X- and Z-directions on the end of the surface of the boom shown in Figure 7–71. Ensure that you leave the Y-direction free. Enter **boom_const** as the constraint name.

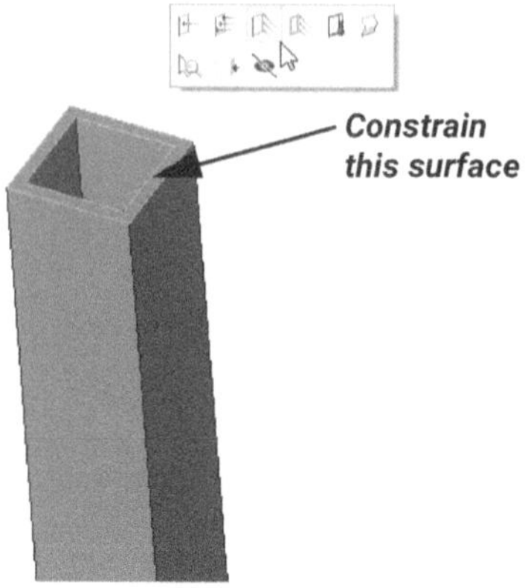

Figure 7–71

Note: *This constraint is required to eliminate the rigid body rotation and sliding motions of the boom about the pin. The contact interface that you defined in Task 4 was frictionless.*

3. Toggle on the loads visibility. The model displays as shown in Figure 7–72.

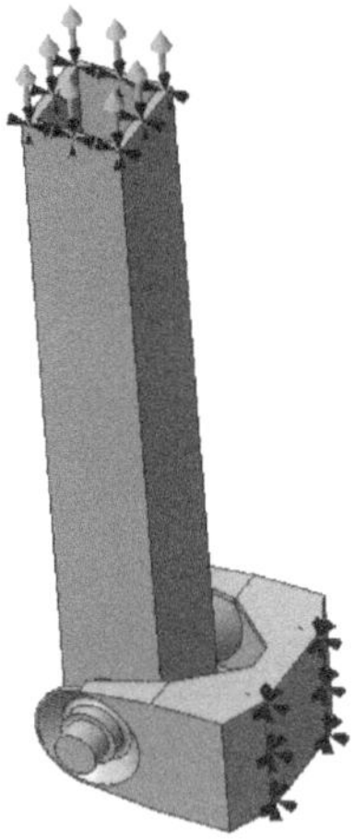

Figure 7–72

Task 9: Mesh the model.

1. Mesh the assembly using the **All with Properties** option. The mesh displays as shown in Figure 7–73.

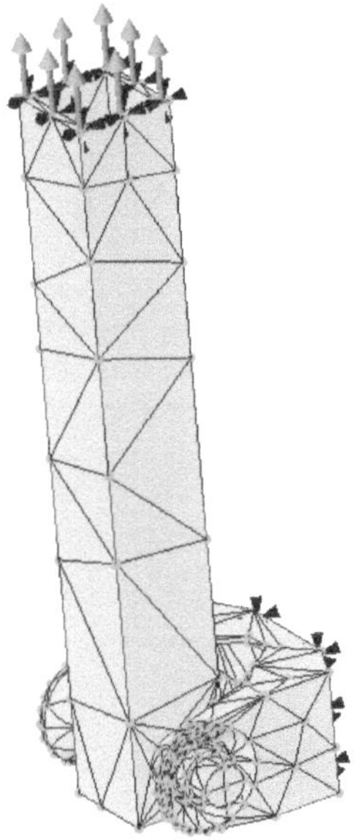

Figure 7–73

2. Close the *AutoGEM* dialog box and save the mesh.

Analysis Tasks

Task 10: Set up and run the analysis.

1. Set up a Single-Pass Adaptive convergence analysis. Enter **hydraulic** as the analysis name and keep all of the other defaults. The *Static Analysis Definition* dialog box displays as shown in Figure 7–74.

Figure 7–74

2. Click **OK** to close the *Static Analysis Definition* dialog box.

   Note: *The **Contacts** option is already selected.*

3. In the **Info** menu, select **Check Model** to check the validity of the model.
4. Run this analysis.

Results Tasks

Task 11: Display the deformation results.

1. Click (Review Results) in the *Analyses and Design Studies* dialog box. In the *Result Window Definition* dialog box, in the *Steps* list, highlight the second row as shown in Figure 7–75.

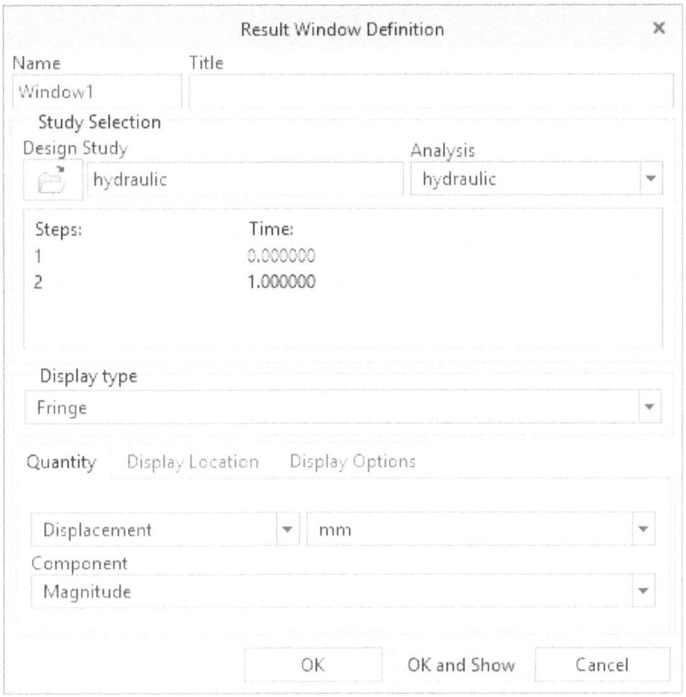

Figure 7–75

2. Select the *Display Options* tab. Select the **Deformed** and **Overlay Undeformed** options, and set the *Scaling* to **5%**, as shown in Figure 7–76.

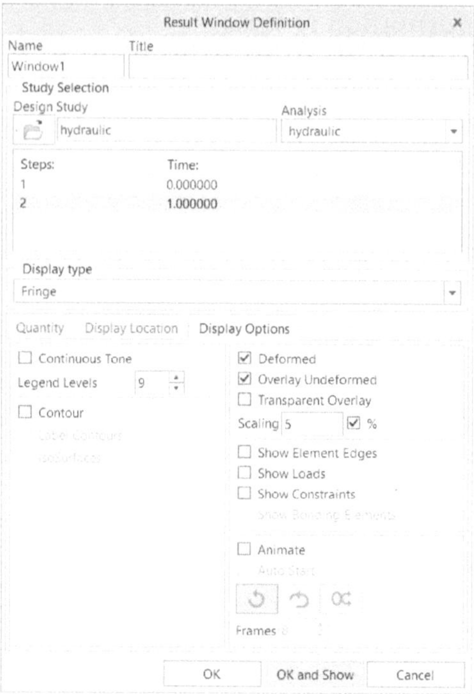

Figure 7–76

3. Click **OK** and **Show** to display the Displacement Magnitude result. The model displays as shown in Figure 7–77.

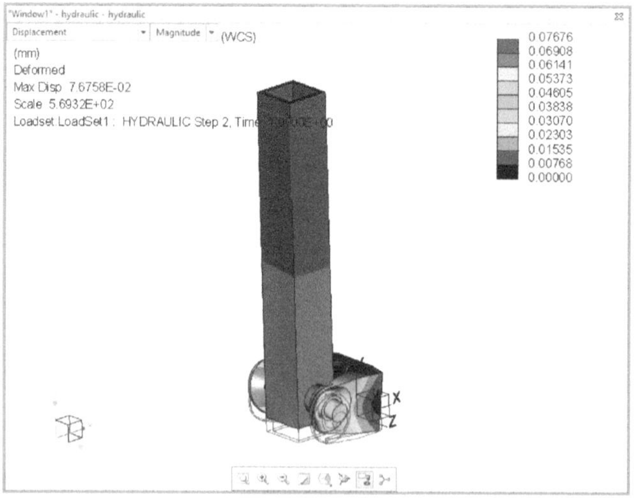

Figure 7–77

4. In the In-graphics toolbar, expand (Saved Orientations) and select **LEFT**. Zoom in on the bottom area. The model displays as shown in Figure 7–78.

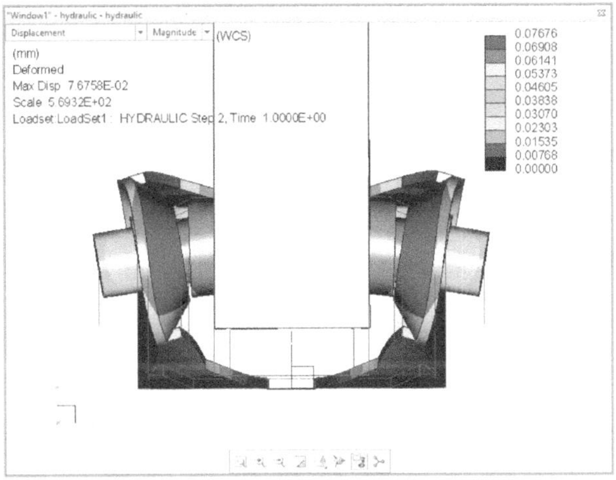

Figure 7–78

Examine the deformation of the parts under the load.

Task 12: Display the stress results.

1. Click (Edit) in the *Home* tab to edit the result window. In the *Steps* area, highlight the last row, and in the *Quantity* tab, select **Stress, von Mises**.
2. In the *Display Options* tab, clear the **Overlay Undeformed** option.
3. Click **OK and Show**. In the In-graphics toolbar, expand (Saved Orientations) and select **DEFAULT**. The von Mises stress plot displays as shown in Figure 7–79.

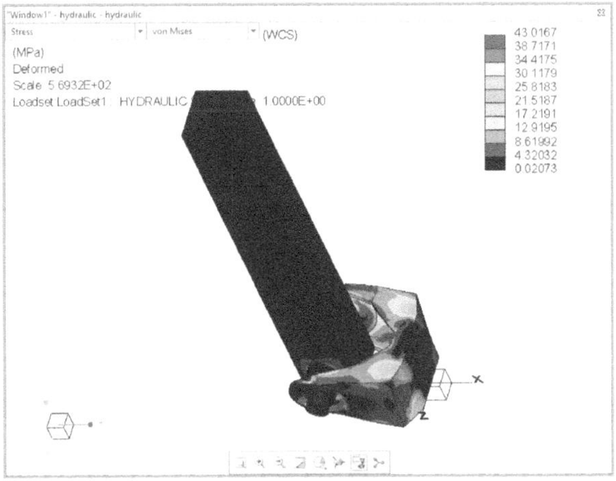

Figure 7–79

4. In the *View* tab, in the *Capping & Cutting Surfs* group, click (New). The *Results Surface Definition* dialog box opens, as shown in Figure 7–80.

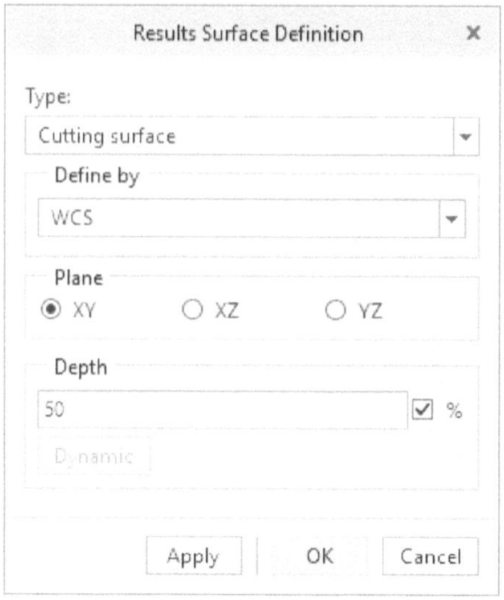

Figure 7–80

5. In the *Plane* area, select **YZ**, and for the *Depth*, remove the check next to **%**, and enter **-190mm** as shown in Figure 7–81.

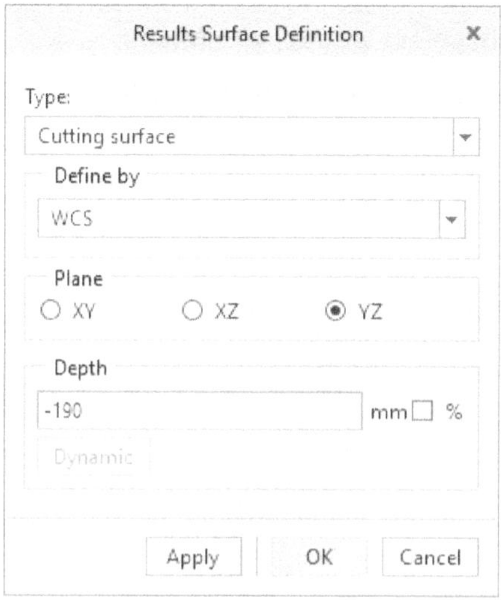

Figure 7–81

6. Click **OK**.
7. In the In-graphics toolbar, expand (Saved Orientations), select **LEFT**, and clear (Shaded). Zoom in on the bottom area. The model displays as shown in Figure 7–82.

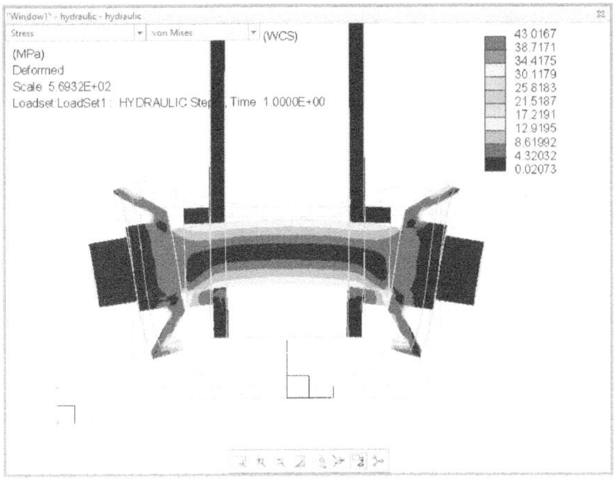

Figure 7–82

Note the well-pronounced bending stress pattern in the pin under the applied load.

Task 13: Display the contact pressure results.

1. Click (Edit) to edit the result window. Highlight the last row in the *Steps* area. In the *Quantity* area, select **Contact Pressure**.
2. In the *Display Options* tab, select the **Overlay Undeformed** option.
3. Click **OK and Show** and rotate the model to view from the bottom. The Contact Pressure plot displays as shown in Figure 7–83.

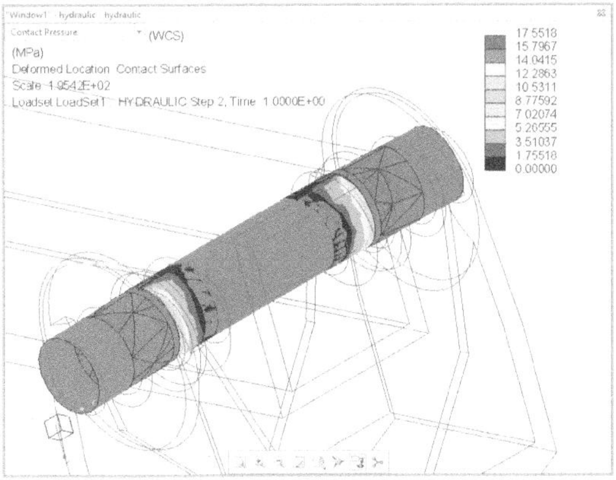

Figure 7–83

Note that the maximum contact pressure occurs at the ends of the boom bushings.

4. Exit the Results environment and save and close the model.

End of practice

Practice 7c
Press-Fit Analysis

Practice Objectives

- Use the **Solidify** tool to simplify the model.
- Create contact interfaces with Infinite friction.
- Set up a static analysis with initial interferences.
- Review results in the cylindrical coordinate system.

In this practice, you will set up a press-fit contact analysis on a shaft and a roller bearing assembly model. The area of interest is the contact between the shaft and the inner ring of the bearing. The assembly that you will analyze is shown in Figure 7–84.

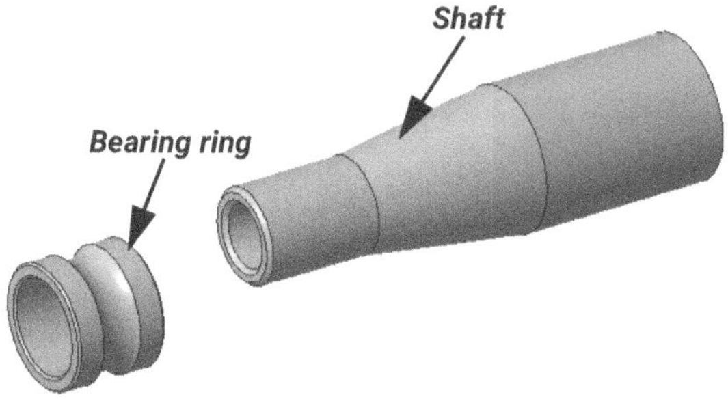

Figure 7–84

The bearing ring is press-fit onto the shaft. The outer diameter (OD) of the shaft is 20mm, and the inner diameter (ID) of the ring is 19.96mm. The objective is to determine radial deformation and hoop stress in the ring due to the press-fit, without applying any other loads.

Modeling Tasks

Task 1: Open the assembly.

1. Set the working directory to **Chapter07**, if required.
2. Open **press_fit.asm**.
3. Set the model display as follows:
   - *(Datum Display Filters)*: All Off
   - *(Spin Center)*: Off
   - *(Display Style)*: (Shading With Edges)

The assembly displays as shown in Figure 7–85.

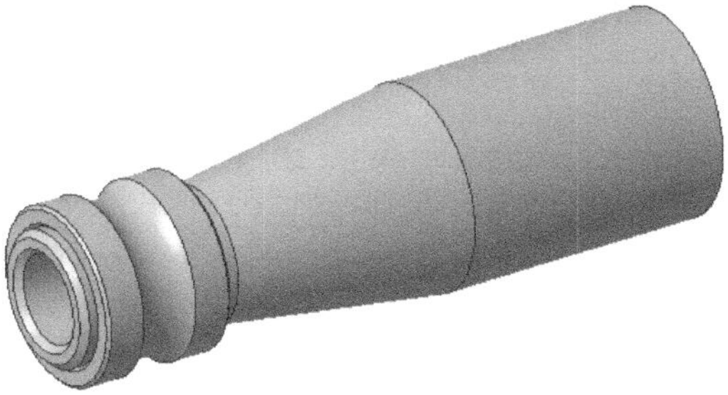

Figure 7–85

4. Do not switch to Creo Simulate yet.

Task 2: Simplify the model.

In this task, you will simplify the model in order to reduce the analysis runtime. Since the model is symmetric, you will analyze a quarter of the assembly.

1. Select **SHAFT.PRT** in the *Model Tree* and select (Open) in the mini-toolbar.
2. In the In-graphics toolbar, enable (Coordinate System) and (Plane Display).
3. In the *View* tab, enable (Plane Tag Display). The shaft displays as shown in Figure 7–86.

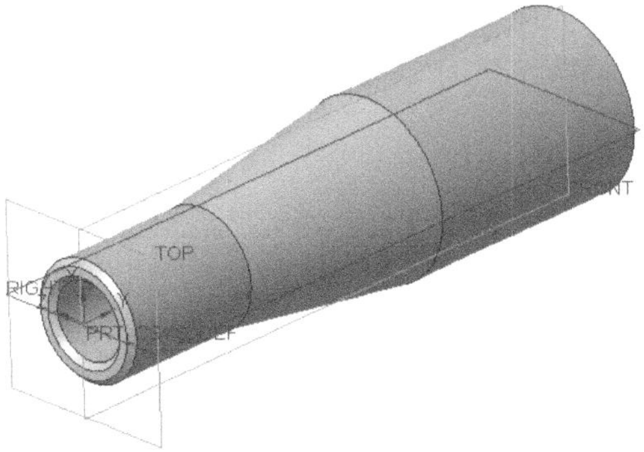

Figure 7–86

4. Select the *Model* tab.

5. Select the **RIGHT** datum plane and click (Solidify) in the *Editing* group. The *Solidify* dashboard opens, as shown in Figure 7–87.

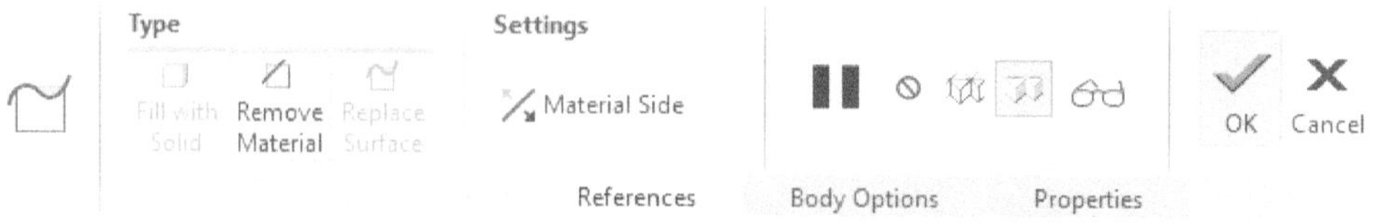

Figure 7–87

6. The **Solidify** tool cuts the part in half using the selected datum plane. Ensure that the tool keeps the side of the part that is in the positive X-direction by clicking (Material Side), if required. The part displays as shown in Figure 7–88.

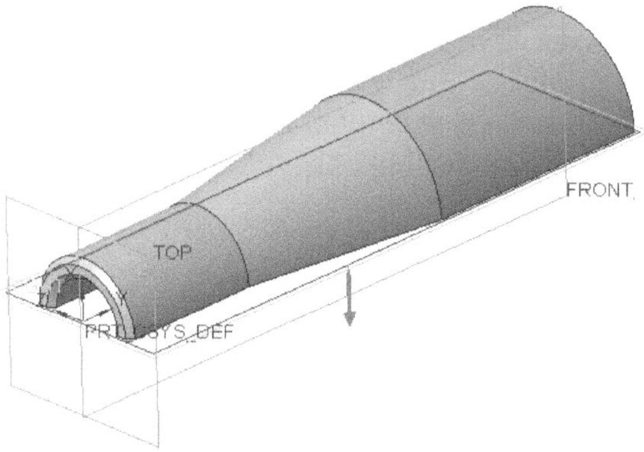

Figure 7–88

7. Click (OK).
8. Select the **FRONT** datum plane and click (Solidify) in the *Editing* section.
9. Ensure that the tool keeps the side of the part that is in the positive Z-direction, as shown in Figure 7–89.

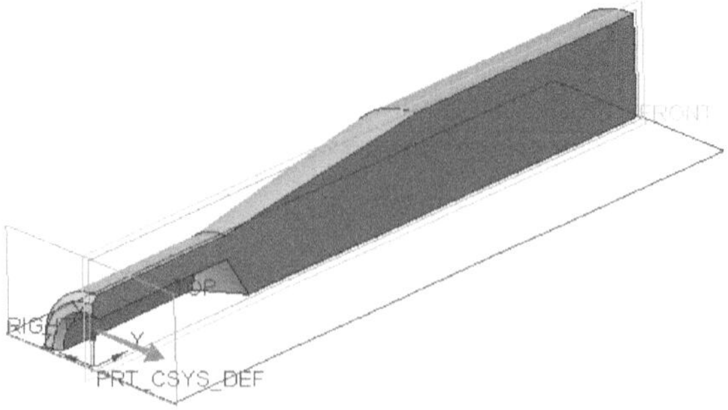

Figure 7–89

10. Click ✓ (OK).
11. Save and close **shaft.prt**. The assembly displays as shown in Figure 7–90.

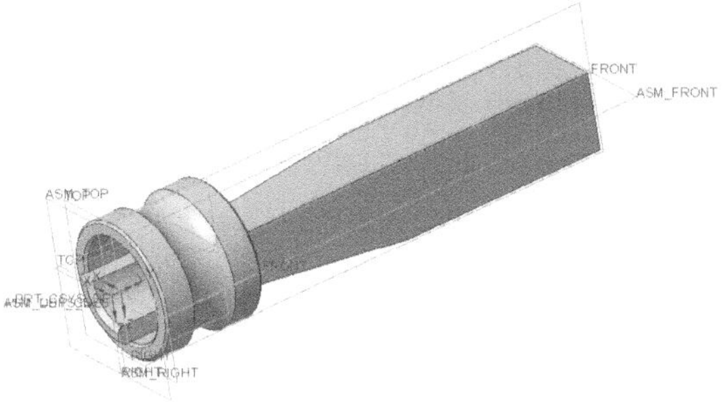

Figure 7–90

12. Open **bearing_ring.prt** and repeat Steps 2 through 8. Use the same datum planes and same directions to make the cuts.
13. In the In-graphics toolbar, disable (Plane Display). The assembly displays as shown in Figure 7–91.

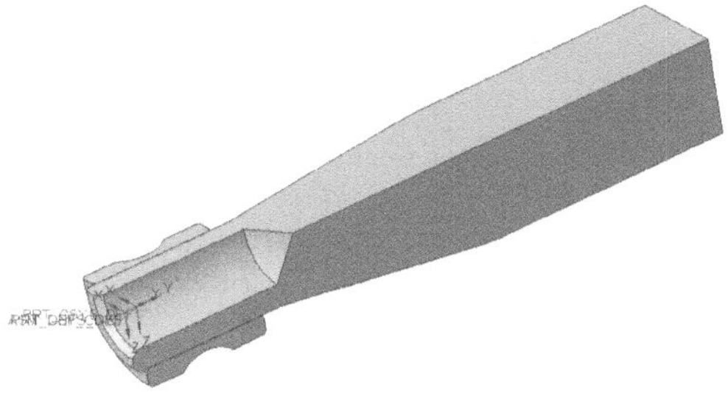

Figure 7–91

Task 3: Apply the materials.

1. Switch to Creo Simulate.
2. Assign materials as follows:
   - *SHAFT:* **AL2014**
     Poisson: **0.33**
     Young's modulus: **73084.4 MPa**
   - *BEARING_RING:* **STEEL**
     Poisson: **0.27**
     Young's modulus: **199948 MPa**
3. Using the *Simulation Display* dialog box, toggle off the display of the **Material Assignments**.

Task 4: Create the interface.

In this task, you will create a contact interface between the shaft and the ring.

1. In the *Refine Model* tab, click (Interface).
2. Expand the *Type* drop-down list and select **Contact**.
3. Expand the *References* drop-down list and select **Component-Component**.
4. Select the **SHAFT** and **BEARING_RING** parts as the references.
5. In the *Friction* drop-down list, select **Infinite**. The *Interface Definition* dialog box displays as shown in Figure 7–92.

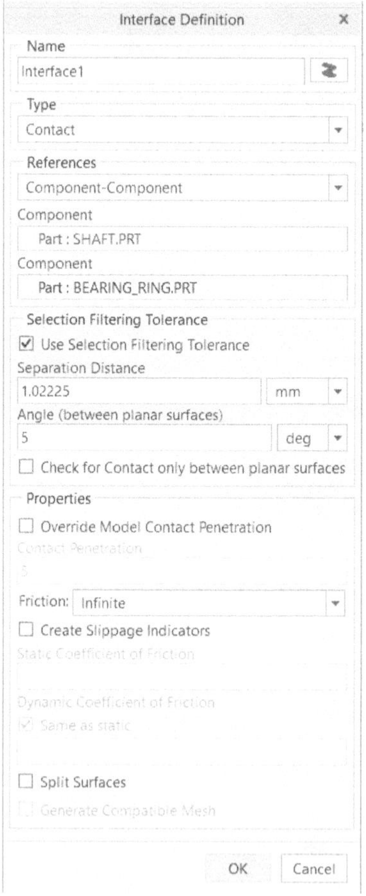

Figure 7–92

Note: *Press fit is a fastening of two parts that is achieved by friction alone. The parts fastened by a press fit are not supposed to slip against each other, which is ensured by using the* ***Infinite*** *Friction option in the contact interface.*

6. Click **OK**.
7. In the *Refine Model* tab, in the *AutoGEM* area, click (Review Geometry) to open the *Simulation Geometry* dialog box.
8. Select the options shown in Figure 7–93.

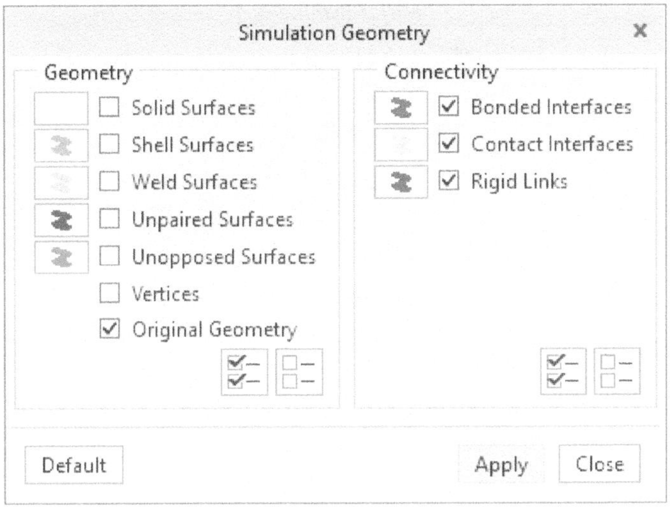

Figure 7–93

9. Click **Apply**. The model displays as shown in Figure 7–94.

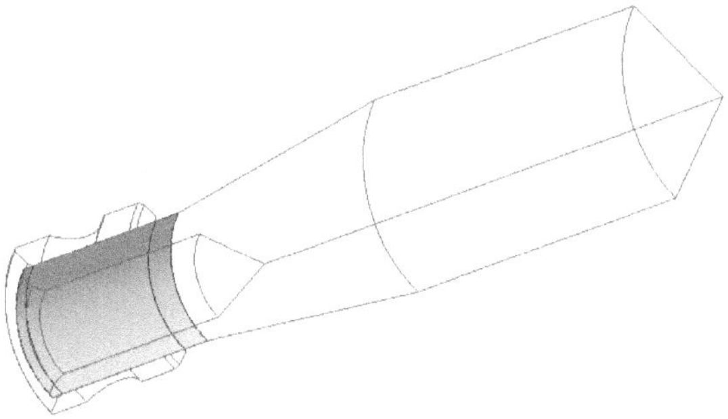

Figure 7–94

Ensure that the contact interface is shown between the shaft and the ring.

10. Click **Close** to finish.
11. Using the *Simulation Display* dialog box, toggle off the display of **Measures** and of **Interfaces**.

Task 5: Apply the constraints.

1. Fully constrain the back end of the **shaft** and apply two Mirror Symmetry constraints on the cutout surfaces, as shown in Figure 7–95.

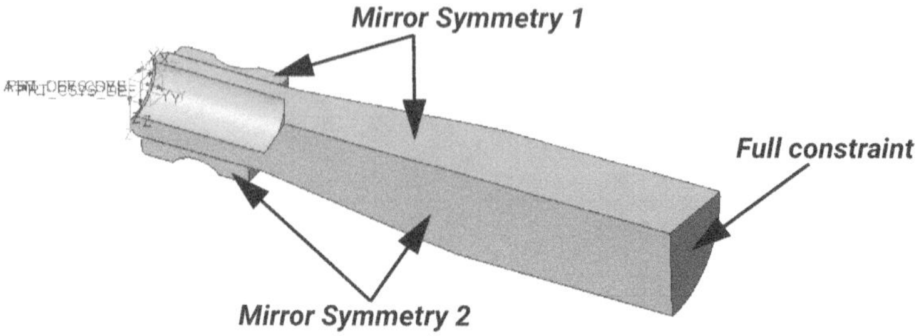

Figure 7–95

The model displays as shown in Figure 7–96.

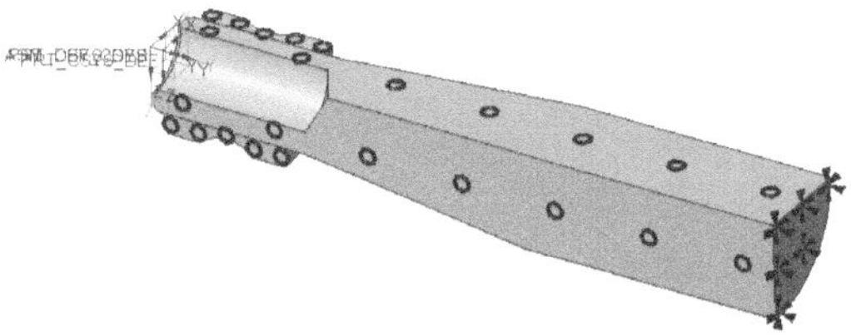

Figure 7–96

Task 6: Apply load.

The goal of this analysis is to determine deformations and stresses due to the press-fit alone, without any other loads. However, Creo Simulate does not permit creating a static analysis without loads. To work around this restriction, in this task you will apply a very small load to the model, which will have no effect on the analysis results.

1. Apply **0.001 N** in the Y-direction to the end surface of the shaft, as shown in Figure 7–97.

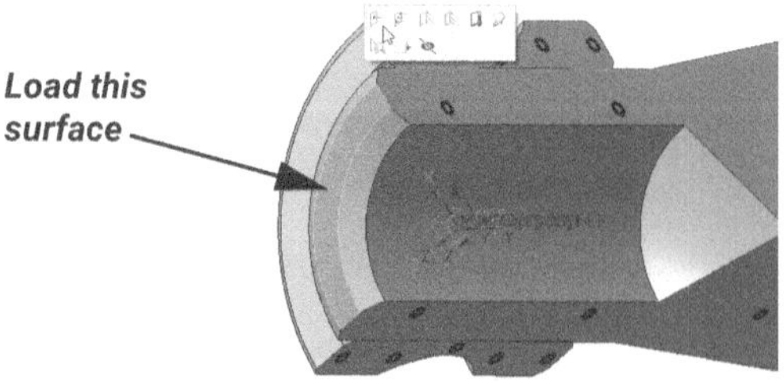

Figure 7–97

The model displays as shown in Figure 7–98.

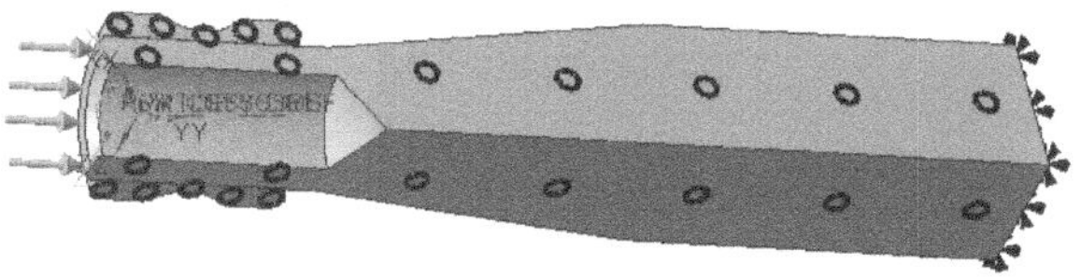

Figure 7–98

2. Using the *Simulation Display* dialog box, hide constraints and loads.

Task 7: Create cylindrical coordinate system.

The quantities of interest in this analysis are as follows:

- Radial expansion of the bearing ring, in order to later determine if the bearing balls might seize due to insufficient clearance between the inner and the outer rings.
- Hoop stresses (i.e., stresses in the direction of circumference) in the bearing ring, which are the main cause of cracking and ruptures of tube- and ring-shaped parts under radial loads.

A Cartesian (XYZ) coordinate system, such as WCS, is not suitable for obtaining the above results. In this task, you will create a cylindrical (RTZ) coordinate system, in which R would be the radial direction on the ring and T would be the direction around the ring's circumference.

1. In the *Refine Model* tab, click (Coordinate System).
2. Select the main assembly as the **Component for Feature**. The *Coordinate System* dialog box opens.
3. In the *Type* drop-down list, select **Cylindrical**.
4. In the *Origin* tab, select the vertex shown in Figure 7–99 as the coordinate system origin.
5. In the *Orientation* tab, select the references shown in Figure 7–99 for the coordinate system axes.

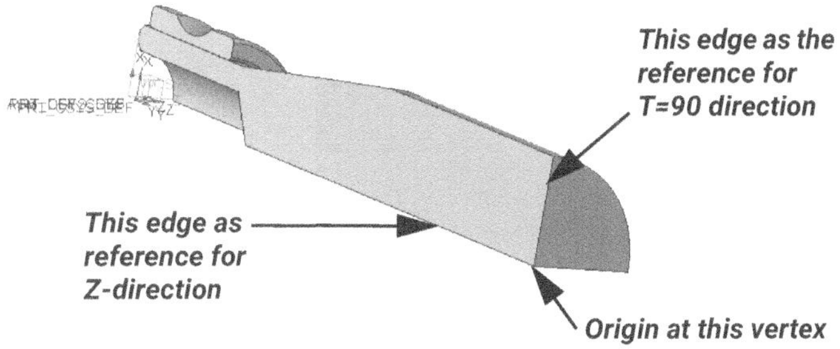

Figure 7–99

The *Coordinate System* dialog box displays as shown in Figure 7–100.

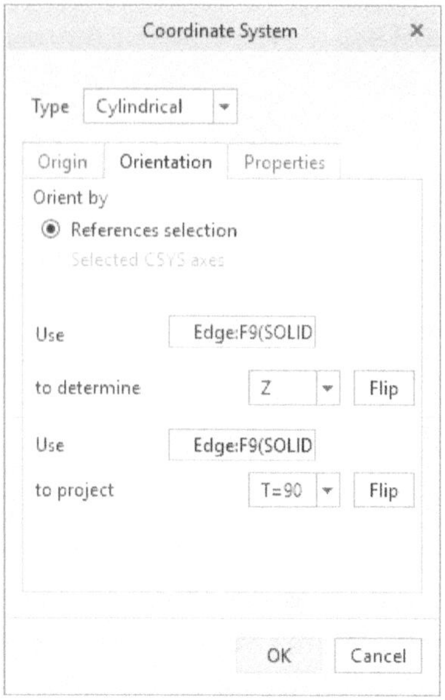

Figure 7–100

6. Click **OK**. The model displays as shown in Figure 7–101.

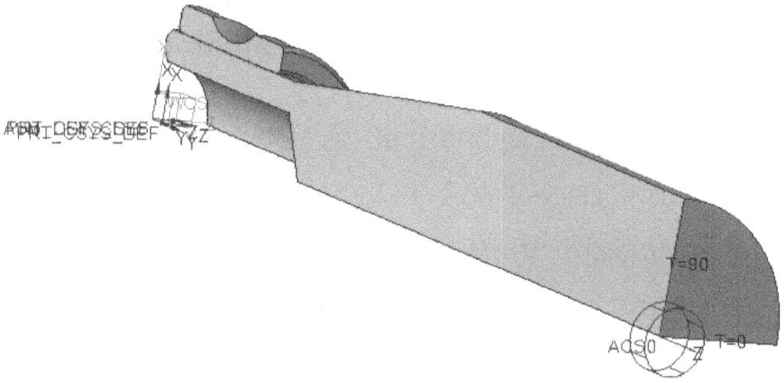

Figure 7–101

Analysis Tasks

Task 8: Set up and run the analysis.

The OD of the shaft is 20mm, and the ID of the ring is 19.96mm. Therefore, the actual initial interpenetration is (20 - 19.96)/2 = 0.02mm. To ensure that this interpenetration is detected in Creo Simulate, you will set the value for detection to be 0.025mm.

1. Set up a static analysis as follows:
   - *Name:* **press_fit**
   - *Contacts:* **ON**
   - *Convergence method:* **Single-Pass Adaptive**
   - *Localized Mesh Refinement:* **ON**
   - *Press fit:* **ON**
   - *Maximum initial interpenetration:* **0.025mm**

   The *Static Analysis Definition* dialog box displays as shown in Figure 7–102.

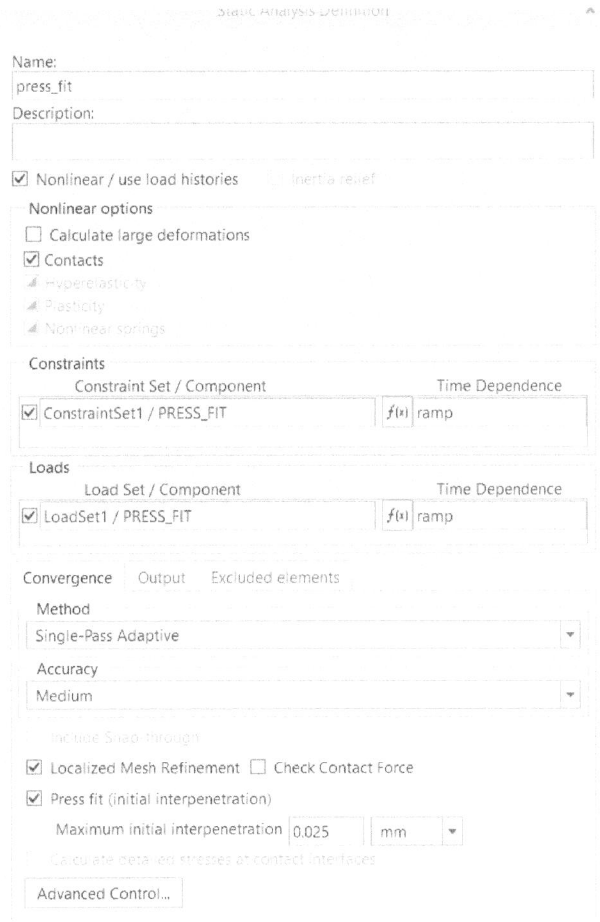

Figure 7–102

2. Click **OK** to close the *Static Analysis Definition* dialog box.
3. In the **Info** menu, select **Check Model** to check the validity of the model.
4. Run the analysis.

Results Tasks

Task 9: Display the deformation results.

1. Click (Review Results) in the *Analyses and Design Studies* dialog box.
2. In the *Steps* column, highlight the second row, and in the *Component* drop-down list select **X**. The *Result Window Definition* dialog box displays as shown in Figure 7–103.

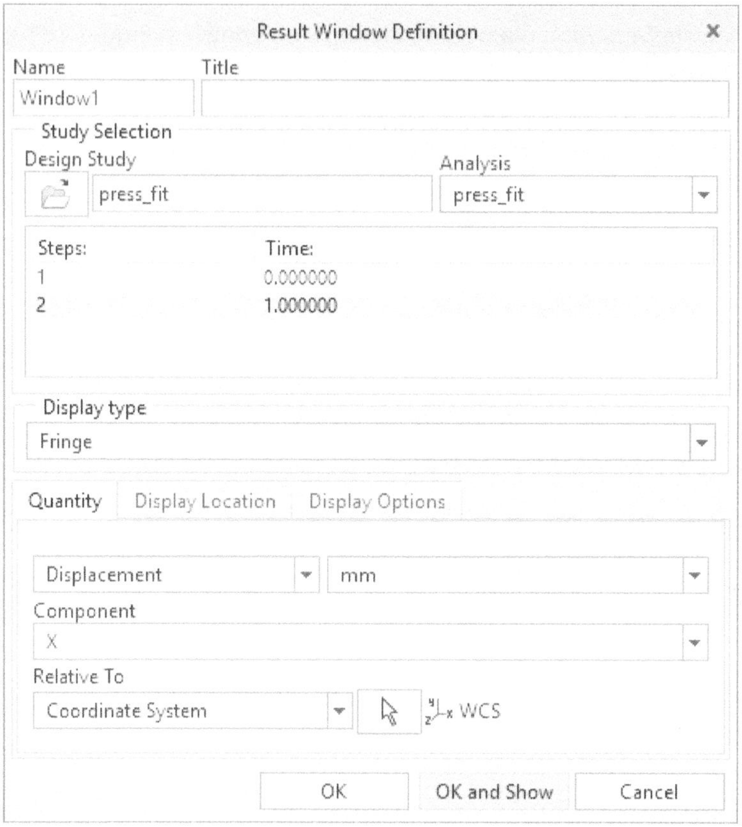

Figure 7–103

3. Click (Select) near the *Coordinate System* drop-down list and select **ACS0** coordinate system in the model. This is the cylindrical coordinate system that you created in Task 7.
4. In the *Component* drop-down list, select **R**, if required. The *Result Window Definition* dialog box opens as shown in Figure 7–104.

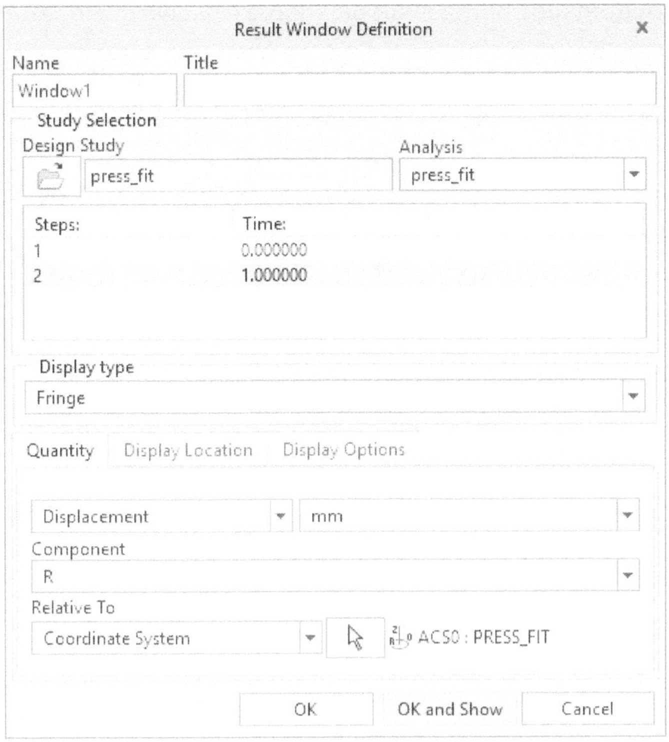

Figure 7–104

5. Click **OK and Show**.

6. In the In-graphics toolbar, expand (Saved Orientations), select **BACK**, and clear (Shaded). The result window displays as shown in Figure 7–105.

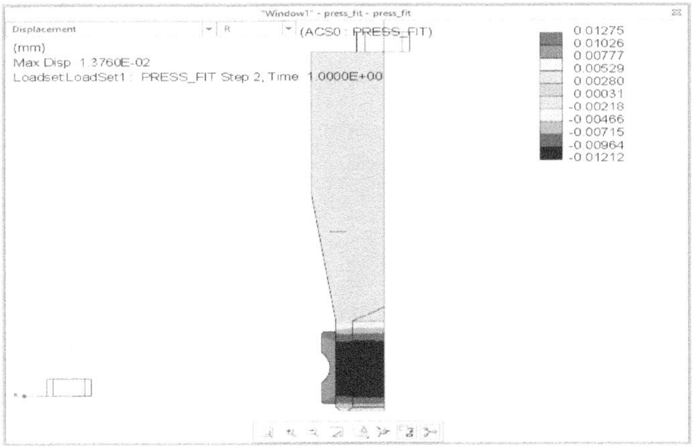

Figure 7–105

7. Zoom in on the bottom area of the shaft and ring, as shown in Figure 7–106.

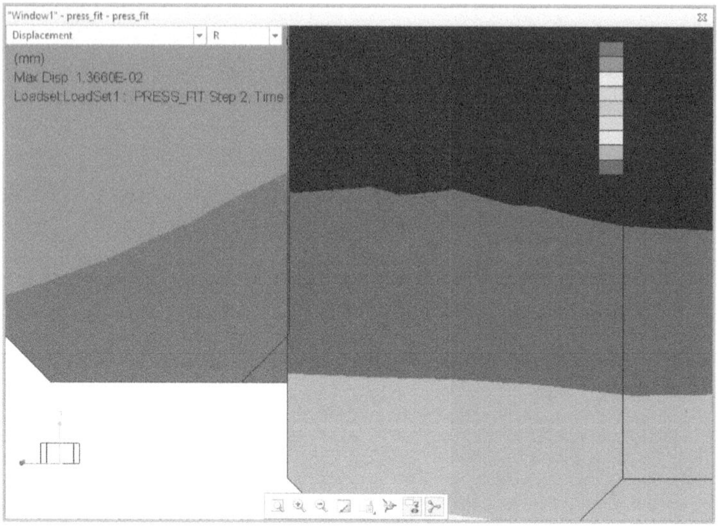

Figure 7–106

Note that there is still a visible interpenetration between the shaft and ring in this area. This is because the result is being displayed on the undeformed model (i.e. the original geometry), as before the analysis.

8. In the *Home* tab, click (Edit).
9. In the *Display Options* tab, select **Deformed** and click **OK and Show**. The result window displays as shown in Figure 7–107.

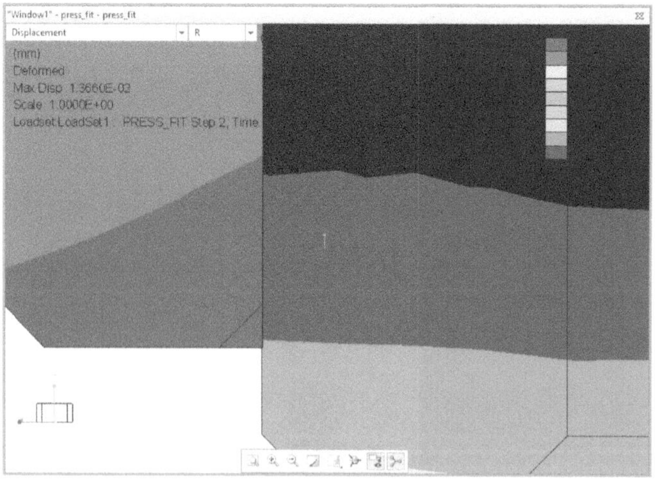

Figure 7–107

Note that now there is no interpenetration between the parts. This is because a contact interface strictly enforces the condition of non-interpenetration; therefore, the detected interference between the parts has been removed during the analysis.

10. Zoom out slightly and use the (Dynamic Query) tool to determine the radial displacement at the bottom of the ball race, as shown in Figure 7–108.

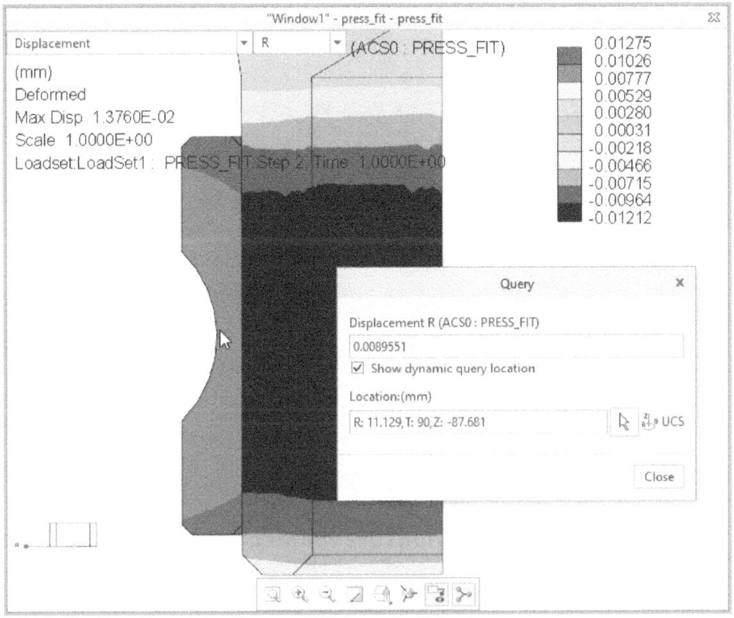

Figure 7–108

The radial displacement at the bottom of the ball race is approximately 0.009mm. Therefore, the increase in the OD of the ball race in the inner ring after the bearing assembly on the shaft is estimated to be 2x0.009 = 0.018mm, and the reduction of clearance between the inner and the outer rings to be 0.009mm.

Task 10: Display the stress results.

1. Select the **DEFAULT** saved orientation.
2. Click (Edit) in the *Home* tab to edit the result window. In the *Steps* area, highlight the last row, and in the *Quantity* area, select **Stress, TT**.

   Note: *T is the Theta direction in the cylindrical coordinate system, which is around the ring's circumference.* ***Stress TT*** *is the hoop stress.*

3. In the *Display Location* tab, select **Components/Layers** and set the **SHAFT.PRT** visibility to (Blanked).
4. In the *Display Options* tab, clear the **Deformed** option.

5. Click **OK and Show**. The hoop stress plot in the bearing ring displays as shown in Figure 7–109.

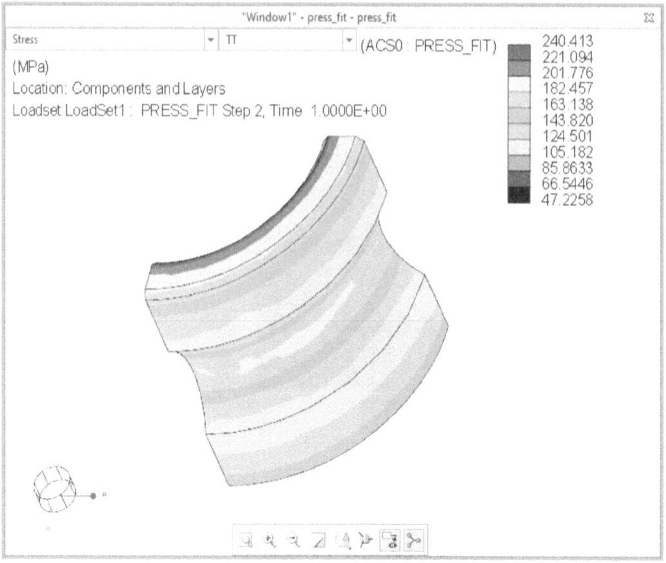

Figure 7–109

6. Using the (Model Max) tool, determine the value and the location of the maximum hoop stress, as shown in Figure 7–110.

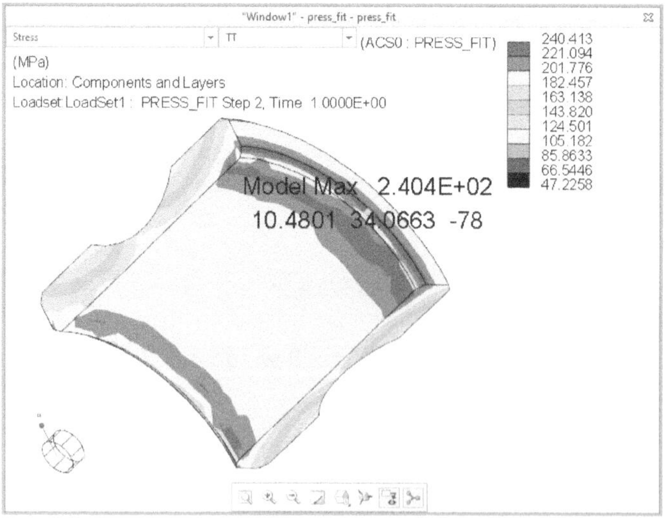

Figure 7–110

Note that the maximum hoop stress occurs on the ID of the bearing ring, and near its ends. The maximum stress is approximately 245 MPa, therefore, the grade of steel used for the ring should have a yield strength greater than 245 MPa.

7. Exit the Results environment and save and close the model.

End of practice

Practice 7d
Contact Analysis of a Skid Shoe

Practice Objectives

- Create contact interfaces.
- Set up contact analysis.
- Display contact analysis results.

In this practice, you will set up and run a static contact analysis of a skid shoe pressing against a plate (shown in Figure 7–111) with minimum instruction.

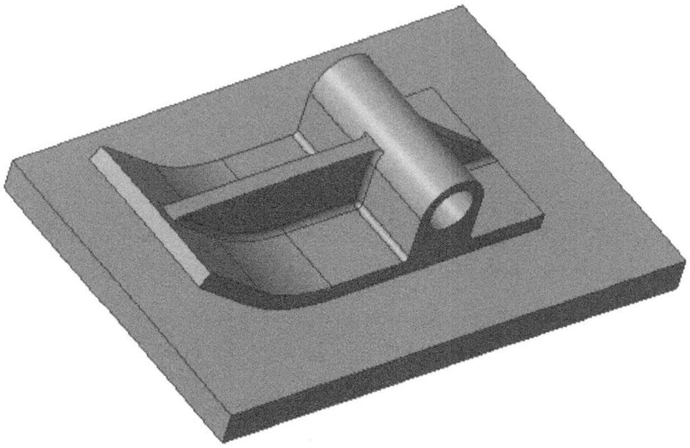

Figure 7–111

Task 1: Prepare the model for analysis.

1. Set the working directory to **Chapter07**, if required.
2. Open **shoe_contact.asm** and launch Creo Simulate.
3. Set the model display as follows:
   - *(Datum Display Filters)*: All Off
   - *(Spin Center)*: Off
   - *(Display Style)*: (Shading With Edges)
4. Apply the **AL6061** material to both parts.
5. Create a frictionless contact interface between the shoe and the plate.

6. Fully constrain the perimeter surfaces of the plate, as shown in Figure 7–112.

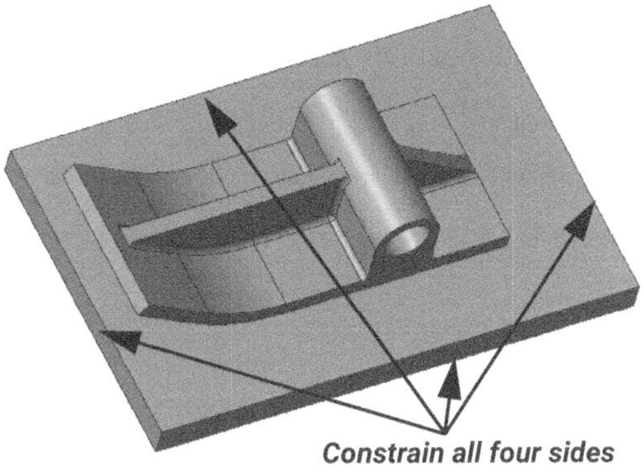

Figure 7–112

7. As contact between the shoe and the plate is set up as frictionless, avoid free sliding of the shoe along the plate by constraining the back surface of the shoe in the X- and Z-directions, as shown in Figure 7–113.

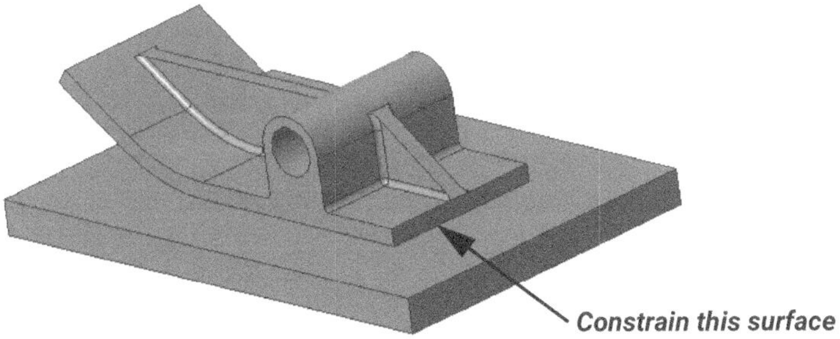

Figure 7–113

8. Apply **10000lbs** bearing load in the negative Y-direction to the hole in the shoe, as shown in Figure 7–114.

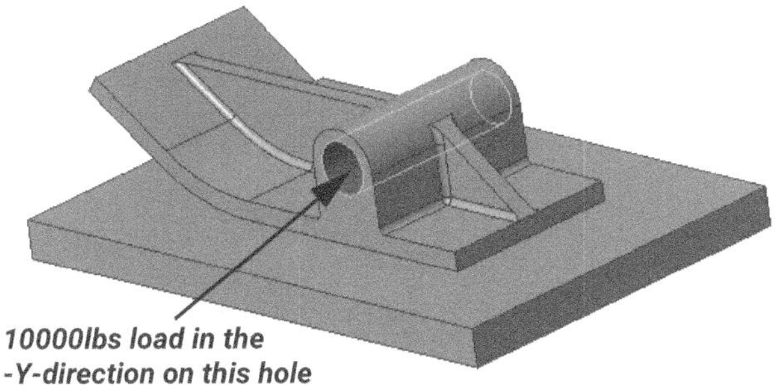

Figure 7–114

Task 2: Set up and run static analysis.

1. Create and run a new static analysis with the following parameters:
   - *Analysis name:* **contact_shoe**
   - *Convergence method:* **Single-Pass Adaptive**
   - *Output Steps:* **User-defined**, 5 steps equally spaced.

Task 3: Examine the analysis results.

1. Display and animate the **Displacement Magnitude** fringe plot. Use a *Scaling* factor of **100** for the deformed shape display.
   - Do the parts deform according to the applied loads and constraints?
2. Display the undeformed **von Mises Stress** plot.
   - In which area in the model are the stresses at maximum?
3. Display the **Contact Pressure** plot.
   - What is the maximum contact pressure and where does it occur?
4. Save and close the model.

End of practice

Chapter 8

Thermal Analysis

You will learn to use thermal analysis to measure the effect of heat transfer rates on a model.

Learning Objectives

- Understand the concept of heat transfer.
- Understand the Creo Simulate thermal analysis steps and options.
- Create idealizations.
- Apply boundary conditions and heat loads.
- Create a thermal analysis.
- Visualize the thermal analysis results.
- Import thermal results into a structural analysis.

8.1 Modes of Heat Transfer

Thermal analyses measure the effect of heat transfer rates on a model. Heat transfer is the flow of heat through a body in which there is a temperature variance. Heat transfer rates are an important part of engineering analysis in many industries. For example, heat transfer rates have a major role in the design of boilers, turbines, and combustion engines. The designer of these systems often needs to maintain high heat transfer rates while staying inside the material's limits for high temperatures. There are three modes of heat transfer: conduction, convection, and radiation.

Conduction

Conduction is the transfer of heat through a solid body or a body of stationary fluid (e.g., water or gas), in which temperature variance occurs. The conduction mode of heat transfer occurs in the atomic and molecular structures of a body. An example of conduction in a gas cylinder is shown in Figure 8–1.

Figure 8–1

The temperature difference between the top and bottom of the gas cylinder is assumed to be 10°C. The molecules of the gas on the top of the cylinder have higher energies (i.e., they vibrate more freely) because of the higher temperature. Therefore, they collide with neighboring molecules and energy is transferred to these molecules. The process continues from high energy molecules to neighboring molecules from the top of the cylinder to the bottom until equilibrium is reached.

Convection

Convection is the transfer of heat from a surface into a moving fluid (e.g., air) with a lower temperature than the surface. The heat must be conducted through material (e.g., heat exchanger) before it can be carried away by the outside air. There are two types of convection heat transfer: free and forced.

In free convection heat transfer, the moving fluid is free-flowing. For example, if a hot plate is left outside to be cooled on a day with little wind, the air in contact with the hot plate has a lower density than the air above the hot plate. This creates a circulation where warm air moves up and cooler air moves down.

In forced convection heat transfer, the moving fluid is pumped or fanned over a surface. Using the previous example, on a windy day, the primary transfer of heat is through the force of wind, while free convection still exists.

Radiation

Radiation is the emission of energy from heated surfaces in the form of electromagnetic waves. Two heated surfaces at different temperatures transfer heat to each other by radiation if there is no other means of transport (e.g., molecular vibration or air). Heat transfer by conduction or convection requires a means of transport. Radiation heat transfer works best in a vacuum.

8.2 Creo Simulate Thermal

Similar to the Structure mode, the Creo Simulate Thermal mode has three components for finite element analysis: analysis, pre-processing, and post-processing. Each component contains steps, as shown in Figure 8–2.

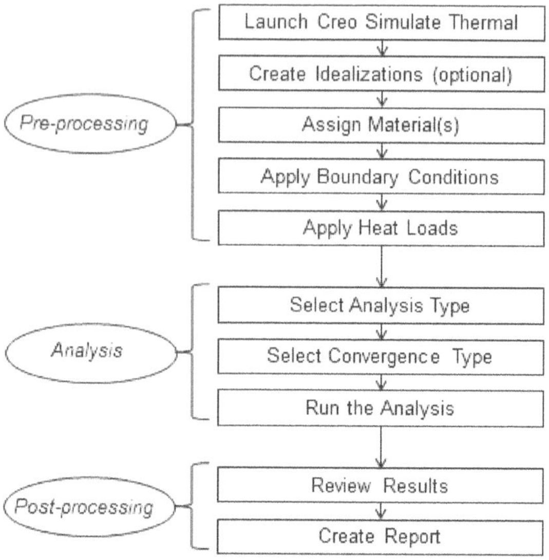

Figure 8–2

After you launch Thermal mode, each step in the model analysis process requires a selection of options. These options are shown as follows:

Model Analysis Steps	**Pro/MECHANICA Thermal Options**	
Model Type	3D 2D Axisymmetric	2D Plate 2D Unit Depth
Element Type	Solid Shells Beams	Connections
Analysis Methods	Steady State Thermal	Transient Thermal
Convergence Methods	Multi-Pass Adaptive Single-Pass Adaptive	Quick Check
Design Studies	Standard Optimization	Sensitivity

> ***Note:*** *Thermal mode is launched in the same way as Structure, but instead of selecting **Structure**, you select **Thermal**.*

Thermal Ribbon

To enter the Thermal mode, click (Thermal Mode) in the Creo Simulate ribbon. The ribbon changes as shown in Figure 8–3. The tools in the Thermal mode ribbon are similar to those in the Structure mode. The *Loads* and *Boundary Conditions* areas are different.

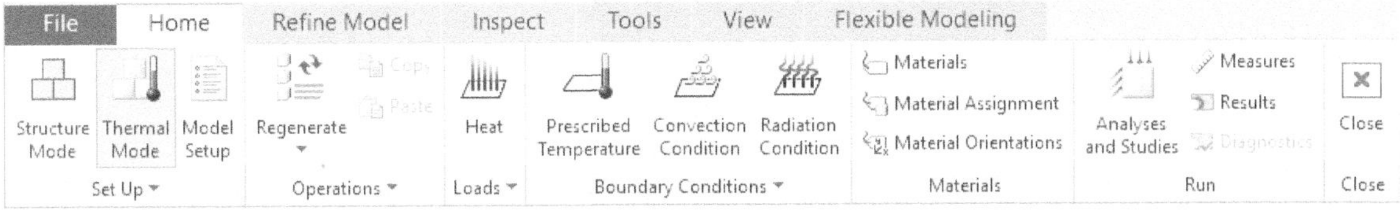

Figure 8–3

8.3 Modeling Steps

The majority of the analysis steps in the Thermal mode are same or similar to those in the Structure mode. The following steps are identical:

- Defining model type
- Applying material
- Simulation features (datums, divided surfaces, etc.)
- Meshing the model
- Convergence methods
- Design studies

The steps and options that are different from their counterparts in the Structure mode, are described below.

Interfaces

Interfaces in Creo Simulate define the treatment of mated or overlapping surfaces in an assembly model.

There are three types of Interfaces in Creo Simulate Thermal:

- **Bonded:** Models a perfect thermal bond, without any thermal resistance, between the interfacing surfaces.
- **Adiabatic:** Disables any heat transfer through the interface.
- **Thermal Resistance:** Models an imperfect thermal bond between the surfaces, where the rate of heat transfer through the interface is determined by a thermal resistance coefficient.

Idealizations

Idealizations are tools that simplify your FEA model, resulting in faster analysis. Idealizations are optional. If your model is not overly complex and solves in a reasonable time, idealizations might not be required.

The following types of Idealizations are available in Thermal mode, as shown in Figure 8–4:

- **Beams:** These are 1D thermal elements (also called thermal rods) in which the temperature variation only occurs in the direction of the element's axis.
- **Shells:** These are 2D thermal elements, in which the temperature variation only occurs within the element's midplane.

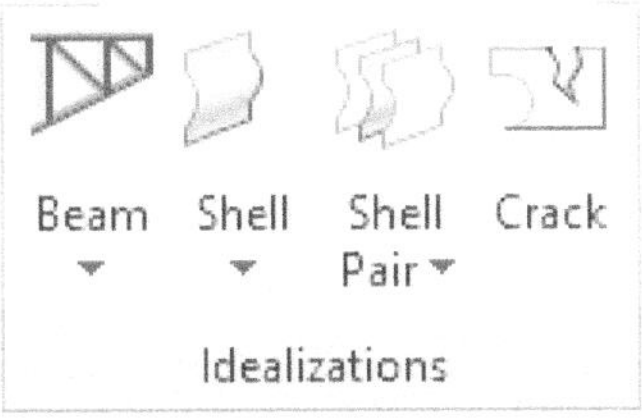

Figure 8–4

Applying Boundary Conditions

In thermal FEA, all of the surfaces default to perfect insulators unless you apply a heat load, specified temperature, convection condition, or radiation condition. A perfect insulator, also called adiabatic surface, means that there is no heat transfer through the surface.

Four types of boundary conditions are available in Thermal mode, as shown in Figure 8–5:

- Prescribed Temperature
- Convection Condition
- Radiation Condition
- Symmetry

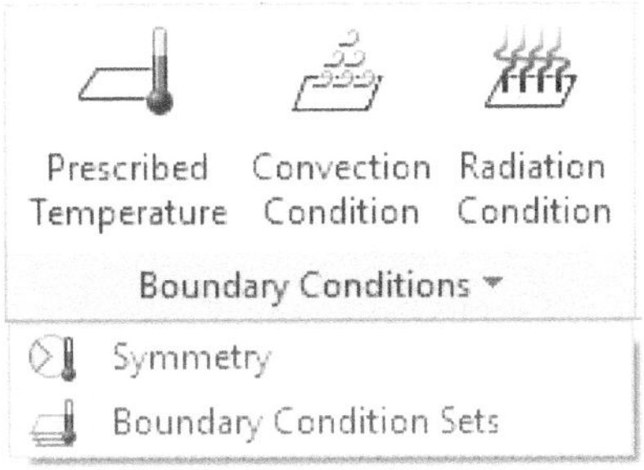

Figure 8–5

__Note:__ Radiation Condition is only available with the Advanced Creo Simulate license.

Prescribed Temperature

Use the **Prescribed Temperature** boundary condition to enforce a specific temperature on one or more geometrical entities in your model. The specified temperature value is strictly maintained throughout the analysis.

The *Prescribed Temperature* dialog box is shown in Figure 8–6.

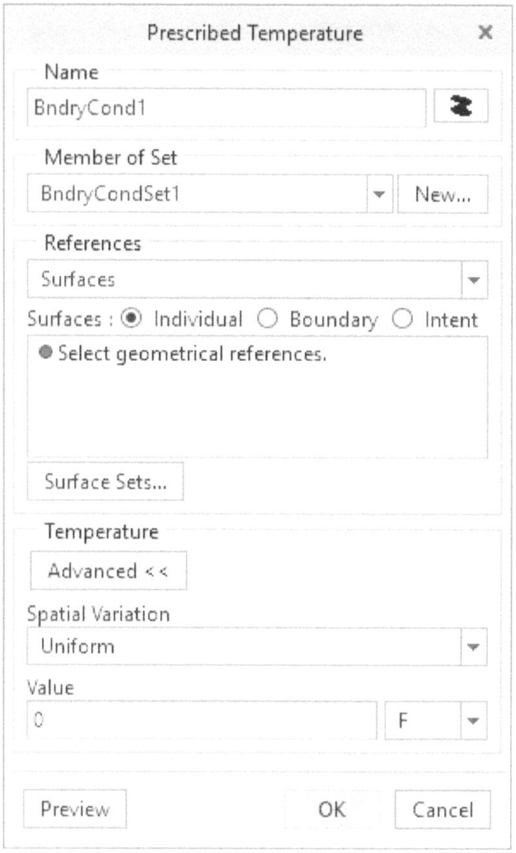

Figure 8–6

Prescribed Temperature can be applied to **Surfaces**, **Edges/Curves**, or **Points**. The options for the *Spatial Variation* are **Uniform, Function of Coordinates**, and **Interpolated Over Entity**.

Convection Condition

Use **Convection Condition** to define a convective heat exchange for one or more geometric entities in your model.

The *Convection Condition* dialog box is shown in Figure 8–7.

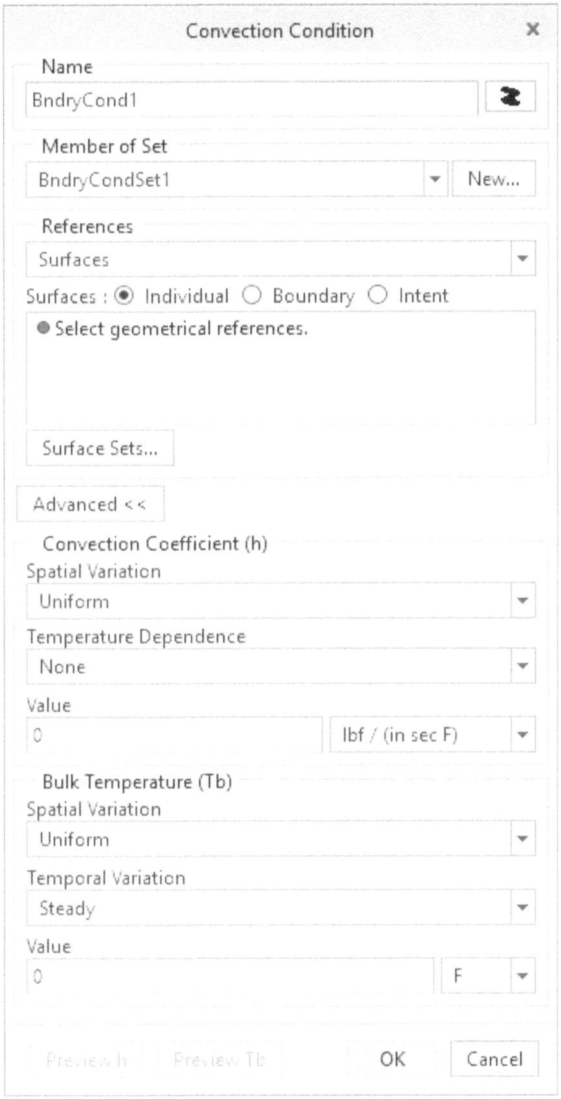

Figure 8–7

Convection Condition can be applied to **Surfaces**, **Edges/Curves**, **Points**, or **Lattice Features**.

The convection coefficient *h* relates the amount of heat *Q* transferred between the boundary surface of area *A* at temperature *T*, and the moving fluid at bulk temperature T_b in the following way:

$$Q = h\,A\,(T - T_b)$$

Radiation Condition

Use **Radiation Condition** to define a radiative heat exchange for one or more surfaces in your model.

> ***Note:*** *Radiation Condition requires an Advanced Simulation license.*

The *Radiation Condition* dialog box is shown in Figure 8–8.

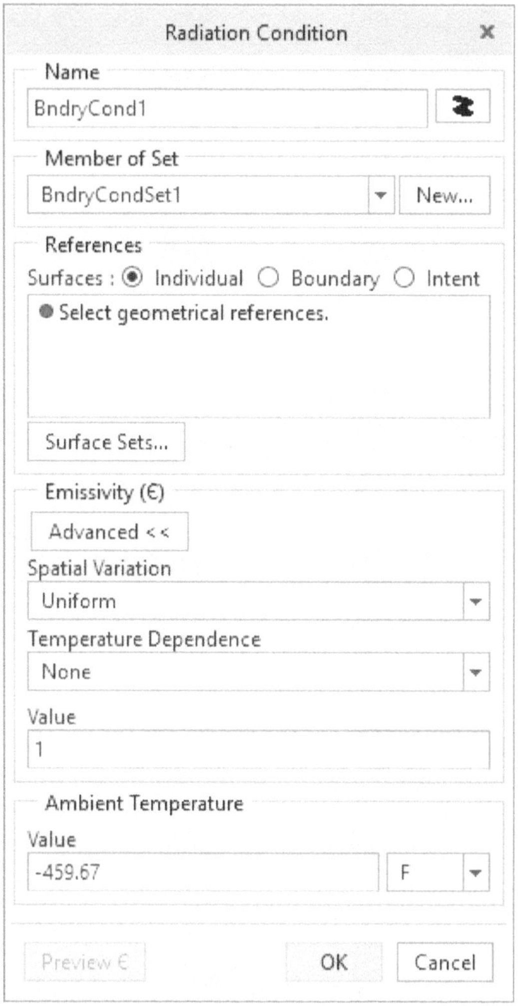

Figure 8–8

The *Emissivity* is the ratio of the energy radiated from a material's surface to that radiated from a blackbody (a perfect emitter) at the same surface temperature and viewing conditions. It is a dimensionless number between 0 (perfect reflector) to 1 (perfect emitter). The *Ambient Temperature* is the absolute temperature of the surrounding medium.

Applying Heat Loads

Heat loads provide local heat sources or heat sinks in your model. The icon to apply heat loads is located in the *Loads* area in the ribbon, as shown in Figure 8–9.

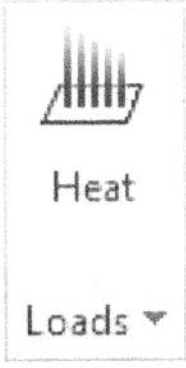

Figure 8–9

The *Heat Load* dialog box is shown in Figure 8–10.

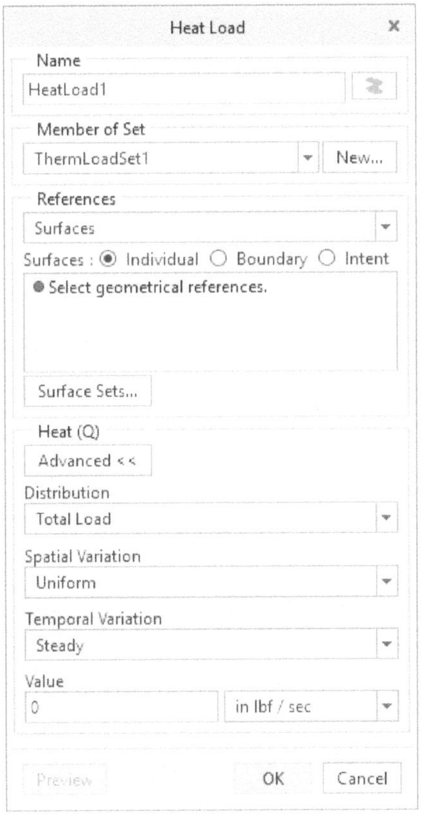

Figure 8–10

Heat loads can be applied to **Components/Bodies/Volumes** (to simulate internal heat generation), **Surfaces**, **Edges/Curves**, **Points**, or **Lattice Features**.

8.4 Analysis

Analysis Types

Creo Simulate enables you to perform two types of thermal analyses on a model. You select an analysis type based on the type of simulation you want to perform. Click (Analyses and Studies) and select the appropriate option in the **File** menu, as shown in Figure 8–11.

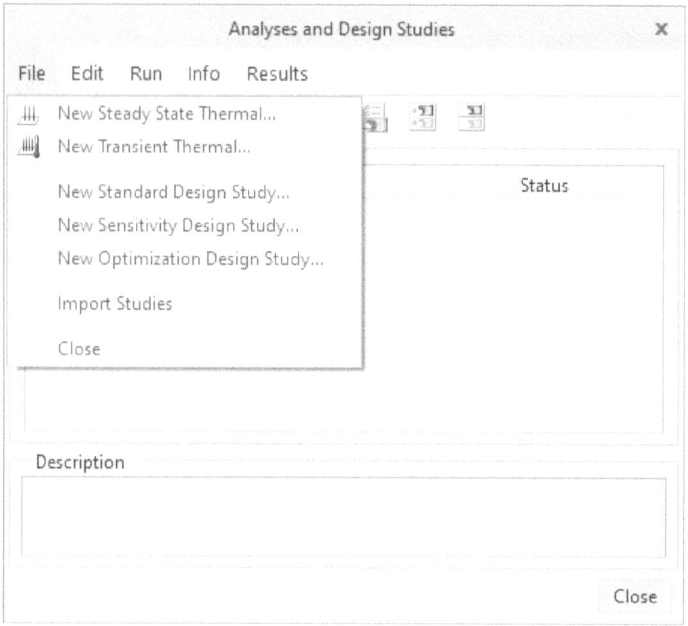

Figure 8–11

A Steady State Thermal analysis calculates the thermal response of a model to a heat load that is constant and does not vary over time. This type of analysis does not evaluate changes in temperature over time. For example, a turbine blade that is turned by steam and generates electricity would require this type of analysis because it is under constant pressure and temperature.

A Transient Thermal analysis calculates the thermal response in your model that is changing with time. The application of a heat load is not typically constant and varies over time. For example, the heat element in a toaster would require this type of analysis because it is time-dependent.

8.5 Results

Result Visualization

Thermal mode enables you to visualize many different types of results:

- Temperatures
- Temperature Gradients
- Heat Fluxes
- P-Levels

The results can be displayed as a fringe plot, as a graph along an edge or a curve. Fringe plots for heat fluxes can be animated for a better understanding of the heat flows.

The results are visualized and manipulated in the Creo Simulate Results environment. An overview of the icons and options in the Results environment is shown in Figure 8–12.

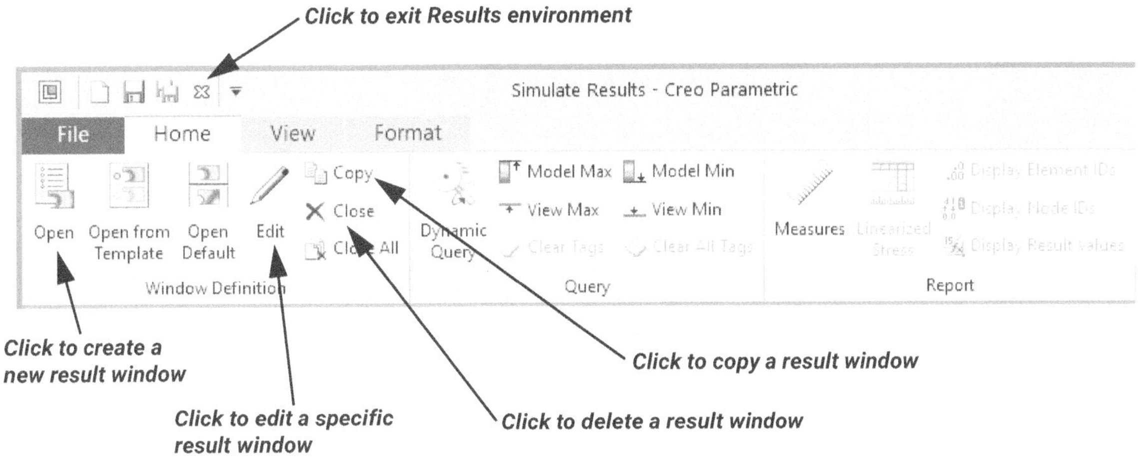

Figure 8–12

8.6 Thermal Load Transfer

You can transfer the temperature field from a thermal analyses to a structural analyses and apply it as a thermal load in your structure. For example, a heat sink is shown in Figure 8–13. The temperature distribution obtained in a thermal analysis can be transferred to structure mode to determine the deformations and stresses in the heat sink as it expands.

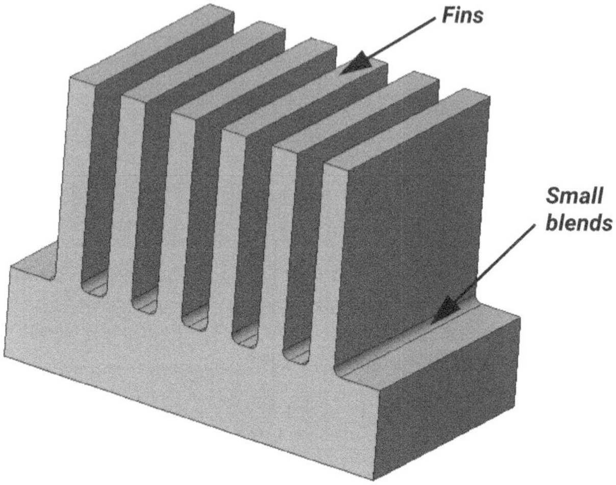

Figure 8–13

To transfer a temperature result from *Thermal* to **Structure**, expand the *Loads* area and select **MEC/T Load**, as shown in Figure 8–14.

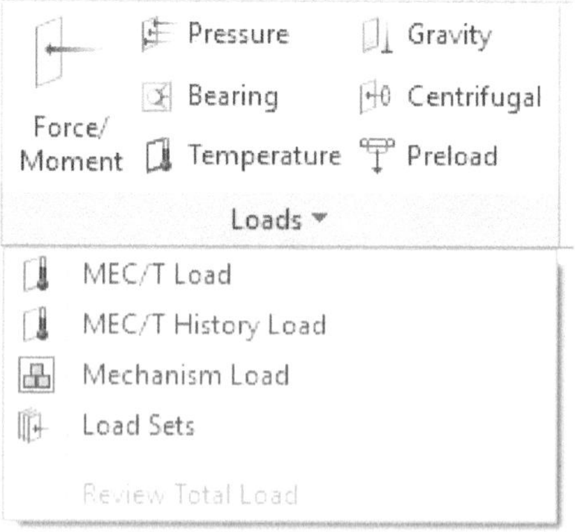

Figure 8–14

The *MEC/T Temperature Load* dialog box is shown in Figure 8–15.

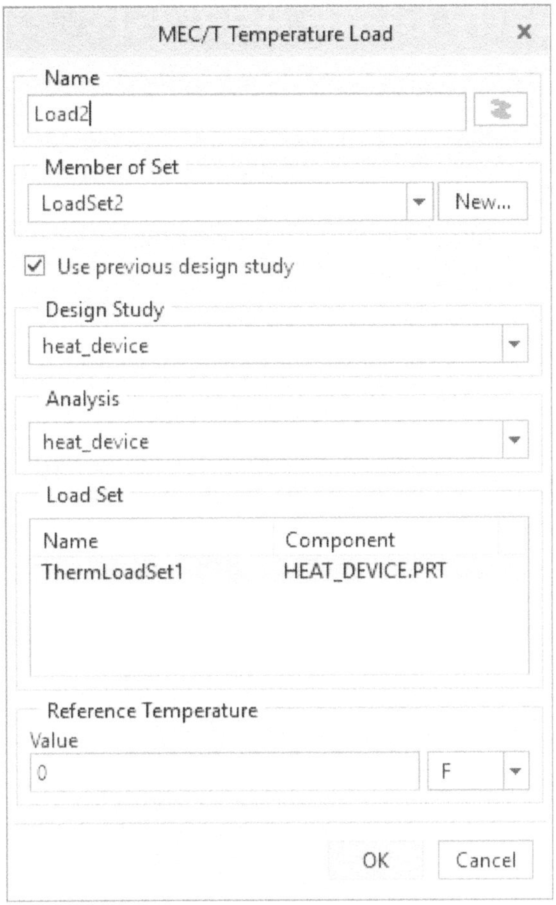

Figure 8–15

Practice 8a
Thermal Steady State Analysis

Practice Objectives

- Set up thermal boundary conditions.
- Set up and run a thermal analysis.
- Display the results of thermal analysis.
- Use the Load Transfer function.

In this practice, you will set up and run a thermal steady state analysis on a heat transfer device, as shown in Figure 8–16. The heat transfer device sits on a 20W CPU (heat source) and a free convection is placed on the long vertical faces of fins. The device is aluminum and has a convection coefficient of 0.01 (lbf/in F$^{\circ}$ sec). Later, you will transfer the heat load to Structure mode to run a static analysis.

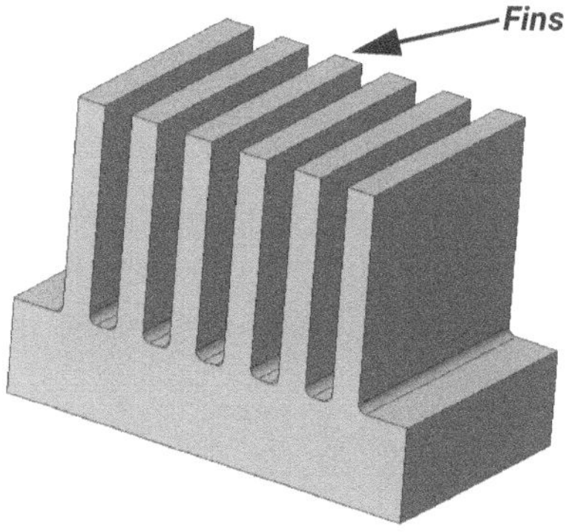

Figure 8–16

Modeling Tasks

Task 1: Open the model.

1. Set the working directory to **Chapter08**.
2. Open **heat_device.prt**.
3. Set the model display as follows:
   - *(Datum Display Filters)*: All Off
   - *(Spin Center)*: Off
   - *(Display Style)*: (Shading With Edges)

The part displays as shown in Figure 8–17.

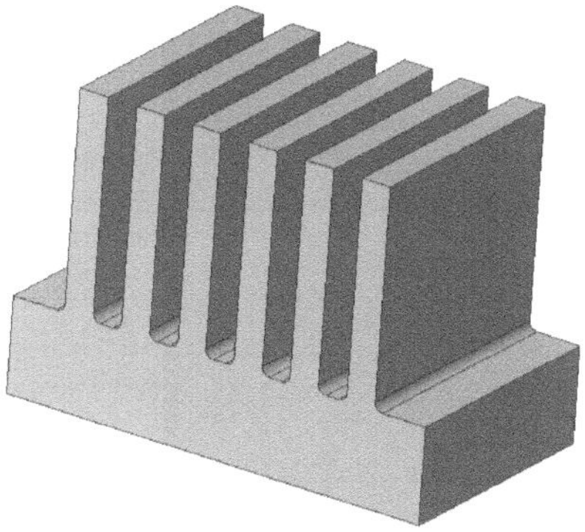

Figure 8–17

4. Ensure that the unit system is set to **IPS**.

Task 2: Launch Creo Simulate.

1. Select **Applications>Simulate**.
2. Click (Thermal Mode) to switch to the Thermal mode.

Task 3: Apply heat loads.

In this task, you will apply a heat load to the bottom surface of the heat device.

1. Select the bottom surface shown in Figure 8–18 and select (Heat) from the mini-toolbar.

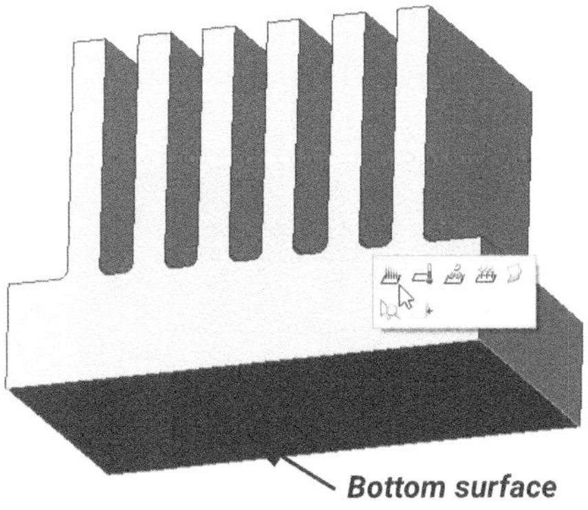

Figure 8–18

2. The *Heat Load* dialog box opens as shown in Figure 8–19.

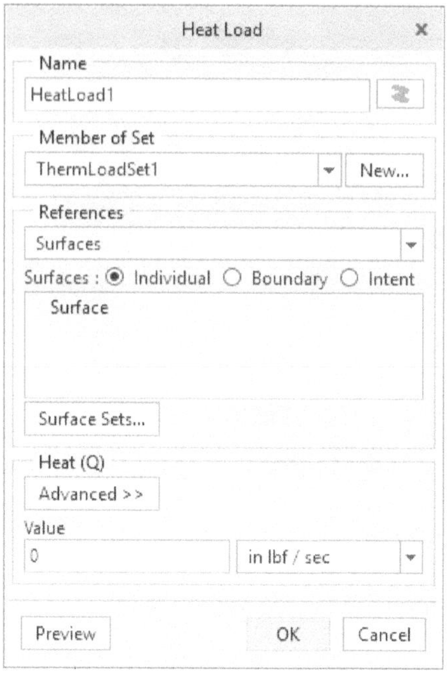

Figure 8–19

3. In the *Name* field, enter **end_heat_load**. For *Member of Set*, accept the default **ThermalLoadSet1** option.
4. In the *Value* field, enter **14.75**.

   Note: *14.75lbf in/sec = 20W*

5. Click **Preview** to preview the applied heat load.
6. Click **OK**. The model displays as shown in Figure 8–20.

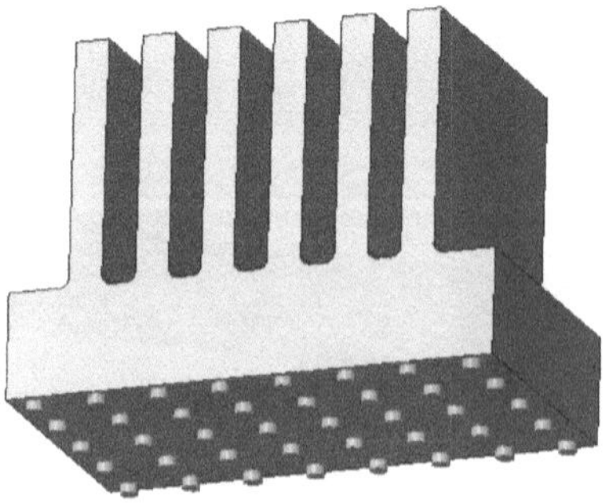

Figure 8–20

Task 4: Apply boundary conditions.

In this task, you will apply boundary conditions to the long vertical faces of the fins, the top faces of the fins, and the side faces, as shown in Figure 8–21.

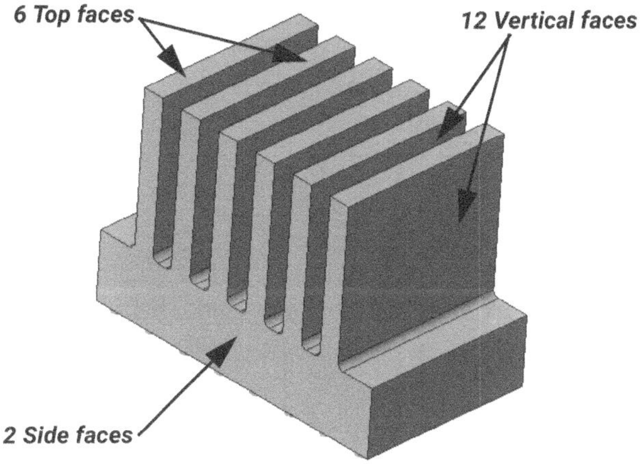

Figure 8–21

> ***Note:*** *Assume that the convection on the smaller surfaces is negligible.*

1. Click (Convection Condition). The *Convection Condition* dialog box opens, as shown in Figure 8–22.

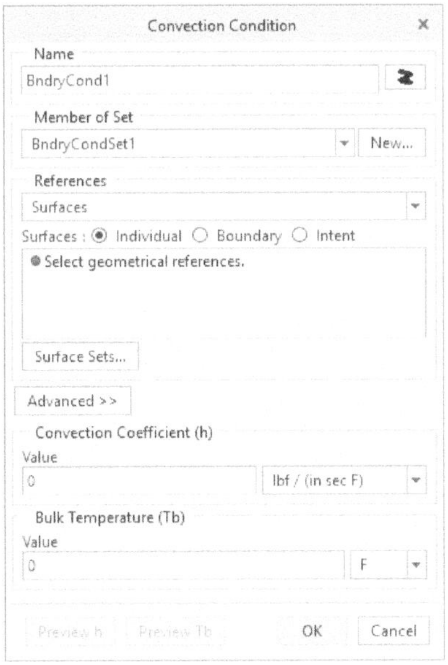

Figure 8–22

2. In the *Name* field, enter **long_face**. For *Member of Set*, accept the default **BndryCondSet1** option.
3. Select the 12 large vertical surfaces of the fins, the six top faces of the fins, and the two side faces. (Hold <Ctrl> to multi-select.)
4. In the *Convection Coefficient* field, enter **0.01**.
5. In the *Bulk Temperature* field, enter **80**.
6. Click **OK**. The model displays as shown in Figure 8–23.

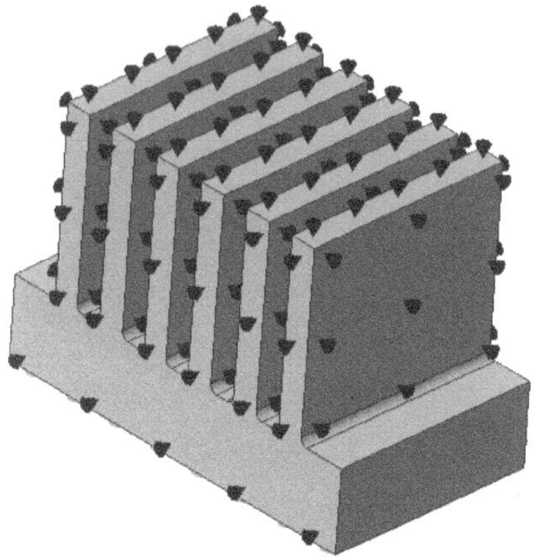

Figure 8–23

Task 5: Apply the material.

1. Assign **AL2014** to the heat device part. The following values are the default material properties for the aluminum alloy AL2014:
   - *Specific Heat capacity:* **829900 in^2/(sec^2 F)**
   - *Thermal conductivity:* **24 lbf/(sec F)**
   - *Density:* **0.0002614 lbf sec^2/in^4**
   - *Poisson's Ratio:* **0.33**
   - *Young's Modulus:* **1.06e+07 psi**
   - *Coeff of Thermal Expansion:* **1.28e-05 /F**

Task 6: Mesh the model.

1. Use the Simulation Display settings to toggle off **Material Assignments**, **Heat Loads** and **Convection Conditions**.
2. Click (AutoGEM). The *AutoGEM* dialog box opens.
3. Expand the *AutoGEM References* drop-down list, select the **All with Properties** option, and click **Create** to mesh the model. The mesh displays as shown in Figure 8–24.

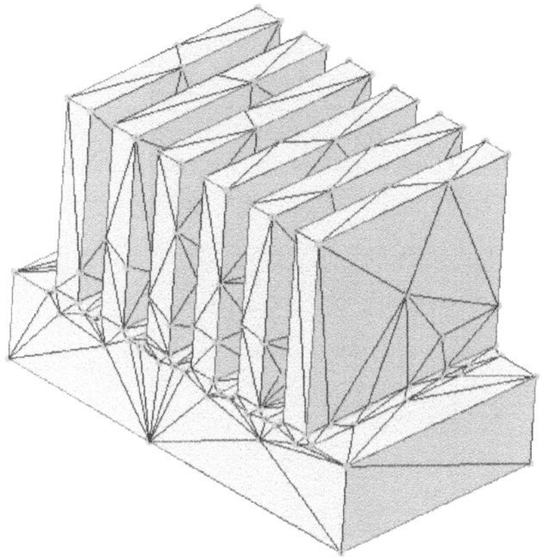

Figure 8–24

4. Close the *AutoGEM* dialog box and save the mesh.

Summary

In the previous tasks, you created the simulation entities required to analyze your model. In the following tasks, you will set the analysis type and the convergence method and run the analysis.

Analysis Tasks

Task 7: Set up and run the analysis.

In this task, you will specify the analysis type. First, the **heat_device** is analyzed using the **Quick Check** convergence option to check for errors. The importance of this option increases with the size of your model (e.g., a model with a large number of elements). The option gives you a general feel for the results and indicates that the model behaves as intended with applied boundary conditions.

1. Click (Analyses and Studies). The *Analyses and Design Studies* dialog box opens.

2. Select **File>New Steady State Thermal**. The *Steady Thermal Analysis Definition* dialog box opens, as shown in Figure 8–25.

Figure 8–25

3. In the *Name* field, enter **heat_device** (heat_device is now the name of a subdirectory containing all of your results files).
4. In the *Description* field, enter **thermal analysis of a heat_device**. This step is optional, but it is helpful for identifying your analysis later.
5. For a thermal analysis, you must specify or select the boundary conditions and heat load sets. These were created in the previous steps. In this case, they are **BndryCondSet1** and **ThermalLoadSet1**. Verify that they are highlighted.
6. For the type of convergence, expand the *Method* drop-down list and select **Quick Check**. This option enables you to determine whether the analysis was set up correctly in your first run.
7. Click **OK** in the *Steady Thermal Analysis Definition* dialog box.

8. Verify that the *Run Settings* are correct, check the model, and run the analysis with interactive diagnostics. Wait until it completes.
9. Expand the *Run Status* dialog box and review the information in the window. Click **Close** when done.

Task 8: Run the analysis using the Multi-Pass Adaptive convergence option.

1. With the **heat_device** analysis highlighted, select (Copy) to create a copy of the analysis.

   Highlight **Copy_of_heat_device** and click (Edit) to edit it. The *Steady Thermal Analysis Definition* dialog box for Analysis opens.
2. For the *Name*, enter **heat_device_multi_pass**.
3. Expand the *Method* drop-down list and select **Multi-Pass Adaptive**.
4. In the *Polynomial Order* area, edit the *Maximum* value to **9**.
5. In the *Limits* area, in the *Percent Convergence* field, enter **10** percent convergence.
6. Click **OK** in the *Steady Thermal Analysis Definition* dialog box.
7. Run the analysis with interactive diagnostics and wait until it finishes.
8. Expand the *Run Status* dialog box and review the following results:
   - The analysis converges on pass two.
   - The flux error is 9.5% of the Max Flux, as shown in Figure 8–26.

```
RMS Flux Error Estimates:

Load Set             Flux Error     % of Max Flux
----------------     -----------    ----------------
ThermLoadSet1         1.02e+01        9.5% of  1.07e+02
```

Figure 8–26

In the *Run Status* dialog box, the *Measures* area is shown in Figure 8–27.

```
Measures:

     Name                 Value        Convergence
--------------        -------------    -----------
energy_norm:            9.831984e+02       0.0%
max_flux_mag:           1.070105e+02       8.0%
max_flux_x:             1.046296e+02      39.1%
max_flux_y:             4.190372e+01     100.0%
max_flux_z:           -1.381975e+01      34.0%
max_grad_mag:           4.458770e+00       8.0%
max_grad_x:           -4.359568e+00      39.1%
max_grad_y:           -1.745988e+00     100.0%
max_grad_z:             5.758227e-01      34.0%
max_temperature:        2.133453e+02       0.0%
min_temperature:        2.127237e+02       0.0%
```

Figure 8–27

Note the maximum temperature (213.3°F) and the minimum temperature (212.7°F). The quantity of interest of the analysis is the temperature. Since the temperature measures converge, you could assume that the result of this analysis is valid, despite the flux convergence index being 8%.

The values that you obtain when you run the analysis might be different than those that have been provided. This is due to the fact that each new build of Creo Simulate produces slight variations in the creation of the mesh.

9. Close the *Run Status* dialog box.

Results Tasks

Task 9: Display the temperature results.

In this task, you will create and display a temperature plot for one of the long vertical surfaces.

1. In the *Analyses and Design Studies* dialog box, highlight the **heat_device_multi_pass** analysis and click (Review Results). The *Result Window Definition* dialog box opens, as shown in Figure 8–28.

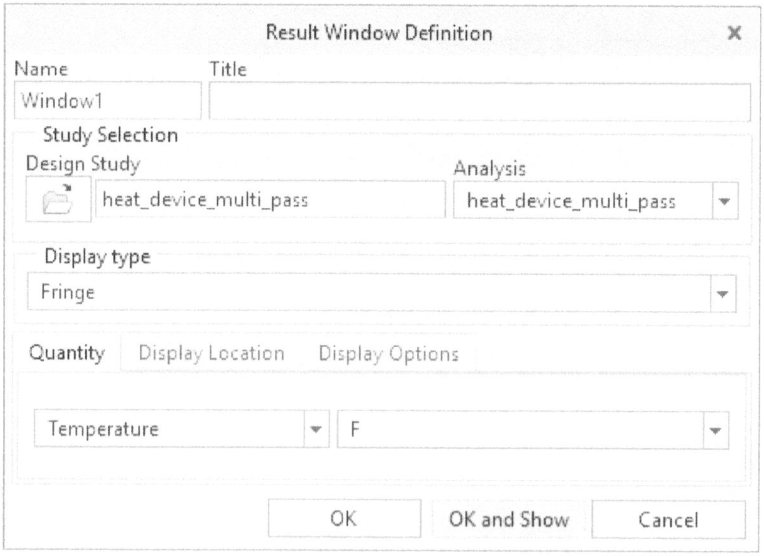

Figure 8–28

2. In the *Name* field, accept the default **Window1**.
3. In the *Title* field, enter **SURFACE_PLOT**.

4. Click **OK and Show**. The Temperature fringe plot displays as shown in Figure 8–29.

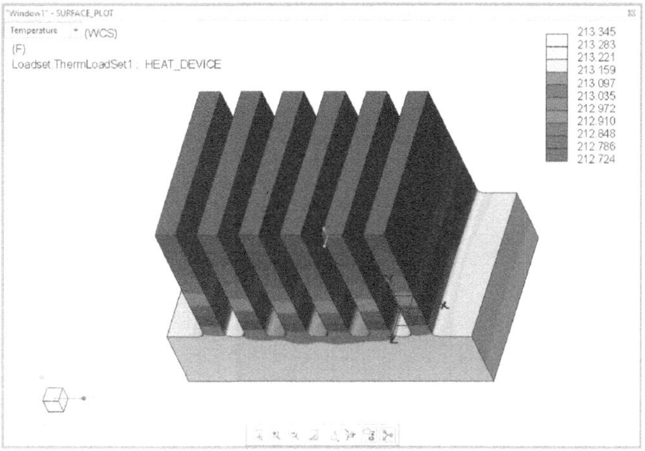

Figure 8–29

Note that the maximum temperature occurs at the bottom of the heat sink, where the heat load is applied. The temperature gradually decreases to the top of the heat sink, due to convection on the fins.

5. Click (Edit). The *Result Window Definition* dialog box opens.
6. Select the *Display Location* tab, expand the drop-down list and select **Surfaces**.
7. Click (Select) and select the right vertical surface of the right-most fin, toward the positive direction of the X axis. Click the middle mouse button when finished.
8. Click **OK and Show**. The result window displays as shown in Figure 8–30.

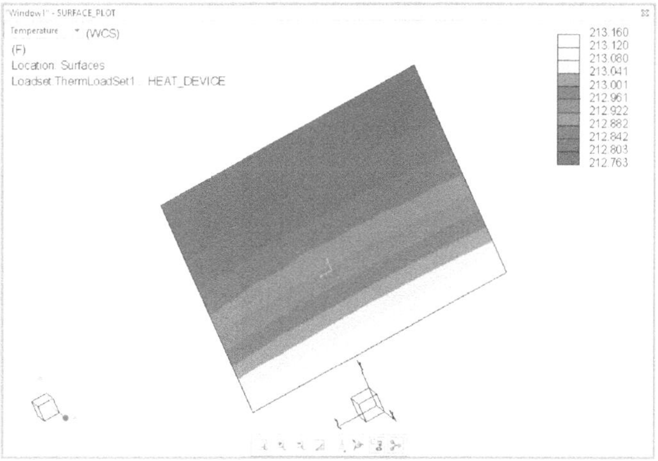

Figure 8–30

The temperature gradient is very small (0.4°F) and the temperature is too high throughout the surface. These results indicate that the heat device is not convecting enough heat to cool the CPU. Possible solutions include either a forced convection by means of a fan or a different heat device with more fins and a higher fin height. A sensitivity study would be useful for the second solution. Additionally, the convection coefficient could be increased by introducing surface roughness to the **heat_device** fins to enhance turbulence.

> ***Note:*** *The higher the temperature gradient, the higher the heat transfer.*

Task 10: Display the heat flux results.

1. In the *Home* tab, click (Edit). The *Result Window Definition* dialog box opens.
2. In the *Quantity* tab, select **Flux**.
3. In the *Display Location* tab, select **All**.
4. In the *Display Options* tab, select **Animate** and **Auto Start**.
5. Click **OK and Show**. Step through the animation. On Frame 5, the result plot displays as shown in Figure 8–31.

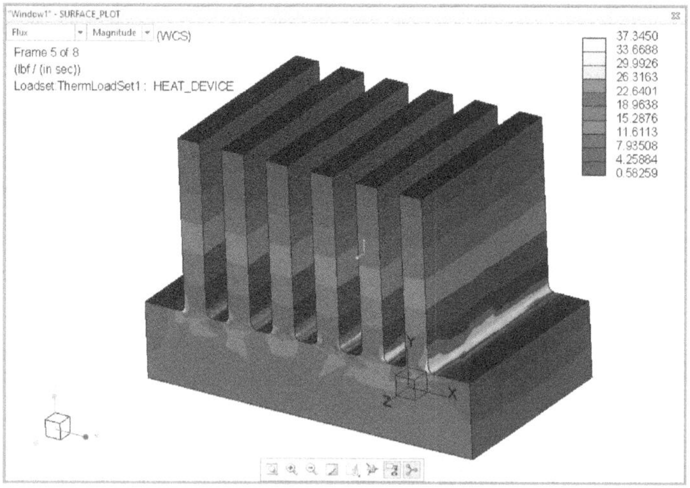

Figure 8–31

Note that the maximum heat flow occurs at the bottom of the fins. This area acts like a funnel, transferring heat from the heat source at the bottom surface to the tops of the fins.

6. Exit the Results environment.
7. Close the *Analyses and Design Studies* dialog box.

Task 11: Transfer loads from thermal to structure.

In this task, you will transfer the temperature distribution from Thermal analysis to Structural analysis and apply the temperature distribution's thermal load in Structure mode.

1. Click (Structure Mode) to switch to the Structure mode.
2. In the *Home* tab, expand the *Loads* group and select **MEC/T Load**. The *MEC/T Temperature Load* dialog box opens, as shown in Figure 8–32.

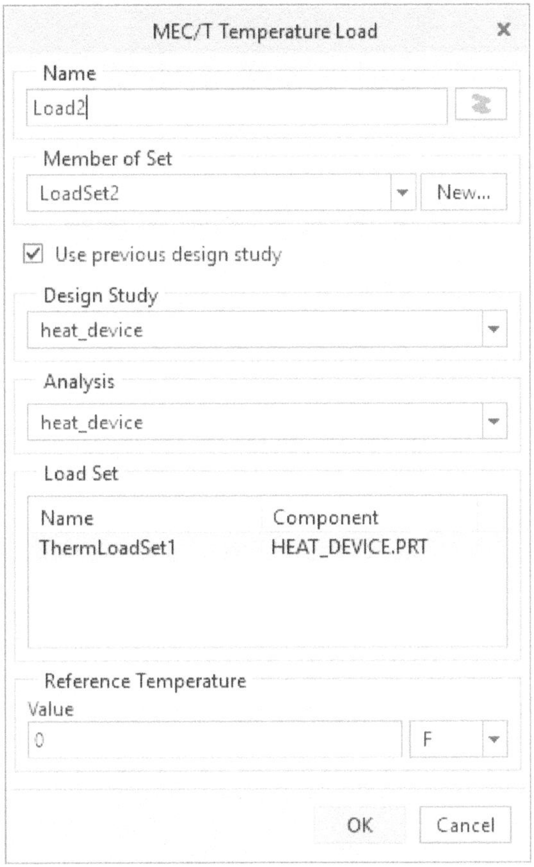

Figure 8–32

3. In the *Name* field, enter **transfer**.
4. For *Member of Set*, accept the default option.
5. In the *Reference Temperature* field, enter **50**.

6. Click **OK**. The model displays as shown in Figure 8–33.

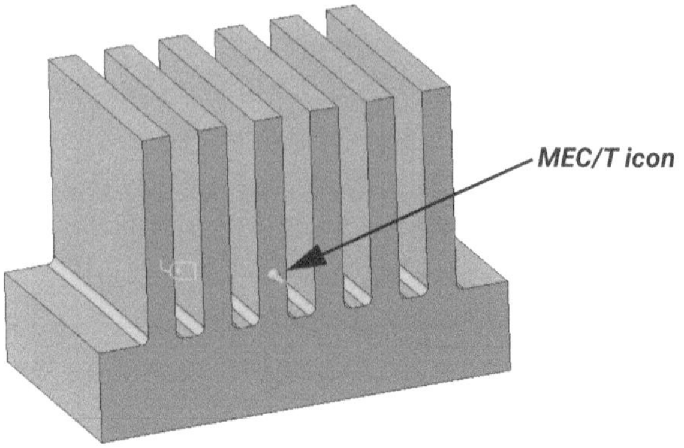

Figure 8–33

Note: *The Reference Temperature is the strain-free temperature. The stresses and strains are computed based on the differential between the temperature calculated in Thermal analysis and the Reference Temperature.*

Task 12: Apply constraints.

The heat sink is bonded to the circuit board. In this task, you will apply the correct constraints.

1. Constrain the bottom surface of the heat sink in all of the translations, as shown in Figure 8–34.

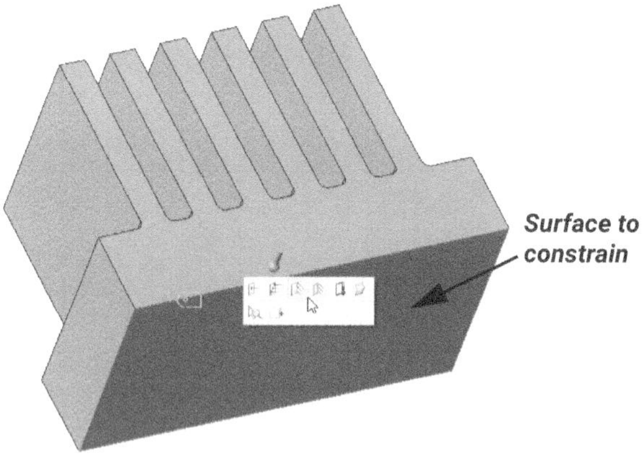

Figure 8–34

Task 13: Run the structural analysis.

1. Set up a static analysis using the **Single-Pass Adaptive** convergence option.
2. For the name of the analysis, enter **heat_structure**.
3. Run the **heat_structure** analysis.

Task 14: Display the results.

In this task, you will create and display two fringe plots: one for displacement and one for von Mises stress.

1. Create the deformed fringe plot for displacement, as shown in Figure 8–35.

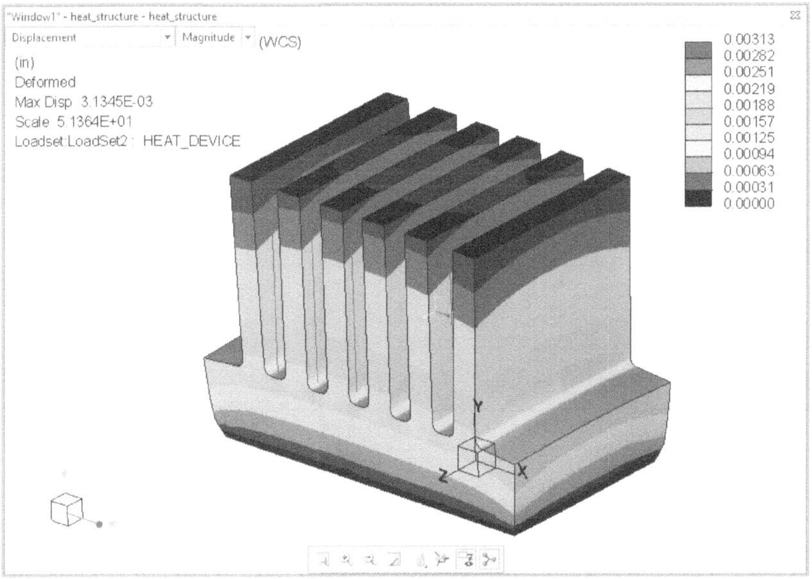

Figure 8–35

Note that the most deformation occurs in the fins, where material expansion due to heating is not constrained.

2. Create the fringe plot for the von Mises stress, as shown in Figure 8–36.

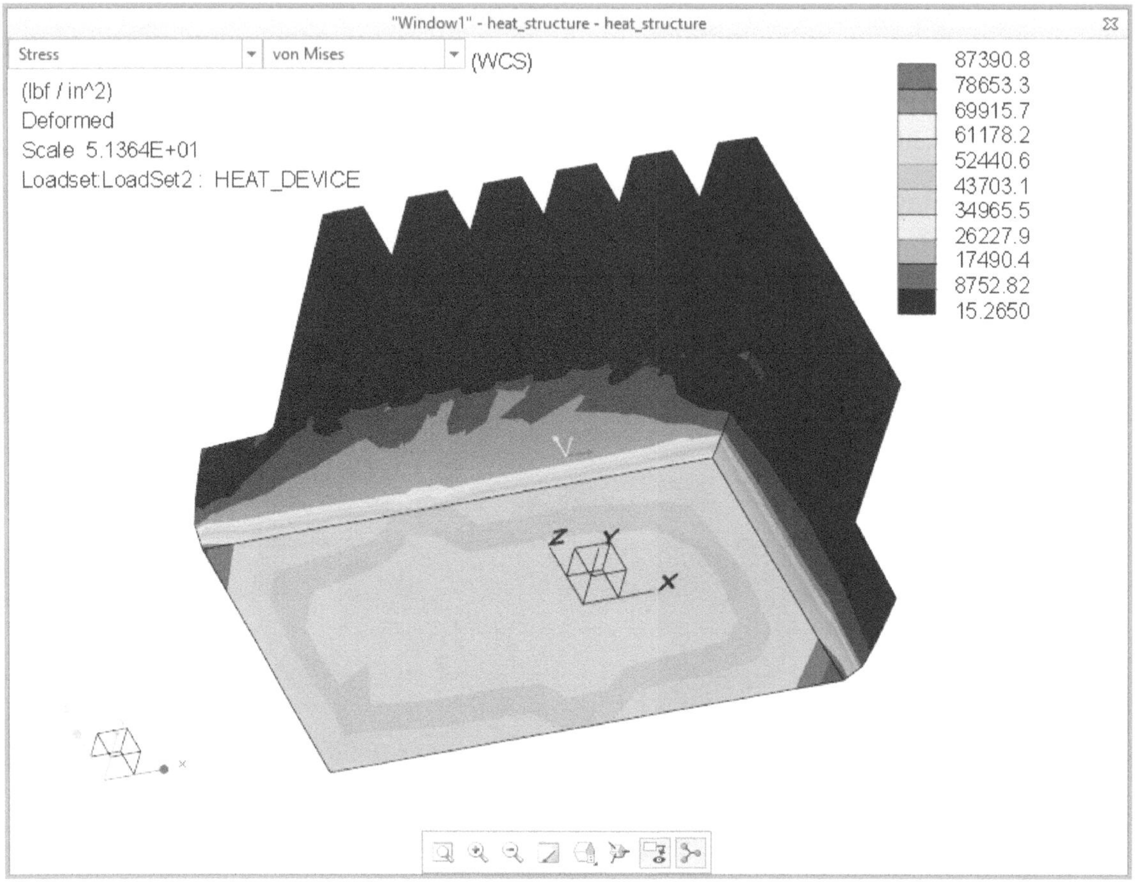

Figure 8–36

Note that the greatest stress occurs at the bottom of the sink, which is due to the constraint that restricts material expansion in that area.

3. Exit the Results environment. Save and close the model.

End of practice

Practice 8b
Thermal Deformation Analysis of an Assembly

Practice Objectives

- Set up and run a thermal analysis on an assembly.
- Create an interface with thermal resistance.
- Import thermal results into structural analysis.

In this practice, you will set up and run a thermal and a structural analyses on the electronic assembly shown in Figure 8–37, with minimum instruction.

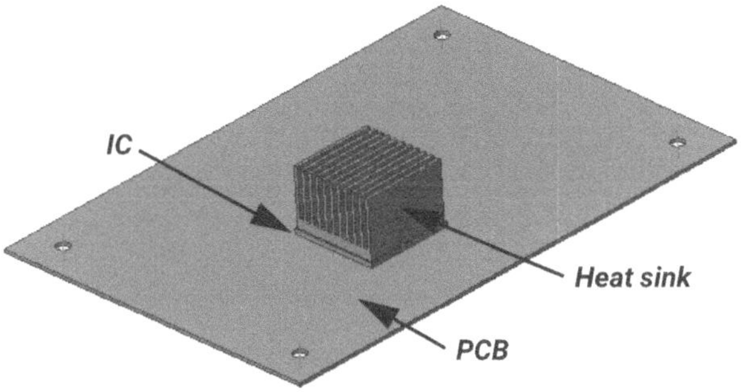

Figure 8–37

The heat source in this simulation is the Integrated Circuit (IC) part, generating 1W of heat. The heat sink is bonded to the IC. The IC is mounted, but not bonded, to the Printed Circuit Board (PCB) part. The generated heat in this design is intended to be dissipated through the means of convection by the heat sink.

Task 1: Prepare the thermal model.

1. Set the working directory to **Chapter08**, if required.
2. Open **PCB.asm** and launch Creo Simulate.
3. Set the model display as follows:
   - *(Datum Display Filters)*: All Off
   - *(Spin Center)*: Off
   - *(Display Style)*: (Shading With Edges)
4. Switch to Thermal mode.

5. Apply the materials as follows:
   - *Heat sink:* **AL2014**
   - *IC:* **EPOXY**
   - *PCB:* **NYLON**
6. Apply the **1W** Heat Load to the IC part.
7. Apply a convection boundary condition on all vertical surfaces and on all top surfaces of the fins of the heat sink, as well as on the top surface of the PCB, as shown in Figure 8–38. Use the following convection parameters:
   - *Convection coefficient:* **0.01**
   - *Bulk temperature:* **30**

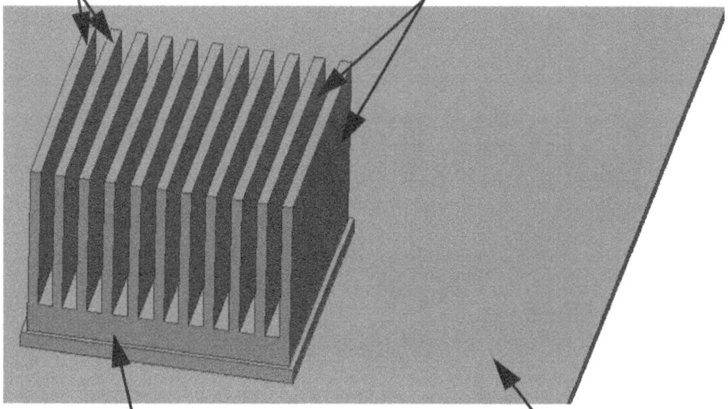

Figure 8–38

8. Create a new Thermal Resistance interface between the bottom surface of the IC and the top surface of the PCB. Use a *Heat Transfer Coefficient* of **0.02**.

   Note: *Since the IC is not bonded to the PCB, there is no perfect conduction of heat between the two parts.*

9. Verify the model's interfaces using the **Review Geometry** tool.

Task 2: Set up and run a thermal analysis and then examine the results.

1. Create and run a new Single-Pass Adaptive steady-state thermal analysis named **pcb_thermal**.

2. Display the **Temperature** fringe plot.
   - Does the temperature field look reasonable?
   - What is the maximum temperature in the Integrated Circuit?
3. Display the **Flux Magnitude** fringe plot.
   - In which areas of the model does the most flow of heat occur?

Task 3: Prepare the structural model.

1. Switch to Structure mode.
2. Fully constrain the inside surfaces of all four holes in the PCB, as shown in Figure 8–39.

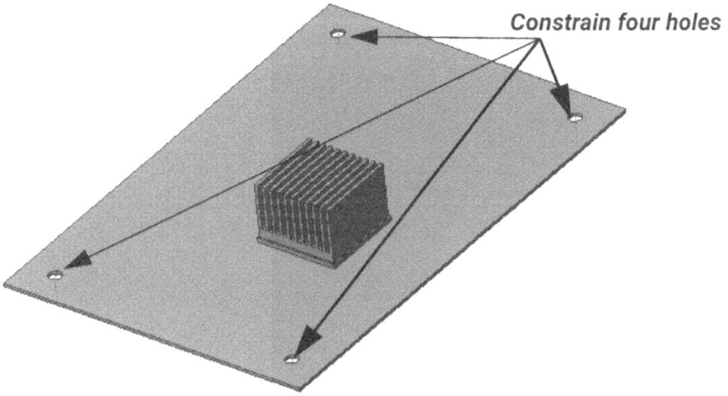

Figure 8–39

3. Apply MEC/T load from the **pcb_thermal** analysis. Use *Reference Temperature* **20**.

Task 4: Set up and run a thermal analysis and then examine the results.

1. Create and run a new Single-Pass Adaptive static analysis named **pcb_struct**.
2. Display and animate the **Displacement Magnitude** deformed fringe plot.
   - Does the deformation display as expected?
3. Display the **von Mises Stress** plot.
   - Can you explain why substantial stresses occur near the mounting holes?
   - Can you think of an alternative set of supports that would decrease the out-of-plane deformation of the model as well as of the stress level?

End of practice

Chapter 9

Modal Analysis

A modal analysis in Creo Simulate helps you to determine the natural frequencies and natural modes of vibration for a model. These factors are important for models that are subjected to cyclic or vibration loads, because resonance occurs at vibrational loads that are at or close to the natural frequencies for the model. You can calculate natural frequencies and model shapes for the following types of parts: a free part (when it has six rigid body modes), a partially fixed part (when the number of rigid body modes is less than six), and a fully fixed part (when there are no rigid body modes).

Learning Objectives

- Understand natural vibration and natural frequency.
- Understand natural modes of vibration.
- Create a modal analysis.

9.1 Natural Frequency

All objects vibrate, when hit, struck, plucked or otherwise disturbed. When an object vibrates, it tends to do so at a specific frequency or set of frequencies. For example, it could be a guitar string or a tuning fork.

The frequency or frequencies at which an object tends to vibrate when disturbed is called the *characteristic* or *natural frequency* of the object.

If a dynamic load is applied to a model close to its natural frequency, the model exhibits a larger than normal oscillation. This phenomenon is called *resonance*. Without correct damping, the resonance can become uncontrollable and cause the model to collapse.

Natural frequencies are numbered (1st, 2nd, 3rd, etc.), with the 1st natural frequency being the lowest. The 1st natural frequency is sometimes called the *fundamental frequency* of an object.

Modal analysis in Creo Simulate predicts the natural frequencies of your model so that you can determine whether or not the applied dynamic loads might cause resonance. The results of a modal analysis also help to determine whether a model requires more or less damping to prevent failure. Use a modal analysis to find the resonant frequencies for a structure under specific constraints.

> ***Note:*** *Resonance occurs when the frequency of the forced vibrations approaches or coincides with the natural frequency of the system.*

9.2 Natural Modes

An object vibrating at a natural frequency creates a physical deformation, or shape, of the object. This shape is called the *natural mode* of vibration.

Using Creo Simulate, you can visualize these shapes and the frequency that is associated with them. Four mode shapes are shown in Figure 9–1. By viewing mode shapes, you can determine how a part reacts to different frequencies.

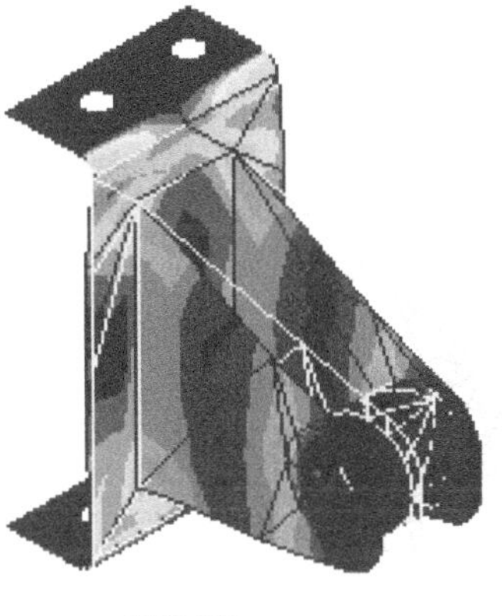

255.6Hz

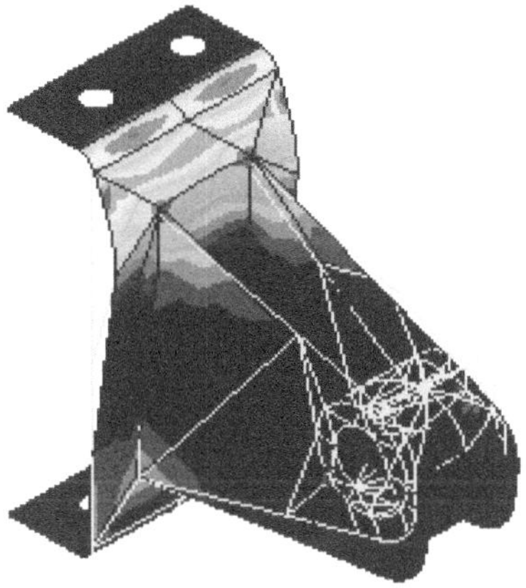

868.8Hz

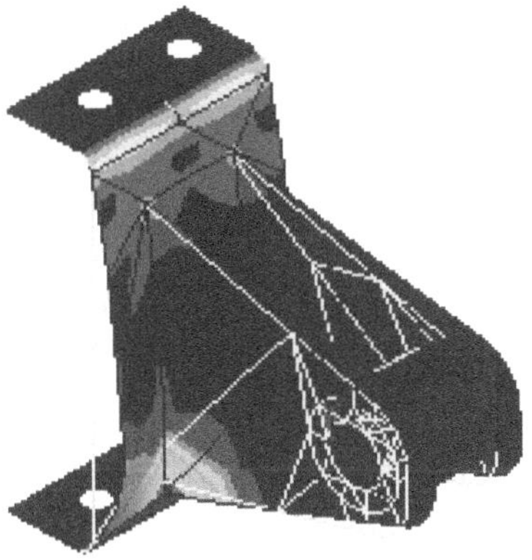

1026.7Hz

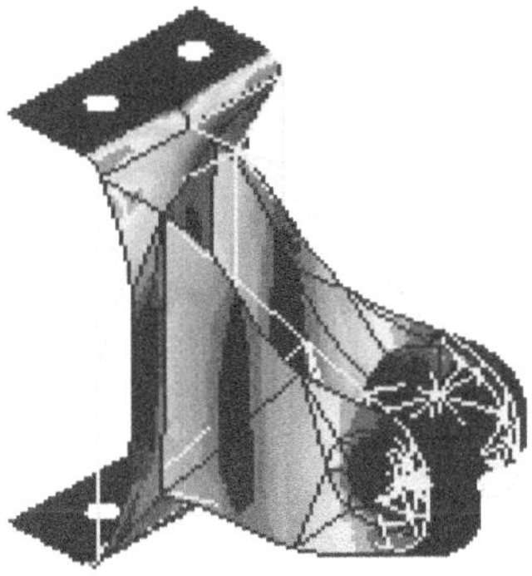

1440.4Hz

Figure 9–1

Note that the equation solved in Modal analysis is the equation of dynamic equilibrium (i.e., Newton's equation) with no loads included in the analysis. Therefore, the mode shapes are essentially dimensionless. When mode shapes display in Creo Simulate, only some imaginary magnitudes display, which are scaled to value 1.0.

9.3 Defining a Modal Analysis

Modal analysis parameters are defined in the *Modal Analysis Definition* dialog box, as shown in Figure 9–2.

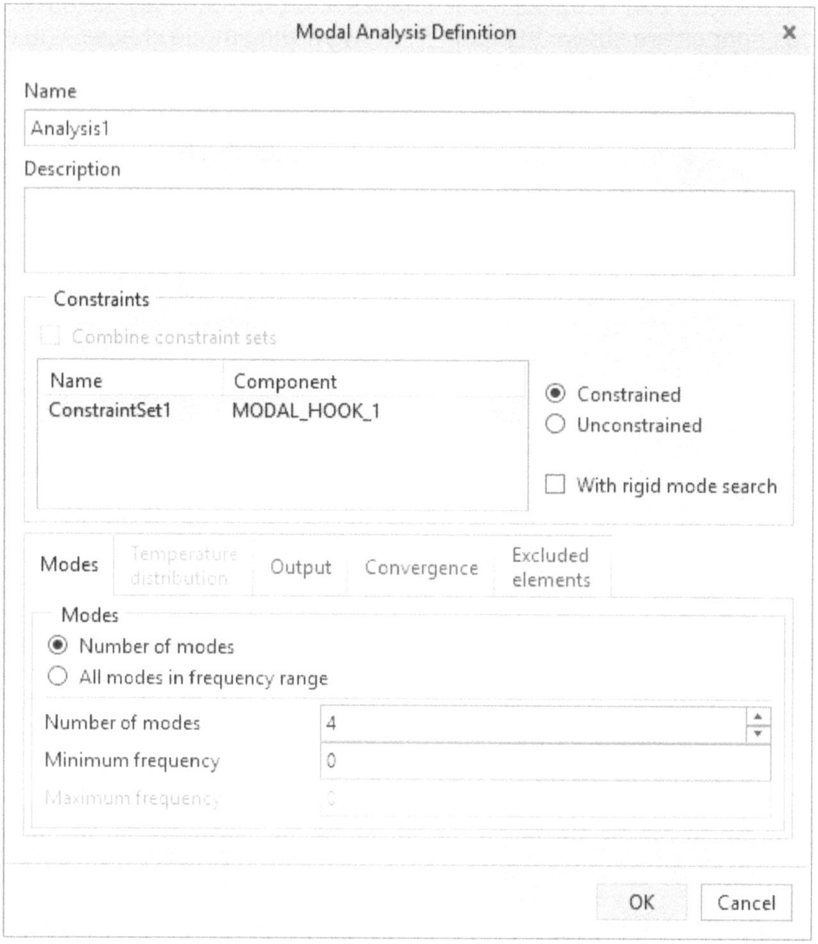

Figure 9–2

The options in the *Modal Analysis* dialog box are as follows:

Option	Description
Name	Enter a name for the analysis.
Description	Enter a description of the analysis (optional).
Constraints	Enables you to define the constraint set using the following options:
Constrained	Solves a fully constrained model.
Unconstrained	Solves an unconstrained or under-constrained model.
With rigid mode search	Use when solving an unconstrained or under-constrained model, if you want to visualize the rigid body modes. Creo Simulate reports any rigid body modes that it finds.
Output	Define the output for the analysis. This tab contains the following options:
Calculate	Select the stresses, rotations, and/or reactions to calculated quantity values.
Plot	Enter a plotting grid density. Creo Simulate calculates and displays quantity values at the intersection of the grid lines on each element.
Convergence	Select a convergence method using the *Method* drop-down list in the *Convergence* tab.
Modes	Define the modes for the analysis in the *Modes* tab. This tab contains the following options:
Number of Modes	Specifies the number of modes and frequencies for Creo Simulate to calculate.
All Modes in Frequency Range	Requests the calculation of all modes within a frequency range in the *Min Frequency* and *Max Frequency* fields.
Minimum Frequency	Specify the minimum frequency of a frequency range. You can only specify this if the **All Modes in Frequency Range** option is selected.
Maximum Frequency	Specify the maximum frequency of a frequency range. You can only specify this if the **All Modes in Frequency Range** option is selected.

Practice 9a
Modal Analysis of a Bracket

Practice Objectives

- Set up and run a modal analysis.
- Display the results.

In this practice, you will set up and run a modal analysis on a bracket model, as shown in Figure 9–3. You will use the shell idealization to represent the thin sections of the model.

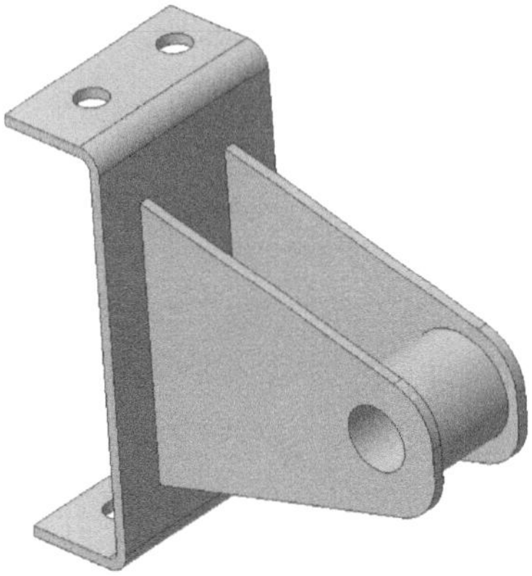

Figure 9–3

Note: *A modal analysis enables you to find the natural frequencies and corresponding natural modes of the bracket under a specific constraint set.*

Modeling Tasks

Task 1: Open the part.

1. Set the working directory to **Chapter09**.
2. Open **modal_hook_1.prt**.
3. Set the model display as follows:
   - *(Datum Display Filters)*: All Off
   - *(Spin Center)*: Off
   - *(Display Style)*: (Shading With Edges)

The part displays as shown in Figure 9–4.

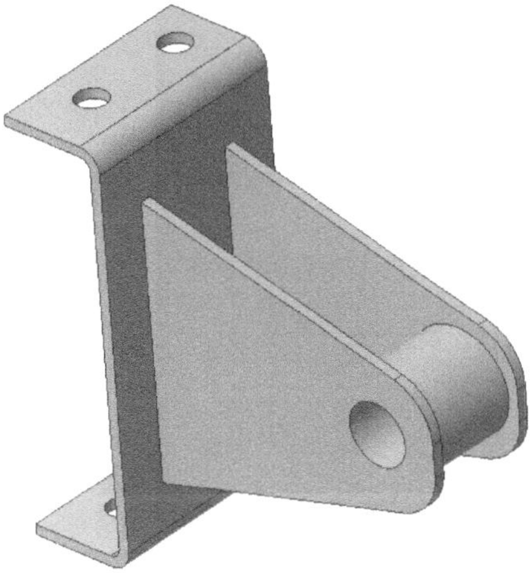

Figure 9–4

4. Ensure that the unit system is set to **mmNs**.
5. Select **Applications>Simulate**.

Task 2: Apply the material.

1. Assign **STEEL** to the model. The following values are the default material properties for HS-low-alloy steel (STEEL):
   - *Poisson:* **0.27**
   - *Young's modulus:* **199948 N/mm2**
   - *Coeff of thermal expansion:* **1.17e-5 /C**
   - *Density:* **7.82708e-9 tonne/mm^3**

   Note: *The model's material properties should be as stated.*

Task 3: Define the shell elements.

1. In the In-graphics toolbar, click (Simulation Display) and toggle off the display of **Material Assignments**.

2. In the *Refine Model* tab, expand the (Shell Pair) drop-down list and select **Detect Shell Pairs**. The *Auto Detect Shell Pairs* dialog box opens, as shown in Figure 9–5.

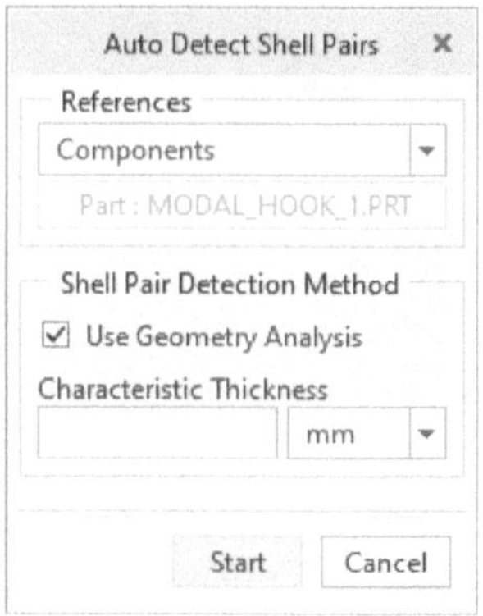

Figure 9–5

3. In the *Characteristic Thickness* field, enter **6** and click **Start**. Creo Simulate runs the automatic detection algorithm and closes the *Auto Detect Shell Pairs* dialog box.

   Note: *The wall thickness in this part is 5mm. Using a Characteristic Thickness of* ***6mm*** *ensures that all thin areas in the part are detected as Shells.*

4. In the *Refine Model* tab, in the *AutoGEM* area, click (Review Geometry) to open the *Simulation Geometry* dialog box. Accept the default options and click **Apply**. The model displays as shown in Figure 9–6.

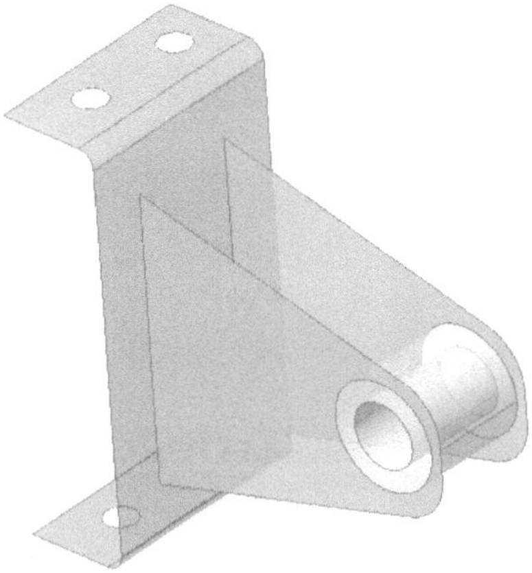

Figure 9–6

   Verify that the boss displays in gray (this is the uncompressed area), while the thin-walled sections display in green (these are the shell pairs compressed to a midsurface).

5. Click **Close** in the *Simulation Geometry* dialog box.

Task 4: Apply the constraints.

In this task, you will apply constraints to the top and bottom surfaces of the bracket.

1. Select (Displacement) to open the *Displacement* dialog box.
2. Select the two outer surfaces shown in Figure 9–7.

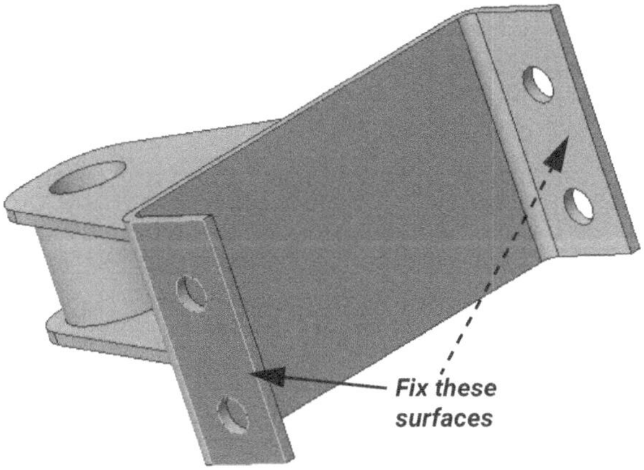

Figure 9–7

3. In the *Name* field, enter **surface_fix**.
4. Constrain the surfaces in all of the translations and rotations. The model displays as shown in Figure 9–8.

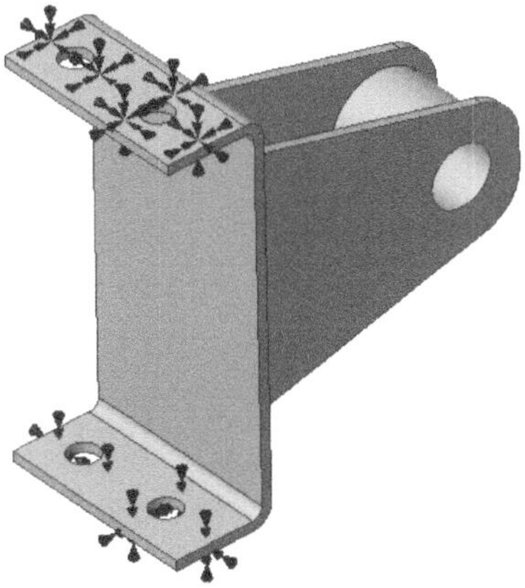

Figure 9–8

Task 5: Mesh the model.

1. Mesh the model using the **All with Properties** option. The model displays as shown in Figure 9–9.

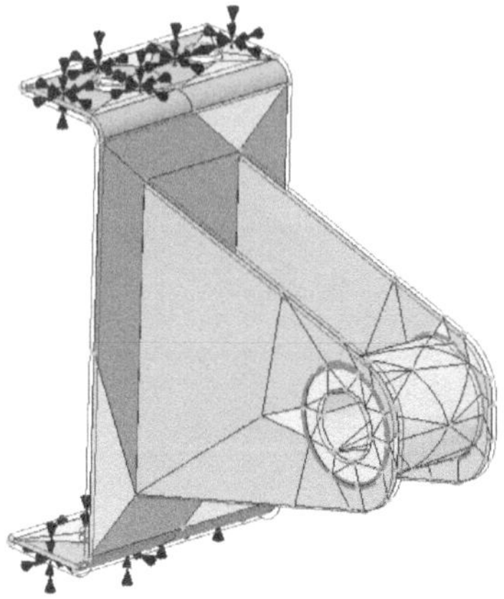

Figure 9–9

Note: *The shell elements (Tri and Quad) display in green and the 3D solid elements (Tetra) display in blue.*

2. Note the warning in the *AutoGem's Diagnostics* dialog box: "Shell compression resulted in loss of some solid material near the following geometry". The warning was due to the need for Creo Simulate to adjust the length of the solid boss to the midsurfaces of the side plates. For this analysis, this is acceptable, therefore, you can ignore the warning and close the *Diagnostics* dialog box.
3. Close the *AutoGEM* dialog box and save the mesh.

Summary

In the previous tasks, you created the simulation entities required to analyze your model. In the following tasks, you will specify the analysis type and convergence method and run the analysis.

Analysis Tasks

Task 6: Run a Quick Check analysis.

In this task, the model is analyzed using the **Quick Check** convergence option, which checks for errors.

1. Click (Analyses and Studies).

2. In the *Analyses and Design Studies* dialog box, select **File>New Modal**. The *Modal Analysis Definition* dialog box opens, as shown in Figure 9–10.

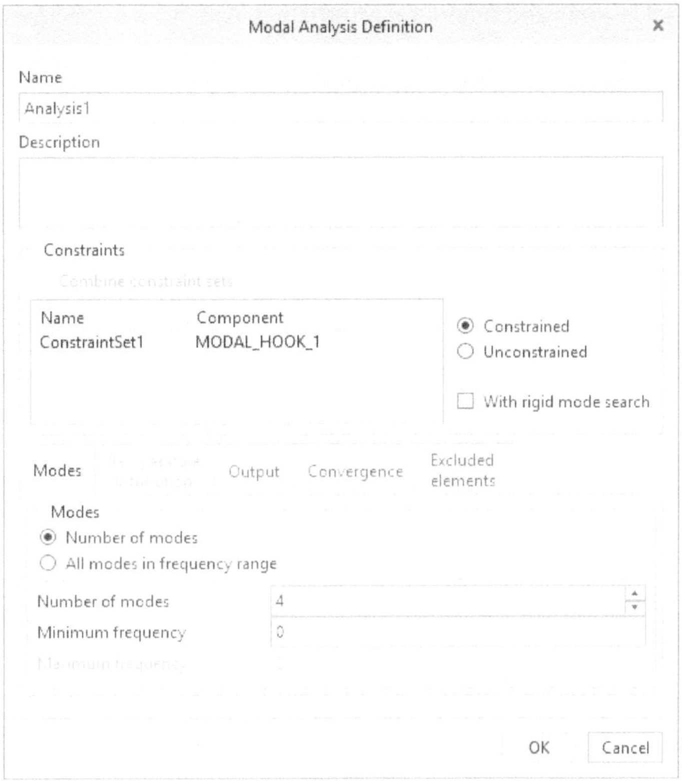

Figure 9–10

Note: *The objective of a modal study is to ensure that the system does not have a resonant frequency near the operating frequency.*

3. In the *Name* field, enter **modal_hook**.
4. (Optional) In the *Description* field, enter a description of the analysis.

Note: *Select the* ***Unconstrained*** *and* ***With rigid mode search*** *options when you are not sure if your model is fully constrained.*

5. In the *Constraints* area, accept the defaults.
6. In the *Number of Modes* field, enter **6**.
7. Select the *Convergence* tab, expand the *Method* drop-down list and select **Quick Check**.
8. Click **OK** to accept the selections and close the *Modal Analysis Definition* dialog box.
9. Check the validity of the model and run the analysis.

Task 7: Run a Multi-Pass Adaptive analysis.

In this task, the model is analyzed using the **Multi-Pass Adaptive** convergence option.

1. Edit the **modal_hook** analysis and change the convergence method to **Multi-Pass Adaptive**. In the *Polynomial Order* field, enter **9**. In the *Limits* area, in the *Percent Convergence* field, accept the default value of **10**.

   Note: *The solution converges on frequency.*

2. Run the analysis and run interactive diagnostics.
3. Expand the *Run Status* dialog box and review the information shown in Figure 9–11.

```
Number of Modes: 6

   Mode   Frequency (Hz)   Convergence
   ----   --------------   -----------
      1    2.607665e+02        3.0%
      2    9.401390e+02        7.5%
      3    1.015977e+03        8.4%
      4    1.467314e+03        3.3%
      5    1.723053e+03        3.6%
      6    1.821113e+03        3.9%
```

Figure 9–11

Note the convergence percentage for the six frequencies. The solution converges on the frequency (you set the convergence in Step 1 of this task). The convergence was obtained on pass six.

Results Tasks

Task 8: Display the results.

In this task, you will create, animate, and display four Displacement Magnitude fringe plots for the first four modes of vibration.

1. In the *Analyses and Design Studies* dialog box, click (Review Results). The *Result Window Definition* dialog box opens, as shown in Figure 9–12.

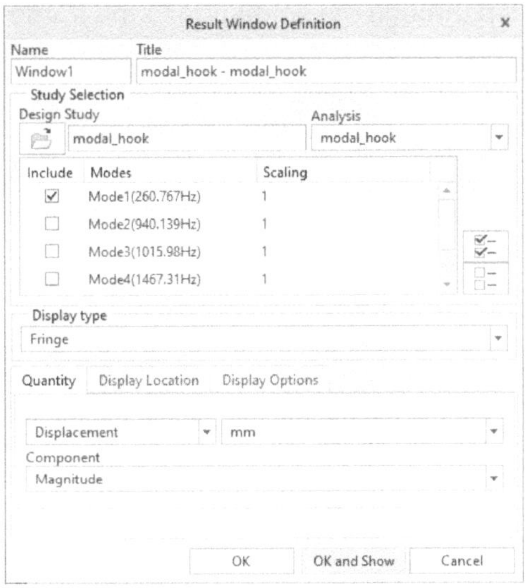

Figure 9–12

2. In the *Name* field, enter **mode1**.
3. Select the *Display Options* tab and enter the information shown in Figure 9–13.

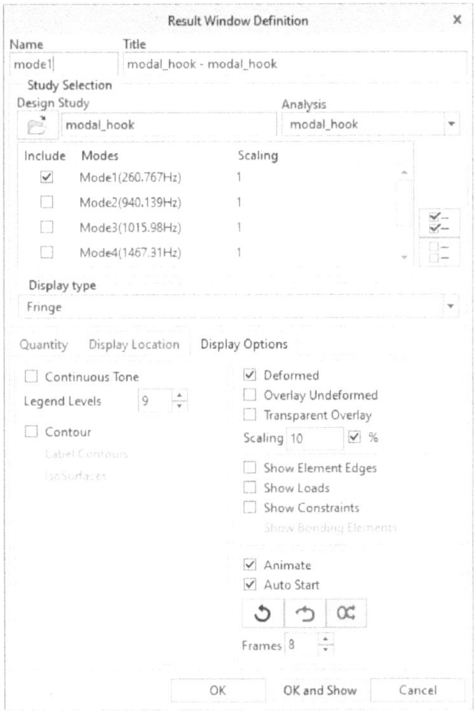

Figure 9–13

4. Display the result plot. Step through the animation to the frame shown in Figure 9–14.

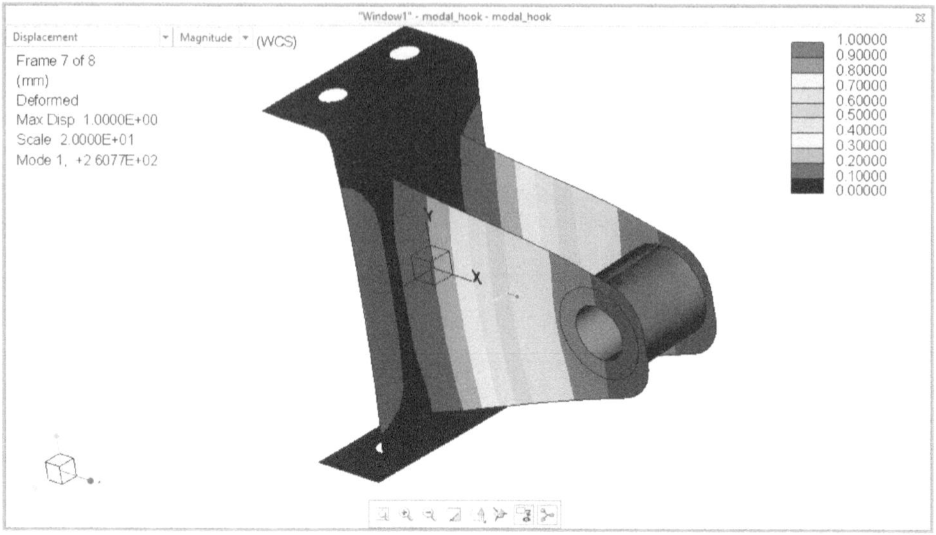

Figure 9–14

5. Create, animate, and display a Displacement Magnitude for mode 2. In the *Name* field, enter **mode2**.
6. In the *Include* column, select the second checkbox as shown in Figure 9–15, and clear the first checkbox.

Figure 9–15

7. Display the **mode2** fringe plot. Step through the animation to the frame shown in Figure 9–16.

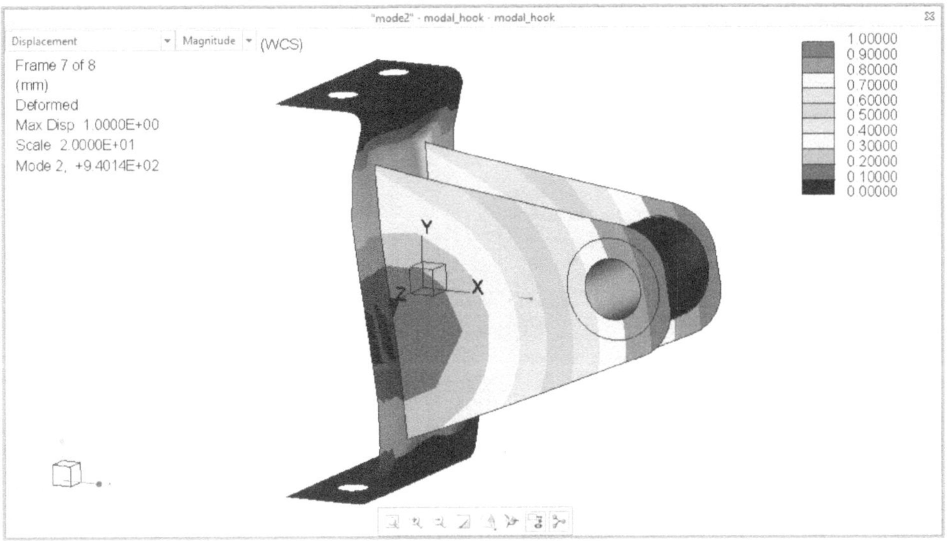

Figure 9–16

8. Create, animate, and display a Displacement Magnitude for mode 3. In the *Name* field, enter **mode3**.
9. In the *Include* column, select the third checkbox and clear the second checkbox.
10. Display the **mode3** fringe plot. Step through the animation to the frame shown in Figure 9–17.

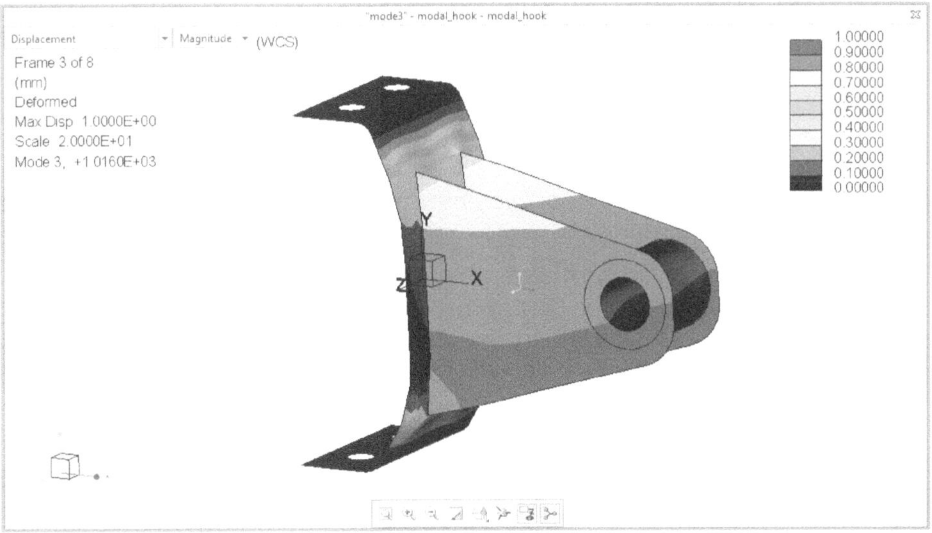

Figure 9–17

11. Create, animate, and display a Displacement Magnitude for mode 4. In the *Name* field, enter **mode4**.
12. In the *Include* column, select the fourth checkbox and clear the third checkbox.
13. Display the **mode4** fringe plot. Step through the animation to the frame shown in Figure 9–18.

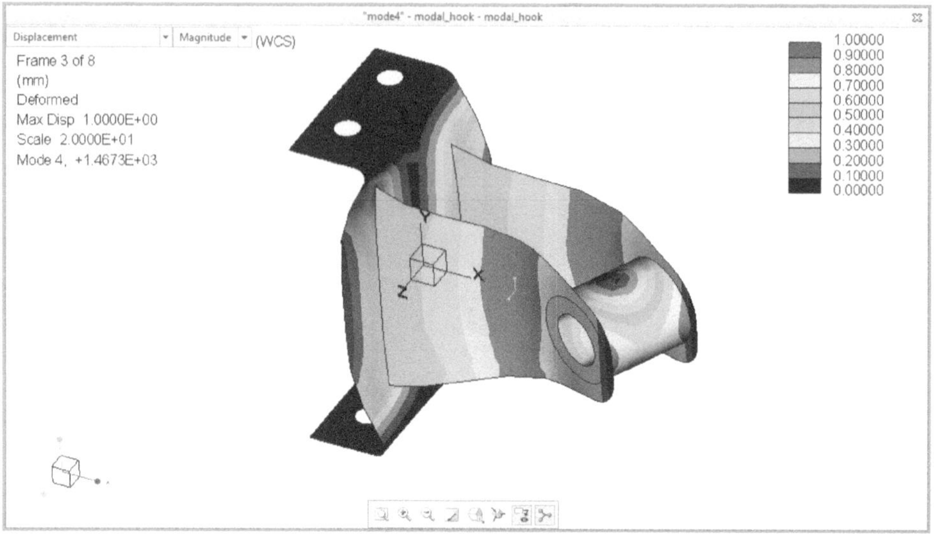

Figure 9–18

14. Exit the Results environment. Save and close the model.

Task 9: (Optional) Set up and run a new analysis.

1. Delete the mesh.
2. Delete the mid-surface shells.
3. Mesh the model with only 3D solid elements.
4. Set up and run a new Multi-Pass Adaptive analysis. Enter a different name for the analysis. In the *Polynomial Order* field, enter **9**. In the *Limits* area and *Converge on* area, in the *Percent Convergence* field, accept the defaults.
5. Compare the results. Note that the first frequency is now by about 2 percent lower than when using the shell model. This is because there was no loss of solid material when the solid mesh was used so the effective mass of the model with the solid mesh was slightly higher than with the shell mesh.

End of practice

Practice 9b
Unconstrained Modal Analysis

Practice Objectives

- Set up and run an unconstrained modal analysis.
- Review the results of the unconstrained modal analysis.

In this practice, you will set up and run an unconstrained modal analysis on the frame shown in Figure 9–19, with minimum instruction.

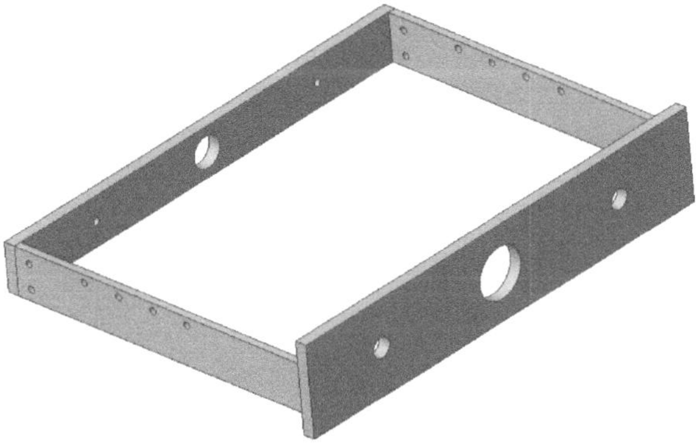

Figure 9–19

Task 1: Prepare the model for analysis.

1. Set the working directory to **Chapter09**, if required.
2. Open **frame.asm** and launch Creo Simulate.
3. Set the model display as follows:
   - *(Datum Display Filters)*: All Off
   - *(Spin Center)*: Off
   - *(Display Style)*: (Shading With Edges)
4. Apply the material **AL6061** to all parts.
5. Do not apply any constraints.

Task 2: Set up and run a modal analysis.

1. Create and run a new modal analysis with the following parameters:
   - *Analysis name:* **modal_free**
   - *Unconstrained:* **ON**
   - *With rigid mode search:* **ON**
   - *All modes in frequency range:* **from 0Hz to 500Hz**
   - *Convergence method:* **Single-Pass Adaptive**

Task 3: Examine the analysis results.

1. Extract the frequency values from the *Run Status* window.
   - How many natural frequencies have been found in the requested range?
   - Did you notice that first six frequencies are zeros or very close to zeros?
2. Examine the deformation plots for frequencies 1 to 6.
   - Do these modes resemble rigid body motions of the model (i.e., without inducing any strain or stress)?
3. Examine the deformation plots for the other frequencies.
   - Which frequency corresponds to the twisting mode of deformation of the frame?

End of practice

Chapter 10

Welds, Springs, and Masses

Idealizations are used to simplify your model and shorten your analysis time. Three other useful idealizations are welds, springs, and masses.

Learning Objectives

- Create spot weld connections.
- Create end weld connections.
- Create perimeter weld connections.
- Understand springs in Creo Simulate.
- Create springs.
- Understand mass elements in Creo Simulate.
- Create mass elements.

10.1 Weld Connections

Weld connections are analysis features that are intended to bridge gaps that occur during the midsurface compression of shell assemblies. The four types of weld connections available in Creo Simulate are spot welds, end welds, perimeter welds, and weld feature welds.

Spot Welds

Spot welds connect parts at datum point locations that you specify. An example of an assembly suitable for using spot welds is shown in Figure 10–1.

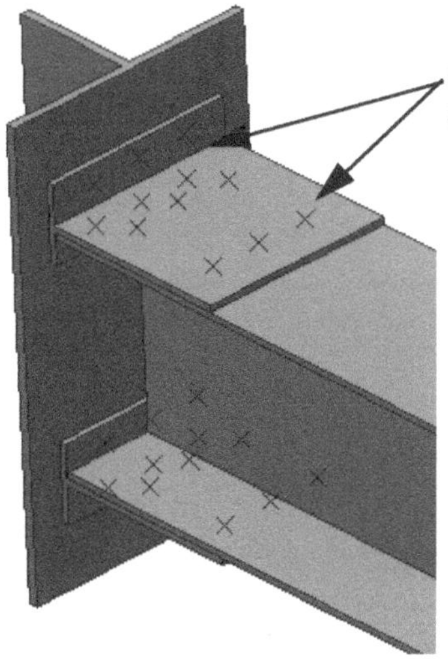

Figure 10–1

A spot weld in Creo Simulate is modeled with a beam element with a round cross-section. This idealization accurately transfers forces from one part to another. However, stress values close to the spot welds might not be accurate.

The following conditions are required for successful spot welds:

- The surfaces being connected by the weld must be within 15° of being parallel to each other.
- One of the surfaces being connected must have datum points that define spot weld locations.

Use the following steps to create a spot weld:

1. In the *Connections* group, click (Weld).
2. Expand the *Type* drop-down list and select **Spot Weld**.
3. Select the two surfaces that you want to connect.
4. Select the datum points where the spot welds are going to be created.

5. Enter the diameter of the weld.
6. Select the material of the weld.

End Welds

End welds are used to connect plates that are joined at right or oblique angles, such as in T or L configurations. An example of an assembly suitable for using end welds is shown in Figure 10–2.

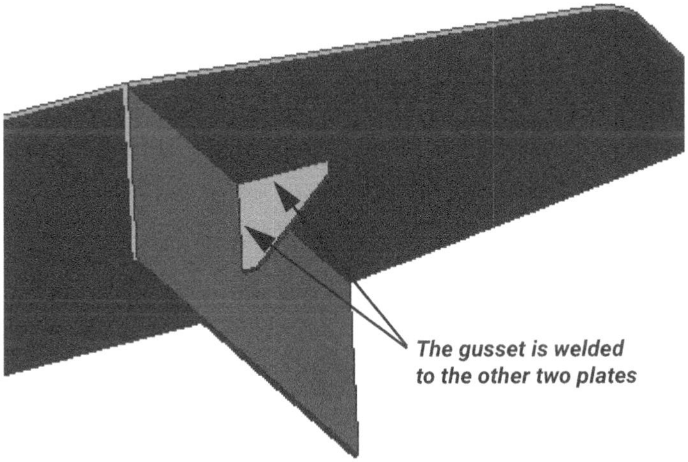

Figure 10–2

When an end weld is created, Creo Simulate creates shell elements to extend the mesh from one plate to join the mesh of a base plate.

Use the following steps to create an end weld:

1. In the *Connections* group, click (Weld).
2. Expand the *Type* drop-down list and select **End Weld**.
3. Select the surfaces to be welded.

Perimeter Welds

Perimeter welds are used to connect plates that are parallel to one another, along the perimeter of one plate. An example of an assembly suitable for using a perimeter weld is shown in Figure 10–3.

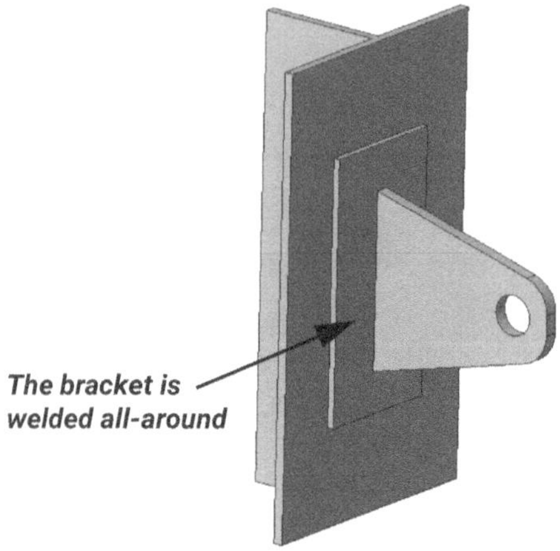

Figure 10–3

Creo Simulate automatically creates a series of new surfaces to extend the edges of one plate to the surface of the other. Shell elements are created on these surfaces.

Use the following steps to create a perimeter weld:

1. In the *Connections* group, click (Weld).
2. Expand the *Type* drop-down list and select **Perimeter Weld**.
3. Select the doubler surface on which you want to place the weld.
4. Select the base surface to which to extend the weld.
5. Select the doubler surface's edges that you want to weld.
6. Enter the thickness of the shell elements that represent the perimeter weld.
7. Select a material for the weld.

Weld Features

This option permits the re-use of welds created with the Creo Parametric Welding application. The following types of welds created with the Welding application can be used to create a simulation weld feature:

- All solid welds. Modeled with solid elements in Creo Simulate.
- Surface welds of fillet or groove type. Modeled with shell elements in Creo Simulate.

Use the following steps to use a simulation weld feature:

1. In the *Connections* group, click (Weld).
2. Expand the *Type* drop-down list and select **Weld Feature**.
3. Select a weld feature created in Creo Parametric Welding.

10.2 Springs

Spring elements are one-dimensional idealizations that are intended to simulate the various elastic components in your model without specifying their geometrical shape.

Springs in Creo Simulate can be linear (constant stiffness) or non-linear (deflection-dependent stiffness). Springs can connect one point to the ground (fixed) or connect two points.

> ***Note:*** *Non-linear springs require an Advanced Creo Simulate license.*

In the example shown in Figure 10–4 one spring connects two points (a point on the frame and the mass point) and a fixed to the ground spring supports the frame at the top.

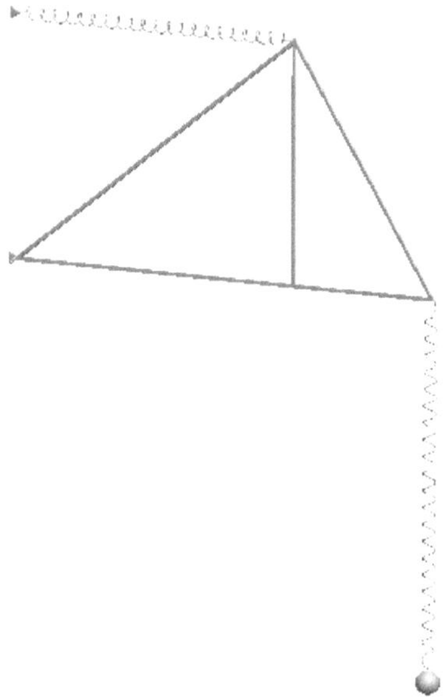

Figure 10–4

In Creo Simulate, you can create three types of springs: **Simple**, **Advanced**, and **To Ground**. Simple and Advanced springs can have any orientation, which is defined by selecting two points. To Ground springs are always parallel to a coordinate system, such as WCS.

> ***Note:*** *Advanced springs require an Advanced Creo Simulate license.*

In the *Idealizations* group, click (Spring). The *Spring Definition* dialog box opens, as shown in Figure 10–5.

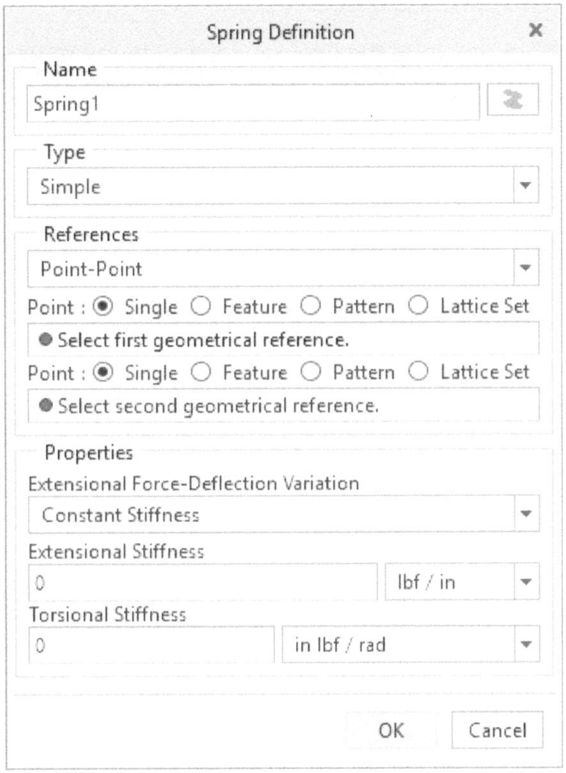

Figure 10–5

Note: You cannot create zero length simple springs.

The options in the *Spring Definition* dialog box are as follows:

Option	Description
Name	Enter the name of the spring or use the default name.
References	Selects geometry references. The following types of geometry references are available: **Point-Point**, **Point-Surface**, **Point-Edge**, and **Point-Point Pairs**.
Type	Selects the type of the spring. The following types of springs are available: **Simple**, **Advanced**, and **To Ground**.
Extensional Force-Deflection Variation	Selects a linear or non-linear spring: • Constant Stiffness (linear spring) • Force-Deflection Curve (non-linear spring)
Extensional Stiffness	Defines the extensional stiffness, (i.e., resistance to stretch) of your spring.
Torsional Stiffness	Defines torsional stiffness (i.e., resistance to twist) of your spring.

Stiffness

Simple springs only have two stiffness properties:

- **Extensional Stiffness:** Acting along the line connecting the two points.
- **Torsional Stiffness:** Acting about the line connecting the two points.

Advanced and To Ground springs require stiffness properties to be defined in the *Spring Properties Definition* dialog box, as shown in Figure 10–6.

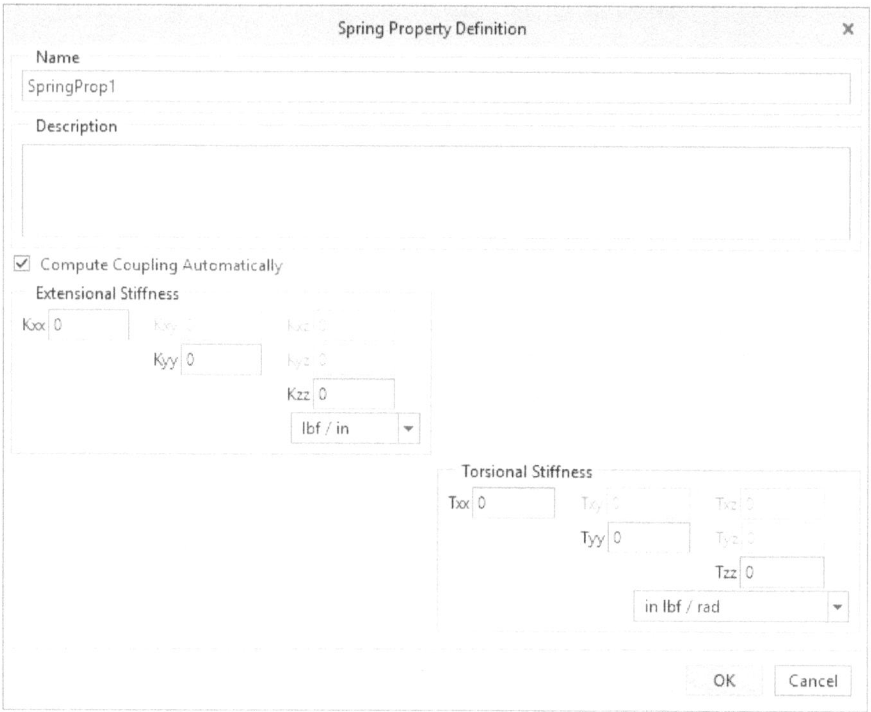

Figure 10–6

The options in the *Spring Properties Definition* dialog box are as follows:

Box	Description
Name	Enter the name of the spring stiffness.
Description	(Optional) Enter the description of the spring stiffness.
Compute Coupling Automatically	Clearing this option enables direct specification of coupling stiffness properties Kxy, Kyz, etc.
Extensional	Enter the stiffness for the principal axes in the *Kxx*, *Kyy*, and *Kzz* fields.
Torsional	Enter the stiffness for the rotation around the principal axes in the *Txx*, *Tyy*, and *Tzz* fields.

Orientation

The spring principal axes, used to specify K_{xx}, K_{yy}, etc. stiffness directions in the *Spring Properties Definition* dialog box, are defined as follows:

- **To Ground spring:** The principal axes are aligned with the axes of the selected coordinate system (the default is WCS).
- **Advanced spring:** The X-principal axis is always along the line between the two points, the Y-axis direction is specified by the user (as is done for Beam elements), and the Z-axis direction is obtained as a cross-product of X-axis by the Y-axis.

10.3 Masses

Mass elements are idealizations that are intended to simulate the mass properties of various components in your model, without specifying the component's geometrical shape. For example, a mass element might be used to simulate the weight of the engine attached to the truck frame, without actually specifying the engine's geometry.

> **Note:** *You can attach a mass to a solid, shell, or beam.*

Masses in Creo Simulate can be **Simple**, **Advanced**, or **Component At Point**. Simple masses only have translational inertia, while Advanced masses can be assigned rotational inertia (i.e., moments of inertia) as well. The **Component At Point** option uses the mass property definition of an assembly component for the mass idealization.

> **Note:** *Advanced masses require an Advanced Creo Simulate license.*

Use the following steps to create a mass:

1. In the *Idealizations* group, click (Mass). The *Mass Definition* dialog box opens, as shown in Figure 10–7.

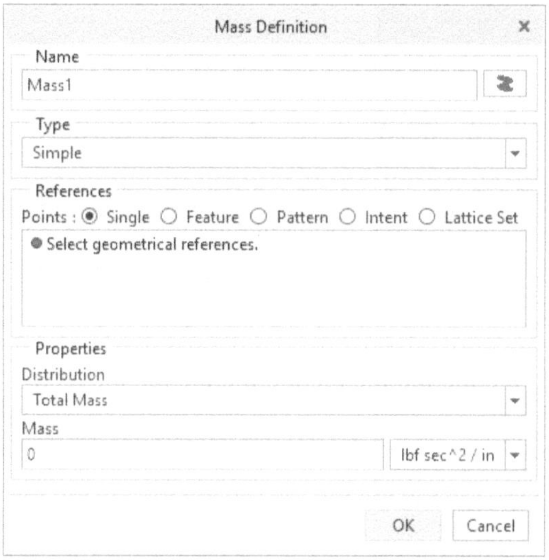

Figure 10–7

> **Note:** *Select* ***Advanced*** *in the Type drop-down list to create an advanced mass.*

2. Enter the *Name*.
3. Expand the *Type* drop-down list and select **Simple** or **Advanced**.
4. Select the *References* (datum points).
5. Select the *Distribution* (**Total Mass** or **Mass Per Point**).
6. Enter the mass value.

Practice 10a
Spot Welds

Practice Objectives

- Create spot weld connections.
- Set up a spot welded FEA model analysis.
- Display the results of the analysis.

In this practice, you will set up and run a spot welded model using the **Spot Weld** option. The assembly model is shown in Figure 10–8. The assembly model consists of four parts. You will use shell idealizations to model the parts.

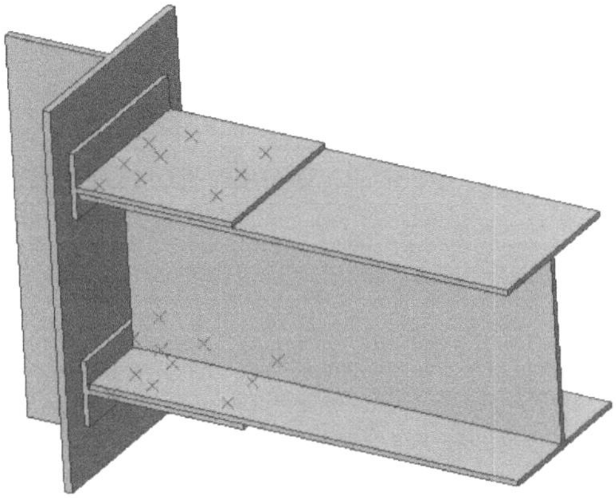

Figure 10–8

> ***Note:*** *Use the* ***Spot Weld*** *option for the small bolts, screws, and rivets in your model, and for the spot welds.*

Modeling Tasks

Task 1: Open the assembly.

1. Set the working directory to **Chapter10**.
2. Open **spot_weld.asm**.
3. Set the model display as follows:
   - *(Datum Display Filters)*: (Point Display)
   - *(Spin Center)*: Off
   - *(Display Style)*: (Shading With Edges)

The model displays as shown in Figure 10–9.

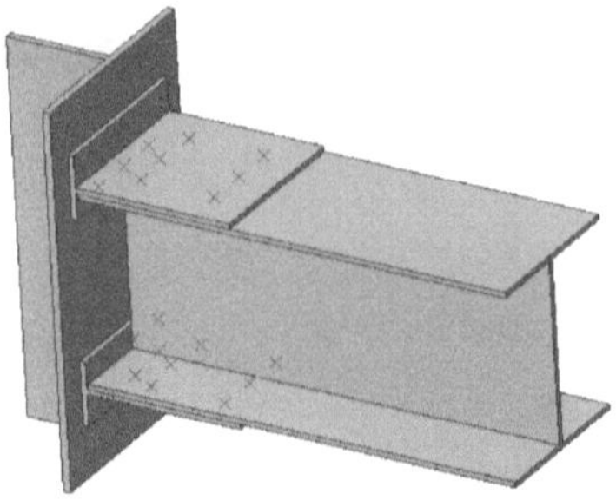

Figure 10–9

4. Ensure that the unit system is set to **mmNs**.

Task 2: Launch Creo Simulate.

1. Select **Applications>Simulate** to launch Creo Simulate.
2. Click (Simulation Display) and clear the **Display AutoGEM Controls** option to unclutter the display.
3. Click (Model Setup). Expand the *Default Interface* drop-down list and select **Free** as shown in Figure 10–10.

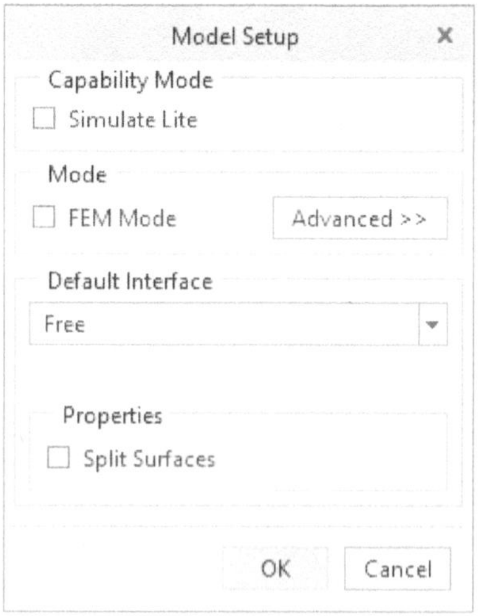

Figure 10–10

Note: *The Free Default Interface ensures that the parts are not bonded over the mated surfaces. Rather, you will connect the parts with spot welds.*

4. Click **OK**.

Task 3: Define shell pairs.

1. In the *Refine Model* tab, expand (Shell Pair) and select **Detect Shell Pairs**. The *Auto Detect Shell Pairs* dialog box opens, as shown in Figure 10–11.

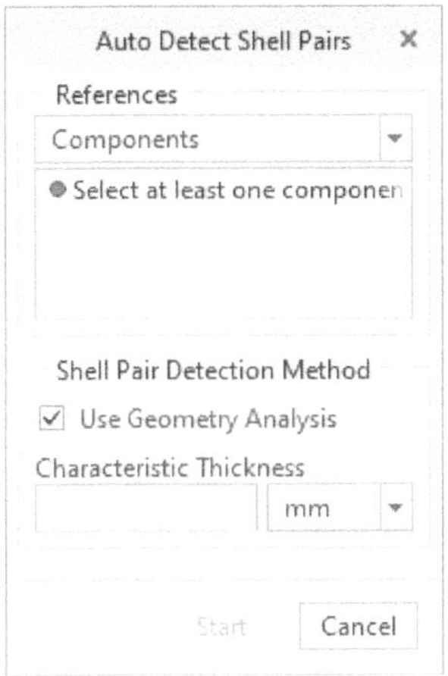

Figure 10–11

2. Select all four parts in the assembly (hold <Ctrl> to multi-select).
3. In the *Characteristic Thickness* field, enter **8**. The *Auto Detect Shell Pairs* dialog box displays as shown in Figure 10–12.

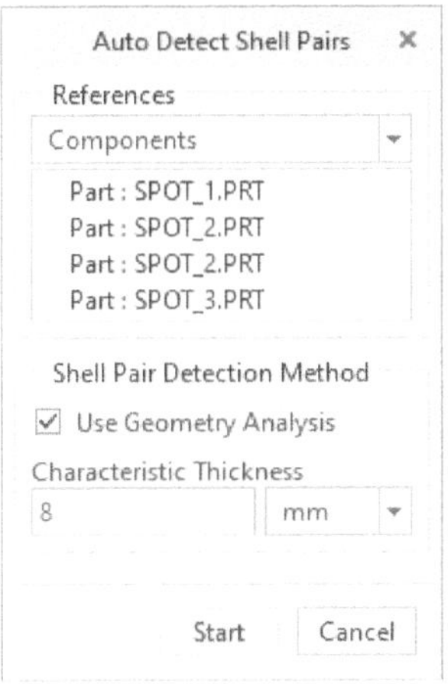

Figure 10–12

Note: *The thickness of the parts in the assembly is* ***5mm****. Using a Characteristic Thickness greater than 5mm ensures that all of the parts are compressed to mid-surfaces.*

4. Click **Start**. Creo Simulate runs the automatic detection algorithm and closes the *Auto Detect Shell Pairs* dialog box.
5. Check the *Model Tree*. There should be nine shell pairs in the *Idealizations* section of the *Model Tree* on the assembly level.
6. In the *Refine Model* tab, in the *AutoGEM* group, click (Review Geometry) to open the *Simulation Geometry* dialog box.
7. Accept the default options and click **Apply**. The model displays as shown in Figure 10–13. Ensure that all of the surfaces are highlighted in green, and that no elements in the model display in a different color.

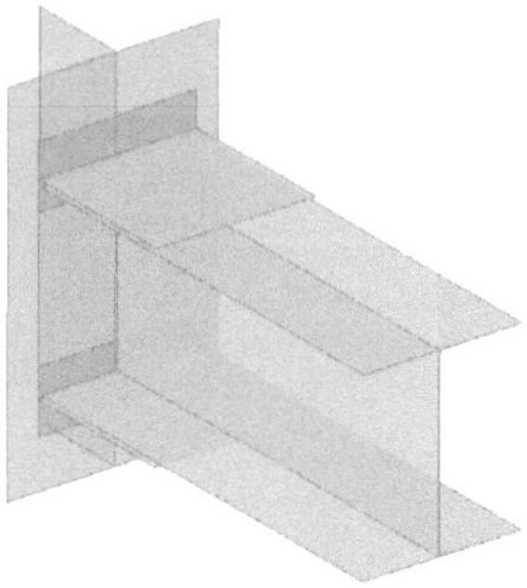

Figure 10–13

8. Click **Close** to close the *Simulation Geometry* dialog box.

Task 4: Apply the material.

1. Assign **STEEL** to the assembly parts as the material. The following values are the default material properties for HS-low-alloy steel (STEEL):
   - *Poisson:* **0.27**
   - *Young's modulus:* **199948 MPa**
   - *Density:* **7.82708e-9 tonne/mm3**

   Note: *The model's material properties should be as stated.*

2. Using the *Simulation Display* dialog box, hide the **Material Assignments** icons.

Task 5: Create spot weld connections.

In this task, you will connect the plates using the **Spot Weld** option.

1. In the *Connections* group of the *Refine Model* tab, click (Weld). The *Weld Definition* dialog box opens.
2. Expand the *Type* drop-down list and select **Spot Weld**.

3. Select the surfaces shown in Figure 10–14 as the *References* for the weld.

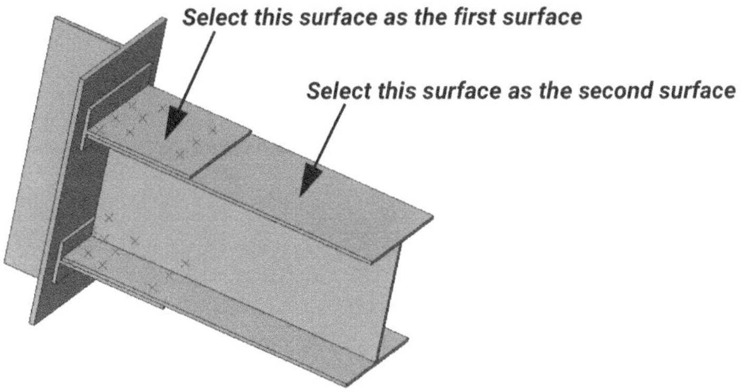

Figure 10–14

4. In the *Properties* area, select **Feature** option and select **PNT0**. Six points (**PNT0** to **PNT5**) are highlighted, since they were created as one feature in Creo Parametric.
5. For the diameter, enter **10**.
6. For the weld material, select **STEEL**. The *Weld Definition* dialog box displays as shown in Figure 10–15.

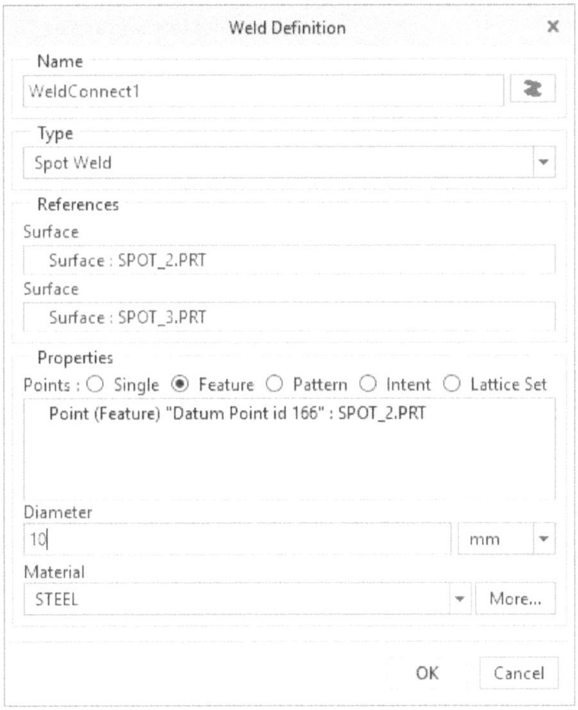

Figure 10–15

7. Click **OK** to close the *Weld Definition* dialog box. **Spot Weld** icons display as shown in Figure 10–16.
8. Repeat Steps 1 to 7 for the other side as shown in Figure 10–16.

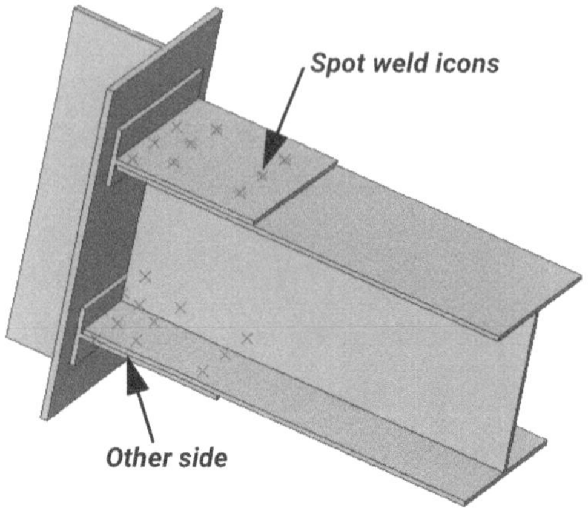

Figure 10–16

9. Repeat Steps 1 to 7 to create spot welds between the surfaces shown in Figure 10–17. Select **PNT6** when selecting the datum point feature.

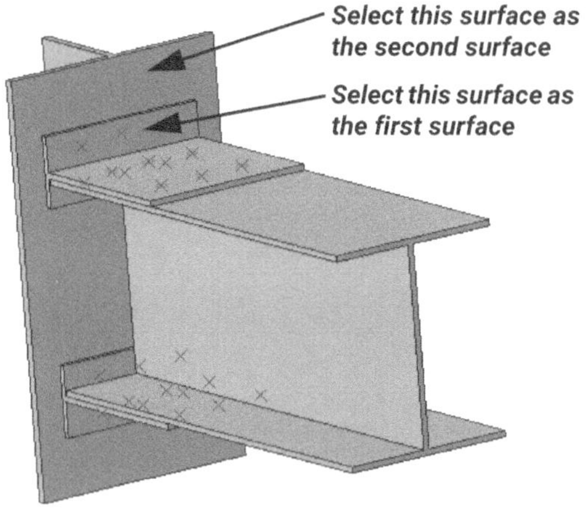

Figure 10–17

10. Repeat Steps 1 to 7 for the other side as shown in Figure 10–18.

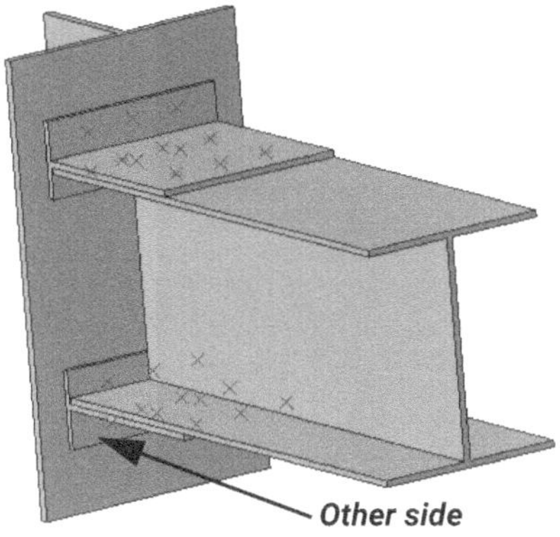

Figure 10–18

Task 6: Mesh the model.

1. Click (AutoGEM) to open the *AutoGEM* dialog box. Accept **All with Properties** and click **Create**.
2. Close the *AutoGEM Summary and Diagnostics* dialog boxes when the meshing finishes. The model displays as shown in Figure 10–19.

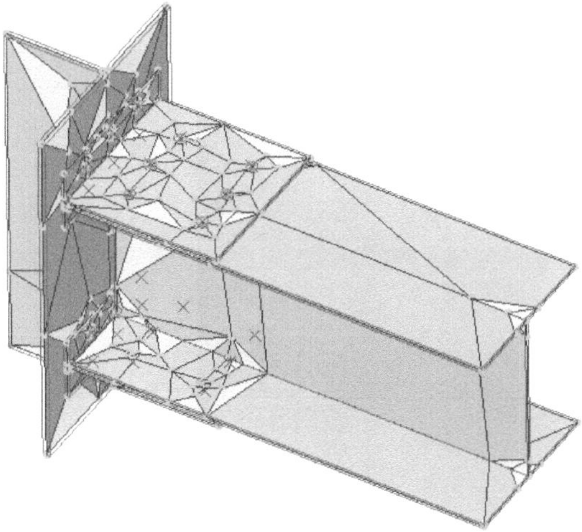

Figure 10–19

3. Zoom in on any spot weld in the model, such as the one shown in Figure 10–20.

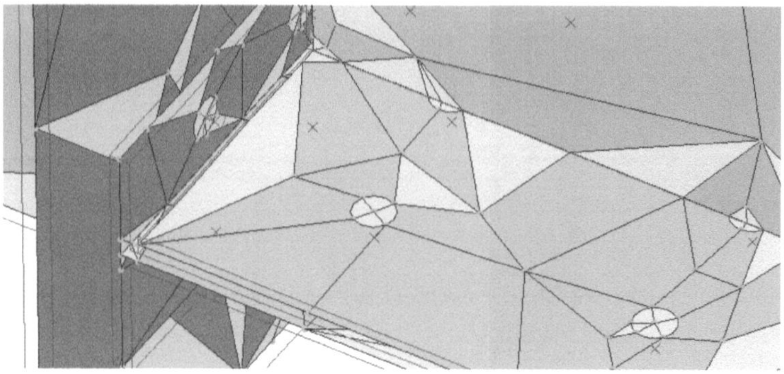

Figure 10–20

Note the small circular regions Creo Simulate created around each spot weld. The diameter of each region is the spot weld diameter that you entered in the *Weld Definition* dialog box.

4. Display the **FRONT** orientation and zoom in on the model to examine the gaps between the midsurfaces, such as those shown in Figure 10–21.

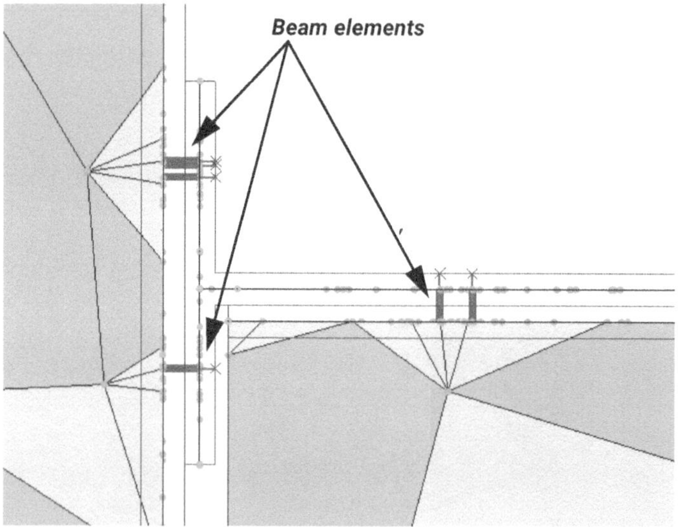

Figure 10–21

Note the beam elements (purple lines) between the parts. These are the elements that Creo Simulate automatically created to connect the midsurfaces at the spot weld points.

5. Close the *AutoGEM* dialog box and save the mesh.

Task 7: Apply loads.

1. In the Z-direction, apply a load of **1000** on the edges (apply it to the edges rather than to the end surface) as shown in Figure 10–22. For the name of the load, enter **edge_load**.

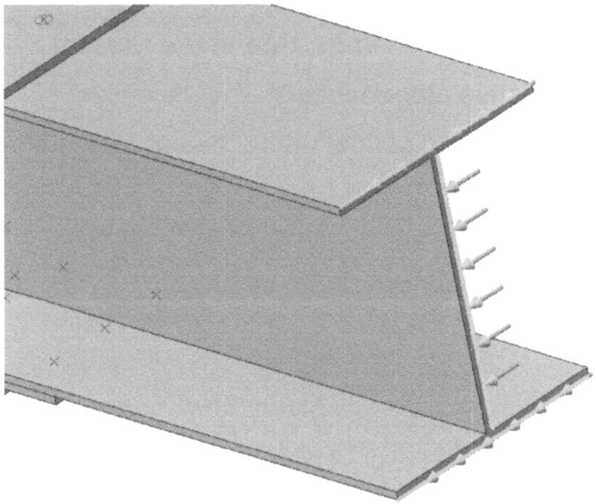

Figure 10–22

Task 8: Apply the constraints.

1. Constrain the T-beam edges (fixed all translations) as shown in Figure 10–23 (constrain the edges rather than the end surfaces). For the name of the constraint, enter **edge_constraints**.

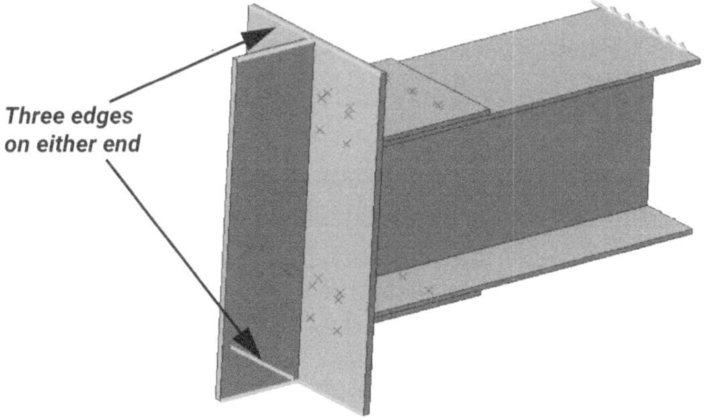

Figure 10–23

Analysis Tasks

Task 9: Set up and run an analysis.

1. Set up a Multi-Pass Adaptive static analysis. For the *Name*, enter **spot_weld**. In the *Polynomial Order* field, enter **9**. In the *Limits* area, in the *Percent Convergence* field, enter **10**.
2. Run the analysis with interactive diagnostics.
3. Expand the *Run Status* window and review the following information shown in Figure 10–24:
   - Analysis converges on pass seven.
   - Stress error is 1.6% of the maximum principal stress.

```
          RMS Stress Error Estimates:

          Load Set          Stress Error  % of Max Prin Str
          ----------------  ------------  -----------------
          LoadSet1            2.34e+00       1.6% of  1.49e+02

          Resource Check                                (18:05:31)
             Elapsed Time      (sec):         8.69
             CPU Time          (sec):        10.44
             Memory Usage       (kb):       351683
             Wrk Dir Dsk Usage  (kb):        52242

    The analysis converged to within 10% on
    edge displacement, element strain energy,
    and global RMS stress.
```

Figure 10–24

Results Tasks

Task 10: Display the results.

In this task, you will create and display a von Mises stress fringe plot and a deformation animation for the model to verify the applied boundary conditions.

1. Create the Displacement Magnitude animation plot. Ensure that the **Deformed**, **Overlay Undeformed** and **Animate** options are selected.
2. Start the animation.
   - Do the applied boundary conditions behave correctly?
3. Stop the animation on Frame 5. The result plot displays as shown in Figure 10–25.

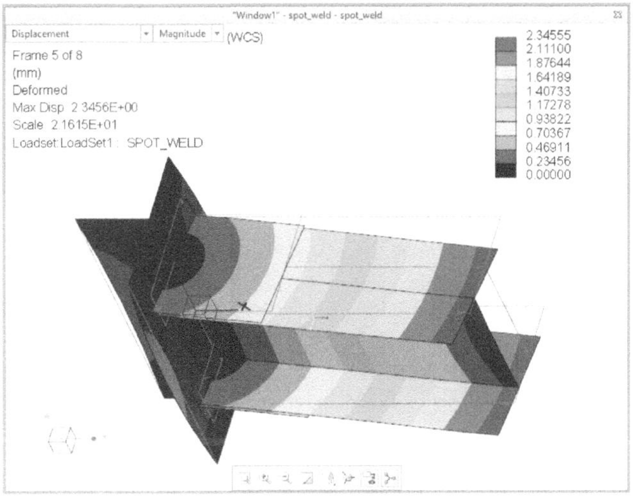

Figure 10–25

4. Create the undeformed von Mises stress fringe plot. Clear all of the **Include contributions from beams** options. In the **Include contributions from shells** group, select **Top and Bottom** in the pull-down list. Change the *Legend minimum* to **0** and *maximum* to **60**. The result plot displays as shown in Figure 10–26.

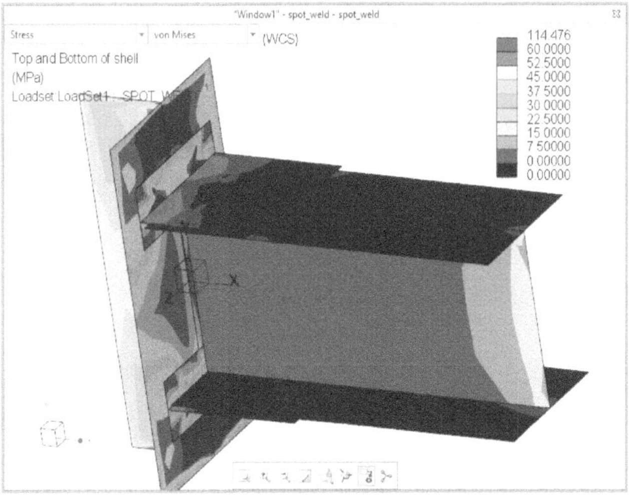

Figure 10–26

5. Locate and examine high stress areas in the model, particularly the welds and the adjacent areas. If a high stress area is located at the weld, a more detailed analysis should be performed, such as using the 3D solid model type.
6. Exit the Results environment. Save and close the model.

End of practice

Practice 10b
Perimeter Welds

Practice Objectives

- Create Perimeter Weld connections.
- Set up a continuous welded FEA model analysis.
- Display the results.

In this practice, you will set up and run a continuously welded model, using the **Perimeter Weld** option. The assembly model is shown in Figure 10–27. It consists of a beam plate and a hook plate.

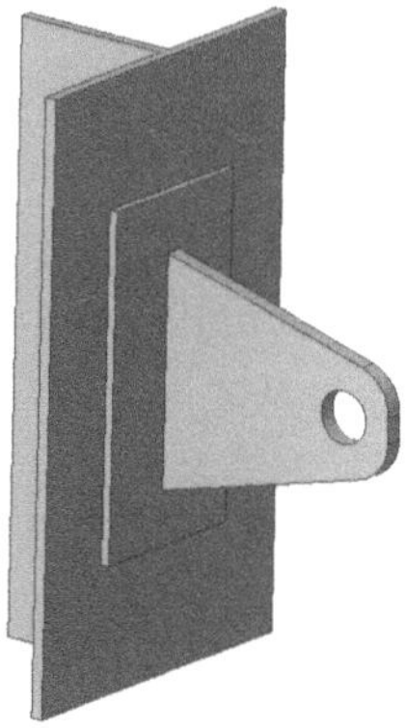

Figure 10–27

__Note:__ Use the __Perimeter Weld__ option to connect parallel plates.

Modeling Tasks

Task 1: Open the model.

1. Set the working directory to **Chapter10**, if required.
2. Open **weld_1.asm**.
3. Set the model display as follows:
    - *(Datum Display Filters)*: All Off
    - *(Spin Center)*: Off
    - *(Display Style)*: (Shading With Edges)

The assembly displays as shown in Figure 10–28.

Figure 10–28

Task 2: Launch Creo Simulate.

1. Select **Applications>Simulate** to launch Creo Simulate.
2. Click (Model Setup). Expand the *Default Interface* drop-down list and select **Free**, as shown in Figure 10–29.

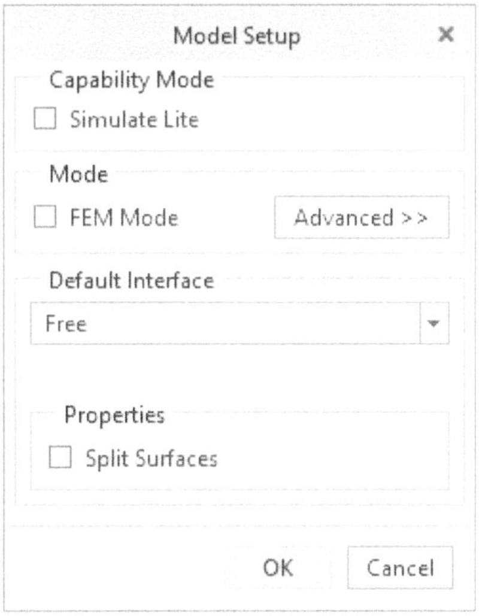

Figure 10–29

Note: *The Free Default Interface ensures that the parts are not bonded over the mated surfaces. Rather, you will use the perimeter weld to connect them.*

3. Click **OK**.

Task 3: Define the shell pairs.

1. In the *Refine Model* tab, expand the (Shell Pair) drop-down list and select **Detect Shell Pairs**. The *Auto Detect Shell Pairs* dialog box opens, as shown in Figure 10–30.

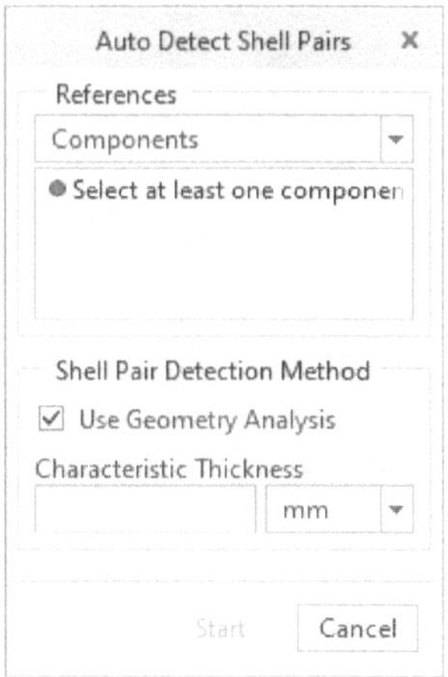

Figure 10–30

2. Select all of the parts in the assembly (hold <Ctrl> to multi-select).
3. In the *Characteristic Thickness* field, enter **10**. The *Auto Detect Shell Pairs* dialog box displays as shown in Figure 10–31.

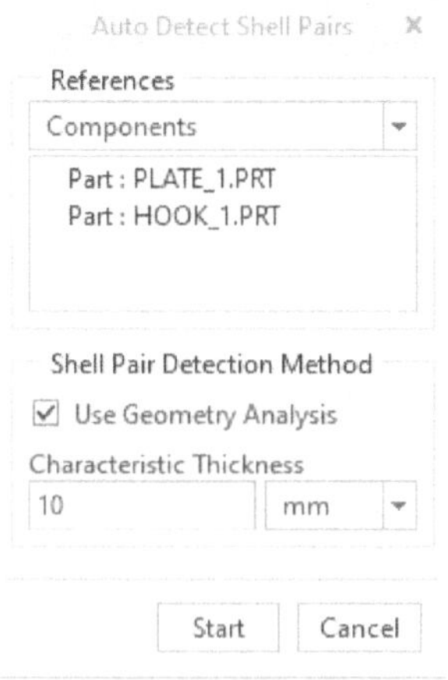

Figure 10–31

Note: *The thickest part in the assembly is 10mm.*

4. Click **Start**. Creo Simulate runs the automatic detection algorithm and closes the *Auto Detect Shell Pairs* dialog box.

5. There should be four shell pairs in the **Idealizations** node of the *Model Tree*.
6. In the *Refine Model* tab, in the *AutoGEM* area, click (Review Geometry) to open the *Simulation Geometry* dialog box.
7. Accept the default options and click **Apply**. The model displays as shown in Figure 10–32. Ensure that all of the surfaces are highlighted in green, and that no elements in the model display in different colors.

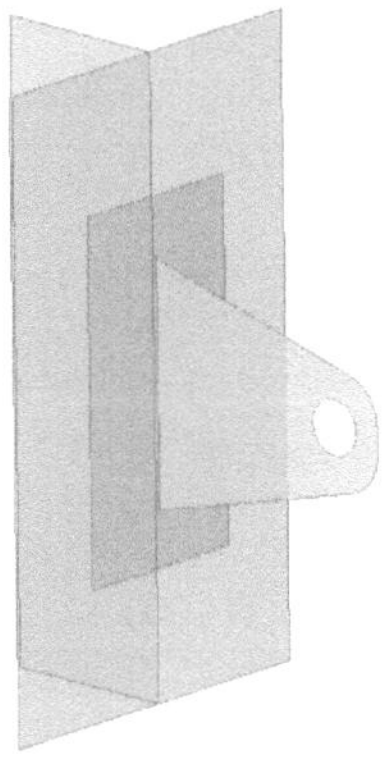

Figure 10–32

8. Click **Close** to close the *Simulation Geometry* dialog box.

Task 4: Apply the material.

1. Assign **STEEL** as the material to the assembly parts. The following values are the default material properties for HS-low-alloy steel (STEEL):
   - *Poisson:* **0.27**
   - *Young's modulus:* **199948 MPa**
   - *Density:* **7.82708e-9 tonne/mm3**

   Note: *The model's material properties should be as stated.*

2. Toggle off the display of **Material Assignments**.

Task 5: Create the weld connections.

In this task, you will connect the two plates using the **Perimeter Weld** option.

Note: *For perpendicular plates, use the* ***End Weld*** *option.*

1. In the *Connections* area in the *Refine Model* tab, click (Weld). The *Weld Definition* dialog box opens.
2. Expand the *Type* drop-down list and select **Perimeter Weld**.

3. Select the top surface of **hook_1** as the doubler surface, as shown in Figure 10–33.

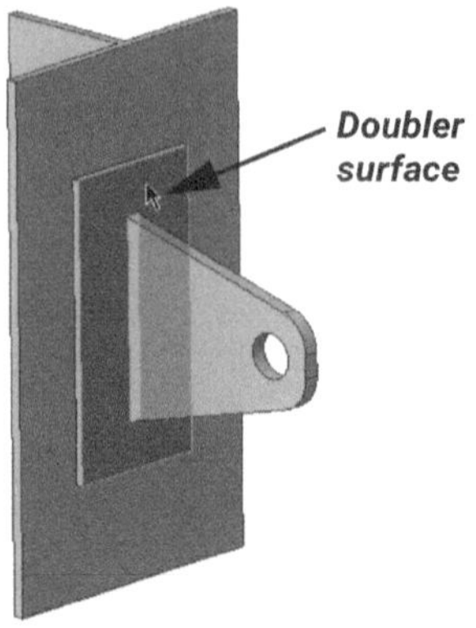

Figure 10–33

4. Select the **plate_1** top surface as the base surface, as shown in Figure 10–34.

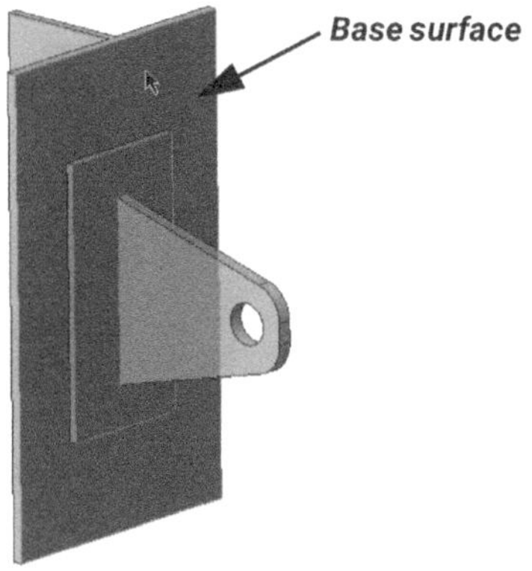

Figure 10–34

5. Select the four edges of the **hook top** surface as the edges of the doubler to define the weld location, as shown in Figure 10–35. Hold <Ctrl> to select all four edges.

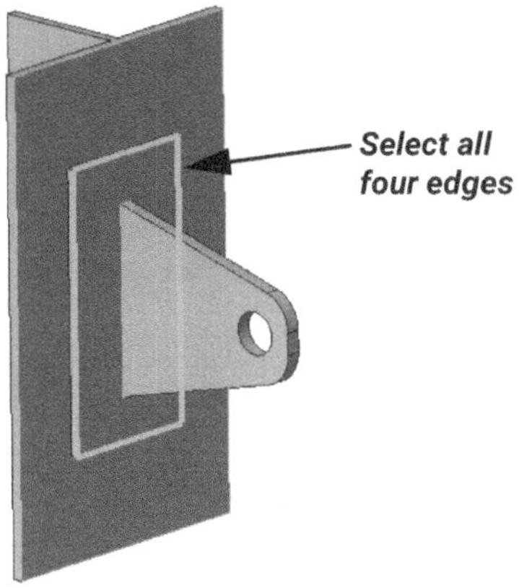

Figure 10–35

6. The thickness of the doubler plate is 7mm. To use the same thickness for the thickness of the weld, enter **7.00**.
7. Accept the default *Material*. The *Weld Definition* dialog box displays as shown in Figure 10–36.

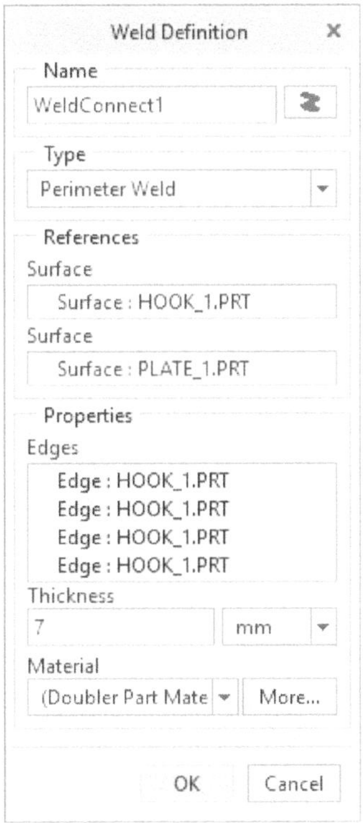

Figure 10–36

8. Click **OK** to finish. Highlight the **Connections** heading in the *Model Tree*. The **Perimeter Weld** icon displays as shown in Figure 10–37.

Figure 10–37

Task 6: Mesh the model.

1. Click (AutoGEM) to open the *AutoGEM* dialog box. Accept **All with Properties** and click **Create**.
2. Close the *AutoGEM Summary and Diagnostics* dialog boxes when the meshing finishes. The model displays as shown in Figure 10–38.

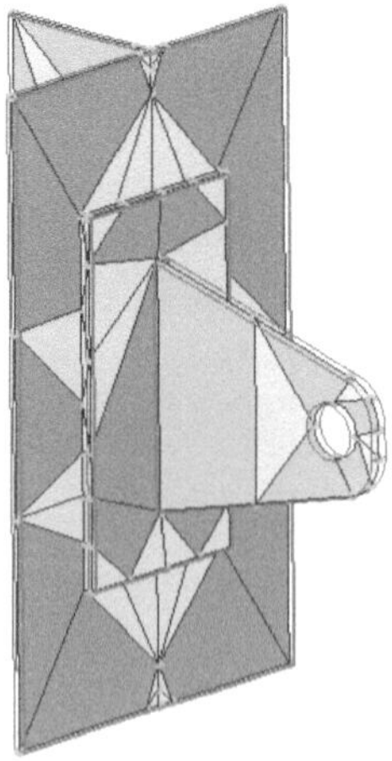

Figure 10–38

3. Zoom in on any perimeter weld area in the model, such as shown in Figure 10–39.

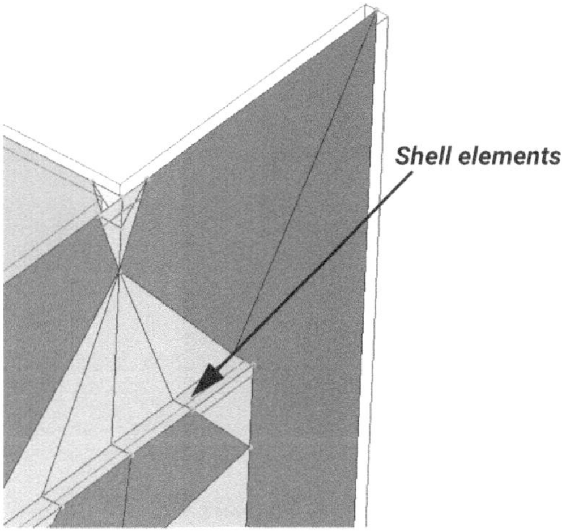

Figure 10–39

Note the shell elements that extend from the hook part edges to the base plate part. These are the elements that Creo Simulate automatically created to simulate the perimeter weld.

4. Close the *AutoGEM* dialog box and save the mesh.

Task 7: Apply the loads.

1. Apply a force of **-8000** in the WCS's Y-direction to the hook's hole edge, as shown in Figure 10–40. For the name of the force, enter **hook_force**.

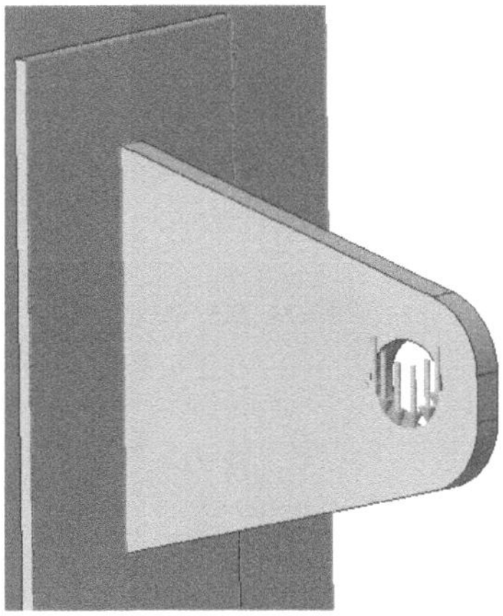

Figure 10–40

Task 8: Apply the constraints.

1. Constrain the edges of **plate_1** (fixed all translations), as shown in Figure 10–41.

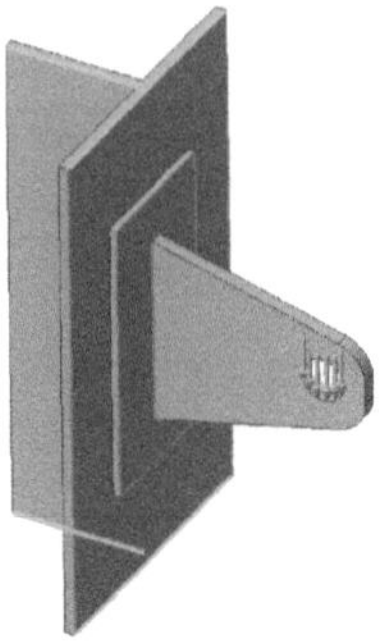

Figure 10–41

Analysis Tasks

Task 9: Set up and run an analysis.

1. Set up a Single-Pass Adaptive static analysis. For the name of the analysis, enter **weld_1**.
2. Run the analysis using interactive diagnostics.
3. Expand the *Run Status* window and review the results:
   - The RMS Stress error is 11.6% of the maximum principal stress, as shown in Figure 10–42.

```
RMS Stress Error Estimates:

Load Set          Stress Error  % of Max Prin Str
----------------- ------------  -----------------
LoadSet1           6.69e+01      11.6% of  5.79e+02
```

Figure 10–42

Results Tasks

Task 10: Display the results.

In this task, you will create and display a von Mises stress fringe plot and deformation animation for the model. This verifies the applied boundary conditions.

1. Create the Displacement Magnitude animation plot. Ensure that the **Deformed**, **Overlay Undeformed** and **Animate** options are selected.

2. Stop the animation on Frame 5. The result plot displays as shown in Figure 10–43.

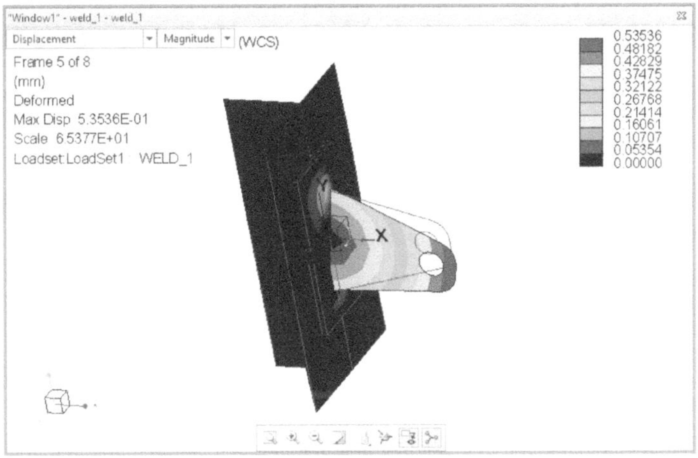

Figure 10–43

3. Create the deformed von Mises stress fringe plot shown in Figure 10–44.

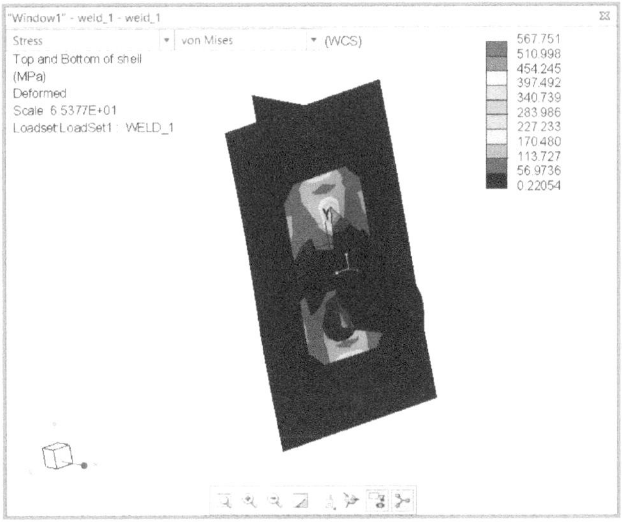

Figure 10–44

4. Locate and examine the high stress areas in the model, particularly the welds and the adjacent areas. If a high stress area is located at the weld, a more detailed analysis should be performed, such as using the 3D solid model type.
5. Exit the Results environment. Save and close the model.

End of practice

Practice 10c
Springs and Masses Analysis

Practice Objectives

- Create beam elements.
- Create spring elements.
- Create mass elements.
- Set up, run, and analyze an FEA model using masses and spring idealizations.
- Display the results.

In this practice, you will use spring and mass idealizations to set up and run an analysis on the model shown in Figure 10–45. The model is composed of beams and two springs. The ends of one beam and one spring are fixed, as shown in Figure 10–45. The beam joints are rigid. A mass is supported by another spring. The only load on the system is due to gravity. You will define three user-defined displacement point measures to determine the displacement of the frame at these points.

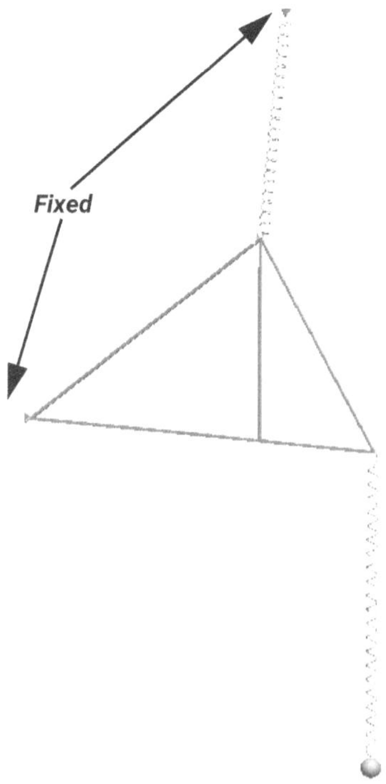

Figure 10–45

The FEA model is shown in Figure 10–46.

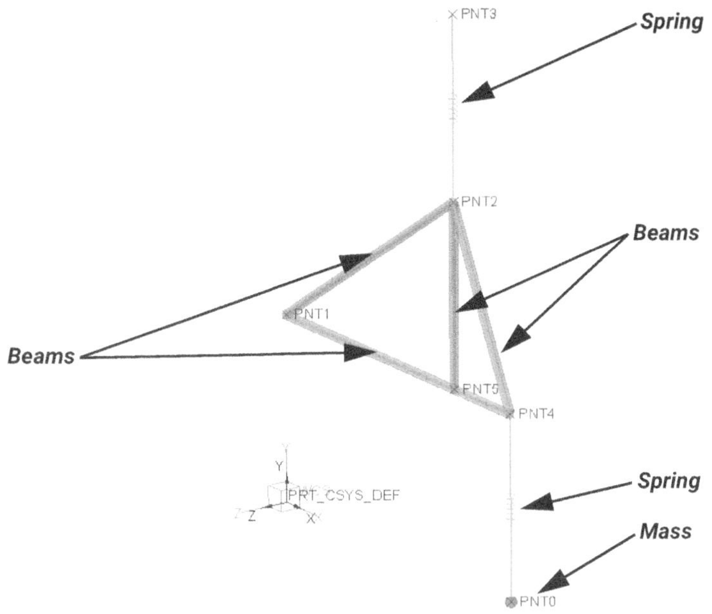

Figure 10–46

Modeling Tasks

Task 1: Open the model.

1. Set the working directory to **Chapter10**, if required.
2. Open **frame_1.prt**.
3. Set the model display as follows:
    - *(Datum Display Filters)*: (Point Display), (Csys Display)
    - *(Spin Center)*: Off
    - *(Display Style)*: (Shading With Edges)
4. In the *View* tab of the ribbon, in the *Show* group, click (Point Tag Display).

The part displays as shown in Figure 10–47.

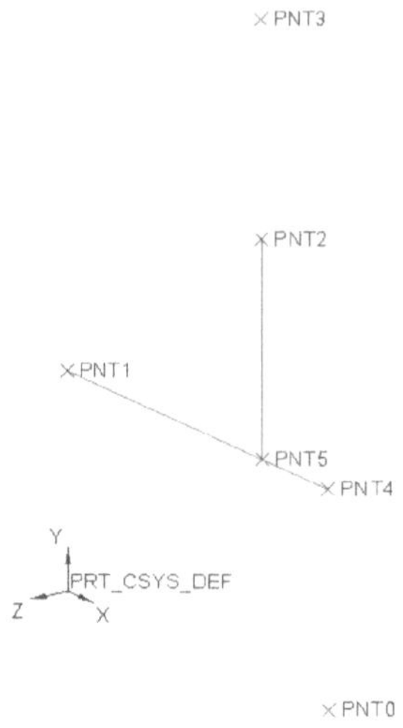

Figure 10–47

5. Ensure the unit system is set to **IPS**.
6. Select **Applications>Simulate** to launch Creo Simulate.

Task 2: Create three beam elements on datum curves.

1. In the *Refine Model* tab, click (Beam). The *Beam Definition* dialog box opens.
2. In the *Name* field, enter **beam_curves**.
3. Select the curves shown in Figure 10–48.

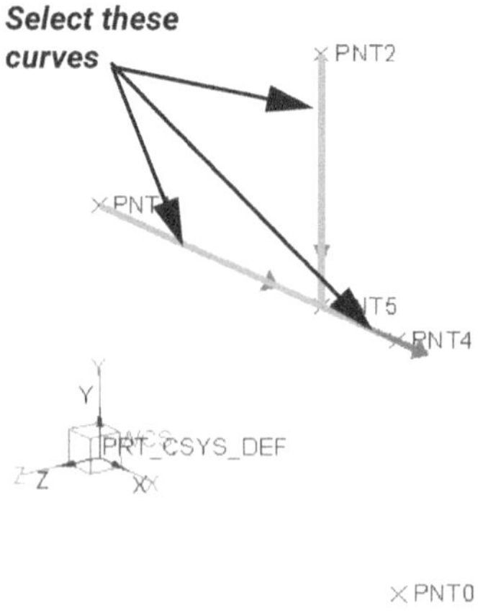

Figure 10–48

4. Assign **STEEL** as the material to the beams. The following values are the default material properties for HS-low-alloy steel (STEEL):
   - *Poisson:* **0.27**
   - *Young's modulus:* **2.9e7 psi**
   - *Density:* **0.0007324 lbf sec^2 /in^4**
5. In the *Orientation* area, in the *X* field, enter **0**, in the *Y* field, enter **0**, and in the *Z* field, enter **1**.
6. Next to the *Beam Section* drop-down list, click **More**. In the *Beam Sections* dialog box, click **New**. The *Beam Section Definition* dialog box opens.
7. For the name of the section, enter **hollow_section**.
8. For the beam section, assign the **Hollow Circle**.
9. For the external radius, enter **0.5** and for the internal radius, enter **0.2**.
10. Return to the *Beam Definition* dialog box.
11. Click **OK** to create the beams. The model displays as shown in Figure 10–49.

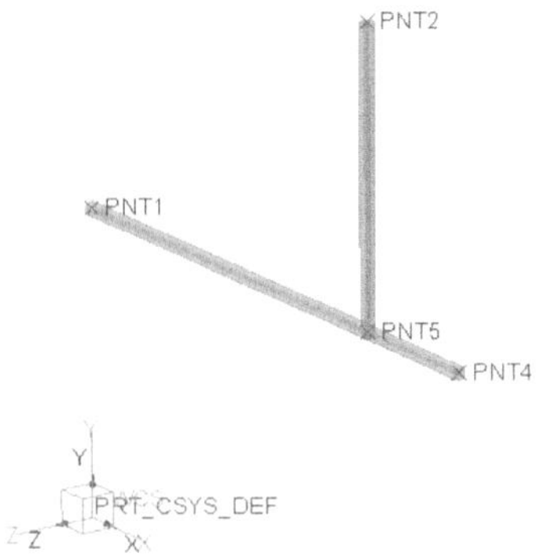

Figure 10–49

Task 3: Create two beam elements on datum points.

1. Click (Beam). The *Beam Definition* dialog box opens.
2. In the *Name* field, enter **beam1_2**.
3. Expand the *References* drop-down list and select **Point-Point**.
4. Select **PNT1** and **PNT2**.
5. For the material for the beam, select **STEEL**.
6. In the *Y Direction* area, in the *X* field, enter **0**, in the *Y* field, enter **0**, and in the *Z* field, enter **1**.
7. Accept the default **hollow_section** beam section.

8. Click **OK** to create the beam. The model displays as shown in Figure 10–50.

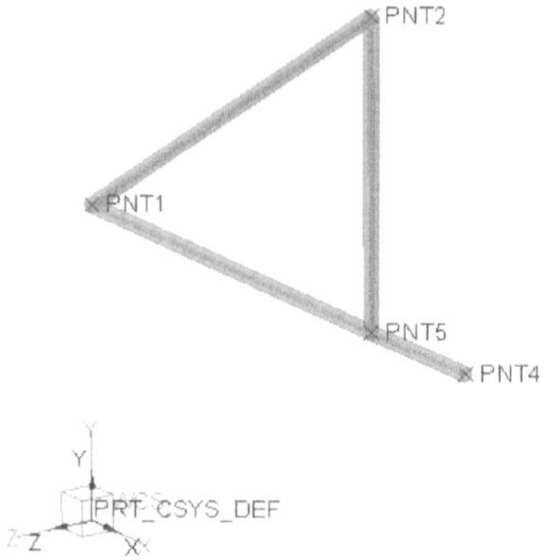

Figure 10–50

9. Repeat Steps 1 to 8 to create a beam element between **PNT2** and **PNT4**. For the name of the beam, enter **beam2_4**. The model displays as shown in Figure 10–51.

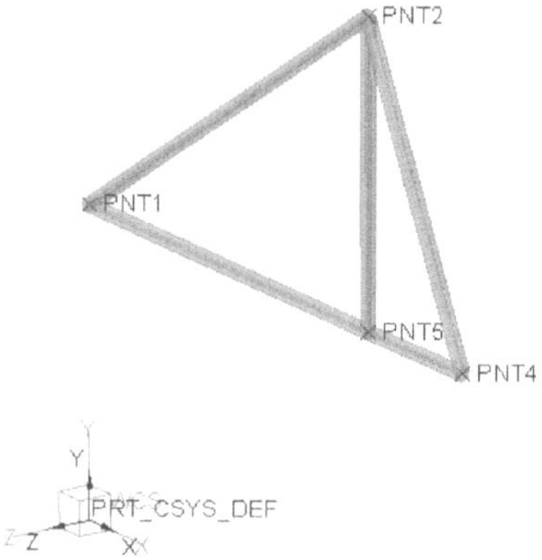

Figure 10–51

Task 4: Create the spring elements.

In this task, you will create two spring elements: one between **PNT2** and **PNT3** and another between **PNT0** and **PNT4**.

1. In the *Idealizations* group, click (Spring). The *Spring Definition* dialog box opens, as shown in Figure 10–52.

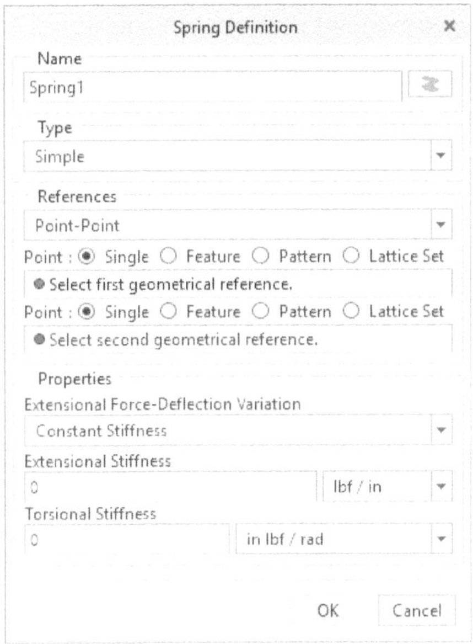

Figure 10–52

2. In the *Name* field, enter **Spring2_3**.
3. Accept the default **References** option.
4. Select **PNT2** and **PNT3**.
5. In the *Extensional Stiffness* field, enter **2500**.
6. Click **OK** in the *Spring Definition* dialog box. A **Spring** icon displays between **PNT2** and **PNT3**, as shown in Figure 10–53.

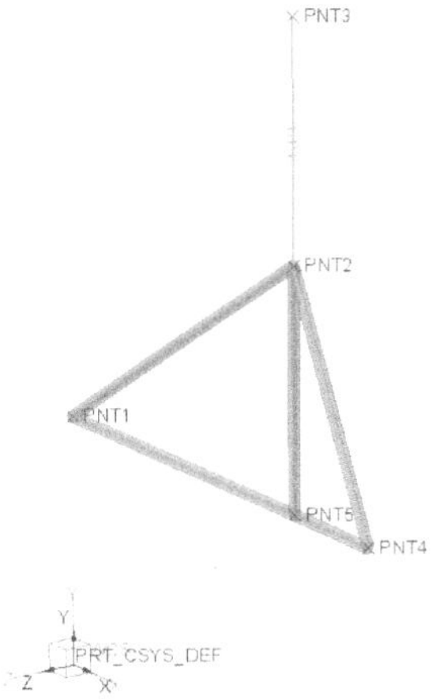

Figure 10–53

7. In the *Idealizations* group, click (Spring). The *Spring Definition* dialog box opens.
8. In the *Name* field, enter **Spring0_4**.
9. Expand the *References* drop-down list and accept the default option.
10. Select the **PNT0** and **PNT4**.
11. In the *Extensional Stiffness* field, enter **1500**.
12. Click **OK** in the *Spring Definition* dialog box. A **Spring** icon displays between **PNT0** and **PNT4**, as shown in Figure 10–54.

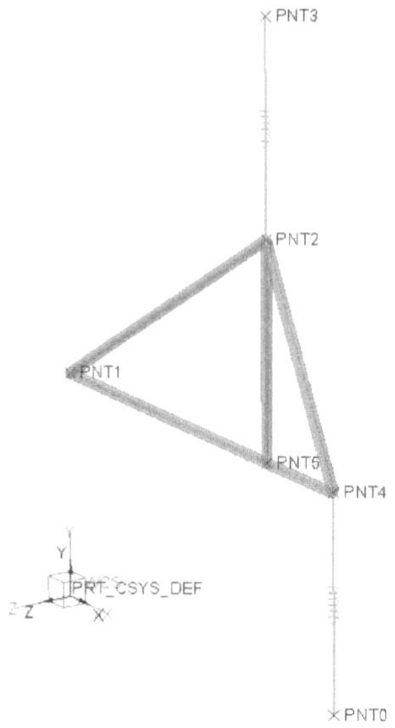

Figure 10–54

Task 5: Create the mass element on PNT0.

1. In the *Idealizations* area, click (Mass). The *Mass Definition* dialog box opens, as shown in Figure 10–55.

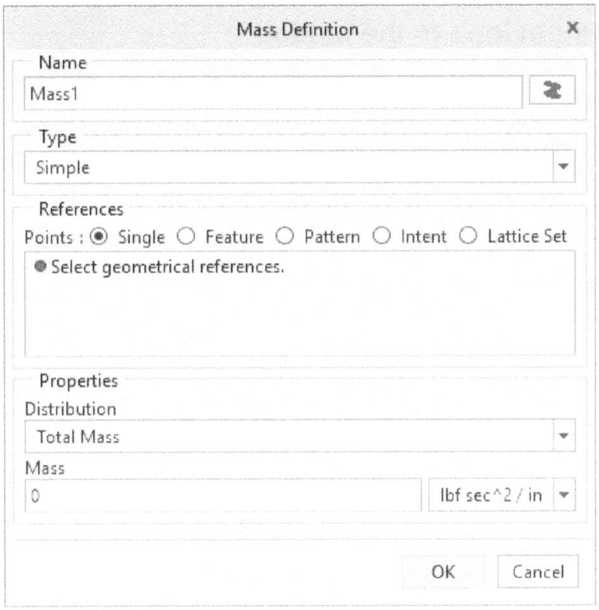

Figure 10–55

2. In the *Name* field, enter **mass_1**.
3. Select **PNT0**.
4. In the *Mass* field, enter **10**.
5. Click **OK**. The **Mass** icon displays at **PNT0**, as shown in Figure 10–56.

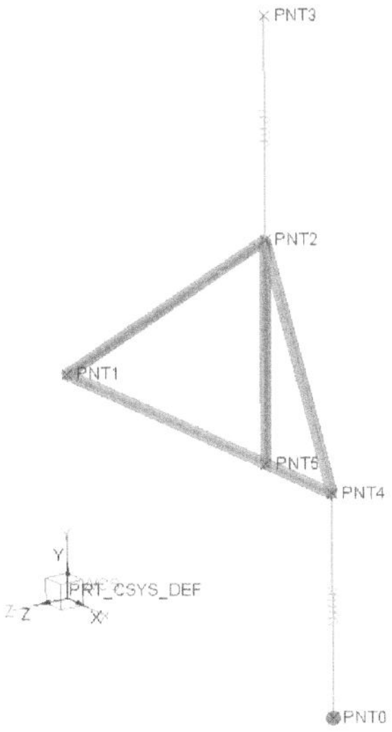

Figure 10–56

Task 6: Apply the weight load to the model.

1. In the *Home* tab, click (Gravity). The *Gravity* dialog box opens.
2. In the *Name* field, enter **gravity**.
3. For *Member of Set*, accept the default **LoadSet1** option.
4. In the dialog box, in the *Acceleration* area, in the *Y* field, enter **-386**.

   *Note: 1G of acceleration is **386 in/sec^2**.*

5. Click **OK** to finish defining the gravity load. The model displays as shown in Figure 10–57.

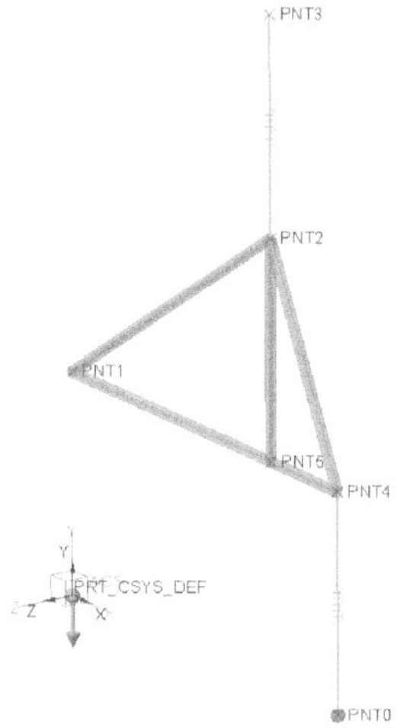

Figure 10–57

Task 7: Apply the constraints.

In this task, you will apply the constraints to **PNT3**, **PNT1**, and **PNT0**.

Note: The beams are cantilevered out from a wall.

1. For the name of the constraint for **PNT3** and **PNT1**, enter **const1**. Fix all of the translation and rotations.
2. For the name of the constraint for **PNT0**, enter **const2**. Leave translation in the Y-direction free, and constrain all other translations and rotations. This way, the point only moves in the Y-direction. The model displays as shown in Figure 10–58.

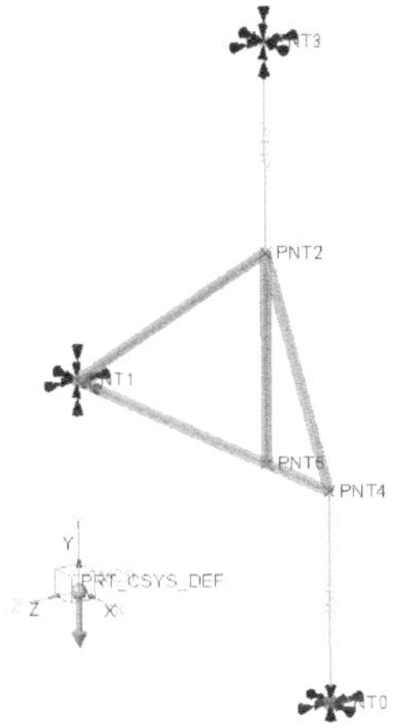

Figure 10–58

Task 8: Define the measures.

1. In the *Home* tab, click (Measures). In the *Measures* dialog box that opens, click **New**. The *Measure Definition* dialog box opens, as shown in Figure 10–59.

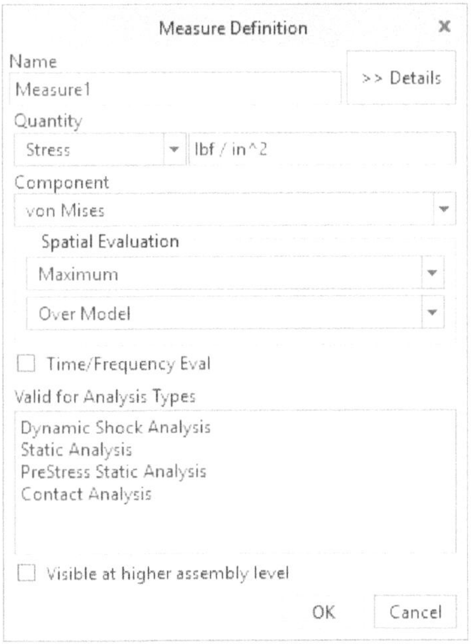

Figure 10–59

2. Name the measure **PNT0**.

3. Select **Displacement** in the *Quantity* drop-down list, and then select **Y** in the *Component* drop-down list.
4. Select **At Point** in the *Spatial Evaluation* drop-down list. Click (Select) and then select datum point **PNT0**. The *Measure Definition* dialog box displays as shown in Figure 10–60.

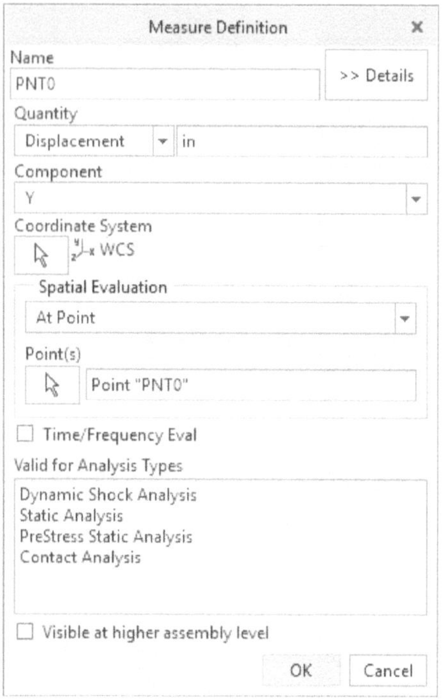

Figure 10–60

5. Click **OK** to complete the measure.
6. Repeat Steps 1 through 5 to create displacement measures in the Y-direction for datum points **PNT2** and **PNT4**. Name the measures **PNT2** and **PNT4**.

Summary

In the previous tasks, you created the simulation entities required to analyze your model. In the following tasks, you will set the analysis type and the convergence method and run the analysis.

Analysis Tasks

Task 9: Set up and run an analysis.

1. Set up a Multi-Pass Adaptive static analysis. In the *Polynomial Order* field, enter **9** and in the *Limits* area, in the *Percent Convergence* field, enter **10**.
2. For the name of the analysis, enter **frame**.

3. Run the analysis using interactive diagnostics.
4. Extract the following information from the *Run Status* window:
   - The pass number on which the analysis converged.
   - The values obtained for the user-defined measures.

Results Tasks

Task 10: Display the results.

In this task, you will create and display a deformation animation for the model to verify the applied boundary conditions.

1. Create the Displacement Magnitude animation plot. The deformation at Frame 5 displays as shown in Figure 10–61.

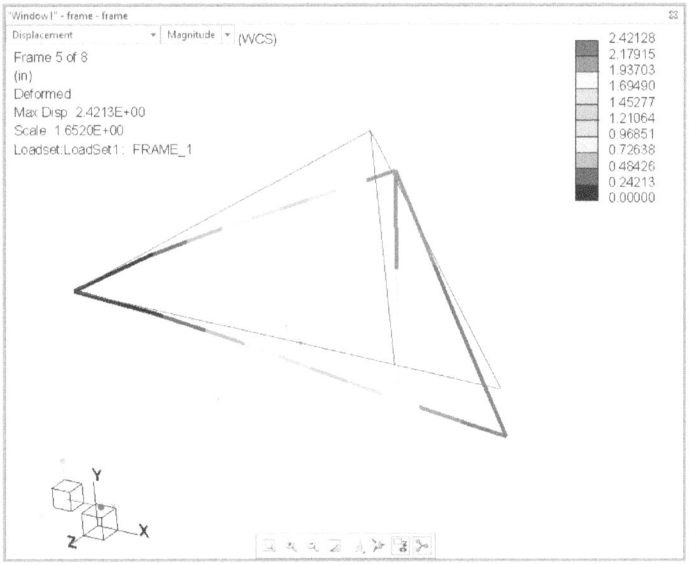

Figure 10–61

2. Start the animation. Do the applied boundary conditions behave correctly?
3. Exit the Results environment. Save and close the model.

End of practice

Practice 10d
Bracket Supported by Rubber Bushings

Practice Objectives

- Create springs.
- Set up and run analysis.
- Display results.

In this practice, you will set up and run a static analysis of the bracket shown in Figure 10–62, with minimum instruction.

The end holes of the bracket are fixed to a rigid foundation, while the middle two holes are supported by rubber bushings in the vertical direction. The bracket is loaded in the horizontal direction at the two holes in the vertical flange.

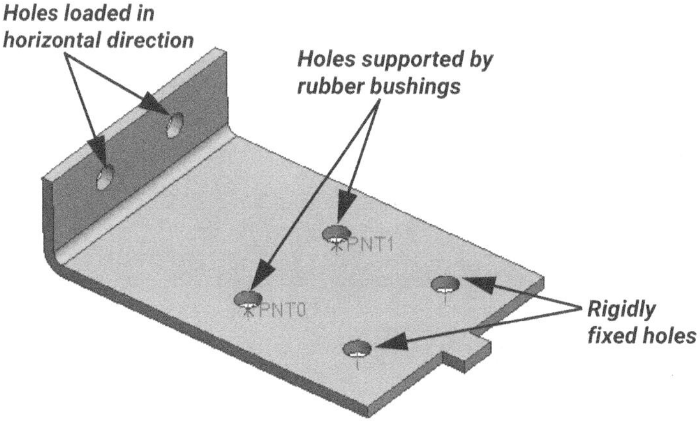

Figure 10–62

Task 1: Prepare the model for analysis.

1. Set the working directory to **Chapter10**, if required.
2. Open **xbracket.prt** and launch Creo Simulate.
3. Set the model display as follows:
    - *(Datum Display Filters)*: (Point Display)
    - *(Spin Center)*: Off
    - *(Display Style)*: (Shading With Edges)
4. If required, in the *View* tab of the ribbon, in the *Show* group, click (Point Tag Display).

5. Apply the **AL2014** material to the part.
6. Fully constrain the inside surfaces of the two end holes, as shown in Figure 10–63.

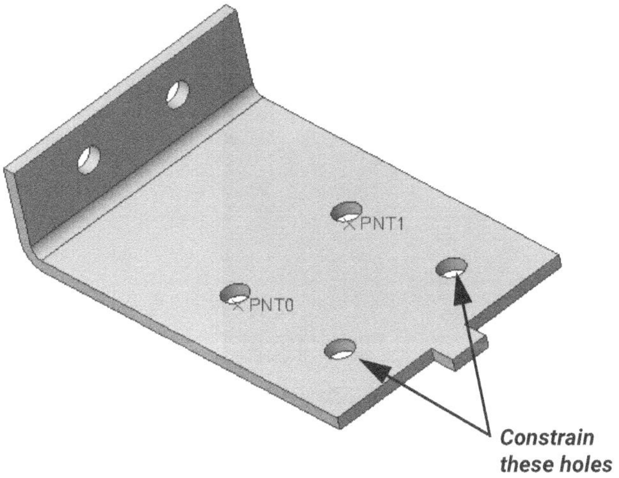

Figure 10–63

7. For the two middle holes, create two **To Ground** springs, as shown in Figure 10–64. Use **PNT0** as the reference for the first spring, and **PNT1** for the second spring. For both springs, use **10000 lbf/in** translational stiffness in WCS X-direction.

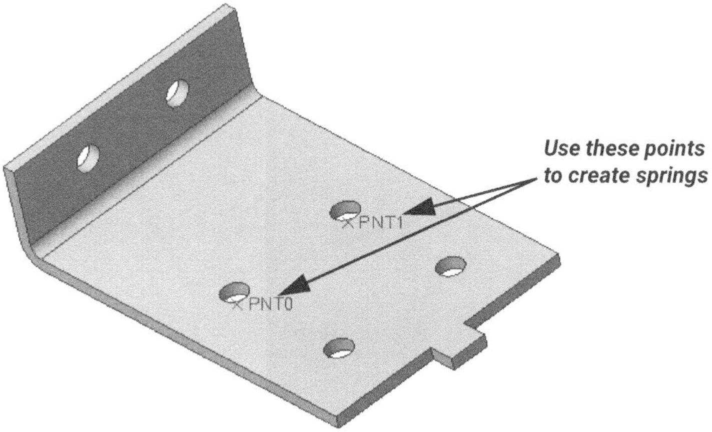

Figure 10–64

Note: Rubber bushings provide compliant supports to the middle holes, which is simulated with springs.

8. To connect **PNT0** and **PNT1** to the holes, create two rigid links, one for each hole. For each rigid link, select the point and the inside surface of the hole as the references, as shown in Figure 10–65.

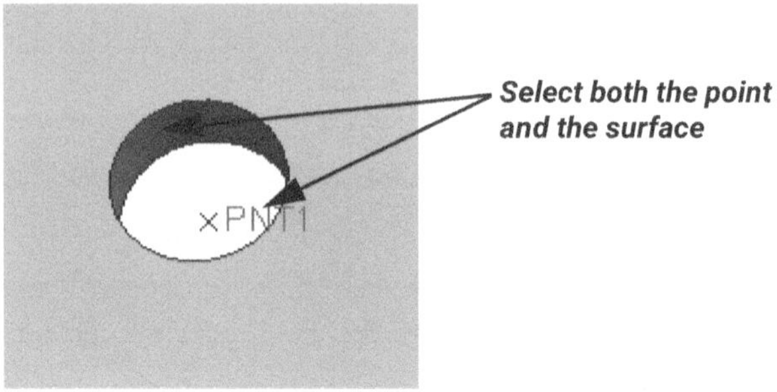

Figure 10–65

9. Apply **1000lbs** combined load in the negative Y-direction to the holes in the vertical flange, as shown in Figure 10–66.

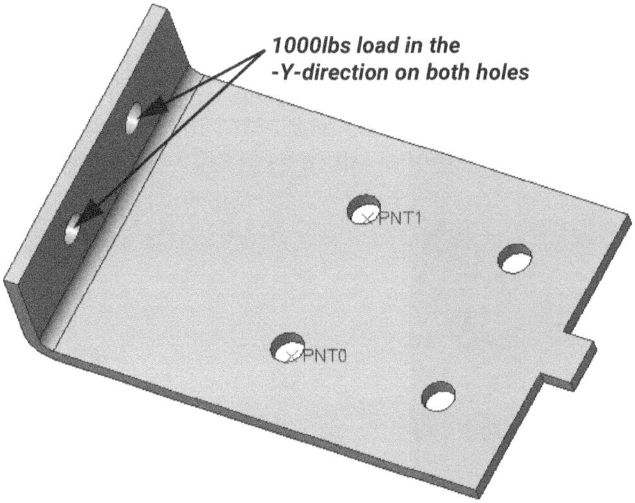

Figure 10–66

Task 2: Set up and run static analysis.

1. Create and run a new Single-Pass Adaptive static analysis. Name it **spring_mount**.

Task 3: Examine the analysis results.

1. Display and animate the **Displacement Magnitude** fringe plot.
   - Do the springs correctly simulate compliant supports on the middle holes?
2. Display the **von Mises Stress** plot.
   - In which area in the model are the stresses at maximum?
   - Would you expect the area of maximum stress to move to a different location if rubber bushings with lower stiffness were used?

Task 4: (Optional) Solve the analysis without compliant supports.

1. Delete springs and rigid links from the model.
2. Fully constrain the two middle holes.
3. Create and run a new Single-Pass analysis. Name it **rigid_mount**.
4. Compare the results with the **spring_mount** analysis.

End of practice

Chapter 11

Fasteners and Rigid Links

When analyzing mechanical assemblies, a correct simulation of the connections and various interactions between the parts is of critical importance. You will learn how to use rigid links and fastener connections in Creo Simulate.

Learning Objectives

- Understand the use of rigid links in Creo Simulate.
- Create rigid links.
- Understand fastener connections in Creo Simulate.
- Create fastener connections.

11.1 Rigid Links

A rigid link rigidly connects geometric entities in your model, such as surfaces, edges, or points, effectively creating a rigid object within your model. A rigid link cannot stretch or deform in any way, which creates a kinematic, rather than elastic, relationship between displacements of the connected entities.

An example of a rigid link connecting two surfaces is shown in Figure 11–1. The rigidly linked surfaces cannot distort or deform but can move together as a rigid body.

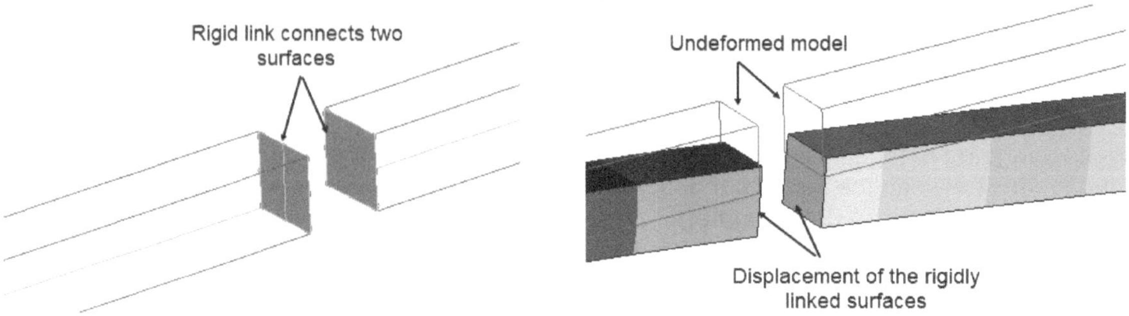

Figure 11–1

A rigid link creates a *constraint equation* that links displacements of the connected entities. A rigid link does not use rigid beams or any other type of finite elements to make the connection.

Since a rigid link cannot deform, it will locally stiffen the mesh on and near the included geometric entities. Therefore, exercise caution when applying rigid links to large areas in your model since this may lead to an over-stiffened model.

The rigid link has a full six degrees of freedom (three translations and three rotations); therefore, it supports rotational constraints and loads.

The rigid link is analogous to the RBE2 element in NASTRAN.

Creating Rigid Links

Use the following steps to create a rigid link:

1. In the *Refine Model* tab, click (Rigid Link) to open the *Rigid Link Definition* dialog box, as shown in Figure 11–2.

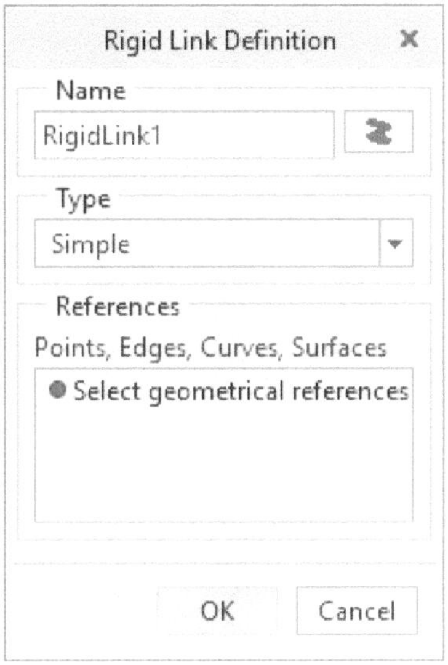

Figure 11–2

2. (Optional) Enter a name.
3. Expand the *Type* drop-down list and select **Simple** or **Advanced**.
    - The **Advanced** type enables you to control the independent degrees of freedom. Requires an Advanced Creo Simulate license.
4. Select the geometrical entities to connect (hold <Ctrl> to multi-select).
    - You can connect the surfaces or edges of your model with a free point that is not otherwise associated with the model geometry.
5. Click **OK**.

Rigid Links Best Practices

One of the typical applications for rigid links is to model a moving rigid structure in your analysis. An example is shown in Figure 11–3. The heat sink/integrated circuit (HS/IC) package is bonded to the printed circuit board (PCB). The heat sink is made of aluminum; therefore, it is much stiffer than the thin PCB, which is made of plastic. The task is to determine the natural frequencies and natural modes of vibration for the assembly, using Modal analysis in Creo Simulate.

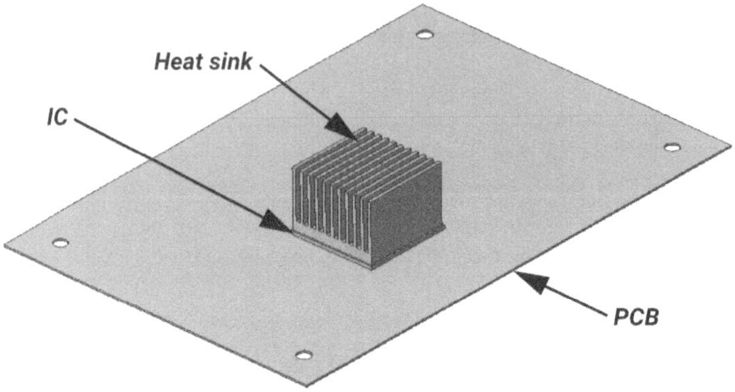

Figure 11–3

It is critical to preserve all of the masses in the system in the Modal analysis, so the mass of the HS/IC package must be included in the simulation. One option might be to model the mass by meshing the HS/IC package with solid elements and applying the material. However, a more computationally efficient approach would be to simulate the mass of the HS/IC package with a concentrated mass located at the CoG of the package, then connecting the mass with the PCB using a rigid link, as shown in Figure 11–4.

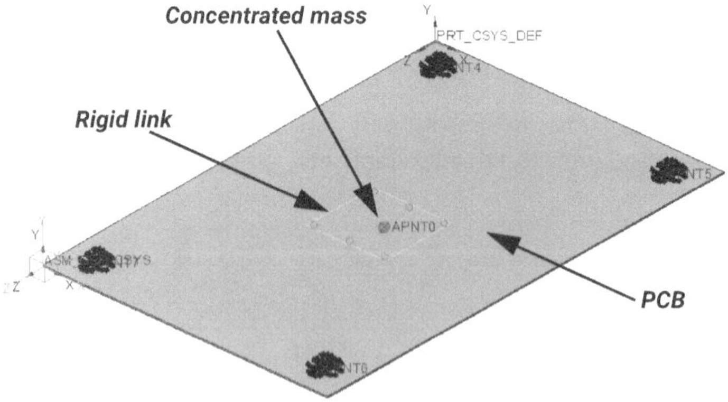

Figure 11–4

Another typical application for rigid links is modeling of small fasteners such as screws or rivets.

An example is shown in Figure 11–5. The lock plate is attached to the door slab with two screws.

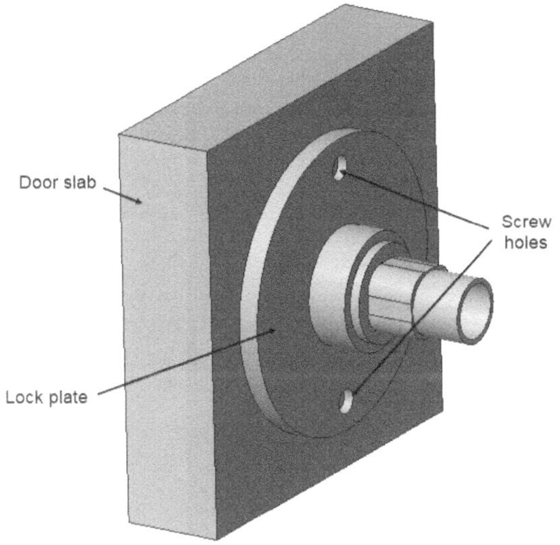

Figure 11–5

One of the ways to model the screws would be to use rigid links connecting the inside surfaces of the two holes in the plate and in the slab, as shown in Figure 11–6.

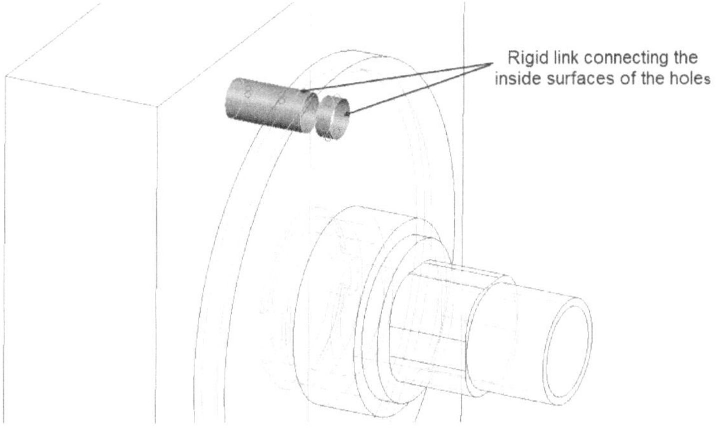

Figure 11–6

> ***Note:*** *Another way to model the screws would be to use the Fastener feature discussed later in this chapter.*

Lastly, rigid links are often used to connect meshes with incompatible degrees of freedom, such as connecting beams or shells to solids.

An example is shown in Figure 11–7. The end point of the beam element must be connected to the entire inside surface of the cylindrical boss in the bracket.

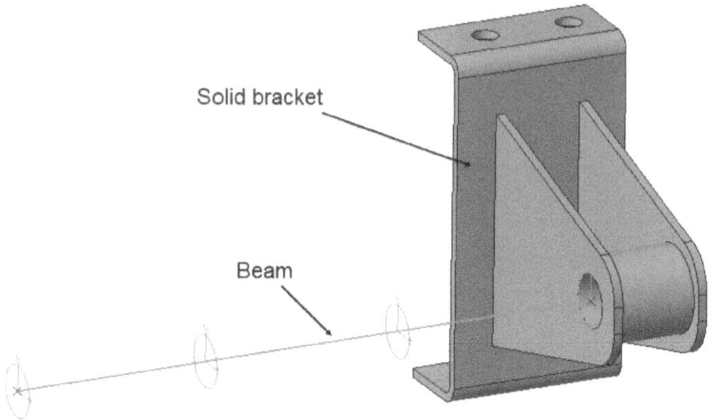

Figure 11–7

> ***Note:*** *Solid elements have three nodal degrees of freedom (translations only), while shell and beam elements have six nodal degrees of freedom (translations and rotations).*

The solution is to use a rigid link to make the connection, as shown in Figure 11–8.

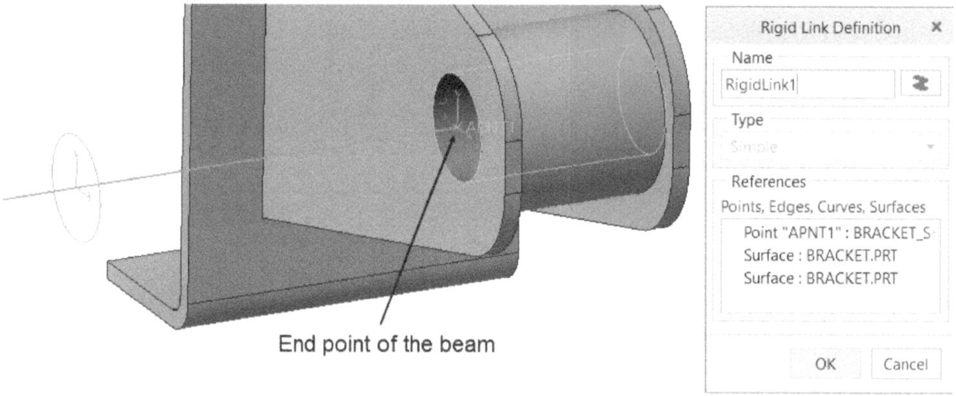

Figure 11–8

When using rigid links, be aware that the connected geometric entities will not be able to stretch, distort, or deform in any other way. For instance, in the example shown in Figure 11–8, the rigid link will effectively render the inside surface of the boss undeformable, and you should consider whether it is acceptable for your simulation.

In general, it is not recommended to apply rigid links to large surfaces since it is likely to over-stiffen your model.

11.2 Fasteners

The Creo Simulate **Fastener** tool creates an idealization of a fastened assembly connection. The fastener is intended to correctly simulate transfer of loads through the structure, as well as to estimate the amount of force carried by each bolt or screw. An important feature of the **Fastener** tool is the ability to apply a preload force on the connection.

You can model both screw or bolt fasteners in solid or shell models. If you plan to add fasteners to your simulation, the model must meet the following prerequisites:

- The model must be an assembly. A fastener must pass through two components.
- You cannot define zero-length fasteners. This may inadvertently happen in shell models if component mid-surfaces that you intend to fasten are in direct contact.
- In solid models, both components to be fastened must have holes through which the bolt or the screw can pass. For bolt fasteners, both holes must be through holes. For screw fasteners, only the component on the screw head side must have a through hole. The hole on the screw tip side can be a through hole or a blind hole.
- In shell models, you can use either holes or points as the fastener's references. If you use points, both components must have points that establish the fastener's axis.
- Any hole that participates in a fastener connection must be a right cylindrical hole (i.e., the hole axis must be perpendicular to the component surface and have straight sides). Slots or oval holes are not permitted.
- The two holes should have approximately the same diameter, and their axes must be coincident within small tolerance.

Creating Fasteners

Use the following steps to create a fastener:

1. In the *Refine Model* tab, click (Fastener) to open the *Fastener Definition* dialog box, as shown in Figure 11–9.

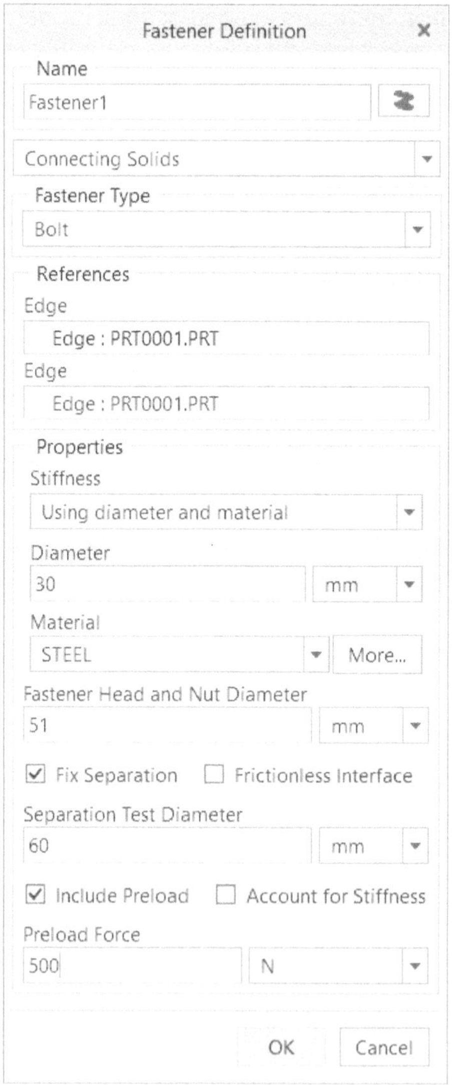

Figure 11–9

2. (Optional) Enter a fastener name.
3. Select **Connecting Solids** or **Connecting Shells**.

4. Select the *Fastener Type*.
5. Selected the fastener *References*.
6. In the *Properties* area, select the required options as shown in the following table.
7. Click **OK** to complete.

Option	Description
Connecting Solids	Creates a fastener connecting two solid parts.
Connecting Shells	Creates a fastener connecting two shell parts.
Fastener Type	**Bolt:** Both holes must be through holes. The first hole you select is associated with the head of the bolt, and the second hole is associated with the nut. **Screw:** The hole on the screw head side must be a through hole, while the hole on the other side can be a through hole or a blind hole. The first hole you select is associated with the head of the screw, and the second hole is associated with the tip of the screw.
References	For the **Connecting Solids** type, select the circular edges of the holes. For the **Connecting Shells** type, select either the hole edges or the datum points that define the axis of the fastener.
Stiffness	**Using diameter and material:** Models the fastener with a beam element. By default, the diameter of the beam's cross-section is assumed the same diameter as the smaller of the two holes. **Using spring stiffness property:** Models the fastener with a spring element using a user-defined spring property.
Fastener Head and Nut Diameter	Defines the head and nut diameter for the fastener. For screws, there is no nut, so the value applies to the screw head. By default, the value is assumed to be 1.7 times the bolt diameter.
Fix Separation	Creates a stiff distributed separation spring over the two annular areas around the fastener's holes between the fastened parts. Can be used instead of contact interface to prevent interpenetration of the fastened parts.
Separation Test Diameter	Defines the diameter of the annular separation spring areas. By default, the value is assumed to be twice the bolt diameter.
Frictionless Interface	If enabled, the shear stiffness component in the separation spring is deactivated. The separation spring becomes shear-soft, and the parts will be permitted to slide along each other over the separation areas.
Include Preload	Enables a preload for the fastener. Not available for the **Connecting Shells** type.
Account for Stiffness	Activates automatic adjustment of the preloads as to compensate for the compression of the fastened parts.
Preload Force	Defines the compressive force on the parts that results from tightening the bolt or screw.

Modeling Fastener with a Beam

If the **Using diameter and material** option is used for the fastener's *Stiffness*, the fastener is modeled as a beam element that connects the opposite surfaces of the parts, as shown in Figure 11–10. The software proceeds as follows:

- Two annular areas are created around the fastener holes on the opposite sides of the parts. The diameter of the areas is set equal to the *Fastener Head and Nut Diameter* value as specified in the *Fastener Definition* dialog box. If the fastener is of the **Screw** type, only one annular area is created on the screw head side.
- Two points ***A*** and ***B*** are created at the centers of the bolt head and nut holes. If the fastener is of the **Screw** type, point ***B*** is created at the centroid of the cylindrical hole on the side of the screw tip.
- The bolt head and nut areas are connected to the points ***A*** and ***B*** with *weighted links*.
- Points ***A*** and ***B*** are linked with a cylindrical *Timoshenko beam* that models the fastener's shank. The *Timoshenko* beam idealization uses a 12x12 stiffness matrix, thus it includes the axial force as well as shear and bending forces in the fastener's deformation.

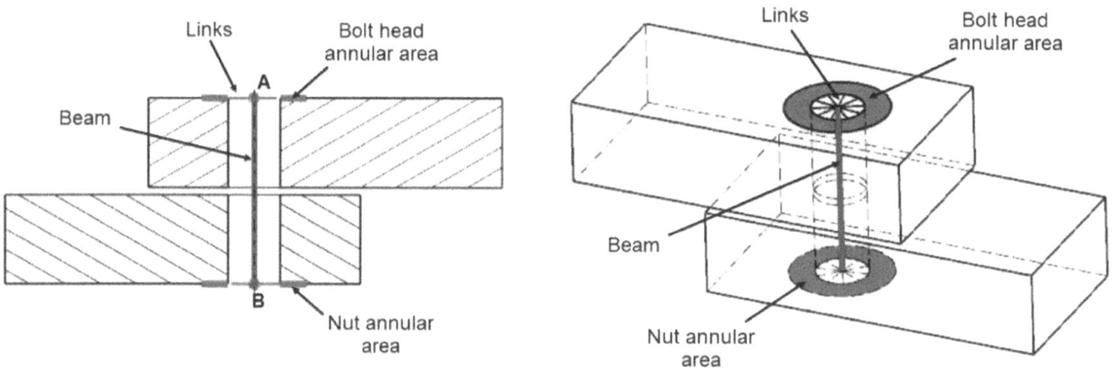

Figure 11–10

Modeling Fastener with a Spring

If the **Using spring stiffness property** option is used for the fastener's *Stiffness*, the fastener is modeled as a *spring*, as shown in Figure 11–11. The software proceeds similarly to the beam option, as far as creating the bolt head and nut annular areas, the center points ***A*** and ***B***, etc. The difference is that the points ***A*** and ***B*** are now connected with a *spring* idealization that models the fastener's shank, rather than with a beam.

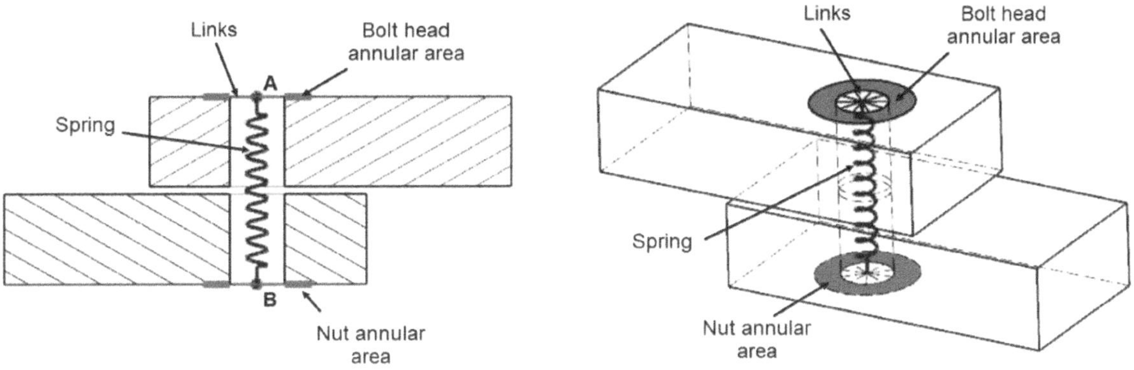

Figure 11–11

The spring's stiffness must be defined in the *Spring Property Definition* dialog box, as shown in Figure 11–12. The spring's X-direction is along the length of the fastener's shank, while the Y-and Z-directions are shearing directions on the fastener. Note that, given the circular cross-section of the fastener shank, the shearing stiffnesses ***Kyy*** and ***Kzz*** must be equal, and the bending stiffnesses ***Tyy*** and ***Tzz*** must be equal too.

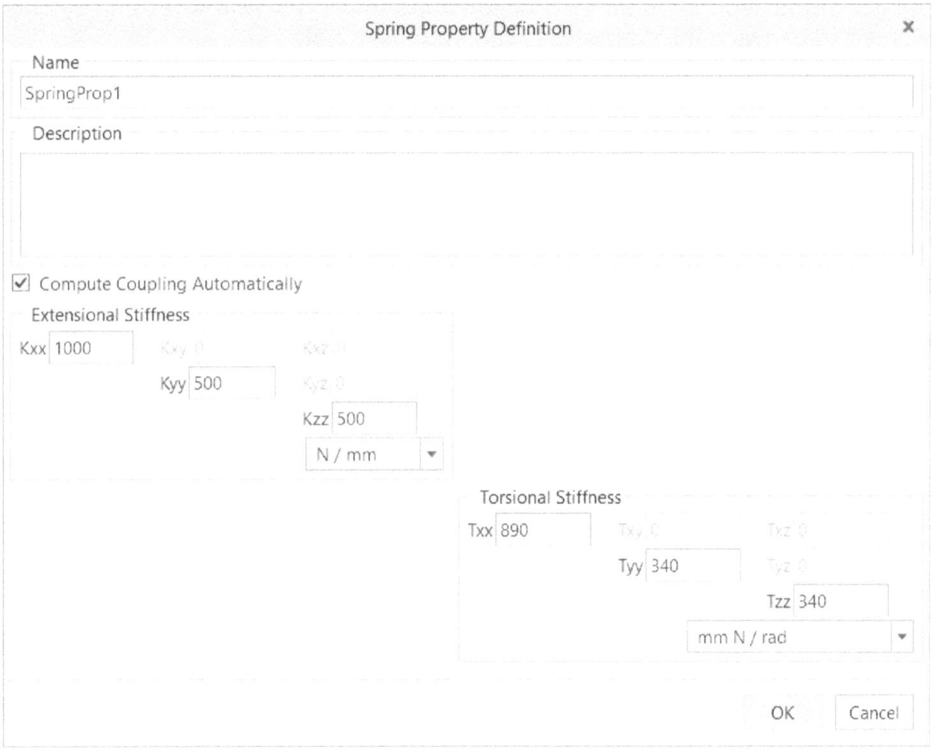

Figure 11–12

Part Separation

The most accurate method for modeling the interface between two fastened parts is to create a true contact interface between the contacting surfaces. When a fastener is used to join two components in the assembly, the components must not interpenetrate, and this is exactly the condition that is enforced by the contact interface.

The problem with using contact interfaces is that it makes the analysis non-linear. Therefore:

- The analysis runtime could be much longer than a comparable linear analysis.
- The model could not be used for modal or any other dynamics simulations because those types of analysis are strictly linear.

The **Fix Separation** option is an alternative and computationally inexpensive approximation of the interface between the two fastened parts.

The option is activated by the **Fix Separation** checkbox in the *Fastener Definition* dialog box. (Note that this option is ignored by the software if a Contact Interface is created between the parts.) The software proceeds as follows, as shown in Figure 11–13:

- Two annular areas, called *separation areas*, are created on the contacting surfaces. The diameter of the separation areas is called ***Separation Test Diameter***, and by default is assumed to be twice the diameter of the fastener's hole.
- A very stiff surface-to-surface distributed linear spring, called the *separation spring*, is created between the separation areas. Since the spring is made very stiff, it enforces the separation areas to stay in contact yet not interpenetrate under the loading (i.e., the separation spring works instead of the contact interface). Yet, since the spring is linear, it is computationally fast.
- Free interface is created on the remainders of the contacting surfaces, so the parts are no longer bonded over areas other than the separation areas.

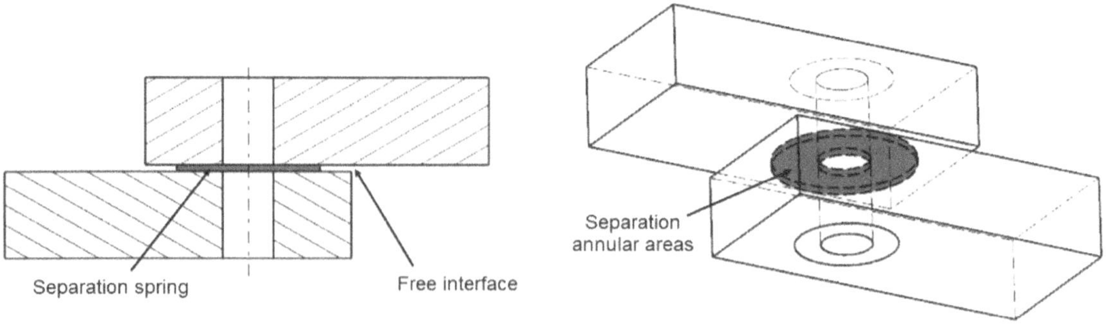

Figure 11–13

The separation spring possesses both normal to the surface and tangent to the surface (i.e., shearing) stiffness components. The former enforces the non-penetration and the latter enforces the non-sliding (i.e., infinite friction) condition between the parts near the fastener. The shearing stiffness, however, can be deactivated by selecting the **Frictionless Interface** option in the *Fastener Definition* dialog box. This makes the separation spring shear-soft, and the parts would be permitted to slide along each other over the separation areas. The shearing force on the connection, in this case, would be fully carried by the fastener itself, rather than the friction in the interface.

The **Fix Separation** mechanism is a good option when parts near the fastener are mostly in the state of compression, and the separation spring acts to enforce the non-penetration condition as it should. However, since the separation spring is a linear spring and thus acts in both compression and tension, it may have the incorrect effect of forcing the separation areas to stay in contact even though the parts should naturally separate under the tensile load that exceeds the fastener's preload. Should this condition occur, Creo Simulate issues a warning message, as shown in Figure 11–14.

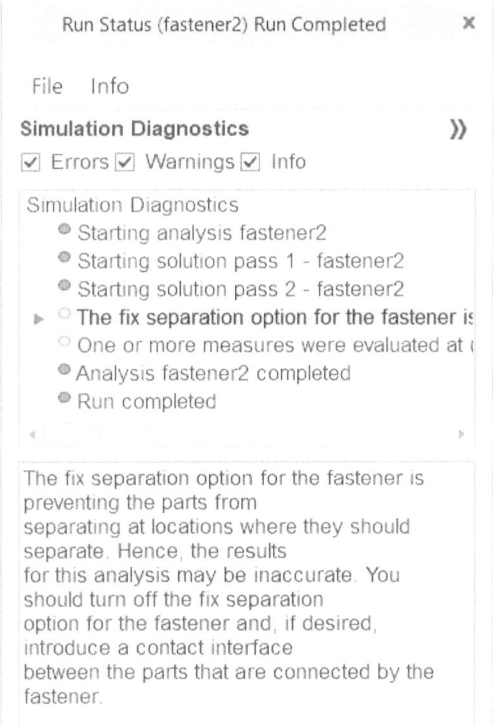

Figure 11–14

Another indicator of whether the **Fix Separation** option is working correctly is the simulation measure *fastenerName_intf_norm_forc*, as shown in Figure 11–15. The measure is automatically created for each fastener, and it tracks the total normal force in the separation spring. A negative value of the measure indicates that there is net compression between the parts, and the Fix Separation mechanism is working correctly. A positive value indicates a net tension in the spring, meaning the parts are incorrectly kept in contact while, in fact, they should separate under the applied load.

```
Fastener1_axial_force:      7.705518e+00
Fastener1_axial_stress:     3.924388e-01
Fastener1_bending_moment:   1.094787e+01
Fastener1_bending_stress:   8.921124e-01
Fastener1_intf_bend_momt:   9.461529e+02
Fastener1_intf_norm_forc:   1.197042e+02
Fastener1_intf_shr_forc:    2.047310e+01
Fastener1_intf_tors_momt: -9.967485e+00
Fastener1_sep_stress:       9.575728e+00
Fastener1_shear_force:      4.704654e-02
Fastener1_shear_stress:     2.396061e-03
Fastener1_torsion_moment:   7.547367e-02
Fastener1_torsion_stress:   3.075074e-03
```

Figure 11–15

Lastly, this condition could also be detected visually when reviewing the analysis results, as shown in Figure 11–16.

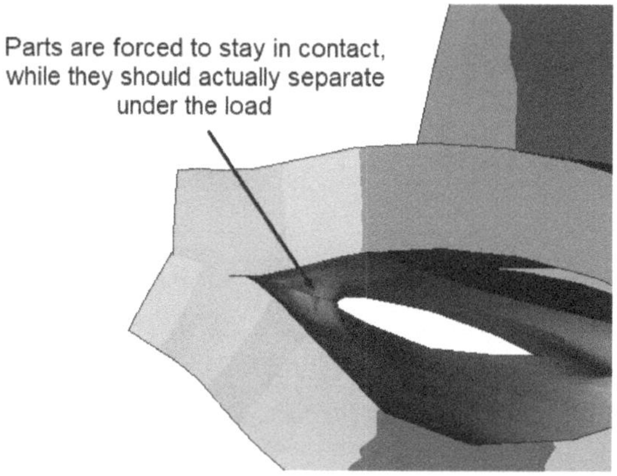

Figure 11–16

Once this condition has been detected, you have two options to correct the problem:

- Create a contact interface between the parts, which automatically turns off the Fix Separation mechanism, or
- Deactivate the **Fix Separation** option in the *Fastener Definition* dialog box.

An example of the part interface around the fastener with the **Fix Separation** option cleared is shown in Figure 11–17.

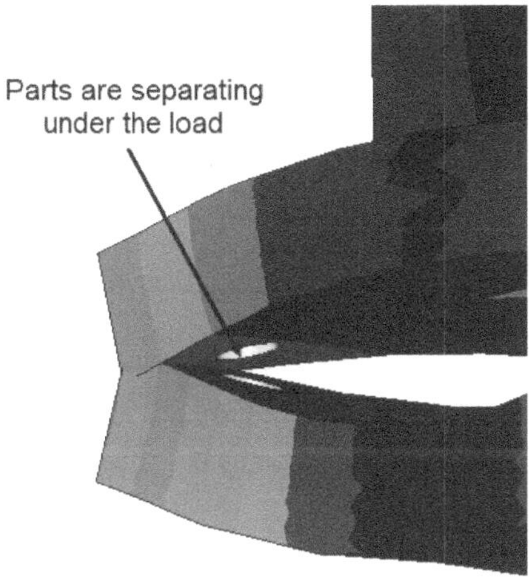

Figure 11–17

Fastener Preload

Most bolted connections in real life are subject to preload that occurs when tightening the bolt. The preload applies a compressive force to both fastened members. When a separation force is applied to the connection, the bolt carries a portion of the load and the member carries a portion. Knowing the total tensile force inside the bolt under such condition is a subject of interest to many engineers involved in design and sizing of bolted connections.

Creo Simulate implements the fastener preload by shortening the initial (i.e., pre-assembled) length of the element that models the fastener's shank (whether it's a beam or a spring), as shown in Figure 11–18. The fastener element is then elastically extended to fit the actual thickness of the parts, which creates tensile force in the fastener and compressive force on the parts, and which clamps the parts together.

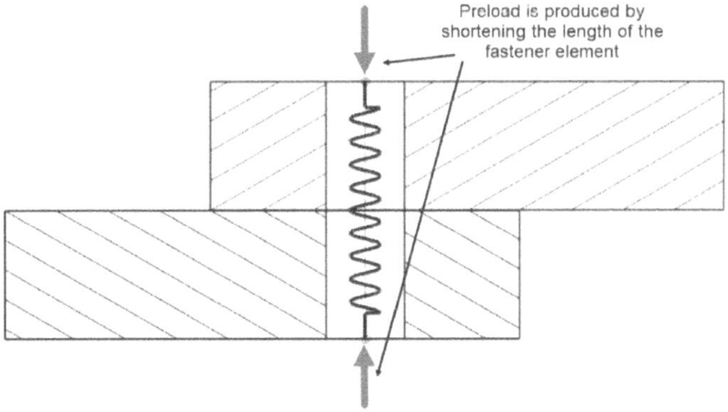

Figure 11–18

The shortened length of the fastener element is calculated by Creo Simulate on the nominal (i.e., undeformed) thickness of the parts as ***L = T – d1***, where ***T*** is the nominal thickness of the parts and ***d1*** is calculated as to produce the nominal preload ***Fn = k * d1*** (***k*** is the tensile stiffness of the fastener), as shown in Figure 11–19.

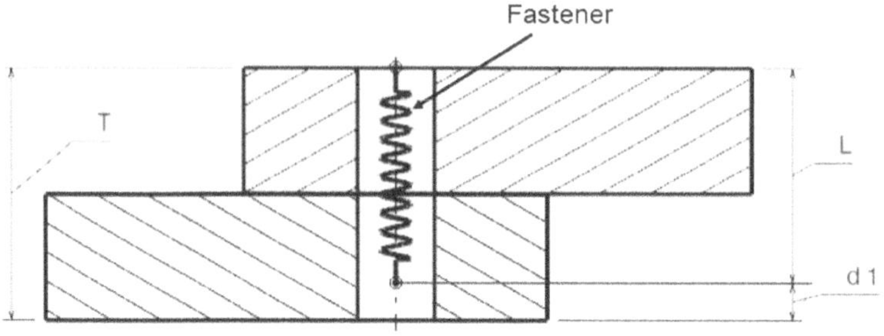

Figure 11–19

As the parts deform under the preload force, the compressed thickness of the parts ***Tc*** becomes smaller than the nominal thickness ***T***, and the actual tensile force in the fastener (i.e., the actual preload) becomes ***Ft = k* (d1- 2*d2)***, as shown in Figure 11–20. Therefore, the actual preload ***Ft*** comes out of the analysis always smaller than the nominal preload ***Fn***.

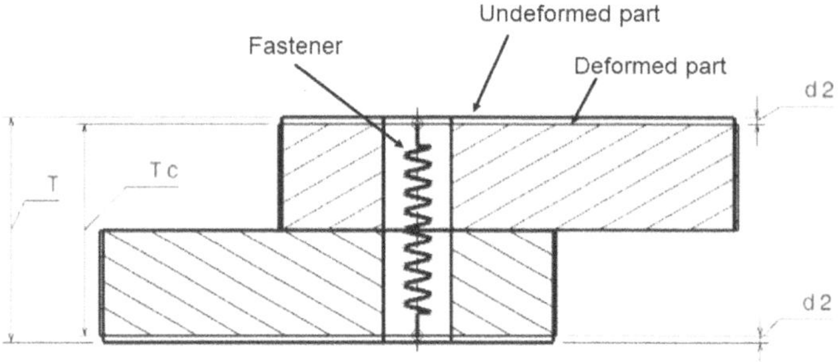

Figure 11–20

Fortunately, the relationship between the nominal preload and the actual preload is linear, so creating the desired preload requires only scaling up the applied in the analysis preload by the factor ***f = Fn / Ft***. In other words, the input preload ***Fi*** must be calculated as ***Fi = f * Fn***. For example, if ***100N*** preload was desired, but the actual preload came out of the analysis as ***80N***, then the scaling factor ***f = 100 / 80 = 1.25***. And to obtain the ***100N*** actual preload, one would have to input ***1.25 * 100 = 125N*** preload in the *Fastener Definition* dialog box.

The actual preload in a fastener is reported as the *fastenerName_axial_force* simulation measure, as shown in Figure 11–21.

Fastener1_torsion_moment	5.89437
Fastener1_torsion_stress	0.0300198
Fastener2_axial_force	501.151
Fastener2_axial_stress	6.38085
Fastener2_bending_moment	3.25921
Fastener2_bending_stress	0.0331981
Fastener2_intf_bend_momt	61.1238
Fastener2_intf_norm_forc	-501.215
Fastener2_intf_shr_forc	89.9117

Figure 11–21

To obtain the desired preloads using a manual correction, first run a static analysis with only preloads applied and compute the preload scaling factors ***f***. Then, re-run the analysis again, now with the preloads scaled up and all other loads applied too.

Alternatively, this process can be automated by activating the **Account for Stiffness** option in the *Fastener Definition* dialog box. In that case, the software proceeds as follows:

- A base analysis is run, with no external loads applied. The preloads ***Fn*** are applied on the undeformed parts, and the actual forces ***Ft*** in the fasteners are obtained.
- Given the actual preload values obtained in the base analysis, the scaling factors ***f*** are computed.
- The second and the final analysis is run, now with all the preloads scaled up as ***Fi = f * Fn***, as well as with all the external loads applied.

Note that the **Account for Stiffness** option requires running two analyses instead of one; therefore, it is computationally more expensive. The upside is that it produces very accurate preloads in the model, should that be desired by the user.

Fastening Three or More Components

The Creo Simulate documentation specifies the following restriction for fastener modeling: "There should not be any interfering or intervening geometry in the fastener path." An example of intervening geometry is shown in Figure 11–22, in which three parts are clamped together with two through-bolts. The middle part in such a case is considered by Creo Simulate as an intervening part.

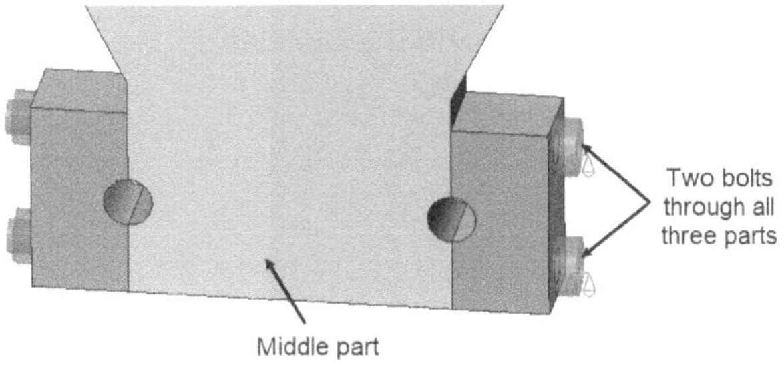

Figure 11–22

If you attempt to solve the model shown in Figure 11–22 with the default fastener options, Creo Simulate fails to start the analysis and issues an error message, as shown in Figure 11–23.

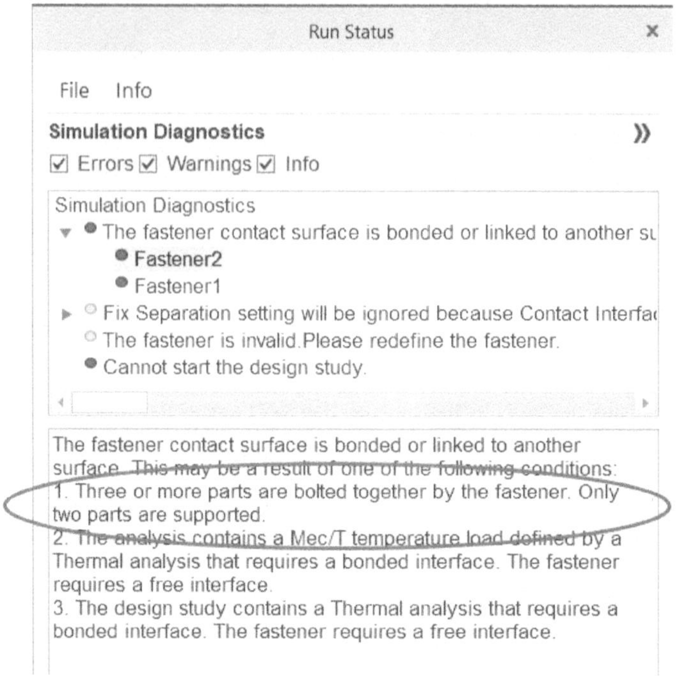

Figure 11–23

In real life, engineers frequently need to deal with designs in which more than two parts are fastened together, such as the model shown in Figure 11–22, and the "no intervening geometry" restriction seems to make it impossible to use the Fastener connection in such cases.

However, we have discovered that the real reason why the analysis fails is that Creo Simulate is unable to execute the default Fix Separation interface between the components, since the software cannot create the separation areas and the separation spring if there is intervening geometry in the fastener's path. Therefore, we have found a workaround for the "no intervening geometry" restriction, which is as follows:

- Use contact interfaces between the fastened parts.
- Deactivate the **Fix Separation** option in the fasteners.

Note: *Although Creo Simulate documentation claims that the Fix Separation option is automatically ignored by the software if a contact interface is detected, we have found that this may or may not work with three parts or more. Therefore, ensure that the Fix Separation option is toggled off manually.*

For example, for the model shown in Figure 11–22, use contact interfaces between the clamped parts, as shown in Figure 11–24.

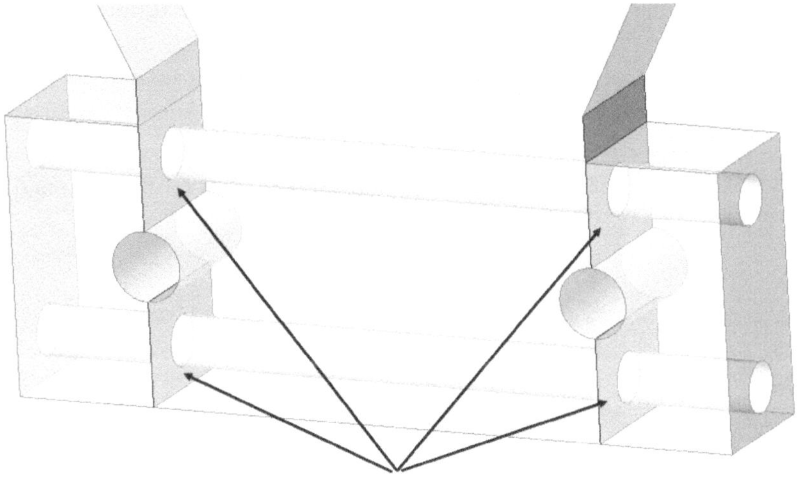

Figure 11–24

When using contact interfaces for bolted connections, consider whether to use the friction option. The *infinite friction* type of interface should be used if the bolt is torqued enough as to disable any sliding motion between the clamped parts, so most of the shearing force in the connection is carried by the interface alone. Alternatively, a *frictionless* interface should be used to model a connection with a loose bolt, in which the shearing force is carried by the bolt alone and small sliding between the connected parts should be permitted.

Fastener Measures

Creo Simulate automatically creates several measures for each fastener. The fastener measures are as follows:

Measure	Description
axial_force	Axial force in a fastener.
axial_stress	Axial stress in a fastener. Calculated for the specified fastener diameter.
shear_force	Shear force in a fastener.
shear_stress	Shear stress in a fastener. Calculated for the specified fastener diameter.
bending_moment	Bending moment in a fastener.
bending_stress	Bending stress in a fastener. Calculated for the specified fastener diameter.
torsion_moment	Torsional moment in a fastener. Calculated if **Frictionless Interface** is enabled. The fastener carries all the torsional moment since there is no friction between the two components.
torsion_stress	Torsional stress in a fastener. Calculated for the specified fastener diameter.
sep_stress	Normal tensile stress over the separation area, calculated as the ratio of the tensile force at the interface to the area in tension. For a valid fastener, the value of this measure should be zero or a small positive number.
intf_bend_momt	Bending moment calculated for the separation area.
intf_norm_forc	Normal force in the separation area. A negative value indicates that there is net compression. A positive value indicates net tension and that the parts should be separating.
intf_shr_forc	Shear force in the separation area. Calculated if **Frictionless Interface** is disabled.
intf_tors_momt	Torsional moment over the separation area. Calculated if **Frictionless Interface** is disabled.

Practice 11a
Modal Analysis of a PCB Assembly

Practice Objectives

- Create masses.
- Create rigid links.
- Set up and run a Modal analysis.

In this practice, you will set up and run a Modal analysis for the PCB assembly shown in Figure 11–25. The PCB is made of plastic, while the heat sink is made of aluminum and is much stiffer than the PCB. You will use a mass and a rigid link to model the heat sink and the IC package.

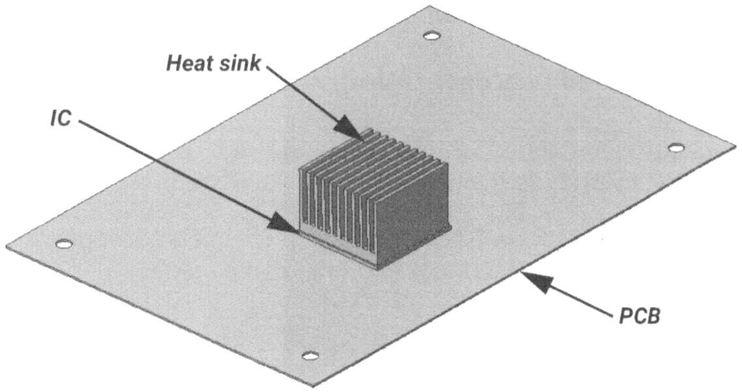

Figure 11–25

Modeling Tasks

Task 1: Open the assembly in Creo Parametric.

1. Set the working directory to **Chapter11**.
2. Open **pcb.asm**.
3. Set the model display as follows:
    - *(Datum Display Filters)*: (Point Display)
    - *(Spin Center)*: Off
    - *(Display Style)*: (Shading With Edges)

4. In the *View* tab of the ribbon, in the *Show* group, enable (Point Tag Display). The model displays as shown in Figure 11–26.

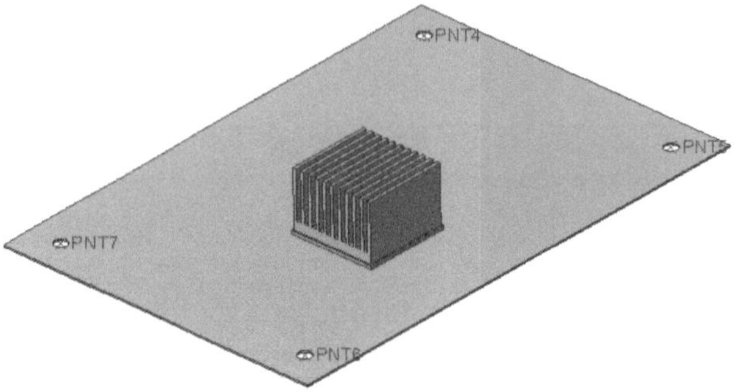

Figure 11–26

5. Ensure that the unit system is set to **mmNs**.

Task 2: Create a simplified representation.

The heat sink/IC package is simulated with a mass and a rigid link. In this task, you will create a simplified representation to exclude the heat sink and the IC geometry from the analysis model.

1. In the In-graphics toolbar, click (View Manager). The *View Manager* dialog box opens, as shown in Figure 11–27. Ensure the *Simp Rep* tab is activated.

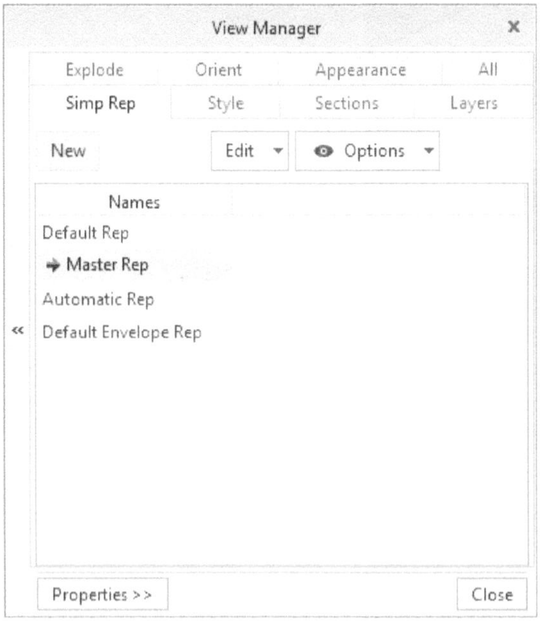

Figure 11–27

2. Click **New**. Rename the new representation as **AnslRep** and press <Enter>. The *Edit:ANLSREP* dialog box opens, as shown in Figure 11–28.

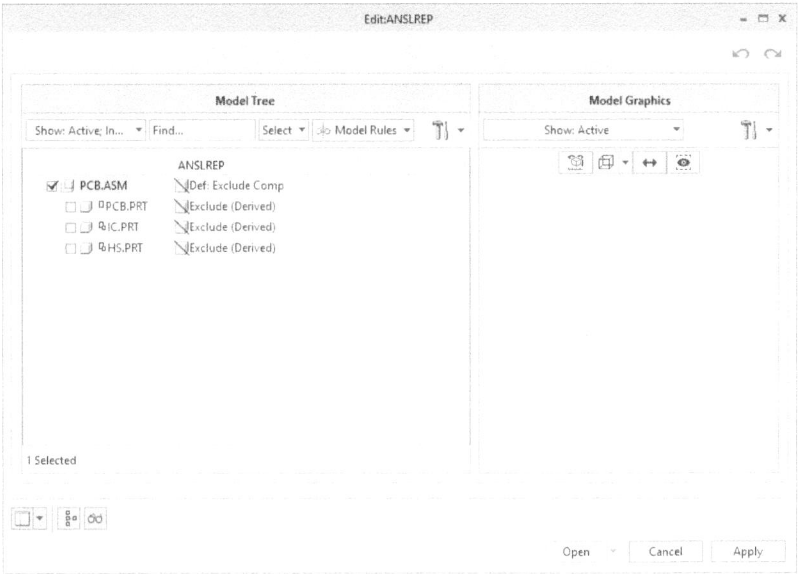

Figure 11–28

3. Set **PCB.ASM** and **PCB.PRT** to **Master Rep**, and **IC.PRT** and **HS.PRT** to **Exclude**. The *Edit:ANLSREP* dialog box updates as shown in Figure 11–29.

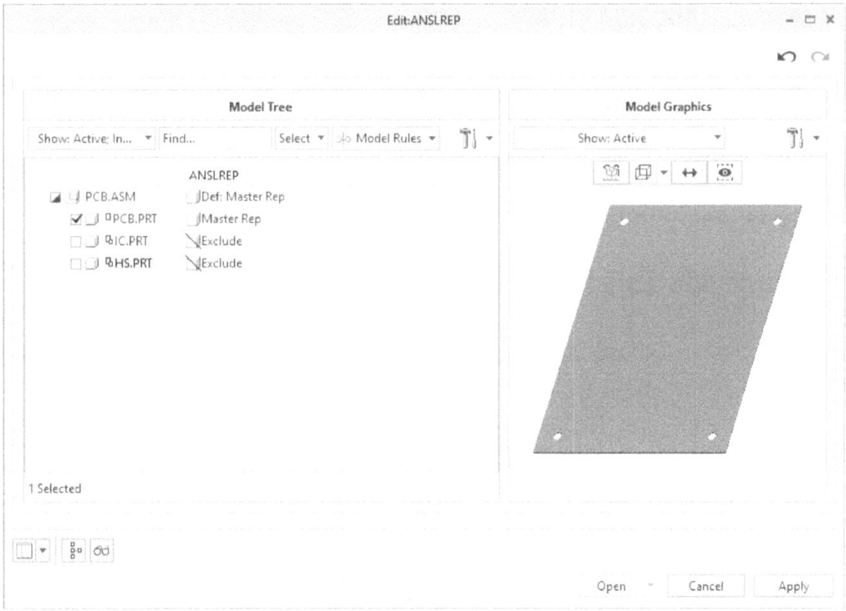

Figure 11–29

4. Click **Open** and **Close** to finish. The model displays as shown in Figure 11–30.

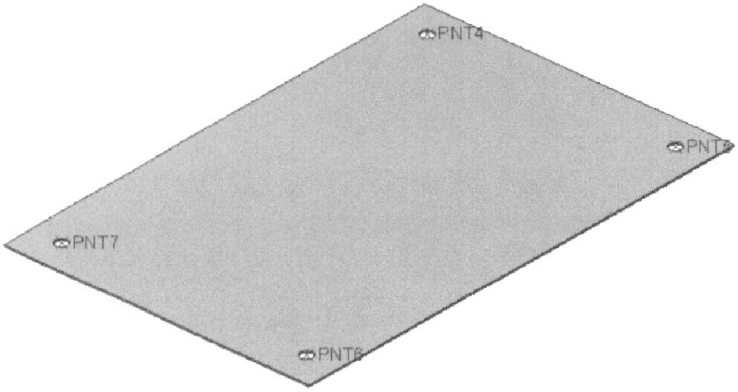

Figure 11–30

Task 3: Launch Creo Simulate.

1. Select **Applications>Simulate** to launch the Creo Simulate environment.

Task 4: Apply the material.

1. Assign **NYLON** to the PCB part. The following values are the default material properties for NYLON:
   - *Poisson:* **0.4**
   - *Young's modulus:* **4000.34 MPa**
   - *Coeff of thermal expansion:* **7.9992e-5 /C**
   - *Density:* **1.20014e-9 tonne/mm^3**

   Note: *The model's material properties should be as stated.*

2. Hide the **Material Assignments** icon.

Task 5: Create a divided surface.

In this task, you will create a divided surface to model the area over which the heat sink/IC package is bonded to the PCB.

1. In the *Refine Model* tab, click (Sketch) and create a sketch on the top surface of the PCB (in the Y-direction up) with the dimensions shown in Figure 11–31.

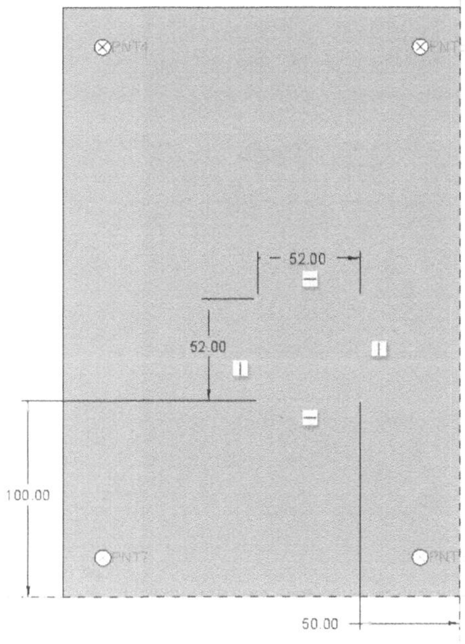

Figure 11–31

2. The model displays as shown in Figure 11–32.

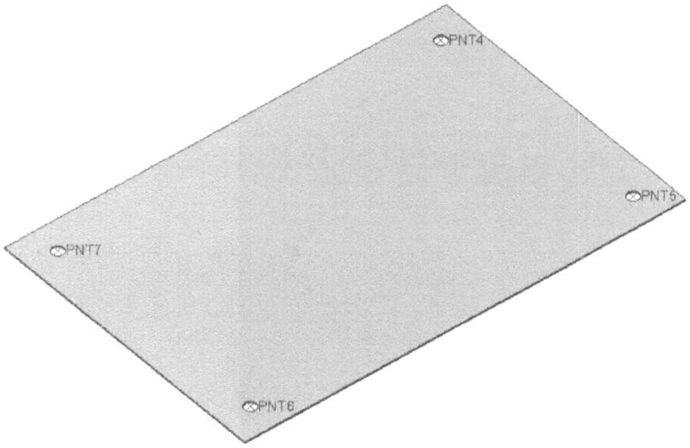

Figure 11–32

3. In the *Refine Model* tab, click (Divide Surface).

4. In the *Select a Component* dialog box, select the **PCB** part and click **OK**. The *Divide Surface* dashboard displays, as shown in Figure 11–33.

Figure 11–33

5. Activate the *Surfaces to divide* field and select the top surface of the PCB.

6. Click (Chain), activate the *Chains* field, and select the sketch. The model displays as shown in Figure 11–34.

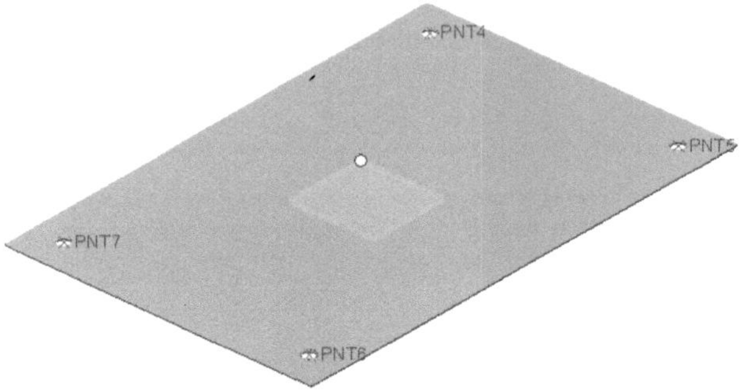

Figure 11–34

7. Click (OK) to complete the divided surface.

Task 6: Create shell pairs.

1. Define the shell pairs using the **Detect Shell Pairs** tool, with a *Characteristic Thickness* of **1**.

   Note: *The PCB thickness is 1mm.*

Task 7: Create a datum point.

In this task, you will create an assembly datum point located at the CoG of the heat sink/IC package.

1. In the In-graphics toolbar, enable (Csys Display).
2. In the *Refine Model* tab, expand (Point) and select (Offset Coordinate System).
3. Click **OK** in the *Select a Component* dialog box.

4. In the *Datum Point* dialog box that opens, select **ASM_DEF_CSYS** as the reference, and enter the new point coordinates as shown in Figure 11–35.

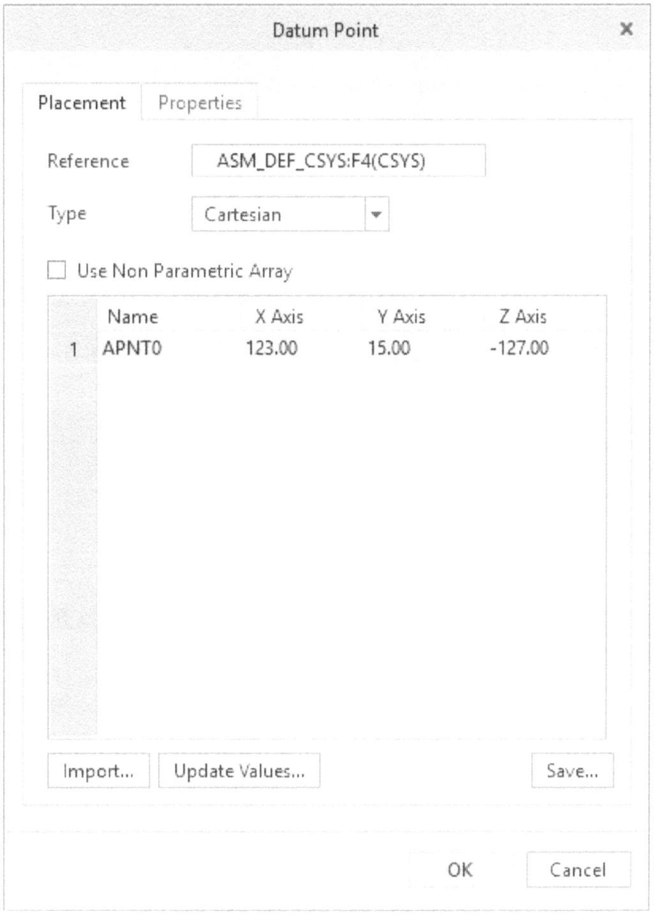

Figure 11–35

Note: *You can use* ***File>Prepare>Model Properties*** *to calculate the CoG coordinates.*

5. Click **OK** to finish.

Task 8: Create a rigid link.

In this task, you will create a rigid link to connect the CoG of the heat sink/IC assembly with the divided surface on the PCB.

1. In the *Refine Model* tab, click (Rigid Link). The *Rigid Link Definition* dialog box opens, as shown in Figure 11–36.

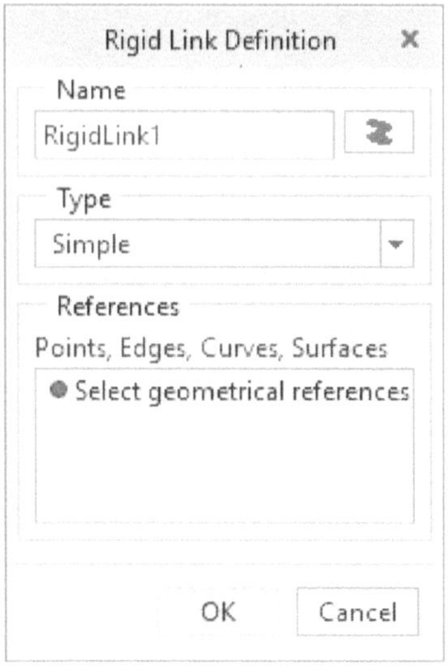

Figure 11–36

2. Select both the **APNT0** point and the divided surface (hold <Ctrl> to multi-select). Click **OK** to finish. The model displays as shown in Figure 11–37.

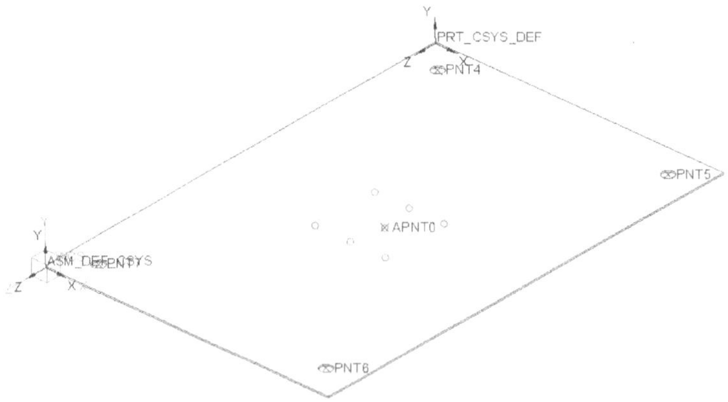

Figure 11–37

Note: Display set to ***No Hidden*** *for clarity.*

Task 9: Create a mass.

1. In the *Refine Model* tab, click (Mass). The *Mass Definition* dialog box opens, as shown in Figure 11–38.

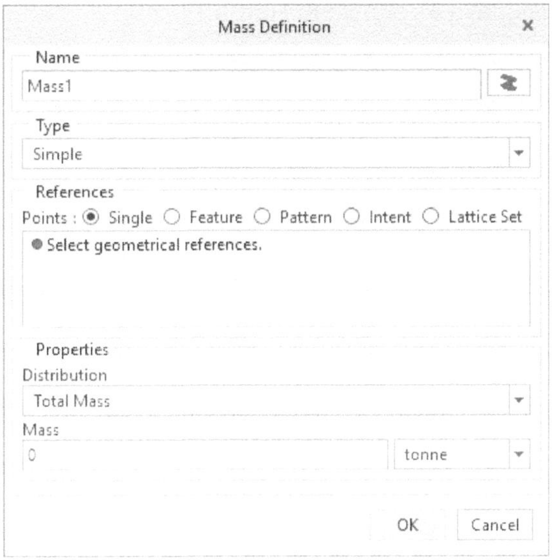

Figure 11–38

2. For the *Name*, enter **HS** and in the *Mass* field, enter **1.3e-4**. For the *Reference*, select the **APNT0** point. The *Mass Definition* dialog box displays as shown in Figure 11–39.

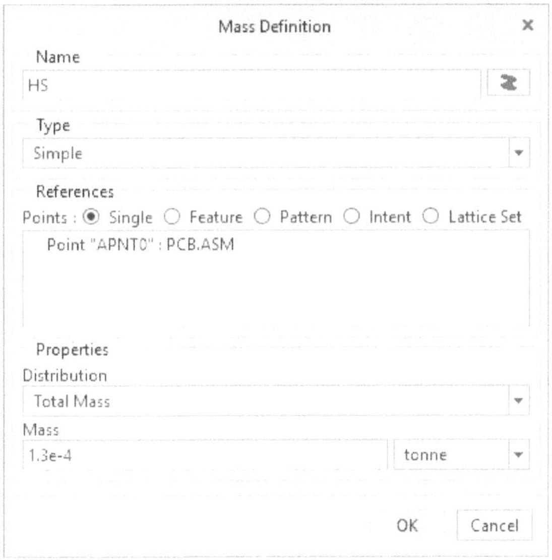

Figure 11–39

Note: *The mass of the heat sink/IC package is 130g (i.e., 1.3e-4 tonne).*

3. Click **OK**. The model displays as shown in Figure 11–40.

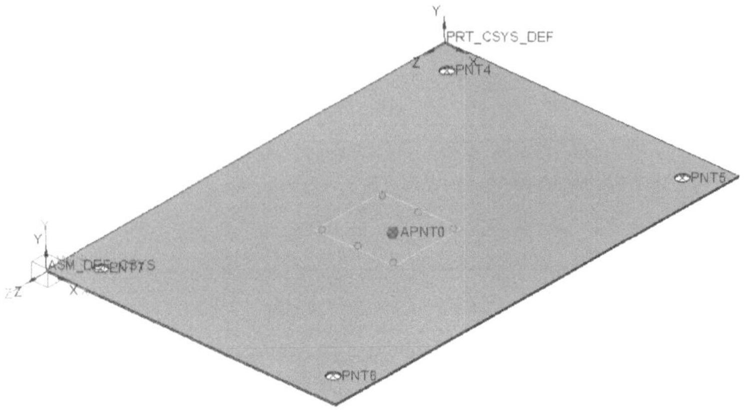

Figure 11–40

Task 10: Apply constraints.

1. Constrain the edges of the four holes in all of the translations. The model displays as shown in Figure 11–41.

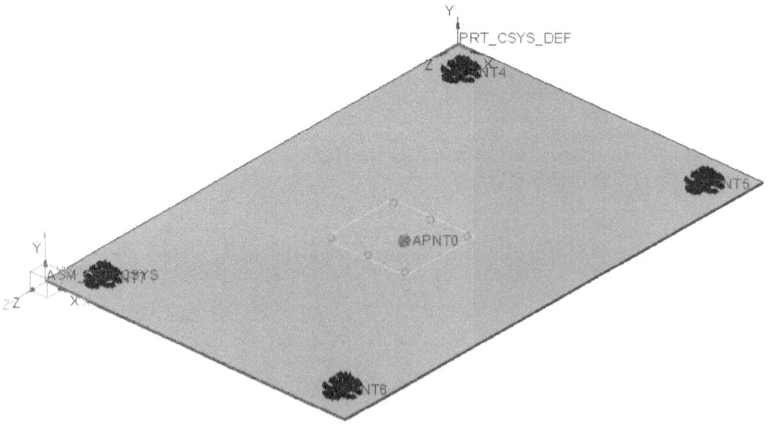

Figure 11–41

Analysis Tasks

Task 11: Set up and run a Modal analysis.

1. Click (Analyses and Studies). In the *Analyses and Design Studies* dialog box, select **File>New Modal**. The *Modal Analysis Definition* dialog box opens, as shown in Figure 11–42.

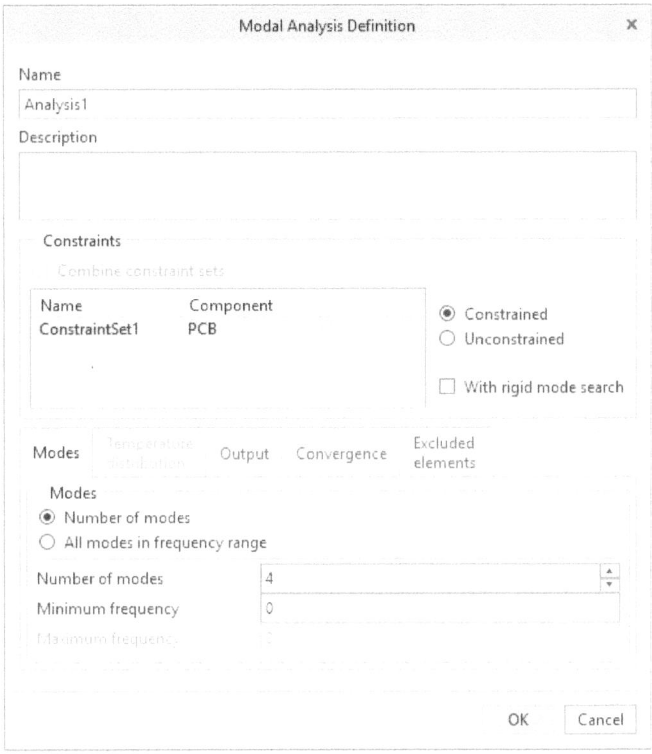

Figure 11–42

2. For the analysis name, enter **PCB**. Accept all of the other defaults and click **OK**.
3. Run the analysis.

Results Tasks

Task 12: Display the results.

In this task, you will create and animate the Displacement Magnitude fringe plots for the calculated modes of vibration.

1. In the *Analyses and Design Studies* dialog box, click (Review Results). The *Result Window Definition* dialog box opens, as shown in Figure 11–43.

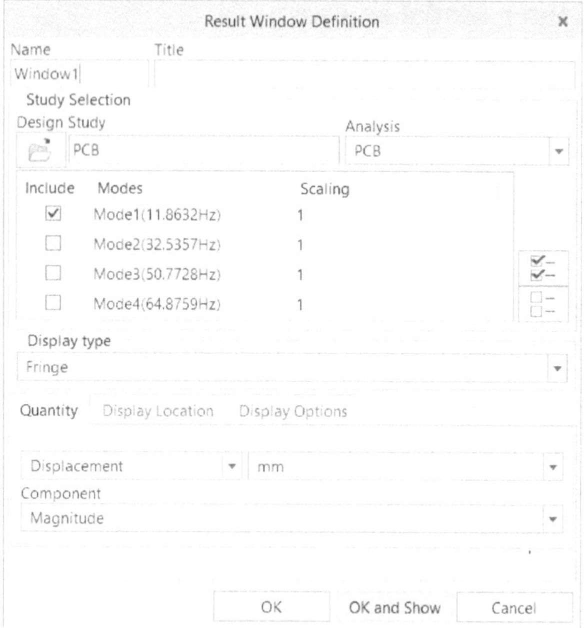

Figure 11–43

2. In the *Name* field, enter **mode1**.
3. Select the *Display Options* tab and select the required options, as shown in Figure 11–44.

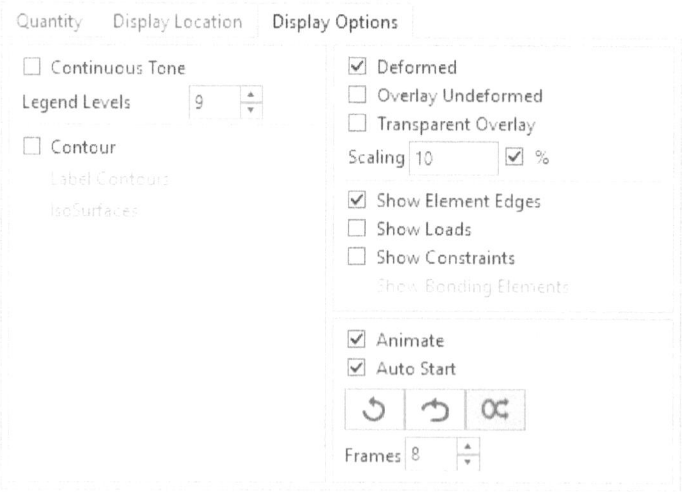

Figure 11–44

4. Display and animate the result plot. Step through the animation to Frame 3, as shown in Figure 11–45.

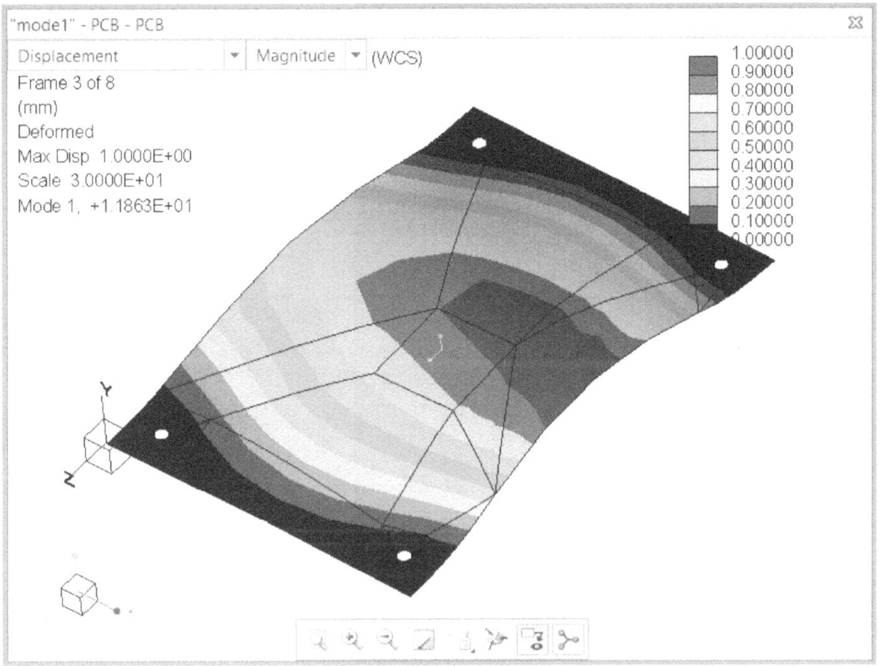

Figure 11–45

Note that the divided surface area remains flat through the deformation. The area has been rendered effectively undeformable due to the rigid link applied to the divided surface.

5. Create, animate, and display the Displacement Magnitude plot for Mode 2. In the *Name* field, enter **mode2**.

6. In the *Include* column, select the second checkbox (as shown in Figure 11–46) and clear the first checkbox.

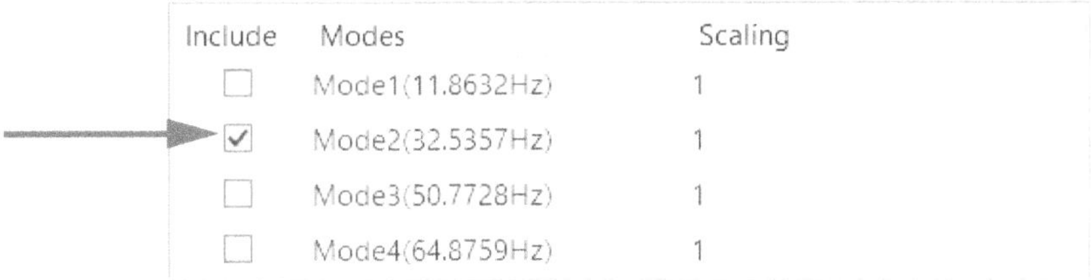

Figure 11–46

7. Display the **mode2** fringe plot. Step through the animation to Frame 3, as shown in Figure 11–47.

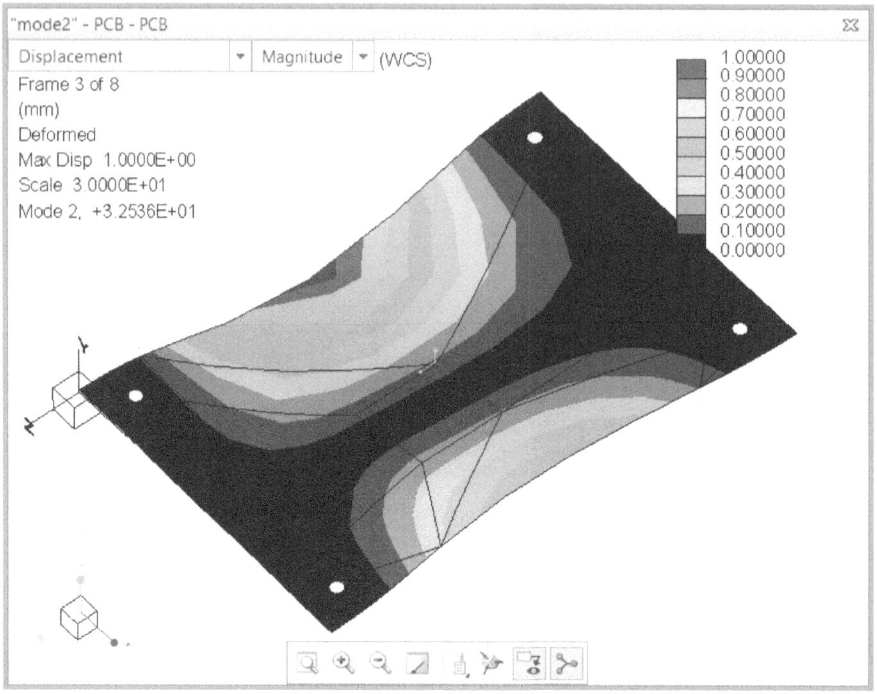

Figure 11–47

8. Create, animate, and display the Displacement Magnitude plots for Modes 3 and 4. Examine the motion of the divided surface area in all of the animations.

9. Exit the Results environment. Save and close the model.

End of practice

Practice 11b
Static Analysis of a Mixed Solid/Shell/Beam Model

Practice Objectives

- Use a combination of solids, shells, and beams in an analysis model.
- Connect a beam to a solid using a rigid link.

In this practice, you will set up and run a static analysis of the bracket assembly shown in Figure 11–48. The shaft is press-fit into the bracket.

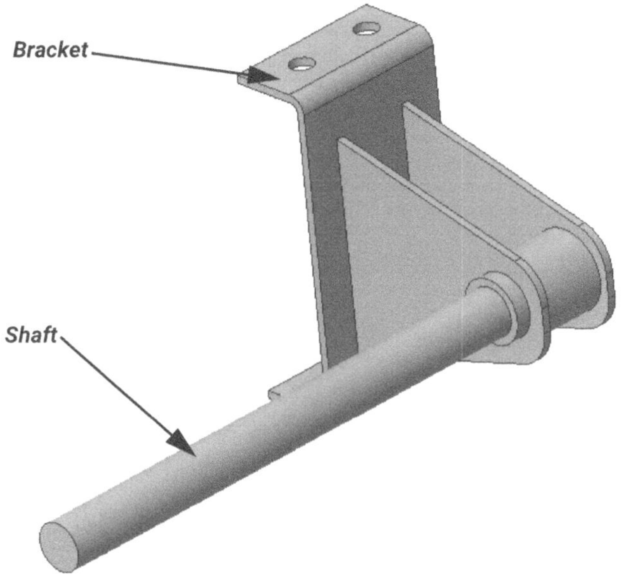

Figure 11–48

You will use the following idealizations for the parts in the model:

- The shaft is modeled with a beam.
- The cylindrical boss, into which the shaft is press-fit, is modeled with solids.
- The bracket is modeled with shells.

You will connect the beam to the solid using a rigid link.

Modeling Tasks

Task 1: Open the assembly.

1. Set the working directory to **Chapter11**, if required.
2. Open **bracket_shaft.asm**.
3. Set the model display as follows:
   - *(Datum Display Filters)*: (Point Display)
   - *(Spin Center)*: Off
   - *(Display Style)*: (Shading With Edges)
4. In the *View* tab of the ribbon, in the *Show* group, enable (Point Tag Display). The model displays as shown in Figure 11–49.

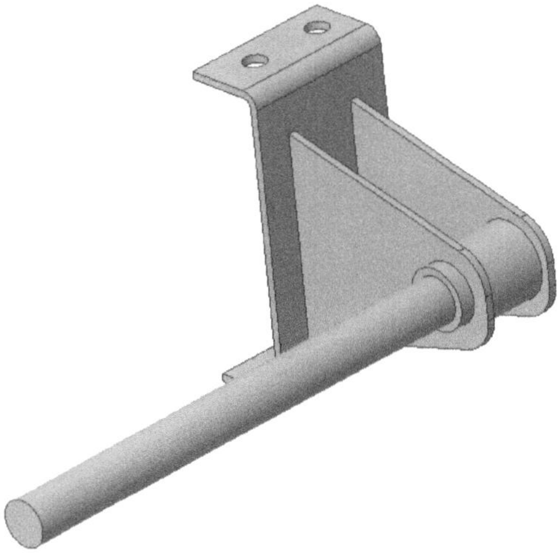

Figure 11–49

Task 2: Create datum points.

The shaft part is simulated with a beam idealization. In this task, you will create two datum points to be used as the reference geometry for the beam.

1. Hide the bracket part.
2. In the In-graphics toolbar, enable (Axis Display).
3. In the *Datum* group in the ribbon, select (Point).

4. Create two datum points as shown in Figure 11–50.

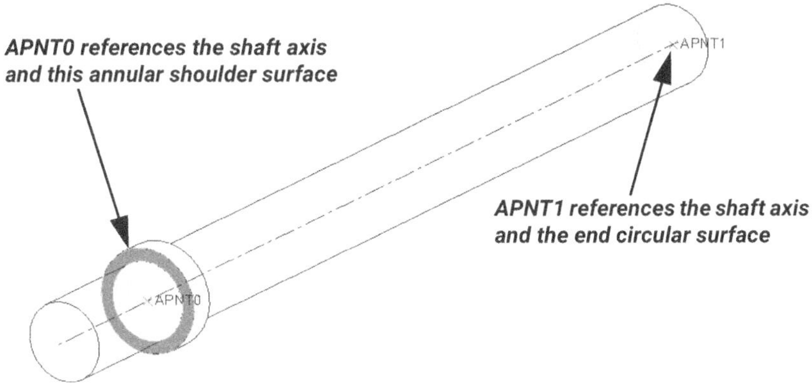

Figure 11–50

5. Show the bracket part.
6. In the In-graphics toolbar, disable (Axis Display).

Task 3: Create a simplified representation.

In this task, you will create a simplified representation to exclude the shaft solid geometry from the analysis model.

1. In the In-graphics toolbar, click (View Manager). The *View Manager* dialog box opens, as shown in Figure 11–51. Ensure that the *Simp Rep* tab is activated.

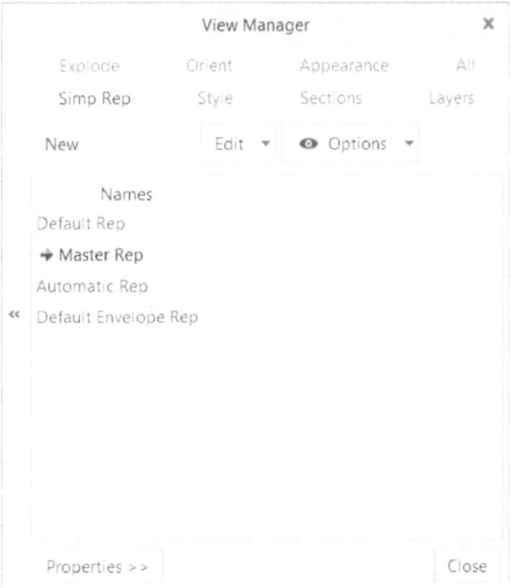

Figure 11–51

2. Click **New**. Rename the new representation as **AnlsRep** and press <Enter>. The *Edit:ANLSREP* dialog box opens, as shown in Figure 11–52.

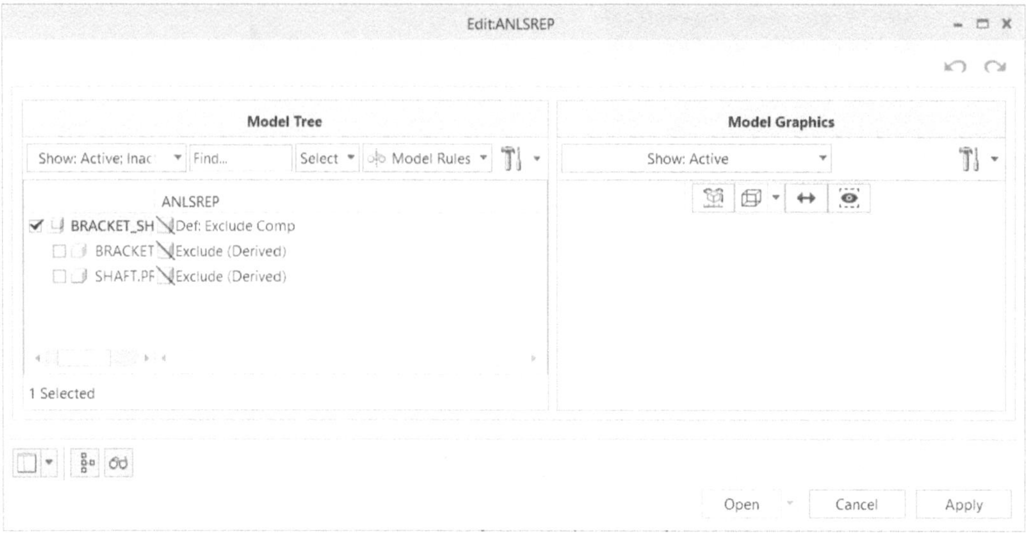

Figure 11–52

3. Set **BRACKET_SHAFT.ASM** and **BRACKET.PRT** to **Master Rep**, and **SHAFT.PRT** to **Exclude**. The *Edit:ANLSREP* dialog box updates as shown in Figure 11–53.

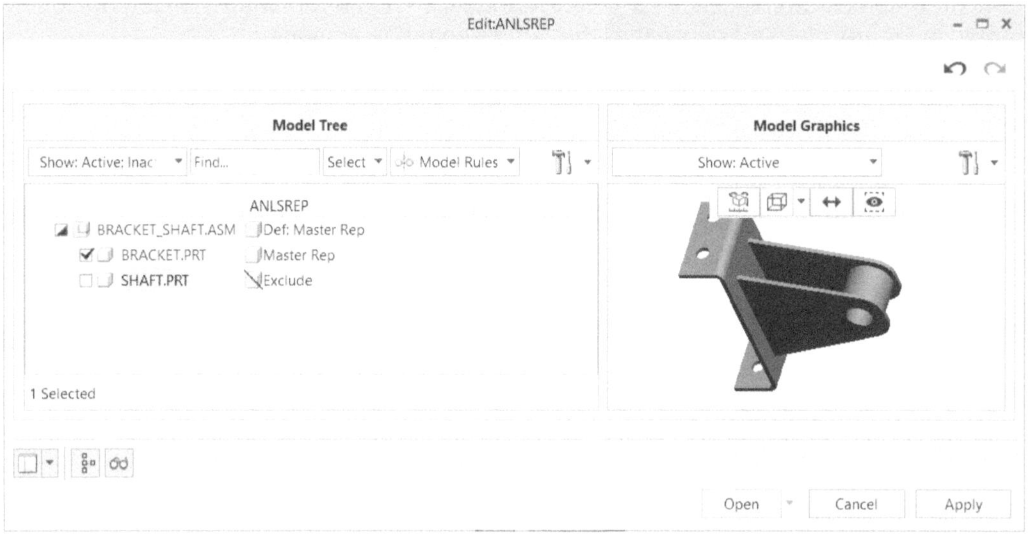

Figure 11–53

4. Click **Open** and **Close** to finish. The model displays as shown in Figure 11–54.

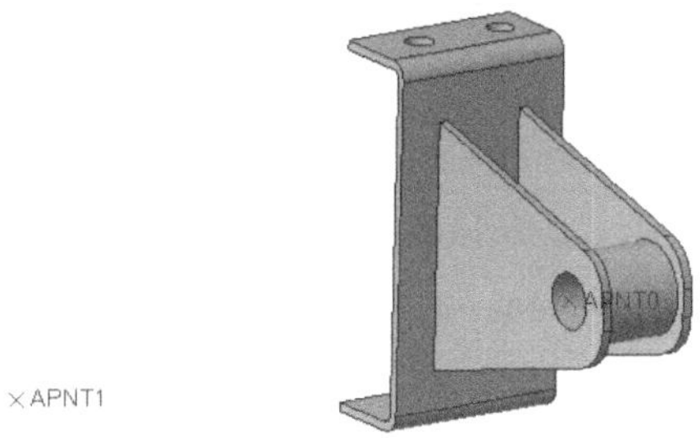

Figure 11–54

5. Switch to the Simulate application.

Task 4: Create a beam idealization.

1. In the *Refine Model* tab, click (Beam). The *Beam Definition* dialog box opens, as shown in Figure 11–55.

Figure 11–55

2. In the *Name* field, enter **beam_shaft**.
3. Expand the *References* drop-down list and select **Point-Point**.
4. Select **APNT0** and **APNT1**.
5. In the *Material* area, click **More** and add **STEEL** to the model.
6. In the *Orientation* area, accept the default X-, Y-, and Z-values.
7. Next to the *Beam Section* drop-down list, click **More**. The *Beam Sections* dialog box opens, as shown in Figure 11–56.

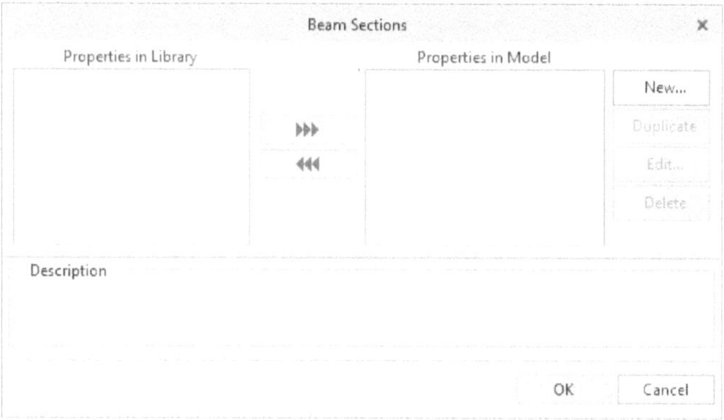

Figure 11–56

8. Click **New**. The *Beam Section Definition* dialog box opens, as shown in Figure 11–57.

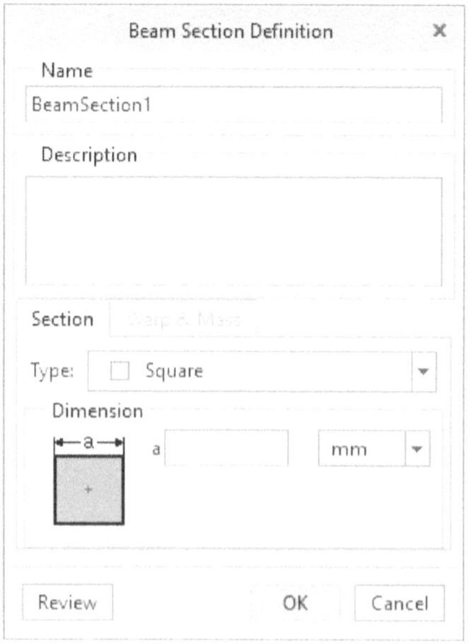

Figure 11–57

9. In the *Name* field, enter **circ_section**.
10. Expand the *Type* drop-down list and select **Solid Circle**. In the *R* field, enter **15**, as shown in Figure 11–58.

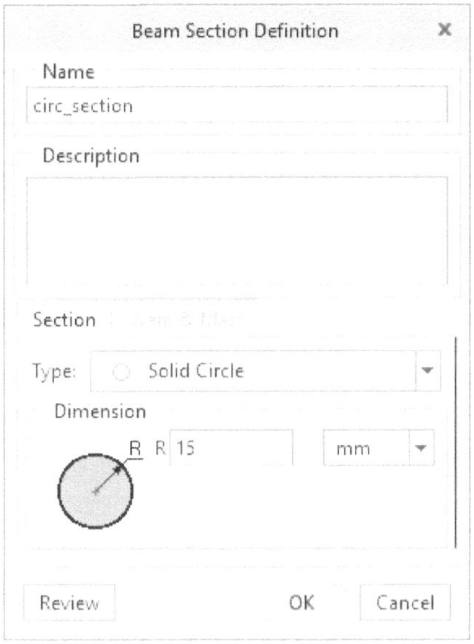

Figure 11–58

11. Click **OK** twice to close the *Beam Section Definition* dialog box and the *Beam Sections* dialog box.
12. Click **OK** to close the *Beam Definition* dialog box. The model displays as shown in Figure 11–59.

Figure 11–59

Task 5: Create shell pairs.

1. Use the **Detect Shell Pairs** tool with the *Characteristic Thickness* set to **5** to define the shell pairs for the bracket part.

   Note: *The bracket thickness is 5mm.*

Task 6: Apply the material.

1. Assign **STEEL** to the bracket part only.

Task 7: Mesh the model.

1. Mesh the model using the **All with Properties** option. The mesh displays as shown in Figure 11–60.

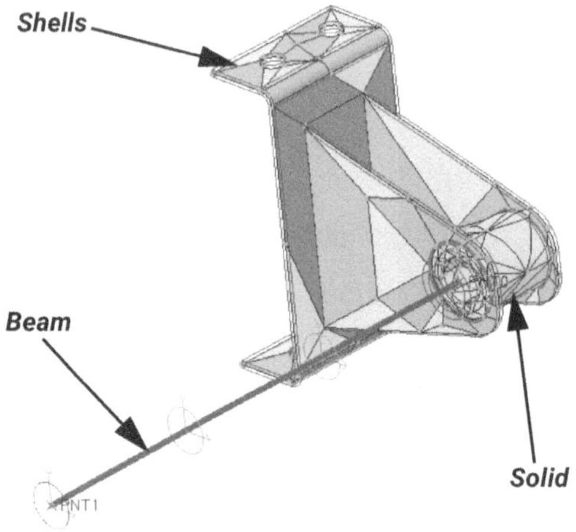

Figure 11–60

   Note that the shaft has been meshed as a beam (purple line), the circular boss has been meshed with solids (blue), and the rest of the bracket has been meshed with shells (green).

2. Exit the *AutoGEM* dialog box without saving the mesh.

Task 8: Create a rigid link.

In this task, you will create a rigid link to connect the end of the beam to the inside surface of the hole in the bracket.

Note: *The end of the beam idealization at **APNT0** is in the middle of the hole in the boss; therefore, it is not yet attached to the solid and shell elements that model the bracket.*

1. In the *Refine Model* tab, click (Rigid Link). The *Rigid Link Definition* dialog box opens, as shown in Figure 11–61.

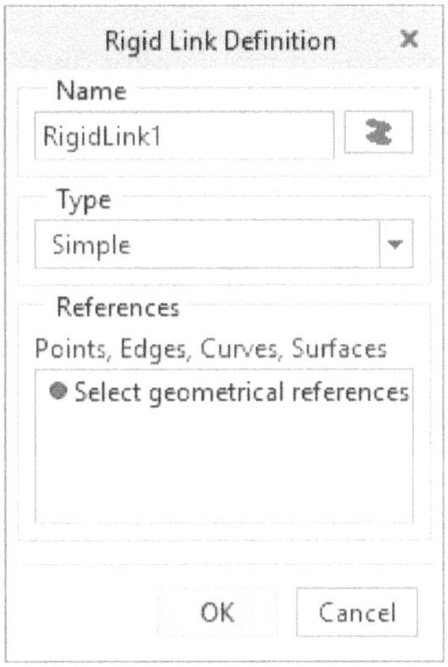

Figure 11–61

2. Select both the **APNT0** point and the inside surface of the hole into which the shaft is inserted (hold <Ctrl> to multi-select). Use the **Pick from List** option to select the surface of the hole.
3. Click **OK** to finish. The model displays as shown in Figure 11–62.

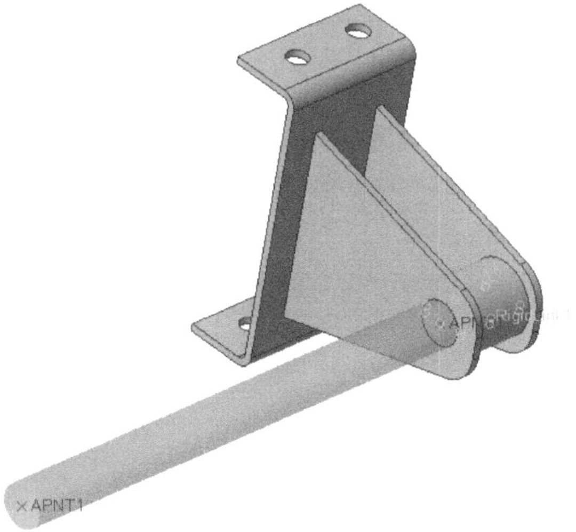

Figure 11–62

Task 9: Apply loads and constraints.

1. Apply force 200N to the **APNT1** point in the negative Y-direction.
2. Constrain the edges of the four holes in the bracket part in all of the translations. Ensure that you only select edges on the outside surface of the bracket. The model displays as shown in Figure 11–63.

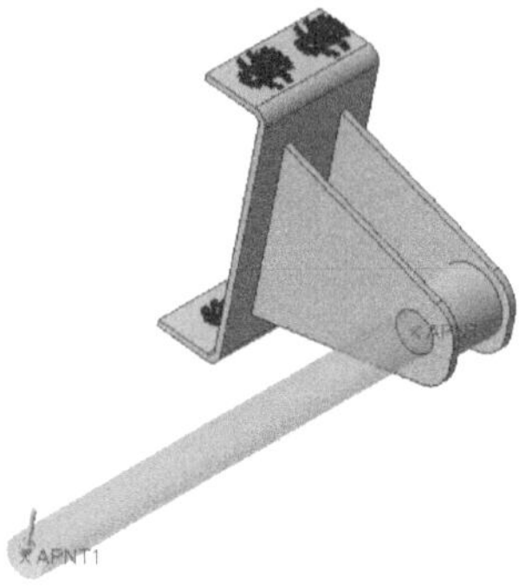

Figure 11–63

Analysis Tasks

Task 10: Set up and run a static analysis.

1. Set up a Multi-Pass Adaptive static analysis. For the *Name*, enter **bracket_shaft**. In the *Polynomial Order* field, enter **9** and in the *Limits* area, in the *Percent Convergence* field, enter **10**.
2. Run the analysis with interactive diagnostics.
3. Expand the *Run Status* window and review the following information:
   - Analysis converges on pass 9.
   - Stress error is 19.0% of the maximum principal stress, as shown in Figure 11–64.

```
RMS Stress Error Estimates:

Load Set             Stress Error   % of Max Prin Str
-----------------    ------------   -----------------
LoadSet1              8.24e+00       19.0% of  4.33e+01
```

Figure 11–64

Results Tasks

Task 11: Display the results.

In this task, you will create and display a von Mises stress fringe plot and a deformation animation for the model to verify the applied boundary conditions.

1. Create the displacement magnitude animation plot.
2. Start the animation. Verify whether the applied boundary conditions behave correctly.
3. Create an undeformed von Mises stress fringe plot. Change the *Legend minimum* to **0** and *maximum* to **40**. The result plot displays as shown in Figure 11–65.

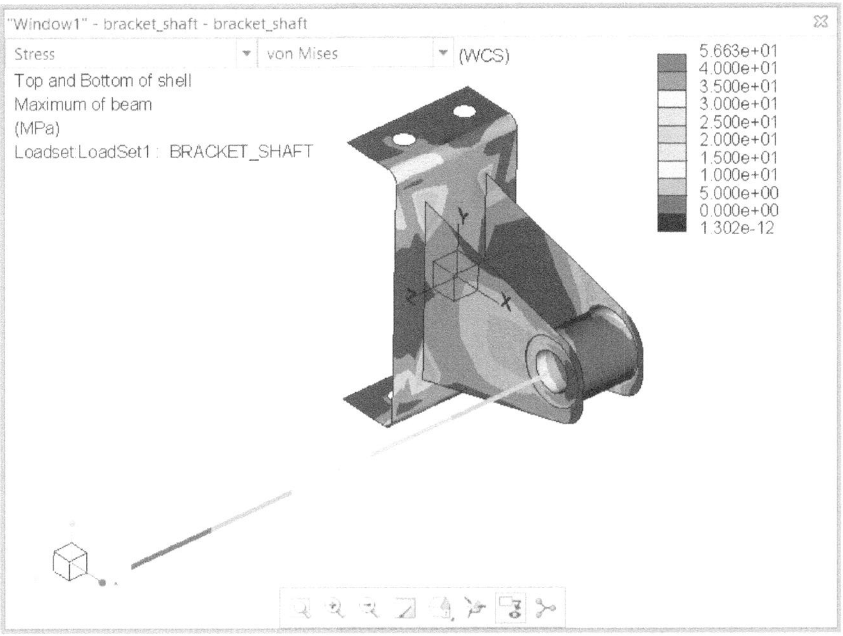

Figure 11–65

4. Locate and examine the high stress areas in the model.
5. Exit the Results environment. Save and close the model.

End of practice

Practice 11c
Fasteners with Preload

Practice Objectives

- Create bolted connections in solid models.
- Apply bolt preload.
- Understand how to control and adjust preload accuracy.

In this practice, you will set up and run a static analysis of the assembly shown in Figure 11–66. The two plates in the assembly are bolted together through the three holes, with a preload of 500N on each bolt.

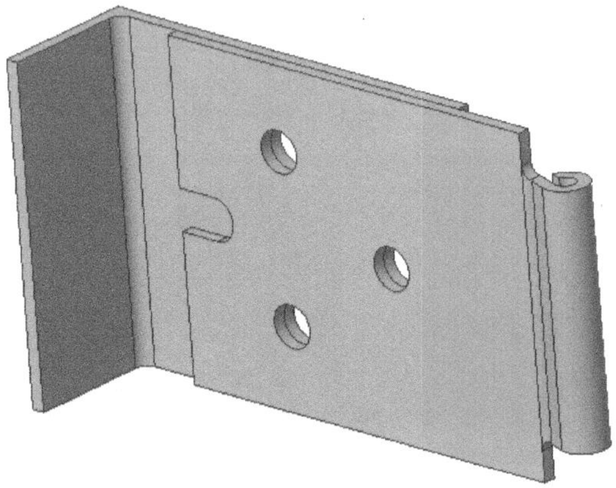

Figure 11–66

You will use the Fastener connection to model the bolted joints. You will solve the model in two iterations:

- In the first and second analyses, you will only apply preloads on the bolts, without applying any other loads in the model. The objective of this analysis is to check how accurately the preloads are simulated, depending on whether or not the **Account for Stiffness** option is activated.
- In the third and final analysis, you will solve the model with the **Account for Stiffness** option toggled on, and with all of the other loads in the model fully applied.

Modeling Tasks

Task 1: Open the model.

1. Set the working directory to **Chapter11**, if required.
2. Open **fastener_ex1.asm**.
3. Set the model display as follows:
   - *(Datum Display Filters)*: (Point Display), (Plane Display)
   - *(Spin Center)*: Off
   - *(Display Style)*: (Shading With Edges)

   The model displays as shown in Figure 11–67.

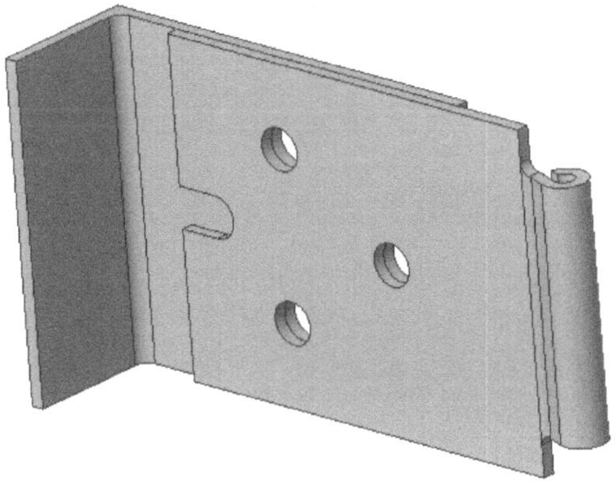

Figure 11–67

4. Select **Applications>Simulate** to switch to the Simulate environment.

Task 2: Apply the material.

1. Assign **STEEL** to both parts. The following values are the default material properties for HS-low-alloy steel (STEEL):
   - *Poisson:* **0.27**
   - *Young's modulus:* **199948 MPa**

   Note: *The material properties should be as stated.*

2. Toggle off the display of the **Material Assignments** icons.

Task 3: Create the fasteners.

1. In the *Refine Model* tab, click (Fastener). The *Fastener Definition* dialog box opens, as shown in Figure 11–68.

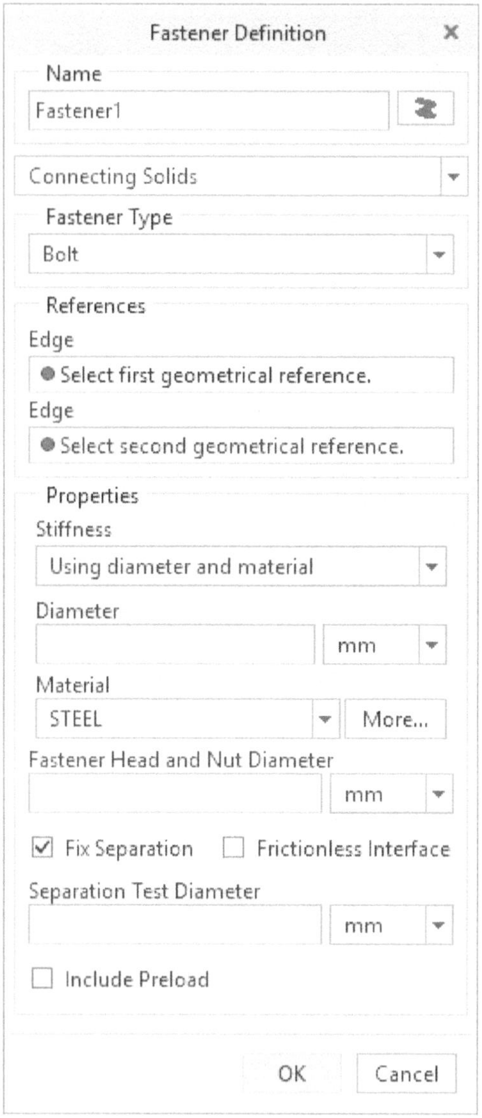

Figure 11–68

2. Select the circular edge of the top hole in the **hinge2** part as the first reference, as shown in Figure 11–69.

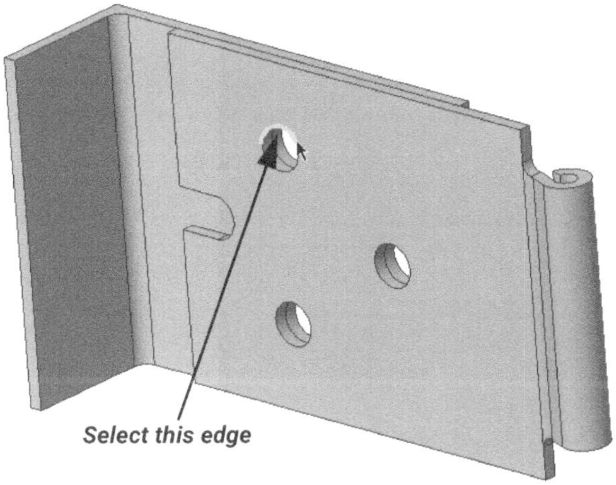

Figure 11–69

3. Select the circular edge of the top hole in the **plate** part as the second reference, as shown in Figure 11–70.

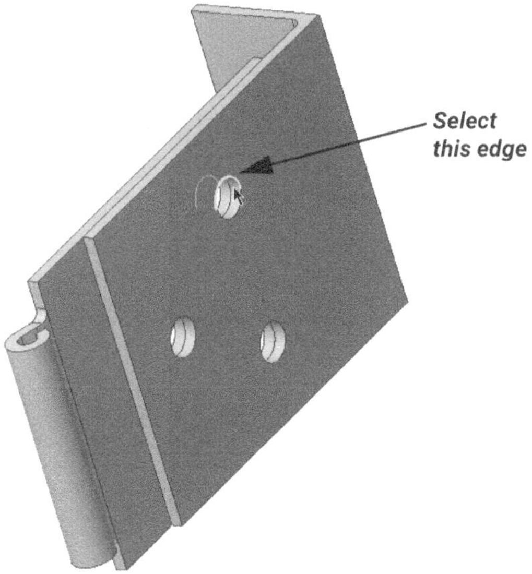

Figure 11–70

4. Select the **Include Preload** option. In the *Preload Force* field, enter **500**, as shown in Figure 11–71.

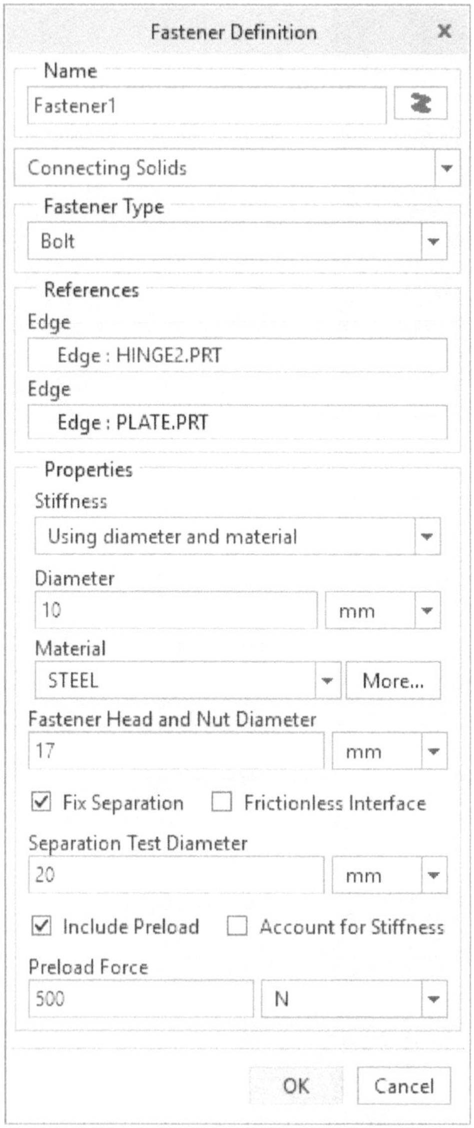

Figure 11–71

5. Click **OK**. A warning message box displays as shown in Figure 11–72, and the two contacting surfaces are highlighted.

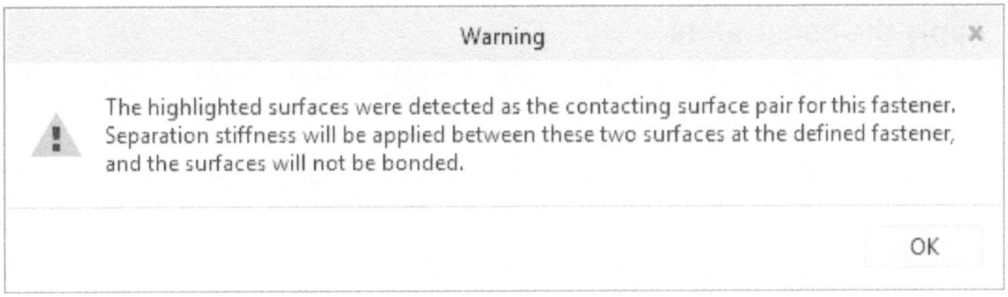

Figure 11–72

Note that the message in the box informs you that the two contacting surfaces will not be bonded during the analysis, due to the application of the fastener.

6. Click **OK** to close the message box. The model displays as shown in Figure 11–73.

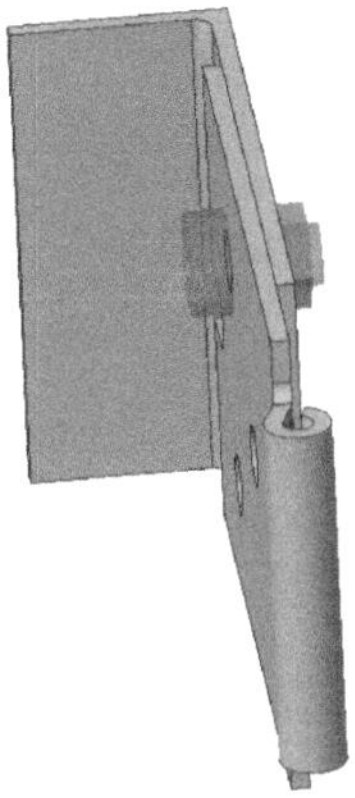

Figure 11–73

7. Repeat Steps 1 to 6 to create fasteners in the second and third holes, as shown in Figure 11–74.

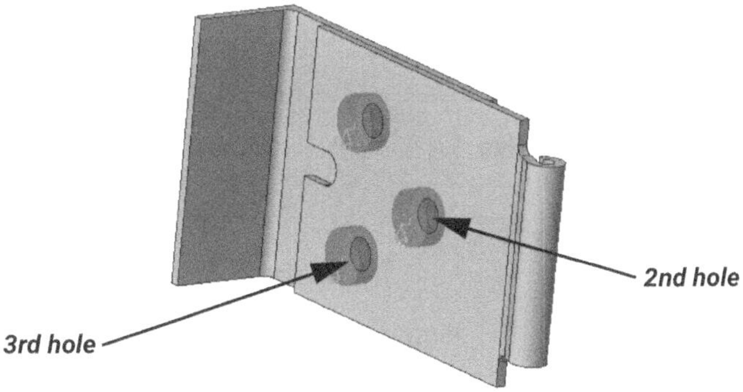

Figure 11–74

Task 4: Apply the constraints.

1. Constrain the surface shown in Figure 11–75 in all of the translations.

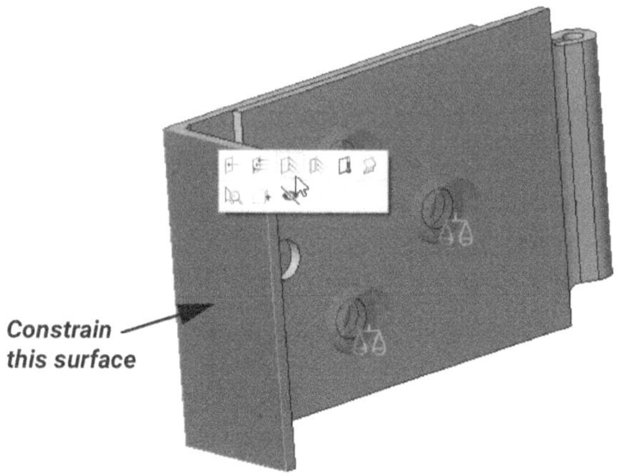

Figure 11–75

Task 5: Mesh the model.

1. Click (AutoGEM). In the *AutoGEM* dialog box that opens, select **Component Volumes** in the drop-down list, and select the **HINGE2** part.
2. Click **Create** and wait until meshing completes. Close the *Diagnostics* and the *AutoGEM Summary* dialog boxes. The model displays as shown in Figure 11–76.

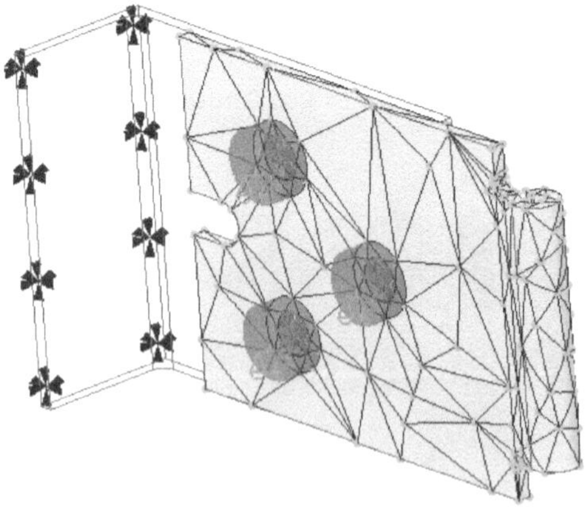

Figure 11–76

3. Click (Simulation Display) and hide the fasteners.

4. Zoom in on the model and note the annular regions under the bolt heads that were created automatically for each fastener, as shown in Figure 11–77.

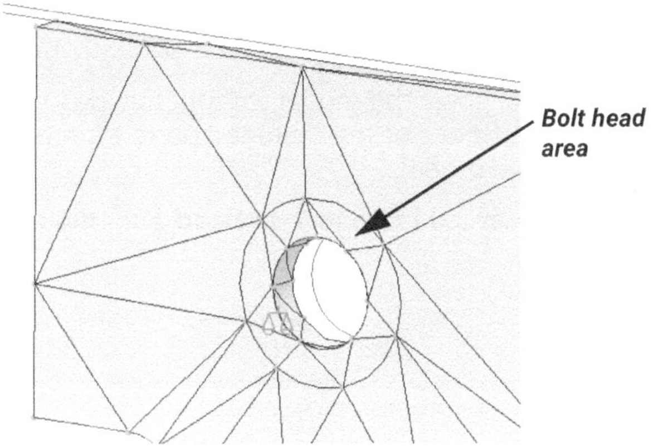

Figure 11–77

5. Rotate the model. Note the annular separation areas around each fastener, as shown in Figure 11–78.

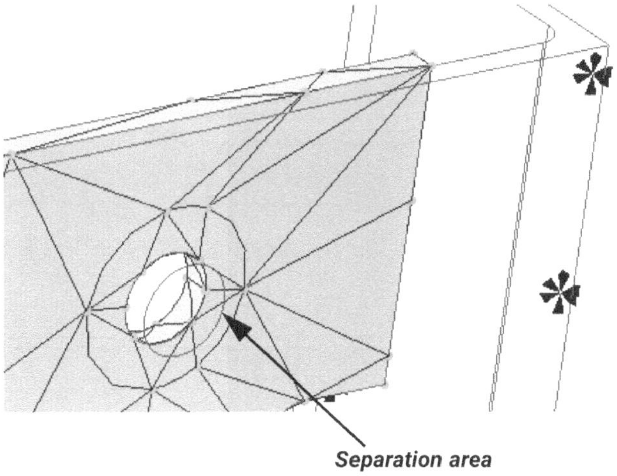

Figure 11–78

6. In the *AutoGEM* dialog box, click **Delete**. In the drop-down list, select **All with Properties** and click **Create** to mesh both parts.
7. Close the *AutoGEM* dialog box and save the mesh.
8. Click (Simulation Display) and unhide the fasteners.

Analysis Tasks

Task 6: Set up and run a static analysis.

In the preliminary analysis, you will solve the model without having any external loads applied. The objective is to test how the stiffness of the fastened parts affects the actual compressive force that a fastener applies on the model.

1. Set up a new static analysis, named **fastener1_preload**, with the options shown in Figure 11–79.

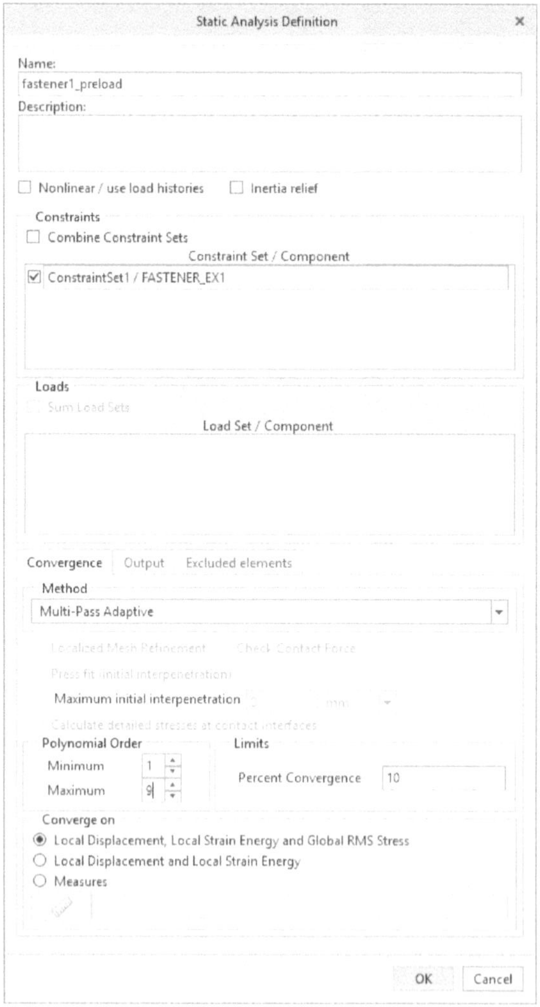

Figure 11–79

2. Run the analysis with interactive diagnostics. It should converge on pass 6.

Task 7: Check the fastener axial forces.

Since no external loads were applied in this analysis run, the force in the fasteners must be equal to the preloads that you applied in Task 3.

1. Expand the *Run Status* window and scroll up to the *Measures* area.
2. Extract the axial forces in the fasteners, as shown in Figure 11–80.

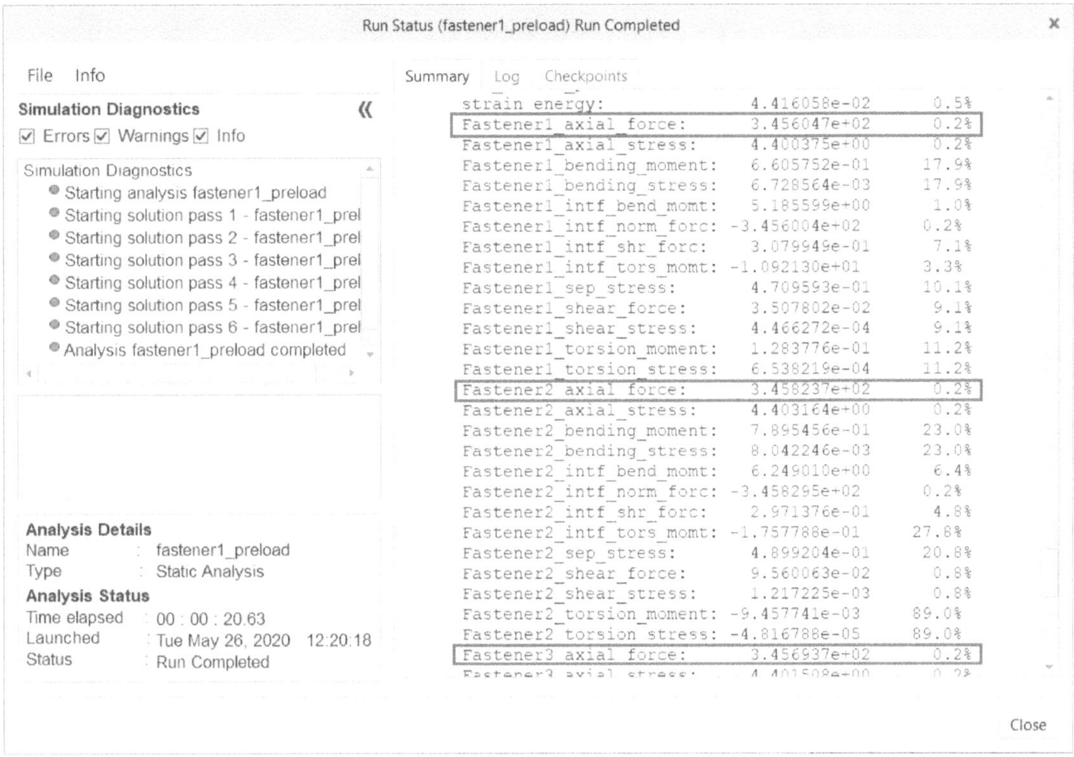

Figure 11–80

Note that Creo Simulate did not get the preloads quite right. The required preloads were 500N, while the actual axial forces in the bolts are approximately 345N. This is because the **Account for Stiffness** option was not selected when the fasteners were created in Task 3. In the next tasks, you will toggle on the **Account for Stiffness** option and re-run the analysis.

3. Close the *Run Status* window and the *Analyses and Design Studies* dialog box.

Modeling Tasks

Task 8: Toggle on the Account for Stiffness option.

1. Select **Fastener1** and select (Edit Definition) from the mini-toolbar.
2. Select the **Account for Stiffness** checkbox, as shown in Figure 11–81.

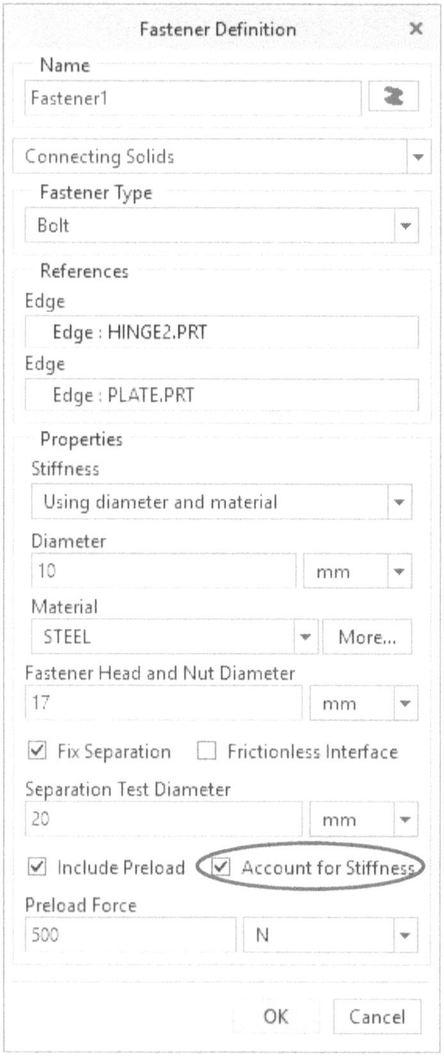

Figure 11–81

3. Click **OK** to finish. Click **OK** in the warning message box that displays.
4. Repeat Steps 1 to 3 for the other two fasteners.

Analysis Tasks

Task 9: Re-run the analysis.

1. Re-run the **fastener1_preload** analysis using interactive diagnostics.
2. Expand the *Run Status* window. Scroll down and note that the analysis began with running the Base Analysis, as shown in Figure 11–82.

```
Base Analysis to scale Fastener Preloads

     Measures:

          Name                  Value        Convergence
     --------------        -------------   -----------
     max_beam_bending:           0.000000e+00       0.0%
     max_beam_tensile:           0.000000e+00       0.0%
     max_beam_torsion:           0.000000e+00       0.0%
     max_beam_total:             0.000000e+00       0.0%
     max_disp_mag:               2.085527e-04       2.5%
     max_disp_x:                 3.431036e-05       0.5%
     max_disp_y:                -2.073626e-04       2.6%
     max_disp_z:                -2.417766e-05       0.4%
     max_prin_mag:              -3.193001e+00      14.0%
     max_rot_mag:                2.251730e-06       3.2%
     max_rot_x:                  2.929513e-07       6.3%
     max_rot_y:                  1.180592e-08       7.6%
     max_rot_z:                 -2.235747e-06       3.2%
     max_stress_prin:            7.102858e-01       6.0%
     max_stress_vm:              2.944639e+00      17.4%
     max_stress_xx:             -1.111410e+00       0.2%
     max_stress_xy:              5.630621e-01       1.9%
     max_stress_xz:              4.038006e-01      18.6%
     max_stress_yy:             -3.183693e+00      14.3%
     max_stress_yz:             -6.111955e-01       4.1%
     max_stress_zz:             -1.078378e+00       4.7%
     min_stress_prin:           -3.193001e+00      14.0%
     strain_energy:              4.416058e-02       0.5%
     Fastener1_axial_force:      3.456047e+02       0.2%
     Fastener1_axial_stress:     4.400375e+00       0.2%
     Fastener1_bending_moment:   6.605752e-01      17.9%
     Fastener1_bending_stress:   6.728564e-03      17.9%
     Fastener1_intf_bend_momt:   5.185599e+00       1.0%
```

Figure 11–82

Note that the axial forces in the fasteners are exactly the same as in the first analysis run, when the **Account for Stiffness** option was off.

3. Scroll down and note that there was also the second analysis run: *Analysis with Scaled Fastener Preloads and External Loads*, as shown in Figure 11–83.

```
Analysis with scaled Fastener Preloads and External loads

Static Analysis "fastener1_preload":

  Convergence Method: Multiple-Pass Adaptive
  Plotting Grid:      4

  Convergence Loop Log:                              (15:43:28)

  >> Pass  1 <<
        Calculating Element Equations                (15:43:28)
           Total Number of Equations:     1242
           Maximum Edge Order:               1
        Solving Equations                            (15:43:28)
        Post-Processing Solution                     (15:43:28)
        Calculating Disp and Stress Results          (15:43:28)
        Checking Convergence                         (15:43:28)
           Elements Not Converged:        1001
           Edges Not Converged:           1854
           Local Disp/Energy Index:     100.0%
           Global RMS Stress Index:     100.0%
```

Figure 11–83

Task 10: Check the fastener axial forces.

1. Scroll down to the *Measures* area. Note that the axial forces in the fasteners are now extremely close to the specified preload 500N, as shown in Figure 11–84.

Figure 11–84

2. Close the *Run Status* dialog box and the *Analyses and Design Studies* dialog box.

Modeling Tasks

Task 11: Apply the external loads.

1. Apply the force 100N in the Z-direction to the surface shown in Figure 11–85.

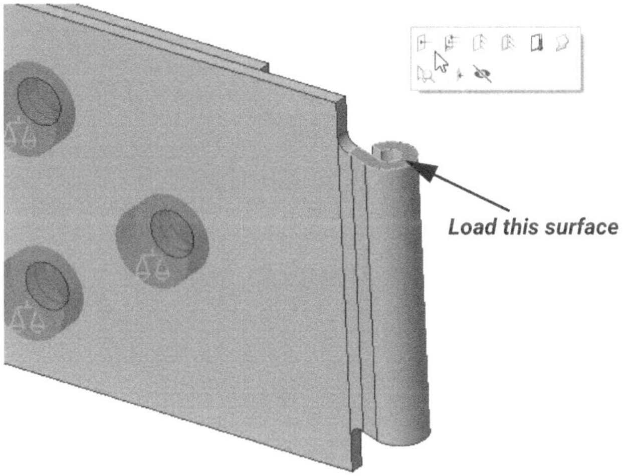

Figure 11–85

Analysis Tasks

Task 12: Re-run the analysis.

1. Open the **fastener1_preload** analysis to edit it.

2. Select the **LoadSet1/FASTENER_EX1** option, as shown in Figure 11–86. This ensures that the external loads are now included in the analysis.

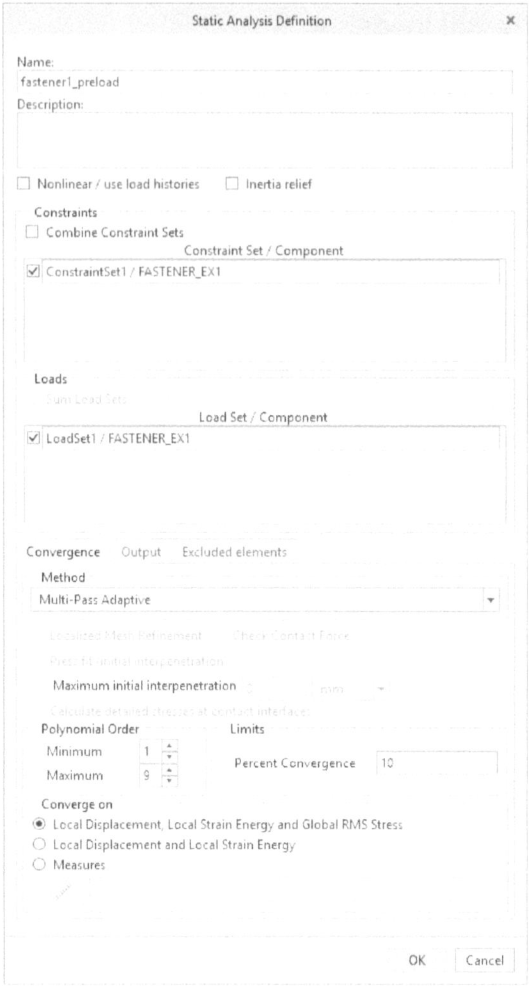

Figure 11–86

3. Run the analysis.

Results Tasks

Task 13: Animate the model deformation.

1. Create the displacement magnitude animation plot.
2. Start the animation. Verify whether the applied boundary conditions behave correctly.

3. Step to Frame 5 of the animation. The result plot displays as shown in Figure 11–87.

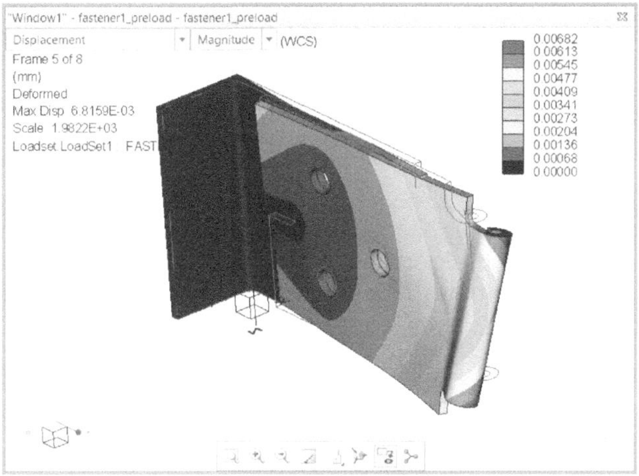

Figure 11–87

Note the interpenetration of the parts in some areas. This is a visual effect due to the deformation exaggeration via the **Scaling** factor in the *Display Options* tab of the *Result Window Definition* dialog box. To visually check if there actually was any interpenetration, set the **Scaling** to **1** and display the result again.

Task 14: Display the stress plot.

1. Create a deformed von Mises stress fringe plot. The result plot displays as shown in Figure 11–88.

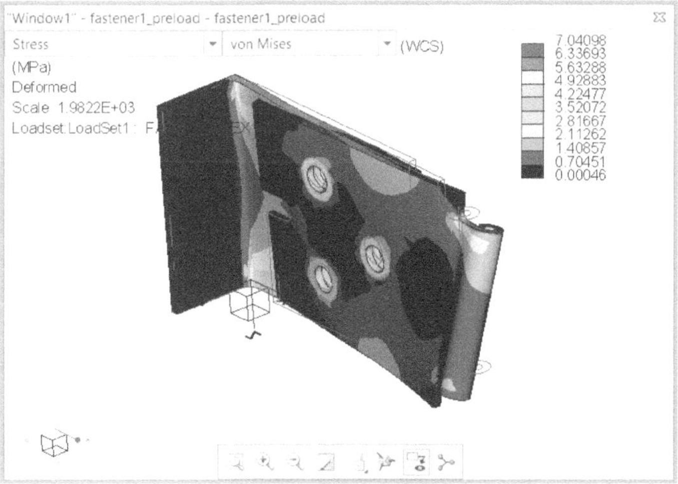

Figure 11–88

2. Examine the areas of maximum stress. Note the higher stresses around the bolt holes, caused by the preloads.
3. Exit the Results environment. Save and close the model.

Summary

In this practice, you learned how Creo Simulate works with the fastener preloads. You performed three analysis runs:

1. **Run 1:** Only bolt preloads were applied, with the **Account for Stiffness** option toggled off. You learned that applying the preload on an undeformed model, without taking into account the relaxation of the preload due to compression of the fastened parts, results in the actual forces in the bolts differing substantially from the specified preload.
2. **Run 2:** Only bolt preloads were applied, now with the **Account for Stiffness** option toggled on. You learned that taking into account the deformation of the fastened parts resulted in extremely accurate actual preloads.
3. **Run 3:** External loads applied along with the preloads, with the **Account for Stiffness** option toggled on. This was the final analysis run that accurately simulated the preloads as well as the effects of the other loads in the model.
4. In practical applications with fasteners, it is not necessary to perform several analysis runs, as you did above. Instead, it is recommended to always use the **Account for Stiffness** option, apply all other loads in the model (as in Run 3 above), and let Creo Simulate do the rest of the work.

End of practice

Practice 11d
Handle Surface Separation Issues When Using Fasteners

Practice Objectives

- Create fastened connections in solid models.
- Check fastener interface forces.
- Understand how to ensure the correct separation of assembly components.

In this practice, you will set up and run a static analysis of the assembly shown in Figure 11–89. The two parts are screwed together using the four holes in the flanges.

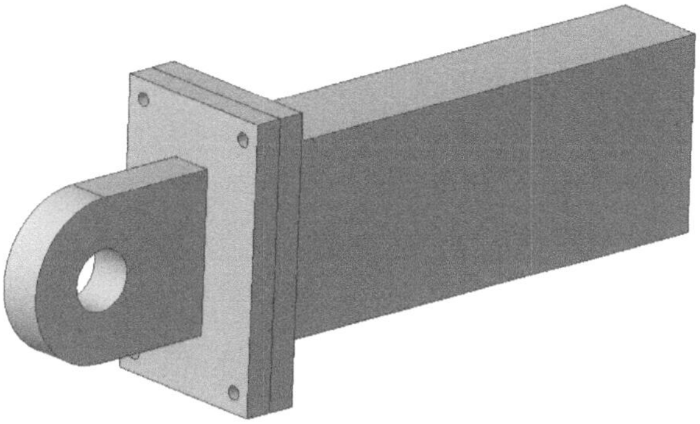

Figure 11–89

Modeling Tasks

Task 1: Open the model.

1. Set the working directory to **Chapter11**, if required.
2. Open **fastener_ex2.asm**.
3. Set the model display as follows:
   - *(Datum Display Filters)*: (Point Display), (Plane Display)
   - *(Spin Center)*: Off
   - *(Display Style)*: (Shading With Edges)

The model displays as shown in Figure 11–90.

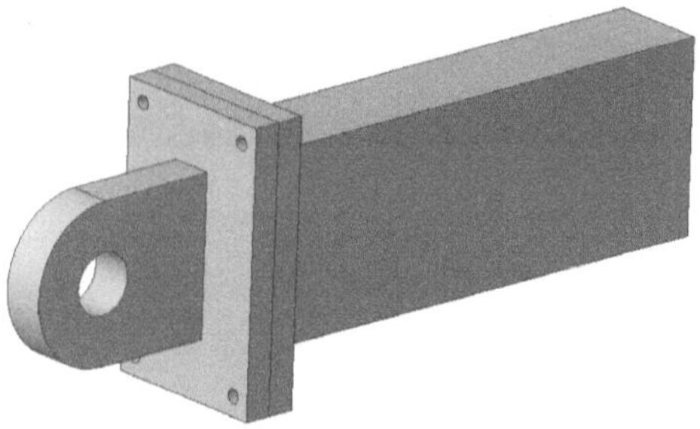

Figure 11–90

4. Select **Applications>Simulate** to switch to the Simulate environment.

Task 2: Apply the material.

1. Assign **STEEL** to both parts. The following values are the default material properties for HS-low-alloy steel (STEEL):
   - *Poisson:* **0.27**
   - *Young's modulus:* **199948 MPa**

   Note: *The material properties should be as stated.*

2. Toggle off the display of the **Material Assignments** icons.

Task 3: Create the fasteners.

1. In the *Refine Model* tab, click (Fastener). The *Fastener Definition* dialog box opens, as shown in Figure 11–91.

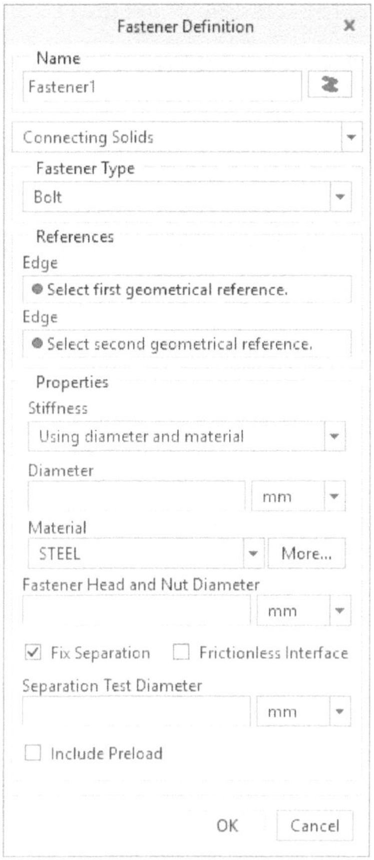

Figure 11–91

2. Select the circular edge of the top left hole in the **part2** part as the first reference, as shown in Figure 11–92.

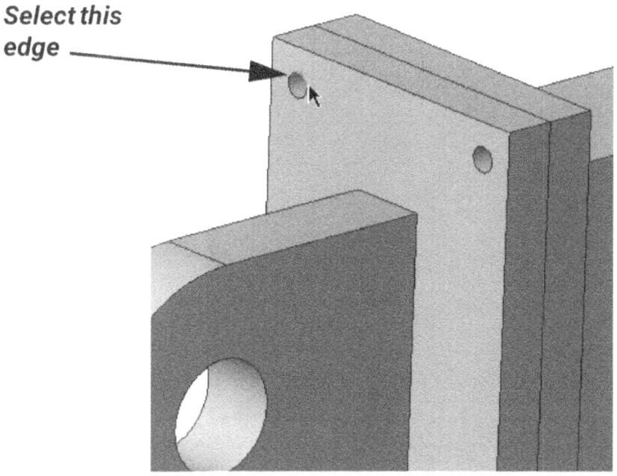

Figure 11–92

3. Select the circular edge of the top left hole in the **part1** part as the second reference, as shown in Figure 11–93.

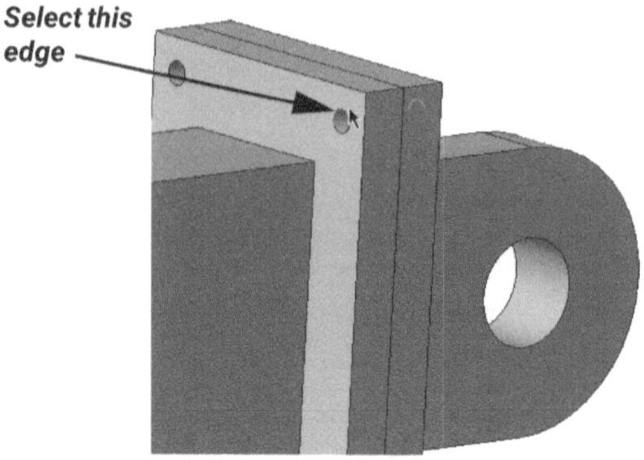

Figure 11–93

4. The *Fastener Definition* dialog box displays as shown in Figure 11–94.

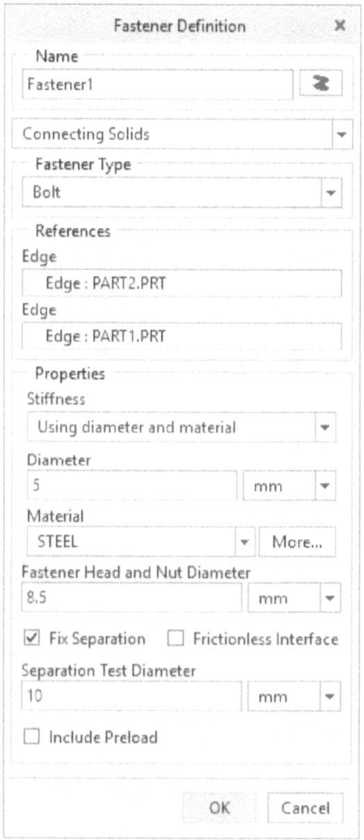

Figure 11–94

5. Click **OK**. A warning message box displays as shown in Figure 11–95, and the two contacting surfaces are highlighted.

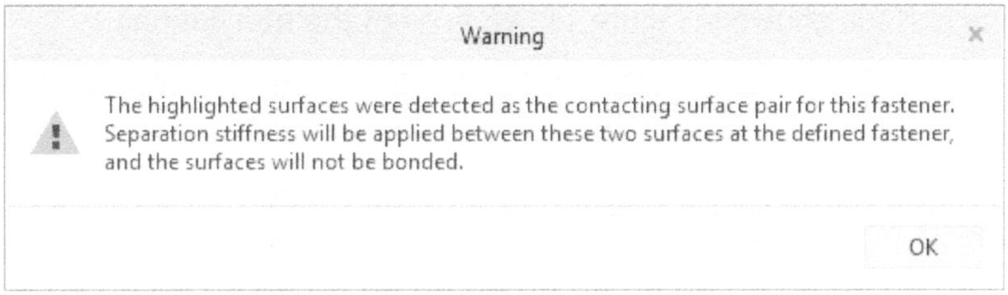

Figure 11–95

Note that the message in the box prompts you that the two contacting surfaces will not be bonded, due to the application of the fastener.

6. Click **OK** to close the message box. The model displays as shown in Figure 11–96.

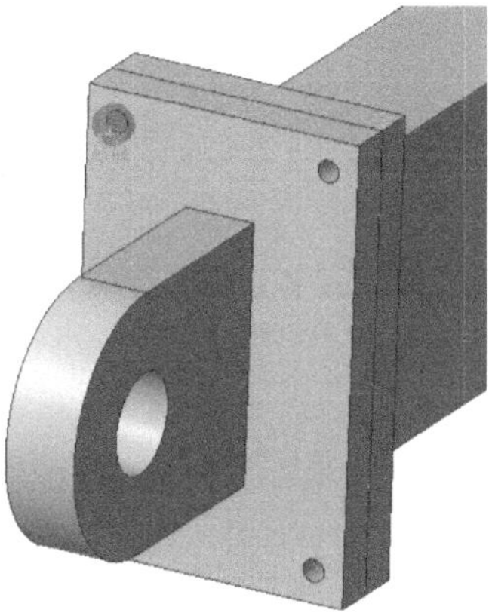

Figure 11–96

7. Repeat Steps 1 to 6 to create fasteners in the remaining holes, as shown in Figure 11–97.

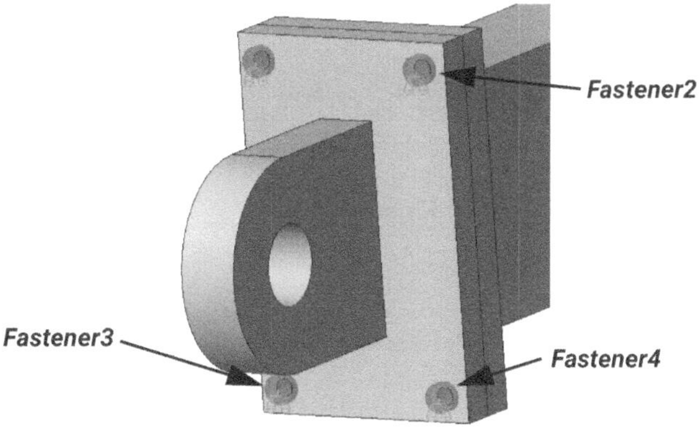

Figure 11–97

Task 4: Apply the constraints.

1. Constrain the surface shown in Figure 11–98 in all of the translations.

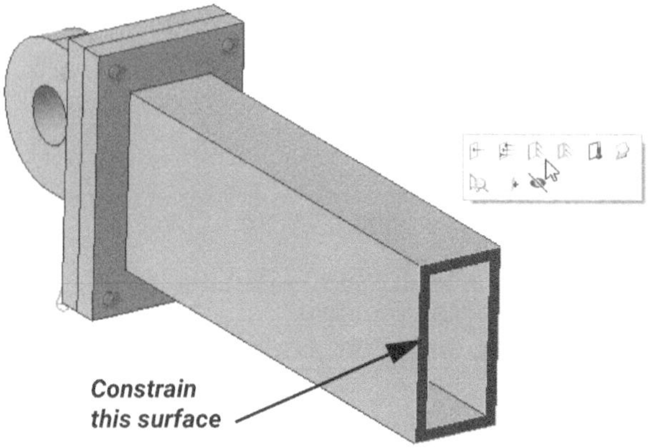

Figure 11–98

Task 5: Apply the loads.

1. Apply the force **-500** in the Y-direction to the large hole, as shown in Figure 11–99.

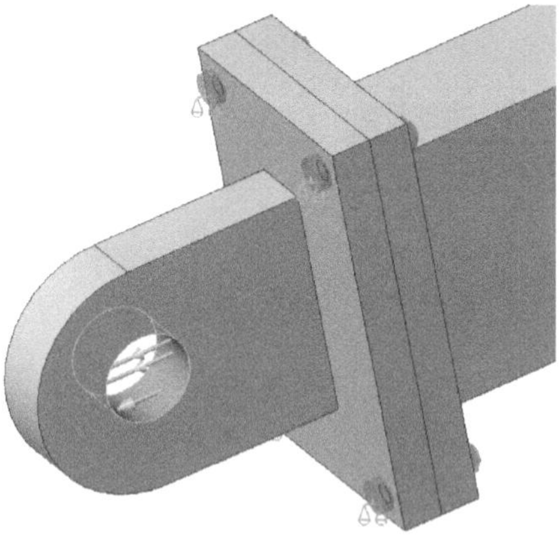

Figure 11–99

Analysis Tasks

Task 6: Set up and run a static analysis.

1. Set up a Single-Pass Adaptive static analysis, named **fastener2**.
2. Run the analysis using interactive diagnostics.

Task 7: Check the fastener separation status.

1. In the *Run Status* dialog box, note that a warning message for all four fasteners displays, prompting you that *The fix separation option for the fastener is preventing the parts from separating at locations where they should separate*, as shown in Figure 11–100.

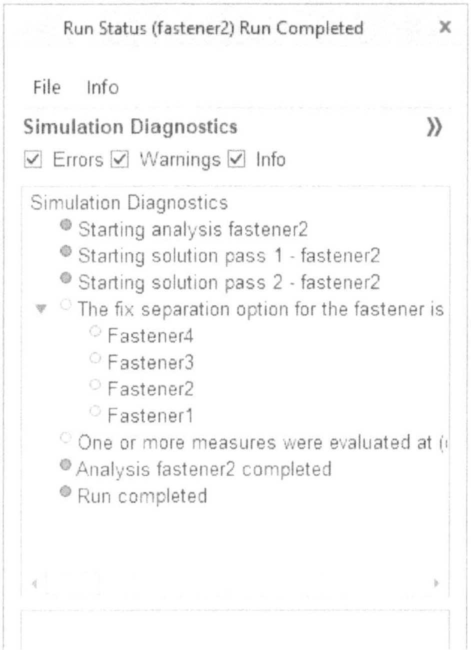

Figure 11–100

2. Expand the *Run Status* window and scroll up to the *Measures* area.

3. Extract the interface normal force (**intf_norm_forc**) measures for the fasteners, as shown in Figure 11–101.

```
Fastener1_axial_force:        7.303252e+00
Fastener1_axial_stress:       3.719516e-01
Fastener1_bending_moment:     1.139909e+01
Fastener1_bending_stress:     9.288814e-01
Fastener1_intf_bend_momt:     9.264600e+02
Fastener1_intf_norm_forc:     1.185485e+02
Fastener1_intf_shr_forc:      1.814293e+01
Fastener1_intf_tors_momt:    -1.202097e+01
Fastener1_sep_stress:         8.237053e+00
Fastener1_shear_force:        1.223051e-01
Fastener1_shear_stress:       6.228946e-03
Fastener1_torsion_moment:     7.991017e-02
Fastener1_torsion_stress:     3.255833e-03
Fastener2_axial_force:        7.332391e+00
Fastener2_axial_stress:       3.734356e-01
Fastener2_bending_moment:     1.055210e+01
Fastener2_bending_stress:     8.598628e-01
Fastener2_intf_bend_momt:     9.268916e+02
Fastener2_intf_norm_forc:     1.161714e+02
Fastener2_intf_shr_forc:      2.019673e+01
Fastener2_intf_tors_momt:     2.246785e+01
Fastener2_sep_stress:         8.547784e+00
Fastener2_shear_force:        8.518501e-03
Fastener2_shear_stress:       4.338437e-04
Fastener2_torsion_moment:    -9.375005e-02
Fastener2_torsion_stress:    -3.819721e-03
Fastener3_axial_force:        7.579593e+00
Fastener3_axial_stress:       3.860255e-01
Fastener3_bending_moment:     1.015827e+01
Fastener3_bending_stress:     8.277705e-01
Fastener3_intf_bend_momt:     9.429991e+02
Fastener3_intf_norm_forc:     1.193551e+02
Fastener3_intf_shr_forc:      1.698343e+01
Fastener3_intf_tors_momt:    -1.415631e+01
Fastener3_sep_stress:         1.090328e+01
Fastener3_shear_force:        9.084610e-03
Fastener3_shear_stress:       4.626754e-04
Fastener3_torsion_moment:    -1.561457e-01
Fastener3_torsion_stress:    -6.361950e-03
Fastener4_axial_force:        7.117430e+00
Fastener4_axial_stress:       3.624878e-01
Fastener4_bending_moment:     1.028671e+01
Fastener4_bending_stress:     8.382366e-01
Fastener4_intf_bend_momt:     9.539942e+02
Fastener4_intf_norm_forc:     1.165924e+02
Fastener4_intf_shr_forc:      1.978054e+01
```

Figure 11–101

Note that the interface forces for all fasteners are positive. This means that the separation springs act in tension (i.e., they incorrectly hold the parts together, while the parts should actually be slightly separating under the applied load).

You will later correct the separation option to enable the parts to naturally separate.

Results Tasks

Task 8: Display the model deformation.

1. Create and display the displacement magnitude deformed plot.
2. Zoom in on the fasteners and examine the deformation, as shown in Figure 11–102. Note that the separation areas around the fasteners are unnaturally kept in contact, as predicted by the interface force signs obtained in Task 7.

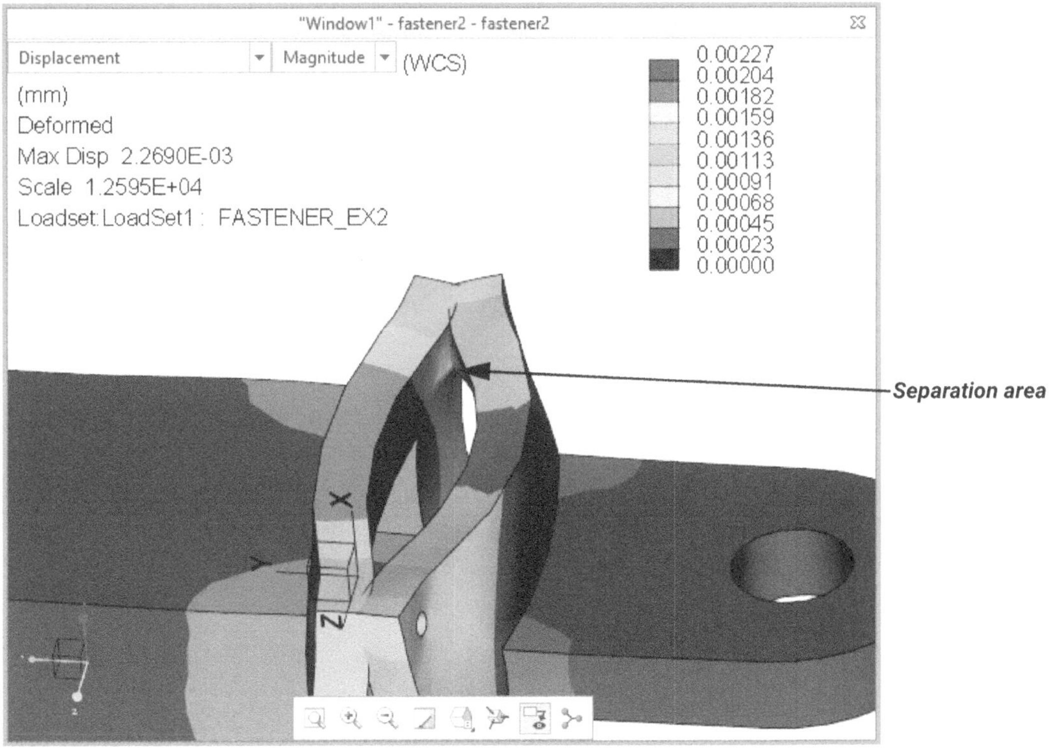

Figure 11–102

3. Exit the Results environment. Close the *Analyses and Design Studies* dialog box.

Modeling Tasks

Task 9: Remove the separation springs.

In this task, you will remove the separation springs from the fasteners to enable the surfaces to separate.

1. Select **Fastener1** and select (Edit Definition) from the mini-toolbar.
2. Clear the **Fix Separation** option, as shown in Figure 11–103.

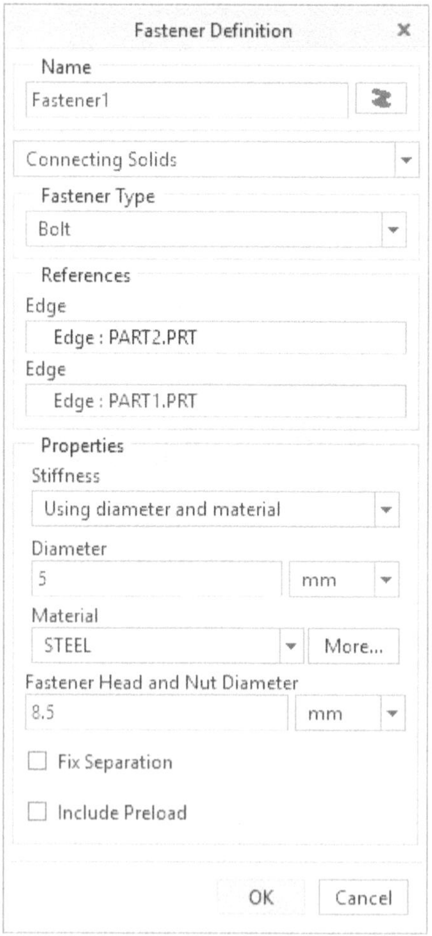

Figure 11–103

3. Click **OK** to finish. Click **OK** in the warning message box that displays.
4. Repeat Steps 1 to 3 for all of the other fasteners.

Analysis Tasks

Task 10: Re-run the analysis.

1. Run the **fastener2** analysis again using interactive diagnostics.
2. Note that the *Run Status* dialog box no longer displays a warning message about the fasteners.

Task 11: Check the fastener separation status.

1. Expand the *Run Status* window and scroll down to the *Measures* area, as shown in Figure 11–104.

```
strain_energy:                1.104766e+00
Fastener1_axial_force:        1.249040e+02
Fastener1_axial_stress:       6.361308e+00
Fastener1_bending_moment:     5.500403e+01
Fastener1_bending_stress:     4.482132e+00
Fastener1_shear_force:        8.114647e-01
Fastener1_shear_stress:       4.132756e-02
Fastener1_torsion_moment:     1.866920e-01
Fastener1_torsion_stress:     7.606516e-03
Fastener2_axial_force:        1.250942e+02
Fastener2_axial_stress:       6.370993e+00
Fastener2_bending_moment:     5.477606e+01
Fastener2_bending_stress:     4.463555e+00
Fastener2_shear_force:        7.822511e-01
Fastener2_shear_stress:       3.983972e-02
Fastener2_torsion_moment: -1.496170e-01
Fastener2_torsion_stress: -6.095943e-03
Fastener3_axial_force:        1.250944e+02
Fastener3_axial_stress:       6.371007e+00
Fastener3_bending_moment:     5.534182e+01
Fastener3_bending_stress:     4.509657e+00
Fastener3_shear_force:        8.291478e-01
Fastener3_shear_stress:       4.222815e-02
Fastener3_torsion_moment: -1.184367e-01
Fastener3_torsion_stress: -4.825547e-03
Fastener4_axial_force:        1.249074e+02
Fastener4_axial_stress:       6.361483e+00
Fastener4_bending_moment:     5.493020e+01
Fastener4_bending_stress:     4.476115e+00
Fastener4_shear_force:        7.671744e-01
Fastener4_shear_stress:       3.907187e-02
Fastener4_torsion_moment:     1.102101e-01
Fastener4_torsion_stress:     4.490364e-03
```

Figure 11–104

Note that the interface measures are no longer recorded since the separation springs have been toggled off.

2. Close the *Run Status* dialog box.

Results Tasks

Task 12: Animate the model deformation.

1. Create and animate the displacement magnitude result plot.
2. Step to Frame 5 of the animation and zoom in on the fasteners. The result plot displays as shown in Figure 11–105. Note that the parts are now slightly separate at the fasteners, which is correct.

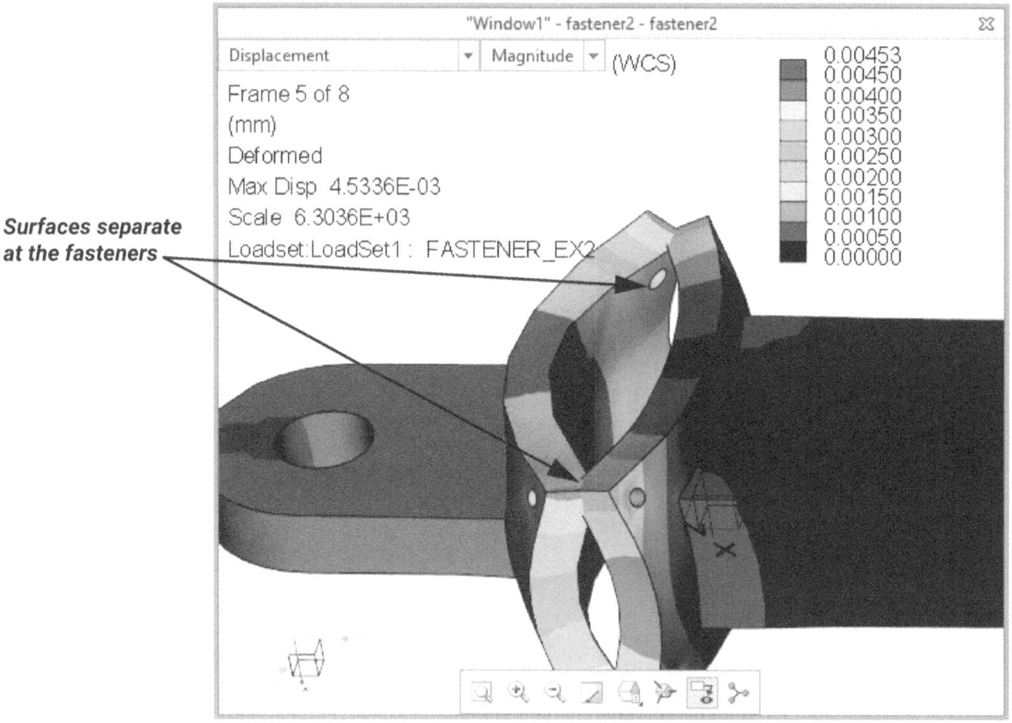

Figure 11–105

Task 13: Display the stress plot.

1. Create a deformed von Mises stress fringe plot. The result plot displays as shown in Figure 11–106.

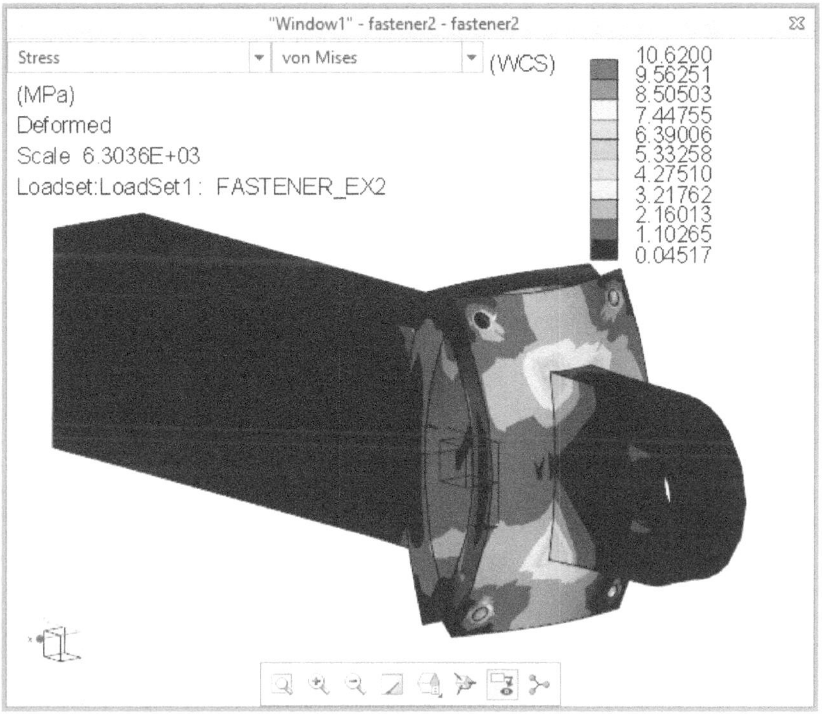

Figure 11–106

2. Exit the Results environment. Save and close the model.

End of practice

Practice 11e
Fasteners in Shell Models

Practice Objective

- Create fastened connections in shell models.

In this practice, you will set up and run a static analysis of the assembly shown in Figure 11–107. The two parts are bolted together at the locations indicated by three datum points.

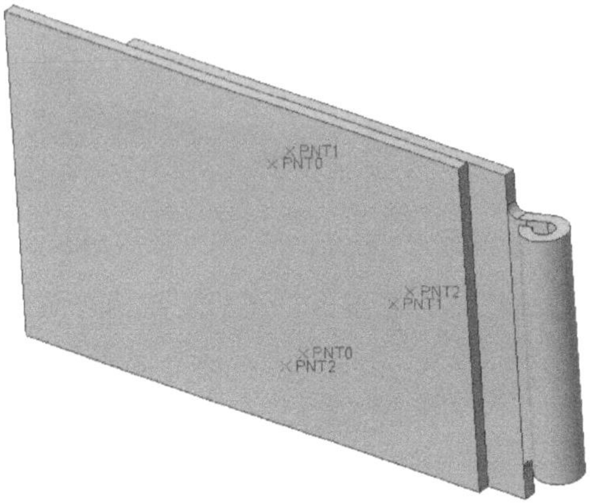

Figure 11–107

Modeling Tasks

Task 1: Open the model.

1. Set the working directory to **Chapter11**, if required.
2. Open **fastener_ex3.asm**.
3. Set the model display as follows:
   - *(Datum Display Filters)*: (Point Display)
   - *(Spin Center)*: Off
   - *(Display Style)*: (Shading With Edges)

   The model displays as shown in Figure 11–108.

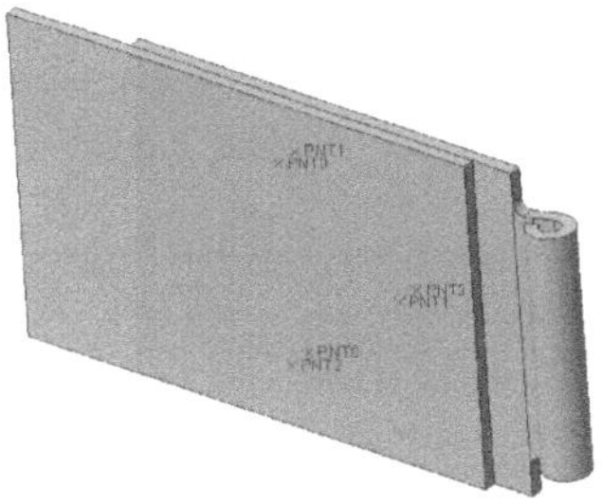

Figure 11–108

4. Select **Applications>Simulate** to switch to the Simulate environment.

Task 2: Apply the material.

1. Assign **STEEL** to both parts. The following values are the default material properties for HS-low-alloy steel (STEEL):
    - *Poisson:* **0.27**
    - *Young's modulus:* **199948 MPa**

Note: The material properties should be as stated.

Task 3: Create shell pairs.

1. In the *Refine Model* tab, expand the *Shell Pair* section and select **Detect Shell Pairs**.
2. In the *Auto Detect Shell Pairs* dialog box, select both parts and enter the *Characteristic Thickness* as **3**. Ensure that the unit **mm** is selected, as shown in Figure 11–109.

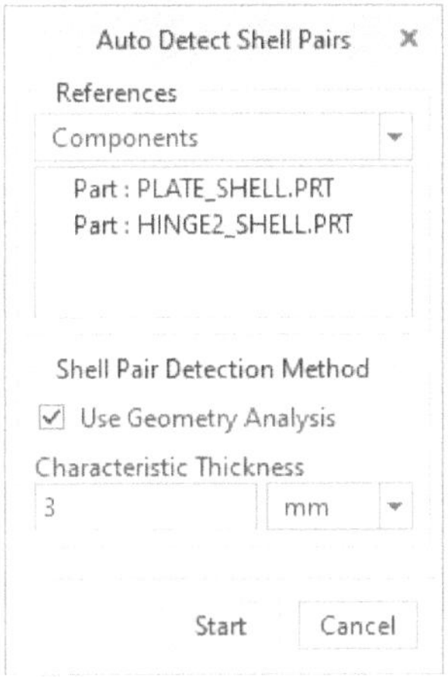

Figure 11–109

Note: The thickness of the parts in this assembly is 3mm.

3. Click **Start** to create the shell pairs and close the dialog box.

Task 4: Create the fasteners.

1. In the *Refine Model* tab, click (Fastener). In the *Fastener Definition* dialog box that opens, select **Connecting Shells**. In the *References* drop-down list, select **Point-Point**. The *Fastener Definition* dialog box displays as shown in Figure 11–110.

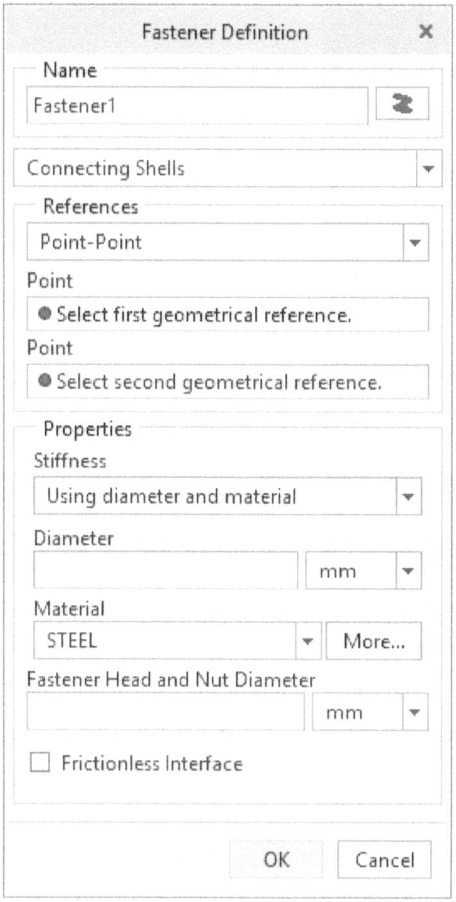

Figure 11–110

2. Select the **PNT0** and **PNT1** datum points as the references, as shown in Figure 11–111.

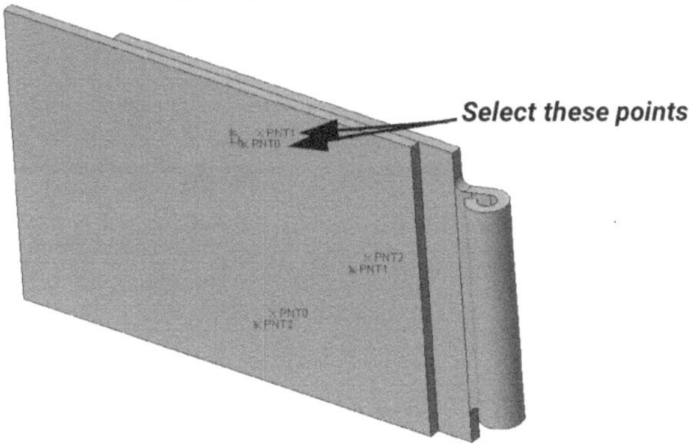

Figure 11–111

3. Enter **10** as the *Diameter* and **17** as the *Fastener Head and Nut Diameter*. The *Fastener Definition* dialog box displays as shown in Figure 11–112.

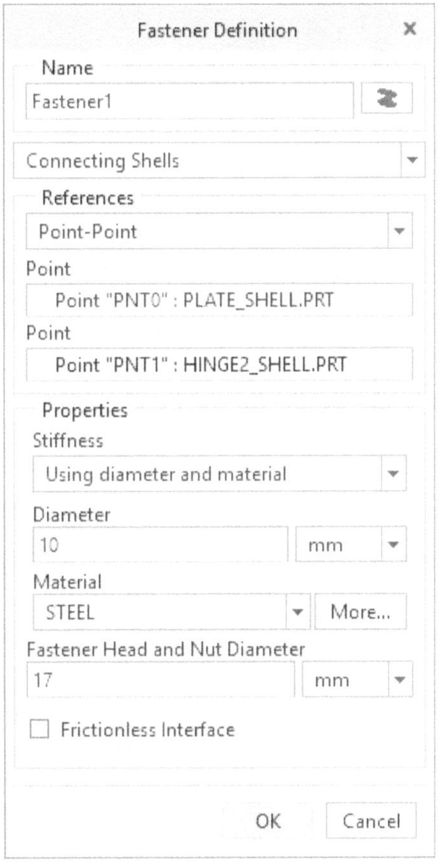

Figure 11–112

4. Click **OK** to complete. Ignore the warning message that opens. The model displays as shown in Figure 11–113.

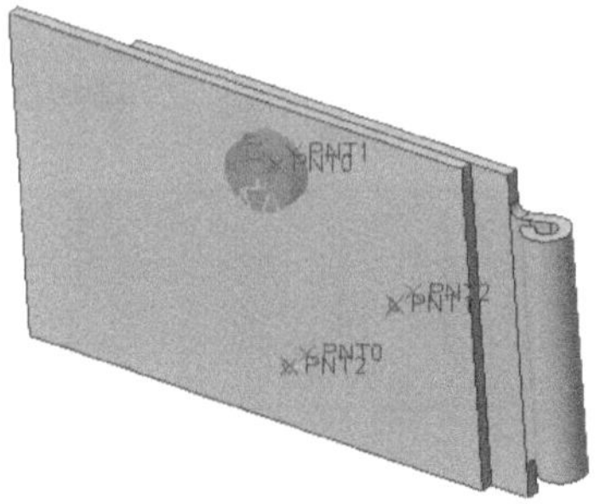

Figure 11–113

5. Repeat Steps 1 to 4 for the other two pairs of points. The model displays as shown in Figure 11–114.

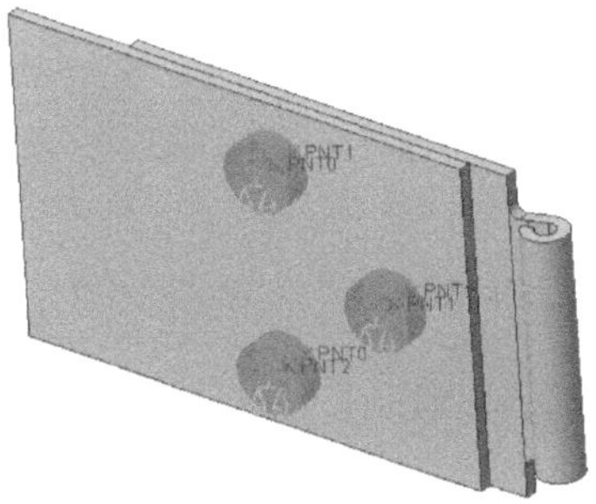

Figure 11–114

Task 5: Apply loads and constraints.

1. Constrain the edge shown in Figure 11–115 for all translations and rotations.

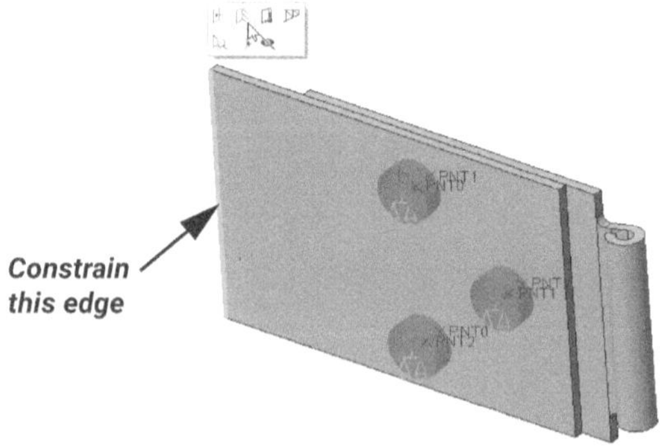

Figure 11–115

2. Apply a **100N** force in the negative Z-direction to the edge of the hook, as shown in Figure 11–116.

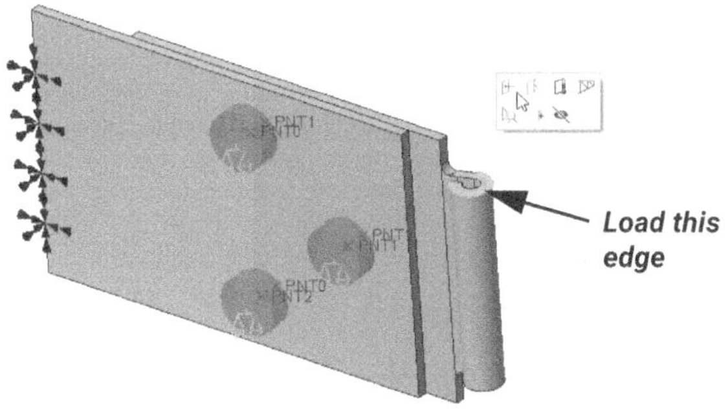

Figure 11–116

3. The model displays as shown in Figure 11–117.

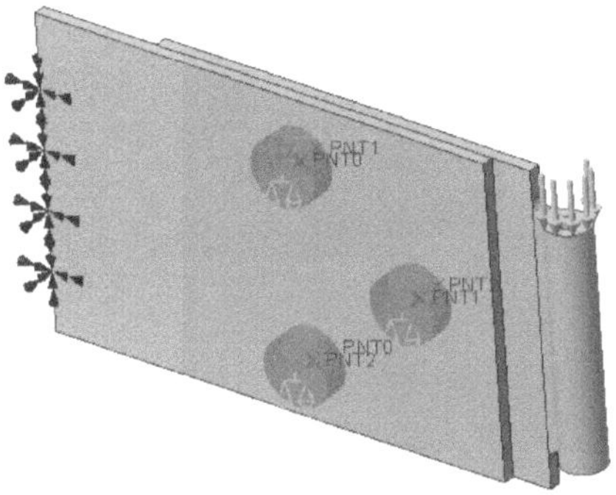

Figure 11–117

Analysis Tasks

Task 6: Set up and run a static analysis.

1. Set up a *Single-Pass Adaptive* static analysis, named **fastener3**.
2. Run the analysis.

Results Tasks

Task 7: Display the model deformation.

1. Create and display the displacement magnitude deformed plot. Select **Show Element Edges** and set *Scaling* to **5%**. The result plot displays as shown in Figure 11–118.

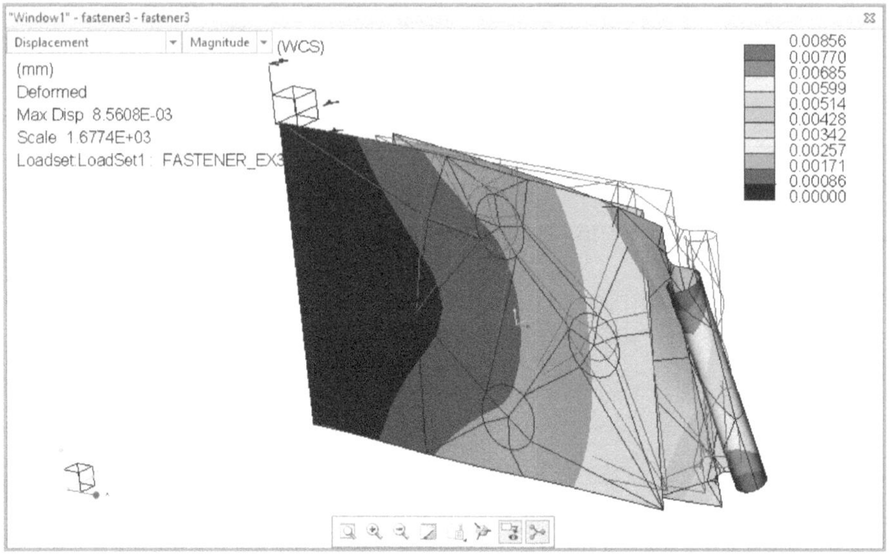

Figure 11–118

Note the circular regions Creo Simulate created around each fastener.

2. In the drop-down lists at the top left corner of the result window, select **Stress** and **von Mises**, as shown in Figure 11–119.

Figure 11–119

3. The result plot displays as shown in Figure 11–120.

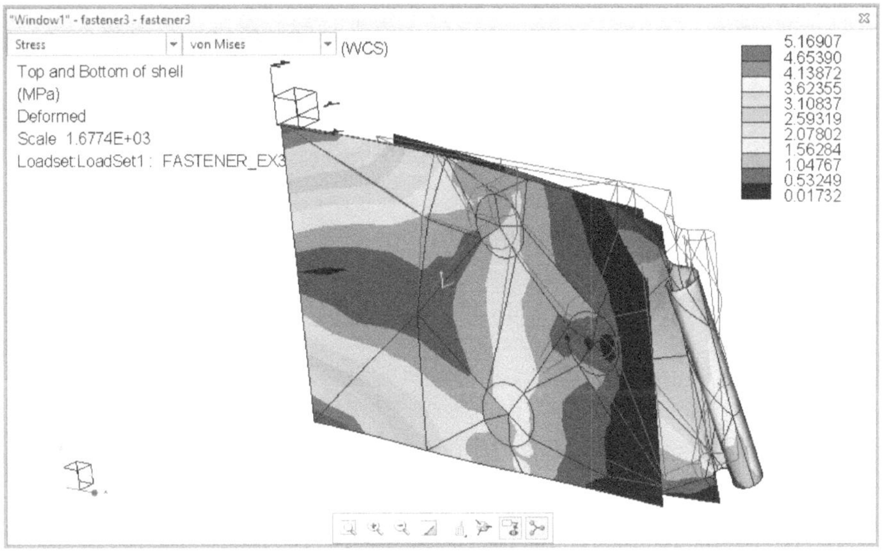

Figure 11–120

4. Exit the Results environment. Save and close the model.

End of practice

Practice 11f
Fasteners Through More Than Two Parts

Practice Objectives

- Understand how to simulate fasteners passing through more than two components.
- Create fasteners with preload.
- Create contact interfaces with and without friction.

In this practice, you will set up and run a static stress analysis on the assembly shown in Figure 11–121.

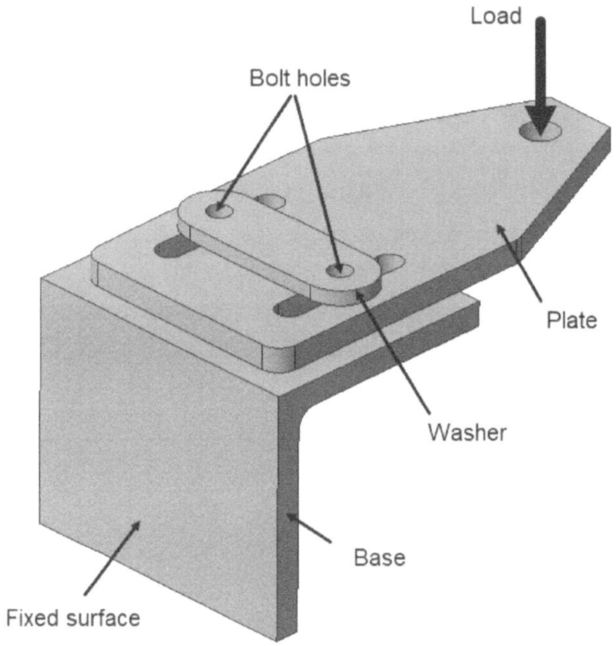

Figure 11–121

The assembly consists of three parts: the base, the plate, and the washer. The plate is fastened to the base with two bolts that pass through the washer, the slots in the plate, and the two holes in the base part. The plate is loaded through the hole located at its free end by a vertical force, as shown in Figure 11–121.

Modeling Tasks

Task 1: Open the model.

1. Set the working directory to **Chapter11**, if required.
2. Open **hanger.asm**.
3. Set the model display as follows:

   - *(Datum Display Filters)*: All off
   - *(Spin Center)*: Off
   - *(Display Style)*: (Shading With Edges)

   The model displays as shown in Figure 11–122.

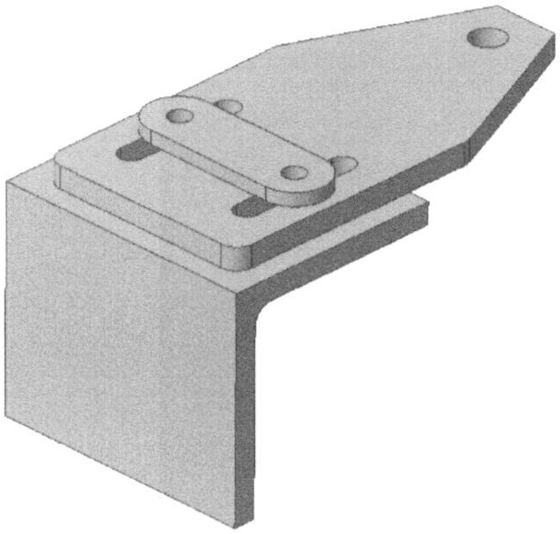

Figure 11–122

4. Select **Applications>Simulate** to switch to the Simulate environment.

Task 2: Apply the material.

1. Assign **STEEL** to all three parts in the assembly.
2. Toggle off the display of the **Material Assignments** icons.

Task 3: Apply the loads and constraints.

1. Constrain the surface shown in Figure 11–123 in all of the translations.

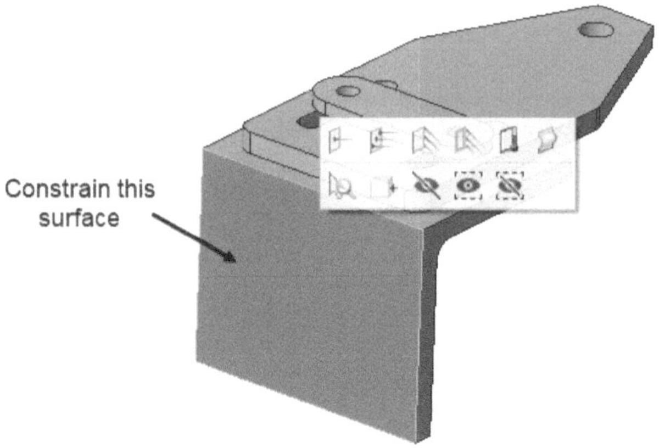

Figure 11–123

2. Apply the force **400N** in the Z-direction to the large hole on the free tip of the plate, as shown in Figure 11–124.

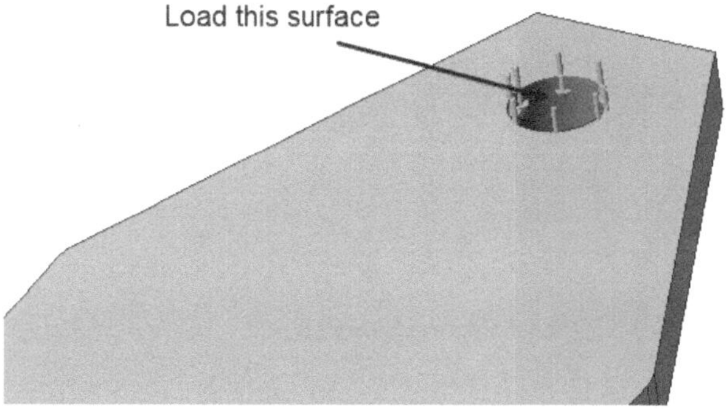

Figure 11–124

Task 4: Create the fasteners.

1. In the *Refine Model* tab, click (Fastener) to open the *Fastener Definition* dialog box.
2. Select the circular edge of the first hole in the washer part as the first reference, as shown in Figure 11–125.

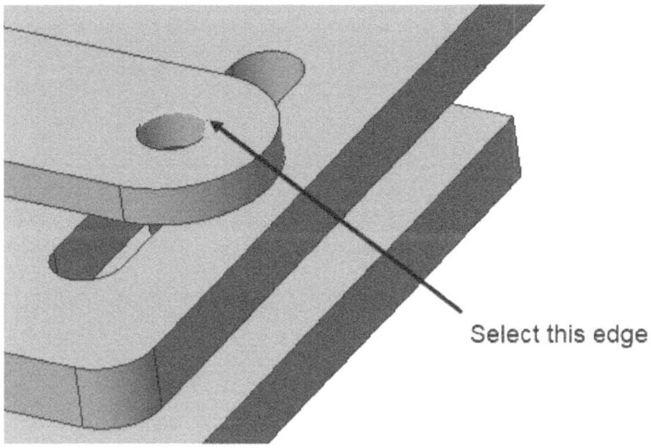

Figure 11–125

3. Select the circular edge on the opposite side of the base part as the second reference, as shown in Figure 11–126.

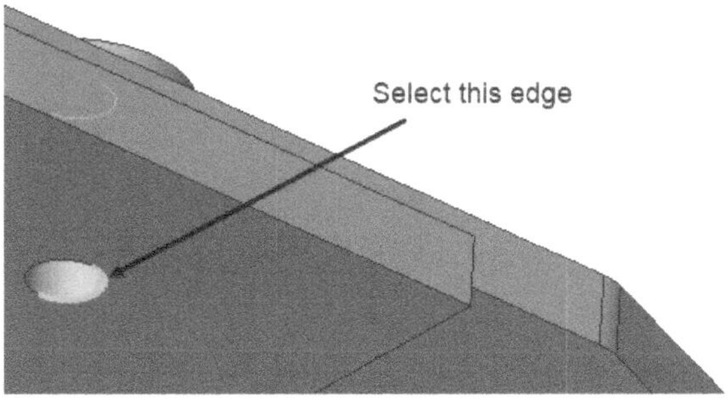

Figure 11–126

4. Toggle off the **Fix Separation** option. Toggle on the **Include Preload** and **Account for Stiffness** options and enter **100** as the *Preload Force*. The *Fastener Definition* dialog box displays as shown in Figure 11–127.

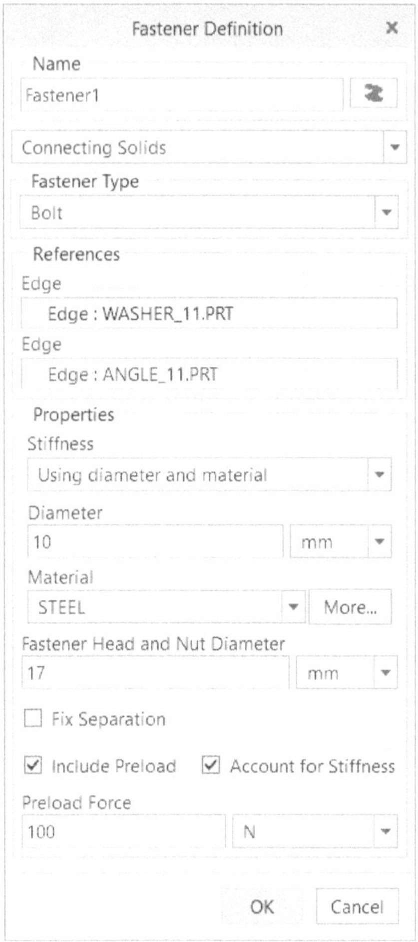

Figure 11–127

Note: *The* ***Fix Separation*** *option must be turned off if the fastener passes through more than two components.*

5. Click **OK** to close the *Fastener Definition* dialog box. The model displays as shown in Figure 11–128.

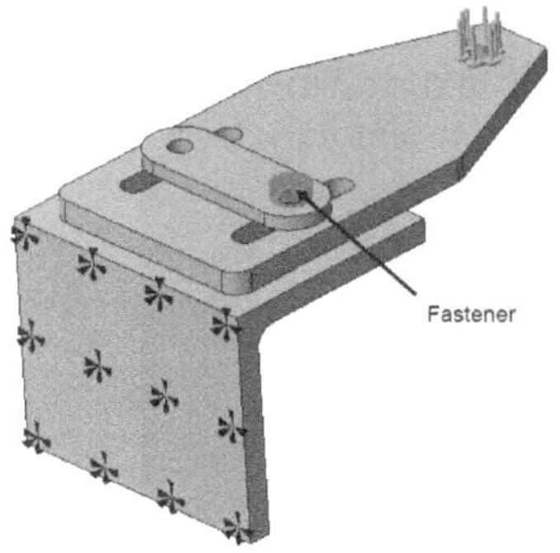

Figure 11–128

6. Expand the *Model Tree*. Select **Fastener1** in the **Fasteners** section, right-click, and select **Copy** in the contextual menu.
7. Select the **Fasteners** heading in the tree, right-click, and select **Paste** in the contextual menu. The *Fastener Definition* dialog box for the copy of the first fastener opens, as shown in Figure 11–129.

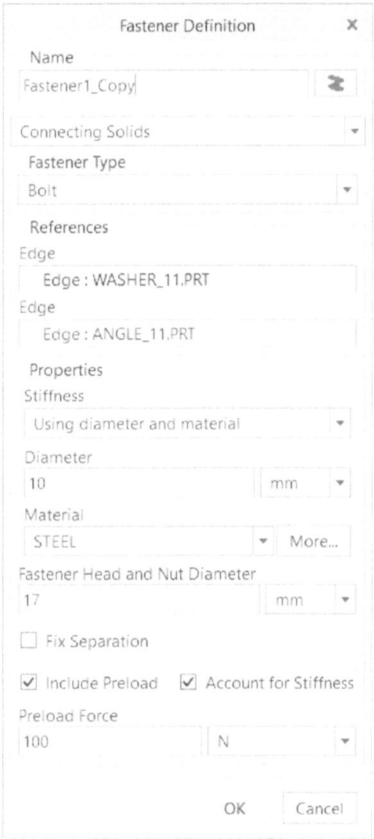

Figure 11–129

8. Rename the fastener to **Fastener2**.

9. For the references, select the edge of the second hole in the washer part and the edge of the second hole in the base part, similarly to Steps 2 and 3. Leave all other options at their default values, which have been copied from the first fastener. The *Fastener Definition* dialog box displays as shown in Figure 11–130.

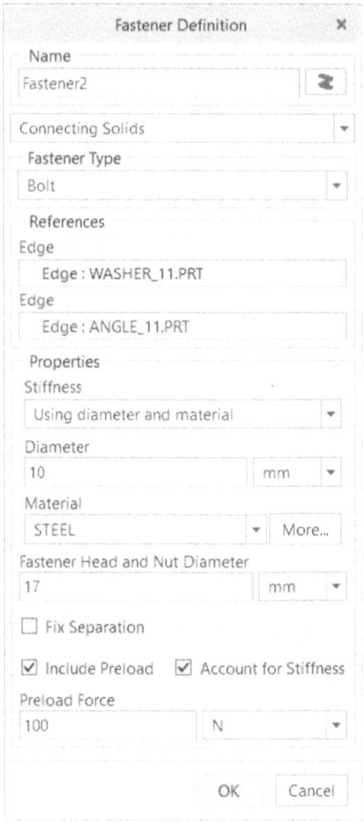

Figure 11–130

10. Click **OK** to close the *Fastener Definition* dialog box. The model displays as shown in Figure 11–131.

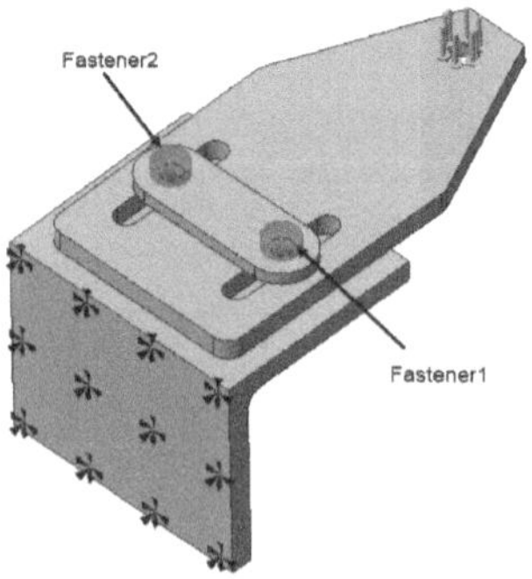

Figure 11–131

Task 5: Create contact interface between the washer and the plate.

Since the **Fix Separation** option has been turned off in the fasteners, contact interfaces must be used between the fastened parts to ensure the parts stay separate, yet do not interpenetrate under the preload and the other loads in the model.

The washer is clamped to the plate with a substantial preload (100N), which ensures that there is enough friction between the washer and the plate so there is no sliding occurring between the parts. This can be simulated with a contact interface with infinite friction.

1. In the *Refine Model* tab, click (Interface). The *Interface Definition* dialog box opens, as shown in Figure 11–132.

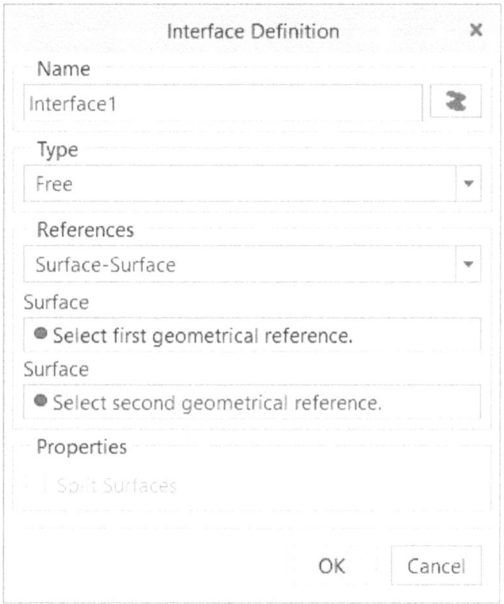

Figure 11–132

2. Rename the interface to **Interface_washer**.
3. Select **Contact** as the *Type* and **Component-Component** as the *References*.
4. Select the washer part as the first component and the plate as the second component.
5. In the *Friction* drop-down list, select **Infinite**.

6. Activate both the **Split Surfaces** and **Generate Compatible Mesh** options. The *Interface Definition* dialog box displays as shown in Figure 11–133.

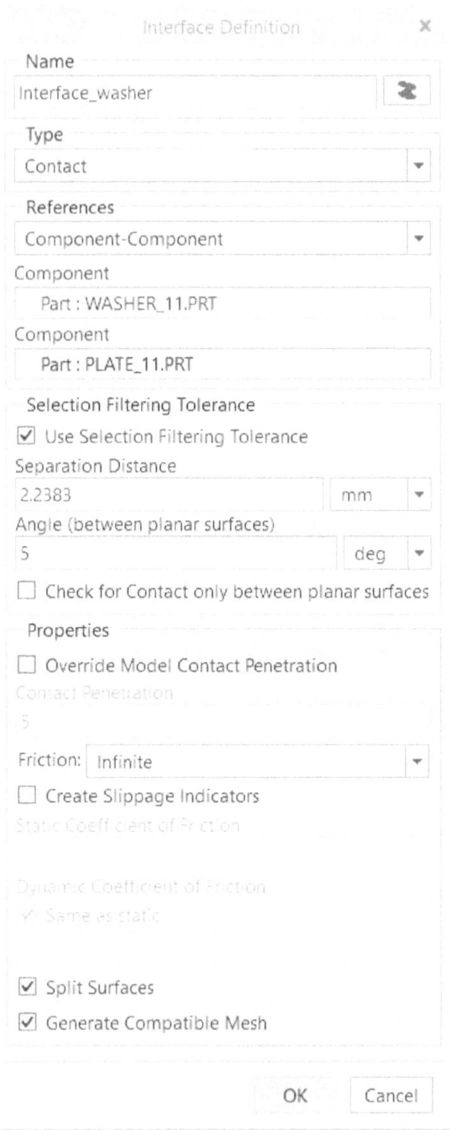

Figure 11–133

Note: *The* ***Split Surfaces*** *and* ***Generate Compatible Mesh*** *options ensure better mesh in the contact area, and therefore more accurate stress results.*

7. Click **OK** to close the *Interface Definition* dialog box.

Task 6: Create contact interface between the plate and the base.

Due to the preload on the bolts, the plate is not supposed to slide along the top surface of the base part. This is the result of the great amount of friction generated by contact pressure near the bolts, which could be simulated with a contact interface with infinite friction.

However, the area of high contact pressure (and hence infinite friction) is expected to be small and highly localized around the bolt holes in the base part. The bulk of the contact interface will experience much smaller amounts of contact pressure; therefore, the assumption of infinite friction over the entire interface would be incorrect.

Ideally, this could be simulated by a contact interface with finite friction. The problem is that this would require running the analysis with the large deformations option turned on, which would make the simulation very expensive in terms of the runtime and which would not be warranted for the purposes of this specific simulation.

Since the bulk of the interface area is not expected to experience the infinite friction condition, an acceptable approximation for this analysis would be to use frictionless contact.

1. In the *Refine Model* tab, click (Interface) to open the *Interface Definition* dialog box.
2. Rename the interface to **Interface_base**.
3. Select **Contact** as the *Type* and **Component-Component** as the *References*.
4. Select the plate as the first component and the base part as the second component.
5. Leave the default **None** in the *Friction* drop-down list.

6. The *Interface Definition* dialog box displays as shown in Figure 11–134.

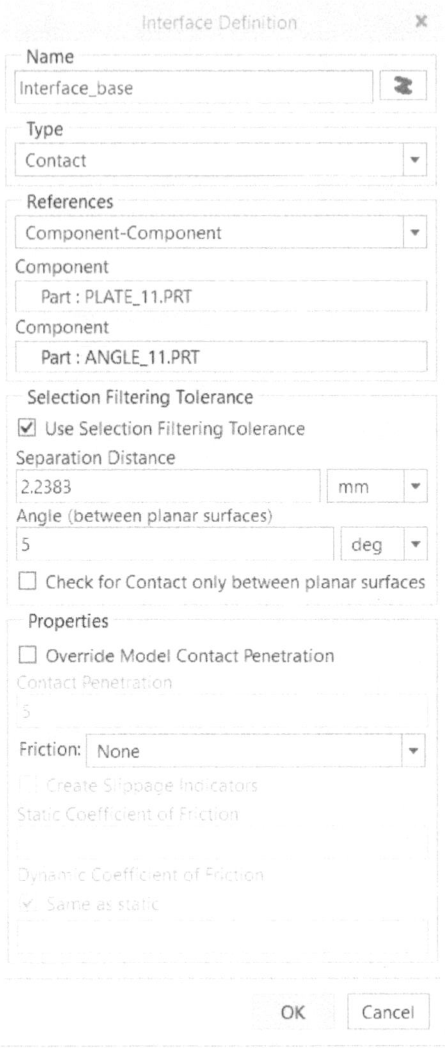

Figure 11–134

7. Click **OK** to close the *Interface Definition* dialog box.

8. Toggle off the display of **Measures**.

9. In the *Refine Model* tab, select  (Review Geometry) to open the *Simulation Geometry* dialog box, and click **Apply**. The model displays as shown in Figure 11–135. Ensure that the contact areas between the parts are shaded in yellow, which is the default color for the contact interfaces.

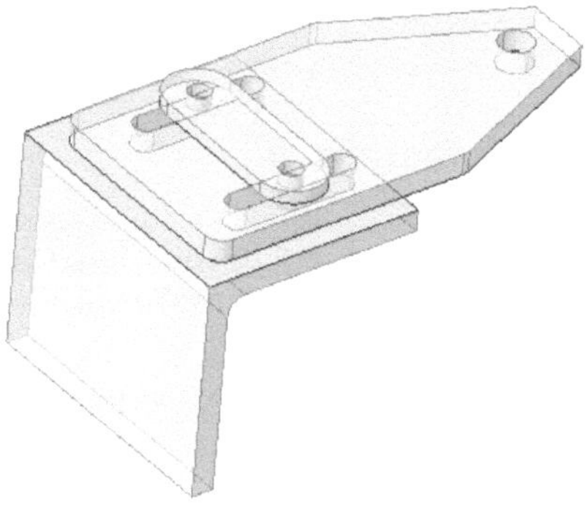

Figure 11–135

10. Click **Close** to close the *Simulation Geometry* dialog box.

Analysis Tasks

Task 7: Set up and run a static analysis.

1. Set up a Single-Pass Adaptive static analysis, named **fastener_three_parts**. Ensure that both the **Nonlinear / use load histories** and **Contacts** options are toggled on, as shown in Figure 11–136.

Figure 11–136

2. Run the analysis using interactive diagnostics, which should take under 5 minutes.

Results Tasks

Task 8: Obtain the forces in the fasteners.

1. Open the *Run Status* window and scroll down to the *Measures* section at the bottom. Note that the axial forces in the fasteners are approximately 490N, as shown in Figure 11–137.

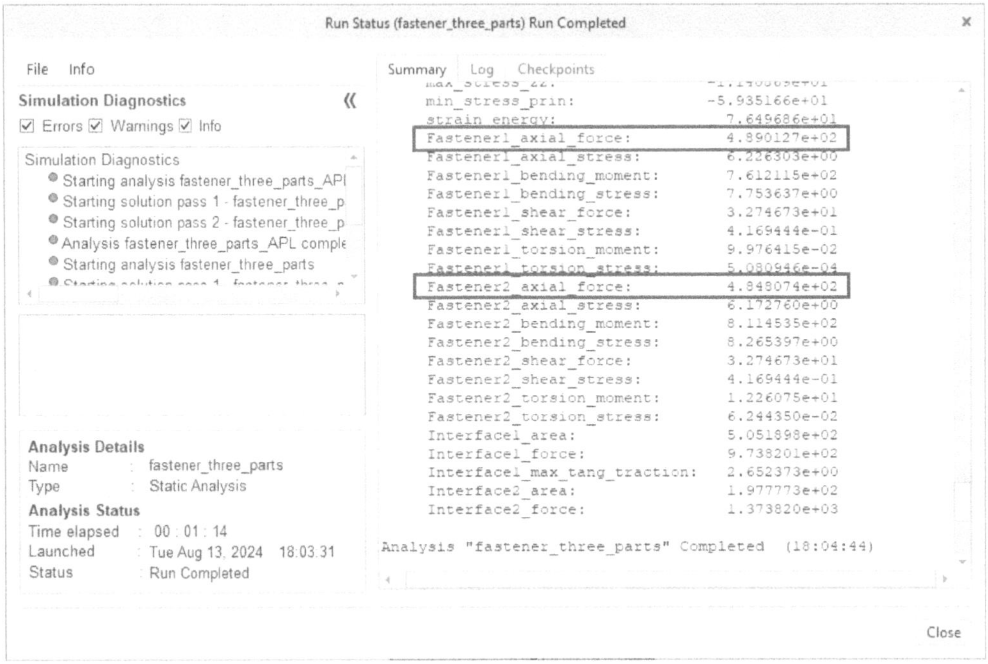

Figure 11–137

Task 9: Verify the forces in the fasteners using hand calculation.

1. Measure the distances from the front edge of the base part to the center of the loaded hole and to the center of one of the bolt holes, as shown in Figure 11–138. Note that the first distance ***Df* = 90mm**, while the second distance ***Db* = 40mm**.

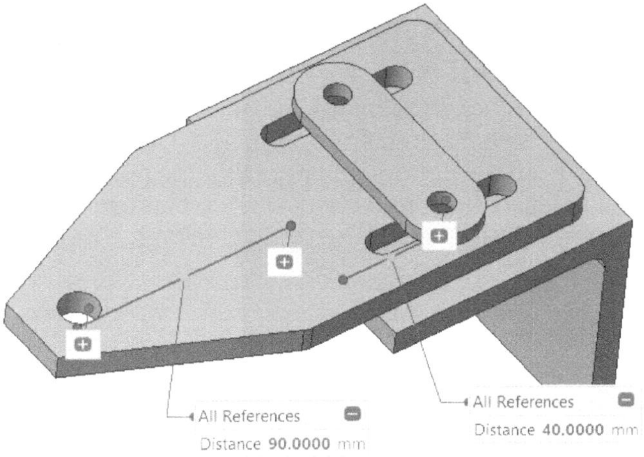

Figure 11–138

2. Given a simple calculation based on the force equilibrium about the front edge of the base part, the total operational force ***Fot*** at the bolt holes exerted by the load ***P = 400N*** on the front hole could be estimated by the formula ***Fot = P * Dl / Df*** (i.e., ***Fot*** **= 400 * 90 / 40 = 900N**). Which makes the operational force ***Fo*** per each bolt approximately **900 / 2 = 450N**.
3. Each bolt is preloaded with a force ***Fp*** **= 100N**. If gapping (i.e., full separation) between the plate and the base part near the bolts was occurring, the operational force ***Fo*** in the bolt would fully add to the preload force ***Fp*** to produce the total force in the bolt ***F*** (i.e., ***F = Fo + Fp*** **= 450 + 100 = 550N**).
4. If no gapping between the fastened parts occurred, then some percentage of the operational force would be absorbed by the fastened plates, and the total tensile force in the bolt should be less than **550N**. In the Creo Simulate analysis, the tensile forces in the bolts were calculated as approximately **490N**, which is indeed about **11%** less than the maximum possible force of **550N**.

Conclusion

- The computed by Creo Simulate bolt forces are within the ballpark estimate obtained by hand calculations.
- No gapping (i.e., full separation) between the plate and the base part near the bolts is expected, so the bolted joint is acting as it should. You will also double-check this finding in the next task.

Task 10: Display the contact pressure.

1. In the *Analyses and Design Studies* dialog box, select (Review results) and create a fringe plot of contact pressure. The result displays as shown in Figure 11–139. Rotate the result to see the model from the bottom and note that the positive contact pressure area extends past the bolt holes in the contact between the plate and the base part, which confirms the conclusion in Task 9 about no gapping between the parts occurring around the bolts.

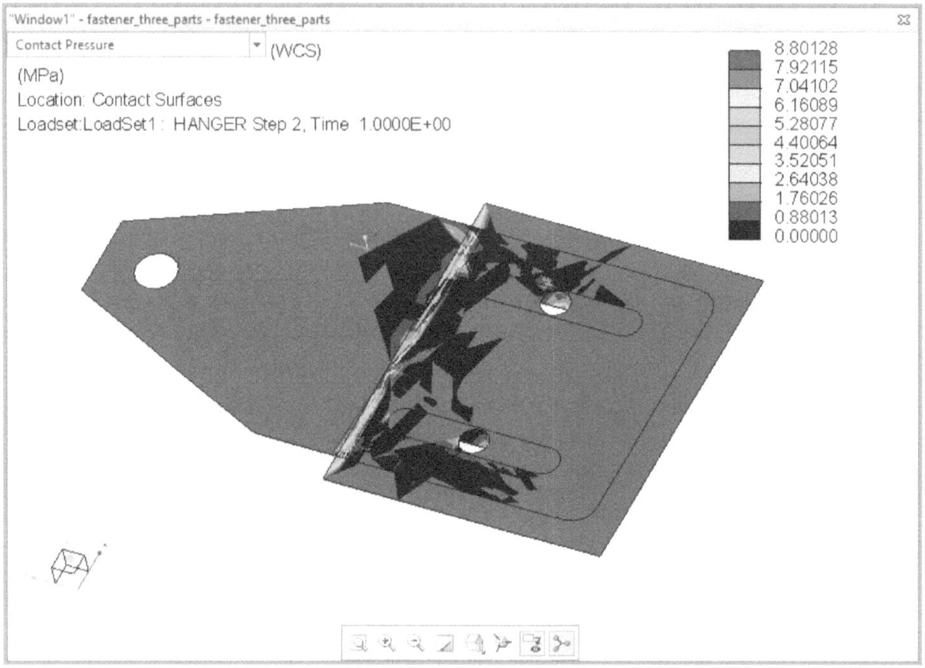

Figure 11–139

Note: *A more accurate and detailed contact pressure plot could be obtained with a finer mesh in contact areas.*

Task 11: Display the model deformation.

1. Create the displacement magnitude result plot, using the **Deformed** and **Overlay Undeformed** options and **10% Scaling**. The result plot displays as shown in Figure 11–140. Does the model deform according to the loads, constraints, and connections between the parts?

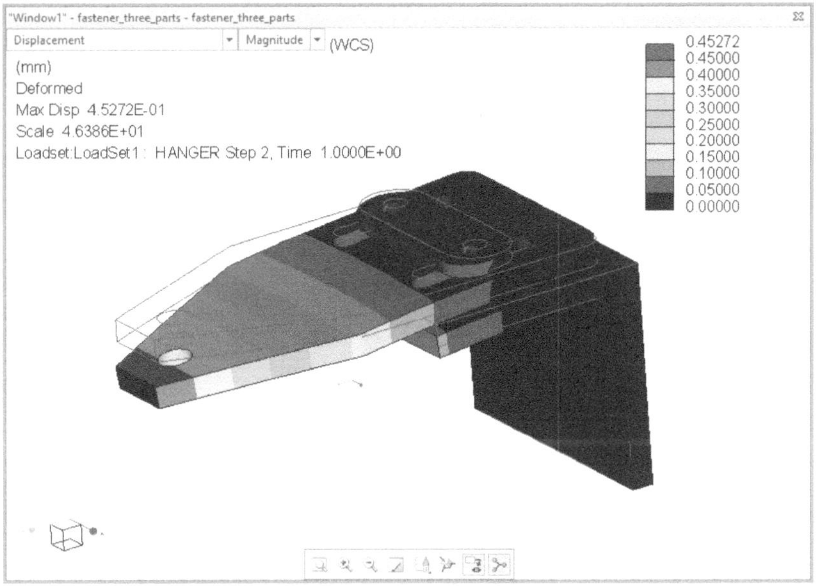

Figure 11–140

Task 12: Display the von Mises stress.

1. Display the von Mises stress plot, as shown in Figure 11–141.

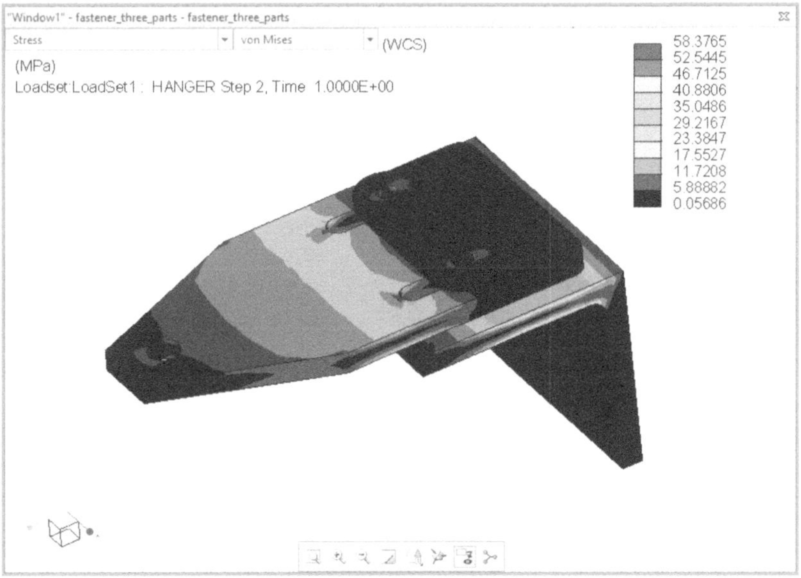

Figure 11–141

2. Using the Model Max tool, find the area of the maximum stress in the model, as shown in Figure 11–142. Note that the maximum stress occurs at one of the bolt holes in the base part.

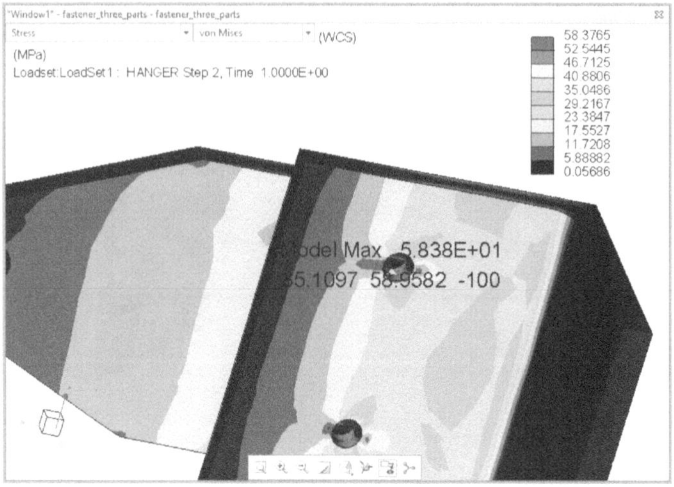

Figure 11–142

3. Exit the Results environment.
4. Save and close the model.

End of practice

Chapter 12

Buckling Analysis

In mechanical design, a column is defined as any member that is loaded in compression. In certain cases, the maximum load a column can sustain is determined by the stiffness of the column, rather than by the yield stress of its material.

Learning Objectives

- Understand the concepts of the buckling analysis.
- Create a buckling analysis.

12.1 Theory of Buckling

Buckling analysis predicts the magnitude of the load at which the loss of stability under compressive loads might occur. It is an important analysis for slender structures that are subject to large compressive stresses. For example, these could be structural columns or posts, bridge trusses, submarine hulls, etc.

Buckling might occur at stresses well below the yield stress. This is called *elastic buckling*. Therefore, it is important to analyze such structures for both stress and buckling.

In the example shown in Figure 12–1, a long slender column AB, of length (L) is constrained at end A and loaded with a centrally compressive load P at end B.

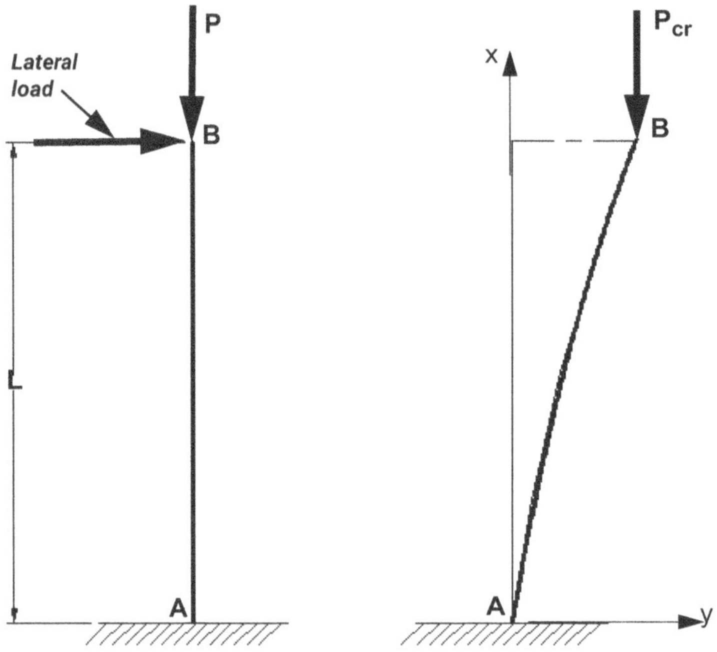

Figure 12–1

Assume that the column has the following characteristics:

- Perfectly straight
- Uniform cross-section
- Homogeneous
- Behaves elastically

When load P is small, the compressive column is laterally stable if end B is pushed slightly to one side. The column returns to its straight form as the lateral force is removed. As load P gradually increases, the straight form of the column becomes unstable and the column, if pushed to one side, remains there even if the lateral load is removed. This occurrence is called *buckling* and the value of the load at which this occurs is called the *critical load* (P_{cr}).

12.2 Creo Simulate Buckling Analysis

The Creo Simulate buckling analysis is a linear i.e. eigenvalue type of buckling analysis. The analysis predicts the critical load under which the structure is neutrally stable. The analysis solution is presented as a load factor called the *Buckling Load Factor* (BLF) and a corresponding buckling mode shape.

> ***Note:*** *The buckling analysis in Creo Simulate is only available for 3D solid models.*

To produce a critical buckling load (P_{cr}), the applied load set is multiplied by the BLF:

$P_{cr} = BLF \times P_{applied}$

Therefore, the BLF is a safety factor for the structure against buckling. A BLF less than 1.0 indicates that the structure is predicted to buckle under the applied load.

The buckling mode shape indicates how the structure deforms at the onset of buckling. The number one mode shape is most likely to be the only one to occur. Therefore, be sure to verify your design for mode 1 as shown in Figure 12–2.

Number of Modes: 3

Mode	B. L. F.	Convergence
1	4.006366e+00	0.0%
2	4.022544e+00	0.0%
3	3.601735e+01	0.0%

Figure 12–2

The linear buckling analysis provides a useful first order approximation of the critical buckling load for designers and generally produces results that are not conservative (the theory calculates a higher critical load than is actually observed in experiments). It also assumes that the initial loading on the model does not change the geometry. Therefore, it is recommended that you use generous safety factors.

Use the following steps to perform a buckling analysis:

1. Set up the model.
2. Assign material properties to the model.
3. Apply boundary conditions to the model (i.e., loads or constraints).
4. Create a static analysis.

   A static analysis must be defined before a buckling analysis can be created because the structure stiffness used in the buckling analysis is obtained from the static analysis. Therefore, the accuracy of the buckling analysis directly relates to the accuracy of the static analysis. You need to set a tight convergence criteria on the RMS stress, displacement, and strain energy.
5. Create a buckling analysis.

6. Run the buckling analysis.
7. Interpret the results.

To calculate the stresses and displacements on the structure at the critical buckling load, multiply the original compressive load by the smallest positive BLF, and rerun the static analysis.

Practice 12a
Buckling Analysis of a Pole

Practice Objectives

- Set up and run a buckling analysis.
- Understand how to determine the Buckling Load Factor.
- Visualize the buckling modes.

In this practice, you will set up and run a buckling analysis on a long slender pole, as shown in Figure 12–3. The pole has a rectangular cross-section (2 x 2) and is 13ft long.

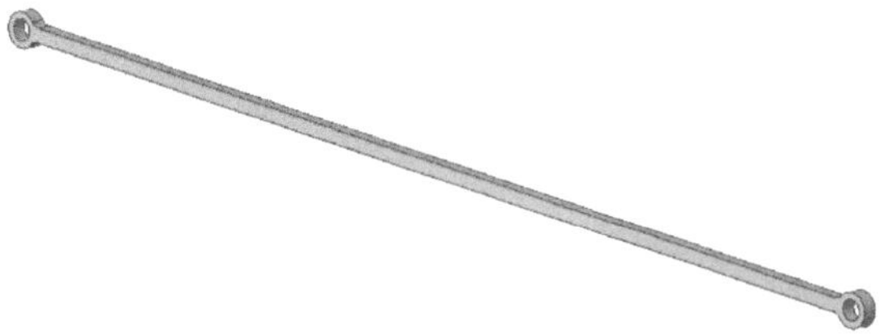

Figure 12–3

Modeling Tasks

Task 1: Open the part.

1. Set the working directory to **Chapter12**.
2. Open **buckle_pole.prt**.
3. Set the model display as follows:
   - *(Datum Display Filters)*: All Off
   - *(Spin Center)*: Off
   - *(Display Style)*: (Shading With Edges)

The part displays as shown in Figure 12–4.

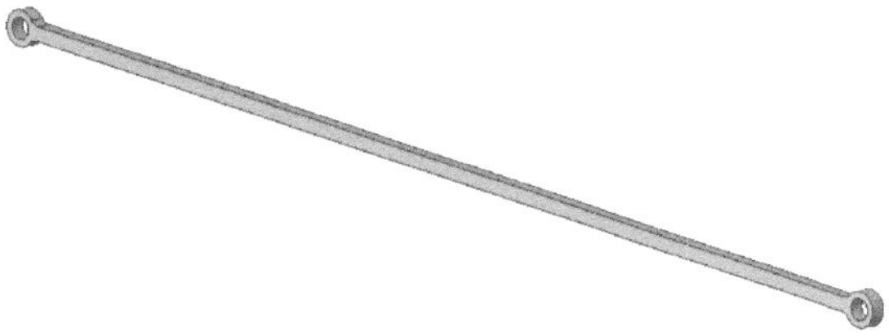

Figure 12–4

4. Ensure that the unit system is set to **IPS**.
5. Select **Applications>Simulate**.

Task 2: Apply the loads.

1. Apply a total and uniform force of **-1000** in the X-direction to the pole's hole surface, as shown in Figure 12–5.

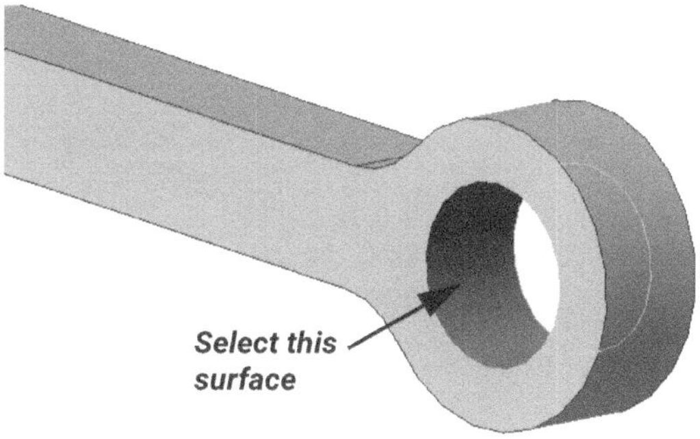

Figure 12–5

Note: *The X-direction is relative to the WCS.*

2. Name the load **buckle_f**. The model displays as shown in Figure 12–6.

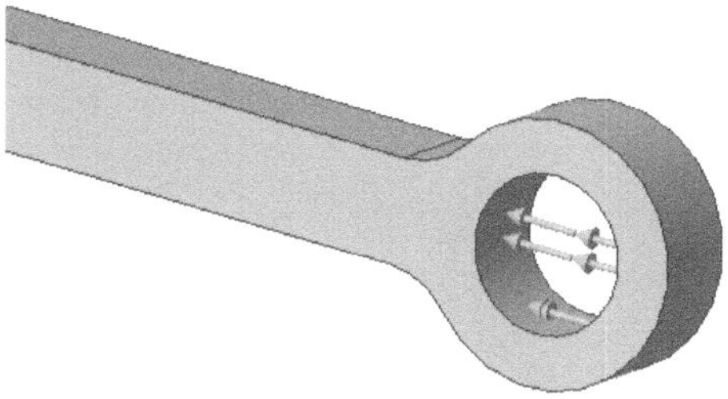

Figure 12–6

Task 3: Apply the constraints.

1. Fully constrain the hole on the other end of the pole (all of the translations), as shown in Figure 12–7.

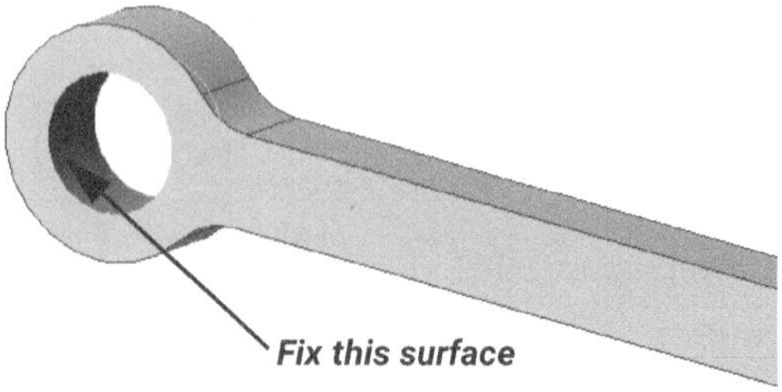

Figure 12–7

2. Name the constraint **pole_const**. The model displays as shown in Figure 12–8.

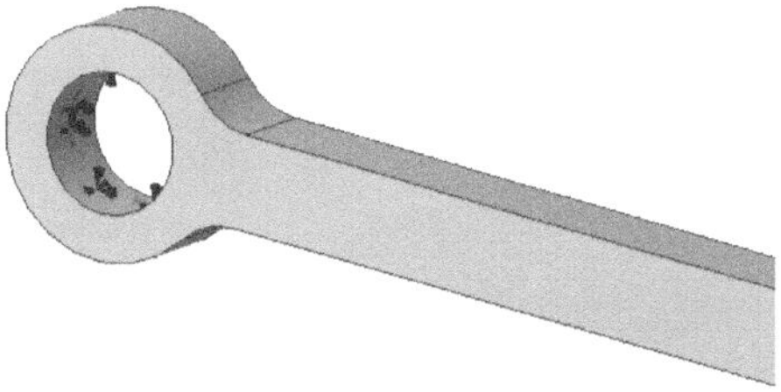

Figure 12–8

Note: *The constraint values are toggled off.*

Task 4: Apply the material.

1. Assign **STEEL** to the **buckle_pole** part. The following values are the default material properties for HS-low-alloy steel (STEEL):
   - *Poisson:* **0.27**
   - *Young's modulus:* **2.9e+07 psi**
   - *Density:* **0.0007324 lbf sec^2/in^4**

Analysis Tasks

Task 5: Set up an analysis.

In this task, you will set up a static analysis and a buckling analysis.

1. Click (Analyses and Studies). The *Analyses and Design Studies* dialog box opens.

2. Select **File>New Static**. The *Static Analysis Definition* dialog box opens.
3. For the analysis name, enter **static_pole**. In the *Static Analysis Definition* dialog box, select the options shown in Figure 12–9.

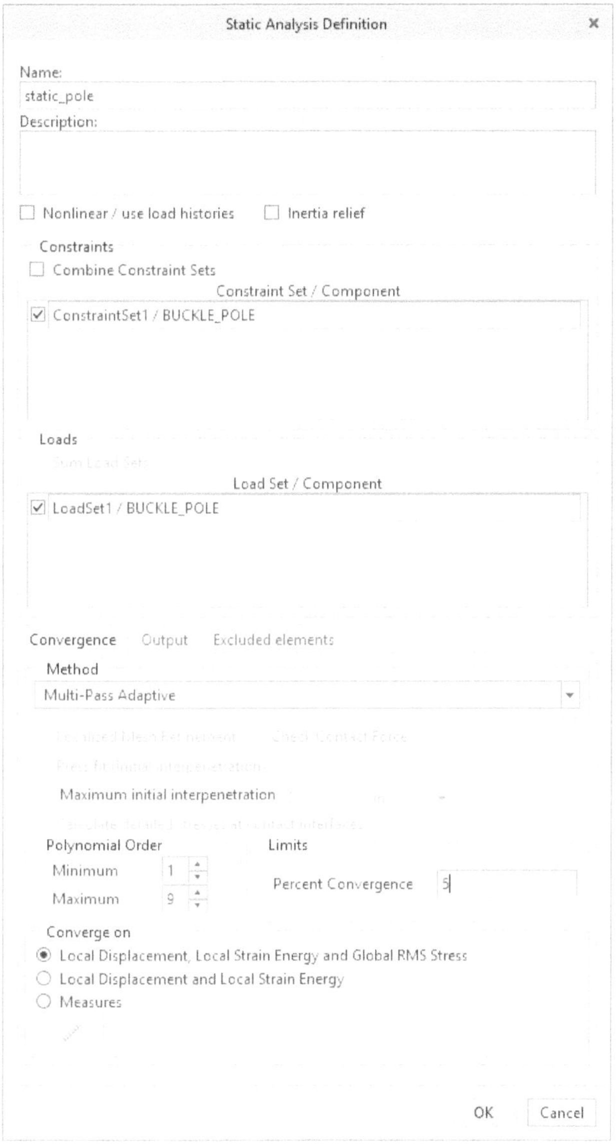

Figure 12–9

4. Click **OK**. The *Analyses and Design Studies* dialog box opens.

5. Select **File>New Buckling**. The *Buckling Analysis Definition* dialog box opens, as shown in Figure 12–10.

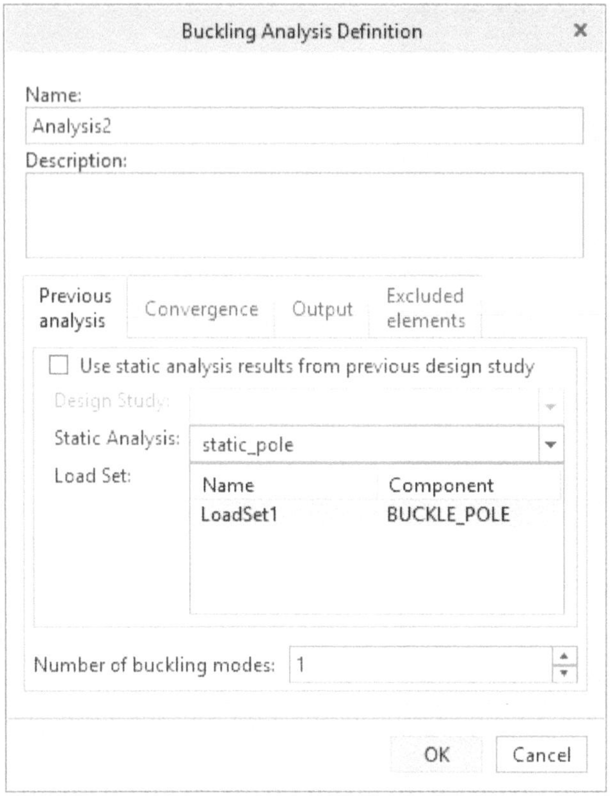

Figure 12–10

6. In the *Name* field, enter **buckle_pole**.
7. In the *Number of Buckling Modes* field, enter **3**.
8. Select the *Convergence* tab and enter the information shown in Figure 12–11.

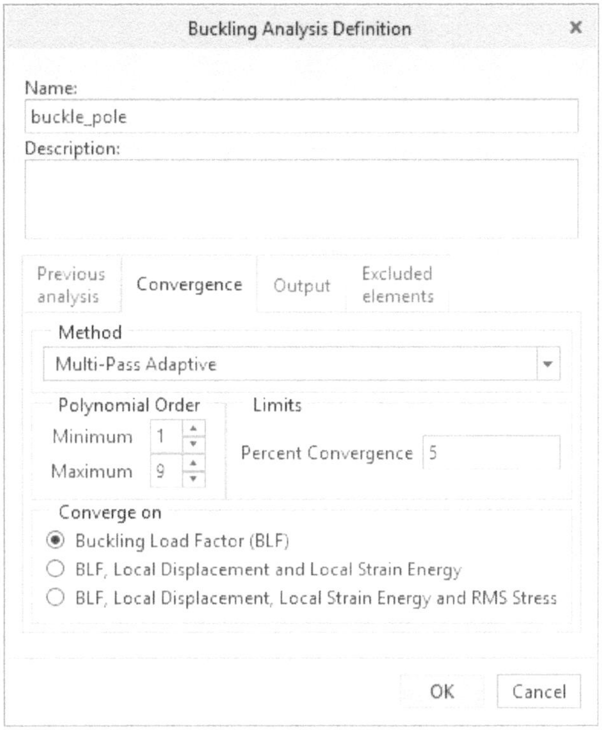

Figure 12–11

9. Click **OK**.
10. Run the **buckle_pole** analysis. Click **Yes** when prompted to run interactive diagnostics.
11. Expand the *Run Status* window and scroll through the *Run Status* window to display the analysis information. Note that the **static_pole** analysis was automatically run before the **buckle_pole** analysis.
12. Locate the BLF values in the *Run Status* dialog box when the run is complete, as shown in Figure 12–12.

```
Number of Modes: 3

   Mode     B. L. F.      Convergence
   ----   ------------   -----------
      1   4.006366e+00        0.0%
      2   4.022544e+00        0.0%
      3   3.601735e+01        0.0%
```

Figure 12–12

Note that the lowest Buckling Load Factor is approximately 4. In Task 2, you applied 1000lbs compressive load. Therefore, the predicted critical load is 4x1000lbs = 4000lbs.

Results Tasks

Task 6: Display the buckling modes.

In this task, you will create and display three deformation animation fringe plots of the three buckling modes.

1. In the *Analyses and Design Studies* dialog box, click (Review Results). The *Result Window Definition* dialog box opens, as shown in Figure 12–13.

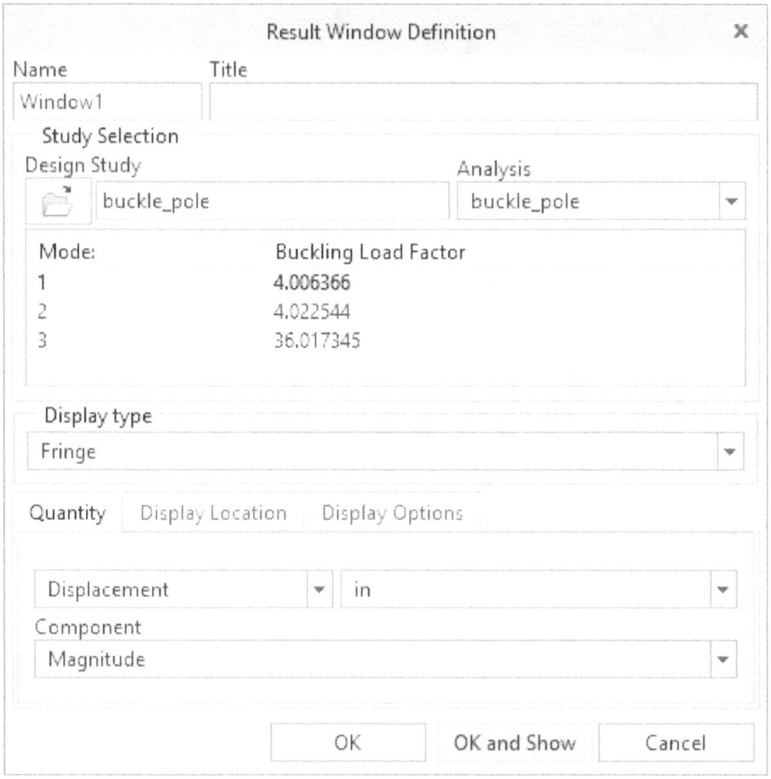

Figure 12–13

2. Ensure that **Mode 1** is highlighted. In the *Display Options* tab, select **Deformed**, **Overlay Undeformed**, and **Animate**. Click **OK and Show**. The Displacement Magnitude result plot at Frame 3 displays as shown in Figure 12–14.

Figure 12–14

3. Click (Edit). Repeat Step 2 to display and animate Buckling modes 2 and 3.

Task 7: Display the static stresses.

In this task, you will examine the stress plot for the static analysis, and determine whether the pole's material might yield before the compressive load reaches the critical buckling value.

1. In the ribbon, click (Open) and select **buckle_pole analysis**. In the *Result Window Definition* dialog box, select **static_pole** from the *Analysis* drop-down list and rename the window to **static_stress**. The *Result Window Definition* dialog box opens, as shown in Figure 12–15.

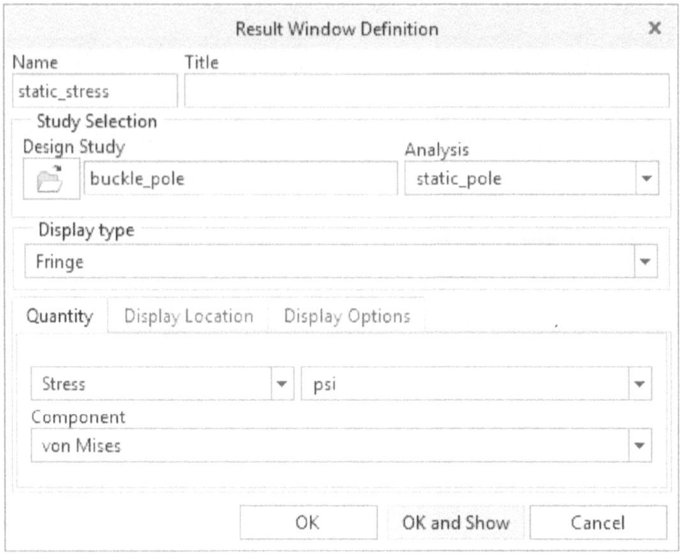

Figure 12–15

2. Click **OK and Show**. In the *View* tab, click (Show). Clear the **Window1** line and then click **OK**. The von Mises stress plot for the static analysis opens, as shown in Figure 12–16.

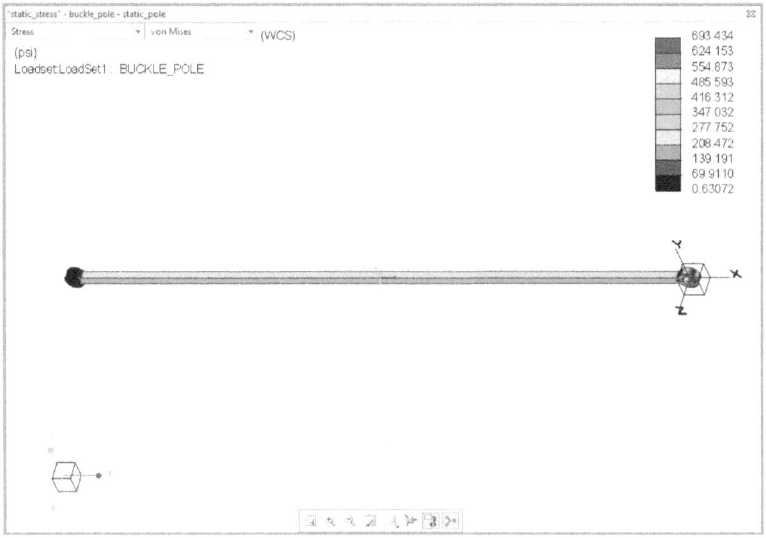

Figure 12–16

3. Using the (Dynamic Query) tool, get a reading of the stress in the approximate middle of the pole, as shown in Figure 12–17.

Figure 12–17

The stress value should be approximately 250psi.

Since the static analysis was linear, the stress value at the critical buckling load can be calculated by linear interpolation. The stress at the critical load is the stress from the static analysis multiplied by the BLF: 250x4 = 1000psi = 1ksi.

According to the ASM standards, the yield stress for HS-low-alloy steels must be greater than 40ksi, which is much greater than the calculated stress value at the critical load. Therefore, we can conclude that this pole is expected to start buckling long before the stress exceeds the material's yield point.

4. Exit the Results environment. Save and close the model.

End of practice

Practice 12b
Buckling Analysis of a Thin Shell

Practice Objectives

- Set up and run a buckling analysis.
- Determine the Buckling Load Factor.
- Determine the safety of the part against buckling and yielding.

In this practice, you will set up and run a buckling analysis on the thin cylindrical shell shown in Figure 12–18, with minimum instruction.

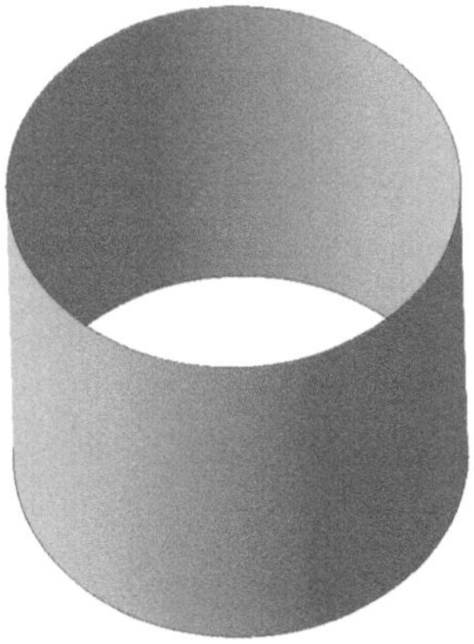

Figure 12–18

Task 1: Prepare the model for analysis.

1. Set the working directory to **Chapter12**, if required.
2. Open **buckle_shell.prt**.
3. Set the model display as follows:
   - *(Datum Display Filters)*: All Off
   - *(Spin Center)*: Off
   - *(Display Style)*: (Shading With Edges)
4. Launch Creo Simulate.

5. Apply the material:
   - *Material:* **STEEL**
   - *Poisson's ratio:* **0.27**
   - *Young's modulus:* **199948 MPa**
   - *Tensile Yield Stress:* **250 MPa**

   Note: *To create a new material that is not in the library, copy an existing material from the library into the model, and then change the material's name and properties.*

6. Use Shell Idealization:
   - *Thickness:* **1mm**

7. Constrain all translations on the bottom edge of the part, as shown in Figure 12–19.

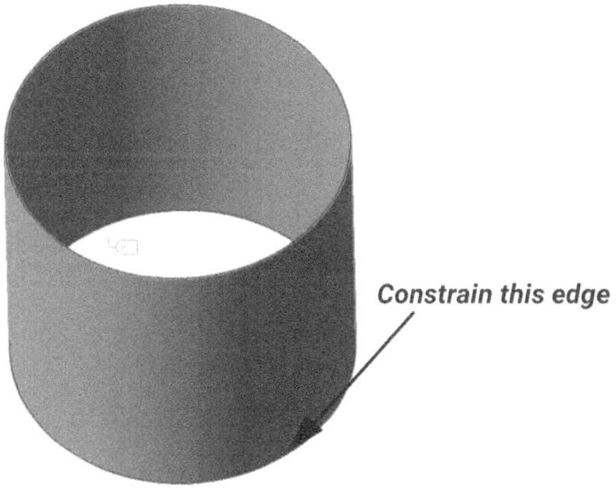

Figure 12–19

8. Apply a **100000N** compressive load (i.e., in the negative Y-direction) to the top edge, as shown in Figure 12–20.

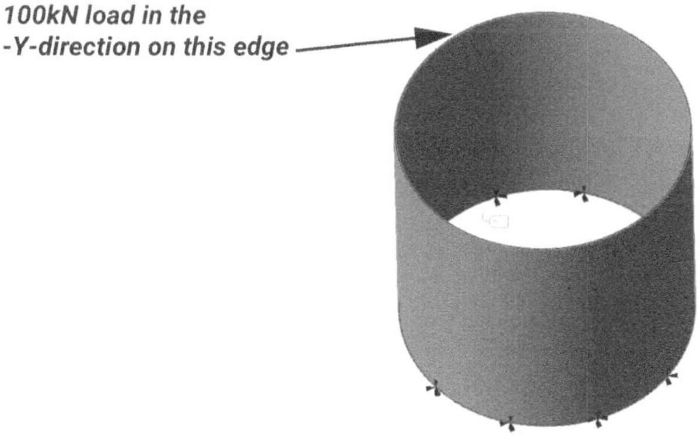

Figure 12–20

Task 2: Set up a static analysis.

1. Create a new static analysis with the following parameters:
    - *Analysis name:* **static_shell**
    - *Convergence method:* **Multi-Pass Adaptive**
    - *Maximum Polynomial Order:* **9**
    - *Percent Convergence:* **10**
    - *Plotting Grid:* **10**
2. Do not run the static analysis.

Task 3: Set up and run a buckling analysis.

1. Create and run a new buckling analysis with the following parameters:
    - *Analysis name:* **buckle_shell**
    - *Static analysis:* **static_shell**
    - *Number of buckling modes:* **4**
    - *Convergence method:* **Single-Pass Adaptive**
    - *Plotting Grid:* **10**

Task 4: Examine the analysis results.

1. Display the **von Mises Stress** fringe plot for the static analysis.
    - Is the part material expected to yield under the given loading?
2. Display the buckling shapes and obtain the lowest Buckling Load Factor from the result.
    - Is the part predicted to buckle?
    - Which is expected occur at a lower load: yielding of the material, or buckling?
3. Save and close the model.

End of practice

Appendix A

Basics of Structural Analysis

You will learn some basics of structural analysis.

Learning Objectives

- Understand quantities and units.
- Understand Newton's laws.

A.1 Quantities and Units

Fundamental Quantities

The fundamental quantities of solid mechanics are Length, Mass, and Time.

Derived Quantities

The derived quantities of solid mechanics are Force, Moment, Weight, Stress, Velocity, and Acceleration.

Units

Units must be consistent to perform valid calculations. The appropriate units for common quantities of the English and Metric systems are shown as follows:

Quantity	English Units	Metric Units
length	Inch, in	Millimeter, mm
time	Second, s	Second, s
mass	Slug $\left(1\text{slug} = \frac{1\text{lbf}}{386.09\text{in/s}^2}\right)$	Tonne, t $(1\text{t} = 1\text{Mg} = 1\text{x}10^6\text{g})$
velocity	in/s	mm/s
acceleration	in/s^2	mm/s^2
force	Pound, lbf	Newton, N
moment	Inch-pound, in lb	Newton-millimeter, N mm
weight	Pound, lbf	Newton, N
stress	Pounds per square inch, psi	Newton per square millimeter, N/mm^2 Megapascal, Mpa $(1\text{Mpa} = 1\text{N/mm}^2)$

A.2 Newton's Laws

Newton's three laws of motion are as follows:

1. An object in motion or at rest stays in motion or at rest unless acted on by an external force.
2. For every action there is an equal and opposite reaction.
3. Force = mass * acceleration ($F = ma$).

Implications of Newton's Laws on Structural Analysis

A body remains stationary or in uniform motion in a straight line unless it is made to change that state by external forces. This is a fundamental assumption when performing a structural Linear Static analysis.

Static implies that there is no movement. It is assumed that the structure being analyzed is not free to move in any direction. Sufficient constraints must be applied to the model to remove all six rigid body degrees of freedom.

Equilibrium and Free-Body Diagrams

Free-body diagrams and equilibrium equations determine the load paths in a structure. Mathematically, this provides six equilibrium equations. The sum of the forces in each direction must equal zero and the sum of the moments in each direction must equal zero.

An example of a cantilever beam is shown in Figure A–1.

Figure A–1

Reactions to a force (F) must exist at the constraints, as shown in Figure A–2.

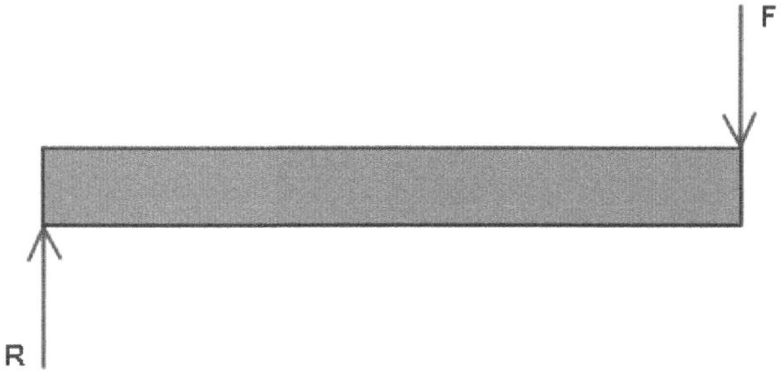

Figure A–2

For equilibrium to exist, the following equation must hold:

$R = -F$

This can be verified mathematically with the following equation:

$R + F = 0$

Moments

If the constraint is a hinge, the entire beam rotates because a hinge cannot react to a moment. A simple hinge would not remove the rotational rigid body degree of freedom. However, a fully fixed constraint can react to moments and you can easily calculate its magnitude.

The ability to calculate the moments acting on and within a structure is useful. Bending often accounts for a part's maximum stress. Therefore, being able to perform a quick hand calculation to validate an analysis model is helpful.

A moment is calculated at a specific location and defined by the following calculation:

FORCE x DISTANCE

An applied force (F) causes moments on a structure as it moves away from the reaction force (R). Alternatively, pure moments might be applied to the structure. Pure moments are transmitted through the system with a constant magnitude.

For static equilibrium to hold for the beam shown in Figure A–3, the sum of moments must equal zero.

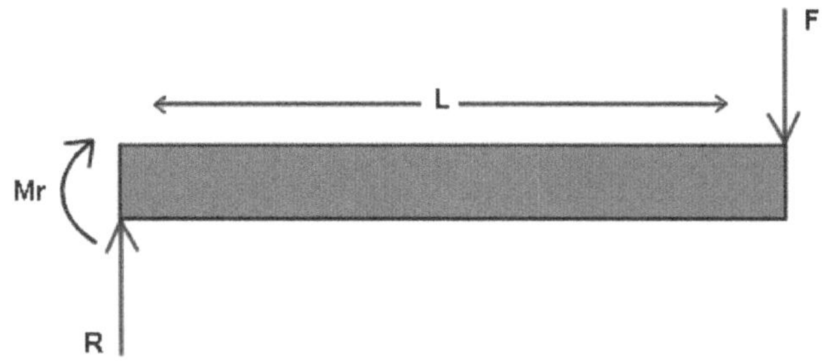

Figure A–3

If a moment is positive in the clockwise direction, the sum of the moments is as follows:

$(F \times L) + Mr = 0$

Since the net moment is being calculated at the location of the reaction force (R) the reaction force itself produces no moment. Therefore, the following equation holds:

$Mr = -(F \times L)$

Another example is shown in Figure A–4.

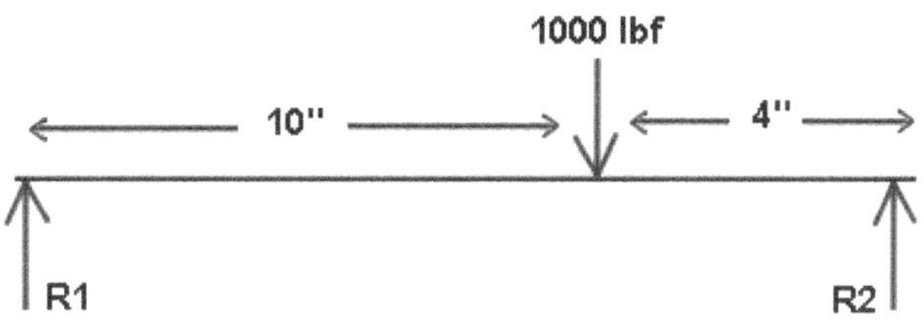

Figure A–4

This beam is supported (pinned) at both ends. Reaction forces exist when an external force is applied. For equilibrium to exist, the following equation must hold (vertical up is considered positive):

R1 + R2 - 1000 = 0

This single equation is not enough to determine the values of R1 and R2. An additional equation from the equilibrium of moments must be used. The following equation calculates the sum of the moments at the location of R1 (clockwise is considered positive):

(R1 x 0) + (1000 x 10) - (R2 x 14) = 0

Using the force and moment equilibrium equations, the values for R1and R2 are calculated as follows:

R2 = 714.3 lbf

R1 = 1000 - 714.3 = 285.7 lbf

In addition to determining reaction loads, engineers typically calculate the shear and moment diagrams for beams. The moment at a beam's cross-section, in conjunction with linear-elastic beam theory, is used to determine the beam bending stresses.

Shears and moments are calculated at a beam cross-section location similar to the way reaction loads were determined. Consider the beam segment on only one side of the cross-section. Imagine the location of the cross-section as a fixed constraint. The beam diagram displays as shown in Figure A–5.

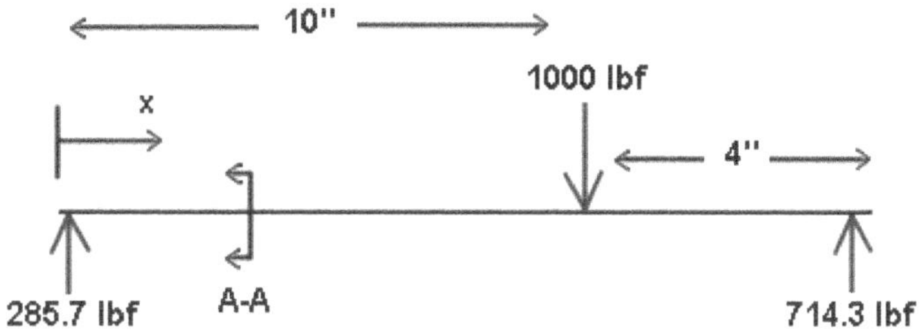

Figure A–5

The only the beam portion to the left of section A-A is shown in Figure A–6.

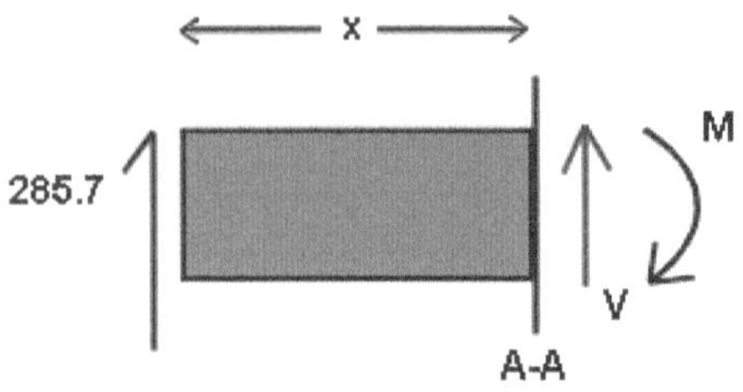

Figure A–6

The value of V is calculated using the following equation:

$$285.7 + V = 0$$

Therefore,

$$M = -285.7x \text{ in} \cdot \text{lbf}$$

The value of M is calculated using the following equation:

$$285.7x + M = 0$$

Therefore,

$$M = -285.7x \text{ in} \cdot \text{lbf}$$

If X is greater than 10in, the equations change due to the extra force. The following equations then apply:

$$285.7 - 1000 + V = 0$$

Therefore,

$$V = 714.3 \text{ lbf}$$

$$285.7x - 1000\,(x - 10) + M = 0$$

$$M = 1000\,(x - 10) - 285.7x$$

Therefore,

$$M = 714.3x - 10000 \text{ in} \cdot \text{lbf}$$

These results can be displayed graphically by creating shear and bending moment diagrams, as shown in Figure A–7.

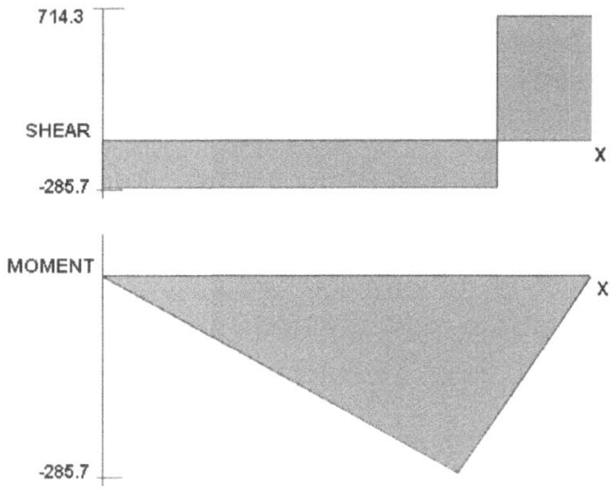

Figure A–7

Graphically, the maximum moment for this beam is directly under the applied load. The value of the moment, in conjunction with the beam bending equation, can be used to calculate the stresses in the beam.

Note that you cannot calculate reaction loads for every structure using only equilibrium. The beam diagram shown in Figure A–8 is similar to the case that you just solved. However, the ends have been fixed instead of pinned.

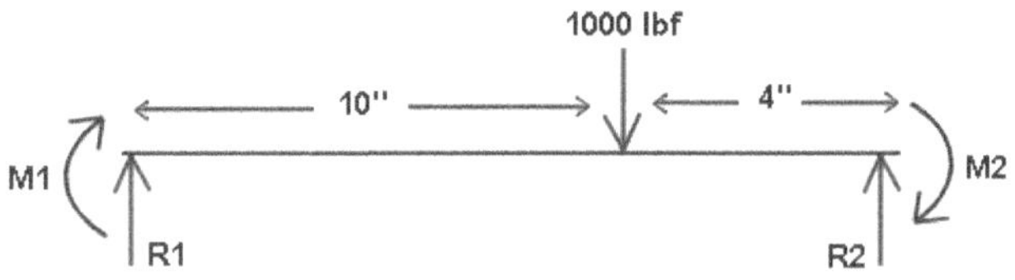

Figure A–8

Two additional unknowns now represent the moments transmitted through the ends of the beam: M1 and M2. A total of four unknowns now exist, but two equilibrium equations are available for each plane.

The following force and moment equilibrium equations (at R1) can be written:

R1 + R2 = 1000

M1 + 10(1000) - 14R2 + M2 = 0

These equations cannot be solved uniquely. Even if you try creating another moment equation at R2, the following equation results:

M1 + 14R1 - 4(1000) + M2 = 0

R1 - 1000 - R2

Therefore,

M1 + 14000 - 14R2 - 4000 + M2 = 0

M1 + 10000 - 14R2 + M2 = 0

The final equation is the same equation that you arrived at earlier. Therefore, creating another moment equation at R2 does not help. This problem is actually solvable by hand but requires additional equations that take into account the stiffness of the structure (elasticity theory). As problems become more complex, the only feasible approach often involves the use of numerical computer methods.

So far, only simple beams in a single plane have been considered. One of the most valuable uses for understanding the equilibrium equations is being able to calculate the reaction loads between different components in an assembly. This skill enables you to analyze single components from an assembly rather than attempting to model the entire structure.

Stresses

The most basic definition of stress is as follows:

$$\text{STRESS} = \frac{\text{FORCE}}{\text{AREA}}$$

Or,

$$\sigma = \frac{F}{A}$$

An example of a tensile test specimen is shown in Figure A–9.

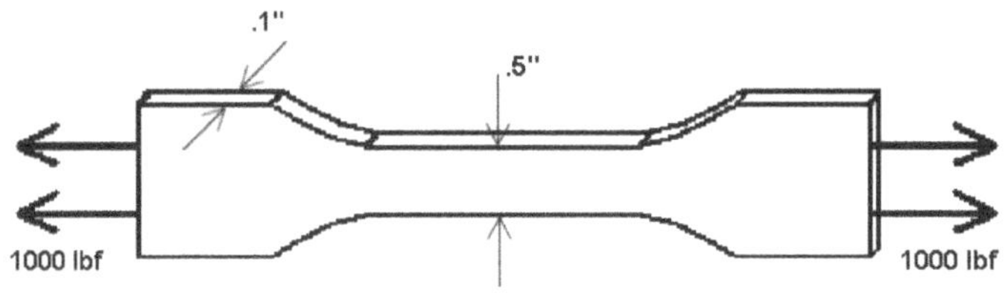

Figure A–9

The following properties apply:

F = 1000 lbf

A = 0.1 x 0.5 = 0.05 in^2

Therefore,

$$\sigma = \frac{1000}{0.05}$$

$(\sigma = 20000)$ psi (20 ksi)

Once a stress has been determined, it can be used to predict the safety of the part, by comparing the stress in the part with the material's strength. A material's yield strength and ultimate strength are typically used for comparison. The yield strength is the amount of stress that a material can sustain before suffering permanent deformation, and the ultimate strength is the stress at which the material ruptures in tension.

Material properties can be displayed using a Stress-Strain diagram, as shown in Figure A–10. Strain relates to the displacements of the structure and is defined as follows:

$$STRAIN = \frac{CHANGEINLENGTH}{LENGTH}$$

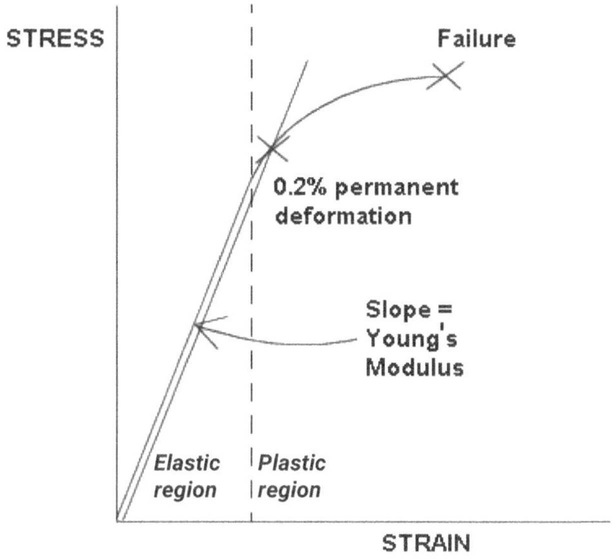

Figure A–10

Note that the initial portion of the curve is a straight line. This is called the *elastic* region. Linear static analysis assumes that the material is *only* being used in its elastic region. The slope of the curve is Young's Modulus, E. By generally accepted standards, the yield strength is determined to be the stress level at which a 0.2% permanent deformation is seen in the material. The ultimate strength is the maximum stress level that is obtained before failure.

The graph shown in Figure A–10 is an idealization. In reality, metals have an essentially linear first segment, but some materials (e.g., plastics or rubbers) do not. Although linear analysis makes the fundamental assumption of the linear material properties, it is still used frequently with plastics and other materials. To be more accurate, a non-linear analysis could be performed, but this is much more complex and costly. It is often quite acceptable to approximate a material's behavior as linear because a valuable insight into the component's behavior can still be obtained.

3D Stresses

So far, only the case of uniaxial stress has been considered. 3D has many components of stress, as shown in Figure A–11.

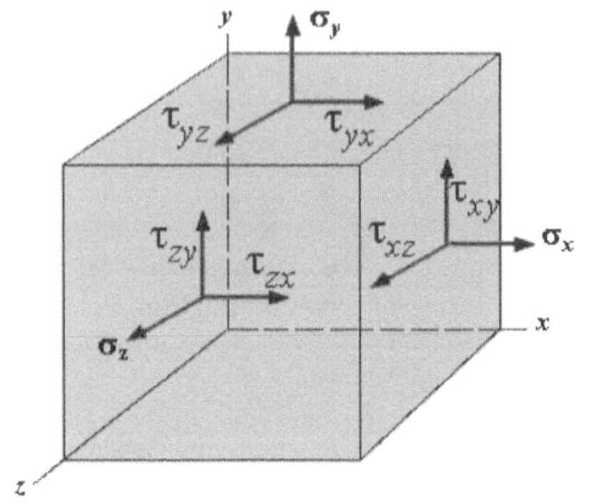

Figure A–11

σ indicates a normal stress parallel to and acting on the plane denoted by the subscript. τ indicates a shear stress acting on the plane denoted by the first subscript and parallel to the plane denoted by the second subscript.

At any point in the component, you can visualize an infinitely smaller cube. Each face of the cube can react to a tensile stress normal to its surface and shear stresses in the other two perpendicular directions. To satisfy the equilibrium of the cube, $\tau_{xy} = \tau_{yx}, \tau_{xz} = \tau_{zx}, \tau_{yz} = \tau_{zy}$.

With multiple stress components, a single value can no longer be compared against a material's yield strength. Furthermore, if the cube is reoriented (i.e., a different coordinate system is used), the stress values change. Consider the 2D example shown in Figure A–12.

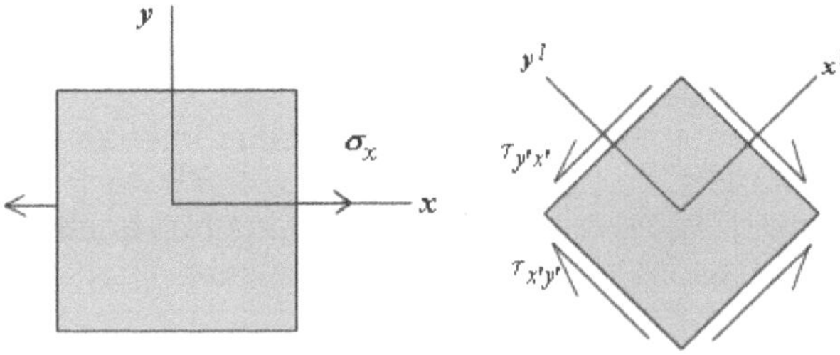

Figure A–12

Only a normal stress is shown on the left in Figure A–12. If the coordinate system is rotated, at least some of the stress in the new system must be reacted in shear. In fact, the normal stresses that must also be present to balance the vertical compression, are not shown on the right in Figure A–12.

Therefore, you cannot simply take a stress value from an arbitrary coordinate system. It is possible to find a coordinate system in which all of the stresses can be expressed as pure normal stresses through trigonometry). This is called the *Principal Coordinate System*, and the stresses expressed in that system are called the *Principal Stresses*. In 3D, three principal stresses are denoted (1, 2, and 3), which are usually arranged in a decreasing order of magnitude.

Failure Theories

Figure A–13 shows three common failure theories:

- Maximum Principal Stress theory
- Maximum Shear Stress (Tresca) theory
- von Mises Stress theory

Each theory tries to predict yielding in a general stress state.

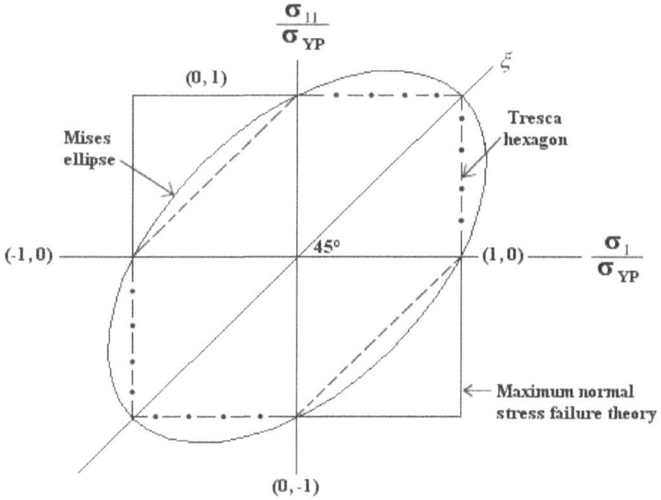

Figure A–13

The Maximum Principal Stress theory states that when the maximum principal stress exceeds the material's yield point, the material yields. The Maximum Shear Stress theory was proposed later when it was understood that yielding resulted from shearing between atoms of the solid. Finally, the von Mises Stress theory (also called *Distortion Energy* or *Effective Stress*) was determined to most closely match the experimental results for ductile isotropic materials.

In most cases, you should compare the calculated von Mises stress to the yield of the material to judge whether a component is capable of withstanding the applied loads without experiencing a permanent plastic deformation.

Appendix B

Poisson's Ratio Project

In this project exercise, you will explore the effect of Poisson's ratio.

Learning Objective

- Apply Poisson's ratio to a model under tensile loading.

B.1 Poisson's Ratio

When a plate is subject to simple tension, the length of the plate increases in the load direction, but decreases in the dimensions that are perpendicular to the load. The ratio of the strain in the lateral direction to the axial direction is defined as *Poisson's ratio*.

$$i.e.\quad Poisson's\ ratio = \frac{unit\ lateral\ contraction}{unit\ axial\ elongation}$$

> **Note:** *Poisson's ratio is a constant for a given material within its range of elastic behavior (e.g., structural steel = 0.3 approx.).*

The following example demonstrates how Poisson's ratio affects a rectangular (14x8) steel plate that is 0.2 thick, has one hole, and is under a simple tension of 20000lbs. You will analyze the plate with a shell model.

You will set up and run two standard design studies with different boundary conditions to indicate the Poisson's ratio effect on the analysis results.

The plate model with hole dimensions is shown in Figure B–1.

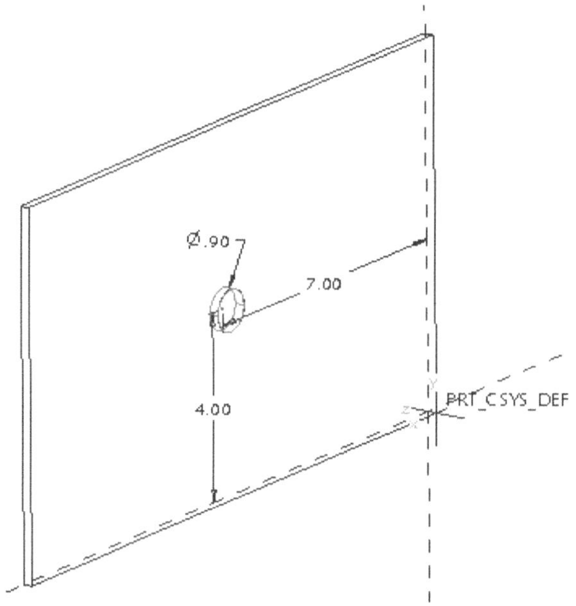

Figure B–1

Modeling Tasks

Task 1: Open poisson_part in Creo Parametric and launch Creo Simulate.

1. Open **poisson_part.prt**. The part displays as shown in Figure B–2.

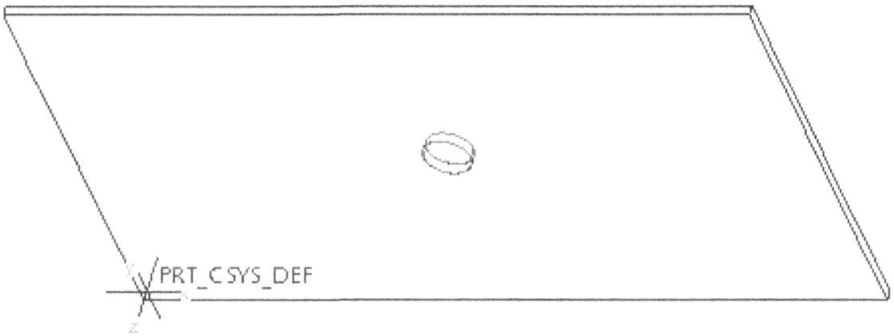

Figure B–2

2. Ensure that the unit system is set to **IPS**.
3. Launch Creo Simulate.

Task 2: Apply the material.

1. Assign **STEEL** to the model. The following values are the default material properties for HS-low-alloy steel (STEEL):
   - *Poisson:* **0.27**
   - *Young's modulus*: **2.9e+07 psi**

   Note: *The model's material properties should be as stated.*

Task 3: Define the shell pairs.

1. Use the **Automatic Detection** tool, with the *Characteristic Thickness* of **0.25** to define the shell pairs.

   Note: *The plate thickness is 0.2 inches.*

Task 4: Apply the loads.

1. Apply a tensile load of **20000lbs** to the edge shown in Figure B–3.

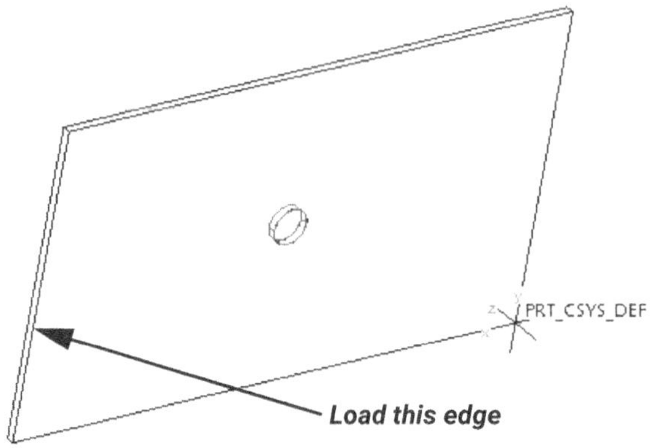

Figure B–3

Note: The model shown in Figure B–3 is reoriented for clarity.

Task 5: Apply the constraints.

1. Constrain the edges shown in Figure B–4, using the following values:

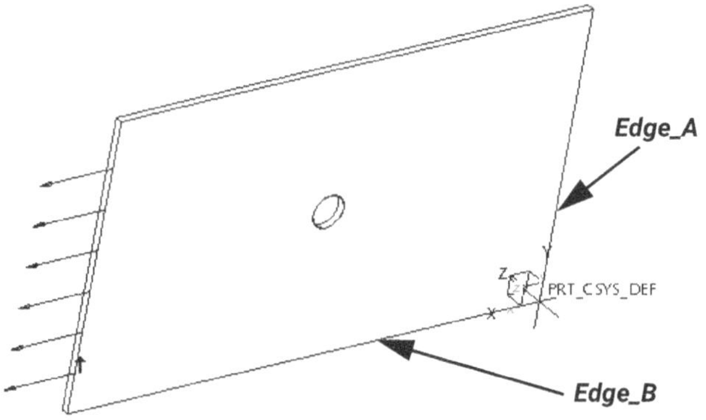

Figure B–4

Constraint Set	Edge_A	Edge_B	Description
const_1	Fixed in all translations and rotations.	Free in all translations and rotations.	The constraint set does not permit the plate to decrease in dimensions perpendicular to the applied load along edge_A. This edge is said to be over-constrained.
const_2	Fixed in X- and Z-directions. Free in Y-direction. Fixed in all rotations.	Fixed in Y-direction only	The constraint set does not constrain edge_A in the Y-direction and edge_B in the X-direction. This permits the plate to decrease in dimensions perpendicular to the applied load, which causes in more realistic results.

The model displays as shown in Figure B–5.

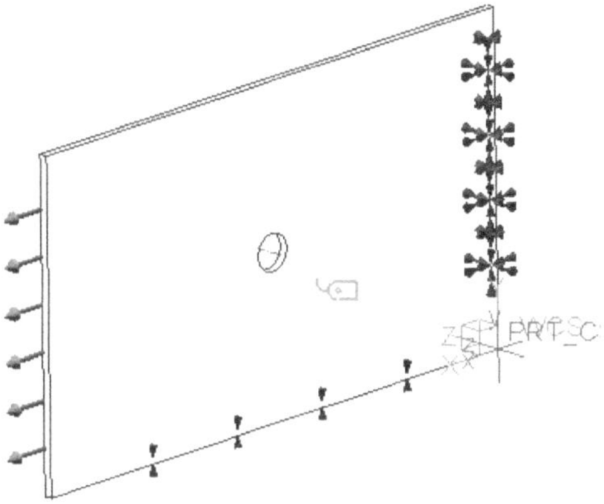

Figure B–5

Analysis Tasks

Task 6: Set up the analysis.

1. Set up the following:
   - A multipass analysis **Max. P order = 9** with a convergence of **1%**. Name the analysis **p_1**. Select **const_1** as the constraint set.
   - A multipass analysis **Max. P order = 9** with a convergence of **1%**. Name the analysis **p_2**. Select **const_2** as the constraint set.

Task 7: Run the analysis.

1. Run both analyses.
2. Once the analyses have finished, open the run status and note the following details:
   - Maximum von Mises stress in the **p_1** analysis = 38.20ksi (approx.)
   - Maximum von Mises stress in the **p_2** analysis= 36.74ksi (approx.)

Results Tasks

Task 8: Display the results.

1. Create and display the following:
   - A deformed fringe color plot of the von Mises stress for analysis **p_1**, as shown in Figure B–6.
   - A deformed fringe color plot of the von Mises stress for analysis **p_2**, as shown in Figure B–7.

The constraint set **const_1** in Figure B–6 does not permit the plate to decrease in dimensions perpendicular to the applied load. This model is said to be overconstrained. Note that the deformation of the plate is restricted and that the plate is not permitted to contract freely in the Y-direction. Therefore, the arched top and bottom edges display.

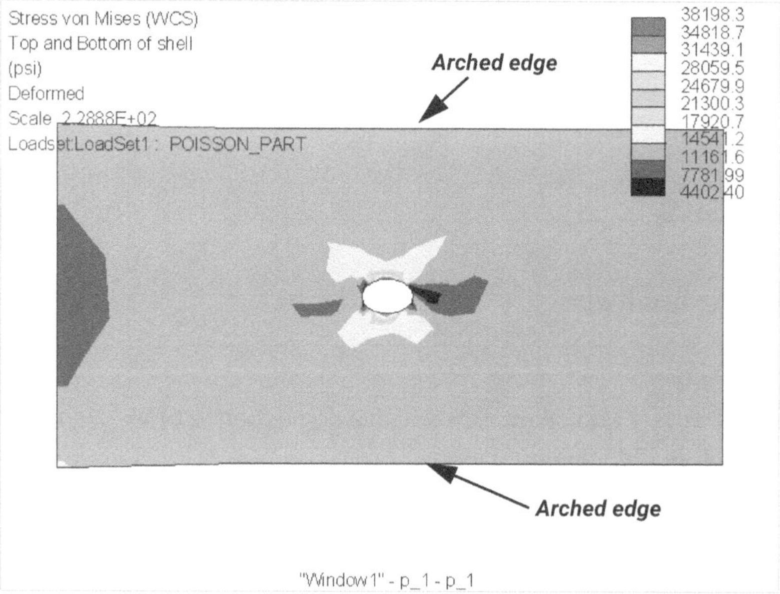

Figure B–6

The constraint set **const_2** in Figure B–7 does not constrain edge_A in the Y-direction and edge_B in the X-direction. This permits the plate dimensions to decrease in the Y-direction. Note that the deformation of the plate is uniform.

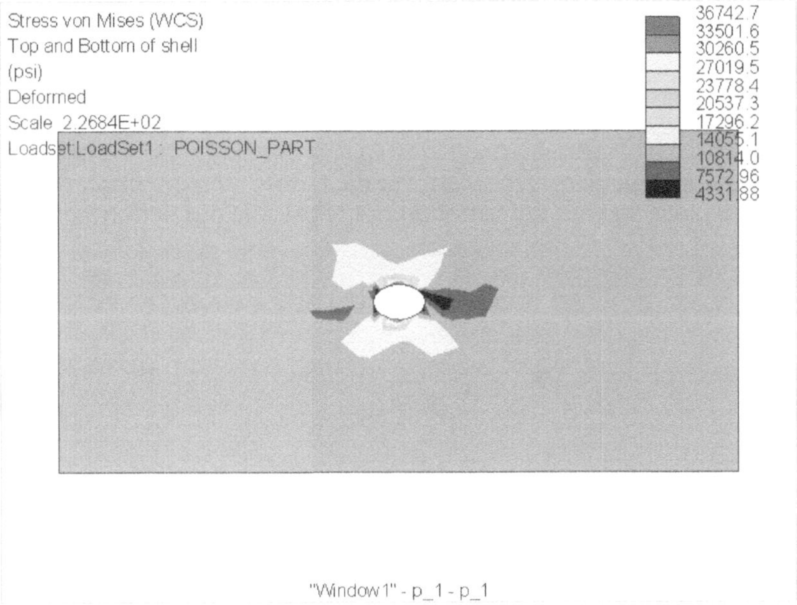

Figure B–7

Task 9: Verify the results with hand calculations.

1. Verify the following results:

   - Cross-sectional area of plate at hole = (8 - 0.9)(0.2) = 1.42 in^2
   - Stress concentration factor for hole = 2.62
   - σ_1 = max. stress at hole = (2.62)(20000)/(1.42) = 36.9ksi

   The plate is under pure tension. Therefore, the principal stresses include the following:

   - σ_1 = 36.9ksi
   - $\sigma_2 = 0$
   - $\sigma_3 = 0$
   - von Mises stress = $\{[(\sigma_1 - \sigma_2)^2 + (\sigma_2 - \sigma_3)^2 + (\sigma_3 - \sigma_1)^2]/2\}^{1/2}$ = 36.9 ksi

2. A comparison of the hand-calculated maximum von Mises value with the values obtained from the FEA analysis is as follows:

Method	vm (ksi)	Error%
Hand-calculated	36.9	0.00
Analysis [P_1]	38.20	3.5
Analysis [P_1]	36.74	0.4

Although the values are close and comparable to each other, the constraint set **const_1** has over-constrained the plate and the deformation of the plate is not uniform due to the effect of the Poisson's ratio.

Appendix C

Verification and Practice Examples

You will review several structural case studies.

Learning Objective

- Review different case studies.

C.1 Structural Analysis

In each of the following cases, create the Creo Parametric model and use the techniques learned in the previous practices to perform the appropriate analysis. Compare the results obtained with the following theoretical values. Note that the theory values also use approximations.

Case	Description	Theory	Creo Simulate	Error %
1A	Cantilever Beam – Bending	d_{max} = .1167 in σ_{max} = 39.4 ksi		
1B	Cantilever Beam – Gravity	$\delta_{max} = 1.7x10^{-4}$ in σ_{max} = 76.54 psi		
2A	Plate w/ Hole – Tension	σ_{max} = 14.6 ksi		
2B	Plate w/ Hole – Bending	σ_{max} = 34.7 ksi		
3A	Step. Cir. Bar – Tension	σ_{max} = 2.14 ksi		
3B	Step. Cir. Bar – Bending	σ_{max} =1.56 ksi		
3C	Step. Cir. Bar – Torsion	τ_{max} = 682.45 psi		
4A	Loaded Hole in Plate	σ_{max} = 9.98 ksi		

Case 1 – Cantilevered I-Beam

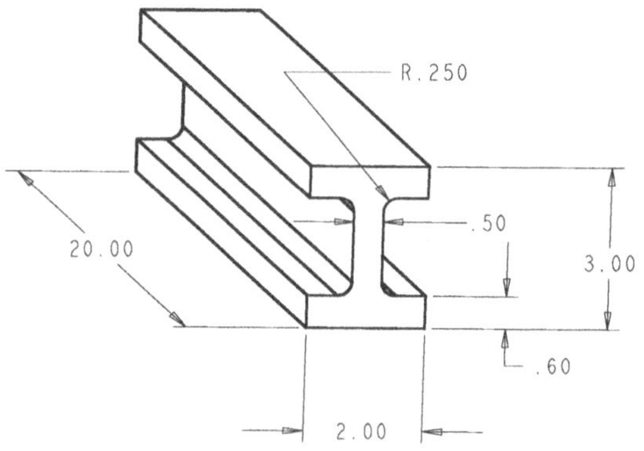

Figure C–1

Loadcase A

- *One end:* **Immovable**
- The other end: **5000 lbf shear** (in the stiffer bending direction)
- *Material:* **Steel**
- Idealize the model with beam elements.
- *Young's modulus:* **E = 3.0e7**
- *Poisson's ratio:* **n = 0.30**
- *Mass density:* **7.5e-4**
- *Bending moment of inertia:* **I = 3.8094 in4**

Loadcase A Analytical Solution

$$\text{maximum deflection, } \delta_{max} = \frac{F \times L^3}{3 \times E \times I} = \frac{5000 \times (20)^3}{3 \times (3 \times 10^7) \times 3.8094} = \mathbf{0.1167\ in}$$

$$\text{maximum stress, } \sigma_{max} = \frac{M \times y}{I} = \frac{5000 \times 20 \times 1.5}{3.8094} = \mathbf{39.4\ ksi}$$

Loadcase B

- *One end:* **Immovable**, 1G gravity load (386.4 in/s2)
- *Cross-sectional area:* **A = 3.35365**
- Idealize the model with beam elements.

Loadcase B Analytical Solution

$$\begin{aligned} w &= \text{mass density} \times A \times G \\ &= (7.5 \times 10^{-4}) \times 3.35365 \times 386.4 \\ &= \mathbf{0.9719\ lbf/in} \end{aligned}$$

$$\begin{aligned} \text{maximum deflection, } \delta_{max} &= \frac{w \times L^4}{8 \times E \times I} \\ &= \frac{0.9719 \times (20)^4}{8 \times (3 \times 10^7) \times 3.8094} \\ &= \mathbf{1.7 \times 10^{-4} in} \end{aligned}$$

$$\begin{aligned} M &= \frac{w \times L^2}{2} \\ &= \frac{0.9719 \times (20)^2}{2} \\ &= \mathbf{194.38\ in \cdot lbf} \end{aligned}$$

$$\begin{aligned} \text{maximum stress, } \sigma_{max} &= \frac{M \times y}{I} \\ &= \frac{194.38 \times 1.5}{3.8094} \\ &= \mathbf{76.54\ psi} \end{aligned}$$

Case 2 – Plate with a Hole

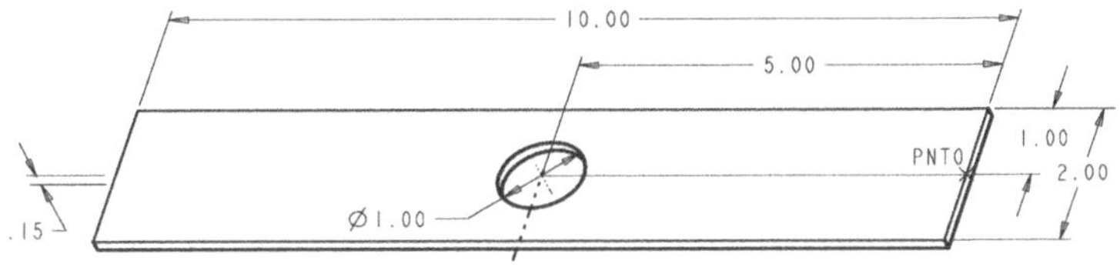

Figure C–2

Loadcase A

- *One end:* **Immovable**
- *The other end:* tensile load of 1000 lbf
- w=2
- d=1

Loadcase A Analytical Solution

$$\sigma_0 = \frac{1000}{(2-1)\times 0.15} = 6667 \text{ psi}$$

$$d/w = 0.5$$

$$K_t = 2.19$$

$$\sigma_{max} = \sigma_0 \times K_t = 6667 \times 2.19 = \mathbf{14.6\ ksi}$$

Loadcase B

- *One end:* **Immovable**
- *The other end:* Bending moment of 100 in lbf

Loadcase B Analytical Solution

$$I = \frac{(2-1)\times(0.15)^3}{12}$$

$$= 2.8125 \times 10^{-4}$$

$$\sigma_0 = \frac{100 \times 0.075}{2.8125 \times 10^{-4}}$$

$$K_t = 1.3$$

$$\sigma_{max} = \mathbf{34.7\ ksi}$$

Case 3 – Stepped Circular Bar

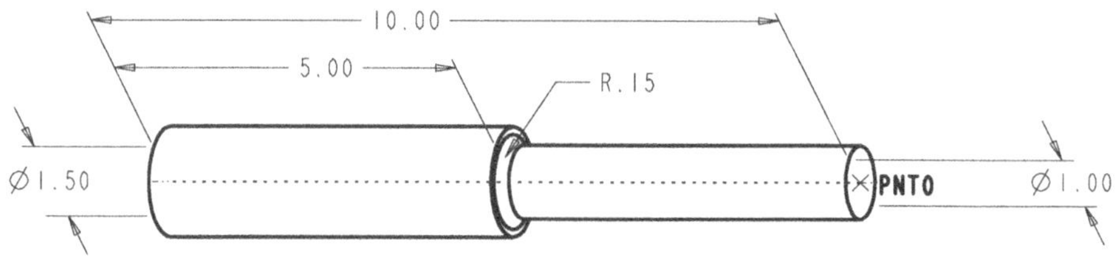

Figure C–3

Loadcase A

- *Large end:* **Immovable**
- *Small end:* **1000 lbf tension**

Loadcase A Analytical Solution

$$\sigma_0 = \frac{F}{A} = \frac{1000}{\left(\pi \times (1)^2 / 4\right)} = 1273 \text{ psi}$$

$$D/d = 1.5$$

$$r/d = 0.15$$

$$K_t = 1.68$$

$$\sigma_{max} = \mathbf{2.14} \text{ ksi}$$

Loadcase B

- *Large end:* **Immovable**
- *Small end:* **100 in×lbf bending**

Loadcase B Analytical Solution

$$\sigma_0 = \frac{M \times y}{I} = \mathbf{1018.6\ psi}$$

$$K_t = 1.53$$

$$\sigma_{max} = \mathbf{1.56\ ksi}$$

Loadcase C

- *Large end:* **Immovable**
- *Small end:* **100 in lbf torsion**

Loadcase C Analytical Solution

$$\tau_0 = \frac{T \times c}{J}$$

$$= \frac{100 \times 0.5}{\left(\pi \times 1^4 / 32\right)}$$

$$= 509.3 \text{ psi}$$

$$K_s = 1.34$$

$$\tau_{max} = \mathbf{682.45\ psi}$$

Case 4 – Loaded Plate with Hole

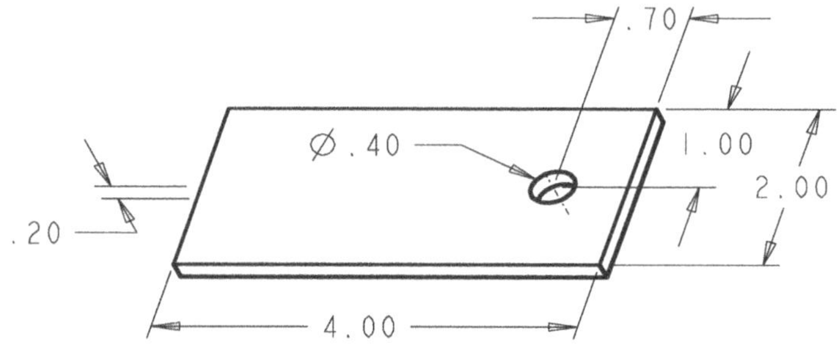

Figure C–4

Loadcase A

- *End farthest from hole:* **Immovable**
- Bearing load in hole of 500 lbf directed towards nearest end of plate.

$$w = 2$$
$$t = 0.2$$
$$h = 0.70$$
$$d = 0.40$$

Loadcase A Analytical Solution

$$\sigma_0 = 500 \times (2 - 0.40) \times 0.2$$
$$= 1.56 \text{ ksi}$$
$$d/w = 0.2$$
$$h/w = 0.35$$
$$K_t = 6.1$$
$$\sigma_{max} = \mathbf{9.98\ ksi}$$

Practice C1
Structural Analysis Examples – Set 2

In this practice, in each of the following cases, you will create the Creo Parametric model and use the techniques learned in the previous practices to perform the appropriate analysis. For each model, define the material as steel with the following properties:

- *Young's modulus:* **E = 3.0e7**
- *Poisson's ratio:* **n = 0.30**
- *Mass density:* **7.5e-4**

Case 1 – Straight Beams

Beams are usually quite easy to solve, but care must be taken when applying boundary conditions. For these straight beam examples, build a 10in long beam with 0.5in x 1.0in cross-section, as shown in Figure C–5.

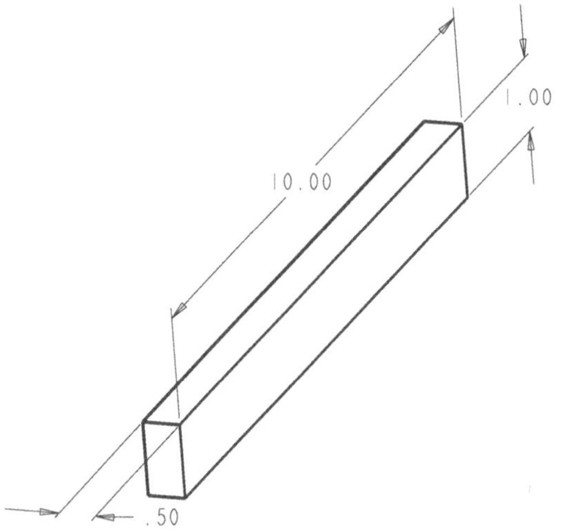

Figure C–5

Task 1: Loadcase A – Fixed-Fixed Beam

1. Apply Immovable constraints to the two ends of the beam.
2. Apply a **200 lbf/in^2** uniform load as the *Load Per Unit* normal to the top of the beam. This equals a **100lbf/in** load along the beam.
3. Solve the model. Compare the results to the table in Loadcase B – All Edges Fixed – Concentrated Load, Step 5.

Task 2: Loadcase B – Pinned-Pinned Beam

In this case, do not use beam elements. Mesh the model with 3D solid elements. To create a pinned connection, you must constrain a curve. Solid analyses do not have an associated moment carrying degrees of freedom. A constrained line is free to spin about the line as required for a pin joint.

1. In Creo Parametric, create a straight datum curve at each end of the beam, as shown in Figure C–6.

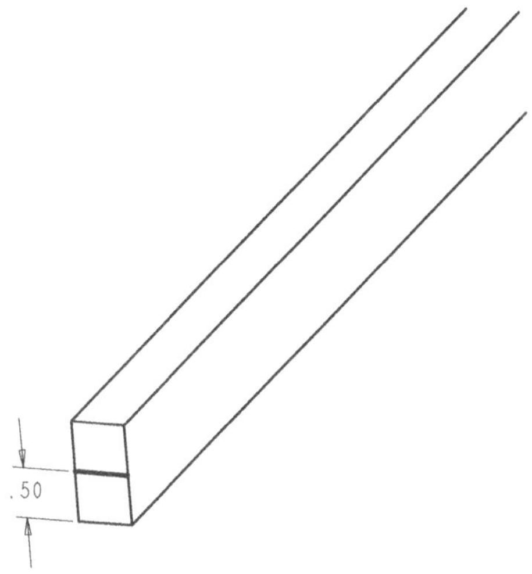

Figure C–6

2. Constrain the curves as **Immovable**.
3. Apply a **200 lbf/in^2** pressure. This is equivalent to the **200 lbf/in2** uniform load (*Load Per Unit*) in Loadcase A.
4. Solve the model. Compare the results to the table in Loadcase B – All Edges Fixed – Concentrated Load, Step 5.

Case 2 – Rectangular Plate

Boundary conditions for plates must be modeled similar to those used for simply supported pinned beam-ends. For these rectangular plate examples, build the following model.

1. Build a 10in x 5in x 0.5in plate. The part displays as shown in Figure C–7.

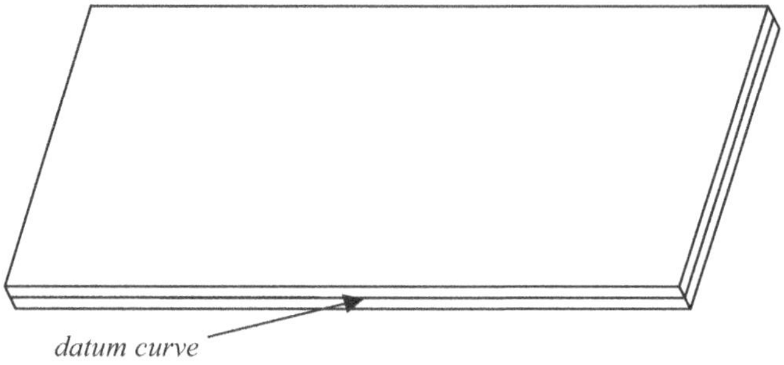

Figure C–7

Task 1: Loadcase A – All Edges pinned – Distributed Load

1. Create datum curves on the four sides.
2. Make the four curves **Immovable** to simulate simple support.
3. Apply a downward **100lbf/in^2** *Load Per Unit* normal to the top surface.
4. Solve the model. Compare the results to the table in Loadcase B – All Edges Fixed – Concentrated Load, Step 5.

Task 2: Loadcase B – All Edges Fixed – Concentrated Load

1. In Creo Parametric, sketch a circular datum curve centered on the top of the plate with a radius of **0.5**.
2. Create a divided surface using the circular datum curve.
3. Set all four side surfaces as **Immovable**.

4. Apply a *Total Force* of **10000lbf** to the small divided surface (normal to surface). The loading should display as shown in Figure C–8.

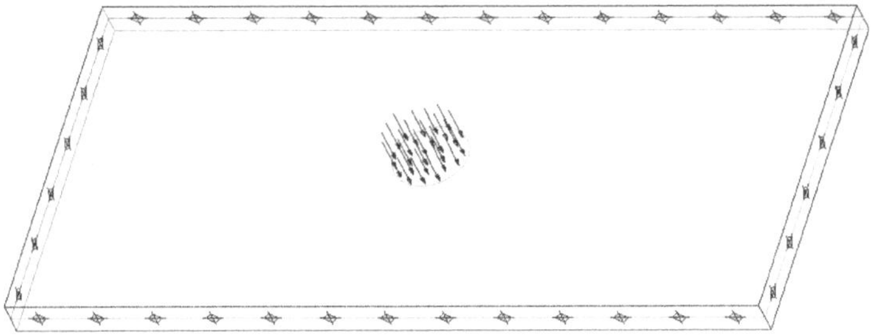

Figure C–8

5. Solve the model. Compare the results to the following table:

Case	Quantity	Roark 6th Ed.	Pro/MECHANICA
1a	Max. Y Disp	-2.083e-3	
	Max. Stress	10000	
	Stress at Mid Beam	5000	
1b	Max. Y Disp	-.0104	
	Max. Stress	15000	
2a	Horz. Disp at left end neutral axis	.69	
2b	Horz. Disp at left end neutral axis	1.58	

End of practice

Made in United States
Cleveland, OH
05 November 2026

47656821R00425